HISTORY OF THE CATHOLIC CHURCH

HISTORY OF
THE
CATHOLIC CHURCH

THOMAS P. NEILL, Ph.D.

DEPARTMENT OF HISTORY, ST. LOUIS UNIVERSITY

AND

RAYMOND H. SCHMANDT, Ph.D.

DEPARTMENT OF HISTORY, LOYOLA UNIVERSITY, CHICAGO

SECOND EDITION
1965

THE BRUCE PUBLISHING COMPANY
MILWAUKEE

NIHIL OBSTAT:

JOHN A. SCHULIEN, S.T.D.
Censor librorum

IMPRIMATUR:

✠ WILLIAM E. COUSINS
Archbishop of Milwaukee
April 14, 1965

Library of Congress Catalog Card Number: 65-17468

© 1965 THE BRUCE PUBLISHING COMPANY
MADE IN THE UNITED STATES OF AMERICA

(4/65)

TO AGNES AND BETTS

PREFACE

THE authors of the following pages believe the student should be advised what sort of a book he is about to read. HISTORY OF THE CATHOLIC CHURCH is a textbook presenting in the small compass of a single volume a synopsis of the history of the Church on this earth. It is not a theological work; it does no more than describe in summary fashion the more important doctrines and moral teachings of the Catholic Church, particularly those on which historical controversy hinged.

One of the most difficult problems in such a work as this is deciding what to omit from the story and what to include. In selecting material for discussion in each period of the Church's history the authors have followed the principle of treating those subjects which seemed important to the good minds of the period under discussion. Thus the political history of the Church is stressed only in those ages when it seemed a most important consideration to contemporaries. In this way we have tried to avoid reading current interests, such as the liturgy or Catholic Action, back into the entire history of the Church.

This text is not a work in apologetics. The authors have tried to follow the advice given by Pope Leo XIII in his encyclical on historical studies of 1883 when he wrote: "It is the first law of history that it dare not say anything which is false nor fear to utter anything that is true, in order that there may be no suspicion either of partiality or of hostility in the writer." The aim of the historian is to write true history; it is not to "defend" the Church by reconstructing the past in a prejudicial light favorable to the Church or any persons or groups within it. The authors believe, with the great majority of historians, that it is almost impossible to write a good history of the Church unless one has a true knowledge of its purpose and its organization, as well as a sympathetic understanding of its doctrines, its moral teaching, its way of life. To draw the proper line between sympathetic understanding and objective history — in so far as history can be considered "objective" — is a difficult task. The authors have conscientiously tried to draw this line as true as they could.

This text is written on the assumption that the history of the Catholic

Church cannot be treated as though the Church exists in a vacuum. Divinely instituted, the Church has nevertheless been guided immediately by human beings, each of whom was the product of his age, who was affected by the standards of his time and his particular locality. Moreover, as an institution the Church has necessarily been concerned with the affairs of the world: with the policies and occasionally even the structure of governments; with the sufferings of the poor, and the ways that men have earned their living; with the civilizing of peoples and the promotion of education. It is therefore necessary to treat Church history as the story of an institution existing in time and space, influenced by the surrounding world, and in turn influencing the course of events that, strictly speaking, fall outside the scope of Church history as such.

The fact that the Church exists in time and space means that it must ever adapt itself to changing conditions in the world. Thus, although divinely founded and never changing in certain respects, the Church develops and grows and adapts itself constantly to the developments of each age. The historian does not deny the unchanging essentials of the Church when he concentrates on the changing accidentals. The latter are his immediate, proper concern.

As historians the authors of HISTORY OF THE CATHOLIC CHURCH try to explain events, in so far as possible, without recourse to providential action or to miracles. In following this rule we do not deny the reality of miracles nor the possibility and the reality of God's direct intervention in human events. But ordinarily God works through men and other secondary causes, and it is the lazy historian — or student — who falls back on "miracle" or "Providence" to explain historical events until he has exhausted all other possible explanations.

A word of description should be offered on what the authors mean by the term "Catholic Church" in the following pages. The Church is a perfect society — a society divinely established by Christ and possessed of all the means necessary to achieve its purpose. It is the Mystical Body of Christ, an entity which exists in both the natural and supernatural orders, as Pope Pius XII explained in his encyclical on *The Mystical Body of Christ*. People also talk and write — though erroneously — of "the invisible Church" in order to include not only baptized Catholics in communion with other Catholics through the sacraments and grace and united under the hierarchy, but also those persons of good will who through invincible ignorance remain "virtually" Catholic although not members of the visible Church.

The visible Catholic Church is a body consisting of members of the hierarchy, the priests who perform their duties under the hierarchy, and the lay faithful organized in dioceses and in communion with Rome. This visible Church has its organization and its institutions, a creed, a code, and a cult to which the faithful subscribe — no matter how much individuals may fall short of adhering to them. It is this visible Church which we treat in the following pages. The Church as such, we shall see, is a spotless institution, but its members are subject to the weaknesses of human nature and the student should therefore not be scandalized to find leaders in the Church making very human judgments and very human mistakes. Nor should he be scandalized to find the visible Church weak and weary at certain times in history, for when Christ breathed on His Apostles and said to them: "Receive ye the Holy Spirit" He did not relieve them of their responsibility and their burden of directing the Church's activity and promoting its mission on earth. That burden and that responsibility have devolved upon their successors and, in less measure, on all Catholics. Their failures in the past are personal failures of individual men or groups of men, not the failure of the Mystical Body of Christ. The following pages, we hope, will bear out the validity of this distinction which we think it advisable to offer to the student before he begins to follow the intensely interesting story of the history of the Catholic Church in its earthly setting.

The suggested readings at the end of each chapter are those which the authors believe students will find both profitable and interesting. Only works in English are listed in these reading lists. A list of more scholarly works in the various Western languages is included in the bibliography at the end of this study. It is sincerely hoped that a fairly large proportion of students reading this short survey of the history of the Catholic Church will be encouraged to read some of the longer and more scholarly works on which it is based.

Some difference in the nature of the Review Aids in Parts I and II will be noted. The questions in Part I can be answered from the text itself. In Part II, however, the student has grown familiar with the subject, and is expected to use material supplementary to the textbook to work out various projects that will increase his mastery of Church history.

ACKNOWLEDGMENT

M ANY friends and associates have contributed to this volume either by their assistance, their counsel, or their generous encouragement. To all of these, the authors extend their sincere thanks. They wish to single out especially Father Florian Guest, O.F.M., of the Old Mission in Santa Barbara, California, and Professor Daniel McGarry of St. Louis University, who have read and ably criticized parts of the manuscript. Mr. Thad Niemira drew up several of the charts, and Mrs. Sarah White performed the arduous task of typing sections of the copy. As indicated at various places in the text, several publishers and owners of copyright material have kindly permitted the use of miscellaneous quotations: Burns, Oates and Washbourne, B. Herder Book Co., Sheed and Ward, The Westminster Press, Professor Leona C. Gabel and Reverend Joseph C. Plumpe. Mr. Aloysius Croft of the editorial staff of The Bruce Publishing Company deserves the gratitude of not one, but two dilatory authors.

T. P. N.
R. H. S.

Feast of St. Raymond of Penafort, 1957

CONTENTS

P A R T   O N E

SECTION I

Christianity Conquers the Graeco-Roman World

SECTION II

Five Centuries of Peril

PART TWO

SECTION V

The Protestant Revolt and Catholic Reform

SECTION VIII

The Contemporary Church

List of Maps

HISTORY OF THE CATHOLIC CHURCH

PART ONE

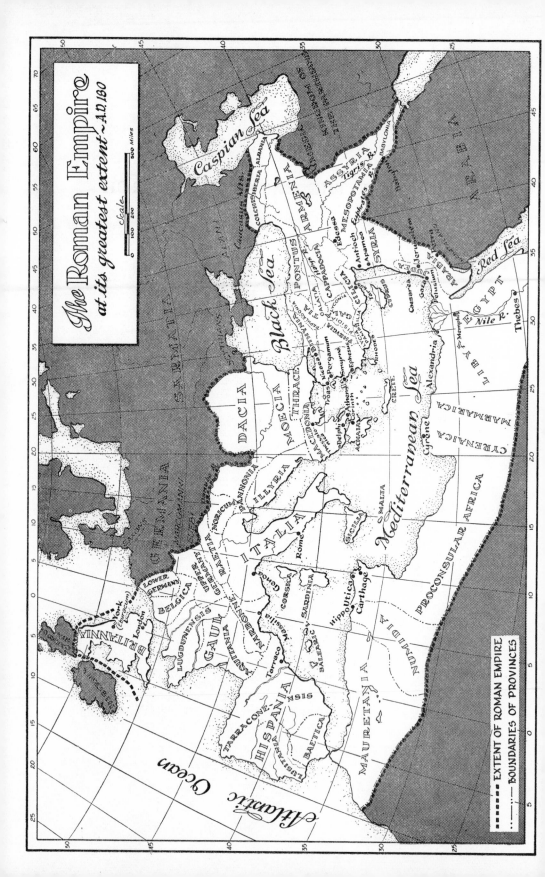

The Roman Empire
at its greatest extent ~ A.D. 180

Scale
0 100 200   500 Miles

EXTENT OF ROMAN EMPIRE
BOUNDARIES OF PROVINCES

CHRISTIANITY CONQUERS
THE GRAECO-ROMAN WORLD

Chapter 1

JESUS AND THE WORLD
AT HIS BIRTH

H OW long mankind has lived upon the earth no one can say with certainty. Historical records extend scarcely sixty centuries into the past, but other types of evidence go much beyond that. Yet only two thousand years ago, after the passing of countless generations, "The Word was made flesh and dwelt among us," and human history received suddenly an entirely new orientation. When he considers this sequence of events, the student of history instinctively asks himself certain questions. Why did the Son of God select this particular moment to come incarnate into the world? What was the world like at the time of His birth? What was the relationship between His life and message and the religious experiences of His contemporaries?

Three Preparations. St. Paul suggested answers to some of these questions when he wrote that the Saviour came "in the fullness of the times." By this concept Paul and the early Christian historians who followed him meant that all history prior to the Incarnation was merely God's plan of preparation for the birth of His Son, which occurred, therefore, when the most fitting human circumstances prevailed. St. Paul's theory does not intend to imply that the world was eager to

3

hail the truth of the Gospel the moment Jesus began to preach. It asserts only that the environment within which Jesus lived contained certain elements, positive as well as negative, which seemed propitious for the foundation and spread of Christianity.

Like concentric circles three cultural spheres impinged upon the life of Jesus, growing in intensity as their geographical area diminished. These were the Roman, the Greek — more exactly, Hellenistic — and the Jewish worlds, representing respectively political, intellectual, and religious factors. In an environment compounded of these elements Jesus preached His Gospel and organized His Church. The visible manifestations of His labors revealed the effect of these conditioning circumstances, as did the attitude of the Apostles and first converts. Although Christianity was meant for all men everywhere, it was greatly influenced by and indeed still shows traces of the milieu in which it arose.

The Roman Empire.   From Syria to the Atlantic, from the English Channel and the Danube to the sands of the Sahara the Western world acknowledged the rule of Rome. Subdivisions existed within the framework of the Empire, permitting vigorous local political life, yet so far as the people of the Mediterranean basin were concerned, Rome was the universal state to which all were subject. Christ Himself and the Apostles owed allegiance to it; St. Paul went so far as to say: "The powers that be are ordained of God." The unity and organization of the Roman Empire, the facility of communication it afforded, and the peace and protection it offered made it truly the "fatherland of Christianity." Even the Roman name and capital city were permanently borrowed by the Catholic Church.

The enduring organization of this Empire was taking shape in the very generation in which Christ was born. A century of social turmoil and civil war ended with the victory of Octavian, known as Augustus, at Actium in 31 B.C. From the point of disintegration he rescued the Roman world, skillfully giving it the government that held it together for the next five centuries. Augustus also inaugurated the *Pax Romana*, that period from his day to about A.D. 180 in which the civilized European world enjoyed its longest period of domestic peace and a high level of prosperity as well. Yet, millions of its inhabitants subsisted in misery. No one raised his voice against the institution of slavery; common freemen suffered at the will of the mighty; brutality was commonplace. Degrading amusements pandered to an already degraded public taste. Charity and a sense of social obligation seemed almost nonexistent.

Hellenism. While Rome held political sway over the Mediterranean, Greece dominated in the intellectual sphere. Yet it was not pure Greek culture but rather an admixture of Greek and Oriental influences that made up the phenomenon called Hellenism.

As a result of Alexander the Great's conquest of the near-eastern states (336–323 B.C.), a veneer of Greek civilization overlaid the indigenous cultures of Egypt, Palestine, Syria, and Asia Minor. The ruling and commercial aristocracy in these areas was often Greek by birth, the Greek language was spoken by all educated men, and Greek ideas and ideals found general acceptance. This was natural, since Greece had produced a civilization higher than anything the ancient world had yet seen. The lower classes, however, usually clung passively to the old ways and resisted Hellenization. The result was not really a fusion of Greek and non-Greek elements, but rather a watering down of Attic civilization through an unconscious adjustment to its new environment.

Rome, too, fell under the spell as soon as it came into contact with Greek settlements in southern Italy and especially after it conquered the East. Being practical men, the Romans recognized the cultural superiority of Greece and proceeded to reshape their society along Greek lines. Looted Greek art adorned Roman homes, Greek slaves tutored their captors' children, and voluntary immigration from the East swelled Rome's cosmopolitan population. Cicero went to Rhodes and Athens for his "university" education, and Vergil and Horace imitated Homer and the Attic poets.

Hellenism was not important except in a negative sense in the immediate life of Jesus. He assiduously avoided contact with Hellenized Jews, and He refrained even from entering the Hellenistic cities in Palestine. Judaism, however, had already been infiltrated by Hellenism; even the Old Testament had been translated into Greek — the Septuagint. Christianity, even before it left its Palestinian cradle, came into contact with Hellenism, and quickly worked out a symbiosis with it. Three of the Gospels, all the Epistles, and other early Christian writings were composed in the vernacular Greek. Systematic Christian theology grew out of the environment of Hellenism. For two hundred years the Church was, in its intellectual life, more Greek than Latin. The universal Empire permitted and the universal Hellenistic culture facilitated the expansion and elaboration of the Christian universal Church.

Religion in the Graeco-Roman World. Religion occupied a vital place in the lives and politics of all inhabitants of the ancient world, but at the time of the birth of Christ the religious condition of the Roman

Empire was far from healthy. Four tendencies can be distinguished: (1) a decline in respect for the old paganism; (2) syncretism, or the fusion of all the pagan religions into an amorphous, all-inclusive unity; (3) attempts to discover substitutes for the decadent cults; (4) the growth of the cults of the state and of the emperor.

Early Roman religion, basically animistic, had contributed to the strength of the State, and had in turn been officially supported and fostered by it. Contact with the more sophisticated Greek religious concepts inaugurated the development of anthropomorphism and idolatry. Henceforth the Romans like the Greeks regarded their gods as merely glorified human beings, subject to all passions and vices that beset mankind. These gods were venerated by certain ritualistic ceremonies which, it was thought, produced the desired divine reaction. Religion was a contractual matter, an affair of prudence rather than of faith or sublime aspiration. There was no connection between morality and religion. Immortality of sorts found general acceptance, but the afterworld was a gloomy, dark, unpleasant habitation for both the good and the wicked. Happiness and pleasure had to be acquired in this world; the next had none to offer.

As the Romans pushed out of Italy and into surrounding lands, they imitated the example of the Hellenistic East in identifying the deities of the states they conquered with their own gods. In this way the highest Roman gods could be adopted by the foreigners, and the foreign gods could be assimilated into the Roman pantheon with no violation of pagan sensibilities. Only when foreign religions became nuclei for anti-Roman patriotism or advocated antisocial practices did the Romans suppress them. This syncretism reached its climax in the early third century when Alexander Severus introduced images of Abraham and Christ into his extensive divine circle. A vague trend toward monotheism is sometimes seen here, with the supreme sun-god absorbing all other gods.

In syncretism lay one reason for Rome's toleration in matters of religion. Indifference, however, seems a better word, for by the time of Augustus the old vitality was fast disappearing from the Roman gods. Augustus and subsequent emperors sought to stem the tide by official decrees and financial support for the temples. They managed to maintain the form and rituals of the ancient cults, but the intrinsic limitations of Graeco-Roman paganism doomed it to further decline. But it was too closely bound up with every aspect of Roman life and politics to disappear without a mighty struggle.

From the first century B.C. efforts were made to discover substitutes that offered more satisfactory answers to religious needs not satisfied by the state cults. Among the educated there arose in consequence of the skepticism induced by moribund paganism a trend toward religious philosophy. Stoicism came first to the fore with its doctrine of natural law and brotherhood of man. Seneca, the leading Roman Stoic, echoed some of the ideas of natural virtues propounded on a higher plane by his contemporary St. Paul, for Stoicism had much to offer a noble mind. Neo-Pythagoreanism and Neo-Platonism later attracted many partisans. Much of Neo-Platonism, redirected by Christian authors, passed into the writings of St. Augustine.

Philosophy, however, held no delights for the ignorant masses, who turned instead to the private, emotional devotions known as the Orphic and Oriental cults or mystery religions. These Greek and eastern religions had penetrated Italy as early as 205 B.C.; in the first three centuries of the Christian era their expansion throughout the Empire was rapid, facilitated by the prevailing syncretism. Such cults combined emotional and sensuous elements into an attractive medley of orgiastic ritual. The Great Mother of Phrygia, the Egyptian pair Isis and Serapis, Atargatis from Syria and Mithra from Persia proved immensely popular. All had certain things in common: belief in a blessed immortality, a symbolic initiation ceremony, sacrifices, a dramatic scene, and a sacred meal.

Christianity, arising also in the East, has been compared to the mystery cults; many Romans regarded it as one of these. However, the rigid ethic and the exclusiveness of the Christian creed had no counterpart in the pagan cults. The analogy is essentially false. Nevertheless, Christianity did borrow terminology and liturgical and organizational features from the mysteries. Celebration of Christmas on the date of the Mithraic feast of the birth of the sun-god is perhaps the most often cited example of this tendency. Christianity, in turn, probably exerted more than a little influence on the mysteries.

Because of its tremendous importance for future Christianity, mention must be made of the imperial cult of Rome and Augustus. In the Hellenistic kingdoms, the custom of deifying rulers served as the theoretical basis of the despotic royal power. After Rome displaced these Hellenistic kings, their former honors were transferred by the people to the new Roman governors and to the goddess Rome as the personification of the Roman State. Emperor Augustus and his successors fostered this veneration because of its political value and as a bond of unity throughout the vast and heterogeneous Empire.

Soon the imperial cult was transplanted to the West. Throughout the

European provinces it found great popularity. About 12 B.C. altars to Rome and Augustus appeared at Lyons and Cologne. Emperor worship did not easily take root at Rome itself; there, the closest approach at first was apotheosis by decree of the Senate after the emperor's death, provided the senators had no grudge against their late master. But worship was rendered to the "genius" of the living emperor. Although adoration of the sovereign and the State was chiefly a political matter, somewhat comparable to saluting the flag, it nevertheless assumed a genuine religious significance for most Romans and thus constituted a major obstacle for Christianity.

Judaism. The third proximate and positive ethical preparation for the Gospels lay in Judaism. This was the ideological and religious source for Christianity, much of which was either explicitly expressed or foreshadowed in the Old Testament. Jesus, Himself a Jew, passed His entire life in an almost exclusively Jewish environment. When the Apostles spread the Gospel beyond the confines of Palestine, Jewish communities scattered throughout the Empire provided the bridge by which contact might be made with the Gentiles. Both Palestinian Judaism and that of the Dispersion must be understood for a proper knowledge of primitive Christianity.

Inextricable confusion of religion and politics characterized the history of the Israelites. For them, existence as a distinct race and state went hand in hand with preservation of the ethical monotheism with which the chosen race had been endowed by God. A threat to the one represented a threat to the other. Patriotism assumed the guise of religious virtue, while the Messias came to be conceived in terms of a national political hero.

The Political Scene in Palestine.   So small a race in such a strategic location could not escape political adversity, which in turn served to purify and crystallize Hebrew religious concepts. Such had been a beneficial effect of the Babylonian captivity. Alexander the Great brought the re-established Jewish state into his empire, but after his death in 323 Egypt and then Syria governed Palestine. In these years the rising tide of Hellenism threatened to submerge Judaism; the Palestinian aristocracy adopted Greek names and the Greek language. King Antiochus Epiphanes even attempted to place a statue of Zeus in the Temple at Jerusalem as part of his Hellenization program. This extreme action provoked the rebellion of the Machabees (165 B.C.). With help from Rome the rebels succeeded, and from 142 to 63 B.C. Judea enjoyed autonomy under its own kings of the Machabean family. An unfortunate dispute led to intervention by the Roman general Pompey in 63 B.C.; his advent marked the beginning of the end of Jewish independence. All the bloody strife that engulfed the Empire until Augustus' victory caught the Jews in its backwash and brought a new and foreign dynasty to the throne in Judea.

Herod of Idumea (40–4 B.C.), a harsh tyrant guilty of the murder of his wife and six of his own sons, reigned at the time of Jesus' birth. His schemes for the material welfare of his state rather than his brutality represented the real threat to Judaism, for he was an avid Hellenist bent on spreading this superior yet pagan culture throughout his realm. Materially Herod did much for his kingdom, even rebuilding the Temple in Jerusalem on a lavish scale. But he represented an alien culture suspect to his conservative subjects who, therefore, distrusted him.

Archelaus, Philip, and Herod Antipas divided Palestine on their father's death. The Jews, however, appealed to Augustus to free them from the hated Herodian dynasty. While the brothers journeyed to Rome to defend themselves, all Palestine erupted in rebellion. Varus, the legate governing Syria, came down and ravaged the land, quashing the revolt by crucifying the leader, Judas of Galilee, and 2000 of the insurgents. Eventually Augustus deposed Archelaus and decided that Judea should be ruled by procurators sent out from Rome (Pontius Pilate, A.D. 26–36, is the best known) with headquarters in Caesarea on the coast. Galilee was allotted to Herod Antipas as tetrarch, who ruled until A.D. 39, while his brother Philip governed Iturea and Trachonitis. Discord continued nevertheless in the form of riots of Jews and Hellenists against each other. The great rebellion of A.D. 66 marked the climax, but instead of winning their coveted independence the Jews only brought the full wrath of Rome upon themselves. After a four year struggle Jerusalem fell to Titus, who leveled it to the ground and scattered its populace.

The turmoil in Palestine during Christ's lifetime defies description. The Gospels pass over most of it in silence. A modern Jewish historian has found scarcely a year between 67 B.C. and A.D. 39 unmarred by bloodshed; at least 200,000 Jews perished by violence in those years. Galilee, where Jesus lived and taught, was always restless, always eager to salute a new upstart as the Messias.

Jewish Monotheism. Behind all this ferment lay the Jews' fear of corruption of their faith through contact with Gentiles. Syncretism meant ruin, emperor worship was idolatry, and Hellenism entailed defilement. Special privileges from the Roman government were intended to afford them protection, but the complete fusion of religion with the whole life of the Jewish community complicated their status beyond even the vaunted Roman genius for government.

From whatever aspect it be considered, Jewish spiritual life far surpassed the puerility that their contemporaries accepted as religion. Nevertheless, obsession with the Mosaic Law often obscured the real spirituality of most of the population. The scribes constituted the group particularly dedicated to study of the Law, and the numerous, influential sect of the Pharisees embodied that study in their rigorous code of conduct. For them religion entailed rigid adherence to an ever multiplying set of minute regulations concerning legal purity and Sabbath observance. As Jesus frequently indicated, they replaced genuine spirituality with mere formalism that robbed religion of value. Still, not all Pharisees deserve censure; sincere, well-intentioned individuals were to be found in their ranks, of whom St. Paul is certainly the greatest. An even more extreme group were the Essenes, a monastic-like band leading an ascetic life in the wilderness near the Dead Sea.

Sharing membership with the Pharisees in the Sanhedrin, the Supreme Council, were the Sadducees, a priestly and lay aristocracy who differed socially, economically, and doctrinally from the Pharisees. These were timeservers, collaborators with the foreign conquerors, compromisers interested in preserving their privileges more than anything else. They were inclined to accept much of the secular Hellenistic culture. Their influence with the Jewish masses was small.

Special strength attached to the Messianic hope during these years of oppression. Little remained of the exalted concepts of the Messias expressed by Isaias and the prophets, for the national crises had disfigured this always vague aspiration. The Jews now thought in terms of a Son of David and king of Israel, a triumphant, conquering hero who should defeat Israel's foes and re-establish the political reign of God's chosen people on earth. In the popular mind the Messias was not divine, although his power was thought to come from the Lord. A humble, suffering Messias who should die on a cross to redeem his people for a kingdom not of this world — such an idea was farthest from their minds.

The Dispersion. Four to five million Jews lived outside Palestine. Almost every major city in the Empire had its Jewish colony, such as Alexandria, Antioch, Ephesus, Corinth, and Rome. The basic difference between the Jews of the Dispersion and those remaining in Palestine

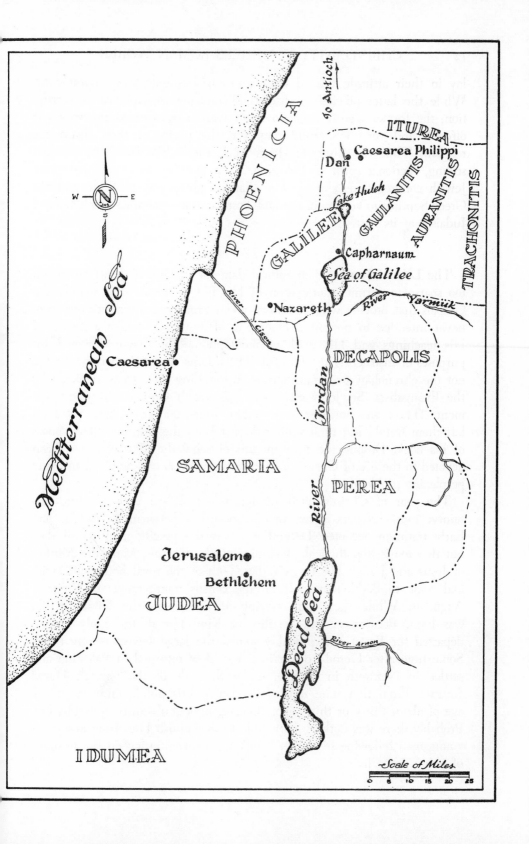

Mediterranean Sea

PHOENICIA

To Antioch

ITUREA

Caesarea Philippi
Dan

Lake Huleh

GALILEE

GAULANITIS

AURANITIS

TRACHONITIS

Capharnaum

Sea of Galilee

Nazareth

River Kison

River

River Yarmuk

DECAPOLIS

Caesarea

Jordan River

SAMARIA

PEREA

Jerusalem

Bethlehem

JUDEA

Dead Sea

River Arnon

IDUMEA

W N E S

Scale of Miles
0   5   10   15   20   25

lay in their attitude toward their non-Jewish intellectual environment. While the latter officially resisted Hellenization as evidence of corruption, the former readily came to terms with it, recognized the values it offered, and yet successfully preserved the purity of their distinctive religion. Thus the dispersed Jews freed themselves from the narrow, stifling, factional spirit of Palestine. Even gentile converts joined these Jewish congregations abroad. The Platonic philosophy of Philo and the Greek Septuagint version of the Old Testament are examples of Hellenized Judaism at its best.

The Life of Jesus. Biographical data for the life of Jesus are much too sparse to permit examination of His life in detail. It is mainly the Gospels that provide what is known about Him, and these writings were never intended to present a biography of Jesus but rather a record of His teachings and His work of redemption. They were designed for purposes of instructing the faithful. The lessons are the important matter, not the chronology or circumstances surrounding each scene depicted by the Evangelists. St. John concluded the fourth Gospel with the statement, "There are, however, many other things that Jesus did," yet John left them untold lest their telling detract from the spiritual effectiveness of his book. Despite the vast amount of scholarly effort that has been devoted to the life of Christ, only tentative answers can be given to many perplexing problems.

The year of Christ's birth cannot be established with absolute certainty; most scholars agree that it occurred between 8 and 4 B.C. Early tradition accepted December 25 as the precise month and day, but that too is hypothetical. According to the Gospels, Mary the Mother of Jesus and Joseph His foster father, both of the royal house of David, had come to Bethlehem to fulfill the census requirements of Emperor Augustus. While they were staying at Bethlehem the Divine Child was born. Because of the hostility of King Herod, the Holy Family departed for Egypt and probably joined the large Jewish colony there. Some time after Herod's death in 4 B.C. they returned to Palestine and settled in Nazareth in Galilee, under the rule of the tetrarch Herod Antipas. From that time until Jesus began His public ministry at the age of about thirty or thirty-five, almost complete obscurity veils His life. Probably there was nothing outwardly to distinguish Him from any other young man following his father's trade and concentrating on the business of eking out a living.

St. John the Baptist. John the Baptist's active career extended for about six months, from the autumn of A.D. 27 to the next spring. His role was that of the divinely commissioned precursor who came from the desert where he had been leading the life of a hermit to announce the imminent approach of the Messias. Accordingly, penance and preparation were the themes he dwelt on in his prophetic discourses. Large crowds flocked about him, a group of disciples joined him and enough excitement was generated to cause the Pharisees to investigate. Everyone at first mistook John for the Messias, but he quickly corrected them. When Jesus appeared before John, there was a public divine manifestation of His mission. Soon several of John's disciples transferred their allegiance to Jesus; probably six of the Twelve came to Jesus in this way. Not long thereafter Herod imprisoned and executed John, ostensibly for personal motives, but perhaps from fear of possible political repercussions of the Baptist's messianic prognostications. From then on Jesus occupied the center of the stage.

Jesus' Ministry. Four different, but of course inseparable, aspects of Jesus' work can be distinguished: (1) He preached a new, higher concept of religion and morality to replace the sterile formalism of the Pharisees; (2) He announced the Kingdom of Heaven which was to be the reward for those who accepted His teachings; (3) He organized the Church as the visible society of the faithful under the guidance of especially trained Apostles, with Peter holding the primacy, in whom He vested all the authority requisite for their task; (4) He established the fact of His own divinity and explained His relationship to each of these — to the Church, to the Kingdom, and to the religion He propounded.

Vague outlines of a definite scheme by which this program was to be achieved can be traced in the gospel narratives. Throughout His ministry Jesus preached only to the Jews. Whenever possible He avoided contact with Gentiles, although this could not always be done. Only after the Resurrection did Jesus specifically instruct the Apostles to "teach all nations"; hitherto He had just as specifically cautioned them to avoid the Gentiles. His original plan logically called for the conquest of Israel first, then, through the Jews, the conversion of the pagans, for Christianity was eventually intended for wider horizons than Palestine. As both the national and the religious capital of Judaism, Jerusalem was the vital point. Whatever should be the reaction of Jerusalem to Jesus would be decisive. Hence Jesus made His initial concerted effort there, and despite rebuff He returned again and again. When this plan failed, when it became clear that official Judaism rejected Him, Jesus adopted an alternate scheme: concentration on a faithful elite, the Apostles and disciples, who would constitute the core and hierarchy of the Church for the proselytizing of the entire world, Judea being abandoned to its fate.

Jesus went to Jerusalem for the Pasch of A.D. 28, several months after His baptism, for His first attempt to convert the capital. At this time probably occurred the incident of the expulsion of the merchants from the Temple — a clear expression of the note of authority so evident in all of Jesus' words and deeds. Except for the conversion of Nicodemus and perhaps a few other timid souls, only opposition showed itself.

After a month Jesus returned to Galilee, where He remained nearly a year. The shore of the Sea of Galilee, especially the town of Capharnaum on its northern side, was the location for many of the best-known incidents related in the Gospels. The Sermon on the Mount sums up what Jesus tried to develop in His audience: deep, interior spirituality that could not be daunted by the unpleasant material circumstances of life. Love of God and of neighbor recurred as constant themes, and miracles accompanied every lesson.

When it seemed that the minds and hearts of His hearers had been sufficiently prepared, Jesus turned to the discussion of the reward for the good life — the Kingdom of Heaven. Being aware of the Jews' natural tendency to interpret everything He said in a materialistic sense, Jesus adopted the parable form of discourse to present this idea. Even so, His followers misunderstood. They wanted to proclaim Him king at once and restore the independence of Israel by revolution under His leadership. The memory of the 2000 insurgents whom Varus had crucified for a similar revolt twenty-five years before must have been still in their minds, but so compelling were Jesus' words and miracles that they were swept away with renewed enthusiasm. If Jesus was the Messias, He had to fit their concept of the messianic role. Their disillusionment was proportionately great when Jesus fled to avoid the dubious honor they wanted to bestow. The crisis in the Galilean ministry came with the sermon on the Bread of Life. This was entirely beyond His audience's comprehension, as St. John records: "After this many of his disciples went back and walked no more with him."

Opposition. Jesus encountered hostility or indifference from various sources. Among the common people it came from those who could not or would not grasp the true nature of His religion, or who were disappointed when Jesus would not fall in with their nationalistic aspirations. His immediate neighbors rejected Him because they knew Him too well; having lived with Him for thirty years in the ordinary routine of life, they concluded that He suddenly had become insane or suffered hallucinations when He began His preaching. To the Scribes and Pharisees Jesus was a fomenter of discord. He attacked them, the recognized authorities, and ridiculed their interpretation of the Law; they replied with hostility. The Sadducees opposed anyone less conservative than themselves, for a threat to the established order was a threat to their power and wealth. Herod too made Galilee unsafe, for he saw in Jesus the ghost of John the Baptist whom he had slain.

The Apostles. From beginning to end Jesus was accompanied by a small core of followers who shared the prejudices and experiences of their countrymen, but who, because of their better preparation, their deeper, more generous faith, received special attention from the Master and hence were able to overcome these obstacles. About seventy of these, although there doubtless were more who feared to disclose themselves, were called disciples. Twelve hand-picked intimate associates made up the inner circle of the Apostles.

Special importance attached to the Apostles, for they constituted the visible structure of the infant Church established by Christ to preserve and spread the Gospels after His own departure. Jesus carefully explained the parables to them when others were left in the dark; they were present at the most solemn moments of His life; Jesus sent them on special missions. At the Last Supper He empowered them to consecrate bread and wine. Always, too, Simon Peter played the leading role. His name heads each of the four complete lists of their names in the New Testament. At Caesarea Philippi he was the spokesman who professed the belief that Jesus was the divine Messias. On him Jesus bestowed the keys and the power of binding and loosing. Although the Church was to consist of all the faithful united in Christ, it was also given a visible form and an hierarchical order as an organized society presided over by the Apostles and resting in a peculiar fashion on Peter.

The Passion and Resurrection. Jesus passed most of His last year in the south in renewed attempts to win the allegiance of Jerusalem. The Evangelist John chronicled this period, and his record especially shows the theological character of the discourses here. The rustic, naïve atmosphere of Galilee has been left behind; Jesus deals now with the shrewd experts in the Law, men qualified to receive such difficult matters as the connection between Himself and the patriarchs and His claims to be the Son of God. But the opposition could not be overcome. Events moved inexorably toward Calvary.

The precise charge on which the Sanhedrin found Jesus worthy of death was the central issue of His work: His claim to be the Messias and the Son of God. To the Pharisees and Sadducees, this was blasphemy, a crime meriting death under their Jewish Law. Since the Roman conquest the Sanhedrin no longer had power of life and death; capital punishment could come only from the civil government. This is the point where Pontius Pilate entered the story. Finding no violation of Roman law, yet fearing the consequences of frustrating the aroused leaders of the ever factious Jews, the hapless procurator tried every expedient to avoid condemning an innocent man. In the end he yielded and sentenced Jesus to the cross as a political revolutionary, although the Jews accepted full responsibility for his decision.

"If Christ be not risen again, your faith is vain." In these words St. Paul described the significance of the Resurrection. Indeed, it is impossible to exaggerate the importance of this miracle, for it proved beyond doubt that Jesus really was the Divine Being He had claimed to be. The care with which the Evangelists depicted the incidents between the Resurrection and Ascension indicates that they recognized how necessary it was to establish this miracle beyond dispute. Incalculable too was the effect of the Resurrection on the Apostles. Despite Christ's predictions, His sudden, horrible death took them completely by surprise. Their whole world collapsed about them, "for as yet they did not understand the Scriptures, that he must rise from the dead." Easter restored hope and raised faith to new heights. Events moved rapidly. A few decisive instructions, the commission to preach to the whole world, and Jesus was gone.

REVIEW AIDS

1. What is meant by St. Paul's expression, "Fullness of the times"?
2. Describe the Roman Empire at the time of Christ's birth.
3. Explain Hellenism.
4. Show how the political and religious condition of the Jewish race influenced the Messianic expectation.
5. Describe the religious condition of the people of the Roman Empire.
6. Explain: syncretism, the imperial cult, religious philosophy.
7. Indicate the difference between Jesus' preaching in Galilee and at Jerusalem.

8. How do you account for Jesus' failure to persuade the Jews to accept His teachings?
9. What function did the disciples and Apostles perform?
10. Why is the Resurrection so important for the history of Christianity?

SUGGESTIONS FOR FURTHER READING

An excellent, brief treatment of all the material in this chapter can be found in Jules Lebreton and Jacques Zeiller, *The History of the Primitive Church*, translated by E. Messenger (New York: 1949), Vol. I, Introduction and Chapter I. On paganism see the two volumes by F. Cumont, *Astrology and Religion among the Greeks and Romans* (New York: 1912), and *Oriental Religions in Roman Paganism* (Chicago: 1911); also H. I. Bell's interesting *Cults and Creeds in Graeco-Roman Egypt* (New York: 1953), and H. J. Rose, *Ancient Roman Religion* (London: n.d.). Excellent for the Jewish background is Giuseppe Ricciotti, *The History of Israel*, trans. by C. Della Penta and R. Murphy, 2 vols. (Milwaukee: 1955). Stewart Perowne, *The Later Herods* (London: 1958) depicts the political background of the New Testament. One of the better concise books on its subject is Jean Daniélou, *The Dead Sea Scrolls and Primitive Christianity* (Baltimore: 1958). Biographies of Christ are numerous, but they are not always good history. The three following are the best in English: Ferdinand Prat, *Jesus Christ, His Life, His Teaching, and His Work*, 2 vols. (Milwaukee: 1950); J. Lebreton, *The Life and Teaching of Jesus Christ*, 2 vols. (London: 1935); L. de Grandmaison, *Jesus Christ*, 3 vols. (London: 1930–1934).

DOCUMENTS

The Catholic Church teaches that Christ not only promulgated a new religion but that He also established a visible Church, under the guidance of the Apostles and their successors, with Peter and his successors holding the primacy, as His representatives on earth, in order to preserve His message intact. The following three selections from the New Testament, the Confraternity edition, are among the most important passages for showing that this was done and hence for proving the divine origin of the power of the Apostles and their successors, the pope and the other bishops.

Peter's Confession. Mt. 16:13–20.

Now Jesus, having come into the district of Caesarea Philippi, began to ask his disciples, saying, "Who do men say the Son of Man is?" But they said, "Some say, John the Baptist; and others, Elias; and others, Jeremias, or one of the prophets." He said to them, "But who do you say that I am?" Simon Peter answered and said, "Thou art the Christ, the Son of the living God." Then Jesus answered and said, "Blessed art thou, Simon Bar-Jona, for flesh and blood has not revealed this to thee, but my Father in heaven. And I say to thee, thou art Peter, and upon this rock I will build my Church, and the gates of hell shall not prevail against it. And I will give thee the keys of the kingdom of heaven; and whatever thou shalt bind on earth shall be bound in heaven, and whatever thou shalt loose on earth shall be loosed in heaven." Then he strictly charged his disciples to tell no one that he was Jesus the Christ.

Commission of the Apostles. Mt. 28:15–17.

But the eleven disciples went into Galilee, to the mountain where Jesus had directed them to go. And when they saw him they worshipped him; but some doubted. And Jesus drew near and spoke to them saying, "All power in heaven and on earth has been given to me. Go, therefore, and make disciples of all nations, baptizing them in the name of the Father, and of the Son, and of the Holy Spirit, teaching them to observe all that I have commanded you; and behold, I am with you all days, even unto the consummation of the world."

The Primacy of Peter. Jn. 21:15–17.

When, therefore, they had breakfasted, Jesus said to Simon Peter, "Simon, son of John, dost thou love me more than these do?" He said to him, "Yes, Lord, thou knowest that I love thee." He said to him, "Feed my lambs." He said to him a second time, "Simon, son of John, dost thou love me?" He said to him, "Yes, Lord, thou knowest that I love thee." He said to him, "Feed my lambs." A third time he said to him, "Simon, son of John, dost thou love me?" Peter was grieved because he said to him for the third time, "Dost thou love me?" And he said to him, "Lord, thou knowest all things, thou knowest that I love thee." He said to him, "Feed my sheep."

Chapter 2

JUDAIZERS AND THE PROBLEM
OF CATHOLICITY

THE Church in the Apostolic Age was a missionary Church. The chief concern of the Twelve was to spread the Faith as widely as possible, among Jews and Gentiles alike. St. Paul, the thirteenth Apostle, achieved spectacular success in this endeavor, but Peter, James, John, and the others performed important if often more obscure tasks. Expansion brought problems, of which the most pressing was the relationship of Jesus' teachings to the Jewish religion which He and His followers had professed. When Gentile converts joined the growing numbers of the faithful, this matter grew serious and occasioned troublesome disputes. A further complication arose when the indifferent attitude of the Jewish authorities toward Christianity changed into active hostility. Gradually, too, the visible organization of the Church was taking definite form.

Pentecost. Obedient to the Master's command, the Apostles returned to Jerusalem after His Ascension to await the coming of the Holy Spirit. Timid and fearful, they assembled together with Mary and over one hundred of the disciples, not knowing what to expect, yet waiting prayerfully and patiently. During these days St. Matthias was designated to fill the vacancy in the Apostolic ranks created by the defection of Judas. On the tenth day of their vigil, the Feast of Pentecost, the Holy Spirit suddenly came upon them amid remarkable visible signs and with even more remarkable spiritual effects. From this time on the Apostles were transformed into fearless, zealous champions filled with an irresistible compulsion to preach what they had seen and been taught by Christ. A complete psychological transformation took place on that Pentecost.

Pentecost being an important Jewish holiday, pilgrims from the Jewish communities of all the eastern provinces of the Empire were in Jerusalem. Attracted by the commotion, a crowd of these visitors hurried to the house where the Apostles were staying. Peter, having received with the rest the gift of tongues, boldly went out to preach his first sermon. About 3000 of his hearers believed and accepted baptism.

For six years the number of believers increased gradually and without incident. All the Apostles apparently remained in Jerusalem. On occasion they addressed public audiences, but much of their proselytizing was carried on in private homes and through personal contact. The *Acts of the Apostles* tell us what little is known of these years.

Since all members of the Church still belonged to the Jewish race, they continued the practices demanded by their national religion such as attendance at the Temple and observance of the Sabbath. In the privacy of their own homes, however, they supplemented these practices with ceremonies that were peculiarly Christian in character — the "breaking of bread" and the Eucharistic feast. Their voluntary poverty and community ownership of property reflected the high degree of charity among them, but it likewise provoked a domestic crisis. Probably the natives of Jerusalem exercised a certain dominance, for soon the Greek-speaking Jews were complaining of not receiving their just share from the common resources. To remedy this seven deacons were appointed to supervise the daily distributions. But as far as any outsider could perceive, the Christians were merely another sect, devout, slightly different, but still faithful Jews.

Opposition at Jerusalem. A second mass conversion resulting from a startling miracle and a speech by Peter within the Temple itself attracted the attention of the priests and Sadducees. Peter and John were arrested, miraculously released, re-arrested and questioned. The officials then forbade further preaching in the name of Jesus but did not harm the Apostles. Since these very officials had been responsible for Jesus' death, and since, moreover, the Sadducees denied the possibility of resurrection after death for anyone, they found reason to object to the Apostles' work. Undaunted, the Apostles persisted in their preaching, whereupon they were all arrested and scourged.

The final break between the Christian community and the Sanhedrin came from the activity of the deacon Stephen. He was a Hellenist, a Greek-speaking Jew, not a native of Palestine. He preached with considerably less restraint than the rest and provoked violent controversy among his audience. When the Sanhedrin looked into the matter, Stephen openly upbraided them and provoked their wrath. An infuriated mob hurried him outside the city and stoned him to death. After Stephen's martyrdom, about A.D. 36, a general wave of persecution began and continued intermittently for eight years.

An immediate result of overt hostility was the dispersal of the community of the "saints." Although the Apostles remained in Jerusalem, most of the Greek-speaking converts at least scattered throughout Judea, Samaria, Phoenicia, and even into Syria. Wherever they went new Christian communities sprang up. A particularly strong congregation arose in Syria in the great metropolis of Antioch. Not only were converts won from among the Jews there but also from the non-Jewish pagan population. Here can be seen the beginning of the separation of the followers of Christ from Judaism. At Antioch the term "Christian" first came into use. To govern the Antiochene Church, the Apostles dispatched Barnabas from Jerusalem and some time later Peter himself went there. Tradition reckons Peter as first bishop of Antioch, a position he presumably held before going on to Rome.

Conversion of St. Paul. Another significant result of the persecution at Jerusalem was the winning of St. Paul to the Church. Born in the Jewish community at Tarsus in Cilicia, a Roman citizen, speaking Greek and conversant with Hellenistic civilization, educated by the rabbi Gamaliel in Jerusalem and hence a Pharisee, Paul (originally called Saul) linked together in his person all the cultural currents of the eastern world. By temperament and training he was a zealot, proud of his race, burning to serve his God. When it seemed that the followers of Jesus were traitors to Judaism, Paul turned on them with his whole being. He abetted those who murdered Stephen. "Breathing threats of slaughter against the disciples of the Lord," Paul hounded them into prison, believing all the while that he was thereby glorifying God.

But the turning point in Paul's life was not far off. As he traveled from Jerusalem to Damascus in pursuit of fleeing Christians, the risen and glorified Christ appeared to him in a vision and informed him of his error. Three days later, in Damascus, he received baptism at the hands of a frightened Christian acting on instructions from the Lord. Paul's conversion probably occurred in the same year as Stephen's death, i.e., A.D. 36.

After a retreat of two years in the desert, Paul returned to Damascus. As eagerly as he had formerly persecuted Christians, he now threw himself into missionary work. Opposition of the Jews and of the city's governor forced him to abandon Damascus. Back in Jerusalem again Paul had difficulty convincing the Apostles of the sincerity of his conversion. Through Barnabas' mediation Peter and James finally consented to receive him. When Paul spoke publicly in favor of Christianity, he fell into arguments just as Stephen had. Threatened with Stephen's fate, Paul departed and went into retirement in Tarsus. Here he remained for several years until Barnabas summoned him to Antioch to aid in administering the Church under the latter's care.

Missions of St. Peter. During this time the growth of the Church in Judea continued slowly yet steadily. The *Acts* tell of Philip the deacon's miracles and conversions in Samaria, and of the visit of Peter and John to this region to lay hands on the converts and give them the Holy Spirit. On the road toward Gaza, Jerusalem's seaport, Philip baptized the servant of the Ethiopian queen and then visited all the cities along the coast. Peter's presence in Lydda, Sharon, Joppa, and Caesarea is also known.

An incident of great significance occurred in Caesarea when Peter baptized the Roman centurion Cornelius, the first clear case of an individual Gentile being received into the Church. The chronology of these early years is obscure; hence it is impossible to date the event precisely. Whether the recorded acceptance of pagans into the Church at Antioch preceded or followed Cornelius' baptism, the fact that the *Acts* emphasize the latter so heavily indicates that it was something very much out of the ordinary.

Cornelius was an uncircumcised proselyte to Judaism, commander of the Roman cohort at Caesarea. In a vision an angel directed him to send to Joppa nearby to summon a certain Simon Peter. In Joppa Peter too received a vision indicating to him by implication that he might disregard the Mosaic Law and associate with Gentiles without fear of contamination. When Cornelius' messengers arrived, Peter accompanied them to Caesarea, entered the centurion's home, and spoke with him about Christ. While they conversed the Holy Spirit descended on them, so Peter set aside whatever hesitation he still felt and baptized Cornelius.

As soon as Peter returned to Jerusalem the disciples chided him for what he had done, for the report of his unusual actions had preceded him. Peter explained the entire incident, and his story was corroborated by witnesses from Joppa. This placated the Jewish Christians and the matter was dropped.

Paul's First Journey. It was not Peter but rather Paul who was destined to be known as the Apostle of the Gentiles. On his last visit to Jerusalem Paul had received a divine command to convert the pagan. At Antioch he worked with Gentiles but he envisaged wider fields. About A.D. 45 Paul embarked on the first of his great missionary journeys. Accompanied by Barnabas and young Mark the future Evangelist, he sailed for Cyprus, Barnabas' birthplace. After converting the Proconsul Sergius Paulus, the trio headed for the southern coast of Asia Minor. Barnabas and Paul evangelized numerous towns in the hinterland and along the coast. Converts from Judaism and paganism were baptized, but hostility too and often physical violence were encountered everywhere. After laboring and planting the Faith in these regions for three years, the missionaries returned to Antioch in A.D. 48.

Persecution of King Herod Agrippa I. With the accession of Agrippa as king of the briefly reconstituted Kingdom of Judea (A.D. 41–44), the persecution in Jerusalem flared up anew. This grandson of Herod the Great, after a strange career in Rome, was sent out by Emperor Claudius to govern the Jews. Anxious to win the affection of his subjects, Agrippa rigidly fulfilled the rites of Judaism and treated the Jews as brothers. To confirm his sincerity the king revived the oppression of the Christians. St. James the Great was executed. Peter too was seized and imprisoned, but an angel released him, whereupon Peter fled Jerusalem. The *Acts* do not reveal where he went. Agrippa's sudden death shortly afterward suspended the persecution. However, before peace could return to the infant Church an internal problem threatened it just as seriously as had the external repression.

The Judaizers. Jesus had come as the Messias to fulfill promises made by God to the chosen people. This was the theme the Apostles and disciples adopted whenever they addressed their fellow Jews. To those Jews who acknowledged Him, therefore, Jesus' teaching represented the perfection of their own doctrine rather than an entirely new and independent religion. In other words, one became a Christian by way of Judaism. It did not suffice merely to believe in Christ and His resurrection; the elaborate ritual of the Mosaic Law concerning circumcision, diet, and purification must also be observed. This attitude was reflected in the lives of the earliest Christians. All being Jews, they continued to frequent the Temple and conducted themselves to all appearances the same as any of their countrymen. Only in the privacy of their own homes did they celebrate the distinctive Eucharistic feast. Indeed, any other conduct would have been impossible in the confines of Jerusalem because of the national as well as religious implications of the Mosaic Law.

As the Church expanded outside of the land of Israel to the great Hellenistic city of Antioch, to the Mediterranean coast, and especially when Paul indiscriminately baptized all who accepted his message without regard for nationality, the matter of the relationship of Christianity to Judaism demanded clarification. The raised eyebrows that questioned Peter's baptism of Cornelius portended serious difficulty. Actually there were two different aspects of the problem: (1) must Jewish Christians continue to live according to the Law? (2) could Gentile converts become Christians without also accepting Judaism?

Extreme Judaizers insisted on the absolute necessity of Judaism as a prerequisite for Christianity. Yet if the Church was to be a universal institution, a Catholic Church, this opinion had to be rejected. An exceedingly great, probably insurmountable obstacle would have been placed in the way of Gentiles if they would have had to become naturalized Jewish citizens — such was the significance of circumcision — before they could become Christians. On the other hand, a schism would have resulted from recognizing two classes of Christians, the perfect who observed the Mosaic Law and the imperfect who did not. If the Jewish Christians continued in the Jewish fold, they would have been forbidden even to associate with other Christians. The only solution, then, was the total emancipation of Christianity from Judaism.

The Council of Jerusalem, A.D. 49. When Paul and Barnabas returned from southern Galatia they found the Church at Antioch in a state of turmoil because of the intervention of Judaizers from Judea insisting on the necessity of circumcision. With his broad background and his contacts with the Gentile world, Paul was ideally suited to be the spokesman for the cause of catholicity against the Judaizers. Going up to Jerusalem, he and his companions laid the matter before the Church there. In private conversations Paul convinced Peter, James, and John, the only Apostles then in the city, of the justice of his own liberal views. A general assembly with the other members of the clergy present confirmed the Apostles' decision. A public enactment was dispatched to all the communities informing them that, except for a few minor matters, the Gentiles were free of the prescriptions of the Mosaic Law.

So firmly was the national religion fixed in the hearts of the Judeo-Christians that they failed to draw from the Jerusalem Council the logical deduction that the Law no longer bound themselves also. It took a personal clash between Peter and Paul to resolve this point. Peter came to Antioch and acted equivocally, first ignoring Jewish customs and then, as if reconsidering, observing them, to the confusion of the Gentile Christians. Paul rebuked Peter openly, pointing out that "we may be justified by the faith of Christ, not by works of the law. . . ." Peter yielded and accepted Paul's catholic views entirely.

Although the Council and the incident at Antioch officially settled the issue, the Judaizers continued surreptitiously to spread their heresy for some time longer. Paul, whom they especially disliked, complains often in his epistles of these "false brethren" undermining his work by demanding more than was necessary from his converts and even attacking him personally. External forces, however, intervened, for when the Roman general Titus destroyed Jerusalem in A.D. 70 and a second Jewish War in 135 ended similarly, the Jewish nation ceased to exist and the prestige of the Judaizers disappeared accordingly.

The Judeo-Christians managed to escape destruction by migrating to Pella beyond the Jordan before the Roman assault, but they never recovered their importance in the Church. Their later history is obscure. Surviving members of Christ's family enjoyed special esteem among them as late as the third century. They had their own mutilated version of St. Matthew's gospel. Occasionally we hear of a prominent figure such as the martyr bishop St. Simeon (62–107), an uncle of Christ, but their isolation from the vital currents of Christianity doomed them to decline and to disintegration into sects. At first the name "Nazarenes" referred to the whole community, but later the term "Ebionites" came into use, although some writers used the latter to designate only an heretical sect among them. There remained among them always a group of strict Judaizers. By the end of the fifth century the Judeo-Christians disappeared. On the site of Jerusalem arose a new Hellenistic city, and its Christian population shared the life of the Gentile Church.

Factors Favoring and Impeding Expansion. Having emancipated itself from Judaism, the Church was free to spread wherever it could take hold in the gentile world. Its progress was rapid. St. Ignatius of Antioch in 110 bestowed on the Church the name Catholic, but three centuries were to elapse before it encompassed a majority of the Empire's population within its fold.

To be sure, the ultimate reason for its success was the Divine Will that Christianity overcome all adversaries. Then too the purity of its teaching and the superior moral principles of its adherents drew others to it. The void left in the minds of common people and educated classes alike by the decay of the Graeco-Roman polytheism caused them to seek new religious experiences. For some this need was supplied directly by Christianity, for others by the Oriental cults or the religious philosophies, both of which might in turn easily lead to Christianity. The privileges granted to Judaism sheltered the Church in its infancy, while strategically located Jewish colonies offered points of penetration into the Gentile world. Finally, the official Roman policy of religious toleration, although cruelly violated during persecutions, and the physical conveniences of a universal state facilitated its spread.

Various circumstances, on the other hand, tended to hamper the dissemination of Christianity. Certainly the difficulty of its sublime truths and the high standards of its ethical code discouraged many who were enthralled by the carnal aspects of paganism. The connection between the Roman State and the official cults led directly to persecution, as it had in Jerusalem when the authorities refused to allow any modification in their national religion. Christian monotheistic exclusiveness seemed like intolerance and wounded the sensibilities of the tolerant, syncretistically inclined Romans. Roman literature and educational ideals held back the educated, and the low social status of many early converts, indeed of Jesus Himself, repelled the aristocracy. So serious in fact were the impediments to the spread of Christianity that the Apologists found in the mere fact of its expansion the surest proof of its divine character.

St. Paul. First rank among the apostolic missionaries belongs to Paul. Immediately after the Apostolic Council he embarked on a second voyage to the pagans, accompanied by Silas and Timothy. Asia Minor was their destination, but after evangelizing Galatia they crossed to Macedonia in Europe and visited Philippi, Thessalonica, and Berea. Athens listened politely, even opening the Areopagus to Paul, but its sophisticated philosophers refused to believe. Eighteen fruitful months were spent in Corinth Paul's success here aroused the Jews who hailed him before Gallio, the Roman proconsul for A.D. 52, but Gallio dismissed their suit. Next spring the Apostle and his comrades returned to Antioch, but soon Paul took the road again. Ephesus on the coast of Asia Minor held him for two years; then he took a long swing through Macedonia and Greece, finally returning to Palestine after five years of travel (A.D. 53–57).

On all these journeys Paul's method followed a definite pattern. First he appeared in the synagogues and addressed the Jews; usually he won a few converts before being ejected, and these established contacts for approaching the proselytes and Gentiles, whom he found more favorable. Time and again the envy of the Jews produced disturbances so that Paul had to move on and begin anew elsewhere. Always Paul kept the incipient congregations under his personal supervision. His fourteen epistles indicate the care he took to preserve them in the Faith.

About A.D. 58 Paul went to Jerusalem. Jews from Asia recognized him in the Temple and provoked a riot leading to intervention of the Roman procurator. For two years Paul lay in prison at Caesarea before being sent to Rome for trial. At Rome he remained under house arrest from A.D. 61 to 63 when he was released unharmed. The details of his trial were not recorded. A possible journey to Spain and another visit to his communities in Asia and Greece preceded his second arrest and imprisonment in Rome. About A.D. 64 or 67 Paul fell victim to Nero's persecution.

St. Peter and the Church at Rome. Because of the survival of the Pauline Epistles and of the prominent place St. Luke assigned to his friend Paul in the *Acts,* our knowledge of the Apostle of the Gentiles is much fuller than of any other Apostles. Nevertheless, the part played by Peter in the original development of the Christian community was of capital importance. Peter was always spokesman for the rest in whatever crises occurred — at Pentecost, in the evangelization of Jerusalem, the conversion of Cornelius, and the Apostolic Council. From the middle of the century Peter's movements become obscure. He is mentioned at Antioch and Corinth. His first Epistle, written to the Christians of Asia Minor, indicates that he visited those parts. But by far the most outstanding fact of his missionary career is his work at Rome.

Who were the first Christians in Rome and when they appeared there cannot be gleaned from the surviving sources. It has been plausibly suggested that the earliest Roman Christians were among those who heard Peter's sermon at Pentecost and who returned to their home after being baptized to found the Christian community in the Empire's capital. Emperor Claudius expelled the Jews from Rome about A.D. 49; among these were two Christians whom Paul met at Corinth. Suetonius narrates the event: "He expelled from Rome the Jews who, led by Chrestus [Christ? Christians?], were the cause of continual agitations." This may signify an outburst of the Judaizing controversy as witnessed by the uncomprehending pagan historian, and if so it proves the existence of a number of Christians among the Roman Jews at an early date. When Paul was brought to Rome in A.D. 61, Christians came to greet him.

Concerning Peter at Rome, two facts are established indisputably: he was there, and he was martyred there under Nero. When he arrived, how long he sojourned there, and what he did are unknown. The tradition of a twenty-five year episcopate is unreliable, albeit possible. Valid evidence substantiating these two facts is found in Peter's first epistle, dated from "Babylon," which is interpreted to mean the "modern" sinful city, i.e., Rome. Peter's martyrdom was always associated with Paul's, and there is no doubt that the latter died at Rome. Between 90 and 110 St. Clement of Rome, Peter's third successor, and St. Ignatius of Antioch both clearly imply Peter's presence in the eternal city. St. Irenaeus, Dionysius of Corinth, St. Cyprian, Origen, and others confirm the tradition in the second and later centuries. Archaeological evidence affords additional confirmation. Excavations at the catacomb of St. Sebastian indicate it. The excavations conducted under the Church of St. Peter's in Rome since World War II have yielded, in the words of Pope Pius XII, "incontestable archaeological evidence" of Peter's burial in that place.

The Other Apostles. James the Less, "the brother of the Lord," held an eminent position in the Church at Jerusalem. He is considered its first bishop, although as long as Peter remained in Judea Peter overshadowed his colleague. James was strongly attached to the Jewish tradition; nevertheless, at the Apostolic Council he helped formulate the liberalizing decree to the Gentiles. For the Jews, however, he favored observance of the Law, perhaps seeing in that the only hope of winning converts in Jerusalem. Paradoxically, it was on a charge of having violated the Law of Moses that the high priest sentenced James to death while the Roman tribune was absent in A.D. 61 or 62. Evidently the protection of the Romans restrained the Jews from doing greater violence to the Christians.

James the Greater suffered martyrdom earlier under King Agrippa. He seems never to have left Judea at all. His brother John the Evangelist lived until about A.D. 100. John attended the Council, but he dropped from sight thereafter, not to reappear until years later in Asia Minor where he composed the Fourth Gospel, the *Apocalypse,* and the Johannine Epistles. During Domitian's persecution John was brought to Rome and then exiled to the island of Patmos. Ephesus provided the refuge where he died.

Of the other Apostles the Gospels and Epistles reveal nothing. At the end of the next century various apocryphal legends came into being to fill this gap. These accounts must be treated with caution; while not historical, they are not to be carelessly dismissed. Agrippa's persecution in A.D. 42 marked the dispersal of the Twelve. Tradition allots Scythia to Andrew, Ethiopia to Matthew, Phrygia to Philip, Edessa to Thaddeus. It cannot be proved that Bartholomew and Thomas labored in Persia or India, the generic Roman designation for the area southeast of the Empire's borders.

Forty-one specific localities are known to have been evangelized before the first century closed. Certainly there were more whose names escape the records demanded by historians. Except for those places associated with Peter, Paul, John, and several disciples, the circumstances of their evangelization are obscure. It must be supposed that Christianity was introduced into many places by the foreign pilgrims baptized by Peter on Pentecost. Thus Alexandria in Egypt, with a great Jewish colony, could scarcely have avoided contact with the Gospel at an early date. St. Mark, Peter's disciple, is said to have labored there after mid-century. Little is known of St. Luke's work after his separation from Paul. Who introduced Christianity into Africa, Gaul, or Britain? Fables such as that relating the journey of Lazarus, his sisters Mary and Martha, and Mary Magdalen to southern Gaul deserve no credence. There is no reliable evidence of Christianity in France until 177, in Africa until 180, and in Britain before 314, but in each case these dates reveal sizable communities already in existence which could not have blossomed overnight. Beyond the Roman Empire, in Armenia, Edessa, and Persia churches existed in the second century, but again the circumstances of their establishment are vague.

The Hierarchy of Jurisdiction. In the organization of the infant Church the Apostles formed a special group. They had witnessed the events of the Lord's life and death, they had close contact with Him after His resurrection, and they received special powers from Him. St. Paul called himself an Apostle by virtue of his vision of the risen Christ on his way to Damascus. Upon the death of the Apostles certain of their prerogatives which were personal died with them; those powers attaching to their office, however, they bestowed upon others before their death, so that apostolic succession soon came to be the accepted touchstone for true Catholicity.

The sources mention three orders: deacons, priests, and bishops. The deacons, or ministers of tables, appeared first as a result of the disputes concerning distribution of common property at Jerusalem. The example of St. Stephen proves that deacons preached also, and Philip was an active missionary, but basically the deacons were charged with the care of the material goods of the churches.

Besides the deacons, the two orders of priests and bishops are found exercising liturgical functions in Jerusalem and in the churches founded by Paul. Some confusion surrounds the early evolution of these orders because it took time to work out the terminology of the hierarchy. Thus St. Paul and St. Luke used the expressions "bishop" (Gk. *episcopos* — overseer) and "priest" (Gk. *presbyteros* — elder) indifferently, regardless of the function involved. These men usually served in groups or colleges, and they were chosen by vote of the congregation, although the necessary ordination was administered by one already in orders.

The clearest indication in the Epistles of the differentiation of functions between priests and bishops is Paul's appointment of Titus and Timothy whom he endowed with authority as his legates over the Greek churches and on whom he conferred power to ordain priests and deacons. In these disciples are seen the true successors of the Apostles. Gradually the custom arose of a single bishop governing each community of priests, deacons, and laity. The sparsity of information does not permit us to know exactly when this happened and how the restricted sense of the word bishop originated. The *Didache,* which provides much information on early Christian life several decades after mid first century, throws no light on the matter, nor does the epistle of St. Clement of Rome near the close of the century. Yet the epistles of St. Ignatius of Antioch about 110 clearly stress an established hierarchical constitution in the order of monarchical bishops, priests, and deacons.

To encourage the faithful and to dispose the pagans to accept Christ, the Holy Spirit endowed certain individuals with charismata, that is, extraordinary graces manifested in prophecy, miracles, tongues, and the like. Such individuals were numerous and spectacular in the infant Church, but they did not on that account possess either orders or jurisdiction. Abuses arose easily because of the subjective nature of the charismata, and they soon became rare. Another office that appeared quite early and eventually disappeared was that of deaconess, women performing duties chiefly in connection with the baptism of female catechumens. As late as the Council of Chalcedon in 451 the office still existed and was treated as an order in the East. Although it survived into the middle ages it was never favored by the West.

Summary. The Apostles built well. The zeal of the convert, closeness to the life of Christ, and the active aid of the Holy Spirit contributed to instill a flourishing life into the scattered communities. In germ at least all essential doctrines and the future organizational structure of the Catholic Church appeared during the Apostolic Age. With the Judaizing heresy overcome and a firm foundation established, the Church was well prepared to prove its mettle in the forthcoming struggle with militant paganism.

REVIEW AIDS

1. Describe the life of the Church in Jerusalem in the years after Pentecost.
2. What was the attitude of the Jewish officials at Jerusalem toward Christianity?
3. Summarize the life of St. Paul.
4. Describe the spread of the Church throughout Palestine and Syria.
5. What was the Judaizing controversy and what was its significance for the history of the Church?
6. How was the Judaizing controversy resolved?
7. What explanation can be offered for the comparatively rapid spread of Christianity?
8. Trace the known facts in the lives of the Apostles.
9. Indicate the evidence for the presence of St. Peter in Rome.
10. Show how the organization of the Church developed in the Apostolic Age.

SUGGESTIONS FOR FURTHER READING

The best brief treatment is again Jules Lebreton and Jacques Zeiller, *The History of the Primitive Church*, Vol. I, pp. 162–370. Very readable is Philip Hughes, *A History of the Church*, Vol. I (New York, 1935), pp. 52–84. A classic, more thorough work is Louis Duchesne, *Early History of the Christian Church*, Vol. I, trans. from the 4th French edition (London: 1950), chapters II–X. The second volume of Giuseppe Ricciotti's *The History of Israel* (Milwaukee: 1955) contains material pertinent to the early Church. Standard volumes on the two great Apostles are C. Fouard, *Saint Peter and the First Years of Christianity* (New York: 1892), and W. L. Knox, *St. Paul and the Church of Jerusalem* (Cambridge: 1925). For the missionary point of view, consult Joseph Schmidlin, *Catholic Mission History*, ed. Matthias Braun (Techny, Ill.: 1933), pp. 34–85. An old Protestant classic is Adolf Harnack, *The Mission and Expansion of Christianity in the First Three Centuries*, trans. and ed. by James Moffat, 2nd ed. (New York: 1908), 2 vols. A more recent Protestant survey is Kenneth Scott Latourette, *A History of the Expansion of Christianity*, Vol. I, *The First Five Centuries* (New York: 1937), Chapter III. The best recent history of St. Paul is G. Ricciotti, *Paul the Apostle* (Milwaukee: 1954). For St. Peter's presence at Rome, see J. Toynbee and J. W. Perkins, *The Shrine of St. Peter and the Vatican Excavations* (New York: 1957). E. Kirschbaum, *The Tombs of St. Peter and St. Paul* (New York: 1959) reports on fascinating excavations under St. Peter's.

DOCUMENTS

Evidence that the hierarchical organization of the Church continued to function after the death of the Apostles can be found among the very earliest Christian writings in existence. Particularly important are the letters of St. Ignatius of Antioch, ca. A.D. 110, a friend of St. John the Evangelist and for that reason a reliable witness to the structure of the Church in Apostolic and post-Apostolic times. From James A. Kleist, translator, *The Epistles of St. Clement of Rome and St. Ignatius of Antioch* (Westminster, Md.: Newman Press, 1946). Used by permission. "Ancient Christian Writers," edited by Johannes Quasten and Joseph C. Plumpe, Series, No. 1.

Ignatius of Antioch to the Smyrnaeans, p. 93.

You must all follow the lead of the bishop, as Jesus Christ followed that of the Father; follow the presbytery as you would the Apostles; reverence the deacons as you would God's commandment. Let no one do anything touching the Church, apart from the bishop. Let that celebration of the Eucharist be considered valid which is held under the bishop or anyone to whom he has committed it. Where the bishop appears, there let the people be, just as where Jesus Christ is, there is the Catholic Church. It is not permitted without authorization from the bishop either to baptize or to hold an agape; but whatever he approves is also pleasing to God. Thus everything you do will be *proof against danger and valid.*

Ignatius of Antioch to the Ephesians, p. 62.

Furthermore: the more anyone observes that a bishop is discreetly silent, the more he should stand in fear of him. Obviously, anyone whom the Master of the household puts in charge of His domestic affairs, ought to be received by us in the same spirit as He who has charged him with this duty. Plainly, then, one should look upon the bishop as upon the Lord Himself.

Chapter 3

FROM THE PERSECUTION OF CHRISTIANITY TO THE PROSCRIPTION OF PAGANISM

FOR 250 years the Church lived under threat of persecution, but there was considerable variation in the times and places of actual attempts by the Roman State to destroy it. Although legally proscribed, the Christians experienced intermittent periods of peace during which they enjoyed freedom from all but the fear of renewed animosity. Much depended on the personality and problems of the various emperors. Not all oppression emanated from the State, however; much of it arose from the common people because of bigotry or prejudice. For their own defense the Christians relied on reasoned explanations of their beliefs by the Apologists and the example of their own uprighteousness to confound the persecutor. In due time a liberator appeared in the person of Constantine, from whom a direct line extends through toleration, then equality with the pagan cults, and finally establishment of Christianity as the State religion by Theodosius at the end of the fourth century.

Causes of the Persecutions. A clash between the Roman government and Christianity was inevitable. Not only was paganism the official religion of the State, fostered, financed, and demanded by it; in addition the rapid spread of the imperial cults created a test of political loyalty that only pagans could meet. Rome maintained a traditional attitude of toleration toward the religions of the people it conquered. Its subjects might worship whatever gods they chose — provided they added the goddess Rome and the divine emperor to their circle of deities. Refusal to venerate these State gods exposed the recusant to the charge of atheism, a capital offense under Roman law, as well as to the charge of treason to the State.

Only the Jewish nation had heretofore found this prescribed worship impossible, but in its case Rome was willing to make exception because of the racial aspect of Jewish monotheism. As long as Christianity was restricted to Jewish nationals, it shared this privileged status of Judaism. When Gentiles began to enter the fold and Christianity lost its national color, it perforce surrendered the protection Judaism offered. Almost from the beginning official Judaism disowned Christianity. Precisely when the Romans recognized the distinction between Christian and Jew cannot be determined, but by the time they did Christianity had already sunk roots deep into the imperial soil.

More important in the long run was the attitude of the Roman people as distinct from that of the government. Popular opinion definitely condemned Christianity. To some extent this arose from ignorance and the bigotry which ignorance engendered. The secrecy surrounding Christian ceremonies gave rise to popular distortions of the Agape and the Eucharistic Sacrifice into execrable rites involving cannibalism, human sacrifice, and incest. "Hatred of the human race" was another charge hurled at Christians, probably in reference to a certain aloofness from society evident among them. Some converts, expecting the imminent second coming of Christ, did turn their back completely on the world, but for most it was merely that so much of the environment of Roman society was repugnant to Christian principles. Incidental and perfunctory acts of homage to the gods pervaded the daily life of the Roman world; popular entertainments, especially the theater and gladiatorial exhibitions, presupposed low moral standards. To avoid contact with what they repudiated, the Christians often found it necessary to avoid social intercourse altogether. The imagination of the ignorant easily interpreted such conduct as misanthropy. Sometimes changes in established habits of the people as a result of conversion provoked ill feeling, as between a convert and his spouse or other members of his family. St. Paul describes the anti-Christian riot provoked at Ephesus by the silversmith Demetrius because of the loss of his lucrative market for idols when the people joined the Church.

The Earliest Persecutions. Emperor Nero (54–68) first turned the authority of the State against the Christians. According to the account in Tacitus' *Annals,* the persecution was almost an accident. A great fire devastated a huge section of Rome in A.D. 64. Popular opinion suspected

Nero of having set it deliberately. To escape blame, Nero and his evil adviser Tigellinus decided that the Christians would make a handy scapegoat. Perhaps Nero knew of already existing anti-Christian sentiment among the populace and hoped to capitalize on it with his trumped-up accusations. Tacitus describes the resulting sufferings of the "immense number" of martyrs: "Some were covered with skins of wild beasts and left to be devoured by dogs; others were nailed to the cross; numbers were burnt alive; and many, covered over with inflammable matter, were lighted up, when the day declined, to serve as torches during the night." St. Peter suffered crucifixion; St. Paul was beheaded. There is no evidence of similar proceedings outside of Rome.

It is usually assumed that Nero issued a decree of condemnation against Christianity as a religion, and that it was on this basis that he punished the faithful. However, no indisputable traces of such a law have survived. Tacitus wrote that the Christians were convicted of "hatred of the human race," not of arson. Suetonius' biography of Nero does not even connect Christians with the fire. Subsequent persecutions, however, seem to rest on some sort of fundamental anti-Christian legislation. At any rate, Christianity from the time of Nero was treated as a forbidden religion and profession of the Christian name was sufficient grounds for prosecution.

There is some evidence of persecution under Domitian (81–96). Members of this emperor's family, his cousin Flavius Clemens and the latter's wife Domitilla, known to have been Christians, were executed for "atheism," but nothing indicates an organized persecution in Rome. In the eastern provinces it was another matter, for executions occurred in Bithynia and Palestine, where the surviving relatives of Jesus were investigated. St. John the Evangelist is said to have suffered in these years; his *Apocalypse* commemorates a persecution but in such vague terms as to be unsatisfactory as an historical source.

The Second Century.   During the second century Rome was ruled by the "good" emperors under whom it attained its peak of power and prosperity. These men of the Antonine family were all capable, cultured rulers of the best type personally, yet their reigns saw no amelioration of the status of the Church. For themselves, they held Christianity in disdain. They did not instigate persecutions, but neither did they repeal Nero's prohibitory legislation. Rather they regulated the Neronian decree in such a way as to encourage attacks by private citizens. Consequently the harrassment of Christians assumed Empire-wide albeit sporadic proportions during the years from Trajan to Commodus.

Correspondence between Emperor Trajan (98–117) and the writer Pliny the Younger provides a clear exposition of the government's attitude toward Christians under the Antonines. Pliny had been sent out in 112 to govern Bithynia where there was a sizable concentration of Christians. Faced with the problem of what to do about them, since he did not relish the thought of large-scale executions and since he found nothing objectionable in their lives beyond their stubbornness in refusing to recant, the governor asked for advice from Rome.

Trajan's rescript containing his instructions (1) acknowledged that the profession of Christianity was a crime meriting death, (2) bade Pliny not to take the initiative in ferreting out Christians but nevertheless to punish those whom private citizens publicly denounced, (3) ordered him to release unharmed any accused who recanted or denied Christianity and proved it by worshiping the emperor's image. Thus modified, Nero's decree remained in force.

Christian Apologists were not slow to point out the illogical elements in this order. Profession of Christianity, a crime against the State, should be ignored by the State unless a private citizen from personal spite or private grudge denounced a specific individual. Then, rather than strive to prove the accused guilty — the usual procedure in courts — and punish the criminal for his crime, the prosecutor should aim only to persuade him to deny the charges. Simple promise of "reform" guaranteed acquittal of all past guilt. Hence the frequent use of torture during persecution was neither for obtaining confession nor for punishment, but to extract a renunciation. The necessity for private denunciation to initiate a prosecution explains why Christians were often seen openly encouraging prisoners, carrying off bodies of martyrs, and appearing in public even during persecutions, for as long as no one denounced them individually they were not touched by the government.

Under these conditions persecution was intermittent throughout the second century. During Trajan's administration Pope Clement, St. Ignatius of Antioch, and St. Simeon of Jerusalem were condemned. Hadrian (117–138) was less severe; in fact, by a rescript to the proconsul of Asia, Minucius Fundamus, calling for "due process" in trials of Christians and punishment for false accusers, he removed abuses stemming from Trajan's procedure. Antoninus Pius (138–161) ruled during the martyrdom of Polycarp of Smyrna and Popes Hyginus and Pius I. Marcus Aurelius (161–180), an eminent Stoic philosopher, did not see fit to moderate the attacks on Christians; the martyrs at Lyons in 177, St. Justin the Apologist, and St. Cecilia in Rome are famous victims of his reign.

Commodus (180–192), the degenerate son of Marcus Aurelius, influenced by his Christian favorite Marcia and other Christians at court, granted pardons to imprisoned Christians and relaxed the rigid application of the law against them, without, however, abrogating it.

The Second-Century Apologists. In the face of the aggressive hostility of paganism, the Christians maintained an attitude of patient resignation. Not once did they attempt to strike back by rebellion. Constantly they heeded the Lord's respectful admonition, "Render to Caesar the things that are Caesar's." Peter and Paul too had counseled obedience to established authority; Paul's Roman citizenship was one of his prized possessions. So the Christians calmly and often eagerly accepted injustice from the State as the surest means of gaining salvation. And this demeanor in turn helped recruit converts more rapidly than the executioners could deplete the ranks of the faithful.

An increasing number of representatives of the aristocracy and of the educated classes found their way into the Church during the second century. Among the latter in particular the need for a more active defense was felt, especially since they themselves possessed all the qualifications to meet anti-Christian philosophers and rhetoricians on equal terms. Because of the caliber of the Antonine emperors there was even hope that they would heed carefully reasoned and well-written expositions of the faith and put an end to persecution entirely. This task of explaining Christianity to the pagans in scholarly fashion was tackled by the first group of Catholic intellectuals, the Greek Apologists.

About a dozen and a half of these Apologists are known, although many survive in name only. Nothing remains of the work of such as Quadratus, Aristo of Pella, Miltiades and Theophilus of Antioch. Others are better known, among them Athenagoras of Athens who addressed his *Supplication for the Christians* to Marcus Aurelius in 177, and Tatian of Syria, author of a *Discourse to the Greeks* (ca. 170). The anonymous *Epistle to Diognetus* explains beautifully the Christian outlook on life. St. Justin Martyr composed two *Apologies* against pagans and a *Dialogue with Tryphon the Jew*. Justin's life exemplifies what manner of men these Apologists were. By profession a teacher of philosophy, he tasted all the Greek systems and found them all wanting. Having discovered Christianity he embraced it enthusiastically as the true philosophy. For thirty years thereafter he taught Christianity as a philosophical system in Rome until a pagan competitor denounced him to the authorities and brought about his death in the arena. Finally, two Latin works deserve mention·

Marcus Minucius Felix's *Octavius* and Tertullian's *Apologeticum,* which vie with each other for the distinction of being the first piece of Christian literature in the Latin tongue.

Whether writing to convince the pagans of the truths of Christianity or to rebut the false charges of formidable literary opponents like Lucian, Fronto, or Celsus, the Apologists followed the same pattern. They challenged the current calumnies against the Church by pointing to the upright, chaste lives of the Christians and by explaining Christian ceremonies. They exposed the immorality and folly of pagan polytheism. They presented Christianity as a philosophical system more perfect and more ancient than all others, tracing its origin back to the Old Testament and offering the fulfillment of its prophecies as proof of its truth. Except for Tatian, the Apologists employed all the resources of Hellenistic learning to drive home their arguments.

There is no way of estimating the impact of these second-century authors on the pagan world. Certainly they failed to end the persecutions, and others took up their work in the next century. Nevertheless their importance for the Church was very great. Although they did not attempt a complete explanation of Christianity, since they were philosophers and not theologians, yet they may be considered the founders of the science of Christian theology in that they were the first to explain Christian doctrine rationally and in an intellectually satisfying guise. Many of their writings specifically concerning doctrinal and liturgical matters have disappeared. Yet, they all, Justin in particular, give much valuable information about contemporary Christian practices and beliefs.

The Severi and the Church, 193–235. The third century was a time of crisis in the Roman Empire. Weakness and signs of decay appeared both in domestic life and in foreign relations. As the control of the Empire shifted into the hands of provincials from Africa, Syria, and the Balkans, the racial strains of the Roman people, already much weakened, became further attenuated. The struggle for power brought dozens of "barrack" emperors to the throne in quick succession. Gradually the republican flavor of the Principate changed into pure autocracy; "lord and god" became the accepted form of address for increasingly tyrannical and suspicious emperors. All these developments had repercussions on the State's attitude toward Christianity. To some extent an amelioration resulted, for the persecutions remained intermittent and long periods of peace now intervened. Yet the later persecutions made up in bitterness what they lost in duration and therefore were much more serious.

Septimius Severus (193–211) continued for a while the toleration introduced by Commodus, but in 201 he unexpectedly issued an edict forbidding conversions to Christianity. The decree did not concern those already in the Church, only converts and catechists. Besides martyrs in Egypt, where the famous catechetical school of Alexandria was disrupted, there were others in north Africa — Felicitas and Perpetua among them — under the proconsul Scapula. Specific data are lacking about other regions. With Septimius' demise persecution ceased and peace reigned for twenty-four years. But a dangerous precedent had been set by Septimius' decree, and a new, more rational approach to the attack on Christianity is evident in the attempt to dry up the stream of converts.

Under the remaining Severi syncretism flourished and toleration was the order of the day. The Syrian dynasty looked for a gradual merging of all religions into a solar monotheism. Alexander Severus (222–235) honored Christ along with pagan gods in his private chapel. His mother Julia Mammaea discussed Christianity with Origen. At this time there is record of the Church owning property and even suing (and winning its case) in a Roman court of law.

The Severian truce collapsed suddenly with the accession of Maximin in 235. Deliberately reversing the policies of his predecessors, Maximin issued orders to renew the persecution, but, according to Eusebius of Caesarea, whose *Ecclesiastical History* is the chief Christian source for the study of the persecutions, Maximin's decree was directed only at clergy and bishops. Pope Pontian was deported to the Sardinian mines, but other important bishops went into hiding. In Cappadocia a popular outburst on the occasion of a destructive earthquake brought private denunciations of Christians and some executions. Peace was restored when Maximin died after six years and the immediately following emperors showed no hostility. In fact, Philip the Arabian (243–249) manifested such a friendly disposition that he was credited, probably without reason, with being himself a Christian.

The General Persecutions. Maximin's action marked a portentous departure from the established procedure, for he let the State take the initiative, not against converts only as Septimius had but against full-fledged Christians, thereby superseding Trajan's order that suits originate only with private individuals. Thus the way was prepared for a change from sporadic, limited attacks to a concerted aggression against Christians simultaneously throughout the Empire, having behind it the full power of the State. The first such general persecution came with Emperor Decius (249–251).

Faced with the threatened total collapse of the Empire, Decius undertook radical measures of recovery, one of which was a total war on Christianity as a subversive element weakening the internal stability of the State. In 250 he issued a general edict ordering all inhabitants of the Empire to perform public acts of worship to the gods of the State. Certificates testifying to compliance had to be obtained from officials in every city. Those who refused suffered death, although the magistrates first applied torture to induce obedience. Decius' motives were as much political as religious; at one stroke subversive and disloyal elements within the citizen body were discovered and the ancient gods under whose tutelage Rome had flourished were propitiated. From the Christian viewpoint, the edict amounted to a threat of extermination.

The accounts of the Decian persecution abound in instances of ferocious torture and heroic martyrdom. Pope Fabian and Origen were eminent victims, the former suffering execution and the latter dying as a result of tortures. Some outstanding figures escaped, however, such as Bishops Cyprian of Carthage and Dionysius of Alexandria, the former by concealment and the latter by being rescued from his captors by pagan Egyptian peasants. As State hostility waxed, that of the people waned, for several sources indicate that the populace openly sympathized with the victims.

How many were executed we do not know, but not all Christians passed the test. Many apostatized, including the Spanish Bishops Basilides of Leon and Martial of Merida. There were different degrees of apostasy: some offered sacrifice, others merely burned a bit of incense, and still others bribed the magistrates to give them the necessary certificates without any act of worship. Fortunately Decius soon had to concentrate his attention on the Gothic war. By the end of 250 the persecution lessened, and after Decius' death Gallus soon allowed it to cease.

The rapid turnover of third-century emperors brought Valerian to the throne from 257 to 261, and with him a vigorous renewal of persecution. His first edict in 257 commanded all Christian bishops, priests, and deacons to sacrifice to pagan gods or suffer exile, ordered the cessation of Christian worship, and closed Christian cemeteries which, especially the catacombs in Rome, might in emergency be used for religious assemblies, although they were not normally used for such purposes. A second edict in 258 condemned the recalcitrant clergy to death and prescribed degradation, exile, slavery, or death for the laity as well. The great Cyprian of Carthage and Dionysius of Alexandria, Pope Sixtus and his deacon Lawrence, and many other priests were slain.

Once again foreign wars saved the Church. In 261 Valerian fell prisoner to the Persians. Although his lieutenant and evil genius Macrienus controlled Egypt and continued to persecute, Gallienus was acknowledged everywhere else. Recognizing the failure of attempts to exterminate the Christian Church, the new emperor not only ended persecution but also promulgated an edict of toleration. Places of worship, cemeteries, and property were restored. For the first time since its foundation Christianity enjoyed full freedom. Isolated acts of hostility marred the next decades. Aurelian in 274 even prepared but did not promulgate new persecuting edicts, but on the whole the forty years from 261 to 302 were peaceful and provided needed respite for the Church before the final grand assault. Gallienus' toleration, it should be noted, was dictated by no love for Christianity. He simply recognized that force could not crush it. He was a syncretist acquainted with the anti-Christian Neo-Platonic circles and he anticipated the conquest of Christianity by these subtle forces rather than by brutality.

Persecution of Diocletian and Galerius. Diocletian (284–305) ranks with the greatest of the later Roman Emperors. His reorganization ensured two centuries more of life to the Empire. In an attempt to end the costly succession disputes he divided the Empire into four prefectures ruled by himself and Maximian as Augusti and Galerius and Constantius with the title of Caesars. Toward Christianity Diocletian displayed no hostility for nineteen years. His wife and daughter were catechumens if not actually Christians. What suddenly turned him against the Church cannot be known, but it probably was the influence of his son-in-law and Caesar Galerius who began a purge of Christians from his army in 302. An unfortunate incident at a pagan ceremony attended by Diocletian and two mysterious fires in the imperial palace, all of which were blamed on the Christians, provided the occasion for Diocletian's bitter persecution.

Four general edicts in 303 and 304 inaugurated the attack. The first ordered the destruction of churches and Christian books, dismissed Christians from all positions in the imperial service, and deprived them of all judicial rights. Two additional edicts soon ordered the arrest and imprisonment of the clergy and commanded them to sacrifice to the gods. Finally, the fourth decree in 304 ordered all citizens everywhere to sacrifice publicly as proof of their paganism.

After forty years of peace during which great progress had been made and churches had risen everywhere (a church even faced the emperor's palace in Nicomedia), Diocletian's declaration of war hit the Church very hard. Except for Gaul and Britain, where Constantius destroyed some buildings but harmed no one, the enforcement of the edicts caused thousands of deaths throughout the Empire. In Egypt the persecution fell with great cruelty. The fortunate victims were executed or drowned quickly; hundreds of others, blinded in one eye and crippled in one leg, were sentenced to penal servitude in the deadly mines. At Rome St. Agnes and Pope Marcellinus were martyred. Disastrous also was the wholesale destruction of Christian books and records such as the library and archives of the Roman bishops.

Diocletian and Maximian abdicated in 305. Their successors in the West immediately halted the persecution, but east of the Adriatic it raged on. Both Galerius and his ferocious colleague Maximin Daia hated Christianity and applied the earlier edicts without mercy. After five years, however, Galerius, real author of the persecution, weakened. Political problems and illness afflicted him so that he was forced to admit defeat. Shortly before his death he proclaimed full liberty for Christians to believe and assemble freely, and he even requested their prayers for himself.

Although Galerius' act of toleration was intended to be as universal as Gallienus' had been in 260, Maximin Daia refused to heed it in his provinces — Asia, Syria, and Egypt. He concocted new schemes for undermining Christianity by resuscitating paganism at the same time that he continued the persecution. A hierarchy of pagan priests was established in imitation of Christian clergy, with a high priest in each city charged with offering daily sacrifice and restraining Christians from public and private services. Efforts were made to incite the common people against the Church. But Daia was trying to stem an irresistible tide; within a year he too yielded and came to terms with Licinius and Constantine, admitting Christianity to the full freedom intended by Galerius.

The Constantinian Peace.   The ultimate triumph of Christianity is bound up with the name of Emperor Constantine the Great (306–337). From his father Constantius, one of the original tetrarchs, Constantine inherited not only jurisdiction over Gaul and Britain but also the former's tolerant disposition toward the followers of Christ, an attitude based on the family's syncretistic and monotheistic tendencies. By the year 310 Constantine shared the Empire with four other Augusti, and a process of elimination began. Constantine found himself pitted against Maxentius. From the decisive engagement at Milvian Bridge (312) Constantine emerged master of the western Empire.

Milvian Bridge marked the turning point in Constantine's progress toward Christianity. According to a contemporary account, some time before the battle Constantine saw in bright daylight a cross in the sky with the Greek words, "Conquer by this." A second story speaks only of a vision during sleep representing the Chi Rho insignia for the name of Christ. Encouraged by these marvels, Constantine hastily marked the shields of his troops with the monogram, won his victory, and professed belief in Christ.

Textual difficulties in the sources, not mere skepticism, provide valid grounds for questioning these tales, but there can be no doubt that Constantine did undergo some sort of intense religious experience at this time and that he did inscribe the shields as narrated. Personally he already leaned toward Christianity before 312. At any rate, the outcome of the battle contributed to the emancipation of Christianity. Immediately Constantine ordered the restoration of Christian property, freed the clergy from certain civil obligations, and took steps against Donatist heretics in Africa. Early in 313 Constantine met his colleague Licinius at Milan for discussions on imperial affairs and on the state of Christianity. When Licinius returned to the East, he defeated Maximin Daia, thereby definitely terminating the latter's persecution. From Nicomedia in 313 Licinius, himself a pagan, then issued the decree known as the Edict of Milan embodying the substance of his agreement with Constantine concerning freedom for the Christians.

Certain points should be noted concerning this edict: (1) it granted toleration and positive encouragement as a civic virtue to everyone, especially Christians, to practice whatever religion he desired; (2) it provided for the return to the Church and to individual Christians of property confiscated from them, with the state treasury in some cases compensating illegal possessors; (3) it is worded in such vague phrases that it does not clearly reveal the religious preferences of its authors.

Constantine and His Sons. Lively debate has raged for decades concerning Constantine's conversion. Some historians insist his acceptance of Christianity was motivated solely by political expediency or a general policy of religious syncretism, while others defend the sincerity of the conversion. Constantine never received instruction as a catechumen, accepted baptism only on his deathbed, retained his *ex officio* title of pontifex maximus in the Roman state cults, and indicated on occasion that Christian morality meant little to him. He always insisted on the legal equality of all religions and made no attempt to suppress paganism. Undoubtedly he perceived the political advantages of alliance with the strong Christian organization; he was too shrewd a politician not to. Nevertheless, Constantine's active share in ecclesiastical affairs like the Nicene Council, his construction of a new Christian capital for the empire at Constantinople, his generosity — he gave the pope the Lateran palace and aided in building the Lateran Basilica and the original St. Peter's in Rome — and the decided Christian flavor of his enactments indicate where his personal preference lay.

In 313 no more than ten per cent of the Empire's population professed Christianity. The percentage was much higher in the East than in the West. In Gaul and Britain practically no one was Christian outside of the few urban areas; and there were few converts within. Although the number of the faithful increased rapidly once fear of persecution disappeared, the Christian emperors' vacillating religious policy reflects the preponderance of paganism and the strength of its hold over large, important segments of the population.

The Edict of Milan prescribed toleration for Christianity but scarcely equality, for paganism continued as the established religion. Licinius' brief departure from this policy ended with his defeat in 324. To the end Constantine himself made no further adjustment in the relative position of Christianity and paganism. But with his sons began a general trend toward suppression of paganism, even though their own Christianity was sometimes of the heretical Arian type. Laws of Constantius II (337–361) forbade idolatry and ordered the closing of pagan temples in 356, but at Rome at least and throughout the West these enactments were not enforced. The pagan Symmachus wrote: "Although he himself followed another religion, he retained this one (paganism) for the Empire."

Pagan Reaction Under Julian. Julian (361–363) was never really Christian and therefore does not deserve the name "Apostate" which history has attributed to him. What slight contact he had with Christianity came through Arians. Libanius his tutor shaped his mental outlook along lines of Hellenistic culture and Neo-Platonic philosophy. Nor did the murder of most of his family by the Christian emperors impress him favorably toward the Church. When Julian assumed the throne he instituted a reaction against the progressive Christianization of the Empire. On the one hand he placed obstacles in the way of the Church: anti-

Christian riots went unpunished; all schools and the teaching profession were closed to Christians; imperial service was restricted to pagans. On the positive side, Julian aimed to rejuvenate paganism along lines suggested by Maximin Daia in 311, that is, by purifying the state cults, instituting a hierarchy of priests dedicated to preaching and austerity, and fashioning a pagan creed. The imitation of Christianity is evident. Even the pagans failed to recognize the old religion in this new guise and did not co-operate. Julian's death on the battlefield rang down the curtain on his brief career.

The Proscription of Paganism. For fifteen years after Julian the Constantinian policy of impartiality between Christianity and paganism again prevailed, although the emperors forbade magical and astrological abuses. Gratian (375–383) finally ended the alliance of Roman paganism with the State by renouncing the title of pontifex maximus and revoking the revenues allotted to the priestly colleges and vestal virgins. Absolute equality now existed, but without governmental support paganism faded rapidly. Theodosius I (379–395) legislated vigorously against paganism. In 391 he forbade pagan ceremonies in Rome and Egypt. The next year a comprehensive edict issued from Constantinople banned all sacrifices, public and private, and even devotions to the household deities. Legally paganism was henceforth dead and, in effect, orthodox Christianity became the official state religion. Nevertheless, since no prosecutions were attempted against individual pagans, generations passed before the old cults disappeared completely.

Conclusion. It is evident that the traditional reckoning of ten persecutions is inexact and also misleading since it ignores important differences in the types and intensity of the persecutions. There is no sure method of calculating the number of martyrs. Formerly it was customary to speak of tens or hundreds of thousands, but the present reaction tending to limit the number of victims to those specifically known is probably too conservative. Paucity of records necessarily prevents our knowing more than a small percentage of those who suffered in one way or another. Apparently there were more apostates than martyrs. The most lasting result of the persecutions was the tradition of heroic fortitude of the early Christians which, magnified, perhaps, by distance and encouraged by the cult of relics and the memory of the saints, has ever since served as an example for the faithful of later centuries to guide them through adversities of their own. But now we must turn to the internal developments within the Church during the age of the persecutions.

REVIEW AIDS

1. Summarize the causes for the opposition to Christianity on the part of the Roman government and of the Roman people.
2. How did the first persecution come about?
3. Explain Trajan's rescript to Pliny.
4. What were the Apologists trying to do? What is the significance of their work?
5. What was the attitude of the Severan dynasty toward religion and toward Christianity in particular?
6. Show how the third stage of the persecutions, the stage of persecution by edict, differed from earlier persecutions.
7. Summarize the events in the persecution of Diocletian and Galerius.
8. Indicate some of the historical problems surrounding Constantine's conversion.
9. What is the Edict of Milan and what does it say about Christianity?
10. Trace the gradual change in the attitude of the emperors from Constantine to Theodosius toward Christianity.

SUGGESTIONS FOR FURTHER READING

A valuable essay by G. E. M. de Ste. Croix in *Past and Present* (Nov., 1963), pp. 193–206, asks "Why Were the Early Christians Persecuted?" The scattered sections on the persecutions in the two volumes of Jules Lebreton and Jacques Zeiller, *The History of the Primitive Church* (New York: 1949) are very soundly written. The same may be said for Louis Duchesne, *Early History of the Christian Church,* Vols. I and II (London: 1950), and Philip Hughes, *A History of the Church,* Vol. I (New York: 1949). Taking up where Lebreton and Zeiller stop, that is, with Constantine, is J. R. Palanque, G. Bardy, *et al.,* *The Church in the Christian Roman Empire,* trans. from the French by E. Messenger (New York: 1953). A good introductory approach to the problems of Constantine's conversion is Problem #2, "The Triumph of Christianity," in Kenneth M. Setton and Henry R. Winkler (eds.), *Great Problems in European Civilization* (New York: 1954). On Constantine see also Norman H. Baynes, *Constantine the Great and the Christian Church* (London: 1929), and the recent short study by A. Alföldi, *The Conversion of Constantine and Pagan Rome* (New York: 1948). For the post-Constantinian period a handy survey of the legal progress of Christianity is Maude A. Huttmann, *The Establishment of Christianity and the Proscription of Paganism* (New York: 1914). See also the fascinating study by L. Hertling and E. Kirschbaum (tr. by J. Costello), *The Roman Catacombs and Their Martyrs* (Milwaukee: 1957).

DOCUMENTS

1. The Roman writer and government official Pliny has given us a view of the Christians in A.D. 113 in the letter he wrote to Emperor Trajan asking advice about the government's policy toward them. He reveals the puzzled attitude of educated Romans toward the new sect, he shows

how Christian services were conducted, he indicates how numerous they were, and he lets us see how the persecutions worked in practice. *C. Plinii Caecilli Secundi Epistularum*, X, xcvi.

Meanwhile I have followed this method in regard to those who were denounced to me as being Christians. I asked them if they were Christian; if they admitted it, I asked a second and a third time, threatening them with death. Any who still persevered I ordered executed. For I had no doubt that, whatever their beliefs, their stubbornness and unbending obstinacy deserved punishment. . . . An anonymous accusation containing many names was proffered. I thought that any of them who denied that he was or ever had been a Christian should be released when they repeated after me prayers to the gods, when they sacrificed with incense and wine to your image which I ordered brought along with the statues of the gods for that very purpose, and especially when they cursed Christ. Rumor has it that no true Christian can be forced to do any of these things. Others named by the informant admitted being Christians, but soon denied it. Some said they had been but had ceased two or more years ago, some even twenty years ago. All these also venerated your image and those of the gods and cursed Christ. However, they insisted that their only crime or error had been their custom of meeting before dawn on a pre-determined day and singing a hymn to Christ as if to a God and that they had bound themselves by oath, not for purposes of performing any wicked deed, but rather to avoid committing theft, robbery, adultery, breaking their word or refusing to give up a trust when called upon to do so. After this they had usually separated but had returned later to take food that was ordinary and harmless. . . . So I postponed the trial and hastened to consult you. The matter seemed worth asking about, particularly because of the number of those endangered. For there are many of every age, of every rank, and of both sexes who are or will be threatened. Not only cities but villages and hamlets have been pervaded by the superstitious contagion, although it seems that it can be checked and cured.

2. Emperor Trajan's reply to Pliny's request for information provides the earliest extant evidence of the official attitude of the Roman government toward Christians. On the whole that attitude was moderate.

You have followed the proper method, my dear Secundus, in prosecuting the cases of those denounced to you as Christians. It is impossible to prescribe a fixed procedure to apply in every such case. They should not be sought out. If they are denounced and found guilty, they must be punished, but with the condition that any one who denies that he is a Christian and proves it by the act of sacrificing to our gods shall receive pardon for his repentance in spite of past suspicion. Anonymous denunciations should not be accepted in any court of law, for that sets a very bad precedent, and it is not in keeping with the spirit of our times.

3. Like any secret society, Christianity was the object of much misunderstanding by credulous Romans. People often had vague notions of Christian practices which they interpreted in strange and unflattering fashion. A

sample of some of the wild stories that circulated regarding the Church and its ceremonies is provided by M. Minucius Felix, *The Octavius* (*The Ante-Nicene Fathers*, ed. Alexander Roberts and James Donaldson, New York, 1890), IV, 177–178.

They know one another by secret marks and insignia, and they love one another almost before they know one another. Everywhere also there is mingled among them a certain religion of lust, and they call one another promiscuously brother and sister, that even a not unusual debauchery may by the intervention of that sacred name become incestuous: it is thus that their vain and senseless superstition glories in crimes. . . . I hear that they adore the head of an ass, that basest of creatures, consecrated by I know not what silly persuasion, — a worthy and appropriate religion for such manners. . . . I know not whether these things are false; certainly suspicion is applicable to secret and nocturnal rites; and he who explains their ceremonies by reference to a man punished by extreme suffering for his wickedness, and to the deadly wood of the cross, appropriates fitting altars for reprobate and wicked men, that they may worship what they deserve. Now the story about the initiation of young novices is as much to be detested as it is well known. An infant covered over with meal that it may deceive the unwary, is placed before him who is to be stained with their rites: this infant is slain by the young pupil, who has been urged on as if to harmless blows on the surface of the meal, with dark and secret wounds. Thirstily — O horror! — they lick its blood; eagerly they divide its limbs. By this victim they are pledged together; with this consciousness of wickedness they are covenanted to mutual silence.

4. Lactantius, a Christian contemporary of Constantine, wrote a history of the persecutions in which we find one of the two surviving versions of the Edict of Milan, A.D. 313, by which the government called off its campaign to eradicate the Church. From Lactantius, *De morte Persecutorum*, ed. Migne, *Patrologiae Latinae*, VII, 267–269.

When we, Emperors Constantine and Licinius, met under happy circumstances at Milan, we conferred about the common good and the public security. It seemed to us that among the various things that would benefit mankind, or which especially ought to be attended to, were those which concerned divine worship. And it seemed that we should grant to the Christians and to all men the free right of practicing the religion that each one desires, so that whatever godhead may be enthroned in heaven may be favorable and propitious to us and to all under our authority.

Wherefore, on the basis of this sound and correct reasoning, we believed it should be ordained that no one be denied the privilege of observing the religion he feels most suitable for himself, either the Christian religion or whatever religion he has accepted, so that the Supreme Godhead, to whose worship we freely devote ourselves, may find it possible to bestow upon us in all things his accustomed favor and benevolence. Wherefore, we hereby inform your Excellency that it is our pleasure that all restrictions imposed on the Christians by former orders be set aside and that each one of them who desires to practice the Christian religion may now continue to do so freely and sincerely, without any fear or hindrance. We thought these things should be brought quite clearly to your attention, so that you may know that we have given these Christians the free and unrestricted right of practicing their religion. Since you discern what we have granted to them, Your Excellency understands that, for the sake of peace in our day, we have also granted to others the same privilege of observing openly and freely their own religion or cult. Everyone may enjoy freedom in practicing what he has chosen, because we do not want to interfere with the right of any religion.

Moreover, in regard to the Christians, we have resolved to decree as follows: if anyone has formerly purchased from the public treasury or from anyone else property consisting of accustomed places of worship which were confiscated in accordance with former instructions, they shall restore it to the Christians without delay and in clear title, freely and without demanding payment. Let those also who received such property as a gift immediately return it in the same way to the Christians. But if any who acquired it either by gift or by purchase shall ask compensation from our generosity, let them petition the Vicar, who in turn will refer their case to our clemency.

Chapter 4

THEOLOGY AND HERESY FROM
GNOSTICISM TO ARIANISM

CHRISTIANITY consists of a body of revealed truths announced by Christ to the Apostles and handed on intact to the faithful. Although the deposit of faith was completed by the time of the death of the last Apostle, St. John, about A.D. 100, the explanation, interpretation, and elaboration of its truths has been a continuous process. This chapter describes the beginning of the precise formulation of Catholic teaching by early learned Christians anxious to believe and understand. Primitive symbols of the Faith such as the Apostles' Creed expressed but did not explain fundamental doctrines; many Christians misunderstood or rejected part of the Church's teaching; finally, the absence of a recognized terminology to express theological concepts in Greek or Latin created difficulties. From such sources arose error, heresy, the corruption of Christian doctrines by Christians themselves from either moral or intellectual causes. Heresy, therefore, was a catalyst contributing to the elucidation of the truth, for the champions of orthodoxy had to combat error with carefully reasoned explanations of traditional doctrine. Meetings of the Church's leaders to discuss doctrinal or disciplinary matters are called councils or synods. These are of two types, local and ecumenical. The former bind only the limited area whence their members come; ecumenical or general councils speak for the whole Catholic world, and their acts, when ratified by the pope, are thereby extended over the universal Church.

Gnosticism. The religious ferment of the Hellenistic world produced the Oriental mysteries, on the one hand, and the religious philosophies, on the other. A syncretistic offspring of these two incompatible parents was the doctrine of Gnosticism, a system of salvation through knowledge which subtly penetrated Christianity and evolved into the first major heresy.

Gnosticism presented such varied forms that it easily incorporated elements of paganism, Judaism, and Christianity. It rested on the idea of an intuitive knowledge (Gk. *gnosis*) possessed by a small elite destined for salvation. Comprehension of this esoteric knowledge as expressed in magical formulas, secret gestures, and mysteries assured salvation. Gnostics entertained an exalted monotheistic concept of a God whom they placed so far above the material world that he lost contact with it except through a series of intermediary beings, the aeons, one of which, the demiurge, produced the world and mankind. They speculated abstrusely about names and numbers of these intermediate agents. All Gnostics professed dualism to a degree: material beings were essentially evil and gave rise to all wickedness; only the spiritual world was good. Yet material man could be saved through an innate divine spark introduced into the human race by the Saviour, one of the emanations from God but not God.

Contact between Christianity and Gnosticism occurred in apostolic times when St. Peter converted the magician Simon Magus and St. Paul encountered Bar-Jesus, but it was during the second and third centuries that Gnosticism really imperiled the Church. Converts from Gnosticism found the way into the Church easy, for a superficial grasp of Christianity seemed to fit in well with their earlier beliefs. Thus they recognized Jesus as the Saviour and the New Testament as a kind of special message for the elect in accordance with Gnostic theories. But they readily fell into errors, the most serious being Docetism, the view that Christ never really suffered in the flesh but only seemed to do so. His human life was a mere phantasm, or else the Divine Being Christ entered the human body of Jesus only at Baptism and deserted it before the crucifixion. Christian Gnostics endeavored to transform Christianity into a system of knowledge rather than of faith. They saw in Christianity only a steppingstone toward the final truth, the Gnosis.

The literary productions of Gnostic Christians far surpassed in number those of orthodox writers. Much of it was apocryphal Acts, Gospels, and Epistles. Schools of the heresy formed about outstanding teachers. Cerinthus represented the Syrian Gnosis late in the first century, Basilides introduced it to Alexandria (*ca.* 130–145), and Valentine in turn brought it to Rome (*ca.* 136–160). The latter gave Gnosticism a particularly attractive form and, despite his excommunication by the Church, gained many followers. Bardesanes (154–223), a Syrian disciple of Valentine, left many important writings in Syriac, including some of the earliest Christian hymns.

Marcionism. A Gnostic of a peculiar sort was Marcion, son of a bishop of Sinope on the Black Sea, who came to Rome about 136 and was excommunicated there eight years later. Whereas other Gnostics established schools, Marcion founded a church with bishops, priests, and a liturgy in competition with the orthodox organization and which endured in the East into the fifth century. He won more adherents than any other Gnostic. Marcionists suffered along with the orthodox during the persecutions. Marcion's teaching developed from his rejection of the entire Old Testament. In the God of the Jews he saw a cruelly just deity subordinate to the God of love revealed in Christ. Marcion was the first of many heretics who "purify" the Bible to make it conform to their ideas. Of the Gospels he kept only Luke, but he cherished the Pauline Epistles, in an expurgated edition, since Paul too had rejected Judaism. Although Marcion did not concern himself with the fantastic speculations of Gnosticism, there can be no question that he belonged in the Gnostic camp.

Montanism. About 172 the sect of the Montanists arose in Asia Minor from the claims of Montanus and his female disciples Maximilla and Priscilla to possession of the charism of prophecy. Not only were prophets now regarded with more suspicion than in the Church's infancy; the circumstances of Montanus' utterances gave reason to question his claims. Local bishops and eventually Pope Zephyrinus condemned the Montanists, but these successfully organized a vigorous propaganda which spread as far as Lyons and Carthage. The African polemicist Tertullian was perhaps the greatest of the Montanists. In Montanism there was no attempt, at least at first, to depart from traditional doctrines but only the error of attributing greater weight to private revelation and alleged personal inspiration by the Holy Spirit than to the teaching authority of the Church — another tendency which will appear time and again in the Church's history and always with the same result.

In both Montanism and Marcionism are to be seen also a leaning toward moral rigorism — Encratism — characteristic of early Christianity, orthodox and heretical. Excessive respect for virginity, prohibition of the use of meat and wine, severe fasts, and an inclination to deny the possibility of forgiveness of sins committed after baptism, especially fornication, murder, and idolatry, found favor with idealistic fanatics. Whence arose the custom of postponing baptism for catechumens until well beyond the age of youthful temptations. The Church frowned upon Encratite exaggerations but was slow to speak its mind. The orthodox *Shepherd* written by Hermas *ca.* 150 conceded only one reconciliation for sinners. Moderation, however, gradually replaced extremism. An important step in this direction occurred when Pope St. Callixtus (217–222) officially mitigated the Church's severe penitential discipline, an action which involved Callixtus in bitter controversy with conservatives like Tertullian and St. Hippolytus but which drew the line more clearly between orthodoxy and heresy.

St. Irenaeus of Lyons. Of those who defended Christianity against heretical attack during the second century, St. Irenaeus (*ca.* 140–202) indisputably holds first place. Irenaeus was an Asiatic Greek, a disciple of St. Polycarp of Smyrna, who in turn had been a disciple of the Apostle St. John. When and why Irenaeus came westward is not known, but after the martyrdom of Bishop Photinus of Lyons in 177 Irenaeus was elected his successor. To defend his flock against Gnosticism he composed his masterpiece *Against Heresies* which has survived in a Latin translation. On the basis of this work Irenaeus has been accorded the title of first outstanding Catholic theologian.

The value of *Against Heresies* stems from its positive approach to the Gnostic heresy. Not only does it refute errors, it also elaborates the content of Catholic dogma. Irenaeus' genius was not of the speculative, philosophical type. He was content simply to state the orthodox view on difficult points and acknowledge mysteries for what they are.

Since Irenaeus witnessed to the faith of the Church early in its history, particular significance attaches to the role he assigned to tradition as the guiding principle in doctrinal matters and in preserving unity among the scattered churches. He describes Christianity as a body of truths handed down from the Apostles, and therefore the test of orthodoxy lies in determining whether disputed points are taught by those churches which through their bishops trace their authority back to the Apostles. Of all such churches, "the greatest and most ancient" is that of Rome, founded by Peter and Paul, and with an unbroken succession of bishops (Irenaeus catalogues them) to guarantee conformity with apostolic tradition. "Because of its superior authority all churches must agree with this church" is Irenaeus' celebrated key to doctrinal unity and orthodoxy and his testimony to the Roman primacy.

The Roman Controversies. By the end of the second century the Roman church emerged into the position of leadership it has ever since enjoyed. Before this time its divinely-established headship, early recognized in letters of Pope Clement and Ignatius of Antioch, remained largely in abeyance since the chief strength of Christianity and the main stream of its history lay in the East. Then came Irenaeus' positive assertion of Roman pre-eminence, followed by a series of disputes during the pontificates of Victor (189–199), Zephyrinus (199–217), and Callixtus (217–222) which brought the primacy into sharper focus.

At Rome Easter was celebrated on the Sunday following the fourteenth day of the Jewish month of Nisan; in Asia Minor Easter commemorated not the resurrection but the crucifixion and came on the fourteenth of Nisan itself, regardless of the day of the week. This discrepancy of feasts and rites seemed undesirable to Pope Anicetus who about 154 requested the Asiatics to conform to Roman usage. Bishop Polycarp of Smyrna journeyed to Rome, protested the equally ancient tradition of Asia sanctioned by the example of the Apostles John and Philip, and persuaded Anicetus to drop his demand. When Victor became Roman bishop he renewed Anicetus' request, backed by many other bishops, but again the resistance of the Asiatics and their spokesman Polycrates of Ephesus thwarted the pope. It was a clear case of conflict of two apostolic traditions. Victor determined to assert the superiority of Rome and excommmunicated Polycrates and the entire Asian Church. Such drastic measures seemed too severe to many Westerners, including St. Irenaeus, so Victor lifted the ban, without, however, yielding on the principle of Rome's superiority. Eventually, under unknown circumstances, the Asian sees accepted peacefully the Roman custom.

Many early errors concerned the divinity of Christ and the union in Him of the divine and human natures, as well as His relationship with God the Father. Adoptionism, for example, denied the absolute divinity of Christ, considering Him a mere man adopted and apotheosized by the Father. This idea originated in the East, but when a certain Theodotus preached it in Rome Pope Victor expelled him from the Church. Some of the defenders of the Trinity under the next pontiff, Zephyrinus, in their zeal to protect Christ's divinity against Theodotus, overshot the mark and ended in the equally false position of identifying Father and Son as a single person. Noetus, Praxeas, and Sabellius defended this concept, known according to its different shades of distinction as Monarchianism, Modalism, Patripassianism, and Sabellianism.

Under Zephyrinus there lived at Rome the remarkably erudite but intolerant scholar St. Hippolytus (*ca.* 170–235). His *Refutation of All Heresies* exposed the errors of others, but his own Christological theories erred in the direction of ditheism. Hippolytus had no patience with Zephyrinus' hesitancy in the face of so many difficult disputes, nor with Pope Callixtus' moderation of the penitential discipline. The latter he also accused of heresy, probably without reason. With a small group of adherents Hippolytus left the Church and procured his own election as pope — the first antipope in history — about 217. He remained in schism until 235 when Emperor Maximin, ignoring the distinction between schismatic and orthodox, exiled both Hippolytus and Pope Pontian to the Sardinian mines. Under these adverse circumstances a reconciliation was effected in time for Hippolytus to merit the crown of martyrdom and sainthood.

Tertullian. Of all the writers involved in the early Trinitarian disputes, the African Tertullian (*ca.* 155–*ca.* 220) was the most capable. A convert trained in law, he became a priest and turned his brilliant mind and facile pen to the defense of Christianity against the pagan State and against heretics from within. Typically Roman in outlook, he deprecated philosophic speculation, to which he attributed the errors of the heretics. "What does Athens have to do with Jerusalem?" he asked. His epigrammatic style produced unforgettable phrases such as the oft-quoted, "The blood of martyrs is a seed." Latin rather than the Greek still officially used by the Roman Church was his language, and the impress of his genius on that tongue earned for him the title "founder of ecclesiastical Latin."

Tertullian's most important productions were apologetic and controversial tracts. His *Apology* reveals him at his eloquent best; here his legally trained, naturally brilliant mind erupts in fiery protest at the patent injustice of the persecutions. Point by point he shows how every part of the established Roman legal procedure was violated in cases against Christians. *The Prescription of Heretics* similarly follows the juridical pattern and is Tertullian's most valuable work. Following Irenaeus he stressed tradition and the witness of the apostolic churches as the key to orthodoxy. In controversial tracts Tertullian attacked the current Trinitarian errors and the Gnosticism of Marcion and Valentine. *Against Praxeas,* while not a wholly satisfactory defense of the Trinity, aided greatly in clearing up confusion by introducing into the theological vocabulary terms such as "consubstantial," "nature," and "person" which subsequently became part of the technical language in Trinitarian doctrine. Tertullian's later years saw him slip into the Montanist heresy which penetrated Africa

—a hard blow for the Church, but one which could not efface his achievements in its behalf.

St. Cyprian of Carthage. Very practical matters: the authority of bishops within their diocese and of the bishop of Rome over the Church Universal were the basic issues involved in the controversies that swirled around a second important African, St. Cyprian, bishop of Carthage from 248 to 258.

Decius' edict instituting a general persecution caught many Christians unprepared and weak from the long peace since Septimius Severus. Many apostatized but, the persecution soon ceasing, repented and begged readmission to communion with the faithful. Cyprian had gone into hiding, although keeping in constant touch with his people, and there were those who murmured at the bishop's conduct. These malcontents, led by the deacon Felicissimus and the priest Novatus, found a cause in the question of readmitting apostates. They maintained that pardons granted by confessors released from prison reinstated the lapsed Christians with the Church. Generous confessors willingly forgave all apostates, so that an air of laxity pervaded the diocese. Cyprian denounced this practice as contravention of the authority of the episcopate and the clergy in disciplinary and ultimately moral matters. "You should understand that the bishop is in the Church and the Church in the bishop and that whoever is not with the bishop is not in the Church," declared Cyprian. The sin of apostasy, he asserted, should be expiated in the regular manner prescribed by the clergy.

At Rome the apostate problem took an opposite twist. Pope Cornelius resisted the theory of rigorists led by the priest Novatian who declared that apostasy was an unforgivable sin. Sixty bishops meeting at Rome condemned Novatian and excommunicated him. Supported by Novatus and others who had appealed to Rome against Cyprian, Novatian organized a schismatic church with himself as antipope. Against Novatianism Cyprian penned *On the Unity of the Church* emphasizing the primacy of Peter and the unity of the episcopate as essential marks of Christ's Church.

Such harmony did not prevail between Cyprian and Pope Cornelius' successor Stephen on the matter of validity of baptisms administered by heretics. African custom regarded such baptisms as invalid. This was the opinion expressed by Cyprian also and by an African synod in 255 and again in 256, for the subject had arisen at this time. Pope Stephen peremptorily bade Cyprian amend his views to bring them into conformity with the Roman theory of the *ex opere operato* efficacy of the sacraments, which discounted the person of the minister. The arguments waxed bitter but Stephen's death and Cyprian's martyrdom in 258 suspended the controversy before it reached the stage of excommunications. Well-preserved documents in the dispute establish the fact that the Carthaginian prelate advanced so far as to deny the primacy of jurisdiction to the Roman bishop, although he undeniably acknowledged the lesser primacy of honor.

The Donatist Schism. The issue at stake in Cyprian's last controversy involved too fundamental an issue not to recur. Indeed, it has revived regularly ever since as one of the most persistent forms of attack on Catholicism. As the Decian persecution first brought it to the fore, so the Diocletian persecution renewed it. Bishop Caecilian of Carthage, elected in 311, was opposed by a hostile group charging that his consecration was invalid because of alleged unfaithfulness of Felix of Aptonga who performed the ceremony. They chose Majorinus in Caecilian's stead, but the ambitious Donatus soon succeeded Majorinus and gave his name to the schism.

In 313 a Roman council under Pope Milziadus pronounced against the Donatists, but these took their case to Emperor Constantine who assembled another council the next year at Arles. Again Donatus was condemned, and the bishops specifically affirmed the validity of sacraments even when conferred by an unworthy minister. But by now the schism was firmly established. Constantine attempted to enforce the conciliar condemnation, even using troops to perpetrate atrocities against the African heretics. Repression only provoking resistance, the emperor in 321 decreed toleration for Donatism. His inglorious intervention failed completely, for the schism was destined to last down to St. Augustine's time.

The Catechetical School at Alexandria. A world of difference separates the pragmatic Africans and Romans from the metaphysical scholars and theologians at the Alexandrian school for catechumens. This city ranked as the intellectual capital of the Empire, a cosmopolitan center where all cultures and intellectual strains met and mixed. Many converts here had previous experience with Hellenistic philosophy and Gnosticism so that a special kind of catechumenate was needed to help them adjust to Christianity. From this need sprang the famous school of Alexandria with its characteristic concern for the philosophical investigation of revelation and its allegorical method of expounding the Scriptures in studying the relation of Old and New Testaments.

Pantaenus created the reputation of the Alexandrian school between 180 and 200, but little is known about him. More firmly established is the fame of Clement of Alexandria, a convert whose youth recalls Justin Martyr. Clement succeeded his master Pantaenus until the persecution of Septimius Severus forced his flight into Cappadocia where he died about 215. Clement's extensive learning in secular and sacred literature eminently qualified him to seek to bridge the gap between Christianity and Hellenism, between faith and reason. He taught that Hellenism had much to offer Christians and that reason was not incompatible with faith, as the Gnostics held, but rather that each had its part to play in the search for true wisdom. The concept of philosophy as the handmaid of theology sums up his position, even though his enthusiasm for the former sometimes carried him too far in estimating the role of intellectual attainment in the approach to God. The Church's ideals of Catholic education owe a great debt to Clement.

Until St. Augustine the Church could boast no theological genius greater than Origen (ca. 185–253), master of the Alexandrian school after Clement. Origen's learning was truly prodigious. St. Jerome numbered his treatises at 2000. Origen attempted a complete systematical analysis of Christian beliefs. *First Principles,* a handbook of dogma, epitomized his labors. A masterly apology, *Against Celsus,* and textual and exegetical volumes on the Scriptures furthered his reputation. Unfortunately, Neo-Platonism, then in its first flower at Alexandria, influenced his philosophy and deceived him into serious error on several important points. For this reason condemnations were pronounced against some of his writings long after his death, which was caused by tortures suffered during Decius' persecution. The Oriental half of the Church continued to regard Origen highly despite his mistakes.

Arianism. Partly in opposition to Alexandria a second theological school arose at Antioch. St. Lucian (martyred in 312) was its founder, but even before him Paul of Samosata, Bishop of Antioch from 260 to 272, had established the reputation and theological tendencies of that city. Certain ideas of both Paul and Lucian had been condemned, but by 320 a number of the latter's students, called Collucianists, attained eminent positions in the eastern Church despite their dangerous tendencies. One of these was the priest Arius. It was from Lucian of Antioch that Arius derived the doctrines he began to preach in Alexandria about 320 and which have since been known as Arianism.

Arianism is a Trinitarian heresy resulting from the attempt to state the precise relationship of the Divine Persons. In emphasizing the unity of God and seeking to reconcile that unity with the Sonship of Christ, Lucian and his disciples such as Arius subordinated the Son to a position where He was deprived of His divinity. The Divine Word, Arius said, is God's foremost creature and creator of all others, but He is not of the substance of God the Father and not eternal. This was certainly a basic issue, for what is Christianity if Christ is not God? Nevertheless, the disputes would never have attained the proportions they did had it not been for the intervention of Constantine and his sons who, by treating the matter as a political problem, complicated it tremendously. Arianism quickly became the most important heresy in the early history of the Church.

Arius preached for some time in Alexandria with popular success before Bishop Alexander ordered him to cease spreading ideas not in conformity with tradition. When Arius refused to be silent, Alexander convoked the Egyptian and Libyan bishops in council where it was agreed almost unanimously that Arius and a dozen priests and deacons with him deserved excommunication. Arius fled into Palestine knowing that he could find refuge among the Collucian bishops of Caesarea, Lydda, Tyre, Berytus, and Nicomedia in Bithynia. His two most ardent partisans were Eusebius of Caesarea, the authority on the history of the primitive Church, and Eusebius of Nicomedia, a politician influential at Constantine's court — whence the name Eusebians often applied to Arius' supporters. Two councils of these sympathetic bishops declared Arius innocent.

Meanwhile Arius engaged in vigorous literary activity. In a book entitled *Thalia* he propounded his opinions on the Trinity. Eusebius of Nicomedia, Eusebius of Caesarea, and Alexander of Alexandria corresponded with other eastern bishops and defended their respective views. Emboldened by the sympathy of many prelates Arius returned to Alexandria, whereupon the city broke into riots and agitation.

At this point Constantine intervened. The emperor understood nothing of the theological implications of the dispute; to him it was mere idle speculation which must be stopped if it provoked public dissension. His attitude is identical with his sentiments in the Donatist affair. After the failure of an attempted mediation by Bishop Hosius of Cordova, Constantine's adviser in ecclesiastical matters, the emperor wrote to all bishops throughout the Church inviting them to a general council to canvass the entire situation.

The Council of Nicaea, 325. Approximately three hundred bishops attended this first ecumenical council, all but four of them Easterners. Carthage, Calabria, Die, and Cordova were the Western sees whose bishops attended, although two Roman priests came as delegates for aged Pope Sylvester. Even Persia and Armenia beyond the boundaries of the Empire were represented.

Arius presented the immediate problem. Twenty-two bishops tentatively defended him, but readings from *Thalia* convinced the assembly of Arius' heresy and his condemnation was unanimously voted. To provide a standard of the true faith it was proposed to formulate a statement of the traditional doctrine. From the discussions emerged the brief original Nicene Creed proclaiming that the Son of God is "of the substance of the Father . . . true God of true God, begotten not made, consubstantial with the Father." The prelates legislated concerning a schismatic Egyptian bishop Melitius, decreed that Easter be celebrated everywhere on the same Sunday, and promulgated twenty canons on disciplinary matters.

Fifty years were to elapse before Arianism ran its course, that is, before the creed formulated at Nicaea won universal acceptance. To judge the Council properly it must be kept in mind that the distinction between a general and a local council was not clearly enough understood in 325 to guarantee complete acceptance of the acts of Nicaea. Moreover, Constantine's presence and known desires played a large part in the decision to accept the creed. Only two bishops refused to subscribe it, but as soon as Constantine's influence was removed three others, including Eusebius of Nicomedia, retracted their signatures. Constantine exiled them at once, but uneasiness remained.

Although the West and Egypt found the creed acceptable, many Greeks, without accepting Arius, did not. The key word "consubstantial" (Lt., *consubstantialis*, Gk., *homoousion*) was perfectly clear in Latin but slightly ambiguous in Greek translation. A half century earlier the East had condemned as a heretic Paul of Samosata who had employed this very word *homoousion,* which to the Greeks smacked of the modalist heresy of Sabellius: a denial of the real distinction between Father and Son. That the danger was more than imaginary is proved by the career of Marcellus of Ancyra, one of the ardent pro-Nicene bishops who was eventually unmasked as a Sabellian. Nevertheless a seeming inability of Greeks and Latins to comprehend the others' difficulties obstructed a peaceful solution to the problems raised by Arius.

St. Athanasius, Constans, and Constantius II. Of the numerous characters involved in the long Arian controversy, none attained such heroic proportions as St. Athanasius, Bishop of Alexandria from 328 to 373. Five times he suffered exile rather than impugn the orthodoxy of the Nicene creed. Athanasius became the touchstone of the true faith. His letters, *Apology against the Arians,* and *History of the Arians* provide much information about the heresy.

While Constantine lived the Nicene creed held firm, for none dared challenge what the emperor considered a personal achievement. But if the Eusebians could not attack the creed, they could strike down its stanchest defenders. This was accomplished by a series of councils, false charges, and pseudo investigations that culminated in deposition and banishment by authority of the State. Even Athanasius was thus removed. A council of carefully selected Eusebian bishops at Tyre in 335 condemned Athanasius and exonerated Arius. When Athanasius appealed to Constantine, his enemies charged him with blocking the normal food exports from Egypt to Constantinople, whereupon Constantine exiled him to Gaul. The Eusebians were on the point of installing Arius as bishop of Constantinople when he died in 336. The next year death claimed Constantine also.

Because the custom of imperial interference in ecclesiastical affairs seemed now well established, the utmost importance attached to the religious views of Constantine's successors. After preliminary skirmishing, Constans, an orthodox Catholic, gained the West (337–350), while Constantius II, a convinced Arian, acquired the East (337–361). A stalemate prevailed — the East Arian, the West orthodox, according to the emperors' personal predilections. Meanwhile Athanasius returned to Alexandria with Constantius' permission in 337, but the Eusebians rallied and appealed to Rome against him. Heretofore Rome had played no part in post-Nicene Arian disputes. To the disappointment of the Eusebians Pope Julius (337–352) at once undertook a canonical investigation. In 340 a council at Rome vindicated Athanasius and other bishops whom the

NICAEA	325	Third Sirmium	357
Tyre	335	Ancyra	358
Rome	340	Fourth Sirmium	358
Sardica	343	Rimini-Seleucia	359
Second Sirmium	351	Constantinople	360
Arles	354	Antioch	379
Milan	355	CONSTANTINOPLE	381

Table of the chief councils during the Arian controversy.
General councils are indicated by capitals.

heretics had displaced. When the Eusebians refused to accept the decision of the Roman synod, another council assembled at Sardica (modern Sophia) in 343 to re-examine the stale charges against Athanasius and to attempt a new formula of the faith. Again the Bishop of Alexandria was vindicated, but the council's effects were limited, for the Eusebian bishops departed in anger in the middle of the proceedings.

The Apogee of Arianism.   Constantius II became sole emperor in 350. At once he threw the full weight of his government into the fray against Athanasius, the soul and the symbol of anti-Arian resistance. To persuade the Western bishops to repudiate their earlier verdicts, Constantius assembled councils at Arles (354) and Milan (355) and in both instances he succeeded. Threat of force combined with shrewd deceit brought the desired signatures to resolutions denouncing Athanasius. Yet ultimate success depended on the attitude of Rome. Pope Liberius (353–366) resisted Constantius to his face in a famous interview where the emperor asserted, "My will is the canon law in this matter." Constantius exiled Liberius and promoted Felix II as antipope, but two years later, in 357, Liberius succumbed, accepted the condemnation of Athanasius, and signed a vague substitute for the Nicene Creed. Here and there voices were heard against Arianism, but the cause of orthodoxy had reached its nadir. Even Germanic barbarians beyond the Empire's frontiers received Arianism from zealous missionaries such as Bishop Ulfilas. All the important sees of Christendom were occupied by heretics or compromised Catholics.

But in the hour of triumph, between 350 and 361, the Arians discovered their own disunity. Three factions now struggled for control: Anomeans insisted the Son is unlike the Father, Homoiousians said the Son is similar to the Father but not of the same substance, while Homoians declared that the Son is similar to the Father but not in substance or in person.[1] Constantius vacillated, while the machinations of the extremists pushed the moderates closer to reconciliation with orthodoxy. Chaos reigned throughout the Eastern Church.

Triumph of Orthodoxy.   At no time were theological principles the decisive factor in the overwhelming strength of Arianism. It flourished when supported by the State; it died when that support was removed.

---

[1] Anomeans or Eunomeans were pure Arians and clearly heretical. The Homoiousians were Semi-Arian, not openly heretical, but not clearly orthodox. The Homoian beliefs, also Semi-Arian, suffered from vagueness, for they defined nothing and might be accepted by anyone according to his own personal interpretation of the theological terminology.

Valens (364–378) was the last Arian emperor. When Theodosius I (379–395) came on the scene, Arianism was doomed. This was the same emperor who made Christianity the State religion of the Empire, and he determined to establish standards of orthodoxy. Three edicts in 380 and 381 enjoined on all his subjects acceptance of the Nicene Creed and also deprived Arians of the right to hold churches and to ordain bishops.

Theodosius' edicts only gave expression to the orthodox sentiment that had prevailed generally in the West when free to declare itself. St. Hilary of Poitiers led the defense in Gaul, while St. Ambrose expelled Arians from Italy. In the East too a strong reaction against Arianism had prepared the way for the emperor's decrees. The reaction here was largely the work of the three Cappadocian Fathers: St. Basil, St. Gregory of Nazianzus, and St. Gregory of Nyssa. Thoroughly orthodox, yet willing to examine dispassionately and to understand the view of their opponents, the Cappadocians succeeded in allaying the fear of Sabellianism among the Semi-Arians by devising formulas stressing the Nicene unity of substance in God the Father and God the Son along with the distinction of the three divine Persons which the moderate Arians had concerned themselves with. Catholic Trinitarian theology was permanently established by the Cappadocians.

To conclude the work of Catholic restoration, the second ecumenical council met at Constantinople in 381. Complete harmony prevailed, for the thirty-six intransigent Arian bishops were refused admittance. To the Nicene creed, accepted without demur, were added statements about the Holy Spirit in refutation of the Macedonians or Pneumatomachi who, carrying Arianism a step further, had lately denied the divinity of the Third Person of the Trinity. This gave the Church the Nicene-Constantinopolitan Creed still used, with a slight later addition, in the Mass.

Summary. The controversies of the second to fourth centuries produced the following results: Trinitarian doctrine, so abstruse yet so fundamental, was established, the objective efficacy of the sacraments was defended, the relationship between Christianity and philosophical truth was explored, and the disciplinary power of bishops and of the pope was sharpened.

REVIEW AIDS

1. Define: theology, heresy, Gnosticism, Marcionism, Montanism, Sabellianism, Donatism, Arianism.
2. Explain the significant achievements of St. Irenaeus of Lyons and Tertullian.

3. What was the circumstance of the schism of St. Hippolytus and the Novatian schism?
4. Analyze St. Cyprian of Carthage's views of the role of the bishop and of the bishop of Rome.
5. What was the general problem faced by the catechetical school of Alexandria, and what solution did Clement and Origen propose?
6. What issue was involved in the Arian heresy?
7. Trace the history of the Arian controversy, and indicate why it was so serious and why it lasted so long.
8. What was accomplished by the General Councils of Nicaea and Constantinople?

SUGGESTIONS FOR FURTHER READING

Most aspects of the Arian dispute are covered in the scholarly old work of H. M. Gwatkin, *Studies of Arianism*, 2nd ed. (Cambridge: 1900). Johannes Quasten, *Patrology*, 3 vols. (Westminster, Md.: 1950–1960), analyzes and surveys all the literature on the Fathers to 451 with impeccable scholarship. All the early heresies and dogmatic disputes are presented lucidly in both Joseph Tixeront, *History of Dogmas*, 3 vols. (St. Louis: 1910–1916), Volumes I and II for this period, and F. Cayré, *Manual of Patrology and History of Theology*, trans. H. Howitt, Vol. I (Paris: 1936). A thorough treatment of Donatism, especially valuable for tracing the nonreligious factors behind such a movement, is W. H. C. Frend, *The Donatist Church: a Movement of Protest in Roman North Africa* (Oxford: 1952). For the general councils and their work see H. J. Schroeder, *Disciplinary Decrees of the General Councils* (St. Louis: 1937). Of the general works on Church history Philip Hughes, *A History of the Church*, Vol. I (New York: 1948), is especially to be recommended for readability and for bringing abstruse theological points down to the level of the average reader. J. R. Palanque, G. Bardy, *et al.*, *The Church in the Christian Roman Empire* (New York: 1953) and L. Duchesne, *Early History of the Christian Church*, Vols. I and II (London: 1950), are also well done.

DOCUMENTS

1. For Catholics the final voice of authority concerning the teaching of Christ is the pope, whose powers rest on the fact that he is the direct successor of St. Peter whom Christ commissioned as head of His Church. Evidence that this appeal to the pope is no novelty but was common among ancient Christians is the statement of St. Irenaeus of Lyons concerning the Apostolic succession of the Church of Rome as the key to orthodoxy. *Against Heresies*, III, c. 3; translated in *The Ante-Nicene Fathers* (New York: 1890), V, 415–416.

It is within the power of all, therefore, in every Church, who may wish to see the truth, to contemplate clearly the tradition of the apostles manifested throughout the whole world. . . . We do put to confusion all those who, in whatever manner, . . . assemble in unauthorized meetings by indicating that tradition derived from the apostles, of the very great, the very ancient, and universally known Church founded and organized at Rome by the two most glorious apostles, Peter and Paul; as also (by pointing out) the faith preached to men, which comes down to our time by means of the successions of the bishops. For it is a matter of necessity that every Church should agree with this Church, on account of its pre-eminent authority, that is, the faithful everywhere, inasmuch as the apostolical tradition has been preserved continuously by those who exist everywhere.

The blessed apostles, then, having founded and built up the Church, committed into the hands of Linus the office of the episcopate. Of this Linus, Paul makes mention in the Epistles to Timothy. To him succeeded Anacletus; and after him, in the third place from the apostles, Clement was allotted the bishopric. . . . In the time of this Clement, no small dissension having occurred among the brethren at Corinth, the Church in Rome despatched a most powerful letter to the Corinthians, exhorting them to peace, renewing their faith, and declaring the tradition which it had lately received from the apostles. . . . To this Clement there succeeded Evaristus. Alexander followed Evaristus; then, sixth from the apostles, Sixtus was appointed; after him, Telesphorus, who was gloriously martyred; then Hyginus; after him, Pius, then after him, Anicetus. Soter having succeeded Anicetus, Eleutherius does now, in the twelfth place from the apostles, hold the inheritance of the episcopate. In this order, and by this succession, the ecclesiastical tradition from the apostles, and the preaching of the truth, have come down to us. And this is most abundant proof that there is one and the same vivifying faith, which has been preserved in the Church from the apostles until now, and handed down in truth.

2. Pope Liberius was subject to tremendous pressure from the emperor who sought to enlist the pope on the side of the Arians. Eventually Liberius weakened somewhat, not to the extent of upholding Arianism but of condemning St. Athanasius, the champion of orthodoxy. The following, the second letter of Liberius while in exile, is the key document for establishing the Pope's position toward Athanasius and Arianism. Conrad Kirch, *Enchiridion Fontium Historiae Ecclesiasticae Antiquae*, 6th ed., ed. Leo Ueding (Barcelona: 1947), pp. 342–343.

Liberius to his dearly beloved brethren, priests and fellow bishops in the East, greetings.

For godly fear your holy faith is known to God and to men of good will. As the law says: "Judge righteous judgments, sons of men," I did not defend Athanasius, but because my predecessor Bishop Julius of blessed memory had received him I was afraid that I might be judged a traitor in something. But when it pleased God that I should know that you had justly condemned him, I soon changed my opinion to conform with yours. Similarly I gave a letter concerning him, that is, about his condemnation, to our brother Fortunantianus to deliver to Emperor Constantius. Now that Athanasius has been removed from communion with all of us and I ought not to receive his letters, I declare that I am at peace and harmony with you all and with all the Oriental bishops in all provinces.

That you may be assured that I am speaking in the true faith in this letter, know that our mutual lord and brother Demophilus has kindly deigned to expound to me your creed which was debated and expounded at Sirmium by many of our brethren and fellow bishops and was accepted by all present. This creed I have freely accepted, I have in no way gainsaid, I have consented to, I follow and I uphold. I trust that I may beg Your Holiness, since you now see that I agree with you in everything, to deign to labor by your mutual advice and effort for my release from exile and my return to the see which was divinely entrusted to me.

Chapter 5

ECCLESIASTICAL ORGANIZATION AND THE GREAT WESTERN FATHERS

I N THE century following Constantine's edict of toleration, the Church organized its government along enduring lines, expanded more rapidly than ever before, and began effectually to mold the society of the Empire into the pattern of Christian life. This was the age also of the greatest of the Fathers and Doctors. The title "Father of the Church" applies to those writers in the early centuries who brilliantly defended or expounded Christian teachings in a generally orthodox manner. "Doctor" designates unusual learning combined with outstanding holiness and implies no particular chronological limits, for the Church bestows this title solely on the basis of merit. All the great Latin Fathers — SS. Ambrose, Jerome, Augustine, and Gregory the Great — are also Doctors. Of these four we consider here the first three, who flourished in the sixty years from 370 to 430.

Ecclesiastical Government: Bishoprics and Provinces. During the fourth century the structure of the Church's government assumed definite shape. When the general Councils of Nicaea and Constantinople legislated concerning organizational matters, more often than not they were only confirming established custom, not prescribing innovations. The main features of administrative organization appeared spontaneously and were conveniently modeled along lines established for the Roman civil administration by Diocletian and the reforming emperors. Although the Church imitated it did so with a spirit of independence, so that the parallels between secular and ecclesiastical organization are often incomplete.

Roman government rested on a large number of municipalities and their surrounding rural areas as units of local administration. These came to be grouped into 120 provinces which in turn constituted a dozen dioceses, five under the western emperor and seven under the eastern. The two lowest levels, municipalities and provinces, were most consistently followed for purposes of ecclesiastical government. In general, each municipality comprised a bishopric as the basic unit. Occasionally, especially in the East, even villages provided a seat for a "country bishop" enjoying limited powers. Everywhere bishops abounded: about A.D. 400 a hundred sees existed in Egypt, almost 500 in North Africa, 200 in southern Italy, and 115 in Gaul. Except for unusual circumstances the early custom of popular election of bishops had given way to election by neighboring bishops. According to Nicene decrees, bishops once chosen were to remain in residence, were forbidden to move to other sees, or to meddle in affairs of municipalities other than their own.

No longer autocephalous, bishoprics were grouped into provinces. The bishop of the civil provincial capital became metropolitan or archbishop with jurisdiction over the rest, his suffragans. Regular meetings of all bishops of a province assembled in local councils under the metropolitan's direction. Circumstances played a large part in determining the role of the metropolitan. In some provinces he wielded great power, in others little.

The pattern of civil government arranging provinces into larger units called dioceses was not accepted for ecclesiastical government. When ecclesiastical dioceses came into existence later they comprised entirely different territory. Nevertheless, certain metropolitans, for one reason or another, extended their influence far beyond the limits of their own provinces. The metropolitans of Rome, Antioch, Alexandria, Constantinople, Jerusalem and Carthage commanded wide respect; all but Carthage eventually gained recognition as patriarchates, i.e., metropolitans of superior rank. Other metropolitan sees such as Milan under St. Ambrose temporarily enjoyed extensive influence during the lifetime of outstanding incumbents. Spain, Gaul, and Britain produced no extraordinary metropolitan sees until after the collapse of the Empire.

Chief Metropolitan Sees.   Carthage owed its power to the fact that no other metropolitan of North Africa could match its political importance. In the other African provinces the title of metropolitan passed to the eldest bishop and hence no other city could develop traditions of rivalry with Carthage. The North African sees always guarded jealously their own rights of local jurisdiction against the centralizing tendencies of

Rome. The case of the priest Apiarius ended with a canon of a local synod in 419 forbidding African priests to appeal to Rome over the heads of their own bishops. We need only recall the Christian writers of Africa — Tertullian, Cyprian, Orosius, Lactantius, Augustine — to realize the importance of these provinces.

Egyptian Church history centered around Alexandria which produced outstanding men of action such as Athanasius, as well as eminent scholars in its catechetical school. So great was the prestige of Alexandria that other eastern metropolitans, fearful of losing their own prerogatives to Egyptian usurpers, agreed at Constantinople in 381 on a law specifically restricting the Alexandrian metropolitan to Egyptian affairs. The Patriarch of Alexandria governed Egypt with an iron hand, supported by fanatical monks. His monopoly on sales of salt and papyrus and a kind of monopoly on funeral ceremonies brought him tremendous revenues.

Resting securely on its apostolic traditions, Antioch dominated more than a hundred bishoprics of the Near East, but a series of disastrous schisms throughout the second half of the fourth century weakened its prestige, as did the heterodox theories of many of its scholars. The rise of Jerusalem, i.e., the Gentile city of Aelia on the site of the old Jewish city, to metropolitan and patriarchical status and freedom from the metropolitan of Caesarea is a tale of ambition and intrigue. Bishop Juvenal (420–458) successfully persuaded the Council of Chalcedon to recognize Jerusalem without reservation as a patriarchate.

Constantinople. The third canon of the Council of Constantinople in 381 declared that "the bishop of Constantinople shall have the prerogative of honor after the bishop of Rome, since Constantinople is the New Rome." This decree marked the beginning of the troubled history of the newest patriarchate. Constantinople definitely became the permanent residence of the eastern emperors at the close of the fourth century. The prelates in 381 raised the ecclesiastical rank of the city correspondingly, and also expressed their respect for the Catholic Emperor Theodosius I. The circumstances of their decision indicated that Constantinople as a bishopric would prosper as a corollary to the city's growing political importance. Instinctively recognizing a threat to the traditional framework of the Church's government, the popes rejected the Council's action. Undeterred, the eastern prelates advanced further at the Council of Chalcedon seventy years later when Constantinople, hitherto a suffragan of Heraclea, received metropolitan rights over the vast area of the civil dioceses of Pontus, Asia, and Thrace. Pope Leo I took issue with this canon which offered as justification the declaration that "the fathers had granted privileges to the See of Old Rome because it was the imperial city," wherefore they could grant similar rights to the new Rome if they wished. Leo insisted that Rome's prerogatives stemmed from St. Peter himself, not from the political significance of Rome or from any act of the "fathers." Nevertheless, as will be seen, Constantinople's rise continued regardless of papal opposition. Only in 1215, when the city was under Latin rule, did the Roman Church acknowledge the patriarchal claims of its eastern rival.

Rome. Head of the Church Universal, Patriarch of the West and Metropolitan of Italy were the titles given the bishop of Rome, each indicating a particular aspect of his jurisdiction. The word "pope," a title of respect applied to any important bishop and even to priests in Asia, first occurs in the sources in reference to the Roman bishop in a decree of a Spanish council at Toledo in the year 400. As metropolitan, Rome's jurisdiction extended originally over all Italy, but after 378 Milan acquired primatial rights in the north, and so soon did Aquileia and Ravenna. Below Tuscany, however, Rome's control remained complete: the sovereign pontiff consecrated all bishops of his province, guided their administration, deposed them if necessary, and summoned them to annual synods at Rome.

The honorary rank as first bishopric of Christendom was universally accorded to Rome in ancient times. The above-mentioned third canon of Constantinople unmistakably reflects the sentiments of the eastern prelates. Occasionally the Roman position suffered temporary eclipse, as when Milan under St. Ambrose overshadowed Rome in the last quarter of the fourth century. Yet the prestige of Milan and of other sees in similar circumstances derived from the illustrious personality of their bishop, while at Rome the pre-eminence of the see clothed even weak incumbents with its own greater authority. This jurisdiction was not impaired by difficulties the popes encountered in Rome itself. Pope Damasus (366–384), accused of murder, opposed by antipope Ursinus, defied by heretical sects, could scarcely control his own see, yet he was an outstanding pontiff. Zozimus (417–418) had a talent for making mistakes, but no one denied the prerogatives of his see for that reason.

More fundamental to the papal position was its jurisdictional authority, as distinct from its honorary position: the right to speak with finality on doctrinal questions and to decide disciplinary matters as a court of last appeal. The fourth century witnessed numerous examples of the acknowledgment and exercise of this power in the West. The first juridical recognition was the formula of the Council of Sardica (343) stating that appeals might be taken from any province to the Apostolic See. Priscillian, a Spanish bishop, turned to Rome for judgment when accused of heresy. During the later fourth century came the earliest papal decretals, authoritative replies to individual questions intended for universal application. Innocent I's letters (409–417) commanded that customs accepted by the Roman Church should be given precedence over local usages elsewhere. St. Augustine's statement, "The case is finished," after Innocent had spoken on the Pelagian question, indicated Africa's position, for the muddled thinking of St. Cyprian in his argument with Pope St. Stephen was never taken as a precedent in the ancient Church.

Candid admission of papal prerogatives of jurisdiction was not so willingly granted by the eastern sees. Petty jealousies, ambition, and political considerations accentuated the desire for autonomy of the Oriental bishops. Tactful diplomacy, therefore, rather than brusque challenge was deemed by the popes to be the proper procedure in relations with the East. Nevertheless, various instances of eastern acknowledgment of papal primacy and "modest interventions" by Rome can be alleged for the fourth century. Emperor Constantius' extreme measures to compel Pope Liberius to concur in the condemnation of Athanasius implied the futility of all such undertakings without Rome's approval. The entire career of Athanasius is eloquent testimony that he regarded Rome as the font of orthodoxy and the supreme court of Christendom.

With the fifth century the popes took a decidedly firmer stand and instances of eastern recognition of Rome's prerogatives became more frequent. Even the bishop of Constantinople, St. John Chrysostom, appealed to the pope in 404 when the emperor and the bishop of Alexandria unjustly deposed him. Pope Innocent I excommunicated John's enemies and compelled them to submit. This is a particularly significant case since it brought about acknowledgment of the papal primacy by all three eastern patriarchs. Subsequent generations reveal other such examples.

Pope St. Leo the Great, 440–461. Of all the popes of antiquity, Leo I seems the one most conscious of his rights and most successful in enforcing them against Orientals and westerners alike. Gifted both in theology and administration, experienced after two decades of service to several popes, Leo brought to his office those practical Roman qualities of energy, perseverance, and understanding of men so necessary for sovereign pontiffs. In Gaul, Spain, Africa, and Illyricum, all the western provinces, Leo regulated discipline and attacked heresy with the absolute confidence of an unquestioned superior. Indication of the pope's mounting secular prestige is his journey to Mantua in 452 to dissuade Attila the Hun from descending into Italy, a task too great for the Roman army and the cowering emperor. When the Vandal chieftain Genseric led his hordes against Rome in 455 Leo again went to meet the barbarian, this time winning the concession that Rome would at least be spared from fire and indiscriminate massacre.

Leo's most striking triumph was registered in the East. When the theological controversy with Eutyches began, Leo plunged in with a positive definition of the traditional faith in his *Tome* or dogmatic letter to Patriarch Flavian of Constantinople. This document was submitted not for debate but as the symbol of the true faith authoritatively expressed. When one council refused to accept his *Tome*, Leo condemned the recalcitrant bishops and convoked the Council of Chalcedon in 451. Here, in the memorable phrase, "Peter has spoken through Leo," the Eastern bishops accepted Leo's definition as the true statement of the Catholic teaching. This identification of the pope with the Prince of the Apostles marked the clearest possible acknowledgment of the Roman primacy by the eastern Church.

Christianization of the Empire. The progress of Christianity was rapid in the fourth and fifth centuries despite the civil wars occasioned by the great heresies. On the one hand removal of threat of persecution and on the other the example and encouragement of the Christian imperial court smoothed the way for many who had formerly held back from human considerations. Converts of this type were not always ideal Christians; in fact as the faithful increased in numbers in these years there was a perceptible decline in their quality. Yet passive resistance to Christianity persisted, especially among two clearly defined groups: the inhabitants of rural areas distant from large cities, and, at the other end of the social ladder, the educated and aristocratic circles.

Forces working in favor of Christianity were numerous. Occasionally Christian mobs rioted against unconverted pagans, at times even abetted by overzealous bishops. In 389 Christians of Alexandria destroyed the famed municipal museum and library, the Serapeum, when pagans sought refuge there in one such outburst. Preaching and teaching, the normal missionary methods, effected many conversions, but few details are recorded except for an occasional outstanding figure such as St. Martin, bishop of Tours from 371 to 397. Without impugning the labors of the missionaries, it can be said that the favorable legislation of the Christian emperors played an integral part in the conversion of the Empire. Gradually all the social pressures which shape every man's life came to work on the Church's behalf.

As the Church triumphed over paganism it found itself in a position to fulfill its social mission by pervading the whole life of the Empire with its principles. This was truly a formidable task and a tremendous accomplishment: to reshape along Christian lines an ancient, great civilization whose every tradition rested on a glorious but pagan past of ten centuries. Imperial laws preserved in the Theodosian and Justinian codes reveal Christian influence working in many directions: public regulation of sexual morality, more humane treatment of slaves, protection of the weak and oppressed, prohibition of the custom of exposing unwanted infants, mitigation of the barbarous penalties inflicted on criminals. Along with these went the bestowal of privileges on the Church and the clergy. Christian churches replaced pagan temples as sanctuaries protecting refugees. Bishops received the right to sit as judges in civil cases, to hear appeals from the ordinary magistrates, and to appeal themselves on behalf of criminals. The reputation for honesty and justice enjoyed by the episcopal tribunals stood in sharp contrast to the corruption and oppression prevailing in the public courts. Further laws exempted clergy from secular jurisdiction entirely, making them responsible solely to episcopal judges.

Church and State. When the rulers of the Empire adopted Christianity, serious problems of practical politics arose concerning the relationship of the Christian prince to his Church. Should the prince employ his political power to further the interests of Christianity? How should the prince treat schismatic or heretical Christians? To what extent would the prince, whose authority recognized no legal limitation, submit himself to the spiritual direction of his Church as represented by her bishops, his own subjects?

Constantine's handling of the Donatist heresy and his part in the Council of Nicaea established precedents for state activity in ecclesiastical matters which his sons eagerly continued to the confusion of Catholicism during the Arian crisis. Ample evidence lay at hand, then, of the danger of political intervention, yet the practice continued since bishops and emperors alike desired it. The State came to be regarded as the secular arm of the Church and the Church accepted the obligation of admonishing its members to obedience to the State, for Church and State were merely two aspects of the one Christian community striving for the eternal salvation of its members. An example of imperial support of ecclesiastical decisions is provided by the joint decree of Theodosius II and Valentinian

III in 445 supporting papal authority on the occasion of a dispute between Pope Leo and St. Hilary of Arles; the decree made the papal primacy the law of the Empire. Laws against heretics are of the same type. The temptation to call on the State for support in ecclesiastical disputes was too great for most of the churchmen to resist. They forgot that the emperors were not theologians and might intervene to uphold an heretical bishop just as easily as an orthodox one, especially when theologians themselves disagreed as to what was orthodoxy and what heresy.

St. Ambrose. Concerning the willingness of secular rulers to accept direction of bishops in cases involving principles of morality, a sharp divergence appeared between the Greek and the Latin worlds. The West derived its heritage in this sphere largely from St. Ambrose, bishop of Milan from 374 to 397. Ambrose was not the first bishop to express himself on the subject, but his example became a major factor shaping Church-State relations. As a Doctor and Father of the Church Ambrose's fame rests on his ability as preacher and author as well as statesman, as attested by his influence on St. Augustine, his hymns, and his book *Duties of the Clergy*, but he is best remembered for his conflicts with the emperors.

Ambrose's life was dominated by the tradition of government service and Roman administrative genius. At the time of Ambrose's birth his father was praetorian prefect, one of the highest imperial offices. Both of Ambrose's parents were Christians. Having decided on a career in the civil service, Ambrose went to Rome for an excellent literary and legal education and then secured appointment as governor of Liguria and Aemilia with residence at Milan. Within a year he won such general acclaim that he was spontaneously chosen bishop. Reluctantly Ambrose accepted, but, still only a catechumen, he had to receive baptism before he could be ordained and consecrated. Immediately he began a diligent study of the Scriptures and theology. His writings reveal how thoroughly he mastered these subjects.

Ambrose's dictum, "The emperor is within the Church, not over the Church," was his guiding principle in four clashes with the imperial authority. With considerable personal risk Ambrose defied young Valentinian II and his Arian mother Justina when they demanded the use of two churches in Milan for Arians. At the urging of prominent Roman pagans Valentinian contemplated restoring an ancient pagan altar removed by his predecessor, but Ambrose insisted that Valentinian would cease to be a Christian if he did so. In 388 the bishop of Callinicon incited a Christian attack on a Jewish synagogue. When Theodosius the Great, a thoroughly Catholic emperor, commanded the bishop to rebuild the synagogue, Ambrose publicly denounced the emperor and forced him to absolve the riotous bishop of the obligation of restoration. Two years later, after an insurrection against the government at Thessalonica, Theodosius punished the rebels by a massacre of 5000 inhabitants of the town. Regarding this brutal act as outright murder, Bishop Ambrose denied the sacraments to the emperor and virtually excommunicated him. Theodosius resisted, but not for long; after performing public penance he was solemnly restored by Ambrose to communion with the Church. The sovereign thus admitted a fundamental restriction on his autocratic power in recognizing that even his public acts must conform to the principles of morality upheld by the Catholic Church.

The Gelasian Theory.   Ambrose's doctrine was taken up and given authoritative expression a full century later by Pope Gelasius (492–496). In a letter to Emperor Anastasius the pope distinguished between the separate spheres of activity of Church and State. On the one hand, he wrote, there is the secular realm which is the proper subject of the emperor, and on the other the spiritual realm over which the bishops hold sway. Neither power must exercise the rights of the other. Yet spirituals are intrinsically superior to temporals, for bishops are responsible to God for the salvation of the emperor. In case of conflict of jurisdiction, therefore, the bishop's decision prevails. Ambrose's examples and Gelasius' theories served as a ready arsenal to be drawn on in future centuries by defenders of the Church's independence. The critical defect of the Gelasian theory was the difficulty of differentiating in practice between the two authorities, since every human act, being a moral act, is subject to ecclesiastical jurisdiction.

St. Augustine, 354–430.   Tagaste in African Numidia was the birthplace of Augustine, second of the triumvirate of Latin Fathers in the closing decades of the fourth century. From childhood he knew of Christ, for his mother, St. Monica, enrolled him as a catechumen at an early age, but he learned little doctrine. His education was in the best pagan Roman tradition. In his sixteenth year he went to Carthage where he pursued advanced studies and dissipation with equal zeal. In 374 Augustine entered upon a brilliant career as teacher of grammar and rhetoric, at Tagaste, Carthage, Rome, and finally at the capital of the western Empire, Milan. During these twelve years his thirst for truth led him successively into the Manichean sect and then to Neo-Platonism, but without satisfaction. At the peak of his career in Milan Augustine came under the influence of St. Ambrose, whose sermons he attended to study the bishop's style of rhetoric. Aided by kindly friends and by his reading of St. Paul, after a hard struggle to free himself from his worldly ties, Augustine was converted. Ambrose baptized him in 387. Having resigned his professorship Augustine returned to Tagaste to take up a monastic life of poverty and prayer. In 391 he was ordained and five years later chosen bishop of Hippo. Here he remained until his death in 430, continually occupied with care of the souls in his charge, with combating heresy, and with the writings that brought him renown.

No Christian thinker has ever surpassed Augustine in the extent of his influence over succeeding generations. For 800 years Augustine alone dominated every aspect of European thought, faith, and theology, and the impress of his genius on Christianity is ineffaceable. Most of his writings were composed in response to immediate problems, but the nature of the subjects treated and Augustine's ability to go directly to the fundamental universal issues behind every conflict have given a permanent value to his work. Two of Augustine's volumes are undisputed classics among the great books of the world.

On the Trinity is Augustine's most profound theological treatise. He attacked the errors of the Manicheans, Donatists, Pelagians, and Arians, composed exegetical works and Scriptural commentaries, and treated educational and psychological subjects also in masterly fashion. Best known among laymen are Augustine's Confessions and City of God. The former narrates his own intellectual and moral development and his progress into the Church. Between 413 and 426 he labored on the City of God to refute the accusations of pagans who tried to blame Christianity for the disastrous Visigothic sack of Rome in 410. Here Augustine treated not only the relationship between the Christian God and the Roman Empire but he went on to explain the full scope of God's relation to the progress and destiny of mankind in terms of a philosophy of history resting on principles of perennial validity.

St. Jerome, 347–419. Jerome's life falls into two distinct periods; prior to 385 he traveled extensively and acquired the wide knowledge which he employed after that date when he settled down to literary pursuits in Bethlehem. Stridon in Dalmatia was his birthplace. His Christian parents sent him to Rome for the best available education in Greek and Latin literature and philosophy. After some youthful dissipation which left a strong impression on his character, Jerome resolved to become a monk. For three years he lived as a hermit in the Syrian desert, busy with study and ascetic practices. St. Gregory Nazianzus' fame attracted Jerome to Constantinople, whence he returned to Rome as the protégé of Pope Damasus. Jerome's austerity, his biting criticism of important people, and his relations with aristocratic ladies whom he introduced to the ascetic life stimulated malicious resentment which caused him to miss being elected to succeed Damasus in 384. Leaving Rome with a select group Jerome returned to the Holy Land. After a short visit to the centers of Egyptian monasticism, he settled at Bethlehem where he passed the remainder of his life surrounded by monks whom he directed along with the convent of women instituted by Paula and the women from Rome.

Scriptural, historical, dogmatic, and controversial works poured from Jerome's fluent pen in amazing quantity, but his outstanding achievement was his translation of the Scriptures. Several different and partly erroneous versions of the Scriptures were then in circulation. At Pope Damasus' suggestion Jerome set himself first to the task of revising current texts; however, it soon became evident that what was needed was an entirely new translation into Latin of the oldest and most reliable Greek and Hebrew manuscripts. To his mastery of the classical languages Jerome therefore added a thorough command of the Hebrew tongue as well as a knowledge of Jewish history, life, and thought. No other Father of the Church could match Jerome in this. His edition of the Scriptures, completed between 385 and 405 with the exception of certain books, gradually superseded all others, but it was not until the thirteenth century that it became known exclusively as the *Vulgate*. In 1546 the Council of Trent decreed that it be considered the authentic version accepted by the Church.

Supplementing the *Vulgate* Jerome composed commentaries on many of the books of the Old Testament in which he displayed his tremendous range of learning in secular and sacred subjects. He prepared the first scientific treatise on Mariology. His controversial writings arose largely from the disputes at the end of the fourth century concerning the errors of Origen whom Jerome first admired greatly but later criticized. Rufinus of Aquileia, a scholar of no mean ability himself, opposed his long-time friend Jerome on this matter. An irascible, suspicious temperament and a tendency to personal abuse in the form of heaped-up epithets marred Jerome's controversial works and embittered his outlook on life.

Heresy in the Age of the Western Fathers. Of the heresies which, after Arianism, troubled the West and occupied the Fathers, four stand out: Donatism, Priscillianism, Pelagianism, and Manicheism. Donatism, having originated in Constantine's day, remained an African heresy, spreading at Rome only among African immigrants. Alternating government persecution and toleration through the fourth century provided martyrs for the sect while failing to destroy it. Not only did the Donatists organize their own church and hierarchy of hundreds of bishops, they also produced an extensive propaganda. For some time in fact the Donatist controversialists met no serious opposition among the Catholics. An alliance between Donatists and a bandit gang called Circumcellians, and schism within their own ranks, weakened them only slightly.

Bishop Optatus of Milevis about 367 undertook a new methodical refutation of Donatism, and subsequently the combined labor of Aurelius of Carthage and Augustine of Hippo finally turned the tide. A group of Augustine's treatises exposed Donatist errors, while a series of conferences climaxing in that at Carthage in 411 held out the possibility of reconciliation. Many preferred schism, however, so that a new series of laws was decreed against them by Emperor Theodosius. Augustine felt qualms about relying on the secular arm until he was convinced that the Donatists had no case in doctrine or discipline. Traces of the heresy survived into the seventh century.

Priscillian, a Spanish priest, began about 370–375 to spread an extreme form of asceticism to which he made numerous converts, including several bishops. His program resembled encratism and smacked of Gnosticism in that it derogated everything concerning the human body and exalted the spirit. Priscillian forbade marriage, for example, unless generation of children was prevented. Condemned at the Council of Saragossa in 380 and banned by edict of Gratian, Priscillian went to Rome and thence to Milan, but both Pope Damasus and St. Ambrose repulsed him. When the usurping emperor Maximus appeared in Gaul, Priscillian appealed to him, but Itacius and Hydacius, Priscillian's chief opponents, brought about his condemnation and execution, the first death penalty for heresy. Thereupon a violent dispute arose over the issue of the use of force against heretics, under cover of which Priscillianism spread further in Spain and Gaul.

Denial of original sin and its consequences and affirmation of man's ability to achieve salvation through the unaided effort of his own will represent the two leading features of Pelagianism. Pelagius, a British monk, and Celestius, a Roman lawyer, advanced these ideas, which were not totally novel with themselves, when they took refuge in Africa after 410. Their chief opponent was St. Augustine, Doctor of Grace, advocate of exactly the opposite theories: so real is original sin that all descendants of Adam are helpless to resist evil without God's grace. Condemned in Africa, Pelagianism reached Palestine. St. Jerome attacked it from his retreat at Bethlehem, but a synod of bishops at Diospolis (Lydda) in 415 found Pelagius innocent of error. Appeal was taken to Rome. Pope Innocent concurred in the condemnation of Pelagius, but Zozimus, who soon followed Innocent, hesitated. A gathering of over two hundred African bishops at Carthage in 418, with Augustine as its guiding spirit, reiterated the earlier African decision, and persuaded Zozimus to do likewise. Meanwhile, Pelagianism spread in Italy and Britain, and did not entirely disappear until the end of the fifth century.

Mani (crucified in 272), the Persian founder of Manicheism, had sought to create a syncretistic religion fusing Greek, Christian, Persian, and Indian elements. Calling himself an apostle of Christ, the Paraclete, or brother of Jesus, Zoroaster and Buddha, he fell strongly under Gnostic influences, which gave his sect its characteristic dualistic theology and orgiastic ritual. Basic to Mani's teaching was the supposition that there existed two ultimate principles, one of good, the other of evil — sources respectively of things of the spirit and of material beings.

Despite Diocletian's prohibition under pain of death by burning, Manicheism seeped into the Empire. Its greatest convert was St. Augustine, whom it held for nine years. After his conversion to Christianity Augustine led the Catholic assault by treatises and public debates with leading Manichees. Pope Leo and the civil authorities at Rome conducted a formal judicial investigation of the sect in 443 which confirmed suspicions of ritualistic sexual perversion practiced by the Manichees. The notoriety of the investigation and Pope Leo's vigilance led to its gradual decline, but Manicheism did not disappear entirely. In the twelfth century it experienced a vigorous revival in the Catharist movement in southern France.

REVIEW   AIDS

1. Describe the organization of the Church in the fourth century.
2. In what way did the growth of Christianity affect Roman society?
3. Indicate the salient factors in the history of the great metropolitan sees.
4. What is the papal primacy? Give some evidence of its recognition in the fourth and fifth centuries.
5. Explain the problem of Church and State in the Roman Empire and the solutions proposed by St. Ambrose and Pope Gelasius.
6. Summarize the chief events in the life of St. Augustine.
7. What was St. Jerome's contribution to the Church?

8. Sketch the beliefs and history of the Donatists, Pelagians, Priscillianists, and Manichees.

SUGGESTIONS FOR FURTHER READING

For the early papacy see E. G. Weltin, *The Ancient Popes* (Westminster: 1964), and M. Winter, *St. Peter and the Popes* (Baltimore: 1960). John Chapman, *Studies on the Early Papacy* (New York: n.d.) retains its importance as a study of celebrated disputes. Popular treatments of the Fathers, emphasizing personalities, are Robert Payne's two books, *The Fathers of the Western Church* (New York: 1951) and *The Holy Fire* (New York: 1957), but for patristic thought a handy survey is P. de Labriolle, *History and Literature of Christianity from Tertullian to Boethius* (New York: 1925). C. N. Cochrane, *Christianity and Classical Culture* (New York: 1957) offers a penetrating analysis. Excellent new biographical studies of the great Western Fathers are now available: Jean Steinmann, *St. Jerome and His Times* (Notre Dame: 1959); F. van der Meer, *Augustine the Bishop* (London: 1961); Angelo Paredi, *Saint Ambrose, His Life and Times* (Notre Dame: 1964).

DOCUMENTS

Many problems were engendered for the Church from the fourth century onward by the claims of the Patriarchate of Constantinople to be a rival to the Bishop of Rome in ecclesiastical matters. The weakness of these claims is revealed by comparing the beginning of the former with the origin of the Roman church. The rise of the Constantinopolitan Patriarchate is chronicled in the decrees of several of the early general councils. These selections are from H. J. Schroeder, *Disciplinary Decrees of the General Councils* (St. Louis: Herder, 1937). Used by permission.

Canon 3 of the First Ecumenical Council of Constantinople, 381.

The bishop of Constantinople shall have the primacy of honor after the bishop of Rome, because the same is New Rome.

Canon 28 of the Council of Chalcedon, 451.

Following in all things the decisions of the holy fathers, and knowing the canon of the 150 most God-beloved bishops which has just been read, we also enact and decree the same things respecting the privileges of the most holy Church of Constantinople, New Rome. For the fathers rightfully granted privileges to the See of Old Rome, because that city was imperial, and the 150 most God-beloved bishops, actuated by the same consideration, awarded equal privileges to the most holy see of New Rome, judging with good reason that the city which is honored with the sovereignty and the senate, and enjoys equal privileges with old imperial Rome, should in ecclesiastical matters also be magnified as she is and rank next after her. And (we decree), therefore, that in the dioceses of Pontus, Asia, and Thrace, the metropolitans only, together with those bishops of the aforesaid dioceses living among barbarians, shall be ordained by the aforesaid most holy see of the most holy Church at Constantinople; while, of course, each metropolitan of the aforesaid dioceses shall ordain the bishops of his province in union with the (other) bishops of the same province, as is prescribed by the holy canons; but the metropolitans of the aforesaid dioceses, as has been said, shall be ordained by the archbishop of Constantinople, after the proper elections have been held according to custom and reported to him.

2. One of the very early attempts to establish the proper theoretical relationship between the Christian Church and the Christian State is Pope Gelasius I's letter to Emperor Anastasius I, 494, on the secular and the priestly powers. Conradus Kirch, *Enchiridion Fontium Historiae Ecclesiasticae Antiquae*, 6th ed. by Leo Ueding (Barcelona: 1947), pp. 548–549.

I beg your Piety not to judge duty to divine truth as arrogance. I implore that it may never happen that a Roman Emperor resents having the truth brought to his attention. There are two powers, August Emperor, by which the world is chiefly governed: the sacred authority of priests and the royal power. Of these the priests' burden is by far the heavier since they have to render account to God for even the kings of men. You are aware, dearest Son, that although by your dignity you preside over the human race, yet you bow your head humbly before those who have charge of divine things and await from them the means of your salvation. In regard to the reception and proper administration of the Sacraments you know that you ought to be subject rather than superior to those in Holy Orders. And so in these matters you ought to depend on their judgment and not want to compel them to follow your will.

If the ministers of religion, recognizing that the right to rule has been bestowed on you by supernatural disposition, also obey your laws as pertaining to public order lest contrary opinions seem to obstruct mundane affairs, with what readiness, I ask you, should you obey those who are empowered to dispense the sacred mysteries? Hence, just as it is hazardous for bishops to keep silent about what is necessary for God's service, so too there is considerable peril for those who (God forbid) refuse when they ought to obey. And if it is proper that the hearts of the faithful be subject to all priests in general who properly administer their divine office, how much the more ought obedience to be given to the incumbent of that see which the Most High has wished to be above all priests and which from the beginning the piety of the whole Church has always respected.

3. The idea quickly developed that the Christian ruler was bound to use his secular power to enforce the laws of the Church regarding discipline as well as doctrine. This is illustrated in a decree issued in 445 by Emperors Theodosius II and Valentinian III making the papal primacy a law of the Roman Empire. It was dangerous because it established precedents for secular interference in ecclesiastical affairs. Translation from James H. Robinson, *Readings in European History*, Vol. I (Boston: Ginn and Co., 1904), p. 72.

Since, then, the primacy of the Apostolic See is established by the merit of St. Peter (who is the chief among the bishops), by the majesty of the city of Rome, and finally by authority of a holy council, no one, without inexcusable presumption, may attempt anything against the authority of that see. Peace will be secured among the churches if every one recognize his ruler. . . .

Lest even a slight commotion should arise in the churches, or the religious order be disturbed, we herewith permanently decree that not only the bishops of Gaul, but those of the other provinces, shall attempt nothing counter to ancient custom without the authority of the venerable father of the Eternal City. Whatever shall be sanctioned by the authority of the Apostolic See shall be law to them and to everyone else; so that if one of the bishops be summoned to the judgment of the Roman bishop and shall neglect to appear, he shall be forced by the moderator of his province to present himself. In all respects let the privileges be maintained which our deified [sic!] predecessors have conferred upon the Roman church.

D.	POPES	WRITERS	HERETICS & HERESY	THE CHURCH	THE WORLD	EMPERORS
				Life of Christ	The *Pax Romana*	Augustus
						Tiberius
				Paul's conversion		Caligula
			Judaizers			Claudius
50	Peter	Epistles		Council of Jerusalem		Nero
		Synoptic Gospels		Paul's journeys	Destruction of	Vespasian
		Didache		Nero's persecution	Jerusalem	
			Gnosticism			Titus
						Domitian
						Nerva
						Trajan
00	Clement I	Clement of Rome		Death of St. John	Consolidation of	
		Ignatius of		Close of the Apostolic	Roman Britain	
		Antioch		Age		Hadrian
				Trajan's rescript		
				Sporadic persecutions	2nd Jewish Revolt	
		Hermas				Antoninus
50	Pius I	Greek Apologists		Continued expansion	Parthian War	
		Justin Martyr				
					Empire at its greatest	Marcus
			Montanus		extent	Aurelius
		Irenaeus of Lyons	Marcion			Commodus
		Pantaenus			Civil war; beginning	
00		Tertullian			of decline	
		Clement of	Sabellius	Schism of Hippolytus		The Severi
	Pontianus	Alexandria				
		Origen			Barrack Emperors	
	Fabian					
50				Decian persecution		Decius
		Cyprian of	Paul of			Valerian
		Carthage	Samosata	Schism of Novatian		Gallienus
				Gallienus' Peace		
					Reorganization of the	Diocletian
					Empire	
		Lactantius			Division of the	
		Eusebius of			Empire	
		Caesarea				
00			Donatism	Anthony of Egypt and		
				beginnings of monas-	Milvian Bridge	Constantine &
		Edict of Milan	Arianism	ticism		Licinius
	Sylvester I			COUNCIL OF		
		Athanasius		NICAEA		Constantius
50	Liberius			Peak of Arianism		Julian
		Pachomius		Cenobitic monachism		
		Hilary				Valens
		Martin of Tours				
		Basil			Battle of Hadrian-	
		Ambrose			ople. Barbarian	
		Jerome	Semi-Arians	COUNCIL OF CON-	invasions begin.	Theodosius I
		Gregory of Nyssa	Macedonians	STANTINOPLE		
		Gregory of	Pneumatomachi			
00		Nazianzen		Paganism outlawed		
	Innocent I	Augustine		Monasticism at Lerins	Visigoths capture	
	Boniface I				Rome	
		Chrysostom				Theodosius II
		Cyril of Alexandria	Nestorius	COUNCIL OF		
				EPHESUS		Valentinian III
		John Cassian		Robber Council		
50			Manicheans		Attila and Huns	
	Leo I, the				Vandals in Rome	
	Great		Eutyches	COUNCIL OF	Anglo-Saxons in	
				CHALCEDON	Britain	
			Monophysitism		Odoacer	
				Encyclion	End of Roman Em-	Romulus
00	Gelasius	Dionysius the			pire in West	Augustullus
		Areopagite		*Henoticon*	Ostrogoths in Italy	Zeno
				Acacian Schism	Clovis unites Franks	

FIVE CENTURIES OF PERIL

Chapter 6

EASTERN CONTROVERSIES
AND COUNCILS

F UNDAMENTAL cultural and intellectual differences between the eastern and western parts of the Roman Empire, minimized by superimposed political unity, reappeared after the fifth century political collapse when the Greek and Latin worlds again went their separate ways. Inevitably this development was reflected in ecclesiastical matters also, so that it is possible to consider as a natural unit the history of the Greek Church from the close of the Arian crisis to the eighth century. This period witnessed the great Christological controversies of Nestorianism and Monophysitism and the four ecumenical councils which examined them: Ephesus, Chalcedon, II Constantinople, and III Constantinople.

Basic Aspects. Certain features characterize eastern Church history and distinguish it from the contemporary West: (1) a deep-seated interest in the most speculative aspects of Christian theology; (2) the rivalry of the two theological schools at Antioch and Alexandria, each with its own special viewpoint, each desiring to dominate the other, especially in regard to control of the new patriarchate of Constantinople; (3) the interplay of religious and political questions; (4) the domination of the State over the Church (caesaro-papism), not only in matters of discipline and of ecclesiastical appointments but even, finally, in doctrinal matters also.

Greek Patrology. The golden age of the Greek-speaking Fathers coincided roughly with the peak of Latin patristic writings. St. Athanasius championed the divinity of Christ in the first half of the Arian dispute. Mention has also been made of the Cappadocian Fathers (so-called from their native province in Asia Minor), St. Basil, St. Gregory Nazianzen, and St. Gregory of Nyssa. Basil, known as "the Great" even to his contemporaries, is especially remembered for his monastic rules. All of his works — dogmatic treatises, homilies, letters — give evidence of high literary ability. Gregory of Nyssa, Basil's brother, surpassed him as a philosopher and mystic. Gregory of Nazianzen alternated between the contemplative monastic life and the active life of a bishop; as patriarch of Constantinople he presided over the great council of 381 but shortly afterward resigned to end his days as a hermit. As a group the fame of the Cappadocians rests on their formulation of Catholic teaching on the Trinity.

The life of St. John Chrysostom (344–407), Doctor and Father, exemplifies almost every facet of eastern Church history. As scholar and author he ranks with Origen both in quantity and quality. His treatise *On the Priesthood* is the finest of his productions, while 250 homilies on the Pauline Epistles are still regarded as the best commentaries ever written on Paul. The name Chrysostom (golden tongue) refers to his oratorical prowess, for it was chiefly by his talent as a moralist that he left his mark on his generation.

Chrysostom's fame caused Emperor Arcadius to nominate him archbishop of Constantinople but immediately the saint ran afoul of the imperial court by fearlessly denouncing the lax morality of Empress Eudoxia and her courtiers. Among the clergy John made enemies by interfering unasked in affairs of dioceses other than his own. Hence it was a combination of forces that brought about John's downfall. Theophilus, a sinister, ambitious archbishop of Alexandria, resentful of the victory of the Antioch school in the elevation of Chrysostom, its greatest figure, to the see of Constantinople, came to the capital in 403 and assembled a group of bishops in a synod at the royal palace called The Oak. On the basis of slanderous charges of his enemies, John was declared deposed by the synod. Arcadius seconded the sentence by ordering John into exile. There followed in quick succession John's recall, renewed intrigue, arrest and a second exile in 404. At St. John's request Pope Innocent I intervened and excommunicated Theophilus and his episcopal colleagues, but by then John was dead. All the protagonists except Theophilus eventually submitted to the Pope.

Nestorianism. A generation after Chrysostom's death Alexandria and Antioch clashed again in the persons of St. Cyril of Alexandria, Theophilus' nephew and successor, and Nestorius, another famed preacher from Antioch who became patriarch of Constantinople in 428. Here there was no question of mere disciplinary measures but one of dogma, and an abstruse one at that.

Nestorianism, advancing from the Nicene affirmation of the divinity of Christ, explained the relationship of the human and the divine natures in Him as a union of two distinct persons, each with its own particular nature, but conjoined only in a superficial, moral fashion. The acts of Christ the man, according to Nestorius, remained distinct from those of Christ as God. Christ was said in effect to have a dual personality.

Theodore of Mopsuestia, Nestorius' teacher at Antioch, fathered the new heresy, and it reflected the particular concern of the entire Antiochene school. Antioch stressed moral theology, Aristotelian realism, literalness in exegesis, and the true humanity of Christ. On the opposite side stood Alexandria: mystic, Platonic, allegorical, and devoted, in the tradition of St. Athanasius, to defending Christ's divinity. In moderate dress both systems were perfectly orthodox even if suspect to each other; when carried to extremes, Alexandria was as prone to heresy as Antioch.

Both abstract theological points of view were entirely beyond the grasp of the ordinary Christian, as such matters always are, until some chance circumstance reduces them to the level of everyday religious practice. This occurred in 428 when Nestorius solemnly informed the faithful of Constantinople that it was incorrect to refer to the Blessed Virgin as Mother of God (*Theotokos*), for she was mother only of the human element in Christ, not of His divine personality. A popular outcry resulted. Without hesitation Cyril of Alexandria, belligerent, imperious, tactless, leapt into the fray with admonitions and denunciations against Nestorius. Both sides appealed to Rome. In August, 430, Pope Celestine I and a synod of western bishops condemned Nestorius' teaching and sent four letters eastward: to Nestorious himself, bidding him retract within ten days; to the church at Constantinople; to Bishop John of Antioch; and to Cyril, commissioning him papal legate to receive the heretic's retraction.

Cyril, exceeding his instructions, drew up in an Egyptian council a statement of twelve propositions for Nestorius to renounce, so as to leave no loophole for the heretic's escape through semantic juggling.

Cyril's phraseology, however, proved highly suspicious, for it was definitely equivocal, especially the expression, "One is the nature of the incarnate Word," a statement found in the writings of a condemned heretic, Apolinaris of Laodicea. Cyril, one of the intellectual giants of the patristic age, could not fairly be accused of heresy, but some of his expressions, taken out of context, left the wrong impression, especially among the Antiochene theologians. Hence Bishops John of Antioch and Theodoret of Cyrus, always ready to criticize Alexandrian thinkers, organized an opposition party, not from any desire to protect Nestorius, but to checkmate Cyril. Since a general conference seemed the only way out of the confusion, Emperor Theodosius II convoked the third ecumenical council to assemble at Ephesus in 431.

The General Council of Ephesus.   The Council convened amid considerable disorder. Under the watchful eye of an imperial magistrate St. Cyril called the assembly of 159 bishops to order. Nestorius declined to attend to defend himself. After an investigation that convinced everyone of his error, Nestorius, still refusing to retract, was condemned and deposed. Theodore of Mopsuestia's death before the Council saved him from a like fate. Shortly after the close of the first session the papal legates arrived and they confirmed the decree against Nestorius. John of Antioch and his suffragans came even later but, distrustful of Cyril and Alexandrian theology in general, the Antiochenes organized their own pseudo-council of forty-three bishops, excommunicated Cyril as a heretic and appealed to the emperor. Theodosius, finding the council unsatisfactory for several reasons, arrested both Nestorius and Cyril. Only after months of backstairs intrigue did Cyril secure his liberty and persuade the emperor to banish Nestorius and accept the twelve propositions as well. With that the Council closed, but not until 433 were Antioch and Alexandria reconciled, and then only through a compromise in which the twelve propositions were passed over in silence.

Nestorianism, condemned, did not die. Numerous adherents of the heresy lived in Syria and Mesopotamia. The theological school at Edessa was a Nestorian stronghold. In 489 when the government closed this school, exiled teachers and students sought refuge among the Persians where a Nestorian or Syro-Chaldean church was organized. From there Nestorianism penetrated central Asia, China, India, and Ceylon where it survived for over a thousand years.

Monophysitism.   Within the Roman Empire the anti-Nestorian movement fell into the opposite heresy of Monophysitism which flourished wherever Alexandrian influence was strong since it claimed to rest on the theology of St. Cyril. Where Nestorius had stressed the separateness of Christ's two natures, the Monophysites stressed the oneness of His Person in such a way that they taught the absorption of His human nature into His divine nature. Eutyches, supervisor of a Constantinopolitan monastery, a man of little education or formal theological training, promulgated this teaching, which is sometimes known as Eutycheanism. Bishop Theodoret of Cyrus, Cyril's opponent fifteen years earlier, published a book, *The Beggerman,* in refutation of the new heresy. Archbishop Flavian of Constantinople summoned a local synod of thirty-two bishops who questioned Eutyches and found his theories erroneous. With that the matter should have ended, but Eutyches had friends in high places.

Dioscorus, bishop of Alexandria since 444, an ecclesiastical ruffian to speak bluntly, intervened to protect Eutyches on the pretext of defending the orthodox faith of St. Cyril against new Nestorians. Emperor Theodosius II also sheltered the monk and furthered his proposal for a new general council. Pope St. Leo I, who had received colored reports of the controversy, consented. Ephesus was again selected as the site, and the date set for 449. Three western delegates represented Pope Leo. To them Leo entrusted a dogmatic letter addressed to Flavian, the so-called *Tome,* propounding Catholic teaching on the disputed point so that the assemblage might have a true standard for judging Eutyches.

The Latrocinium. The council turned out to be a travesty. Pope Leo dubbed it a *latrocinium* or robber council and history has retained the name. Dioscorus presided in highhanded fashion. Ignoring the papal legates and Leo's instructions, he first reinstated Eutyches, over whom he personally had no jurisdiction whatsoever, then packed a jury to hear the monk's trial. Eutyches was of course acquitted. Next Dioscorus turned the council against Flavian, whose condemnation and deposition were voted. At this point the meeting broke up in a riot of Syrian monks in which Flavian was fatally injured. Emperor Theodosius solemnly ratified the conciliar acts and threatened deposition and banishment to any bishop who dared protest.

Pope Leo indignantly denounced the robber council as soon as he received his legates' reports — they had barely escaped Ephesus with their lives — and appeals from a few Oriental bishops, but as long as Theodosius lived nothing could be changed. In 450 Theodosius died and Marcian assumed the throne; the atmosphere cleared at once. Exiles returned,

Eutyches was jailed, and many bishops rescinded their approval of the acts of the council. Desiring a final settlement, Marcian convoked a new council, to which Leo reluctantly consented, to meet at Chalcedon across the Bosphorus from Constantinople.

The Council of Chalcedon, 451.   During three weeks 630 bishop sat in the largest ecumenical council until that of 1870. Practically all were Greeks. Five papal legates attended, Paschasinus of Lilybaeum in Sicily presiding. Doctrinally the work of the Council was to reverse the acts of the robber council. This was accomplished, but only with considerable struggle. Dioscorus now stood trial and suffered deposition as a heretic. A formula of faith was accepted based on creeds of the three earlier ecumenical councils plus Leo's *Tome,* reading in part: "We confess one and the same Christ Jesus, the only-begotten Son, whom we acknowledge to have two natures, without confusion, transformation, division or separation between them . . . the attributes of each nature are safeguarded and subsist in one person." Thus the middle way was mapped out between Nestorianism and Monophysitism. Also enacted were divers disciplinary canons, of which the twenty-eighth raised Constantinople to the rank of second see in Christendom.

Spread of Monophysitism.   As far as theological questions were concerned, Chalcedon settled the Monophysite heresy once for all. What the attitude of the Monophysites would be was another matter. These insisted that the Chalcedonian formula for the two natures in Christ contradicted the decision of the ecumenical Council of Ephesus where Nestorius' theory of two persons had been anathematized. They rested their case on St. Cyril's twelve propositions, forgetting that Cyril himself had discarded them on realizing their equivocal wording. At the root of the matter lay a confusion of the theological terms "person" and "nature."

However, theology was not the sole consideration. Questions of politics and culture entered into the picture, just as the long stubbornness of the African Donatists originated in social and economic motives. Monophysitism exercised a strong attraction in Syria and Egypt precisely at a time when these provinces were feeling a desire for independence of the Roman Empire. National and social instincts, long suppressed by foreign rule, re-emerged as the Empire's weakness became apparent and fastened upon Monophysitism as a means of furthering these secular aims. Thus along the Nile Greek began now to disappear as the liturgical language and the Monophysites substituted the native Coptic, while

Syriac became the official language of the Syrian Monophysites. For over a century the most powerful man in Egypt had been the Patriarch of Alexandria, and in the victories of Athanasius, Theophilus, Cyril, and Dioscorus over Constantinople their people saw a kind of revenge for Greek political domination and an expression of their own independent spirit. Hence in the Monophysite dispute they continued to rally around the heretical patriarch rather than admit defeat at the hands of the Greeks and Romans. Egyptian bishops at Chalcedon declared that they were afraid to return home with the report of Dioscorus' deposition. When Alexandria heard the news it rose in revolt, massacred the imperial garrison, and tore to pieces the orthodox patriarch whom Constantinople appointed. From the emperor's viewpoint, then, Monophysites were rebels against his political authority as well as against the authority of the Church, and the preservation of the Empire demanded an end to the dispute.

Attempts at Reconciliation. For twenty years after Chalcedon the Monophysites of Syria, Palestine to a lesser degree, and Egypt resisted attempts of Emperors Marcian and Leo II to impose on them the doctrine of two natures, while virtual civil war raged in these provinces. With the attempted usurpation of the imperial throne by Basiliscus in 476–477 a new policy was introduced, for Basiliscus recalled the Monophysite exiles, including Timothy the Cat and Peter the Fuller, Monophysite bishops of Alexandria and Antioch, and tried to arbitrate the dispute. Although his dogmatic formula, the *Encyclion*, succeeded temporarily, his defeat by Emperor Zeno ended the matter. Zeno, however, taking a leaf from Basiliscus' book, promulgated in 482 his own formula of reconciliation, the *Henoticon*, drawn up by Acacius, patriarch of Constantinople. This was a statement of the minimum requirements of faith Zeno expected from his subjects; it simply ignored Chalcedon and established a test of faith based on the earlier councils. Many accepted the *Henoticon*, Catholics as well as Monophysites, but many too did not, and among these latter was the pope. Under the circumstances, to ignore Chalcedon meant an implicit denial of the Council's work, and this impression Pope Simplicius had to avoid.

Because of Acacius' pro-Monophysite tendencies Pope Felix condemned and deposed him and all his followers who accepted Zeno's act of union. Acacius thereupon went into schism, taking many but by no means all Catholics under his jurisdiction with him. During the thirty-five years of the Acacian schism Monophysitism flourished. Zeno's tactics tacitly favored the heretics; Emperor Anastasius (491–518) boldly declared for Monophysitism in a desperate attempt to recover his eastern provinces. If the Catholics could not vanquish the heretics, Anastasius reasoned, perhaps the Monophysites could overcome the Catholics. Anything for the sake of unity. But Anastasius only alienated his Catholic subjects who wanted to remain orthodox even if schismatic while the heretics stayed unconvinced.

In 518 the Acacian schism came to an end. As soon as Emperor Anastasius died, the stanchly Catholic populace of the capital raised such an outcry that Emperor Justin had to reopen negotiations with Rome. Hormisdas occupied the chair of Peter and proffered a formula of reunion that was accepted by the Constantinopolitan patriarch and the bishops of his province acknowledging the guidance of the pope in ecclesiastical disputes. Not only was the Formula of Hormisdas a recognition of the papal primacy of jurisdiction, it also voiced the claim that "Christianity has ever been kept undefiled in the Apostolic See," a reference to papal infallibility.

The Age of Justinian. Caesaro-papism gained ground within the Eastern Roman or Byzantine Empire under Justinian (527–565) and his successors. No longer is the State satisfied to be the secular arm for executing decisions of the Church; from now on the State makes all major decisions itself. Not only that, the emperor appoints and deposes patriarchs and bishops and supervises ecclesiastical administrative detail. Although Justinian embodies caesaro-papism he certainly did not create it. Actually it was inherent in the type of despotic government headed by Justinian, for absolute rulers from the ancient world down to the most modern totalitarian governments have always reacted in identical fashion toward the Church.

Yet Justinian seemed always sincerely religious, so much so that some historians have seen religious fervor as the guiding principle in his every undertaking, judging even his reconquest of the West as an attempt to defeat the Arianism of the barbarian kings holding sway in Africa, Spain, and Italy. Whole sections of the famous Justinian code deal with religious topics such as proper qualifications for bishops and episcopal prerogatives. With a lavish hand he built monasteries and churches, of which the church of the Holy Wisdom (St. Sophia) in Constantinople has ever since been considered a wonder of ecclesiastical architecture. Nor can his support of Christian missionaries be disregarded.

Obsessed with the despot's love of uniformity, Justinian sought to quash all dissident religious groups. Dying paganism received its *coup de grâce* when Justinian closed its last stronghold, the public school of Athens, in 529. Repressive measures hampered the Jews. Christian heretics — Montanists, Manicheans, Nestorians — felt his harsh hand, but the most pressing heresy, Monophysitism, defied him to the end. This was due partly to factors already noted as contributing to this heresy's strength and also to the Monophysite leanings of Justinian's virile wife Theodora, without whom Justinian's reign would have been an entirely different thing.

Justinian and the Monophysites. In dealing with the Monophysites Justinian followed Theodora's whims and tried first a policy of reconciliation. He permitted exiles to return, housed 500 heretic monks in one of his own palaces in the capital, and by employing pressure secured the election in 536 of Anthimus, a concealed Monophysite, as patriarch. Severus of Antioch, a leading Monophysite, figured openly in ecclesiastical politics in Constantinople. Jacob Bardaeus, bishop of Edessa, reorganized the Syrian Monophysites and gave his name to their so-called Jacobite church. When it seemed as if the heretics were about to triumph completely, Pope Agapetus arrived in Constantinople on a diplomatic mission from the Ostrogothic king in Italy. Agapetus unhesitatingly opposed Anthimus and brought about his deposition. Toward Agapetus as toward all the popes in the early years of his reign Justinian showed great respect, on one occasion addressing the pope as "head of all holy churches" in acknowledgment of the papal primacy.

Justinian's second attempt at a rapprochement with Monophysitism concerned the Three Chapters. These were selected passages from the writings of Theodore of Mopsuestia, Theodoret of Cyrus, and Ibas of Edessa, all dead nearly a century, who had been involved in the Nestorian controversy, the first as Nestorius' teacher, the other two as opponents of St. Cyril. Theodore had died before Chalcedon but the Council investigated and reinstated Theodoret and Ibas. Justinian demanded the condemnation of Theodore personally as well as the passages he cited as a way of freeing Chalcedon from the stigma of Nestorianism which the Monophysites attached to it and thus facilitating the Monophysite acceptance of its decisions. Theodore of Askidas, Archbishop of Caesarea in Cappadocia, suggested this scheme to Justinian in order to divert him from a contemporary Origenist dispute in which the emperor was meddling.

When Justinian issued a decree condemning the Three Chapters as heretical and calling upon the bishops to subscribe to his dogmatic statement, he encountered opposition, for Catholics saw in the emperor's act a dangerous derogation of an ecumenical council. Many eastern bishops acquiesced, however, either with reservation or under compulsion, since the Chapters as they stood isolated from context did express heretical opinions. The West denounced the whole thing. Pope Vigilius (537–555), a pitiful creature who owed his office to Theodora, added his protest. Thereupon Justinian had Vigilius kidnaped and brought to Constantinople in 547. For eight years pope and emperor thrust and parried in a duel to outwit or outlast the other; neither escaped the contest with his honor vindicated.

After lengthy discussions with Justinian, during which time he was not mistreated, Vigilius was won over to the emperor's view. In 548 he published his *Judicatum* concurring in Justinian's edict but specifically upholding the authority of the Council of Chalcedon. Immediately the West objected strenuously. An African synod excommunicated Vigilius while the bishops of Dalmatia and Illyricum went into schism. Thoroughly confused, Vigilius reversed himself and by a *Constitutum* recalled the *Judicatum*. Justinian angrily condemned the Three Chapters a second time, with approval of the Greek bishops, and turned wrathfully against Vigilius. On one occasion when the emperor's soldiers tried to drag the pontiff from a church where he had taken refuge Vigilius clung so tightly to the columns supporting the altar that the whole thing toppled over. Public opinion would not stand for such treatment of the pope whom the people rescued from Justinian's police. Justinian had to moderate his tactics, and it was finally agreed to summon a general council.

Fifth Ecumenical Council, 553. The second general Council of Constantinople was highly unusual. Justinian and Vigilius had each consented to calling it in hopes of dominating its proceedings, but the emperor outmaneuvered the pope and controlled the Council closely. Vigilius, therefore, and a dozen or so western bishops who happened to be in Constantinople refused to attend. At its final session the Council voted to anathematize the Three Chapters along the lines of Justinian's edict. Living in exile on an island in the Sea of Marmora, ill-treated and deprived of counselors, Vigilius early in 554 concurred in the Council's decision. After eight years' absence the pope was permitted to return to Rome, but he died en route. Fifty years later Pope Gregory I recognized the Council as ecumenical in so far as "nothing was violated or in any way changed in the matter of religion." Yet despite Justinian's efforts in their behalf the Monophysites remained aloof. In fact, Justinian personally veered more and more toward heresy in his later years.

Heraclius and Monothelitism.　Justinian's immediate successors vacillated between toleration and brutal persecution of the Monophysites. The political significance of the religious dissensions became manifest in the period 611–617 when Byzantium's hereditary foe Persia swept victoriously into the southern Monophysite provinces which the debilitated Empire could not defend. Jerusalem fell in 614, the invaders destroying Christian sanctuaries and carrying off the Holy Cross. Within ten years Emperor Heraclius (610–641) recovered everything including the Cross but the series of calamities recalled the need for religious unity and impelled a new attempt at reconciliation. The tale is the same: Catholic emperors granting concessions to intransigent heretics and being foiled by popes who objected to imperial meddling in theological disputes and who, far from the scene of conflict and with no political interests at stake, were in a better position to judge projected compromises objectively.

Patriarch Sergius of Constantinople advanced the scheme adopted by Heraclius which is known as the heresy of Monothelitism. Because the disputed points of person and natures in Christ could not be arbitrated, Sergius hoped to find common ground for heretic and orthodox in the as yet not explicitly or officially considered question of the operation and will of Christ, which Sergius declared to be one despite His two natures. The Monophysite patriarchs of Alexandria and Antioch were won over by 633 and five years later Heraclius sought to put his official stamp on the reunion of the churches by his decree, the *Ecthesis,* drawn up by Sergius professing belief in one will, summoning all Christians to do likewise, and forbidding further discussion.

Opposition to the *Ecthesis* came from St. Sophronius, Patriarch of Jerusalem, and St. Maximus Confessor, the most capable theologian of the time. Anticipating trouble, Sergius appealed to Pope Honorius I (625–638) who apparently misunderstood the issue. Honorius' reply upheld Sergius' opinion and commended the patriarch for trying to silence those who spoke of two principles of operation in Christ. Yet when the *Ecthesis* appeared, even though two synods at Constantinople approved it, it encountered nothing but opposition from the Latins. Pope Severinus denounced it in 640 and a Roman synod outlawed Monothelitism.

As an attempt to pacify the Monophysites the *Ecthesis* and Monothelitism failed. The very year of their promulgation witnessed the loss of Syria and Palestine to the all-conquering Moslems, and Egypt followed them into bondage shortly. The Arabs did not persecute Christianity after the initial rush of conquest and resistance, but they definitely favored the Monophysites since orthodoxy was more closely linked to allegiance to the Roman Emperor. For their part the Monophysites preferred the tolerance of the Arabs to the imperial policies. Thus Monophysitism triumphed but it was a hollow victory, for all vigor gradually disappeared from Christianity in Moslem lands and eventually many Monophysites apostatized to Islam. An incidental further result of the Moslem advance was a great augmentation of the prestige of the Patriarchate of Constantinople, which alone of the four eastern patriarchates survived under Christian rulers in a Christian state.

But Monothelitism had made a convert of Emperor Constans II (641–668) who kept the artificial heresy alive. Following established custom, Constans in 648 issued his own religious edict, the *Typos,* a disciplinary measure forbidding all criticism of Monothelitism. Nevertheless, Pope Martin I (649–655) condemned the *Ecthesis,* the *Typos,* and Monothelitism after careful investigation by a Lateran synod. Rome being still under imperial rule and the pope a Byzantine subject, Constans ordered his officials to send Martin to Constantinople to stand trial for alleged treason against the State. Amid great suffering and humiliation, the pope was falsely convicted and given the death sentence, but this was commuted to banishment to Cherson in southern Russia where Martin soon died. For a generation Rome and Constantinople refused communion with each other until Constantine IV took the initiative and requested that papal legates be sent to negotiate a reconciliation.

Sixth Ecumenical Council. Before the Roman legates departed great care was taken that the papal position be fully clarified. Pope Agatho endeavored unsuccessfully to procure the services of Theodore of Tarsus, the Greek archbishop of Canterbury, to match wits with Byzantine theologians. A lengthy doctrinal letter similar to Leo's *Tome,* prepared by a Roman synod of 125 bishops, explained the Roman faith in Christ's two wills. Although the assembly in Constantinople was not intended by the emperor to be ecumenical, it subsequently was recognized as such by the Church. All five patriarchates participated personally or by representatives, but less than a hundred prelates attended some of the early sessions.

The Council sat from November, 680, to September, 681. It devoted itself exclusively to Monothelitism. On the basis of Agatho's epistle and the passages cited there from Latin and Greek Fathers, the Council recognized the doctrine of two operations and two wills in Christ as the true teaching of the Church. Proceeding to the names of specific upholders of the Monothelite heresy the Council pronounced anathemas against Sergius, three other bishops of Constantinople, and against Pope

Honorius. The patriarch of Antioch, Macarius, was deposed and excommunicated for having defended Monothelitism at the Council and for refusing to recant. In its official report to Pope Agatho the Council addressed him as "bishop of the first see of the Universal Church . . . since you willingly take for your standing ground the firm rock of the faith. . . ."

Constantine IV's ecclesiastical policies marked the definite abandonment of the trend instituted by Justinian. No longer is there need to conciliate the Monophysites, now under Arab rule and written off as lost, so the eastern church returns to solidarity with the head of the Church in Rome. The similarity between the fourth and the sixth ecumenical Councils, Chalcedon and III Constantinople, confirms the impression of the unity of Christendom under the See of Peter.

Political considerations were also involved in Constantine's actions. A factor in Byzantine ecclesiastical politics since Justinian was the Greek desire to maintain control of Italy. From 568 barbarian Lombards gradually reduced the Italian lands acknowledging Byzantine sovereignty, but the popes protected Greek interests and commanded the only effective resources left to the Empire in the peninsula. Every religious aberration of the emperors, therefore, concerned the popes in a dual capacity: as head of the Church and as a subject of the emperor. Similarly, shrewd emperors avoided losing the good will of the Roman clergy lest there occur a political reaction. In surrendering the Arab conquests, Constantine IV found it expedient to re-establish amicable relations with Rome to hinder further losses to the Empire in its western outposts.

The Trullan Council. Caesaro-papism by this time was such an ingrained Byzantine habit that it could not be surrendered as easily as could the imperial patronage of a particular heresy. This became evident in the reign of Justinian II, Constantine IV's successor, under whom relations with Rome were again strained. In 691 Justinian summoned the Council called Trullan from the domed hall (Gk. *trullos*) in which it met, or Quinisext because its avowed purpose was the completion of the fifth and sixth general Councils. These Councils had enacted no disciplinary canons, and some eastern bishops felt their doctrinal work should be supplemented with such measures. What the Trullan assembly accomplished was to re-enact and invest with an ecumenical character decisions of various earlier councils, general and local, and add to them certain Greek practices. Because of the latter in particular Pope Sergius refused to endorse the Trullan canons and apply them to the Church Universal. When Justinian ordered the arrest of Sergius the army in Italy mutinied and the people drove the imperial commissioners out of Rome. Chastened by this experience and by a political revolution at home, Justinian a decade later invited Pope Constantine to visit Constantinople voluntarily. Contantine came, the last sovereign pontiff to visit the city on the Bosphorus, was received with enthusiasm and devotion by people and emperor alike, and worked out a suitable compromise concerning the Trullan enactments.

Conclusion.   On this amicable note we can break off in order to turn back and pick up the thread of contemporary western developments. The disputes and the succession of great councils in the Greek world fixed for all time the Christological doctrine of the Church, and this was an important achievement. But the cost had been high and the results serious. In Egypt and the Middle East splinter Christian churches now existed cut off by heresy from the Universal Church. Some were Nestorian, and in four districts national Monophysite churches existed: the Egyptian Coptic, the Syrian Jacobite, the Abyssinian, and the Armenian. A thirteenth-century Greek historian, trying to assess the beliefs of the various eastern communities, expressed the opinion that they all believed alike but differed only in terminology. In some ways he was not far from the truth.

REVIEW AIDS

1. Enumerate the chief characteristics of eastern Church history in the fifth to seventh centuries.
2. Name the Greek Fathers and indicate their achievements.
3. Explain Nestorianism; show how it arose from the views of the Antioch school and how Antioch differed from Alexandrian theology.
4. Describe the Robber Council.
5. What was the work of the Council of Chalcedon? Why did Monophysitism survive after its condemnation at Chalcedon?
6. Define Caesaro-papism. Show how Justinian embodied this theory.
7. Compare the Third General Council of Constantinople with the Council of Chalcedon.
8. Summarize the role of the popes in the eastern controversies.

SUGGESTIONS FOR FURTHER READING

For the general background, the best volume is A. A. Vasiliev, *History of the Byzantine Empire 324–1453*, 2nd ed. (Madison: 1952). George Every, *The Byzantine Patriarchate 451–1204* (London: 1947), is a short but at times confusing survey. F. Cayré, *Manual of Patrology*, Vols. I and II, *passim*, is indispensable. Philip Hughes, *A History of the Church*, I, 285–375, is, as usual, remarkably lucid and well written. For the general councils and the background of each consult H. J. Schroeder, *Disciplinary Decrees of the General Councils* (St. Louis: 1937). An older, more scholarly work is C. J. Hefele, *A History of the Councils of the Church*, 5 vols. (Edinburgh: 1896). Two recent studies take up the most important of the early councils: Francis X. Murphy, *Peter Speaks Through Leo* (Washington, D. C.: 1952), and R. V. Sellers, *The Council of Chalcedon: A Historical and Doctrinal Survey* (London: 1953). The former is brief; its author is Catholic. The latter, by an Anglican, is more detailed. For the general councils, Philip Hughes, *The Church in Crisis* (New York: 1961) combines scholarship with a wide appeal.

DOCUMENTS

1. The formula which Pope Hormisdas submitted to the Greeks in A.D. 518 for their acceptance as the condition for being received back into communion with the Church is important not only for ending the Acacian schism but for the much more significant reason that it so clearly expresses the papal primacy and infallibility. H. Denzinger, *Enchiridion Symbolorum*, 24–25th ed., J. Umberg (Barcelona: 1948), pp. 83–84.

The first condition of salvation is to preserve the rule of the true Faith and to deviate in no way at all from the decrees of the Fathers. Because it is impossible that the statement of our Lord Jesus Christ when He said: "Thou art Peter, and upon this rock I will build my Church, etc.," should not be verified and these words are proved by the course of events since religion has ever been kept undefiled in the Apostolic See. Desiring therefore to be in no way separated from this hope and faith and following in all things the decrees of the Fathers, we anathematize all heretics. . . . We accept and approve all the letters written by blessed Pope Leo concerning the Christian religion, as we have said, in all things following the Apostolic See and proclaiming its decrees. And so I hope that I may be deemed worthy to be with you in the one communion which the Apostolic See proclaims. In this is the whole, true and perfect solidarity of the Christian religion. . . . I have subscribed this my profession with my own hand, and I have sent it to you, Hormisdas, holy and venerable pope of the city of Rome.

2. While Pope Hormisdas laid claim to infallible powers in determining the dogma of the Church, Pope Honorius I's attitude toward the Monothelite heresy seemed to impugn those powers. The fact that the third general Council of Constantinople condemned Honorius seemed to indicate beyond doubt that Honorius had been guilty of error. The following four selections shed some light on the question. (Translation adapted from C. J. Hefele, *A History of the Councils of the Church*, ed. and trans. by W. R. Clark [Edinburgh: 1896], V.)

First letter of Honorius to Patriarch Sergius, A.D. 634 (pp. 28 ff.).
Under God's leadership we arrive at the measure of the true faith which the Apostles of truth have spread abroad by the rule of the holy Scriptures:

We confess that the Lord Jesus Christ, mediator between God and men, worked the divine works by means of the humanity hypostatically united to the Divine Word, and that the same (Christ) worked the human works, since the flesh was assumed by the Godhead in an ineffable, unique manner. . . . In agreement with this the Apostle says, "They crucified the Lord of Glory," while yet the Godhead could neither be crucified nor suffer; but on account of that ineffable union we can say both: "God has suffered"; and, "the Manhood came down from heaven with the Godhead." Wherefore also we confess one will of the Lord Jesus Christ, because clearly our nature, not the sin, was assumed by the Godhead, that is, that nature which was created before sin, not that which was corrupted after the sin.

Second letter of Honorius to Sergius. (*Ibid.*, p. 50.)

Thus keeping away, as I said, from the vexation of new expressions, we must not maintain or proclaim either one or two energies, but, instead of one energy which some maintain, we must confess that the one Christ, the Lord, truly works in both natures; and instead of the two energies they should prefer to proclaim with us the two natures, i.e. the Godhead and the assumed manhood, which work what is proper to them in the one Person of the only-begotten Son of God, unmingled and unseparated and unchanged.

Condemnation of Honorius by the Third General Council of Constantinople, 681. (*Ibid.*, p. 167).

After we had read the doctrinal letters of Sergius of Constantinople to Cyrus of Phasis and to Pope Honorius, as well as the letter of the latter to Sergius, we find that these documents are quite foreign to the apostolic dogmas, also to the declarations of the holy Councils, and all the Fathers of repute, and follow the false teachings of the heretics; therefore we entirely reject them, and execrate them as hurtful to the soul. But the names of these men must also be thrust forth from the Church, namely, that of Sergius, who first wrote on this impious doctrine, further, that of Cyrus of Alexandria, of Phyrrhus, Paul, and Peter of Constantinople, and of Theodore of Pharan, all of whom Pope Agatho rejected in his letter to the Emperor. We anathematise them all. And along with them, it is our unanimous decree that there shall be expelled from the Church and anathematised, Honorius, formerly Pope of Old Rome, because we found in his letter to Sergius that in all respects he followed his view and confirmed his impious doctrines.

Letter of Pope Leo II to Emperor Constantine IV, confirming the acts of the General Council.

Similarly we anathematize the inventors of new error, that is Bishop Theodore of Pharan, Cyrus of Alexandria, Sergius, Pyrrhus, Paul, Peter, subverters rather than heads of the church of Constantinople, and also Honorius, who did not purify this Apostolic Church by the doctrine of apostolic tradition, but by dark treachery permitted the immaculate faith to be corrupted.

Chapter 7

EARLY MONASTICISM

MONASTICISM denotes the manner of life of those who live in seclusion from the world, usually under vows and a fixed rule, in order to devote themselves to prayer and the achievement of salvation. Ascetic renunciation is entirely consistent with the message of the Gospels and hence it appeared instinctively wherever Christianity spread. Further causes of its popularity were the expectation of an imminent second coming of Christ and the difficulty of living uncontaminated amid the society and politics of pagan Rome. Gradually becoming organized, monasticism grew with the Church, taking many different forms before settling down along lines marked out by great rules such as those of St. Basil and St. Benedict.

St. Anthony of Egypt. Egypt was the birthplace of organized Christian monasticism and St. Anthony (251–356) is usually called the first monk. There had been ascetics before Anthony — St. Paul of Thebes, for example — who withdrew in spirit from the world to devote their lives to prayer and charity, either remaining in their own homes or living as hermits. But Anthony is the recognized originator of monasticism as a definite way of life completely in its own right. Various factors have been suggested to explain why Egypt should have provided the breeding ground for monasticism: geographical features, severity of persecution, influence of mystical Neo-Platonism. Whatever may have been the reason, by the end of the third century Anthony was established in solitary asceticism along the banks of the lower Nile.

After twenty years in the loneliness of an abandoned fort, Anthony yielded in 305 to the importunities of a group of other hermits and came forth to guide them on the basis of his personal experience. Anthony composed no rule, simply supervising loosely the activities of his disciples. Ten years later, however, Anthony again tired of human company and sought a new, distant retreat where he passed the remaining four decades of his life. But his influence and example had been decisive. Northern Egypt soon had a hermit population in the thousands collected about the hills of Nitria and the deserts of Scete and Cellia.

Anchoritic Monasticism. Anthony exemplifies one of the two basic types of monachism, the eremitic or anchoritic variety. The hermit or anchorite lived alone in some desert place, often on the outskirts of a village, for he depended on admirers to provide an occasional modicum of food. No fixed rule guided him; he was his own superior. Sometimes groups of anchorites assembled on week ends for divine services, although some preferred no contact at all with others. Most anchorites were not priests; not uncommonly they considered their way of life superior to that of ordained clergy.

A semi-anchoritic life evolved when hermits lived in separate cells but close to each other, meeting regularly for prayer or mutual support yet retaining their essential autonomy. It commonly happened that the reputation of a particularly saintly monk such as Anthony attracted neophytes hoping to learn from him the way to perfection. The semi-anchoritic life naturally suited their purposes best. Although pure anchoritic monachism never disappeared entirely, by the sixth century it was largely supplanted by the semi-anchoritic type.

Either the pure or modified anchoritic pattern offered a maximum of flexibility and individuality. This characterized Antonian monasticism and was at the same time its greatest weakness. With each monk setting his own standards, eccentricities developed. Naïve enthusiasm untempered by experience often led to disaster, especially since the majority of the first monks had little education. Often they erred in the direction of excessive severity. The early monks had to be "spiritual athletes" trained to endure extreme feats of asceticism: protracted fasts, severe penances, and self-inflicted bodily punishment. A spirit of rivalry at times replaced genuine asceticism as the motive for picturesque practices. In fifth-century Syria some hermits ate nothing but grass; others hobbled their legs with iron chains; still others took to living atop pillars reaching up to fifty feet in height, whence their name "pillar saints" or stylites. St. Simeon Stylites (395–461) achieved the record of thirty-six years on his tiny platform.

Cenobitic Monachism. Community life is the essential feature of cenobitic monasticism which includes as a usual concomitant an established rule of conduct. This second type grew out of the anchoritic form, but it did not necessarily represent a revolt or reform. St. Pachomius (290–345), an Egyptian like his friend Anthony, founded cenobitism about 320 when he established the first monastery at Tabennisi in southern Egypt. Twenty years later his sister organized a house for women. Soon monasteries were to be found throughout the Nile Valley but cenobitism flourished particularly in the southern Thebaid.

Pachomius' Rule eventually was observed in nine large monasteries for men and two for women, comprising about 7000 members by A.D. 400. The rule provided definite organization under recognized superiors. Prayer, fasting, manual labor, and study of the Scriptures were provided for, the greatest innovation being the importance attached to regular and diversified types of labor, including agriculture. Since the traditional independent spirit of Egyptian monks could not be tampered with too much, the Pachomian rule permitted considerable freedom. In general, Pachomius set a minimum standard of asceticism attainable by all, but he allowed and even encouraged each monk to set whatever goals of mortification or austerity he could achieve over and above that prescribed by the rule.

The Basilian Rule. From Egypt monachism spread quickly over the Near East. In Asia Minor it found its most important Greek promoter in St. Basil, the Cappadocian father, whose ideals were reflected in all monastic life of the Greek world. Basil's attention was turned to monasticism by his sister Macrina who fostered the monastic life on family estates at Annesi near Neocaesarea in Pontus. After visiting the disciples of Eustatius of Sebaste who first introduced monastic life into that region, Basil journeyed to Egypt, Syria, and Mesopotamia to observe the monks there. Returning home in 357 Basil became a hermit near Annesi but was soon joined by others so that a community arose. For this community Basil composed his *Longer Rules* and *Shorter Rules* consisting of ascetical and moral precepts on various aspects of monastic life. They do not make up a rule in the sense of a constitution but rather a core of principles around which a monastic group might develop.

Basil believed firmly that the cenobitic life was much superior to the eremitic. "If you always live alone whose feet will you wash?" he wrote. Hence the Basilian rule went further than the Pachomian by strengthening the community element: meals, work, and prayer all in common within the same house. The number of monks per monastery was considerably reduced from the hundreds in Pachomian houses. Obedience definitely took its place alongside poverty and chastity as cardinal virtues of cenobitism. Furthermore, Basil emphasized charitable service to others as part of the monk's routine, and to this end he introduced the practice of monks laboring in hospitals, providing hospices and teaching. Excessive asceticism was frowned upon. A system of regular prayer seven times daily was prescribed. Basil's own monastery was built about 360 near Neo-caesarea. When he moved into Cappadocia as bishop of Caesarea he promoted monasticism in that province also.

Despite Basil's efforts cenobitism never entirely displaced the looser anchoritic life in the Byzantine Empire; probably the Greek spirit was too much akin to the Egyptian to surrender all individual freedom. But monasticism became very popular in the East, and when a Rule was observed at all it was usually Basil's.

Palestine. Hilarion, a disciple of Anthony, inaugurated monachism in Palestine about the year 307. He favored the hermit life, but very soon cenobitism appeared also as colonies of monks collected about the holy places. Rufinus of Aquileia, after visiting Egypt, established a monastery on the Mount of Olives where the copying of books was an honored occupation. Rufinus counseled Melania, an aristocratic Roman lady, and collaborated with her in the foundation of a convent for women. St. Jerome's monastery at Bethlehem and that of his follower Paula followed shortly. Some of these Palestinian institutions corresponded to the Antonian semi-anchoritic foundations but there were true cenobia among them also. No rule emanated from Palestine or Syria although Jerome translated Pachomius' into Latin, thus assuring it wider circulation.

Western Monasticism. St. Athanasius and the Egyptian monks who accompanied him on his journeys during the Arian crisis introduced monasticism to the West. In 335 Athanasius was exiled to Trier; in 341 he was in Rome. Wherever he went Athanasius spread the monastic ideals. His biography of St. Anthony, translated into Latin in 380, immediately found a wide audience and enkindled the spirit of pious emulation. In the later fourth century monachism progressed rapidly and in a variety of ways as different individuals made their own adaptations of Egyptian customs. Practically all Christian biographies of the late fourth and fifth centuries show traces of monachism. Both anchoritic and cenobitic types found favor, but naturally isolated hermits usually left fewer traces of their activity than did the communities.

Eusebius, Bishop of Vercelli (340–371), combined monasticism with the clerical state by prescribing community life for his cathedral clergy.

St. Augustine described a monastery outside Milan. During St. Jerome's stay in Rome from 382 to 385 he acted as spiritual adviser to Marcella, Paula, and other women ascetics who met together for prayer, although they did not share a communal life.

St. Augustine was not a monk before his return to Africa but he can be called one immediately thereafter. As bishop he turned his episcopal residence into a monastery, probably the first in North Africa, wherein dwelt his friends and clergy. Two of Augustine's writings specifically concern monachism. One, the letter numbered 211 in his collected epistles, addressed to a convent of nuns under his sister's direction, discusses monastic life in general and the principles on which it is based, with little in the way of detail of conventual routine. At a later date this letter was interpreted as a rule and was adopted by groups of monks and nuns calling themselves Augustinians after its author. Augustine's treatise *The Work of the Monks* exposes the evils to which unregulated anchoritic life was prone and indicates that Augustine, like Basil, preferred cenobitism.

Gallic Experiments. In Gaul monasticism quickly took root. St. Martin of Tours, the former soldier of popular legend, became almost a patron saint for Gallic monachism. His life as portrayed in Sulpicius Severus' widely read biography did much to stimulate enthusiasm and emulation. Martin became a hermit after leaving the army. Elected bishop of Tours in 371, Martin resolved to continue his way of life unchanged and found a hut for himself in an inaccessible place outside the city. Others clustered around him and soon a colony of about eighty disciples existed following a semi-anchoritic system. Out of this group arose the monastery of Marmoutier. Needless to say, Martin's episcopal duties often took him out of his hut for he played a prominent part in Gallic Christianity.

Interesting and significant experiments in monasticism were undertaken in southern Gaul by St. Honoratus, John Cassian, and St. Caesarius of Arles. Honoratus exchanged wealth and position for monastic austerity on the island of Lerins opposite Cannes in Provence about A.D. 400. A monastery soon arose and a rule was composed, of which fragments survive. Egyptian influence is evident: loose organization, preference for anchoritic over cenobitic life, an atmosphere of severity. The reputation of the Lerins group caused neighboring cities to turn to it for bishops. Honoratus himself was elevated to the see of Arles; St. Hilary and St. Caesarius occupied the same see; St. Lupus of Troyes, St. Eucherius of Lyons, and St. Faustus of Riez were graduated from the school of Lerins to the episcopate. Duchesne called Lerins a "nursery of bishops and saints," and he might have added "of scholars too," for Lerins monks participated vehemently in fifth-century theological controversy concerning St. Augustine's and Pelagius' teachings on grace and salvation.

A contemporary of Honoratus and one of the most influential writers in the history of early monachism, John Cassian founded the monastery of St. Victor at Marseilles about 410. Cassian's experience with monasticism included a sojourn in a cenobium in Bethlehem and ten years among the Egyptian anchorites. Cassian's contribution to monachism lay in his writings on asceticism. His *Institutes* and *Conferences* propound the theory behind monasticism, ascetical theology, and they remained recommended reading for monks of all kinds throughout the middle ages. Most of the pre-Cassian literature on monachism dealt with the marvelous, heroic, or miraculous deeds of individual monks which might incite to emulation but which offered little help as to precisely how such sanctity might be achieved by a neophyte. While Cassian wrote partly in this same tradition he presented more of an analysis of monastic ideals and of the way to attain them.

At St. Victor's Cassian endeavored to adapt Egyptian ideals to the environment of the West. As much as he personally admired the eastern hermits, he realized that criteria of asceticism at Nitria or Scete did not suit the West without modification. At the same time Cassian turned his back on Basil and Pachomius for he upheld the eremitic as the more perfect life. Still, aware of the difficulties facing the hermit, he advocated long preparation within a cenobium before embarking on the anchoritic life.

St. Caesarius of Arles (470–543) figured in the development of monasticism with a pair of rules. Five years at Lerins taught him the ideals of that school which are reflected in his rule for men, while that for women, written after Caesarius became archbishop in 503, rested largely on Augustine's rule. For two centuries Caesarius' rules were widely used in southeast Gaul.

Double Monasteries and Lauras. Along with the more common single houses we also find double monasteries, joint communities of both men and women situated within separate compounds but sharing the same church. Sometimes there were separate superiors and at other times an abbot or abbess ruled both sexes. Double monasteries appeared in all western lands. In the East the monastic type called the laura became popular. This represented a semi-anchoritic organization: the monks lived in separate cells grouped about a central building used by the community for Saturday and Sunday services and as the house for novices. St. Sabas founded seven such lauras in Palestine during the fifth century.

Celtic Monasticism. During the sixth century monasticism blossomed forth exuberantly among the Celts. St. Patrick, who had apparently spent some time at Lerins, brought monasticism into Ireland but not until fifty years after his death (461) did it assume significant proportions. Contact with monastic institutions founded by St. David and St. Ninian in Celtic Wales and Scotland stimulated Irish monachism into rapid and luxurious growth. Within three generations monasteries dotted the Irish landscape, numbering their inmates in the thousands, and the whole Irish church became an appendage of monasticism. Practically all Irish saints for centuries were products of the monasteries.

Kildare	St. Brigid	c. 470
Aran	St. Enda	c. 484
Clonard	St. Finnian	c. 520
Derry	St. Columba	c. 540
Clonmacnois	St. Kieran	544
Kells	St. Columba	554
Clonfert	St. Brendan	557
Bangor	St. Comgall	559
Iona	St. Columba	563
Annegray	St. Columban	c. 585
Luxeuil	St. Columban	590
Bobbio	St. Columban	612

Some important early Celtic monasteries and their founders.

Monasticism dominated Irish Catholicism because of the tribal organization of primitive Irish society. Normal usage dictated the establishment of bishoprics only in populous centers. Patrick endeavored to follow custom, but owing to the lack of towns his episcopal system functioned poorly. The rural environment of the monasteries, however, made them natural centers of tribal religious life. Consequently Ireland came to be ruled ecclesiastically from monasteries rather than urban bishoprics. Areas which normally would have constituted dioceses were administered by the abbot of the local monastery, who in about half of the largest monasteries was himself a bishop, but where the abbot possessed only priestly powers a consecrated bishop was always to be found among the brethren of the community. These bishops did little more than ordain priests, for jurisdictional powers were vested in the abbot.

Characteristics of Irish Monachism.   Three features distinguish Celtic monasticism: intellectual pursuits, great austerity, and missionary zeal. There existed among the Celts a tradition of intellectual leadership by the native pagan priests, the druids, whose literary schools had served as centers of national culture. Celtic Christian monks thus were merely carrying on ancient traditions in the schools attached to their convents, although at first that tradition was suspect because of its pagan background. But a second, foreign root of Celtic monasticism stretched back by way of Britain to Lerins, and from this source was drawn Christian concern for learning which combined with the national element represented by the druidic heritage. Naturally monks and nuns concerned themselves mostly with sacred sciences — theology, exegesis, patrology — but surviving works prove that Celtic monks did not ignore profane authors. The cultural prosperity of Ireland in the period 650–750 derived entirely from monasticism.

In asceticism Irish monks rivaled the austerity of the Syrians and Egyptians. A popular saying described their life as "the white martyrdom." Although customs differed from monastery to monastery because of the absence of a uniform rule, general similarity prevailed. Food was scant and never included meat or fowl, fasts were long and frequent, sleep was curtailed and disrupted by many prayers. Celtic monks often prayed with arms extended in the form of a cross. The intensely penitential nature of Celtic monachism demanded a severely rigorous routine. In general the spirit of Irish monachism harked back to Egypt and Syria.

As soon as Irish monasteries were securely planted at home the monks started traveling abroad. Instead of fleeing the world they fled their native land. Many went on pilgrimage to the Holy Land, not a few of whom ended their days in Italy such as St. Fredian who died in 588 as bishop of Lucca. Others traveled in groups to pagan lands. Iceland and the northern islands received colonies. St. Columba and a dozen companions founded Iona in 563 as an advance base for work among the Picts of Scotland and the Northumbrians. St. Columban (540–615) left Bangor at the age of forty with a dozen monks and journeyed into eastern Gaul. In the Burgundian area he preached and established monasteries, the most important being at Luxeuil on land granted by King Guntram. Here Columban composed a rule for the guidance of the new houses. After further wanderings through Gaul and Switzerland Columban arrived in Italy, where three years before his death he founded Bobbio, one of the great monasteries of upper Italy, on land donated by the Lombard King Agilulf.

St. Benedict of Nursia, 480–547. The European monastic system *par excellence* is that formed by St. Benedict early in the sixth century. In many ways Benedict's religious career followed the pattern of most monks of his time. Born of an important family at Nursia north of Rome, he received a good education in Rome but decided to abandon the world in which he saw much wickedness. All that was required to become a monk was to discover a retreat in the wilderness and take up the eremetical life. Subiaco about forty miles from Rome offered a suitable cave, and there Benedict remained for three years, known only to another monk nearby who aided him in small ways. But eventually others learned of Benedict and came to Subiaco for his guidance. There was even a monastery in the vicinity at Vicovaro whose inmates begged him to become their abbot. Benedict accepted, but before long his administration proved too strict and the monks tried to poison him. Returning to Subiaco, Benedict governed twelve monasteries of his own, each housing a dozen of his more sincere disciples. This time it was the jealousy of a local priest who tried to undermine Benedict's work that compelled him to flee. In 529 he found refuge at Monte Cassino, midway between Rome and Naples, where Benedict and his brethren erected the mother house of Benedictine monasticism. Here too out of his personal experience and his familiarity with ascetic literature of East and West he composed his rule which was so excellent and so widely adopted that Benedict has been honored with the title Patriarch of the Monks of the West.

The Benedictine Rule. The fundamental quality that assured the success of Benedict's rule was its spirit of moderation. Herein lay the most radical departure from traditional monachism which had heretofore tended to consider eastern austerities and the anchoritic life the acme of asceticism. Benedict urged his monks to read the older monastic literature along with Scripture. The Rule quotes Cassian some ninety times while specifically repudiating his eastern ideals. In the prologue Benedict wrote: "We are going to establish a school of God's service in which we hope we shall establish nothing harsh or burdensome." The first chapter characterizes cenobites as "the highest type of monk." Certainly the Rule was hard and provided many opportunities for exercise of heroic virtue, but it was not supposed to be beyond the capabilities of the average man.

In regard to food and drink Benedict wrote: "Some say monks should not drink wine at all, but since in our day we have been unable to persuade monks of this, let us at any rate agree that it should be used in moderate amounts." All meat is forbidden, but as to other food, "in general, the rule should be to eat sparingly." Even then the abbot was empowered to increase the amount allowed if the monks were engaged in hard labor. An average of eight hours of sleep a day was permitted. In short, for those who followed St. Benedict's rule, there was no place for that spirit of individualism which led eastern hermits into bizarre experiments in asceticism. The Benedictine system preferred the anonymity of the cloister and a thoroughly sane, normal conduct.

Monastic Vows. The Rule specifies six vows: poverty, chastity, obedience, observance of the Rule, moral reform, and stability. The last is Benedict's most tangible contribution to monasticism. By it he meant that a monk should be bound to the monastic life and that he should spend his life in the community which he joined. Heretofore the line between the lay and the monastic vocation had been too easily crossed and there was a constant temptation to return to the world at the first waning of enthusiasm. Moreover, foot-loose monks wandering from place to place begging, getting into mischief, attracting the unfit to imitate them in a life of some apparent ease with a religious gloss plagued many parts of the Catholic world and made a mockery of the whole monastic institution. Benedict tried to remedy this with exact provisions for a novitiate to weed out those who did not have a true vocation. The organization of the monastery was to be such that everything necessary was located inside the walls to reduce contact with the outside to a minimum.

Routine of the Monastery. Life at Monte Cassino revolved about the three obligations of prayer, manual labor, and spiritual reading. Prayer — the "Work of God" is Benedict's phrase — consisted of recitation in common of the divine office. "Let nothing take precedence over the Work of God," Benedict wrote, and he ordered the day around the canonical hours. Prayer consumed five hours a day and approximately eight on Sunday.

Although the rule indicated six hours daily of manual labor, it did not specify what this work should be. The arts and crafts were practiced, including building, there were always miscellaneous chores, and a garden was worked within the enclosure. But heavy agricultural work was ordinarily performed by slaves, coloni, or serfs. The requirement of labor helped the monastery achieve self-sufficiency at the same time that it balanced the contemplative features of the monk's life.

Spiritual reading occupied four or more hours. The Rule indicated the Scriptures, Fathers, and early monastic literature, for it was to be reading of a truly spiritual nature, not an intellectual occupation, although its intellectual benefits could not be denied. Characteristically the Rule permitted substitution of manual work for those who are unwilling or unable to benefit from reading.

Numerous ideas contained in the Rule were not original with Benedict. What was original was the moderate tone and the form of the Rule. All earlier rules were essentially treatises on monastic virtue with few regulations covering daily routine. Custom, therefore, provided the only guide and much discretionary power was vested in the abbot. Benedict, with the legislative instinct native to the Roman mind, approached the subject differently. He established a sound framework by specifically regulating the duties of superiors, occupations for every hour of the day, procedure for admitting novices and checking refractory members, and much other detail. The result was a real legislative code or constitution. Homiletic sections of the Rule and the required spiritual reading were intended to furnish the flesh to fill out the skeleton.

Cassiodorus and Vivarium.   One additional early experiment deserves mention: the monastery of Vivarium established at Squillace in southern Italy by Cassiodorus (c. 475–570), the "Father of literary monasticism." Cassiodorus had been a statesman and author before retiring at the age of sixty to devote himself to monastic life. Vivarium resembled a literary academy with monastic overtones. At great expense Cassiodorus collected a fine library for his monks who copied manuscripts and studied the Scriptures and profane letters as an aid to the understanding of sacred literature. The decline of learning and its consequences for the Church motivated Cassiodorus' undertaking, which contrasted sharply with contemporary Benedictine system wherein manual labor was prescribed but no mention was made of scholarship. But in time Cassiodorus' scholarly aims fused with the devotional aspects of Benedictine monachism, and it was in the Benedictine houses that Cassiodorus' projects attained fruition.

Spread of St. Benedict's Rule.   Benedict legislated for Monte Cassino. Whether or not he intended his rule for wider circulation cannot be determined. Nor did Benedict found an order: any monastery adopting his Rule constituted an independent self-sufficient unit, entirely separate from other houses. In the sixth and early seventh centuries Celtic mona-chism prospered and through its missionaries spilled over onto the Con-tinent so that a contemporary observer would probably have predicted that, if one set of practices was destined to displace the other, it would be the Benedictine that would disappear. But the intrinsic merits of Benedict's Rule and a concatination of circumstances led to its eventual spread. Between 600 and 700 it paralleled Celtic customs in popularity, but from the eighth century until the eleventh the Benedictine Rule had the field to itself except for Ireland.

The beginning of Benedictine expansion occurred when the Lombards destroyed Monte Cassino about 581. Its refugee monks found haven in Rome and the patronage of Pope Gregory the Great. Gregory, himself a monk, established the monastery of St. Andrew in Rome and six others in Sicily, perhaps after the Benedictine pattern. In 596 Gregory sent St. Augustine and forty Benedictine companions to convert England; thus the first Benedictine house outside Italy arose at Canterbury. In turning the Benedictines into missionaries the pope also brought more of them into the ranks of ordained clergy. Missionaries from England, St. Boniface in the forefront, then carried the Rule into the Low Countries, Germany, and Gaul. Frankish synods in 742 and 743, presided over by Boniface, urged that the Rule be adopted throughout France. St. Benedict of Aniane's reorganization in the early ninth century completed the work of making European monasticism a Benedictine thing by persuading the emperor and all abbots to outlaw other rules.

Monasticism and the Church.   Although there are some indications of sporadic opposition to monasticism as an institution, it easily vindicated itself in the eyes of most Christians. More important was the question of discipline and control of the monks, an acute problem in areas where anchorites abounded. Eastern monks in particular were prone to fanatic outbursts of physical violence during the theological disputes of the fifth century — Origenism, Nestorianism, and Monophysitism. Often under-standing little of the problems, the monks at times became stout champions of heresy. Yet during the Acacian schism the monks of Constantinople steadfastly adhered to the papacy. Alexandrian patriarchs found a private bodyguard in the monks of Nitria who swarmed into the city to strike down opposition to their archbishop. In 431 they had to be expelled from Ephesus for endangering the ecumenical council. St. Flavian was beaten so severely by monks at the Robber Council that he died. St. Augustine and St. Benedict criticized *gyrovagi* and *sarabites,* wandering, unworthy monks whose "law is their own desires."

The advance of cenobitism corrected some abuses, while synodal decrees established the principle that monks and monasteries belonged under the supervision of the local bishop. This, however, occasionally led to trouble of a different sort, when the monks found themselves oppressed by unworthy bishops. Individual monasteries, therefore, were sometimes removed from diocesan jurisdiction and placed directly under papal control. A letter of Pope Hormisdas about 515 to a monastery near Arles is the earliest instance known of the granting of papal protection and exemption to a monastery. The Celtic method of adjusting monastic and episcopal jurisdiction remained peculiar to Ireland. The frequent practice of electing bishops from among the monks or, following St. Augustine, organizing the clergy into a community, obviated much potential friction. The Greek world depended heavily on monasteries for its bishops, since these had to be celibate and most of the secular clergy were married.

Accomplishments of Monasticism. Monachism aims primarily at the personal salvation of its own members but in ways that are incidental to this purpose it has contributed enormously to European civilization. For centuries the only means of education available anywhere were monastic schools and the only educated men were monks. The copying of manuscripts in monastic scriptoria preserved practically all that is now extant of ancient Roman literature, sacred and profane, while few but monastic chroniclers recorded events of their own day for the benefit of future historians. Since the State provided no social services for the alleviation of the misery of the poor, the sick, travelers, or pilgrims, monasteries undertook such tasks. By their agricultural endeavors they brought extensive areas of virgin soil into useful cultivation. In converting and civilizing pagan barbarians the monks proved remarkably successful. Monasteries furnished qualified incumbents for episcopal sees and for the papacy. Every religious revival in the medieval world originated with the monasteries or allied groups.

Summary. The countless experiments of hermits from Anthony in Egypt to Martin in Gaul seemed to lead inevitably to some form of community life as more suitable for the social nature of man. All authors of significant monastic rules, after personal experience or investigation, drew the same conclusion: Pachomius, Basil, Augustine, Cassian, Columban, and Benedict. In providing a legalistic framework for true monasticism

Benedict produced a code that embodied the best elements of his predecessors' achievements, thereby making possible the tremendous services to mankind which medieval Europe so desperately required. Of the four basic rules still used by the Church — Augustinian, Basilian, Benedictine, and Franciscan — all but the Franciscan date from the formative period of monasticism.

REVIEW AIDS

1. Explain the two types of monasticism and the origin of each.
2. What are the characteristics of St. Basil's Rule?
3. Trace the spread of monasticism in Italy and the West.
4. How did monasticism reach Ireland? Name several of the monasteries under the Celtic observance and some of the Celtic monks.
5. What features characterized Celtic monasticism?
6. Summarize St. Benedict's life and experience with monasticism.
7. Show the meaning of moderation and stability as these ideas are found in Benedict's Rule.
8. In what way did Benedict's Rule differ from earlier rules?
9. How can we account for the spread of the Benedictine system?
10. Describe Cassiodorus' contribution to monasticism.
11. Indicate some of the achievements of monasticism.

SUGGESTIONS FOR FURTHER READING

A thorough treatment of the beginnings of monasticism is to be found in Palanque, Bardy *et al., The Church in the Christian Roman Empire,* Vol. II (New York: 1953). Owen Chadwick, *John Cassian* (Cambridge: 1950), analyzes the ideals of one of the early important figures in monastic history and ties them in with the fifth-century framework. A thoroughly satisfactory treatment in scholarly fashion of Celtic monasticism is John Ryan's *Irish Monasticism* (Dublin: n.d.), while a more popular, enthusiastic treatment is contained in John Healy, *Ireland's Ancient Schools and Scholars,* 5th ed. (Dublin: 1908). The best biography of St. Benedict is Ildefonso Shuster, *Saint Benedict and His Times* (St. Louis: 1951). Cuthbert Butler's *Benedictine Monachism,* 2nd ed. (London: 1924), is a masterly analysis of Benedict's Rule and a brief history of Benedictine monasticism. Eleanor Shipley Duckett has a chapter on Cassiodorus as well as chapters on other phases of early monasticism in *The Gateway to the Middle Ages* (New York: 1938).

DOCUMENTS

1. In 451 the Council of Chalcedon undertook to regulate the life of the monks who, especially in the East, were not properly submissive to normal ecclesiastical disciplinary procedures. Especially significant is the positive statement that monks were subject to the bishops. Canon 4, from H. J. Schroeder, *Disciplinary Decrees of the General Councils* (St. Louis: Herder, 1937), p. 65. Used by permission.

Those who lead a true and sincere monastic life ought to enjoy due honor. Since, however, there are some who, using the monastic state as a pretext, roam about aimlessly in the cities, and even undertake to establish monasteries for themselves, it is decided that no one shall build or found a monastery or a house of prayer without the consent of the bishop of the city. It is decided furthermore, that all monks in every city and country place shall be subject to the bishop, that they love silence and attend only to fasting and prayer, remaining in the places in which they renounced the world; that they shall not leave their monasteries and burden themselves either with ecclesiastical or worldly affairs or take part in them unless they are commissioned to do so for some necessary purpose by the bishop of the city; that no slave shall be received into the monasteries and become a monk without the consent of his master. Whosoever transgresses this decision of ours shall be excommunicated, in order that the name of God be not blasphemed. The bishop of the city, moreover, shall exercise a strict supervision over the monasteries.

2. Western monasticism first followed the anchoritic pattern, but there was a constant tendency toward the cenobitic type. This is seen in the Life of St. Martin of Tours, founder of the monastery of Marmoutier, as recorded by Sulpicius Severus. Translated by F. R. Hoare, *The Western Fathers* (New York: Sheed and Ward, 1954), pp. 23–25. Used by permission.

What Martin was like, and his greatness, after entering the episcopate, it is beyond my powers to describe. For with unswerving constancy he remained the same man as before. There was the same humble heart and the same poverty-stricken clothing; and, amply endowed with authority and tact, he fully sustained the dignity of the episcopate without forsaking the life or the virtues of the monk.

For a time he occupied a cell next to the cathedral. Then, when he could no longer endure the disturbance from his many visitors, he made himself a hermitage about two miles from the city. The place was so secluded and remote that it had all the solitude of the desert. On one side it was walled in by the rock-face of a high mountain, and the level ground that remained was enclosed by a gentle bend of the River Loire. There was only one approach to it, and that a very narrow one.

His own cell was built of wood, as were those of many of the brethren; but most of them had hollowed out shelters for themselves in the rock of the overhanging mountain. There were about eighty disciples there, being trained in the pattern of their most blessed master. No one possessed anything of his own; everything was put into the common stock. The buying and selling which is customary with most hermits was forbidden them. No craft was practised there except that of the copyist, and that was assigned to the younger men. The older ones were left free for prayer.

It was seldom that anyone left his cell except when they assembled at the place of worship. All received their food together after the fast was ended. No one touched wine unless ill-health forced him to do so. Most of them wore clothes of camel's hair; softer clothing was looked upon as an offence there. This must be regarded as all the more wonderful because there were many among them of noble rank, who had been brought up to something quite different before forcing themselves to this lowliness and endurance. Many of them we have since seen as bishops. For what kind of city or Church would it be that did not covet a bishop from Martin's monastery?

3. This selection from the Rule of St. Benedict, Chapter 48, illustrates the role of labor and of reading in the monks' lives. It also shows the spirit of moderation which is one of the chief characteristics of the Rule. Conradus Kirch, *Enchiridion Fontium Historiae Ecclesiasticae Antiquae*, 6th ed. by Leo Ueding (Barcelona: 1947), pp. 560–561.

Idleness is the enemy of the soul; therefore the brothers should be occupied with manual labor at certain times and with spiritual reading at others. We believe that both periods should be regulated according to this schedule: i.e., from Easter to the first of October let them go out in the morning and labor from the first almost to the fourth hour as shall be necessary. From the fourth hour to the sixth let them be free for reading.

Rising from dinner after the sixth hour, let them rest in their beds in complete silence, or if anyone wishes to read, let him read to himself in such a way that he disturbs no one else. Let Nones be observed properly at the middle of the eighth hour; and let them work again at whatever has to be done until Vespers. If the condition of the place and poverty make it necessary that they work longer, as at harvest time, let them not be sad, because then truly are they monks, if they live by the labor of their hands as did our fathers and the Apostles. Yet everything should be done with moderation because some are faint-hearted.

From the first of October to the beginning of Lent, let them be free for reading until the end of the second hour. Let Terce be said at the second hour and until the ninth let all labor at the task that is enjoined upon them. When the first signal for the ninth hour is given, let them each finish up their work for the day and let them be prepared until the second bell sounds. . . .

During Lent let them be free for reading from morning until the end of the third hour, and let them labor to the end of the tenth hour at their assigned tasks. During Lent let each receive his own books from the library which they should read from beginning to end. The books should be distributed at the beginning of Lent. Above all, let one or two of the older brothers be assigned to go about the monastery at the hours assigned for reading to see lest perchance any brother be found carelessly idling away his time or chatting and not paying attention to his reading, not only wasting his own time but also disturbing others. If anyone such as this be found (Heaven forbid!), let him be rebuked the first and the second time; if he does not mend his ways let him be punished with a staff as a lesson to the rest. . . .

On Sunday let all be free for reading except those who are assigned various tasks. If anyone is so negligent or lazy that he does not wish to meditate or to read or is unable to do so, let some task be assigned to him so that he may have something to do. Let tasks or an occupation be assigned to sick or weak brothers that they be not idle, but these should not overtax them or be beyond their strength. The abbot must take their weakness into consideration.

Chapter 8

THE IMPACT OF THE
BARBARIANS AND THEIR
CONVERSION

EVEN before a majority of its citizens professed Christianity the Roman Empire was tottering toward its grave. The lifetime of the Latin Fathers witnessed the beginning of the barbarian invasions. From Jerusalem St. Jerome lamented the sack of Rome in 410; Augustine died during the Vandal siege of Hippo. In addition to the tangible blows of the barbarians, more subtle forces — maladjusted social and economic systems — undermined the Empire. The eastern world was spared much of the misery that afflicted the West; hence the Greeks were free to expend their energies on deep theological controversies. But the Latins as usual faced more practical difficulties: the relations between barbarian invaders and the Church, the preservation of Christian morality and discipline amid general decadence, and the conversion of the pagans both within and without the Empire's boundaries.

Historical Task of the Church. In addition to its mission of helping men save their souls the Church was called upon to perform a vital function of a nonreligious nature in serving as the medium through which basic ingredients of European civilization passed from enfeebled Rome to the barbarians of the later European states. Just as Rome preserved Greek civilization by conquering Greece, the Church preserved Roman civilization by conquering Rome. When the political world of Rome disappeared from the West in the fifth and sixth centuries the Church survived. By then it had embraced and made its own much of the culture of the

Graeco-Roman world in which it was born and matured, so that in converting the Teutonic, Slavic, and Celtic races the Church also instinctively presented them with the heritage of classical civilization. Naturally the process was slow, lasting almost a millennium, for conversion did not automatically make gentlemen out of the barbarians. Nevertheless it was finally accomplished so that we can truthfully say that Western civilization owes to the Church its very existence.

Conversion of Ireland.   The inability of the fifth-century Empire to defend its citizens was a factor in the conversion of Ireland. A pirate band raiding Britain carried off an irresponsible sixteen-year-old British Catholic named Patrick and sold him into slavery in Ireland. For six years Patrick tended sheep and turned for solace to religion. After escaping he determined to return to the scene of his captivity as a missionary. Patrick received his religious training in Gaul, at Lerins, Marmoutier, and finally at the church of Auxerre, then ruled by its famed bishop St. Germanus. In 431 Palladius was commissioned by the pope to become Ireland's first bishop, for there were scattered Christian communities there, but Palladius' death led to the appointment of Patrick in his stead. Patrick's arrival in Ireland is placed in the year 432. By concentrating on the conversion of the pagan chieftains, forming a native clergy, and organizing dioceses with his own metropolitan see at Armagh, St. Patrick effected the conversion of practically the entire island by the time of his death in 461.

The Teutonic Invaders.   Preceding the migration of nations there was considerable contact between Germans and Romans, one aspect of which was Christian missionary enterprise. A certain Theophilus "bishop of the Goths" attended the Council of Nicaea, but the celebrated Bishop Ulfilas holds the title Apostles of the Goths. About 340 he commenced his work beyond the Danube frontier, even translating the Scriptures into the Gothic tongue for his converts. Unfortunately, Ulfilas and his unknown colleagues were semi-Arians, and the result of their fruitful labor was that Christianity in this heretical form became something like a national religion to the Visigoths, Ostrogoths, Vandals, and Burgundians. When these tribes carved out their kingdoms inside the Empire the religious difference between themselves and the Romans exacerbated an already tense situation and obstructed the fusion of the races.

Visigothic Kingdom in Spain.   Arian Visigoths, after defeating Emperor Valens at Hadrianople in 378, drifted westward. In 410 they captured Rome; a decade later they were established in southern Gaul; Spain finally became their permanent home. In the excitement of the invasions some churches were plundered and clergy murdered but there was no genuine persecution. Since the Visigoths had their own Arian bishops and priests, they appropriated various churches for their own use but otherwise left the Catholics unmolested.

This situation among the Visigoths remained undisturbed until the reign of King Leovigild. About 584 Leovigild decided to enforce religious uniformity in the Arian faith on his subjects. His motives were more political than religious. Catholicism had already won some of the Visigoths, including the king's son Hermenegild, a convert of St. Leander, Bishop of Seville. Some of these Catholics became involved in a conspiracy against the king, who was already worried about pressure from the Sueves, another Germanic tribe with a kingdom in northwest Spain whom St. Martin of Braga, an Oriental hermit, had converted by 560. For two years Leovigild pursued his anti-Catholic policy. Hermenegild was murdered, Leander exiled, and the Sueves overwhelmed. But as soon as Recared ascended the Visigothic throne in 586 everything changed. Recared, many of his nobles, and eight Arian bishops accepted Catholicism at the third Council of Toledo in 589. St. Leander himself baptized the king.

From 589 the closest co-operation prevailed between the Church and the Visigothic government. National church councils, convened at Toledo at the king's summons eighteen times between 589 and 701, were as much secular congresses as ecclesiastical synods, for their membership included laymen and they legislated on civil and ecclesiastical matters. The king, acting through the archbishop of Toledo as primate of the Spanish Church, appointed bishops freely and without opposition, and intervened at will in ecclesiastical affairs. On their part the bishops endeavored to stabilize the monarchy and check political turbulence.

A striking feature of the Visigothic Church was its isolation from outside contacts, even with Rome, which imparted a self-sufficient atmosphere to Spanish Catholicism. Yet St. Isidore of Seville (560–636), the foremost scholar of Visigothic Spain, gained a European-wide reputation for his *Etymologies,* an encyclopedic epitome of all knowledge. Saints Braulio, Ildephonsus, and Julian are additional eminent Spanish bishops and authors of the seventh century. Spain shared in the popularity of monasticism. The monastery of Agli at Toledo rivaled Lerins. SS. Leander, Isidore, and Fructuosus composed rules, the latter sometimes being called the Spanish Benedict.

Vandal Persecutions. Only in the Vandal kingdom in Africa did the Arian invaders persecute orthodoxy as a matter of fixed policy. As soon as he had completed his conquest Genseric (d. 477) expelled bishops, confiscated property, banned public Catholic worship, and did everything in his power to entrench Arianism at Carthage and throughout the northern part of the old Roman province. Huneric, a fanatical Arian, commenced his reign peacefully in 477 but shortly embarked on a bitter attack on Catholicism. Bishops and clergy were banished, often under circumstances of great cruelty. A decree of 484 abolished Catholic worship and turned all churches over to the Arians. Three years later the persecution was relaxed only to be renewed under King Trasimund (496–523). St. Fulgentius, the West's outstanding theologian, was among the bishops deported to Sardinia at this time. With Trasimund's death the persecution ceased. A decade later the Vandal kingdom disappeared and Africa acknowledged the rule of Catholic Byzantium. Few if any of the Vandals ever accepted orthodox Catholicism.

The Ostrogothic Kingdom and the Roman See. Theodoric (493–526), king of the Ostrogoths and master of Italy, pursed an enlightened religious policy, making no effort to force his own Arianism on the Italians, but at the same time discouraging any Ostrogoths from becoming Catholic. Only toward the end of his reign did he oppress the Church, and that was in retaliation for measures taken by Emperor Justin against Arianism. Theodoric dispatched Pope John I to Constantinople to intervene on behalf of the Arians. When the pope's unenthusiastic efforts failed, Theodoric imprisoned him on his return. John died in prison and is venerated as a martyr.

The Roman See experienced troubled times early in the sixth century, not because of the Ostrogoths but because of the turmoil of the era. The Acacian schism and simony in papal elections caused the difficulties. Pope Gelasius (492–496) having failed to restore unity with Constantinople, Anastasius II adopted a more conciliatory attitude toward the schismatics and thereby incurred the displeasure of a strong group of Roman clergy. At Anastasius' death the intransigents elected Symmachus, while a pro-Greek faction, possibly bribed by a wealthy senator, voted for Laurence. Both candidates appealed to the heretic Theodoric. With the king's approbation Symmachus was consecrated pope while Laurence submitted and received a bishopric.

Within a short time Laurence's partisans brought charges of immorality and malfeasance against Symmachus and recalled their antipope. Theodoric refused to intervene beyond summoning a synod of 150 Italian bishops to examine the charges against Symmachus. For a year the bishops temporized, insisting that God alone could judge the pope, thus in effect acquitting Symmachus. For several years the Roman schism continued until Laurence finally admitted defeat.

Of the succeeding popes, Hormisdas ended the Acacian schism, John died a prisoner of Theodoric, and Felix IV was the appointee of the Ostrogothic monarch. A novel feature of the decade after Theodoric's death was the attempt to establish the principle of the pope designating his successor during his own lifetime. Felix IV actually appointed Boniface II, averring that the Church could not bear the expenses of an election. Another schism threatened when the electors chose Dioscorus, but Dioscorus died within a month. Boniface then rashly designated his successor but in the face of mounting opposition he quashed his nomination. With that the practice was nipped in the bud.

In 535 Justinian's army landed in Italy to reconquer it from the Ostrogoths. The popes found themselves in a difficult position. Agapetus departed for Constantinople to mediate on behalf of the Goths; in this he failed, but while in the East he struck a blow at Monophysitism by deposing the heretical patriarch of Constantinople, Anthimus, the friend of Empress Theodora. When Agapetus died in Constantinople Silverius, the nominee of the Ostrogothic king Theodahat, secured the suffrage of the Romans. Theodora, however, sent the pliable deacon Vigilius back to Italy with a letter of recommendation to the Byzantine General Belisarius who then dominated Rome. On the basis of Theodora's nomination and in consideration of a sizable bribe Belisarius deposed Silverius and induced the clergy to recognize Vigilius. Silverius died, perhaps of starvation, on a remote island in the Mediterranean. Vigilius disappointed Theodora in refusing to aid the Monophysites as she wished. In 545 he suffered the indignity of being carried off to Constantinople where he played his role in the controversy of the Three Chapters.

Conversion of Clovis, King of the Franks. Gaul became the home of the Franks in the course of the fourth and fifth centuries. In 496 King Clovis accepted baptism from St. Remigius and as usual among the barbarians the king's example was followed by most of his people. This entailed a rapid fusion of the Gallo-Romans with the Franks since there were now no insurmountable obstacles and the Gallic bishops wholeheartedly supported Clovis' policies within Gaul and in his wars of expansion against Arian Visigoths and Burgundians. At the same time the bishops relinquished control over the Church to the king who pursued the identical erastian policy of the Catholic Visigothic monarchs. This was illustrated at the Council of Orleans in 511 which met at Clovis' command, considered an agenda compiled by him, decreed that none might become a cleric without royal consent, and submitted its legislation to Clovis for confirmation.

St. Caesarius of Arles (470–543), an alumnus of Lerins, was the outstanding bishop of the early Merovingian period in Gaul. Although his prime interests were monasticism and moral questions Caesarius occupies a place in the history of dogma for his decisive part in the Semi-Pelagian controversy. This debate concerned original sin, grace, and predestination as treated by St. Augustine and the heretic Pelagius. Through Caesarius' efforts and the co-operation of Pope Felix IV the second Council of Orange in 529 defined the Church's teaching, upholding in general but moderating in some points the theories of Augustine. Arles' claim to be the primatial see of Gaul was furthered by Caesarius' prestige but it never became effective. The political situation tried the bishop's skill severely because control of Arles was disputed between Ostrogoths, Visigoths, Burgundians, and Franks. Since the Franks were Catholic Caesarius favored them, thereby incurring suspicion of treason when the Arian Visigoths captured his city. In this respect Caesarius' position was no different from that of many other bishops during the barbarian invasions.

In the Burgundian kingdom on the upper Rhone St. Avitus held the see of Vienne from 490 to 519. Through his efforts the Arian King Gundobald tolerated Catholicism and prince Sigismund accepted baptism. Avitus is known for his poetical talents, especially a long epic-like production based on *Genesis,* and for his devotion to the papal primacy.

Frankish Catholicism. St. Gregory, bishop of Tours (d. 594), presents in his *History of the Franks* a graphic description of Merovingian society and of the impact of the barbarians on the Church. Officially the Franks were Catholic but their Catholicity was often the thinnest veneer over their barbarian habits. Kings, queens, and nobles were monsters of cruelty, selfishness, and ambition. Constant civil war, the result of the custom of dividing the realm among all sons of a deceased sovereign, provided opportunity unlimited for display of brutality. Piously denouncing simony the kings disposed of bishoprics at a handsome profit and introduced men of their own caliber into the Church. St. Gregory's history describes bishops and abbots guilty of every crime: Cautinus of Clermont buried alive a priest who refused to give up property unjustly demanded;

Gunther of Tours was a chronic drunkard; Salonius of Gap and Sagittarius of Embrun were accused of adultery and manslaughter; Abbot Degulf died at the hands of the husband of one of the women he debauched. Among the people superstitious use of relics and of the cult of the saints abounded. Roman and Celtic pagan rites continued to be observed.

Among the eleven archbishops and 118 bishops in the Frankish kingdom at the time Gregory was writing, there were many good men along with their more notorious colleagues. St. Gregory himself and St. Nicetius were excellent bishops. St. Venantius Fortunatus, one of Gregory's successors at Tours, was the most learned man of his generation; he composed poetry and hymns that are still used, such as *Vexilla regis*. St. Arnulf of Metz in the next century has been praised highly. Local synods met regularly and legislated against abuses, but without a reform in the royal house and because of the lack of trained clergy local disciplinary canons accomplished little. The better men found it expedient to continue associating with reprobate kings and courtiers to do what they could to ameliorate conditions without a futile open clash. St. Columban coming from Ireland and indignantly denouncing royal misconduct soon found himself expelled from Frankland. In time of crisis resolute bishops did threaten ecclesiastical punishment and prevent crimes but tact and patience were required in abundance.

Despite the shortcomings of certain members of their class and the obstacle of state domination the bishops were the one force in Frankish society standing between order and absolute chaos. They did accomplish tremendous good. Often they were members of the old Roman aristocracy, hence men of some culture, rulers and administrators by nature. They protected the helpless population against the rapacious Frankish nobility, conducted just trials, granted haven to refugees, provided education, served the king as adviser, judge or diplomat, built aqueducts and dykes, straightened the course of meandering rivers. "In short, the bishops were invaluable members of a community poor in valuable men."[1] If their theological learning was limited, society then needed administrators and men of action rather than scholars.

Monasticism flourished in Frankish Gaul, the number of houses increasing from about forty to near 200 in the sixth century. As a result of donations from repentant aristocrats the material wealth of the Church increased rapidly, reaching an estimated one-third of the land of Gaul

---

[1] O. M. Dalton (trans.), *The History of the Franks by Gregory of Tours*, 2 vols. (Oxford: 1927), Vol. I, "Introduction," p. 268.

by the end of the seventh century. This fact accounts for the attraction ecclesiastical careers offered to many of the unworthy clergy.

Pope St. Gregory the Great. In the midst of the Church's efforts against barbarism a truly great man ascended the Apostolic Throne in the person of Pope Gregory I (590–604). Scion of an aristocratic ancient Roman family, Gregory had entered on an unusually successful public career, attaining at an early age the position of Prefect of Rome, the highest office in the city. Abruptly abandoning his worldly achievements Gregory disposed of most of his wealth and became a monk in a monastery he founded in his own house in Rome. Although Gregory always remained a monk at heart, the Church needed his great talents in the active life, first as one of the Roman deacons and then as apocrisiarius or nuncio in Constantinople, a position he held for seven or eight years. During a devastating plague at Rome that carried off Pope Pelagius Gregory was immediately chosen his successor.

As pope, Gregory's attention was divided between the demands of his ecclesiastical office and the necessity of providing for the secular needs of the city. Since 568 Italy had been ravaged terribly by the Lombards, pagans tinged with Arianism. The exarch at Ravenna, representative of the sovereign Byzantine power, found himself helpless before the barbarians, incapable of checking the Lombards and unwilling to make peace. But an end to the horrors of war was essential, so Gregory took the initiative and negotiated a truce. When the exarch disregarded the truce and provoked King Agilulf to attack Rome Gregory inspired the city's defense. By 599 Gregory brought about a new truce. Henceforth the popes eclipsed the exarch in Lombard politics.

Gregory was a zealous defender of the prerogatives of the Roman See. He remonstrated with the bishop of Constantinople who had begun to style himself "universal patriarch," lest this innovation injure the prestige of Rome. Within his own metropolitanate Gregory appointed bishops, reproved others, readjusted dioceses, and urged lax clergy to their duty. He corresponded with bishops of Spain, Africa, Ravenna, Milan, Illyricum, seeking to end schism or repress heresy. He discussed the improvement of the Frankish Church with Queen Brunhildis. He seconded St. Leander's work in converting the Visigoths, urged the Lombards to accept Christianity, and dispatched St. Augustine of Canterbury to England to bring the Angles and Saxons into the Church. Benedictine monasticism owed its first expansion to him and much of its fame from his biography of St. Benedict. With detailed instructions Gregory supervised the administration of the Patrimony of St. Peter, the vast estates belonging to the Church scattered throughout Italy, Sicily, and the north — the Church's endowment and source of the funds Gregory dispensed freely for charity, defense, and feeding the destitute people of Rome. Ecclesiastical music and liturgy also were permanently influenced by Gregory.

Gregory the Great's writings justify his title "fourth Father of the Church," for they were tremendously popular throughout the middle ages. Gregory was not a speculative theologian but rather a moralist. His *Moralia,* in the form of a commentary on the book of Job, expounded moral theology. The *Pastoral Care* treats of the virtues and duties of the clergy. It was translated into all the vernaculars and served almost as a textbook for training priests and bishops. Gregory's *Dialogues,* inspirational lives of the saints, set the pattern for medieval hagiographers.

The Conversion of England. The Anglo-Saxon invaders of Britain obliterated Christianity along with the rest of Roman civilization. Refugee Britons re-established themselves and their churches in the western parts of the island but bitter mistrust and sporadic border wars of the sixth century prevented any thought of converting the hated invaders. Hence the conversion of Angles, Saxons, and Jutes had to come from outside, and it arrived in two streams, one from Rome, the other from Ireland.

Gregory the Great took the work in hand. St. Augustine and forty Benedictine monks whom the pope recruited from his own monastery of St. Andrew in Rome arrived in 597 in southeast England in lands of King Ethelbert of Kent, one of the seven kingdoms comprising Anglo-Saxon England. Ethelbert, a pagan, had married a Catholic Frankish princess who brought priests to England with her, so the king had some familiarity with Christianity. Within a few months Ethelbert was baptized with many of his subjects. On the ruins of a Roman chapel at Canterbury Augustine built Christchurch cathedral, over which he presided as bishop, and nearby a monastery dedicated to SS. Peter and Paul, later known as St. Augustine's. The monk Mellitus, one of a group of reinforcements from Rome, converted the king of the East Saxons and became bishop of London; another see at Rochester was entrusted to Justus. When Augustine died in 604 Christianity was firmly established in southeast England. Within a generation Wessex and East Anglia too had been evangelized, and a bitter pagan reaction in Essex had been stayed by Laurence of Canterbury. The chief failure of the early years was the lack of co-operation between the Roman and native British clergy of Wales and Cornwall.

Celtic Missionaries in Northumbria. When Ethelbert of Kent's daughter Ethelberga married Edwin of Northumbria Paulinus was consecrated bishop and accompanied her northward as her chaplain. Paulinus' eloquence quickly overcame King Edwin who was baptized along with his thanes in 627. Paulinus organized his see about York and began an ambitious program of missionary activity. In 633, however, the heathen King Penda of Mercia destroyed Edwin's kingdom, wiping out Paulinus' work and forcing the bishop and Edwin's widow to flee.

Penda's rule was short. In 635 Oswald conquered Northumbria and he was already a Catholic. But Oswald had received his religion from the Celtic monks at Iona, and to them he turned for new missionaries. St. Aidan accepted Osward's invitation and from the monastery he founded at Lindisfarne Aidan soon brought the entire north into the Church. Mercia too was converted by the Celts after a marriage between a Catholic Northumbrian princess and Penda's son opened that pagan stronghold to Christian penetration.

Between the Celtic northwest and the Roman southeast, united as they were in doctrine, there stood several differences of a constitutional nature: their methods of calculating the date of Easter and hence the whole ecclesiastical year, the form of tonsure, the ceremonies of administering baptism and consecrating bishops. In the seventh century these discrepancies loomed large and while they continued there could be no ecclesiastical unity. More troublesome was the Irish practice of organizing dioceses around their monasteries with the abbot of Iona exercising vague primatial rights, and, because of its monastic environment, the rigorous tone of Irish Catholicism.

Under the leadership of St. Wilfrid of York a party arose in Northumbria advocating conformity with Roman customs of the south. After much debate a synod assembled at the monastery of Whitby in 664 to thrash out the issue. When the Roman cause triumphed St. Colman and many Celtic monks departed from England rather than submit, but already parts of Ireland had begun changing over to Roman practices and eventually the problem subsided. At any rate, unity was secured in England.

Theodore of Tarsus and St. Bede. With the end of Celtic dominance in the north came opportunity for a thorough reorganization of the English church. Gregory the Great had prescribed the basic pattern for St. Augustine, but it was left for Theodore of Tarsus, Archbishop of Canterbury from 669 to 690 and a papal appointee, to take the matter in hand. Theodore secured recognition of Canterbury as the primatial see. He increased the number of suffragans from six to fourteen, he fixed geographical boundaries for all sees, and he secured endowment for them. In 673 he convoked the first national council at Hertford which legislated on numerous administrative matters. Somewhat later York became the second English archbishopric with jurisdiction over the entire north.

Besides his administrative work Theodore and his friend the African Abbot Hadrian fostered education. An important school began at Canterbury and others at Benedict Biscop's Northumbrian monasteries of Wearmouth and Jarrow. In every instance the new learning retained close touch with Mediterranean civilization. One of the glories of the Anglo-Saxon church is its scholarship, and the greatest of its scholars is St. Bede (672–735). This erudite Benedictine monk spent his entire life at the monastery of Jarrow teaching and writing on a multitude of subjects, preserving the learning of Greece and Rome on the borders of Scotland. But Bede's outstanding work is his *Ecclesiastical History of the English People* to which we are indebted for the story of England's conversion as well as for most of our secular information about early England. In his personal life Bede also mirrored the high caliber of the Anglo-Saxon clergy, among whom there was nothing like the decay rampant in the Frankish church.

Early Missions in Germany. Christianity reached the different tribes and sections of Germany from a number of sources. Some bishoprics survived in the old Roman lands west of the middle Rhine and south of the Danube, but most of central Europe remained pagan until the seventh century. Frankish bishops were not noted for missionary zeal, but some priests from Gaul visited Bavaria — SS. Rupert, Emmeran, and Corbinian. The conversion of the Alemanni was an Irish project begun by Fridolin in Alsace before 538, but the real impetus came with St. Columban. Monasteries such as St. Gall and Reichenau in Switzerland and Murbach in Alsace are among the four dozen or so Celtic foundations scattered throughout the Rhineland area. Celtic missionary effort, however important and widespread, lacked co-ordination, discipline, and organization. It followed customs different from the rest of Christendom, it stressed asceticism and it had almost no contact with Rome.

The English Church resembled the Celtic in missionary zeal but possessed those qualities of order and administrative genius wanting to the Irish. Its missionaries too were monks but of the milder Benedictine

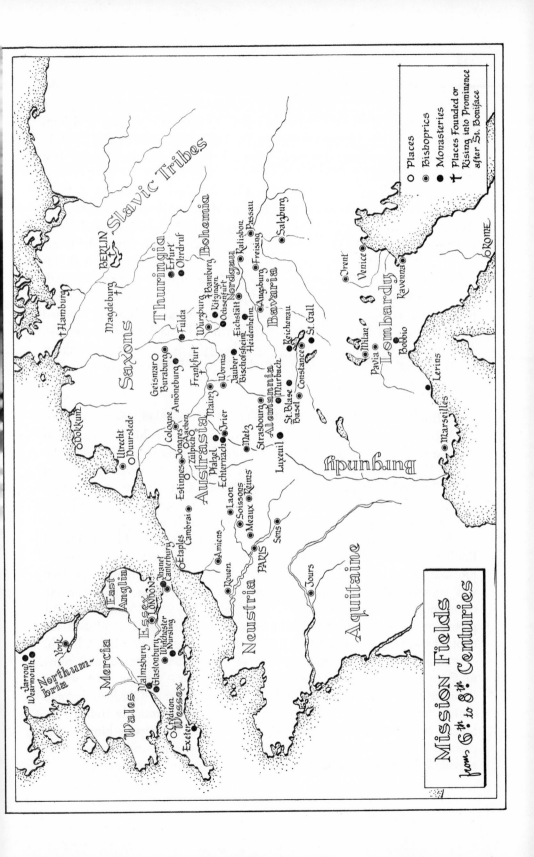

Mission Fields
from 6th to 8th Centuries

Places ○
Bishoprics ◉
Monasteries ●
Places Founded or
Rising into Prominence
after St. Boniface †

Slavic Tribes

BERLIN †
Magdeburg †
Hamburg †

Saxons

Thuringia
Erfurt
Ohrdruf

Bohemia
Würzburg † Bamberg
Kitzingen
Fulda
Geismar○
Buraburg○
Amöneburg
Frankfurt †
Ochsenfurt
Eichstätt Nordgau
Heidenheim
Ratisbon
Passau
Freising
Augsburg
Salzburg
Bavaria

Utrecht ◉
Duursiede ○
Dokkum ○

Cologne ◉
Jonges
Aachen
Zülpich
Estinges
Austrasia
Pfalzel
Echternach
Trier ◉
Mainz ◉
Worms ◉
Tauber
Bischofsheim
Metz ◉

Strasbourg ◉
Alemannia
Murbach
St. Blase
Basel ◉
Constance ◉
Reichenau
St. Gall

Trent ◉
Venice ◉
Milan ◉
Pavia ◉
Lombardy
Bobbio ●
Ravenna ◉
ROME ○

Lérins ●

Marseilles ○

Burgundy

Luxeuil ●

Laon ◉
Soissons ◉
Cambrai ◉
Amiens ◉
Meaux ◉ Reims ◉
PARIS ◉
Sens ◉
Étaples ○
Rouen ◉
Neustria

Tours ◉

Aquitaine

Jarrow ●
Wearmouth ●
York ◉
Northumbria
Mercia
Wales
Malmsbury ●
Glastonbury ●
Winchester ◉
Nursling ●
Wessex
Crediton ○
Exeter ◉
East Anglia
Essex
LONDON ◉
Canterbury ◉
Thanet

type and they consciously linked themselves through the papacy to the Universal Church. The typical Celtic missionary was an itinerant monastic bishop while the Anglo-Saxons preferred to establish territorial bishops as soon as feasible. Hence the Celts were really precursors of the English. Columban may be called a new John the Baptist, but Boniface is best compared to Paul.

Across the North Sea from England lay the Frisians. Wilfrid of York, shipwrecked in 679, briefly preached to them only eighty years after Augustine's advent in England. The permanent Christianization of Frisia commenced with St. Willibrord and his eleven companions. At Rome in 695 Willibrord was consecrated archbishop of the Frisians with his see at Utrecht. However, the conversion of the Frisians was tied up with the question of their freedom or subjugation to the Franks, and their princes harried the monks and impeded their work. Willibrord founded the monastery of Epternach as a refuge when Frisia became impossible. Nevertheless by the time of the missionary's death in 739 southern Frisia at least was firmly Christianized and provided an advance base for further penetration of Germany.

St. Boniface of Crediton (680–754).   St. Boniface (Wynfrith by his Anglo-Saxon name), the "apostle of Germany," left behind a reputation for learning and certain advancement in the monastic ranks when he joined Willibrord in Frisia in 716. At that time, however, the pagan Duke Radbod was in process of rooting out Christianity, so Boniface returned to England. In 719 he took a momentous step in going to Rome to secure from Gregory II a commission to preach to those "still in the bondage of paganism." After several successful years with Willibrord Boniface transferred his activity to central Germany, declining Willibrord's proposal to be his successor at Utrecht. In Rome again in 722 Boniface was consecrated bishop for his German converts. Pope Gregory wrote commending Boniface to Charles Martel, and thus it was under the joint protection of pope and Frankish prince that Boniface accomplished his twofold task of evangelizing Germany and reforming the Frankish Church.

Boniface's success attracted a flood of Anglo-Saxon monks and nuns to Germany. Benedictine monasteries at Fritzlar — on the spot where Boniface cut down an oak tree sacred to Woden — and Ohrdruff became centers for the missionaries. Convert monks were thoroughly trained. St. Sturm, for example, was sent to Monte Cassino to prepare him for his position as abbot of Fulda, Boniface's most important monastery which provided the Church with bishops and scholars for centuries.

In 732 Pope Gregory III appointed Boniface archbishop, still without a see, and empowered him to consecrate bishops as needed. In 738, on a third visit to Rome, Boniface, now almost sixty years old, was entrusted with the task of revitalizing the Church in Bavaria with powers of a papal legate. This he accomplished through synods and the administrative reorganization of the area around the sees of Salzburg, Passau, Regensburg, and Freising. These bishoprics were filled with English monks as were Boniface's four sees in Franconia and Hesse: Würzburg, Eichstett, Buraburg, and Erfurt.

Next Pope Zachary requested Boniface to restore the Church in Frankland and to that task the saint turned his attention as soon as the cooperative Carloman and Pepin the Short became Frankish mayors (741). The Frankish Church had reached its nadir in the time of Charles Martel (717–741). This prince pillaged the property of bishoprics and monasteries to equip and pay his army — for the defense of Europe against the Moslems, it must be admitted — and had appointed relatives and friends to high offices in the Church, men who knew how to fight, hunt, and feast but who had no interest whatever in ecclesiastical matters. Numerous sees remained vacant for years at a time. Reformers retired to monasteries in despair. The entire disciplinary machinery of the Church collapsed. Metropolitans lost their jurisdiction, bishops made little effort to supervise the lower clergy, and synods ceased to meet.

Boniface undertook his epoch-making reform with a series of councils over which he presided in 742, 743, and 744. Legislation was enacted against clerical immorality, heresy, and pagan superstitions, ecclesiastical organization was restored, and the Benedictine rule was recommended to all monks. In 747 a final synod declared its fidelity to the pope. About this time Boniface took up residence as archbishop of Mainz. But, missionary to the last, he resigned the sedentary life after five years to pass the last year of his life among a remnant of pagan Frisians. While waiting to confirm a group of converts Boniface, his disciples, and the new Christians were martyred at Dokkum, June 5, 754.

Conclusion. The conversion of the Celts, Franks, Anglo-Saxons, and Germans brought the Church safely through a major crisis. It increased the prestige and the resources of the papacy. It also preserved European civilization by starting the process whereby the barbarians assimilated the spiritual and intellectual achievements of antiquity and thus guaranteed their perservation. But most significant of all is the shift in the center of gravity of Christianity toward the north and west of Europe, for the ancient strongholds of the faith were rapidly lapsing into Byzantine stagnation or else were succumbing to the new paganism of Islam.

In the pontificate of Gregory the Great Mohammed began formulating his religious concepts in Arabia just as St. Augustine was setting out for England. Between 636 and 641 Syria, Palestine, and Egypt fell into Moslem hands. Carthage was swept away while Willibrord was laboring in Frisia, and five years before Boniface crossed the channel Spain sank beneath the flood. These were the lands that had witnessed the great events of primitive Christianity, that had produced the Church's scholars and martyrs, but now they were lost and Christianity there was destined to wither away. By pushing back the frontiers of Christendom the missionaries of the eighth and ninth centuries helped offset the serious losses and prepared a new foundation for the Church.

REVIEW AIDS

1. What is the historical task of the Church in the formation of European civilization?
2. Explain the problems raised by Arianism among the Germanic invaders.
3. Summarize the history of the papacy under the rule of Theodoric the Ostrogoth.
4. Describe the relations between the Church and the converted Germanic kings.
5. How did the barbarian background of the Franks influence the Church in Gaul?
6. What accomplishments of Pope Gregory I merit for him the title "the Great"?
7. Summarize the outstanding events in the conversion of England.
8. In what way did the Celtic missionaries in England and Germany differ from the Roman and Anglo-Saxon missionaries?
9. What factors shaped St. Boniface's missionary career?
10. What is the relationship between the conversion of the Germanic peoples and the expansion of Islam?

SUGGESTIONS FOR FURTHER READING

Christopher Dawson, *The Making of Europe* (New York: 1932), is an excellent survey of this period; Chapters V and XI are especially pertinent. L. Bieler, *The Life and Legend of St. Patrick* (Dublin: 1949), is aimed for the general reader but has a sound basis of scholarship. The classic work on Pope Gregory I is F. H. Dudden, *Gregory the Great, His Place in History and Thought,* 2 vols. (London: 1905). For the Frankish Church, there are good sections in Samuel Dill, *Roman Society in Gaul in the Merovingian Age* (New York: 1926), pp. 88 ff., 178 ff., and 476 ff.; also the introductory volume to O. M. Dalton's translation of Gregory of Tours's *History of the Franks,*

2 vols. (Oxford: 1927). Historiographic, archaeological, and literary themes are treated in Hartman Grisar's *History of Rome and the Popes in the Middle Ages*, trans. L. Cappadelta (St. Louis: 1912), 3 vols., of which Vols. II and III may be consulted. Very small yet comprehensive and enthusiastically written is S. J. Crawford, *Anglo-Saxon Influence on Western Christendom* (Oxford: 1933), which treats of the conversion of England and of Germany. The section on Boniface is well done. G. W. Greenaway's *St. Boniface* (London: 1955) is very brief but eminently satisfactory as a historical summary of Boniface's work. Satisfactory for factual information but poorly written is Joseph Schmidlin, *Catholic Mission History*, ed. Matthias Braun (Techny, Ill.: 1933). A more interpretative approach is found in the scholarly Protestant work of Kenneth Scott Latourette, *A History of the Expansion of Christianity*, Vol. II: *The Thousand Years of Uncertainty* (New York: 1938). An important article that shows the peculiarly Catholic features of the missionary work of these centuries is Richard E. Sullivan, "The Papacy and Missionary Activity in the Early Middle Ages," *Mediaeval Studies*, XVII (1955), 46–106.

DOCUMENTS

1. Pope Gregory the Great's instructions to the missionaries in England reveal the technique so successfully followed in the conversion of the pagan Germans. They show the psychological insight of the Pope and establish precedents that have proved fruitful in many other circumstances since the sixth century. Translated by James Harvey Robinson, *Readings in European History*, Vol. I (Boston: Ginn and Co., 1904), pp. 100–101.

When Almighty God shall bring you to the most reverend Bishop Augustine, our brother, tell him what I have, after mature deliberation on the affairs of the English, determined upon, namely, that the temples of the idols in that nation ought not to be destroyed, but let the idols that are in them be destroyed; let holy water be made and sprinkled in the said temples; let altars be erected, and relics placed. For if those temples are well built, it is requisite that they be converted from the worship of devils to the service of the true God; that the nation, seeing that their temples are not destroyed, may remove error from their hearts and, knowing and adoring the true God, may the more familiarly resort to the places to which they have been accustomed.

And because they have been used to slaughter many oxen in the sacrifices to devils, some solemnity must be substituted for them on this account, as, for instance, that on the day of the dedication, or of the nativities of the holy martyrs whose relics are there deposited, they may build themselves huts of the boughs of trees about those churches which have been turned to that use from temples, and celebrate the solemnity with religious feasting, no more offering beasts to the devil, but killing cattle to the praise of God in their eating, and returning thanks to the Giver of all things for their sustenance; to the end that, whilst some outward gratifications are permitted them, they may the more easily consent to the inward consolations of the grace of God.

For there is no doubt that it is impossible to efface everything at once from their obdurate minds, because he who endeavors to ascend to the highest place rises by degrees or steps and not by leaps. Thus the Lord made himself known to the people of Israel in Egypt; and yet he allowed them to use the sacrifices which they were wont to offer to the devil in his own worship, commanding them in his sacrifice to kill beasts to the end that, changing their hearts, they might lay aside one part of the sacrifice, whilst they retained another; that whilst they offered the same beasts which they were wont to offer, they should offer them to God, and not to idols, and thus they would no longer be the same sacrifices.

2. Bede's *Ecclesiastical History* provides the record of the Synod of Whitby in 664 which resolved the Irish-Roman controversy concerning the celebrating of Easter. The solution to the problem paved the way for a new epoch in the history of the Church in England. The advocates of the Roman observance argued from the basis of tradition as well as the divine commission of St. Peter as head of the Church. *Ibid.*, pp. 103–105.

"The Easter which I keep (Bishop Colman speaking for the Celts) I received from my elders, who sent me hither as bishop; all our forefathers, men beloved of God, are known to have kept it after the same manner; and that this may not seem to any contemptible or worthy to be rejected, it is the same which St. John the Evangelist, the disciple beloved of our Lord, with all the churches over which he presided, is recorded to have observed. . . ."

Then Wilfrid was ordered by the king to speak for the Roman practice: "The Easter which we observe we saw celebrated by all at Rome, where the blessed apostles, Peter and Paul, lived, taught, suffered, and were buried; we saw the same done in Italy and in France, when we traveled through those countries for pilgrimage and prayer. We found that Easter was celebrated at one and the same time in Africa, Asia, Egypt, Greece, and all the world, wherever the Church of Christ is spread abroad, through the various nations and tongues; except only among these and their accomplices in obstinacy, I mean the Picts and the Britons, who foolishly, in these two remote islands of the world, and only in part even of them, oppose all the rest of the universe. . . .

"You certainly sin if, having heard the decree of the apostolic see, and of the universal Church, and that the same is confirmed by Holy Writ, you refuse to follow them; for, though your fathers were holy, do you think that their small number, in a corner of the remotest island, is to be preferred before the universal Church of Christ throughout the world? And though that Columba of yours (and, I may say, ours also, if he was Christ's servant) was a holy man and powerful in miracles, yet should he be preferred before the most blessed prince of the apostles, to whom our Lord said, 'Thou art Peter, and upon this rock I will build my church; and the gates of hell shall not prevail against it. And I will give unto thee the keys of the kingdom of heaven?' "

When Wilfrid had spoken thus, the king said, "Is it true, Colman, that these words were spoken to Peter by our Lord?" He answered, "It is true, O King!" Then said he, "Can you show any such power given to your Columba?" Colman answered, "None." Then added the king, "Do both of you agree that these words were principally directed to Peter, and that the keys of heaven were given to him by our Lord?" They both answered, "We do." Then the king concluded, "And I also say unto you, that he is the doorkeeper, whom I will not contradict, but will, as far as I know and am able, in all things obey his decrees, lest when I come to the gates of the kingdom of heaven there should be none to open them, he being my adversary who is proved to have the keys." The king having said this, all present, both great and small, gave their assent and, renouncing the more imperfect institution, resolved to conform to that which they found to be better.

Chapter 9

THE FORMATION OF THE
PAPAL STATE

FROM 754 to 1870 the bishop of Rome was both head of the Church Universal and secular ruler of the territory of central Italy known variously as the States of the Church, the Papal State, or the Patrimony of St. Peter. Within this area the pope's power was the equivalent of that of a king within his kingdom; he possessed sovereign authority in all secular matters. This situation developed imperceptibly without deliberate forethought over a period of two centuries. Four factors contributed significantly: (1) the Lombard wars, (2) the weakness of the Byzantine Empire, (3) various religious disputes, especially that known as iconoclasm, (4) the alliance between the papacy and the Franks.

The Patrimony of St. Peter. In its original usage the term "Patrimony of St. Peter" designated private property in the form of landed estates owned by the Roman Church as its endowment. These estates had accumulated over the centuries since Constantine's decree in 321 permitting the Church to own property. Constantine's own generosity and the donations of wealthy Romans built the Patrimony into considerable holdings in the vicinity of Rome, in northern Italy, Dalmatia, southern Italy, and Sicily. The Church became in fact the largest landholder in Italy. From the Patrimony, either farmed by papal stewards or leased to tenants, the popes drew revenues for ecclesiastical administration, construction and maintenance of buildings, charity, defense, and a multitude of other necessities. Gregory the Great, as we have seen, made serious efforts to manage the Patrimony profitably. The Patrimony, however, was private property over which the popes did not possess sovereignty. After mid-eighth century when much of the original Patrimony had been lost, the term continued in use as one of the designations of the area over which the popes exercised political sovereignty, in particular the Duchy of Rome.

Lombards and Greeks in Italy. The Lombard invasion in 568 had two results: it permanently disrupted the unity of Italy, and it brought the pope to the fore as the most prominent figure in Italian affairs. Italy belonged to Byzantium, but the eastern emperors were too occupied with the Persians and Moslems to defend their western possessions adequately against the Lombards. Constans II's expedition in 663 was the last time a Byzantine emperor set foot on Italian soil. The exarch residing in impregnable Ravenna was vested with plenipotentiary powers as Byzantine governor of Italy but his actual resources were too limited to permit him to drive out the invaders. Other Byzantine officials were stationed elsewhere in the peninsula but usually they occupied themselves chiefly with fleecing their subjects in order to line their own pockets. Consequently the area of effective Byzantine rule was restricted to littoral regions organized into duchies under military rule. The Exarchate of Ravenna, the Pentapolis, Venetia, Apulia and Calabria, the Duchies of Naples and Rome comprised the regions of more or less Byzantine control. For their part, the Lombards, too, were divided against themselves. Their king controlled only the Po valley and Tuscany with his capital at Pavia, while practically independent Lombard dukes carved out two great dominions around Benevento to the south and Spoleto to the northeast of Rome. Thus was Italy partitioned.

Within the Duchy of Rome the pope emerged as the man to whom all turned for leadership. Gregory the Great effected the first treaty with the Lombards after vainly imploring the exarch for assistance, and even though Byzantium denounced him for it his treaty became permanent in 599. By the seventh century the Roman senate disappeared, the Greek officials were impotent, and the exarch unable or unwilling to exercise his authority. By default, therefore, the pope found himself in the position of unofficial representative of the Byzantine government. And from Gregory the Great's time to 754 there was no more effective upholder of the empire's rights than the pope. It had even become customary for a pope-elect to postpone his consecration until the emperor in Constantinople confirmed his election.

The growth of the pope's political influence paralleled the development of secular responsibilities of bishops everywhere in these troubled times when people turned instinctively to anyone with talent or prestige to give them the protection which the State could not provide. The Romans desired freedom from the threat of Lombard domination and the safe-guarding of their Roman citizenship, and only the pope seemed able to secure these things for them. As a result of the influence of the Bavarian Catholic princess Theodelinda over her Lombard consorts King Authari (584–590) and Agilulf (590–616), plus the missionary endeavors sponsored by Gregory the Great, Catholicism had become the official Lombard religion as early as 650. Nevertheless the Romans and the popes, too, preferred to be ruled by distant emperors who might at times be heretics but at least were far away. The Lombard kings subjected their bishops to the same close control as the Frankish and Visigoth monarchs. Better, the pope felt, to owe allegiance to a distant than to a local tyrant.

Religious Complications — Iconoclasm. Although the seventh century witnessed comparative political stability in Italy the religious disputes concerning Monothelitism played their part in weakening Byzantine influence. The popes, striving to protect orthodoxy against the heretical aberrations of the emperors, enjoyed the solid support of most Romans. When Justinian II's agents tried to kidnap Pope Sergius I in 692 for rejecting the Trullan council, the imperial army in Italy, consisting of local recruits, mutinied and defended Sergius instead. The Italians refused to acknowledge Emperor Bardanes when Pope Constantine (708–715) condemned him as a heretic. By the time of Pope St. Gregory II (715–731) the duchy of Rome was already an independent state under papal jurisdiction. Yet forty years of intermixed political and religious crises intervened before the *de facto* situation became a *de jure* reality.

Emperor Leo III (717–740) secured the Byzantine throne by virtue of his military prowess during the great Moslem siege of Constantinople in 717–718. Devoid of cultural background, education, or theological training, Leo none the less felt impelled to meddle in ecclesiastical business in typical Byzantine caesaro-papist fashion. The project to which he devoted himself is called iconoclasm, i.e., the destruction of images (icons) or representations of Christ, the Blessed Virgin, the cross, or the saints in certain forms, chiefly paintings on a wooden surface. Iconoclasm aimed at the total destruction of Christian art despite the fact that the use of icons could be traced back to primitive Christianity. The cult of the martyrs and the veneration paid to their relics had long ago promoted the employment of images in private and public services, particularly among the

Greeks whose production and use of images greatly exceeded Latin customs.

Various hypotheses have been suggested to explain the motivation of the iconoclastic emperors. Since the controversy extended from 726 to 780 and again from 813 to 843, different causes can be alleged for the rulers involved. The obvious religious basis was the charge that images were another form of idolatry and hence a contamination of Christianity. This issue had been discussed thoroughly before the eighth century and Christian art had been vindicated. The fact that the iconoclastic emperors directed the severest measures against the monks, who unlike the episcopate often refused to be cowed by the imperial power and thus represented a check on caesaro-papism and autocracy in general, renders it probable that at least one issue in the controversy was the political situation.

In 726 Leo III issued the first edict prohibiting the use of images. When his soldiers smashed to pieces a prominent statue of Christ in Constantinople the people rioted in protest and some were killed. More serious was the opposition of Pope Gregory II, the refusal of the Patriarch Germanus to endorse Leo's campaign, and the three *Apologetic Discourses against Those Who Reject Holy Images* penned by the eminent theologian St. John of Damascus, "last of the Greek Fathers." John developed the Catholic position by pointing out the difference between worship and veneration and describing the utility of pictures in stimulating piety and instructing the unlearned. But the emperor persisted. In 730 Germanus resigned and was followed by Patriarch Athanasius, Leo's creature, who lent the support of his office to the emperor's iconoclasm.

Not until Constantine V (741-775) did a really thorough attempt begin to root out the veneration of images and relics. At Hieria on the Asiatic side of the Bosphorus a council of 338 bishops assembled in 753. Taking their cue from Constantine the bishops pronounced that "there shall be rejected and removed and cursed out of the Christian Church every likeness which is made out of any material whatever by the evil art of painters." With the apparent sanction of the Church the desecration of statues and effacement of pictures commenced and together with that a fierce persecution of those who dared resist. Since the strongholds of Orthodoxy were the monasteries Constantine directed a steady stream of violence and ridicule against the monks. Many suffered death or mutilation and an estimated 50,000 fled to Italy.

The Seventh General Council.   Irene, wife of Leo IV (775-780) and regent for her son Constantine VI, finally brought the first iconoclastic persecution to a halt. She joined the new patriarch St. Tarasius in a request to Pope Adrian for a general council. Adrian complied, sending two Latin representatives. The Council met at Nicaea in 787 and restored the veneration of images and the display of mosaics, painting, and the like inside of churches as a legitimate form of devotion. Most striking is the docility of the Greek bishops in condemning as heresy their own solemn pronouncement of 753.

Only indirectly did iconoclasm help sever the ties between Italy and Byzantium since no earnest effort was made to enforce the heresy in the West. However it did aggravate the situation by offending the Italians and the popes and it gave another example of what Italy might expect from Byzantium.

Pope St. Gregory II (715–731). Gregory, a Roman pope after a series of seven Greeks and Syrians, presided over the destiny of the Church during troubled years. His contemporary Liutprand (712–744), greatest of the Lombard kings, set himself the task of conquering all Italy, while Emperor Leo III harassed rather than defended his Italian subjects. Italy was already restless because of Leo's new, heavy taxes — which Gregory led in protesting — when the iconoclastic edict of 726 was promulgated. Rebellions broke out and the exarch was assassinated, but Pope Gregory, while denouncing iconoclasm, prevented an attempt to elect a new emperor for Italy. As soon as the next exarch, Eutychius, established himself he tried unsuccessfully to procure Gregory's assassination because of the pope's stand against the emperor's law concerning iconoclasm and taxation. Failing in this Eutychius allied with Liutprand in 729 to capture Rome. Liutprand, however, yielded to Gregory's entreaties and withdrew. The next year Gregory co-operated with Eutychius in suppressing a revolt against the emperor. The obvious conclusion from the facts of Gregory II's pontificate were that the exarch was helpless without papal aid, yet despite provocation the pope remained the empire's loyal subject.

Pope St. Gregory III (731–741). A Lateran synod in 731 decreed excommunication for the iconoclasts, whereupon Emperor Leo dispatched a fleet to attack Rome and capture the pope. An Adriatic storm destroyed the fleet, so Leo then confiscated valuable papal estates in Calabria and Sicily. More than that, he detached southern Italy, Sicily, and all the Illyrian provinces from the patriarchical jurisdiction of Rome and transferred them to Constantinople.

Politically Gregory III continued to uphold the Byzantine cause, even to the extent of persuading Liutprand to surrender the captured fortress of Sutri and inducing Venice to expel the Lombards from Ravenna which they held briefly. Liutprand, a pious Catholic, always treated Rome with greater respect than Ravenna, but the Romans blundered in supporting the Duke of Spoleto in a rebellion against the Lombard king. Liutprand then invaded the Roman territory, seized four strategic towns and ravaged up to the gates of Rome.

In desperation the pope resorted to diplomacy. In 739 he sent messages across the Alps to Charles Martel, mayor of the palace and the real power among the Franks, begging for military aid. Since the Franks were technically still *foederati* or allies of the empire Gregory had reason to hope for a hearing, although he based his plea on religious rather than legal grounds. Moreover, Martel was co-operating effectively with the pope's legate St. Boniface in Germany. However, relations between Martel and Liutprand were too harmonious to be suddenly ruptured, for the Lombards had just assisted Martel in driving the Moslems out of Provence. The Frankish mayor respectfully declined to come to the aid of the Romans.

Gregory III's death brought Pope St. Zachary (741–752) to the throne. Zachary quickly improved the situation by inducing Liutprand to turn aside from Rome in return for abandonment by the Romans of their alliance with the ungrateful duke of Spoleto. Liutprand accepted the proposal, restored the four towns, and concluded a treaty promising peace for twenty years. Then Liutprand turned against Ravenna. At the request of the population of the helpless Exarchate Zachary again approached the king and again persuaded him to desist. Liutprand's death the next year eased things greatly for his successor Ratchis (744–749) was peacefully inclined. However, at the insistence of his warlike nobles Ratchis reopened the campaign against the Exarchate in 749. Zachary immediately demanded an interview with the king. So decisive was the pope's moral ascendancy that Ratchis not only gave up his campaign, he even laid down his crown to become a monk at Monte Cassino.

Frankish Intervention. The *status quo* of 749 was too delicate to endure long. Aistulf, the new Lombard king (749–756), cherished ambitions of conquest which he immediately set out to realize. By 751 Ravenna and the Exarchate were his, as was the Pentapolis soon afterward leaving only Venetia acknowledging Byzantine sovereignty in the north. The Duchy of Rome was Aistulf's next objective, and although he did not move against it at once, neither would he guarantee its independence. Dreading the thought of imminent subjugation to the Lombards, even though these were Catholics, the Romans and the pope began to search for a protector to deter Aistulf and maintain the position of nominal Byzantine suzerainty.

Gregory III had approached the Franks in vain in 739 but Zachary, by bringing the son of Charles Martel into his debt, took the step that directly paved the way for the temporal sovereignty of the papacy. Pepin the Short, like his father Martel, held the office of mayor of the palace and ruled Frankland in all but name. For a century the insignificant Merovingian "do-nothing" kings had lived briefly and died young with nothing to justify their existence. Pepin aspired to the royal title, but he felt the need for some sanction before undertaking a palace revolution. In 751 he sent Bishop Burchard of Würzburg and Abbot Fulrad of St. Denis to lay the matter before the pope as a problem in morals. Zachary's reply, that he who exercised the royal power should wear the crown, suited Pepin's purposes exactly and convinced the Frankish nobles to acknowledge Pepin king. The last Merovingian was sent into a monastery. Some historians believe that St. Boniface in his capacity as papal vicar anointed Pepin in a religious ceremony at the coronation. These events occurred the year of Aistulf's conquest of Ravenna, 751.

Pope Stephen's (752–757) desperate pleas for military aid against the Lombards elicited from Emperor Constantine V the admonition to seek an alliance with another Germanic tribe against them, the time-honored Byzantine practice in such circumstances. Direct negotiations with Aistulf failed to turn him from his purpose of annexing Rome, although at one point he consented to a forty years' truce — which he violated six months later. Stephen thereupon secretly contacted Pepin requesting an escort for a journey into France. Pepin sent ambassadors to accompany the pope, but just before they set out from Rome legates from Constantinople arrived ordering the pope to visit Aistulf personally to try again to win back the Exarchate. Stephen, his Roman associates, and his two Frankish companions, the illustrious Bishop St. Chrodegang of Metz and Duke Autchar, made no impression on Aistulf in their interview at Pavia. Either Stephen did not possess the persuasive talents of Pope Zachary or Aistulf was immune to any argument but that of the sword. Crossing into Gaul the papal entourage met Pepin at Ponthion in January, 754. Stephen was the first Roman pontiff to venture over the Alps.

Pepin received Stephen very respectfully and listened to his pleas "to put in order the cause of blessed Peter and the republic of the Romans." To this the king consented, and there is evidence that the agreement was sealed by a pact signed at Quierzy. Pepin then joined Stephen in an exchange of notes to Aistulf demanding the peaceful surrender of lands taken from the Empire. Stephen bestowed on Pepin the Byzantine honorary title of Patrician and reanointed him Frankish king. More than that, the pope also consecrated Pepin's sons and forbade the Franks under penalty of excommunication to recognize any king outside of Pepin's family.

Since Aistulf persisted in refusing to relinquish his conquests, Pepin gathered the Frankish army and invaded Lombardy. After a short campaign the Lombard king now yielded and promised to "restore" Ravenna and other areas, but the restoration was not to be to Byzantium but to the pope. Pepin's disposition of the disputed territories rested on a realistic appraisal of the situation. Byzantine power in northern Italy was a thing of the past and there were no valid arguments to urge its revival. By right of conquest the Exarchate belonged to Pepin to do with as he chose. Since the Romans under papal leadership had managed to retain their lands by their own efforts, some equilibrium might be attained by adding the Exarchate and Pentapolis to the Duchy of Rome under the independent rule of the one man who might be able to hold them with Frankish support. All these events of 754 indicate that the pope had finally resolved to cast off allegiance to Constantinople and to embark on a career of independence in alliance with the Franks. The iconoclastic canon pronounced by Constantine V's council at Hieria the year before had probably helped Stephen to reach this resolution.

Whether or not Pepin was consciously motivated by gratitude for papal support of his *coup d'état* in 751, all the sources indicate a religious basis for his action. When Greek diplomats visited him and protested that Byzantine jurisdiction should be re-established, Pepin insisted that he had acted only out of love for St. Peter and the Church and had no intention of restoring Byzantine rule. He felt that he was endowing the papacy in the same way that he endowed monasteries and bishoprics in Gaul.

The Donation of Pepin. Pepin's departure was the signal for Aistulf to return to his old ways. Not only did he refuse to fulfill his promised concessions, he even advanced on Rome in January, 756, and put the city under siege. Pope Stephen's three appeals in Pepin, the last in the form of a letter from St. Peter himself, did not go unheeded. For a second time the Franks overwhelmed the Lombards. This time a document was prepared repeating Pepin's promises at Quierzy and enumerating specific cities to be turned over by the Lombards to the pope. This charter, called the Donation of Pepin, was deposited in Rome by the indefatigable Abbot Fulrad who visited each city with Lombard envoys,

Romagna (*EXARCHATE*)

Lombard
Kingdom

Ravenna

Tuscany

Pentapolis

Corsica

Perugia

Patrimony

of
St. Peter

Spoleto

Rome

Sardinia

Naples

Tyrrhenian Sea

Sicily

States of the
~ Church
about 770 ~

collected the keys to their gates, and presented them also to the pope.

Aistulf's death that same year provided opportunity for the acquisition of more territory by Stephen II. Aistulf had surrendered all parts of the Exarchate and the Pentapolis which he had conquered; other sections taken by Liutprand were apparently not included, such as the cities of Bologna and Ferrara. When rival candidates claimed the Lombard throne Pope Stephen through Fulrad extracted further concessions from Desiderius in exchange for assistance in winning the throne. Once securely in possession, however, Desiderius (756–774) forgot his promises. Diplomatic haggling with an occasional show of force continued until the end of Desiderius' reign.

St. Paul I (757–767), Stephen's brother, upheld the claims against Desiderius, but with Pepin declining to intervene again the issue was stalemated. More serious were the efforts of the Greeks to effect an antipapal alliance with Pepin, which was very unlikely, or with Desiderius, another matter indeed. Within the Duchy of Rome Pope Paul acquired a reputation for harshness. The sources speak of death sentences and full prisons, extortions and "iniquitous satellites." The flare-up following Paul's death reveals considerable dissatisfaction arising from confusion because of the dual function of the pope as religious and secular head of Rome.

Roman Controversies.   From the Church's viewpoint the prime advantage of an independent papal state was the freedom it entailed in the consideration of ecclesiastical policies without regard for the whims of a secular sovereign. The dangers of an effective secular sovereignty over Rome had been made abundantly clear during the Byzantine period: Belisarius' deposition of Pope Silverius in 537, the kidnaping of Vigilius in 545 at Justinian's orders, Martin I's arrest in 653 and his fatal exile after a fraudulent trial by Constans II. The domination exercised over the Church by the German princes in Spain, Gaul, and Lombardy showed the same tendencies. One possible solution for the papacy had been the anomalous situation of the early seventh century when the popes were virtually independent but acknowledged emperors too weak to interfere in Italian ecclesiastical debates. When this system broke down under Lombard attack the only alternative seemed to be the Frankish protectorate over a nominally independent papal state.

However, political sovereignty was no unmixed blessing. For one thing, it made the papacy a very attractive office to men who would never have desired it for its religious prestige. Then too, with the disappearance of the external danger of the Lombard aggression, the pressure was removed which had formerly served as a cohesive force over the Romans. The pope, no longer a savior, became in their eyes a new oppressor in his capacity as secular governor. A spirit of factionalism became evident. A natural division existed in Rome between the military aristocracy and the numerous clergy backed by the militia organized on the papal farms near Rome, each considering itself the fittest agent for administering the temporal affairs of the papal state. Pope Paul's severity brought the issue to the surface at the very beginning of the history of the papal state.

Both Stephen II and Paul had leaned heavily on the primicerius or chief notary of the Roman Church, a man by the name of Christopher who had guided papal undertakings of the preceding decade. Christopher discovered a plot by a certain Duke Toto and his three brothers to seize the papal throne, and the loose procedure governing papal elections prevented Christopher from thwarting them. As soon as Pope Paul was dead they forced their way into the Lateran and installed Toto's brother Constantine, a layman, on the papal throne. The bishop of Palestrina consecrated him under compulsion. Christopher, marked out for destruction, found sanctuary in St. Peter's and was permitted to leave Rome alive only on the understanding that he would enter a monastery. Instead, Christopher hastened to the Lombard court to procure Desiderius' aid in ridding the Church of the anti-pope. Desiderius jumped at the chance of winning a foothold in Rome.

Led by the priest Waldipert a Lombard force entered Rome and ended Constantine's thirteen months' reign by summarily deposing him. Toto was killed. Before Christopher reached Rome the Lombards advanced their own anti-pope, a venerable priest Philip, but the primicerius persuaded him to resign. Through Christopher's efforts a valid election resulted in the choice of Stephen III (768–772). Philip withdrew unharmed, but Waldipert, Constantine, and others had their eyes torn out by the Roman mob. Those who survived were imprisoned. In 769 Stephen III convoked a Lateran synod which annulled all ordinations performed by Constantine and decreed that henceforth none but the cardinal clergy might be elected pope and the laity were to have no voice in elections.

King Desiderius, resentful of the mistreatment of his countryman Waldipert and of Christopher's efforts to keep Rome out of Lombard hands, organized a jealous group at the papal court to undermine the influence of the primicerius. Paul Afiarta, a papal chamberlain, became Desiderius' tool and began to play on the weak-willed pope. In 771 Desiderius came with troops to Rome — on pilgrimage, he asserted.

Christopher cautiously readied the city's defenses. In the crisis the pope, "morally a Lombard prisoner," abandoned Christopher who fell into his enemies' hands and was murdered. Afiarta then dominated Stephen III until his death the next year. Desiderius returned to Pavia to be dealt with shortly by Charlemagne.

The Donation of Constantine. A celebrated document in papal history from the second half of the eighth century is the Donation of Constantine. This charter, proved to be a forgery at the time of the Renaissance but generally considered genuine until that time, purported to be a deed by Constantine the Great granting to Pope Sylvester I (314–335) temporal sovereignty over the entire western Empire and primacy within the Church. The forged Donation was drawn up by its anonymous author to lend an air of greater legality to the *de facto* sovereignty by the papacy in the course of the Lombard wars or to provide an added inducement to Pepin to rescue the papacy and restore to it the independence that was rightfully its prerogative. Some medieval writers used the Donation of Constantine as proof for arguments that all of Europe belonged under the political jurisdiction of the papacy. The popes occasionally used it along these lines, but not until after 1054. No pope ever saw in the Donation the basis of his spiritual supremacy.

Summary. In the total inability of Byzantium to perform for the people of Italy the first duty of government, i.e., defense against external aggression, lies the fundamental reason for the independent course adopted by, in fact forced upon, the popes. The alliance between the papacy and the Franks, a matter of mutual convenience in 751–756, brought together the two strongest forces then shaping European history and gave a fruitful new impulse and direction to both. The events of Stephen III's pontificate raised the question of whether the popes had escaped domination by Byzantium and the Lombards only to succumb to the more pernicious control of petty Roman factions.

REVIEW AIDS

1. Explain the term "Patrimony of St. Peter."
2. Describe the political situation in Italy about the year 700.
3. Define Iconoclasm and trace its history in its first phase.
4. Summarize the pontificates of Popes Gregory II and Gregory III.
5. What factors explain the alliance between Pepin and Stephen II?
6. Explain the Donation of Pepin and its significance.

7. What advantages and disadvantages resulted for the Church from the establishment of the temporal sovereignty of the papacy?
8. Discuss the Donation of Constantine.

SUGGESTIONS FOR FURTHER READING

The best work on the subject is the English translation of Louis Duchesne's French volume, *The Beginnings of the Temporal Sovereignty of the Popes A.D. 754–1073*, trans. Arnold Mathew (New York: 1908). Horace K. Mann, *The Lives of the Popes in the Early Middle Ages*, 2nd ed. (London: 1925), Vol. I, part II, is a thorough piece of work. Also worth consulting is the article "States of the Church" in the *Catholic Encyclopedia*, Vol. XIV. There is a good brief treatment in Chapter VII of Jeremiah O'Sullivan and John F. Burns, *Medieval Europe* (New York: 1943). An old work that is still worth consulting is Thomas Hodgkin's *Italy and Her Invaders*, 2nd ed. (Oxford: 1899), Vols. VI and VII. For Iconoclasm see C. J. Hefele, *A History of the Councils of the Church* (Edinburgh: 1896), Vol. V. *The Dumbarton Oaks Papers*, especially No. VII (1953) contain several scholarly articles on the Iconoclastic controversy. Also see appropriate chapters in H. Daniel-Rops, *The Church in the Dark Ages* (London: 1959).

DOCUMENTS

1. When the Lombards threatened to overwhelm central Italy and bring the pope under their rule, the pope was forced to seek aid. Since the Byzantine Empire was no longer capable of defending territory in Italy which it legally claimed, the pope was forced to look to the barbarian Franks for assistance. Reproduced here is one of the letters of Pope Gregory III requesting help (from Charles Martel) against the Lombards in the year 739. Migne, *Patrologia Latina*, XCVIII, 67–68.

Pope Gregory to his most excellent son Charles, sub-king:

Because of our tears and the great sadness of our heart we have thought it necessary to write to Your Excellency again, confident that you are a loving son of Blessed Peter prince of the Apostles and of us, and that out of respect for him you may obey our commands to defend the Church of God and the chosen people who now cannot bear the persecution and oppression of the Lombard race. They have taken away all gifts offered in honor of the prince of the Apostles by your parents or by yourself. Because after God we flee to you, they hate us bitterly and oppress us. Hence the church of St. Peter is plundered and reduced to great desolation. We have orally explained all our sorrows to the bearer of this message, your faithful subject, which he ought to narrate to Your Excellency. You, my son, will share with the prince of the Apostles here and in the next life in the presence of Almighty God according as you hasten to take steps to fight for His Church and for our defense. In this way all nations will recognize your pure faith and the love you have for Blessed Peter prince of the Apostles by your zeal in defending us and God's chosen people. In this way you can win for yourself lasting fame and eternal life.

2. During the Iconoclastic controversy the Greek Church formed and then changed its opinions several times according to the wishes of the successive emperors. This decree of the Greek synod of 753 is one of those that upheld Iconoclasm. C. J. Hefele, *A History of the Councils of the Church* (Edinburgh, 1896), V, 310–313.

. . . It is the unanimous doctrine of all the holy Fathers and of the six Ecumenical Synods, that no one may imagine any kind of separation or mingling in opposition to the unsearchable, unspeakable, and incomprehensible union of the two natures in the one hypostasis or person. What avails, then, the folly of the painter, who from sinful love of gain depicts that which should not be depicted, that is, with his polluted hands he tries to fashion that which should only be believed in the heart and confessed with the mouth? He makes an image and calls it Christ. The name Christ signifies God and man, and consequently he has in his foolish mind, in his representation of the created flesh, depicted the Godhead which cannot be represented, and thus mingled what should not be mingled. Thus he is guilty of a double blasphemy, the one in making an image of the Godhead and the other by mingling the Godhead and manhood. Those fall into the same blasphemy who venerate the image, and the same woe rests upon both, because they err as did Arius, Dioscorus, and Eutyches. When, however, they are blamed for undertaking to depict the divine nature of Christ, which should not be depicted, they take refuge in the excuse: We represent only the flesh of Christ which we saw and handled. But that is a Nestorian error. For it should be considered that that flesh was also flesh of God the Logos, without any separation, perfectly assumed by the divine nature and made wholly divine. How could it now be separated and represented apart? . . . Supported by the Holy Scriptures and the Fathers, we declare unanimously, in the name of the Holy Trinity, that there shall be rejected and removed and cursed out of the Christian Church every likeness which is made out of any material whatever by the evil art of painters.

Chapter 10

THE CHURCH UNDER THE CAROLINGIANS

T HE Carolingian Empire was the result of the papal-Frankish alliance, the missionary and the reform activity of St. Boniface, and the personality of Pepin and Charlemagne. It marked the closest cooperation between the spiritual and the temporal powers. Charlemagne and his son Louis the Pious wanted to create a genuinely Christian society that embraced elements of the Christian Roman Empire and the divinely ordained monarchy of the Old Testament. In this they enjoyed the complete support of the Church, even though their theocratic tendencies threatened religious freedom within their realm. In reviving the Roman Empire, Pope Leo III and Charlemagne cemented the entente between the Franks and the papacy but also sowed the seeds of many future conflicts of jurisdiction.

Carolingian Catholicism; Pepin the Short. The starting point for the history of the Frankish Church under the Carolingians is the restoration begun by the Anglo-Saxon missionaries. Since the first significant act of Pepin's public career was his collaboration with St. Boniface at the great councils of 743 and 744, we would naturally look for the same reform motif in his reign as king. To a certain extent Pepin did continue Boniface's program. Four synods between 755 and 757 and two later in Pepin's reign concerned themselves with the enforcement of earlier decrees on marriage laws and the Sunday observance, strengthening the episcopate and regenerating the monasteries.

Pepin, however, departed from the Bonifacian program in two significant respects: he did not revive the jurisdiction of metropolitans, nor did

148

he hinge the Frankish Church's hierarchical organization on the papacy, which really represented the heart of Boniface's endeavors. Pepin allowed no change that might weaken his control of the Church. In the matter of the restoration of secularized Church property Pepin at first sought to alleviate hardship along lines specified by the Council of Lestines in 743, that is, the lay lord holding former Church land was obligated to make a small annual payment to its original owner to relieve financial distress of the churches and to keep alive the memory of the Church's ownership. But in the end Pepin himself outdid Martel by further confiscations that often left churches and monasteries in greater distress than ever. To provide new revenue for impoverished parishes Pepin by public law imposed the tithe, heretofore largely voluntary, as a fixed tax on all agricultural products, thus largely passing on to the faithful the obligation of supporting their church. In short, Pepin's program resulted in improvement of clerical and lay morality but left everything ultimately dependent on the monarchy.

Charlemagne's Theocracy. It is inexact to say that Charlemagne's reign (768–814) witnessed the complete subjugation of the Church to the State; rather there occurred under Charlemagne such a thorough fusion of temporal and spiritual matters that the distinction between them practically disappeared. Most of the early Germanic kings had tended to dominate the Church within their realms after the Byzantine caesaropapist fashion, that is, they used the Church as a prop for their political power. Charlemagne did likewise but he surpassed his predecessors here as in everything else, for he justified his actions by an exalted theocracy that recalls Justinian or Constantine rather than Clovis or Recared.

Charlemagne considered himself a new David commissioned by God to guide the chosen people to their eternal salvation. He thought of himself as more a priest than a layman, to some extent even the equal of the pope. His strong sense of duty compelled him to take the affairs of the Church into his own hands and to write to Pope St. Leo III his famous letter explaining that it was the pope's business to pray and the emperor's to handle the external affairs of the Church. In his capitularies Charlemagne legislated on clerical discipline, the liturgy, the baptismal rite, monasteries, and religious instruction. His *missi*, royal inquisitors, were instructed to investigate the private lives of the clergy and to examine their knowledge of canon law and the liturgy. At the same time the *missi* were to see that the laity knew the Lord's Prayer and Credo and paid their tithes promptly.

At least sixteen Frankish synods assembled during Charlemagne's reign and the king played the decisive role in all of them. Archbishops reappeared but like all members of the hierarchy they were virtual appointees of Charlemagne. St. Boniface had favored the exemption of monasteries from episcopal jurisdiction but Charlemagne preferred otherwise. Uniformity in ecclesiastical practices was one of Charlemagne's goals. To that end he received from Pope Hadrian I a copy of Dionysius Exiguus' code of canon law as the norm for Frankland. He encouraged all monks to follow the Benedictine Rule and he sent to Monte Cassino for an authentic copy. For cathedral clergy he favored the rule of St. Chrodegang of Metz (d. 766) which grouped into a semi-monastic community all the multitude of lectors, choristers, students, clerics of all ranks, and priests who comprised the "family" of a Carolingian bishop.

Charlemagne's missionary campaigns were as much political as religious endeavors. He waged war against the Moslems in Spain, against the Avars and Slavs in eastern Europe, and against the Saxons who were the last pagan tribe of northwestern Germany. The Saxon wars were his most determined undertaking. The safety of his frontier demanded the subjugation of the Saxons, yet submission to Frankish rule entailed acceptance of Christianity. So Charlemagne baptized the Saxons at the point of the sword and blanketed Saxony with monasteries and bishoprics to hold them in check. Again and again the Saxons rebelled, and their revolts always had the character of wars against Christianity since bishops and monks were among the first victims. Often it was the insistence of the missionaries that the Saxons submit to ecclesiastical exactions such as tithes that goaded them into rebellion. In 802 Charlemagne's Capitulary for the Saxons decreed death for any who postponed baptism, cremated bodies, continued pagan practices, injured clergymen, or damaged Church property. Abbot Sturm of Fulda, St. Ludger bishop of Münster, St. Lebuin, and the English missionary Willehad mitigated in practice the emperor's harshness, the first two among the Saxons, the latter two among the remnant of pagan Frisians.

Doctrinal Questions. Three doctrinal controversies arose during Charlemagne's reign. The veneration of images, sanctioned by the seventh ecumenical council in 787, met with little favor among the Frankish bishops, partly from their fear of reawakening idolatry so recently suppressed among their people, partly from a faulty translation of the acts of the council which gave a false impression of its decisions. A synod at Frankfurt in 794 condemned the Second Council of Nicaea, and not until the tenth century was it recognized as ecumenical among the Franks.

From Spain came the heresy of Adoptionism, a derivation of Nestorianism, which asserted that Christ was not divine at birth but only became God when adopted by God the Father at the time of His baptism in the Jordan. Bishop Felix of Urgel (d. 818) did not orginate Adoptionism but he was its chief exponent, while Alcuin took charge of the Catholic defense. Felix's doctrine was prohibited by two Frankish councils and a Roman synod before he agreed at the council of Aachen in 800 to renounce his error. One of Felix's opponents estimated that the heresiarch had 20,000 followers in southern Gaul.

The Frankish liturgy had incorporated the *filioque* clause into the Nicene-Constantinopolitan Creed sung at Mass. This differed from the eastern and the Roman usage where the expression was not used since it was not found in the original Creed. An argument between Frankish and Greek monks occasioned an inquiry by the Franks to the pope. Leo III earnestly requested that the Franks omit the disputed *filioque*, even though it expressed orthodox theology, in order to avoid difficulty with the Greeks, but the Franks ignored the pope's wishes. As Leo foresaw, the matter later became very troublesome.

The Carolingian Renaissance. The Carolingian period witnessed a significant revival of intellectual activity involving the three areas of England, Frankland, and central Germany. Now that these lands were Christianized and the political climate was temporarily favorable it was possible to turn attention to things of the mind. The most obvious feature of Carolingian scholarship is its clerical environment and ecclesiastical interests. Alcuin of York, Peter of Pisa, Paulinus of Aquileia, Einhard, and Paul the Deacon were all clergymen in either major or minor orders. One of the reasons for Charlemagne's patronage was to assure an educated clergy. The capitularies commanded that schools be attached to every monastery and bishopric as the means for spreading education. Those trained at the palace school at Aachen received bishoprics or monasteries in every part of the Empire and they in turn became the foci for spreading the influence of the new learning over the Frankish Empire. The bishoprics and abbeys at Lyons, Reims, Corbie, Fulda, St. Gall, and Reichenau were particularly important.

Alcuin's (735–804) works indicate the interests of the Carolingian scholars. He treated theological questions during the Adoptionist dispute, prepared a corrected edition of the Vulgate, commented on the Scriptures, composed four lives of saints, and wrote liturgical treatises. In the second generation Rabanus Maurus (776–856), abbot of Fulda and then arch-bishop of Mainz, holds first place. Under him the monastic school of Fulda attained eminence. Rabanus' most prominent works are extensive commentaries on Scripture and a treatise *On the Education of the Clergy*. From Fulda came Walafrid Strabo, author of part of the *Glossa Ordinaria*, the early series of Scriptural commentaries. Paschasius Radbertus of the monastery of Corbie wrote the "first scientific monograph on the Holy Eucharist," entitled *The Body and Blood of the Lord*. Bishop Hincmar of Reims combated the predestination taught by the monk Gottschalk and worked for the acceptance in Frankland of the decrees of the seventh general council. John Scotus Eriugena (d. c. 877), a Neo-Platonic philoso-pher and theologian, was the most original thinker of the century, even though somewhat heterodox. He translated into Latin the works of the fifth-century Syrian known as Pseudo-Dionysius, the source of a long strain of mysticism in the popular spiritual writings of medieval Europe.

The Papacy. Three thorny problems remained unsettled concerning the Papal State: (1) its geographic boundaries, (2) its relations with the Lombards, (3) the conflicting claims of papal autonomy and Frankish sovereignty. King Desiderius' blunders precipitated a solution to the first two, but it required many years to resolve the third.

Adrian I (772–795), who ruled longer than any other medieval pope, is the last of the remarkable sovereign pontiffs of the eighth century. By birth a member of the aristocracy, by profession an ecclesiastical civil servant, Adrian suited both factions whose conflicts had disgraced the reign of the preceding pope. Moreover, he was a man of action, energy, and unquestioned probity. Adrian's first decision was to rid the papacy of the pro-Lombard sentiment of Stephen III's pontificate and to punish those responsible for the recent disturbances. Afiarta's removal and the general reaction to Desiderius' aggression against papal lands produced the desired new atmosphere. Soon Adrian was corresponding with Charlemagne begging for aid.

The Franks heeded Adrian's request, for Desiderius had offended Charlemagne also by harboring Frankish fugitives. While his army be-sieged Pavia in 774 Charlemagne came to Rome — something his father Pepin had never done — and while there he not only renewed the Dona-tion of Pepin, he also granted his own Donation enlarging the Papal State with territory he hoped to conquer from the Lombards. However, after Desiderius' surrender Charlemagne decided to put an end to the Lombard problem once for all by himself assuming the title King of the Lombards and annexing Lombardy to his own domains. Under such circumstances it is understandable that Charlemagne did not carry out the terms of his Donation. Pope Adrian recognized the situation in 781 and again in 787, and in return Charlemagne granted him a segment of old Roman Tuscany by way of compensation. For all practical purposes the Papal State under Adrian had reached the maximum limits it was to retain until 1861.

Charlemagne did not regard the Papal State as an independent political entity. That his title Patrician of the Romans entailed some kind of jurisdiction in Rome he did not doubt, and he expected all Romans to be loyal to the Frankish monarchy. Nor could the pope dispute the fact that the Frankish protectorate likewise gave the king certain prerogatives in the civil government. On several occasions the king judged cases appealed to him over the pope's protest, but Charlemagne and Adrian's mutual esteem kept them from arguments that might have resolved more satisfactorily the question of sovereignty in central Italy.

Pope Leo III and the Revival of the Roman Empire.   Immediately after his election Pope St. Leo III (795–816) notified Charlemagne and sent him the flag of Rome and the keys to the tomb of St. Peter in recognition of the rights of the Frankish king. Pope Leo was soon in need of Frankish protection. Apparently Adrian had filled important positions in the government of Rome and of the Church with his own relatives and when Leo, not of the nobility, curtailed their privileges, they struck back. In 799 Leo was assaulted in the streets of Rome. Although his assailants failed in their attempt to cut out the pope's eyes and tongue, Leo did suffer serious wounds. As soon as possible he hastened to Germany to enlist Charlemagne's help.

Charlemagne detailed an escort to see Leo safely back to Rome and to open an investigation. Leo's enemies thereupon charged him with some kind of crime so Charlemagne came in person to look into the case. The result was a repetition of the proceedings against Pope Symmachus in 501; since no one was deemed competent to judge the pope he could be neither convicted nor acquitted. To break the impasse and clear himself Leo took a public oath of purgation in the presence of Charlemagne, insisting, however, that no precedent for the future should be thereby established. A few days later, on Christmas day of the year 800, while Charlemagne was attending Mass in St. Peter's, Pope Leo placed a crown upon his head and the crowd in the church hailed Charlemagne as the new Roman Emperor.

Significance of the Revival of the Empire. Although no tangible changes resulted, the revival of the Roman Empire in the West was tremendously important. It was the political side of the Carolingian Renaissance; it showed the Church acting as the intermediary linking the new Germanic Empire with the ancient roots of Western civilization. The revival of the Empire created both a partner and a rival to the papacy in the government of Christendom. It emphasized the jurisdiction of the pope by contrasting his position as spiritual head of Europe with the emperor's role as temporal head. Medieval man was accustomed to think of Europe as a unit, as Christendom, a single entity overshadowing differences of race and ignoring the existence of lesser kingdoms. Both the one Church and the one State were felt to be divinely ordained as the two aspects of Christendom, the heavenly and the temporal cities of God. Each complemented and in turn drew strength from the other.

Pope Leo perceived from his own experience the pope's inability to govern his state without the resources of the Frankish monarchy at his disposal. He considered the bestowal of the imperial title on the Frankish king a means of guaranteeing a closer protectorate by the Franks over the papacy. In this Leo judged correctly. Whatever prerogatives accrued to the king from his coronation as emperor — and no attempt was made to define them — they undoubtedly exceeded the equally obscure privileges bestowed by the office of patrician. From this time on the Franks intervened more willingly in Roman affairs and more directly to their own advantage, whether the popes liked it or not.

A source of later friction was the question of the right of Charlemagne's successors to use the imperial title without papal confirmation. The princes objected to being indebted to the pope for a temporal office, which was the impression created by the papal anointing, while the popes refused to relinquish the privilege for that very reason. This is probably the cause of that displeasure which one of the sources attributes to Charlemagne when Leo crowned him, since Charlemagne may have been contemplating independent means of acquiring the imperial title. To inaugurate a tradition of hereditary right Charlemagne before his death crowned his own son Louis the Pious, but Louis agreed to a repetition of the ceremony at the hands of Pope Stephen in 816. Louis then crowned his son Lothair, but again Pope Paschal duplicated the emperor's action in 823.

Monasticism and Missions Under Louis the Pious. Charlemagne's stabilization of Europe was premature. Everything depended on himself and could endure only if a man of his own outstanding ability followed him. The fact that his son and successor Louis the Pious (814–840) possessed lesser talents accounts largely for the turmoil of the next generation. Louis' sobriquet indicates his more sincere spirituality than Charlemagne's, whose uninhibited sexual morality was a blot on his reputation. Although Louis' first undertaking was to remove from court the more notorious figures of the preceding regime, in general he followed Charlemagne's policies whenever possible.

In his religious program Louis at first leaned heavily on St. Benedict of Aniane (d. 821) for whom he built the monastery of Kornelimünster near Aachen. This "second" Benedict instituted the first reform of Benedictine monasticism by attempting to restore the primitive observance. Because of the nature of the Rule and the autonomy of each Benedictine house, numerous customs and accretions, not all reprehensible by any means, had accumulated alongside the Rule. Benedict of Aniane proposed to unify all observances by the adoption of a common code of supplementary regulations. His program was accepted at a meeting of abbots at Aachen in 817 and promulgated by the emperor as imperial law, thus establishing the modified Benedictine Rule as obligatory for all monasteries within the Empire. The same tendency toward uniformity is evident in the emperor's support of the proposal to impose the rule of St. Chrodegang on all canons. Similar measures were begun for nuns also, but the disruption of society in the later ninth century nullified most of these reforms.

Missionary activity continued under Louis, minus the political implications of the Saxon conversions. Louis and Pope Paschal combined in support of Archbishop Ebbo of Reims who betook himself without success to the heathen Danes in 823, nor were the labors of St. Ansgar among the Swedes any more fruitful. Louis founded the Archbishopric of Hamburg for Ansgar's base of operations, but Scandinavia was not yet ripe for conversion. In the southeast the Bavarian bishops, encouraged but not greatly assisted by the emperor, had better results among the Slavic tribes.

Decay of the Carolingian Empire. The progressive disintegration of the Carolingian Empire occupied the attention of all the magnates of the realm, whether laymen or clergy. Louis the Pious' innate weakness and the subdivisions of the empire among his sons occasioned rebellions and civil war which continued throughout the ninth century. In all disputes the Frankish bishops were prominent, for Charlemagne's generation had produced some outstanding men and had accustomed them to an active life. Archbishop Hincmar of Reims (845–882), the right arm of Charles the Bald and the very center of ecclesiastical and political government in West Frankland, exemplified the role of the Frankish episcopate.

Although bishops were to be found in every camp during the civil wars, they were almost invariably actuated by a general desire to keep alive the traditions of unity and strong government as the best means of preserving social order. Only the great churchmen seem to have fully recognized the dangers inherent in the collapse of the central monarchy and their efforts to secure peace and good government contrast sharply with the greedy, shortsighted ambition of the nobility. Naturally the bishops disagreed among themselves as to which of the various factions offered the best possibilities of attaining their goal. Until the weakness of Louis the Pious became evident they supported him, but thereafter they cast their prestige behind Lothair. After the division of the empire by the treaty of Verdun in 843 each of the three kings found his stanchest supporters among the clergy of his realm.

As the empire declined the Church was liberated from the theocratic domination instituted by Charlemagne. In fact, the collapse of the political order seemed at first to enhance the theoretical position of the Church. Charlemagne had emphasized the necessity of the unity of State and Church so that the former's failure left the latter the chief agent for governing Christendom. By mid-ninth century the reaction had progressed so far that Hincmar of Reims and Jonas of Orleans were boldly asserting the bishop's superiority over the king. In 868 Hincmar wrote to Charles the Bald that the royal power derived solely from the king's coronation and anointing by the bishop. Nevertheless in this barbarous age theories meant little and the destruction of the empire hurt the Church in many ways. The spoliation of ecclesiastical property, usurpation of prerogatives, lay control of monasteries, and acts of violence against the clergy continued apace. The close of the Carolingian period found the Church in as distressed a condition morally and materially as it had been in before the appearance of St. Boniface 150 years earlier.

Canon Law: The False Decretals. One of the most important ecclesiastical documents of the later ninth century is the so-called False Decretals, a spurious collection of canon laws composed in northwestern France between 847 and 852. Although there were no authorized collections of universal canons before the twelfth century, numerous semiofficial or private codes existed from very early times, for the Council of

Nicaea had imposed on every bishop the obligation of teaching the Church's laws to those under his jurisdiction. Ecclesiastical law derived from Scripture, tradition, papal pronouncements, and decrees of councils. The Oriental Church had drawn up the first codes, which the Latins also accepted. Due to the political disturbances in the West from 400 onward and the resultant large measure of autonomy actually enjoyed by the "national" churches, the codes in vogue in every diocese presented a mixture of general and local matter. Among these early collections of limited application may be mentioned the Canons of the African Councils, the *Itala* or *Prisca* in Italy, and the Spanish *Hispana,* all dating from the fifth century.

Early in the sixth century the Scythian monk Dionysius Exiguus compiled the general collection for the Roman Church: 213 Greek canons, fifty apostolic canons, and the 138 canons of the African collection. Dionysius also collected thirty-eight decretals of the Roman pontiffs from Siricius (384–399) to Anastasius II (496–498), for these "authoritative replies" were always held in high esteem among the Latins. Theodore of Tarsus and Caesarius of Arles, among others, made small collections of canons for use in England and southern France. When Charlemagne wrote to Pope Adrian for an authoritative copy of the laws of the Church he received in reply the Dionysian code which a council at Aachen in 802 adopted for the empire, thus making it the most widely used collection in the West.

The anonymous author of the False or Pseudo-Isidorian Decretals wanted to protect the Church from the wholesale spoliation of its prerogatives by the Carolingian nobility. To this end he forged laws strengthening the authority of bishops and, as the final source of authority, the papacy. Thus he declared that a layman could not accuse a cleric in court, local councils required papal license for convocation, and bishops might appeal to the pope against deposition by a metropolitan.

The False Decretals were a clever mingling of genuine with forged materials. Pope Nicholas I accepted them as did almost everyone until the fifteenth century. Basically they were the *Hispana* to which were added letters assigned to very early popes on the basis of mere mention of such decretals in the *Liber Pontificalis,* an ancient and sketchy collection of lives of the popes. In this way an aura of antiquity and veracity pervaded the False Decretals. Actually few novelties were introduced; rather customs and practices already accepted were given a more solid legal foundation. Forgeries of this type were common in the middle ages. Although the False Decretals failed to impede the decline of the Frankish

Church in the ninth century, they were incorporated into the code of
canon law and played a part in the later centralization of papal administration.

The Papal State Under Louis the Pious. The constitutional status
of the Papal State was certain to change when the Frankish empire
declined, but in the early part of Louis' reign there was nothing to indicate that Frankish sovereignty in Italy had weakened. In fact, Louis
curtailed papal prerogatives more specifically than his father had done.
At Pope Paschal's request Louis in 817 renewed the traditional papal-
Frankish compact and on this occasion granted a charter, the oldest of
the various "donations" that has survived in original form, spelling out
in detail the geographic limits of the Papal State. The emperor also
guaranteed protection and allowed the pope a free hand in his government except that certain major offenses were to be justiciable in imperial
rather than papal courts.

Pope Eugene II's (824–827) tumultuous election confirmed Louis'
resolve to take measures to protect imperial rights in Italy. To his son
Lothair he entrusted the task of visiting Rome and restoring order. The
"Constitution of Lothair" which was then imposed on the pope provided
for imperial supervision of the papal government, allowed the pope's
subjects to choose which law — Frankish, Lombard, or Roman — they
preferred to be judged under, restored to the laity the right to participate
in papal elections which they had lost in 769, obligated the pope to swear
allegiance to the emperor before consecration, and removed certain papal
subjects from the jurisdiction of the papal courts. Lothair's constitution
left no doubt who was the superior partner in the papal-Frankish alliance.
Moreover, papal elections were now subject to royal veto, but most
mischievous of all was the restoration of lay participation in papal elections. It remained to be seen whether this Frankish predominance would
last.

Papal Politics. The chief obstacle preventing the popes from throwing
off Frankish overlordship during the decline of the Empire was the
need for protection. Pope Gregory IV (827–844), who had fruitlessly
intervened in the domestic strife in France, passively awaited the end
of the disputes he could not stop. Sergius II (844–847), as if feeling out
the situation, did not request imperial confirmation before his consecration,
but Emperor Lothair quickly sent his son Louis to Rome to insist on
his prerogative. Sergius' reign was stigmatized by simony and the tyranny

of his brother Benedict, bishop of Albano, "a rustic boor of vicious habits." The need for Frankish protection increased when the Moslems from Africa started raiding Italy. A band landed at the mouth of the Tiber in 846 and looted the basilicas of St. Peter and St. Paul and other property outside the city walls. Emperor Lothair sent money to pay for extending the Roman walls to include St. Peter's and at the same time he dispatched Louis, henceforth the real ruler of Italy, to expel the Moslems from their bridgehead in southern Italy.

Louis, successful against the Saracens, entertained a scheme for incorporating the weak Papal State directly into his own Lombard Kingdom, and to that end he built up a party among the papal officials. In the election of 855 he tried unsuccessfully to foist one of his friends on the Romans. When he heard of Benedict III's death in 858, Louis hastened to Rome and this time saw to it that his candidate, different from the one three years previous, was chosen. In this way Pope Nicholas I ascended the papal throne.

Pope Nicholas the Great. Nicholas I (858–867), last of the three popes to be given the title "the Great," held a high opinion of his office. He possessed great talent and force of character, and brooked no interference from his royal patron in ecclesiastical affairs. The problems Nicholas encountered did not concern petty Roman politics or even politics in general but rather far-reaching dogmatic and disciplinary questions which he energetically faced as champion of Catholic faith and morals. Not since Gregory I had papal influence extended so widely as under Nicholas. His part in the schism of Patriarch Photius of Constantinople will be described in the next chapter; here we can only sketch his Carolingian relations.

Emperor Lothair wanted to be rid of his wife Theutberga so that he might marry his mistress Waldrada. Despite Theutberga's protestations, a synod of German bishops in 860 annulled her marriage. Theutberga appealed to Pope Nicholas, who quashed the annulment and called for a new, fair investigation. A second council, rigged like the first in the emperor's favor, reiterated the earlier verdict. Again Nicholas set aside the synodal decree, deposed the archbishops of Cologne and Trier and threatened Lothair with excommunication. The king yielded and took back Theutberga.

Powerful Archbishop Hincmar of Reims crossed swords unsuccessfully with Nicholas I over the right of an archbishop to depose a suffragan bishop who appealed to Rome. Hincmar's theory would have broken the pope's control of bishops by interposing the jurisdiction of archbishops between the papacy and the episcopate. However, the next year, 864, Nicholas supported Hincmar in demanding that the emperor remove an unworthy appointee he had intruded in the see of Cambrai. The archbishops of Ravenna had been a source of friction since the end of the Exarchate; Nicholas in 861 excommunicated Archbishop John and quelled his rebellious spirit. Such instances of firm, decisive action by the pope indicate how complete was the reaction against the passive role Charlemagne had assigned to the papacy.

Conclusion. The Carolingian epoch provided Europe with a breathing spell between two waves of barbarism, and the Church benefited as much as did society as a whole. Religious life was raised to a higher level and was able to exert a greater influence on the world because of the sincere co-operation of the kings. Whatever civilization and culture existed in Frankland bore the imprint of Catholicism. The revival of the Roman Empire raised the dignity of the Church both in fact as well as in theory. At the same time that the Carolingians created the circumstances for an independent, sovereign papacy they also left a legacy of theocratic domination of the Church from which it could escape only with the collapse of the Frankish State.

REVIEW AIDS

1. How did St. Boniface's program fare under Pepin the Short?
2. Explain the Carolingian controversies concerning iconoclasm and the filioque.
3. What was Charlemagne's opinion of his own position within the Church?
4. In what way was the Carolingian Renaissance significant for the history of the Church?
5. Summarize the history of the Papal State under Charlemagne and Louis the Pious.
6. Describe the religious significance of the revival of the Roman Empire.
7. Show how the decay of the Carolingian Empire affected the Church.
8. What is the origin and importance of the Pseudo-Isidorian Decretals?
9. Describe missionary activity under the Carolingians.
10. Show why Pope Nicholas I deserves to be called great.

SUGGESTIONS FOR FURTHER READING

A new book of great importance for the study of the basic principles of the Church's government is Walter Ullmann, *The Growth of Papal Government in the Middle Ages* (London: 1955), of which sections III to VI concern the

Carolingian period. Louis Duchesne, *The Beginnings of the Temporal Sovereignty of the Popes* (New York: 1908), continues into the period. There is much material in Volume I, part 2, and Volumes II and III of H. K. Mann, *Lives of the Popes in the Early Middle Ages* (London: 1925). Eleanor Shipley Duckett's *Alcuin, Friend of Charlemagne*, gives a good picture of the intellectual life of the Carolingians. On this point there is also the excellent *History of Christian Philosophy in the Middle Ages* (New York: 1955), by Etienne Gilson. An old but still well worth reading biography of Pope Nicholas I is that by J. Roy (English version, London: 1901). A more specialized study is the brief book by Allen Cabaniss, *Agobard of Lyons* (Syracuse: 1953), a biography of a Frankish bishop under Louis the Pious. There is a good essay on St. Benedict of Aniane in Watkin Williams, *Monastic Studies* (Manchester: 1938). J. M. Clark's *The Abbey of St. Gall* (New York: 1926) provides a glimpse of one of the great monasteries in European history. For the Pseudo-Isidorian Decretals and the early history of Canon Law see Amleto Giovanni Cicognani, *Canon Law*, 2nd ed. (Westminster, Md.: 1949), Part II, Chapters 7 and 8. Also see G. Ellard, *Master Alcuin, Liturgist* (Chicago: 1956).

DOCUMENTS

Charlemagne interpreted his power as extending to all visible aspects of the life and organization of the Church as well as of his State. In some respects he treated the pope the same way he treated the local bishops of Frankland. In this famous letter of Charlemagne to Pope St. Leo III in A.D. 796 the Emperor's attitude is readily apparent. Migne, *Patrologia Latina*, XCVIII, 307–309.

Charles, by the grace of God King of the Franks and Lombards and Patrician of the Romans, to His Holiness Pope Leo, Greetings in Christ.

In the same way that I entered into an agreement with Your Holiness' blessed predecessor I now desire to conclude an inviolable treaty of the same fidelity and love with you, so that the divine grace of the saints may be called down upon me by Your Holiness' prayers and the apostolic blessing may be with me everywhere, and that with God's help we may always defend the most holy See of the Roman Church. It is our duty everywhere to defend with divine aid the Church of Christ: externally by our arms from the incursion of the pagans and the devastation of infidels, internally to fortify it by the acknowledgment of the Catholic Faith. It is your duty, most Holy Father, with hands raised to God in prayer like Moses, to help our warfare, so that by your intercession, by the guidance and gift of God, the Christian people may everywhere be victorious over the enemies of His holy name, and the name of our Lord Jesus Christ may be glorified in all the world. Prudently abide by the canons in all things that examples of your sanctity may be manifest to all with whom you come into contact, that holy admonition to sanctity may be heard from your lips, that your light may shine before men for them to see your good works and glorify the Father who is in Heaven. May almighty God deign to preserve Your Holiness unharmed for many years to the exaltation of His Holy Church.

Chapter 11

THE CHURCH UNDER LAY DOMINATION

FOR the two centuries from 850 to 1050 the chief feature of the history of the Church is the dominance of the laity and of lay interests. This situation, certainly not a novelty except in degree, extended from parish churches to the papacy itself. What brought it about was the breakup of the Carolingian Empire and the devastating raids of a new group of barbarian invaders of Europe, plus certain defects in the administrative machinery of the Church. The two institutions embodying lay control are feudalism and the proprietary church system. As a result there is evident a general religious decline, only faintly relieved by continued missionary activity and an occasional monastic oasis of spirituality.

Barbarian Attacks. Europe in the ninth and tenth centuries presented the appearance of a fortress besieged from three sides: south, east, and north. In the south the Moslems ventured up the Rhone in 842; fifty years later they ravaged the Mediterranean coast of France; in 940 they advanced as far as the monastery of St. Gall in Switzerland; in 972 they ambushed and captured the abbot of Cluny in an Alpine pass. Since the attack on Rome in 846 Moslems continually harassed Italy and gained a stronghold in Sicily and Calabria. To the east the Magyars or Hungarians, sweeping out of northern Asia, debouched into the Hungarian plain about 896 and for a long half century thereafter they ravaged Lombardy and the German countryside as far westward as Utrecht and Reims. Most serious of all were the Northmen who from about 830 swept up every navigable river of Europe to loot and destroy. London, Paris, Cologne, Bordeaux, Nantes, Reims — no significant town escaped their ravages. "From the fury of the Northmen deliver us, Oh Lord!" is a plea found in many prayer books of this time.

All three of these peoples quickly discovered that monasteries and churches offered excellent opportunity for plunder: gold and silver orna-ments or chalices, jewels, precious cloth vestments, and the like, with the result that such places suffered terribly. Not only the destruction of property but the killing or enslavement of monks and clergy disrupted the normal ecclesiastical routine of many parts of Europe for long periods at a stretch. Much of the obvious decline of religion and of clerical disci-pline and education is due at least in part to the devastation caused by this second wave of barbarian invaders of Europe.

Internal Confusion.   At the same time domestic discord of an equally serious nature added to the turmoil. The unified Carolingian Empire split into three sections by the Treaty of Verdun in 843 and for the next century these domains in turn crumpled into numerous smaller units each jealously ruled by counts, dukes, or weak kings. Left to their own devices in this turbulent age, the bishops and abbots as well as the material goods of the Church fell into dependence upon one or the other of the aristocratic feudal princes, each of whom posed grandly and often sincerely as the defender of the Church in the tradition of the Carolingians.

The crux of the matter was the endowment in land possessed by every parish church, bishopric, or monastery. Canon law forbade the erection of any ecclesiastical institution unless means of supporting it were pro-vided, and this normally meant an endowment of land furnished through the generosity of the laity. Extensive areas of land, therefore, became Church property. Under the feudal regime that replaced the centralized Carolingian government the possessor of land also enjoyed political juris-diction over it; not only was he the owner or tenant, he was also in large measure the ruler. This situation had two results: on the one hand secular lords striving to obtain or increase their political power eyed the lands of the Church as an available means to that end; on the other hand the bishops and abbots who administered Church property them-selves became feudal lords and hence secular rulers in their own right.

Means of Lay Domination.   Because of the Roman and Carolingian traditions of the State's obligation to protect the Church, there was very little opposition to secular encroachments under this pretext of protection. In Charlemagne's day all bishoprics and most monasteries were at the king's disposal. When the Empire splintered into smaller units, each ruler claimed to inherit the Carolingian rights, but whether or not he succeeded in making good his claim depended on circumstances. In the German part of the Frankish Empire the king kept control of all bishoprics and large abbeys, while in France only about one third of the bishoprics remained under royal tutelage. The duke of Normandy controlled seven bishoprics, the duke of Brittany an equal number, the count of Roussillon one, and so on. The distribution of monasteries followed roughly similar proportions.

Lay control of ecclesiastical offices meant simply that the office was treated like any other fief and its occupant like any other feudal lord with rights and obligations dictated by custom. Sometimes a nobleman might confiscate Church property outright and turn it entirely to his own use, but this was unusual. As long as the bishop or abbot fulfilled his feudal obligations to his lord, the lay lord would not disturb his vassal. And the ecclesiastical fief might be disposed of like any other: in 990 Count William of Toulouse gave the bishopric of Beziers to his daughter as her dowry, and later bequeathed the bishopric of Agde to his wife. The changed circumstances meant only that the money and services owed by the bishops concerned went to a new lord.

The most important right — the one that permitted much lay control of bishoprics — was the right to influence the choice of bishops. Canon law specified that elections of bishops be by priests and people. Whereas the cathedral canons spoke for the diocesan clergy, the aristocracy of the diocese represented the laity. Medieval elections in general were irregular affairs since they did not proceed according to the majority principle but on a qualitative basis whereby the vote of one important individual outweighed those of a number of ordinary men. If the bishop was a vassal of a lay lord, the latter's voice could not be ignored. He might exercise his prerogative by directly nominating his candidate, either unasked or at the clergy's request, or he might veto the clergy's choice. No election was complete without the form of acceptance by the canons although this usually followed as a matter of course after the lord had indicated his preference. If the bishop was practically an independent sovereign without a strong overlord, elections resembled a contest between the nobility of the area anxious to secure an influential position for a younger son. Thus law and custom sanctioned secular intervention, and since the papacy was itself in the same position at this time, no protest could be expected. In 921 Pope John X scolded the archbishop of Cologne for ignoring the wishes of King Charles the Simple in an election for the archbishop's suffragan see of Liége: "We have not ceased to wonder," the pope wrote, "that you have dared to act against all reason and without the king's order; you should not have done that. Remember that no bishop can be consecrated in any diocese without the king's consent."

Feudalism and the Church. Feudalism, the system of government that arose in the ninth and tenth centuries, transformed everyone who possessed land into a sovereign over his own acres, owing certain obligations to those higher than himself in the feudal scale, yet enjoying prerogatives which could not be taken from him. We have already seen that bishops and abbots became involved in feudalism on the basis of the lands they administered. This development followed the same line whereby ecclesiastical officials, especially bishops, had, ever since the Edict of Milan, been vested with some degree of public authority. Feudalism, however, defined more precisely and imparted a clearer legal title to the present position than had often been the case earlier.

The feudal abbot or bishop enjoyed the following rights over his barony, an area distinct from the diocese or monastery over which his spiritual jurisdiction extended: protection by his lord, greater or lesser judicial powers including fines accruing therefrom, tolls and miscellaneous revenues, sometimes the right to coin money and very often secular jurisdiction over the city in which the cathedral was located. The temporal overlord enjoyed the right to bestow the ecclesiastical fief on virtually whomever he wished, to invest that individual with his office, and to receive from him an oath of fidelity. There was no difference between the temporal services of an ecclesiastical and a lay vassal. These included: the obligation to attend the lord's court, military service, hospitality and entertainment, aids and relief.

Military service seems most incompatible with the ecclesiastical vocation yet it underlay the entire feudal system and could not be avoided. Every lord had his own small corps of fighting men to defend his territory. Some of the episcopal armies reached sizable proportions, such as the 1700 knights of the archbishop of Cologne in 1184. These knights were the bishop's vassals and they occupied parts of his land as fiefs in payment for their services. A certain number of them accompanied the bishops when they went to fulfill their personal obligation of armed assistance to their prince. Seldom were bishops excused from military obligations and their knights made up the largest contingents in the royal armies. Ecclesiastical troops comprised about seventy per cent of the armies that Frederick Barbarossa took on his Italian wars. Since many monasteries employed a layman called an advocate to handle their secular affairs, he rather than the abbot fulfilled the monastery's military obligations. But very often bishops were not loathe to take part in campaigns, despite the Church's prohibition on the shedding of blood by anyone in orders. When we consider that most bishops were noblemen, who as a class were born and bred to military life, it is not surprising that they could not free themselves from the influence of heredity.

One reason for the prominence of bishops in secular affairs of the middle ages is the fact that they were normally the most loyal vassals a lord could find, precisely because they were most amenable to control. Bishops who held their bishoprics not by virtue of hereditary right but by nomination of a king were usually in sympathy with the king's aims, were personally known to him if not a member of his family, and very probably had served many years as royal chaplain, chancellor, or courtier of some kind. The German empire presents the outstanding examples of secularistic bishops of great wealth and power. This came about because the emperors pursued a deliberate policy of bestowing huge grants of land on the bishops in feudal tenure, in order to build up the bishoprics as a counterbalance to the power of the great lay nobles who defied the kings with impunity. With the aid of the bishops the German emperors ruled their empire; without episcopal services, the emperors would have been reduced to impotence.

Medieval bishops charged with the dual functions of serving both Church and State were usually inclined to devote more attention to politics than to the business of saving souls. SS. Bernward of Hildesheim, Ulrich of Augsburg, and Norbert of Cologne are among the exceptions that prove the rule. So long as the enfeebled papacy also lay under secular influences there was no one to protest a wholly unsatisfactory situation.

The Proprietary Church.   Lay domination reached the level of the parish through the proprietary or private church system, an outgrowth of the Germanic mentality which tended to fix concepts of all kinds with as much concreteness as possible. The parish church with all its property and revenues was conceived as a piece of property that had to be owned by a specific person acting in the name of the patron saint to whom the church was dedicated. That person was the founder or donor of the church, or his descendant. Since most parish churches were built and endowed by laymen they were regarded as the layman's property, although the proprietor might also be a bishop or an abbot if the parish originated from those sources. Records indicating sixty or more parishes in the hands of a single count reveal the extent of the system. In the Swabian bishopric of Chur under Louis the Pious thirty-one of 230 churches were episcopal, most of the rest were lay property.

Under the proprietary system the proprietor appointed the priest, whom a bishop ordained, of course, but often with no serious investigation of his qualifications. Although legally the priest was not entirely at the proprietor's mercy, in practice he approached that condition. Episcopal surveillance of such clergy was limited. The priest might pay the proprietor for his appointment and the lord had almost complete control over tithes, stole fees, burial fees, and all other parish income. Decrees of synods attempting to prevent complete usurpation of parish revenues proved futile. The right to collect such revenues could be assigned to others, sold, exchanged, or alienated in any way whatsoever, provided the church building and altar were not put to secular use. All responsibility rested with the proprietor, and while the conduct and motives of some were above reproach, all too often noblemen founded churches as lucrative investments. Under such circumstances the spiritual aspects of parish life were not likely to receive proper attention. Monasteries and sometimes bishoprics too were exploited as part of the proprietary system and fared no better than parishes.

The Papacy. Inevitably the Carolingian collapse dragged the papacy down from the heights of Nicholas I's pontificate. The disappearance of the strong if distant hand of the Frankish kings exposed the papacy to the same forces that were everywhere bringing ecclesiastical offices into the power of the lay aristocracy. Papal temporal jurisdiction and wealth were worthwhile prizes. The exalted position of the office and the peculiarities of the Italian temperament disgraced the papacy more scandalously than other bishoprics, although there were a few statesmen and reformers among the occupants of the Holy See. Of the forty-four popes between 867 and 1048, nine met violent deaths: two by poison, four by murder or execution in prison, one by strangulation, and two under suspicious circumstances. It was a time of shame and disgrace for the Roman pontiffs. The one significant relieving feature is that however wicked the popes were personally and however scandalous their conduct, none of them attempted to promulgate false doctrine or teach heresy. The infallibility of the See was preserved despite the sins of its occupants.

The Case of Pope Formosus. John VIII, successor to Adrian II in 872, on two occasions exercised decisive influence in the choice of em-

s, for the title was kept alive even though effective authority dis-
eared. But John failed, a victim of circumstances, in his efforts to
uncover a papal champion, and his murder opened the gates to a flood
of barbarism and savagery at Rome.

Pope Formosus (891–896) had been prominent in papal politics for
years but not always wisely. His most pressing problem was the ambition
of Duke Lambert of Spoleto at Rome's back door to bring all Italy
under his scepter and re-create something like the aggressive Lombard
monarchy of Aistulf. Formosus unwillingly crowned Lambert king and
emperor, but at the same time he appealed to King Arnulf in Germany.
Arnulf came and Formosus bestowed upon him the imperial title without
bothering about the fact that he had already given it to Lambert. Illness
forced Arnulf to retreat before dealing with Lambert. By the time Lambert
was in possession of Rome, Formosus had died leaving weakling Pope
Stephen VI to face the wrathful Lambert.

Stephen had Formosus' nine months old corpse exhumed, propped
on a throne clad in papal vestments, and tried by a council as a false
pope. The judges found Formosus guilty, annulled his acts and ordinations, removed his name from the list of popes, and cast his body into
a public grave from which the mob tossed it into the Tiber. Rome then
divided into violent Formosian and anti-Formosian factions and many
priests and even bishops were in a quandary because of the annulment
of Formosus' ordinations. The uproar continued until John IX (898–900),
a peacemaker, finally rehabilitated Formosus' reputation. To prevent new
disputes John decreed anew that the emperor's approbation must be received before a pope-elect could be consecrated. John's hopes for an entente
with Emperor Lambert as a means of restoring a semblance of order
perished when the youthful emperor died of a hunting accident. His
demise marked the end of the brief Empire of Spoleto.

The Dynasty of Theophylact. Events following the removal of the
royal power from central Italy at once made it clear that some other
strong hand was needed to avoid complete chaos in Rome. Pope Leo V
was imprisoned by an antipope, Christopher, whom Pope Sergius III
(904–911) sent to join Leo in prison; then "out of pity" he executed them
both. Sergius had belonged to the anti-Formosian faction and irritated
old wounds. Out of the melee arose the wealthy papal official and senator
Theophylact who, with his wife Theodora and two daughters Theodora
and Marozia, dominated Rome for two generations. Marozia captivated
Sergius by her charms and cemented her family's power.

To the House of Theophylact John X (914–928) owed his elevation. He was a vigorous man of action who personally led the army to victory against the Saracens and made his influence felt in both Germany and France. John XI (931–935), son of Marozia and Pope Sergius III, gave his mother free rein in affairs of the Roman government, but before long the pope's brother Alberic seized control. This prince gave Rome effective government for twenty years, but only at the price of personally designating five successive popes. Through the influence of Alberic's friend, St. Odo of Cluny, a concern for spiritual reform reappeared in Rome. Unfortunately, the fifth pope whom Alberic designated on his own deathbed was his son, John XII (955–964), with whom the papacy sank to the lowest level in its history. Not yet twenty years old, John gave himself up entirely to the pursuit of pleasure in its manifold forms. But a new chapter in papal history was dawning, for a powerful prince was emerging north of the Alps and he was watching Italy with interest.

The German Popes. Otto I of Germany was the most powerful European monarch since Charlemagne. When Pope John XII found himself threatened by enemies he had foolishly provoked he turned to Otto for deliverance. Otto had already been entertaining imperialist dreams and hence did not hesitate to venture over the Alps. By February, 962, he was in Rome and John XII crowned him Roman emperor. The scene was reminiscent of the first revival of that Empire in the year 800. Rome now had a new lord protector who issued a new constitution in which it was promised that the Papal State should be preserved intact and that no pope would be consecrated without the emperor's consent. And again the perplexing problem arose of the extent of the German overlordship.

John XII had desired a protector only, not a suzerain. Quickly he realized that Otto envisaged a permanent occupation of Italy for he took the Lombard title also and installed German bishops in the north Italian sees to rule their dioceses in the interests of the emperor. Pope John began an intrigue against Otto who thereupon returned and placed John on trial *in absentia,* since the pope had fled. John XII's scandalous life provided ready charges and the assembled bishops proceeded to depose him and install another, forgetful of the precedents that none may judge the pope. As soon as Otto departed John returned and expelled the antipope.

In this way the stage was set for eighty more years of Roman turmoil. Whenever the German emperors were in Rome they set up popes to suit themselves; the Romans, however, hated German domination and their liberty became a rallying cry for native factions. Until about the turn of the century the aristocratic Crescentii controlled the non-German popes, but they were then displaced by the Counts of Tusculum. Both families sprang from the House of Theophylact and their motives and means had a like origin. But by this time a current of reform was sweeping across Europe and occasional eddies rippled the surface of central Italy. Pope Benedict VII (974–983) took measures against simony and encouraged monasticism. Sylvester II (999–1003), Otto III's mentor, was the most learned man of his day. Benedict VIII (1012–1024) labored to recover some of the dissipated papal dignity.

Synod of Sutri.   But one final shock preceded the general reform so long delayed at Rome. Pope Benedict IX (1032–1044), variously estimated at twelve to twenty years old, returned to the spirit of revelry and sacrilege until even the Romans had had enough. In 1044 the Crescentii rose in revolt and installed Sylvester III in the Lateran. Although soon restored by his Tusculan relatives, Benedict longed for peace to pursue his pleasures, so he sold the papacy to his godfather and abdicated. Gregory VI was not a bad sort, discounting his simony which was not publicly known, but Sylvester was still vaunting his claims and Benedict IX soon grew bored in retirement and reclaimed the throne. Since no one had thought to consult the emperor about these transactions, Henry III swooped down into Italy in 1046, summoned a synod of the clergy at Sutri, and disposed of the lot, introducing a German as Pope Clement II. At this point the new era began.

The Greek Church: Iconoclasm.   Lay domination, i.e., caesaropapism, was endemic at Constantinople and it occasions no surprise to see the Greek Church in the ninth century sorely tried by government meddling. First came a revival of iconoclasm which a new dynasty again made official policy. The facile Greek bishops, having promulgated iconoclasm in 754 and condemned it in 787, found no difficulty in insisting anew that the veneration of images was tantamount to idolatry. The Patriarch St. Nicephorus, however, preferred exile to iconoclasm, and the champions of traditional usages were again the monks, especially those of the monastery of Studium in Constantinople and their learned Abbot St. Theodore. Empress Theodora finally ended the destruction of images by appointing a new patriarch in 842 and convening a synod the next year which solemnly re-established the veneration of images.

The Photian Schism. Of much more serious import because of its ramifications was the schism of the Patriarch Photius (857–867; 877–886). St. Ignatius, a sincere but naïve patriarch, incurred the wrath of Emperor Michael the Drunkard's powerful minister Bardas to whom Ignatius publicly refused Holy Communion, since it was common knowledge that Bardas was living in incest. Ignatius either resigned under pressure or was outright deposed and in his place Michael raised Photius, an imperial secretary, a layman, but the most erudite scholar of his day. Gregory Asbestas, the excommunicated archbishop of Syracuse, consecrated him. Pope Nicholas I refused to countenance Photius' elevation and insisted that both Photius, whom he excommunicated, and Ignatius come to Rome for a hearing. Emperor Michael's insulting letter to Nicholas drew from the pope a splendid defense of the Roman primacy. Photius himself expressed his views in 867 in an encyclical circulated throughout the East vehemently assailing the claims of Rome and condemning all Latin Catholics as heretics. A Greek synod declared Pope Nicholas excommunicated.

Caesaro-papism broke the impasse, however, when a usurper named Basil murdered Bardas and Michael and seized the Byzantine throne. He cleared the court of Bardas' friends and persuaded Photius to resign. Basil then reinstated Ignatius and asked the pope for a general council to settle the matter. Pope Adrian II and a Roman synod condemned Photius and delegated representatives for the Fourth Ecumenical Council of Constantinople. Harking back to the Acacian schism, Adrian extracted from the Roman archives the Formula of Pope Hormisdas for the Greek bishops to subscribe as proof that they acknowledged the Roman primacy. Although the eighth general council (868–870) was poorly attended, it wholly vindicated the Roman position by accepting the Formula and Photius' condemnation.

By the time of Patriarch Ignatius' death Emperor Basil had changed his policies and now offered the patriarchal throne to Photius who again accepted. Photius immediately moved to exonerate himself. A magnificent council was assembled in Constantinople in 879 which dutifully annulled the anti-Photian acts of the Council of ten years earlier. Even the Roman legates accepted the acts of the new Council despite its defiance of Rome. Pope John VIII tried to defend his position but he was murdered and the subsequent turmoil in Rome prevented a new crisis. However the situation was so tense that many historians have felt that a second schism actually occurred. As for Photius, he was not destined to die in possession of the coveted patriarchal chair for a new emperor, Leo VI, wanted that position for his brother Stephen.

Slavic Missions.   By mid-ninth century all the Germanic peoples except those in Scandinavia had accepted Christianity. Stretching eastward from the Elbe River and the Alps, occupying more than half the European continent, were the Slavs: Poles, Czechs, Moravians, Slovenes, Croats, Serbs, Bulgarians, and Russians. Since all but a minute portion of these were still pagan, the missionaries had an extensive field to cultivate.

The Slovenes living between the Danube and the Drave Rivers were the first Christian Slavs. Their conversion stemmed from Frankish political hegemony established over them by Charlemagne and it was the joint work of the archbishops of Salzburg and Aquileia. Frankish control also introduced missionaries to the Croats in Dalmatia between 800 and 850. The fate of these two tribes seemed to warn the others that Christianity and subjection to the Germans of East Frankland went hand in hand.

As a result other Slav princes ready to accept Christianity turned to Constantinople for missionaries and a Greek-Latin rivalry began in central Europe which was often as much political as religious, but was also very significant culturally. The Latins insisted on a single liturgical language and submission to the papal authority, while the Greeks permitted the use of the native language among the people they evangelized and in general allowed greater freedom from outside control. These issues manifested themselves distinctly in Moravia and Bulgaria.

SS. Constantine and Methodius.   Prince Rostislav of Moravia, which then included most of modern Czechoslovakia, fearful of subjection to King Louis the German, dispatched ambassadors to Constantinople in 862 with a request for missionaries. Michael III and Photius selected the brothers Constantine (known to the West as Cyril) and Methodius, experienced missionaries, Greek by birth and well educated. Before their departure Constantine prepared an alphabet for the Slavs, who till then had no written language, and translated selections of the Bible for them. Once established in Moravia he also translated the Latin Missal into the new language for use at Mass. Despite the success of Constantine and Methodius and the approbation of Popes Adrian II and John VIII for the use of the Slavic language, the new liturgy did not flourish because of the intense hostility of the neighboring German bishops of Passau,

Freising, and Salzburg. Rostislav's successor Svatopluk was also under German influence and did not co-operate with the Greek missionaries. Constantine died in Rome in 869 and when Methodius died in 885 the issue was still undecided. Pope Stephen V, mistrusting Greek influences in central Europe because of the Photian schism, forbade the Slavic liturgy. The expulsion of the Slavic and Greek clergy completed the destruction of the work of Constantine and Methodius. Moravia and Bohemia too became Latin Catholic in religion and German in culture.

Conversion of Bulgaria. The Slavonic liturgy, however, did not perish, for it found a new home in Bulgaria. Emperor Boris (852–889) of the large, Slavicized Bulgarian state was baptized in 864 by Greek priests and he forced many of his people to imitate him. But Boris worried about Byzantine political domination more than German so he wrote to Pope Nicholas I and asked for Latin clergy. This transfer of allegiance by Boris sharpened the hostility of Photius for the papacy and was the occasion for his bitter encyclical of 867. However, it did not last. Boris soon switched back to the Greeks since they offered the better hope for the independent, national Church which he desired. When the Greeks sent the Slavic clergy trained by Methodius into Bulgaria with their vernacular liturgy they were enthusiastically welcomed. In 918 Emperor Simeon erected an autonomous Bulgarian patriarchate at Okhrida free of Byzantine ties yet culturally linked to the Greek world. The Serbs, alternately under Bulgarian or Byzantine rule, also accepted the Greek Church.

Russia. Constantinople was the source also of Russian Christianity. Christian churches existed in the Viking-Russian principality of Kiev by the middle of the tenth century. In 955 Princess Olga of Kiev was baptized at Constantinople amid great pomp, but Christianity progressed slowly until the great Prince Vladimir was converted in 988. He then used every means to spread Christianity among the Norse and the Slavic population. Kiev became a metropolitan see and many churches and monasteries were erected. The Slavonic liturgy mingled with Byzantine elements in shaping Russian Christianity.

Hungary and Poland. Latin Christianity triumphed north of the Danube. The Mongolian Hungarians, having settled down after 955, came under the influence of German missionaries. Bishops Pilgrim of Passau and St. Adalbert of Prague were active in Hungary, but thorough conversion occurred only after the accession of King St. Stephen (997–1038).

The major Slavic unit north of Moravia was the Poles. The first recorded Polish convert was Duke Mieszko who was baptized in 966. Rapid progress was made under Mieszko's son Boleslav the Brave (992–1023). He encouraged the preaching of St. Adalbert and when the latter was martyred by the Prussians, Boleslav brought his body back to Gnesen as a national hero. German influence pervaded Polish Christianity. The first bishopric at Posen was a suffragan see of Magdeburg and the Polish metropolitanate at Gnesen was set up in the year 1000 by Emperor Otto III.

Finally, between the Elbe River and the Polish lands lay many small Slav tribes such as the Wends, Obodrites, and Wilzi. These owed their Christianity to Germany also but, since the Germans destroyed their political liberty, the Slavs rebelled and returned to paganism as often and as desperately as had the Saxons. Not until the twelfth century were they reconciled to Christianity.

REVIEW AIDS

1. In what way did lay domination of the Church in the ninth and tenth centuries differ from Charlemagne's domination?
2. Explain the impact of feudalism on the Church.
3. Show how electoral practices and the proprietary church system made possible lay control of the Church.
4. How do you account for the decline of the papacy in these years?
5. Give examples of the papal decline and explain the problems raised for the Church by the lives of some of these popes.
6. Describe the Photian schism and explain its significance.
7. What factors influenced the course of missionary activity among the Slavs?
8. Summarize the achievements of the missionaries in eastern Europe.

SUGGESTIONS FOR FURTHER READING

Sections III–VI of Walter Ullmann, *The Growth of Papal Government in the Middle Ages* (London: 1955), contain much valuable information. A classic study recently made available in English is Ulrich Stutz, "The Proprietary Church as an Element of Mediaeval Germanic Ecclesiastical Law," translated by Geoffrey Barraclough in his *Mediaeval Germany, 911–1250* (Oxford: 1948). Volumes 3–5 of H. K. Mann, *Lives of the Popes in the Middle Ages* (St. Louis and London: 1906–1910), offer about the only biographical material on the popes of this age. An excellent picture of the impact of feudalism on the Church is contained in Edgar N. Johnson, *The Secular Activities of the German Episcopate 911–1024* (Lincoln, Neb.: 1930–

31). A good biography of one of these bishops is Francis J. Tschan, *Saint Bernward of Hildesheim*, Volume I, *His Life and Times* (Notre Dame, Ind.: 1942). Two other volumes of Tschan's study concern the artistic achievements of Bishop Bernward. Another interesting monograph is Sarell E. Gleason, *An Ecclesiastical Barony of the Middle Ages* (Cambridge, Mass.: 1936). Revolutionary is the only word for Francis Dvornik, *The Photian Schism* (Cambridge: 1948), a scholarly study of great merit which overthrows the traditional historical opinion of its subject. For missions in eastern Europe see Kenneth Scott Latourette, *A History of the Expansion of Christianity*, Vol. II, *The Thousand Years of Uncertainty* (New York: 1938). See also the latter part of Richard E. Sullivan's excellent article, "The Papacy and Missionary Activity in the Early Middle Ages," *Mediaeval Studies*, XVII (1955), pp. 46–106.

DOCUMENTS

During the feudal period the Church was subject to many stresses and strains. These manifested themselves particularly in the lives of bishops who were both churchmen and important secular rulers. The following selection shows how ambitious men fought to secure bishoprics and then devoted their lives to secular pursuits. It describes the election and death of Bishop Henry of Augsburg (973–982). Chapter 28 of *Vita Oudalrici episcopi Augustani, M.G.H. Scriptores*, IV, 415–418.

After the death of the holy Bishop Udalrich, Henry, son of Count Purchard, succeeded him, but he did not enter the shepherd's place properly but rather in an irregular fashion. On the advice of Duke Purchard who had married his cousin and of many others, especially also of some knights who slyly wanted to increase their fiefs through him, he began to give serious thought to how he might acquire this position, even though he was informed that Udalrich had designated Abbot Werinhar to succeed. . . .

Some of the clergy, accompanied by the advocate and several knights of the bishopric, rode to the emperor's court to deliver the bishop's staff . . . but they returned home. . . . Shortly afterwards a messenger of the Duke came and announced that the emperor would hold court in the specified place and that they should come there. They hastened at once to take other brethren and to journey to that place, and when they had arrived at a spot called Baden they met another messenger who said, "Henry, son of Purchard, whom the emperor with his vassals and Duke Purchard have designated bishop of Augsburg, will be here shortly.". . . And on this very day when the knights who had come with Henry from Duke Purchard arrived at their camp they began to importune the clergy to elect Henry bishop of their city unanimously and on the spot. These demanded a delay until all the brethren could meet in general chapter at home. When the knights refused, some of the canons, following a long dispute, accepted Henry and elected him bishop; but others, disagreeing, went to Augsburg to their brethren.

When they arrived and had assembled with the rest for an election, a certain Count Wolverad came with some others pretending to have a message from the emperor for the group and said to them, "The Emperor demands that you do not refuse to elect this Lord Henry whom he and his vassals have designated the shepherd of this Church.". . . When Henry realized that it was in the canons' power to elect or reject him, he humbly begged that they would not refuse to elect him, and he promised them all sorts of favors if they would do as he requested. Since they believed his promises . . . they unanimously elected him bishop. . . .

With all his energy he strove to serve the emperor and win his favor to avert through his command all opposition threatening him. Therefore he often came to court with rich gifts and tried to win over his favorites with suitable presents. Moreover he followed him on campaign so that, as he calculated, he might please him most of all.

In the year of the Incarnation of our Lord Jesus Christ 983 (*sic*), the emperor with his army invaded the province of Calabria and Bishop Henry accompanied him. In a battle against the Saracens many fell on both sides, and alas! Bishop Henry also remained behind, either killed or taken prisoner. His loss is the more lamentable because neither his clergy nor his relatives and friends could discover what became of him.

A.D.	POPES	WRITERS	HERETICS & HERESEY	THE CHURCH	THE WORLD	SECULAR RULERS
500		Dionysius Exiguus				Anastasius Justin I Theodoric
	Hormisdas John I	Code of Canons Boethius			Restoration of the Empire Justinian Code	Justinian
		Cassiodorus		Irish monasticism Monte Cassino		
	Vigilius	Rule of St. Benedict		Benedictine monas- ticism COUNCIL OF CON- STANTINOPLE II		
550			Conflicts with Nestorians and Mono- physites	Three Chapters	Lombards invade Italy	Justin II
600	Gregory I the Great	Pope Gregory	Monthelitism	Conversion of Visi- goths and Anglo- Saxons	Mohammed	Ethelbert of Kent
		Sophronius of Jerusalem			Persians capture Jerusalem	Phocas
	Honorius I	Maximus Con- fessor		Irish missionaries	Hegira	Heraclius
					Moslems capture Jerusalem and Alexandria	Penda of Mercia
		Isidore of Seville		*Ecthesis*		
650	Martin I			*Typos* Theodore of Tarsus in Britain Synod of Whitby COUNCIL OF CON- STANTINOPLE III Pope Honorius I condemned Trullan Council		Do-nothing kings of Franks
						Justinian II
700		Bede			Moslems in Spain	
	Gregory II Gregory III		Iconoclasm	Anglo-Saxon mis- sionaries	Battle of Tours	Charles Martel
				Conversion of Germany by Boniface	Lombard advances in Italy	Leo III
	Zachary			Papal-Frankish alliance	Byzantine Empire weakening in West	Liutprand
				Reform of Frankish Church		Aistulf
750	Stephen II (III)	John Damascene		Donation of Pepin Papal State		Pepin the Short
	Adrian I		Adoptionism	COUNCIL OF NICAEA II		Charlemagne
				filioque dispute	Carolingian Empire End of Lombards	
	Leo III	Alcuin		Conversion of Saxons in Germany		Desiderius
800				Benedict of Aniane	Revival of Roman Empire	Irene Louis the Pious
		Hincmar of Reims Walafrid Strabo Rabanus Maurus False Decretals John Scotus Eriugena		Constitution of Lothair Destruction by Northmen Scandinavian missions	Viking invasions begin Treaty of Verdun divides Carolin- gian Empire	Sons of Louis
850	Nicholas I the Great Adrian II	Anastasius the Librarian Photius		Church feudalized	Development of feudalism	Michael the Drunkard Bardas
	Adrian III	Slavic liturgy of Constantine and Methodius		Proprietary system Photian Schism COUNCIL OF CON- STANTINOPLE IV	Moslems attack Italy Magyars harry east Europe	Basil
900	Formosus			Photian Council Conversion of Bohemi- ans and Bulgars Monastery of Cluny Conversion of Normans House of Theophylact controls papacy	Dark Ages of Europe	Alfred of Wessex
950	John XII			Crescentii and counts of Tusculum control papacy Dunstan's reforms	Invasions end Recovery begins Second revival of Roman Empire	Otto I
		Gerbert of Aurillac		Conversion of Rus- sians, Poles, Hungarians	German ambitions in Italy	Otto III Hugh Capet Stephen of Hungary

APOGEE OF MEDIEVAL CATHOLICISM

Chapter 12

THE MEDIEVAL REFORMATION

HOWEVER serious the decline of religious life as the result of the twin evils of barbarian devastation and secular domination, there were never entirely wanting, somewhere in every generation, saints to keep alive spiritual ideals or monasteries where better traditions refused to die. It was only a matter of time before their efforts and the innate regenerative powers of the Church produced a general revival. The most significant of the early reactions against conditions of the tenth century was the monastery of Cluny and its Congregation, but the ideals of Cluny were monastic and limited. Only when the reformers gained a hold on the papacy was it possible to co-ordinate all lesser efforts and challenge effectively the very principle of lay control. This was the task of Pope St. Gregory VII.

The Monastic Renaissance. Most medieval reform movements were monastic in nature or origin, and this is true of the first reformation. Various monastic experiments of the tenth and eleventh centuries may be singled out as paving the way for the Gregorian reform. In England where organized monastic life ceased entirely in the ninth century a triumvirate of dedicated souls — SS. Dunstan, Oswald, and Ethelwold — revived the Benedictine life. About 970 they prepared the *Concordance* *of the Rule,* the customs which English houses followed until the suppression in 1539. In Lorraine the monasteries of Gorze near Metz (*c.* 933), Brogne near Namur (*c.* 920); and St. Vannes in the diocese of Verdun (1005) became centers of a revival that permeated the Rhineland.

Italy saw the establishment of Camaldoli by St. Romuald in 1012 and Vallombrosa by St. John Gualbert in 1038, both following the semi-anchoritic rather than the cenobitic Benedictine life since Italy always felt a strong attachment to the hermit tradition. Although neither Romuald nor John composed a rule they found many imitators, and orders in the proper sense of the word sprang up. Vallombrosa introduced the idea of lay brothers as a supplement to the monks, a practice which most orders thereafter copied. St. Peter Damian (1007–1072), a Doctor of the Church and one of the most influential men of the century, became prior of Fonte Avellana and restored several dozen Italian houses. Damian also reverted to the austere ideals of the desert Fathers. St. Nilus (d. 1005), a Calabrian Greek, founded the monastery of Grottaferrata near Rome according to the Basilian rule.

Cluny. Foremost among the monastic reforms was Cluny and its Congregation. In 910 Duke William of Aquitaine, in co-operation with Abbot Berno of Baume, founded Cluny near Macon in Burgundy, an area that was something of a monastic oasis to which other houses had been transplanted to escape Viking attacks. Cluny owed its greatness, on the one hand, to a succession of saintly and long-lived abbots: Berno (910–926), Odo (926–942), Maieul (954–994), Odilo (994–1049), and Hugh the Great (1049–1109), who played prominent roles in ecclesiastical affairs of all Europe. But the abbots were able to accomplish their work because of Cluny's freedom; the foundation charter removed all lay control by Duke William or his descendants and placed the house directly under papal jurisdiction. And for all their decadence the popes of the tenth century patronized and protected Cluny and its abbots as if aware of the monastery's destiny.

Life at Cluny rested on the Benedictine Rule as modified by St. Benedict of Aniane. Thus Cluny discarded manual labor and made recitation of the divine office almost the sole occupation of the monks. Study and copying of manuscripts remained; Abbot Peter the Venerable once wrote that "it is more noble to set one's hand to the pen than to the plough." But the simplicity of traditional Benedictinism disappeared; in its place arose an elaborate ceremonial. Yet Cluny became a mecca men in search of spiritual perfection.

Cluny's influence extended over a wide area either through daughter houses or houses reformed by Cluniac monks. This task of reform was not always easy, as demonstrated by the fate of the abbot of Lobbes in Flanders, whose monks cut off his hands and gouged out his eyes rather than submit to stricter discipline. Fleury, St. Benigne of Dijon, Marmoutier, and St. Denis were among the French monasteries reformed by Cluny. Hirsau in southwestern Germany spread Cluniac ideals over the Black Forest area, while Spain, England, and Italy too felt the reforming hand of Cluny. From the time of Abbot Odilo monasteries reformed by Cluny were placed under its immediate control and came to form a congregation governed directly by the abbot of Cluny and exempted from episcopal jurisdiction. Subordinate houses were headed by an appointed prior responsible to the abbot of Cluny, the only full abbot in the entire organization. At its peak the Cluniac congregation numbered hundreds of houses. This was a clear departure from the Benedictine custom of autonomous monasteries but the experiment in centralization was an intelligent endeavor to reach the causes of spiritual decline through greater unity and cohesion. Cluny's example in this respect was imitated by all later orders and even by the pure Benedictines.

Nonmonastic Reforms. The enthusiasm of the monastic reformers overflowed the monasteries and penetrated the secular clergy and the laity. Bishops chosen from the ranks of the reformed monks carried the new zeal into their dioceses, while the extensive travel of the abbots of Cluny and the fame of outstanding monks brought them into contact with important laymen. We have already seen the close connection between Alberic, lord of Rome, and Odo of Cluny whom Alberic summoned in 936 to reorganize the Roman monasteries.

Among the great princes of Europe too were to be found those who used their position to improve the state of religion in one way or another. Alfred the Great of England (871–899) tried to restore education among his clergy; he is reported to have remarked that there was scarcely a priest in all England capable of understanding Latin. William the Conqueror (1066–1087) did much to end abuses in his Norman Duchy and in England after the conquest. In bestowing the primatial see of Canterbury on Abbot Lanfranc of Bec William brought to England an outstanding prelate and scholar. Emperor Henry II of Germany (1002–1024) has been canonized for his efforts to revive the spiritual life among the corrupt German clergy and Henry III (1039–1056) imitated him. A considerable group of reformed monasteries in Germany persuaded their proprietary lords to renounce their rights and grant freedom or immunity to the communities after the fashion of Cluny, thus striking a blow at the proprietary system.

The Reform and Feudal Society.   An immediate result of the monastic renaissance was a greater awareness by churchmen of the social mission of the Church, and this led to measures to check the greatest scourge of feudalism, the constant, petty but destructive warfare of the nobility. The influence of Cluny in particular contributed directly to the promulgation of the first Peace of God about 990. This was an agreement binding those who swore to it under pain of excommunication to refrain from attacking noncombatants and neutrals, specifically clergy, peasants, and townsmen, and their property. A generation later appeared the Truce of God which prohibited warfare outright during certain times of the year such as Lent, Advent, holydays, and week ends. Although the effect of these institutions was sometimes slight, they contributed to the stabilization of society and they offer proof of the perennial efforts of the Church to aid society according to its needs.

Aims of the Reformers.   For the sake of convenience we can divide the medieval reformation into two periods, the Cluniac and the Gregorian, the first stressing moral regeneration, the second characterized chiefly by the raising of political questions along with the moral program. The year 1058 is the dividing point. In the Cluniac period emphasis was placed on simony and clerical marriage, besides the general program of monastic revival. After 1058 secular domination of the Church as expressed in lay investiture became the leading issue.

Simony, the sin of trafficking in sacred objects or offices, arose from the possibility for laymen to profit from the disposition of the ecclesiastical positions within their jurisdiction. The evil was compounded when simonist prelates tried to recover the price of their office by extracting money from other clergy. Thus the archbishop of Milan, who owed his position to the emperor, established a fixed scale of twelve, eighteen, and twenty-four denarii as the price of ordination of subdeacons, deacons, and priests respectively. The ancient canons of the Church, many times renewed, were ignored. Some sincere laymen such as Emperor Henry II disapproved of simony in the strict sense of an exchange of money, but even he still insisted on having free disposition of bishoprics to reward service to himself. Humbert of Moyenmoutier's *Three Books Against Simonists* (1058) was the most outspoken attack on simony; he went so far as to deny the validity of ordinations performed by simonist bishops.

There was general agreement on the need for a moral regeneration of the clergy. St. Peter Damian in his *Book of Gomorrah* depicted in lurid and perhaps exaggerated phrases the existence of vice among the clergy. However, the most prominent concern of this moral revival was the lax observance of the law of clerical celibacy. Western canonical tradition, dating back to the synod of Elvira about 306, prescribed celibacy for priests or continence if they had been married before ordination. This law applied to those in major orders only and did not bind the numerous minor clergy who had no intention of advancing further. Despite frequent repetition the law had largely fallen into desuetude during the period of anarchy and married or concubinary priests and bishops were often accepted as the normal thing. This was true of both secular and regular clergy. Sometimes the priestly office was handed on from father to son like any hereditary benefice. Abbots, bishops, popes labored to restore celibacy, but there were practical difficulties involved such as the fate of priests' wives and children. One bishop complained that if he degraded all married priests he would have no one left to say Mass in his whole diocese.

Political Problems of Reform. The political act of lay investiture involved the bestowal by laymen of the insignia of office on a clergyman. This practice symbolized secular domination, the extirpation of which became the third major aim of the reformers and the phrase which has given its name to the most bitter part of the reformation, the Investiture Controversy. Bishops, to speak of the most prominent rank, held a temporal as well as spiritual office, and the two had become confused. "Receive this church," was the formula of investiture as the king granted the bishop-elect his crozier and ring. The whole ceremony left the impression that the layman was bestowing a spiritual power upon his vassal. Because of the confusion of the dual functions of bishops any attempt to change customary procedure seemed an attack on the prince's authority. For it must be remembered that the power of all kings, and especially of the German emperor, depended on their control over the powerful prelates of their lands.

Lay investiture in itself did not become a major issue until after 1085. Actually it was only the symbolic manifestation of royal rights over the Church and the first question was whether or not to abolish royal rights at all. On this point the reformers disagreed among themselves. Ever since the Edict of Milan, and very obviously in the theocratic

Carolingian Empire, it had been the accepted prerogative of kings to exert extensive influence and control over the Church. Royal theocracy had existed unquestioned for centuries. Kings recognized their obligation to protect the Church and churchmen acknowledge the need of royal protection. Had not God set up the Old Testament kings to help His people observe the Law? Objections were raised against abuse of the power, but seldom against the principle of the thing. To the medieval mind the monarch was both king and priest and therefore his control was not secular domination at all.

Humbert's book *Against Simonists* was the first attack on the principle of active lay participation in ecclesiastical administration, and this marked a revolution in reforming circles. When Humbert's theory was broached Damian, the stanchest advocate of moral reform, denounced it as political meddling, and the abbot of Cluny, St. Hugh, stood by as a neutral observer during the papal-imperial controversy over the issue. But logical reformers like Humbert and Hildebrand pointed out the precariousness of any reformation which depended on the unpredictable succession of hereditary lay rulers. As they saw it the only answer was to strike at the root of the matter and eliminate the cause of spiritual decadence: lay domination.

The Reformed Papacy. Having begun on the monastic level, the reformation gradually crept upward until in 1049 it made its way to the papacy. This happened through the action of Emperor Henry III who, at the synod of Sutri, set aside three claimants to the papal throne and imposed the first of three successive German popes, the third of whom was St. Leo IX (1049–1054). Leo came from Lorraine — he was bishop of Toul — and in this region the reform current had been running strong for half a century. Around him the new pope collected a coterie of like-minded men: Humbert of Moyenmoutier, Frederick of Lorraine, Halinard of Lyons, and the monk Hildebrand, the personalities who were to develop and effect the epoch-making ideas of the next thirty-five years. Leo set out to put Rome at the head of the reform and to re-establish the tarnished authority of the papacy. His pontificate was one long journey that took him throughout Italy and over the Alps three times into France and Germany. Everywhere councils assembled to reform abuses, outlaw simony, enforce celibacy, and depose the unworthy. With the emperor, Leo remained on the best of terms for Leo eschewed political problems. But the reign ended in a disaster, for Leo took up arms against the Norman brigands in southern Italy and suffered a decisive defeat.

Victor II (1055–1057), another imperial nominee, continued the reform under difficult circumstances, while Stephen IX (1058–1059), choice of the Roman clergy, did not wait for the imperial sanction before being consecrated. Stephen's short reign was followed by a disputed election as the clergy chose Nicholas II (1059–1061) while the counts of Tusculum attempted unsuccessfully to recover lost authority by imposing a candidate of their choice as they had done so often before.

The Acts of Nicholas II. Nicholas II's three years were tremendously important for the cause of reform. Emperor Henry IV (1056–1106) was a child and the confusion of the regency provided opportunity for the pope to act boldly. The disputed election had raised the possibility of a renewal of secular dominion over the Apostolic See by the local aristocracy. To prevent such a disaster a new election law was proclaimed by a Lateran synod in 1059 declaring that only the cardinals had a direct voice in papal elections, the Roman clergy and people being permitted to express their consent but nothing more. To the emperor was reserved a vague right of confirmation. Although the decree aimed specifically at the Roman nobility, it was also a step in the direction of emancipating the papacy from imperial domination. A further point of note is that the same synod formulated the first absolute prohibition of lay investiture.

To offset possible hostility of the Romans or Germans because of the election law, Nicholas took the step of securing military aid. A treaty with Robert Guiscard, leader of the parvenu Normans in southern Italy, legalized Guiscard's right to rule as duke in return for his becoming a vassal of the pope and binding himself to protect the papacy from its enemies.

The first test of the new election law came in 1061. Through the efforts of Hildebrand, now archdeacon of the Roman Church, Alexander II was selected by the cardinals and enthroned. But the Roman nobles appealed to the German court. The empress-regent designated Bishop Cadalus of Parma whom a group of German and Lombard bishops then acknowledged as Pope Honorius II. After three years Alexander II secured general recognition, although he had to appear before a largely German council and swear that his election was untainted by simony. Although little was accomplished in Alexander II's pontificate because of his precarious situation, the schism had the effect of separating those reformers who were still willing to collaborate with the civil authorities from those who turned vigorously now in the opposite direction.

Pope St. Gregory VII. Gregory VII (1073–1085) is one of those tremendous personalities who appear in history at what seems to be the precise climax of a long evolution and who so shape events of their day that all future generations cannot escape their influence. As the monk Hildebrand he had been a power behind the scenes at the Curia for fifteen years prior to his elevation. During Gregory VII's reign the reformation definitely attained the political stage and brought the papacy into a headlong clash with Henry IV of Germany. Gregory sought to avoid political conflict. For two years he concentrated on purely moral problems, and whenever his opponents showed good will he readily reciprocated. But he refused to budge from his principles. He was no great lawyer or scholar, but intuitively Gregory VII possessed a better understanding of the true nature of the Church than did most of his contemporaries.

Gregory VII's favorite expression was "righteousness," by which he understood the "right relationship between Church and State." For Gregory this meant the emancipation of the Church from lay control so that it could perform its proper task unhindered. Gregory can be called a revolutionary, for he overthrew the existing order of secular domination of the Church, a condition sanctioned by centuries of usage. Yet in another sense Gregory deserves to be known as a conservative. He realized the unsatisfactory nature of the present situation and sought to return to the fundamental tenets of Christianity, which inherently posited the pre-eminence of the divinely established Church over all human institutions. St. Ambrose and Pope Gelasius had enunciated this idea long ago. Reduced to the level of everyday affairs, the Investiture Controversy involved a question of jurisdiction over the hierarchy: whether king or pope should appoint bishops and prescribe their qualifications and duties.

Conflict With Henry IV. The occasion of the clash between Gregory VII and Henry IV was an election to the archbishopric of Milan, a city where the reform forces, the Patarines, clashed violently with the vested interests of simonist bishops and married clergy. Milan was also an essential base of German power in Italy and Henry determined to keep it in his grip. He rejected Archbishop Atto whom Pope Alexander II had consecrated and, despite his solemn promises, invested the anti-reform candidate Tedald. Moreover, the king refused to dissociate himself from five of his councilors under sentence of excommunication for simony. ~~ ^ in general showed little respect for ordinary standards of m~~ ^

At the Lenten synod of 1075 Gregory VII passed a decree prohibiting lay investiture (although the prohibition was not published), suspended a handful of German bishops, and forbade the laity to hear Masses of married priests. On December 8, 1075, Gregory wrote to Henry admonishing and threatening him. Henry retaliated by calling a synod at Worms in January where his bishops, ever restive under the new pope's sharp eye, declared Gregory a usurper and called upon him to resign the papacy. Henry's letter to the pope took a very vituperative tone: "I, Henry, king by the grace of God, with all my bishops, say to you, 'Come down, come down, damned throughout the ages.'"

Gregory excommunicated Henry at the Lenten synod of 1076 and took the unprecedented step of declaring him deposed and his subjects free from all obligations to him. At once the German nobility seized the opportunity to enhance their power at the king's expense. When the diet met at Tribur in October, 1076, they forced the king to accept his suspension until Gregory should come into Germany to settle the king's fate. Thus the pope found himself allied with the German princes, interested not in reform or the liberty of the Church but in their own aggrandizement.

Canossa and Beyond. To forestall the meeting of his enemies the king hurried over the Alps in midwinter and intercepted the pope at Canossa, a castle belonging to Countess Matilda of Tuscany, Gregory's friend. The dramatic scene is well known. Henry is said to have stood in the snow for three days begging forgiveness as a humble penitent. As a priest Gregory had no choice but to accept the king's protestations of contrition and lift the ban. But the German princes nevertheless proceeded to the election of Rudolph of Swabia as anti-king and a civil war commenced. Gregory refused to take sides until it became apparent that the unscrupulous Henry had no intention of keeping the promises made at Canossa. In 1080 Gregory repeated the excommunication and renewed the king's deposition. Now Henry advanced on Rome and set up an antipope, Clement III. Rome finally fell, but the Normans rescued the pope. Gregory died at Salerno in the Norman duchy in 1085. Obviously Gregory VII's greatness does not rest on his ability to solve the problems he raised, but rather on the fact that he dared to bring up the questions of the role of the laity in the Church, the relationship of Church and State, and the pre-eminence of the pope.

With the civil war continuing in Germany and the antipope unable to maintain himself in Rome, the reform party took heart. After the short reign of Victor III, Pope Urban II (1088–1099) was elected, a pontiff who resembled Gregory in zeal for the Church's freedom and who, as a former monk of Cluny, felt all the Cluniac hatred for moral laxity. Urban continued adamantly to regard Henry IV as deposed, while Henry would acknowledge no pope but Clement III. But gradually a shift in emphasis in the issues at stake occurred and prepared the way for a future settlement. Gregory VII had chiefly desired free episcopal elections, but Urban II and his successors regarded the investiture cere-mony as of greater significance. Hence lay investiture now came to the fore and Urban II officially and publicly forbade laymen to invest bishops with their office.

Henry IV's position weakened as the German bishops slowly came around to the Roman view. The king's own son rebelled against him also and the Empire approached a state of anarchy. As soon as the emperor's antipope was driven from Rome, Urban embarked on a series of journeys reminiscent of Leo IX. At Piacenza in March, 1095, a well-attended council renewed decrees against simony and clerical marriage. Then Urban crossed into France for the council at Clermont, best known for the beginning of the crusades but important also for the disciplinary measures enacted. At Clermont Urban forbade churchmen to take an oath of homage to a layman. Rome (1097), Bari (1098), and Rome again (1099) witnessed further synods that swelled the stream of reform. At Urban's death the papal prestige was at a higher peak than ever before.

The Concordat of Worms. Although a sincere reformer, Pascal II (1099–1118) lacked strength of character and almost ruined the reform. His reign opened with fair prospects but these were dashed when the new king Henry V (1106–1125) proved little different from his father. When Pascal excommunicated him Henry invaded Italy. Pascal refused to retreat but rather tried to negotiate. In 1111 he offered to surrender completely all the feudal rights of the Church in Germany — temporal jurisdiction, lands, endowment, privileges, and all — in return for Henry's abandonment of lay investiture. Whether or not the proposal would have worked, and nothing indicates that it could, it had to be discarded be-cause of opposition from cardinals and other churchmen more perspica-cious than Pascal II. Henry then arrested the pope and coerced him to cease all opposition to lay investiture. Again the vehemently unfavorable reaction of the reform party all over Europe forced Pascal to back down. Saved by a new rebellion in Germany, the pope publicly confessed his weakness. Before long Callixtus II (1119–1124), a Cluniac monk, was pope. Negotiations for a settlement dragged on for three years before the Concordat of Worms was accepted in 1122.

The Concordat represented a logical compromise that left victory in the hands of the papacy but in fact did not eliminate imperial domination of the Church. Extreme Gregorians had tended to consider every aspect of the German bishops' activity from a strictly ecclesiastical viewpoint just as the imperialists viewed everything from an essentially secular angle. A logical compromise would recognize the duality of the bishop's office and draw a distinction between the two kinds of powers in the investiture ceremony. This was accomplished by the Concordat.

The emperor guaranteed free, canonical episcopal elections. In return Callixtus permitted Henry V to be present at elections, provided no simony or violence were involved, and to have a voice in settling disputes that arose. In recognition of the secular duties of the bishops they were allowed to swear homage to the emperor who, in turn, invested them with their temporalities by means of the scepter. Ring and crozier, however, and with them the ecclesiastical authority, came from the metropolitan. Although the bishops still professed two masters, and the Concordat represented a compromise, still the reformers gained a victory in principle.

To ratify the Concordat Callixtus convoked the first ecumenical council to meet in the West. Known as the First Lateran Council, it sat in Rome in 1123. The Council concerned itself with disciplinary measures. By its eighteenth canon it sought to bring the proprietary church system under control, although the right of lay patronage was never absolutely abrogated. And it accepted the Concordat.

Investiture Outside the Empire. In France, where reform sentiment was strongest, secular rulers weaker, and bishops less important than in the Empire, the investiture question never assumed major proportions. England, however, provided a striking example of the clash between the old and the new ideas.

William I (1066–1087), Hildebrand's contemporary, embodied the traditional concept of royal rights over the Church. He did a thorough job of improving the English Church by restoring discipline and removing corrupt Anglo-Saxon prelates whom he replaced with outstanding Normans without taint of simony. Yet William ruled the Church with a hand of iron. Local synods met only with his approbation, bishops could not leave England without permission, papal legates and letters were excluded without royal consent. All of this William justified on the basis of established custom, and despite minor irritations Gregory VII made no attempt to change the situation. The king successfully interposed a barrier between England and the revolutionary reformers on the continent who were insisting on an end to this type of domination.

William II (1087–1100), a despoiler of churches and abuser of his power, had an entirely different reputation from his father. In a moment of compunction he gave Canterbury to St. Anselm but before long he was up to his old tricks and fell afoul of his archbishop. Anselm fled to Italy where he attended the last of Urban II's councils where the leading papal decrees against the laity were renewed. Anselm for the first time came into direct contact with the full papal program of ecclesiastical independence, hitherto unknown in England because of William I's isolation. When Henry I (1100–1135) readmitted him to England, Anselm refused to perform homage or deal with bishops who accepted investiture — all according to Urban II's decrees. After bitter and protracted negotiations the king gave up investiture and Anselm agreed to the performance of homage by the king's ecclesiastical vassals. Thus the Gregorian program took root in England. The London Concordat of 1107 provided the model for the Concordat of Worms in 1122.

The Greek Schism. While the papacy was fully engaged with the reformation, a new Greek schism exploded. Michael Cerularius occupied the patriarchal throne at Constantinople from 1043 to 1059 and the schism was his personal doing. He was a very ambitious prelate who had become patriarch after the failure of his scheme to become emperor, but as patriarch he practically ruled the State as well as the Church. In 1053 he suddenly attacked the Latins for the "horrible infirmities" of using unleavened bread in the Eucharist, for insisting on clerical celibacy, and for fasting on Saturdays. Cerularius also closed all Latin churches in Constantinople, including the chapel of the papal legate.

Pope Leo IX sent Cardinals Humbert and Frederick and Archbishop Peter of Amalfi to investigate. Cerularius abused the legates and excommunicated the pope. Cardinal Humbert replied with an excommunication of the patriarch (July, 1054). Before the legates departed Emperor Constantine IX, who had good political reasons for desiring amicable relations with the pope, gave them gifts for Leo and protected them against personal assaults.

Obscurity veils the subsequent events that transformed the personal schism of Cerularius into a general break between Greeks and Latins. The antipapal forces among the Greeks drew upon the precedents of Photius' attack on the papal primacy, and soon the Greeks hit upon the western insertion of the *"filioque"* in the Creed as a sign of heresy. At the council of Bari in 1098 an attempted mediation failed completely. Although further negotiations were conducted in later centuries, the schism has never been healed. The Greek Orthodox Church remains schismatic to this day.

In the final analysis it was social and cultural rather than religious issues that produced the schism. The inability of East and West to understand each other had been a source of difficulty ever since the Arian crisis. Byzantium's more advanced civilization in the early middle ages caused them to depreciate westerners as barbarians. The restoration of the western empire and the clashes that occurred during the crusades pushed them further apart all the time.

Conclusion. The medieval reformation, in emancipating the Church from secular domination, revolutionized the relationship between the Church and medieval society. Although it did not wholly eliminate abuses, the reform movement did create a better atmosphere among the clergy and it shaped the disciplinary machinery for the continued prosecution of its aims. It stimulated a new, energetic Catholic life which manifested itself in many ways throughout the next centuries. Since the papacy had embraced the reform and had seen it through to its conclusion, the papacy reaped immediate advantages in terms of prestige. From now on the leading thread in the history of the medieval Church is the self-confident development by subsequent popes of their now unquestioned leadership in ecclesiastical affairs. This position was not damaged by the loss of the Byzantine Church which made little impression on Europe in general at the time. Rather than injuring the Latins, the Greek schism proved fatal to Byzantine Catholicism.

REVIEW AIDS

1. Explain the characteristic features of Cluny and its congregation.
2. In what way did Peter Damian and Cardinal Humbert contribute to the reform?
3. Show how lay investiture was the root of the reform problem.
4. How did the reform make its way to Rome?
5. Discuss the aims and methods of the Cluniac phase of the reform and show how it differed from the Gregorian program.
6. What reform measures were taken by the papacy before Gregory VII?
7. Explain Gregory VII's aims and describe his conflict with Henry IV.
8. Summarize the events in the Investiture Controversy to the Concordat of Worms.

9. Analyze the attitude of the papacy toward England in the matter of reform.
10. Why did the Greeks break from the Catholic Church in 1054?
11. Discuss the significance of the medieval reformation for the history of the Church and of the papacy.

SUGGESTIONS FOR FURTHER READING

The outstanding work on the reform is G. Tellenbach, *Church, State and Christian Society at the Time of the Investiture Contest*, trans. by R. Bennett (Oxford: 1948). Also very important is Walter Ullmann, *The Growth of Papal Government in the Middle Ages* (London: 1955), of which sections VII and VIII pertain to the Investiture Controversy. Volume IV of R. W. Carlyle and A. J. Carlyle, *History of Mediaeval Political Theory in the West*, 6 vols. (London: 1928–1936), gives a thorough analysis of the views of both papalist and imperialist writers.

Less theoretical than the above are Joan Evans, *Monastic Life at Cluny 910–1157* (Oxford: 1931) and J. P. Whitney, *Hildebrandine Essays* (Cambridge: 1932). Sketches of the reform popes are to be found in H. K. Mann, *The Lives of the Popes in the Middle Ages* (St. Louis: 1910), Volumes 6, 7, and 8. There are numerous biographies of Gregory VII, of uneven merit. A brief sketch is W. R. Stephens, *Hildebrand and His Times* (London: 1914). Adrian Fortescue, *The Orthodox Eastern Church* (London: 1924), Chapter V, gives a Catholic view of the schism of Cerularius, while Steven Runciman, *The Eastern Schism* (Oxford: 1955) analyzes political and cultural factors.

DOCUMENTS

The Investiture Controversy inevitably raised the question anew of the relationship between the Christian emperor and the possessors of spiritual power. Pope Gregory VII took up the matter in a letter to Bishop Hermann of Metz in 1081 in order to justify Gregory's deposition of Emperor Henry IV. Gregory showed his low opinion of secular rulers. James H. Robinson, *Readings in European History*, Vol. I (Boston: Ginn and Co., 1904), pp. 284–285.

Shall not an office instituted by laymen — by those even who did not know God — be subject to that office which the providence of God Almighty has instituted for his own honor, and in compassion given to the world? For his Son, even as he is unquestioningly believed to be God and man, so is he considered the chief of priests, sitting on the right hand of the Father and always interceding for us. Yet he despised a secular kingdom, over which the men of this world swell with pride, and came of his own will to the priesthood of the cross. Whereas all know that kings and princes are descendants of men who were ignorant of God, and who, by arrogance, robbery, perfidy, murder — in a word by almost every crime — at the prompting of the prince of this world, the devil, strove with blind avarice and intolerable presumption to gain the mastery over their equals, that is, over mankind.

To whom, indeed, can we better compare them, when they seek to make the priests of God bend to their feet, than to him who is chief of all the sons of pride and who tempted the highest Pontiff himself, the chief of priests, the Son of the Most High, and promised to him all the kingdoms of the world, saying, "All these will I give thee, if thou wilt fall down and worship me"?

Who doubts that the priests of Christ should be regarded as the fathers and masters of kings and princes, and of all the faithful? Is it not evidently hopeless folly for a son to attempt to domineer over his father, a pupil over his master, or for any one, by iniquitous exactions, to claim power over him by whom he himself, as he acknowledges, can be bound and loosed both on earth and in heaven. . . .

Armed accordingly with such decrees and authority, many bishops have excommunicated, in some cases kings, in others emperors.

Chapter 13

THE AGE OF ST. BERNARD
OF CLAIRVAUX

I N TERMS of institutional development, social impact, and depth of
spirituality, medieval Catholicism reached its peak between 1073 and
1274. In part this was the result of the momentum of the eleventh-
century reformation, in part of the general stabilization of Europe. Since
the Church matured more rapidly during this period than any other
institution — except perhaps the revived Empire — its pre-eminence was
virtually unchallenged. This pre-eminence expressed itself in many ways:
in the continued expansion of monasticism, the crusades, the further elaboration of papal government, and a tremendous burst of intellectual and
social activity. In the first half of the twelfth century all lines of spiritual
and ecclesiastical development converged in the towering figure of St.
Bernard of Clairvaux.

Monasticism. Twelfth-century monasticism presents a variegated
appearance but, however different in externals, the new experiments had
certain common characteristics: intense fervor, simplicity, respect for manual labor, and the desire to return to primitive customs. Cluny no longer
satisfied the ascetic mood of the times; it fell on evil days under its
unworthy abbot Pons and its splendor, wealth, and way of life lost their
attraction. The new foundations, therefore, reacted against Cluniac usages
and sought to restore either the original Benedictine observance or, with
the more extreme, the ideals of the Egyptian and Syrian hermits who
preceded Benedict.

Many of the new small congregations and individual foundations disappeared within a short time. Of the less prominent groups attaining

local importance were the Orders of Sempringham and Fontevrault (both maintaining double monasteries), Grandmont and Savigny, all of which originated within the first twenty-five years of the eleventh century. At this time also the Augustinian Hermits began to emerge from the obscurity which surrounds their early history.

Canons Regular. Priests attached in groups or "chapters" to particular churches, especially cathedrals, were called canons. Attempts to amalgamate the lives of these essentially secular (i.e., "in the world") clergy with the monastic habits of the regulars (i.e., living "according to a rule") date back to the fourth century. St. Chrodegang's scheme popularized by the Carolingians broke down after about 840 and from then on the regular life vanished among the secular clergy. Even the chapter's endowments were divided up and specific portions or "prebends" were allotted to each canon.

Cluniac reformers, judging that community life offered better safeguards for clerical morality, began a campaign to revive it among the seculars. Local councils took up the idea and the community life again became popular for the canons. While some chapters adopted the Benedictine Rule outright and became full-fledged monks, many others took the rule of St. Augustine. These Canons Regular of St. Augustine, to be distinguished from the Augustinian Hermits, became quite numerous. Although living a regular life they were not enclosed and their work was essentially pastoral: preaching, teaching, and in general administering to the needs of the parish. Provost or dean, scholasticus, chancellor, treasurer, and precentor comprised the chapter officers. The Victorines, so-called from their house in Paris dedicated to St. Victor, were canons founded by the eminent teacher William of Champeaux (1070–1121), and were unique among the orders in sharing in the full tide of early scholasticism.

Premonstratensians. From Prémontré their first home, or from St. Norbert (d. 1134) their founder, another group of canons are known as Premonstratensians or Norbertines. Norbert, himself a worldly canon who underwent a sudden conversion, was laughed out of his chapter at Xanten and became a wandering missionary before settling down in 1120 at a swampy meadow at Prémontré near Laon. Not Norbert but his friend Hugh composed a rule, an eclectic constitution that drew heavily on the Augustinian, Cistercian, Victorine, and Benedictine rules, so that the new order stood halfway between monasticism and the life of the Augustinian Canons. Its members engaged in missionary and parochial work. When the emperor compelled Norbert to accept the archbishopric of Magdeburg he took some of his canons along and soon eastern Germany, Prussia, and Poland became the most important scene of Premonstratensian endeavors. They supplied many bishops and contributed immeasurably to the civilizing and Christianizing of these eastern areas. St. Norbert also added nuns and laymen to his order, the latter composing the first "Third Order." Premonstratensians rivaled the Cistercians in popularity during the twelfth century.

Carthusians.   "Never reformed because never deformed" is the boast of the Carthusians, the extreme ascetic order in the Church. They took their name from their first home at Chartreuse in southeastern France founded by St. Bruno in 1084. Bruno was one of that body of men of his day who longed for the perfect monastic life, in search of which he left a promising teaching career at Reims. However, Bruno soon had to leave Chartreuse when the pope summoned him to Rome and he never returned. The fifth abbot, Guigo (1110–1136), put the customs of Chartreuse into writing and attracted many recruits. Chartreuse took its inspiration from Egypt and the desert Fathers, sharing the monastic instinct of Italy that had evoked Camaldoli, although Chartreuse never cut its ties with the West as completely as had the Italian hermits. Its life was semi-anchoritic; the monks lived in solitude in their individual huts with their own gardens, assembling for only a portion of the daily office and an occasional meal. Silence, solitude, mortification, and a meager diet shaped an essentially contemplative life. Lay brothers, called *conversi,* handled most of the outside contacts. Carthusian expansion proceeded slowly but eventually they were to be found widely scattered. St. Hugh, Bishop of Lincoln (d. 1200), is probably the best known after Bruno himself.

Cistercians.   In its beginnings nothing distinguished Citeaux from a host of comparable monastic ventures. It was founded in 1098 by St. Robert of Molesme, a restless monk who had wandered in and out of a score of monasteries in search of perfection before establishing his own house with a handful of followers. Soon Robert was recalled to Molesme leaving Citeaux beset by many difficulties and overshadowed by its great neighbor Cluny. Citeaux's prosperity began only with its third abbot, the Englishman St. Stephen Harding (1109–1133), one of the original band of pioneers, a man motivated by the same idealism as Robert. Stephen was a vigorous administrator. He lost no time telling the Duke of Burgundy,

Citeaux's only real benefactor, that his visits were no longer welcome since they disturbed the peace of the monastery. The real change in the fortunes of Citeaux began in 1112 with the arrival of St. Bernard and thirty companions to ask admission of the monks who were just then praying desperately for recruits. The very next year Citeaux established its first daughter house at La Ferté, followed by Pontigny, Clairvaux, and Morimond within the next two years. At Bernard's death in 1153 the Order possessed 343 houses all over Europe. By 1300 the number reached almost 700.

The Cistercian Rule. Stephen Harding, author of the Cistercian rule, the Charter of Charity, approved by the Cluniac Pope Callixtus II in 1119, gave the Order a fine constitution. Although the professed purpose of Citeaux was the return to the original observance of the Benedictine Rule as a reaction against Cluny's interpolations and additions to it, the Cistercians nevertheless copied certain features of their great predecessor and also deviated unconsciously from the Rule. The shortened conventual liturgy, the simplicity and poverty of the monastic buildings, and the clothing of the Cistercian monks were Benedictine. One innovation was the use of a white habit instead of the traditional black, whence the designation "white monks" to distinguish Cistercians from Benedictine "black monks." No one under fifteen was to be admitted; educational opportunities were not available for outsiders. Unlike the Cluniac centralization under a single abbot, the organ of government of the Cistercians was the General Chapter, the annual meeting of all abbots, chiefly to secure disciplinary uniformity. Each monastery was visited annually by the abbot of its parent house, while Citeaux's visitors were the abbots of its first four daughters. Exemption from episcopal jurisdiction was not sought by the earliest Cistercians.

Manual labor in the fields was an important Cistercian characteristic, although the Order used *conversi* who joined in large numbers. These lay brothers usually came from the peasant class, while the monks themselves represented the nobility or at least the middle class. Cistercian property became extensive; its estates were never organized after the manorial system but were directly and efficiently managed as granges by the monks. Cistercian agricultural practices contributed significantly to European civilization, not only in bringing new land under cultivation — the constitution specified that monasteries be erected in remote, desolate places — but especially in cattle breeding and sheep raising. Cistercian simplicity in architecture also influenced the early development of the Gothic style.

St. Bernard of Clairvaux. The expansion of Citeaux is inseparably linked with the personage of St. Bernard, just as Bernard is linked with every aspect of European history in his day. Bernard was a Burgundian aristocrat, born in 1090, well educated, and early resolved to become a monk. When he decided to enter Citeaux he persuaded thirty others, including his uncles and almost all his brothers, to accompany him. In 1115 at the age of twenty-five he became abbot of the new foundation at Clairvaux which, before Bernard's death in 1153, comprised 700 monks and sixty-five daughter houses. Bernard was a great mystic in the true sense of the word. His widely read sermons on the *Canticle of Canticles* and his extensive correspondence are as much responsible for his influence as his political activity.

Although always a monk at heart, Bernard was summoned again and again into the arena of the active life. In Church councils he strove for reform. He exposed the heresy of Abelard and Arnold of Brescia. Abbot Suger of St. Denis became one of the outstanding French prelates under Bernard's spiritual direction. When the papal schism of 1130 threatened the peace of the Church, Bernard persuaded the kings of England, France, and the Empire to accept Innocent II. Pope Eugene III (1145–1153) was Bernard's protégé; the abbot wrote a book *On Consideration* warning Eugene of the pitfalls of his office. The second crusade was Bernard's work, at the instance of the pope, and he personally persuaded Louis VII of France and Conrad III of Germany to take the cross. In an age that admired the monastic vocation as the highest of human undertakings, Bernard of Clairvaux was everywhere esteemed as the most perfect representative of that life.

The Papacy After the Concordat of Worms. Papal history in the generation following 1122 recalls to mind the biblical story of the giant with feet of clay. Having triumphed over all the kings of Christendom the popes suddenly discovered that their hold on the city of Rome was none too secure. It was the old problem of the temporal sovereignty obtruding itself again through the growth of new factions striving to lay hold of the papacy for their own advantage, and, in the second place, an insurrection of the Roman people against their temporal ruler.

Rivalry between the aristocratic Frangipani and Pierleoni families threatened to overwhelm the papacy on the death of Pope Callixtus in 1124. The factions clashed and the Pierleoni triumphed with the elevation of Celestine II, but during the ceremony of installation the Frangipani broke in, tore the papal mantle from Celestine's shoulders and forced him to resign. In terror the cardinals chose Honorius II who, after all of Celestine's adherents had acquiesced, was more canonically elected a few days later. Despite its inauspicious inception, Honorius' six year reign was peaceful. His major triumph occurred in Germany when Henry V died without heirs; the pope's influence helped secure the crown for Lothair of Saxony on the latter's pledge not only to safeguard the Concordat of Worms but even to extend it by renouncing the right of royal presence at elections.

The Schism of 1130. While Honorius lay dying, whatever unanimity existed among the cardinals was sundered by the determination of Cardinal Peter Pierleoni to be the next pope and the equally resolute intention of his enemies of the Frangipani faction to prevent this. A further complication stemmed from the electoral procedure as outlined by Nicholas II in 1059, for it seemed to give cardinal priests and deacons merely a right to consent to an election completed by cardinal bishops. The cardinal priests and deacons insisted that all cardinals should have an equal vote, and in 1130 they were willing to force the issue.

Schism resulted despite attempts to prevent it. Fourteen or fifteen cardinals, including a majority of the cardinal bishops, elected Innocent II, while twenty-four cardinals — two bishops, thirteen priests, and nine deacons — voted for Cardinal Peter who styled himself Anacletus II. Both were consecrated pope on the same day. Through the financial and military resources of his clan Anacletus mastered the city while Innocent fled into France. Anacletus' strength in Italy was not seriously questioned. Typical of the fickle Romans, the Frangipani also joined the Pierleoni as soon as Innocent departed. The Norman vassals of the papacy were won for Anacletus when he permitted Duke Roger to assume the ardently desired title King of Sicily.

At this time the greatest moral force in Europe was Bernard of Clairvaux and it was to him that Innocent II owed his recognition north of the Alps. Assembled at a national council at Étampes, the French hierarchy voted to appoint Bernard sole judge of the disputed papal election and the abbot named Innocent pope. Canonically Bernard might have decided either way but, as Suger of St. Denis reported, Bernard's consideration hinged "upon the character of the person elected rather than on the election itself," and there was no doubt about Innocent's personal superiority over Anacletus.

Henry I of England acknowledged Innocent after a visit from Bernard, who is said to have asked the King: "What are you afraid of? Are you afraid of sinning by obeying Innocent? Just think of how many other sins you have to answer to God for, and leave this one to me." Although St. Norbert had already helped Lothair of Germany to make up his mind, that king and Innocent met for a formal submission. At the last instant Lothair tried to bargain: for his support he suggested that Innocent abrogate the Concordat. Again St. Bernard came to the rescue. "The holy abbot opposed himself like a wall and boldly resisted the king." Lothair meekly withdrew his proposal and promised, as the natural protector of the pope, to escort Innocent to Rome with the royal army.

The Second Lateran Council. Despite Bernard's indefatigable campaigning and Lothair's military aid, it was not until Anacletus' death in 1138 that Innocent succeeded in establishing himself in the Lateran. To clear up problems raised by the schism and to put the Church back on the track of reform, Innocent convoked the tenth ecumenical Council in 1139. Almost all its thirty canons reproduced decrees of earlier synods; they concerned simony, clerical marriage, excommunication, the Peace and Truce of God, and a condemnation of usury. The Council also excommunicated Roger of Sicily who still refused to recognize Innocent II lest he lose his royal title. Ecclesiastical censures failing, Innocent went to war against Roger but the papal force suffered defeat and Innocent fell into Roger's hands. The pope remained a prisoner until he lifted the excommunication and confirmed Roger's royal title.

The Revolutionary Roman Republic. Eugene III (1145–1153), formerly a monk of Clairvaux (during his pontificate men said that St. Bernard pulled the strings in Rome), and Hadrian IV (1154–1159), the only English pope, displayed courage and sound judgment but new temporal problems arose to impede their spiritual programs. Already by mid-eleventh century Italy was fast becoming a land of city states. The Investiture Controversy had weakened the hold of the emperor on northern Italy, and the revival of trade and commerce, one of the most potent factors in European history at this time, transformed the Lombard towns into wealthy, self-confident, republican city states. In the process most Lombard bishops lost their temporal authority.

Rome occupied a unique position in the middle ages. It was a poor, unhealthy city which derived its prestige and its livelihood solely from the fact that it was the capital of the Church. Yet Rome subsisted amid the decay of a more splendid day. Periodically in Italian history there have arisen demagogues who agitate the Romans by appealing to their sense of history and provoking an ephemeral desire for a renewal of the ancient glory. This motive combined with the communal spirit seeping down from Lombardy to produce the revolution of 1143. In the last weeks of Innocent II the Romans rose in revolt, repudiated the papal temporal rule and organized a Republic. Three factors however complicated Roman aspirations for independence: their ruler was not only bishop but also pope, the interests of the emperor, and the total absence of a middle class of merchants and artisans such as the Lombard communes depended on as the solid foundation for republican government.

For twelve years, 1143–1155, the Republic lasted. Pope Lucius II attacked the rebels unsuccessfully, while Eugene III found himself too busy with the second crusade to pay much attention to Rome. Meanwhile the Republic attracted the services of Arnold of Brescia, a talented priest and friend of Abelard who had fallen into heresy from excessive zeal for reform. Tracing all the evils afflicting the Church to clerical greed, Arnold insisted on the abolition of all temporal rights of the Church, including the surrender of the temporal power of the popes.

Arnold remained the most prominent man in Rome for some eight years before Pope Adrian IV and Frederick Barbarossa brought down the Republic. In reprisal for an assault on a cardinal in Rome and for the Romans' refusal to recognize him as pope, Adrian placed an interdict on the city, forbidding all church services of any kind until Arnold was expelled. The interdict produced the desired effect. At this point Emperor Frederick appeared, and by his help the heretic republican was captured and executed. Papal temporal authority was re-established, but the Romans never lost their taste for self-government.

The Twelfth-Century Renaissance.   Three features characterized the burst of intellectual activity in the late eleventh and early twelfth century which historians have named the Renaissance of the Twelfth Century: the growth of institutions within which learning could flourish, the rediscovery of Aristotelian logic as the guide to the new learning, and the creation of a new technique for systematic study.

Between the Carolingian period and the rise of universities shortly after 1200, education was carried on in monastic and cathedral schools. Great monasteries such as St. Gall, Reichenau, Bobbio, Fleury, and Bec taught their own novices as well as oblates. But the rurally situated monasteries and the tendency, as exemplified in the Cistercians, to exclude all but their own members, caused the eclipse of the monastic by the cathedral schools during the twelfth century. Every cathedral was supposed to maintain facilities for education. The *magister scholarum,* later called chancellor, ranked after the bishop and the dean among cathedral dignitaries and retained control of education within the diocese throughout the middle ages. Chartres above all, but also Cologne, Laon, and Paris had outstanding episcopal schools.

The revival of philosophy, the study of Aristotle's logic and the application of a new method of reasoning to the study of revealed truths revolutionized the study of theology and eventually almost displaced the long prevailing Augustinian, i.e., Platonic, cast to theological speculation. Here too the age of St. Bernard marked the preliminary stages of a process that was not completed until the thirteenth century.

Progress of Theology. Lanfranc (d. 1089), a Lombard, later archbishop of Canterbury, was the first in the long line of eminent theologians of the high middle ages, but both in content and in method his work remained traditional. St. Anselm (d. 1109), another Lombard who also became primate of England, first opened up new vistas and is usually conceded the title "founder of scholasticism." Anselm, like all medieval thinkers who were both philosophers and theologians, investigated the relationship between the two sciences just as the Alexandrian scholars had done long before, and he came to the same conclusion as they, namely that there could be no conflict between revealed truth and truth discovered through rational speculation. *Why God Became Man,* the first formal treatise on the Redemption, and his famous proof of the existence of God based on the possibility of conceiving a being than whom there is no greater, are Anselm's significant accomplishments. Anselm also inaugurated the controversy concerning the reality of universal concepts in his refutation of Roscelin whose nominalism led to a heretical interpretation of the Trinity.

Abelard (d. 1142), a stormy petrel throughout his life, undertook to compress all theology into a brief compendium, an *Introduction to Theology,* a favorite occupation of subsequent scholastics. But Abelard is remembered for two other reasons, his methodology and his clash with Bernard of Clairvaux. *Yes and No* was the provocative title Abelard gave to his novel collection of arguments pro and con from the Fathers of the Church on 150 theological propositions. By this pedagogical technique Abelard proposed to indicate the need for a rational approach to theology rather than mere dependence on authority as the source of belief. His opponents charged him with fostering disbelief instead.

Along with many of his contemporaries who were also sailing uncharted waters, Abelard struck a reef occasionally and ran into serious trouble. His errors on the Trinity, the Incarnation, and original sin brought him into conflict with St. Bernard, the defender of the Faith, and led to Abelard's condemnation as a heretic at the Council of Sens (1140). Gilbert of la Porrée (d. 1154), bishop of Poitiers, was another whose errors merited the saintly abbot's censure. Bernard typified the conservative wing among the Church's thinkers who feared the new science and condemned it because of its mistakes without really understanding what it was all about. Gilbert refused to argue with Bernard unless the abbot first studied logic, while Bernard himself declined to debate with Abelard, whom he insisted the bishops should condemn without argumentation.

The outstanding systematizer and one of the very important theologians of the early twelfth century, Peter Lombard (d. 1164), bishop of Paris, showed little originality in his *Four Books of Sentences*. The work consisted of an orderly classification of patristic and conciliar texts on all points of doctrine, along with the opinions of all his contemporaries. While giving first place to the argument from tradition, Peter admitted dialectic as a means of reconciling or criticizing contradictory opinions. Thus Peter carried Abelard's method a step further, attempting to solve rather than merely present conflicts among the authorities. The conciseness and clarity of the book and the plethora of carefully chosen excerpts suited the needs of the schools so well that the *Sentences* became the leading theological textbook for centuries.

Canon Law. Corresponding to the advance of theological studies was the progress of canon law. The newly won pre-eminence of the Church demanded a solid legal basis lest the Church's position be again undermined. A mass of material had accumulated through the decrees of the many councils of the reform period and this required systematic study and organization. About forty collections of canons had been made since the False Decretals and some of them, such as the books of Ives of Chartres and Burchard of Worms, showed distinct progress. But the example of the rediscovered Roman Law and its intensive cultivation at Bologna proved the decisive factor in the emergence of the science of canon law and its differentiation from theology.

Gratian, a Camaldolese monk who taught at Bologna, produced about 1148 the *Decretum* or *Concordance of Discordant Canons,* the book that did for canon law what Peter Lombard's *Sentences* did for theology. It was a systematic arrangement of over a thousand canons with Gratian's comments to reconcile apparent contradictions. Although never more than a private collection the *Decretum* was greeted with enthusiasm and rapidly became the only manual used in teaching and in court practice. Because of its wide usage and apparent acceptance by the popes it came to be considered the first part of the later *Code of Canon Law.*

The Crusades. Although the crusades involved numerous factors besides religion, the religious motive was the mainspring and most important sustaining element in the holy wars against Islam. Essentially the crusades aimed to liberate the Holy Land from the infidel; they were, in effect, pilgrimages in a military guise. Baser motives, intolerance, and deeds of tremendous wickedness sullied the idealism of the venture. Permanent results were far less important religiously than politically, socially, or economically; nevertheless, without the religious ingredient there would have been no crusades.

Since the second quarter of the eleventh century the Christian recovery of Spain and the Mediterranean islands from Moslem hands had been proceeding apace, but no thought had been given to a Christian counter-offensive in Palestine. True, the Byzantine Empire had long been waging war against Islam and the Greeks considered their effort the equivalent of a crusade for the defense of Christendom. But the West had no cause for complaint since pilgrims were permitted to visit Palestine without difficulty provided they purchased a permit, something like a modern visa, from the Arab officials. After 1050, however, the Seljuk Turks took control of the Holy Land and, having recently accepted Islam, manifested all the intolerance of the fanatical convert. The Turks massacred Christian pilgrims and desecrated sacred shrines. Reports of these atrocities and the entreaties of the Byzantine emperors for mercenary soldiers to join their army, decimated by the Turks at Manzikert in 1071, provided the occasion for the Christian attack just at the time of the reorganization of the Church by the Cluniac and Gregorian reforms.

First Crusade. Pope Gregory VII planned a Christian counter-offensive but Urban II actually inaugurated the first crusade with his closing address at the Council of Clermont in 1095. In his famous speech Urban proposed many reasons why European Christians should embark for the Orient, but the basic appeal was to the religious sentiment of the listening throng. A number of favors, temporal and spiritual, were offered to those who would take the cross, among them a plenary indulgence, the first such ever offered. Christ died for men; Christians should not shrink for material considerations from the hardship and danger of the attempt to rescue the places hallowed by His life. The people responded with tremendous enthusiasm. Cries of "God wills it," rang out, thousands pressed forward to take the crusader's vow, and cloth crosses were fastened to their clothing as a sign of their intention. (Crusader means "one signed with the cross.") Popular preachers like Peter the Hermit spread the tidings across Europe.

The success of the first crusade arose largely from the internal divisions among the Moslems. Palestine in 1099 was a no man's land between the warring caliphs of Cairo and Bagdad, hence the crusaders were able to take Jerusalem with a minimum of effort. The Latin Kingdom of Jerusalem was organized with vassal dependencies and a Latin hierarchy was set up alongside the Greek and Monophysite Churches. Latin patriarchates at Jerusalem, with four archbishops and nine bishops, and Antioch, with four archbishops and seven bishops, provided the ecclesiastical framework.

One of the tragedies of the crusades was the crusaders' ignorance of the existence and status of the many eastern Christians formerly under Moslem rule. These people suffered more from their fellow Christians than they had from the infidels. Only one group, the Maronites of Syria, returned to permanent union with Rome. The crusaders also exhibited the usual Latin inability to understand Byzantium in either its politics or its religion. The Byzantine Empire had for centuries been a bulwark protecting Christendom from the Moslems and the Greeks resented the crusaders' ingratitude.

Military Monasticism. Monasticism adapted itself to the cause of the crusades by producing the military orders. These were orders of monks, mostly unordained, and lay brothers obeying the usual vows of poverty, chastity, and obedience, but having as their special purpose the military defense of the Holy Land. Since the Latin Kingdom suffered from a constant shortage of man power, the military orders became the backbone of the Christian army in the East, both in field operations and in garrison duty. As knights they were all noblemen. Recruited all over Europe they attracted eastward a stream of first class fighting men.

The Knights Hospitallers, the earliest foundation, originated before the crusades, about 1023, as a nursing group for the care of pilgrims in Jerusalem. About 1120 they transformed themselves into the Knights of the Hospital of St. John in Jerusalem and became purely military. The Templars were founded by Hugh de Payen, a Burgundian knight; they derived their name from their headquarters near the Temple of Solomon at Jerusalem which they received in 1118. With the collaboration of St. Bernard, Hugh drew up a rule modeled on Cistercian practices. The Templars remained active in medical work, and their red cross on a white field is still used as a symbol of mercy. German Knights established the Order of St. Mary, popularly known as the Teutonic Knights, about 1190; they are famous for their forcible Christianization of the Prussians among whom they were active after 1227. Military orders abounded in Spain also because of the lengthy Moorish wars.

Second and Third Crusades.   In 1144 the County of Edessa, eastern-most of the crusading states, fell to the Turks. When Pope Eugene III learned of the disaster he commissioned St. Bernard to preach a second major crusade. Bernard persuaded Louis VII of France and Conrad III of Germany to lead the hosts whom he encouraged to take the cross, but neither king accomplished anything. The halfhearted siege of Damascus, high point of the crusade, failed completely. Saladin's capture of Jeru-salem in 1187 after practically annihilating the Christians at Hattin evoked the third crusade. Pope Clement III's strenuous labors finally induced Richard I of England and Philip II of France to stop fighting long enough to rescue the Holy City, but even with the initial co-operation of Frederick Barbarossa the third crusade accomplished next to nothing: the recovery of a few coastal cities and a treaty permitting Christians to visit Jerusalem. The days of the Latin Kingdom of Jerusalem seemed numbered.

REVIEW AIDS

1. What are the special features that characterized monasticism in the twelfth century?
2. Briefly summarize the early history and peculiar features of the Canons Regular, Premonstratensians, and Carthusians.
3. Explain the leading features of the Cistercian way of life.
4. Summarize the career of St. Bernard of Clairvaux.
5. Describe the papal schism in 1130.
6. What is the significance of the revolutionary Roman Republic?
7. Explain the significance for Catholic learning of St. Anselm, Abelard, Peter Lombard, and Gratian.
8. In what way are the crusades of concern to the student of Church history?

SUGGESTIONS FOR FURTHER READING

Although concerned chiefly with one country, Dom David Knowles' *The Monastic Order in England*, 2nd ed. (Cambridge: 1949) contains a great deal of information about monasticism in general. Louis J. Lekai, *The White Monks* (Okauchee, Wis.: 1953) is a concise history of the Cistercians. A detailed study of Citeaux and its first four daughter houses is Archdale A. King, *Citeaux and Her Elder Daughters* (London: 1954). Many aspects of Cistercian history are treated in a scholarly fashion by Watkin Williams, *Monastic Studies* (Manchester: 1938). The same author has produced the best English biography of *Saint Bernard of Clairvaux* (Manchester: 1935), but for the spirituality of St. Bernard the student should consult Etienne Gilson, *The Mystical Theology of St. Bernard* (New York: 1940). A thoroughly erudite treatment of developments in the intellectual area is Etienne Gilson, *History of Christian Philosophy in the Middle Ages* (New York: 1955), which supersedes anything of comparable scope. George Greenaway, *Arnold of Brescia* (Cambridge: 1931) discusses the republican revolution and its most prominent figure. H. Daniel-Rops, *Cathedral and Crusade, Studies of the Medieval Church* (London: 1957), covers this period well.

DOCUMENTS

1. St. Bernard of Clairvaux was one of the most influential men of his times, and his opinions carried great weight. The first two selections show the wide range of matters that came under his scrutiny; they also reveal his strong opinions. The first represents St. Bernard's estimation of the Roman people and their rebellion against papal government. It is taken from the *De Consideratione*, IV, ii, Migne, *Patrologia Latina*, Vol. CXXXVII, c. 773.

What shall I say about the people? It is the Roman people. I cannot tell you more briefly nor more specifically what I think of your parishioners. What is as well known to history as the impudence and pride of the Romans? They are a race that is not accustomed to peace but to rioting; a race to this very day wild and unmanageable, not knowing how to obey unless deprived of all power to resist.

2. This excerpt gives Bernard's position on the spiritual and material power of the Church. *Ibid.*, IV, iii, c. 775.

What tempts you again to lay claim to the sword you were once ordered to put back into its scabbard? Yet if anyone denies that that sword is yours, he apparently is not paying enough attention to the word of the Lord when He said, "Put up your sword into the sheath." Therefore it is yours and it may perhaps be unsheathed if you desire but not by your own hand. Otherwise if it did not belong to you at all, when the Apostles said, "Lo, here are two swords," the Lord would not have answered them, "It is enough," but "It is too much." Therefore both the spiritual and the temporal sword belong to the Church; the latter should be used on behalf of the Church, the former by the Church; the former by the priest, the latter by the soldier but with the consent of the priest and at the emperor's order.

3. Fundamentally the crusades were a religious undertaking; however, other motives entered in from the very beginning. Even Pope Urban II at the Council of Clermont in 1095, when he initiated the crusading movement, offered nonreligious inducements to persuade Europe to take up the cross. This is the version of Urban's speech as given by Robert the Monk, translated in *Translations and Reprints from the Original Sources of European History*, published by the Department of History of the University of Pennsylvania, Vol. I, No. 2, pp. 6–7.

But if you are hindered by love of children, parents and wives, remember what the Lord says in the Gospel, "He that loveth father or mother more than me, is not worthy of me." "Every one that hath forsaken houses, or brethren, or sisters, or father, or mother, or wife, or children, or lands for my name's sake shall receive an hundred-fold and shall inherit everlasting life." Let none of your possessions detain you, no solicitude for your family affairs, since this land which you inhabit, shut in on all sides by the seas and surrounded by the mountain peaks, is too narrow for your large population; nor does it abound in wealth; and it furnishes scarcely food enough for its cultivators. Hence it is that you murder and devour one another, that you wage war, and that frequently you perish by mutual wounds. Let therefore hatred depart from among you, let your quarrels end, let wars cease, and let all dissensions and controversies slumber. Enter upon the road to the Holy Sepulchre; wrest that land from the wicked race, and subject it to yourselves. That land which as the Scripture says "floweth with milk and honey," was given by God into the possession of the children of Israel.

Jerusalem is the navel of the world; the land is fruitful above others, like another paradise of delights. This the Redeemer of the human race has made illustrious by His advent, has beautified by residence, has consecrated by suffering, has redeemed by death, has glorified by burial. This royal city, therefore, situated at the centre of the world, is now held captive by His enemies, and is in subjection to those who do not know God, to the worship of the heathens. She seeks therefore and desires to be liberated, and does not cease to implore you to come to her aid. From you especially she asks succor, because, as we have already said, God has conferred upon you above all nations great glory in arms. Accordingly undertake this journey for the remission of your sins, with the assurance of the imperishable glory of the kingdom of heaven.

Chapter 14

CHURCH AND STATE IN THE
HIGH MIDDLE AGES

THE concordats closing the Investiture Controversy marked a compromise rather than the definitive end of the disputes between Church and State, or *sacerdotium* and *regnum* to give them their medieval designations. The two powers were too closely entangled to avoid continuous friction, and the clashes between them are among the most spectacular events of the high middle ages. Thanks to the efforts of Gregory VII and the moral regeneration of Europe expressed in the new monasticism the papacy now felt strong enough to assert unhesitatingly what it considered to be the Church's prerogatives. Moreover, Gratian's *Decretum* and the canon lawyers it nourished established the Church's position with a precision and clarity lacking to its secular opposition. Although in every instance the conflicts sprang from specific issues, the question of theoretical relationships was always simultaneously raised and this lent an air of bitterness that made it practically impossible to attain mutually satisfactory solutions.

The Ideological Basis. During the Investiture Controversy many writers had re-examined the matter of Church-State relationships, and their thinking developed along divergent lines. The papalists stressed increasingly the moral superiority of the spiritual over the temporal power and translated this into a more active papal jurisdiction over secular monarchs, often through appeal to the Donation of Constantine. The imperialists countered with the assertion that temporal power also derived from God and therefore in the exercise of their own duties kings were responsible to God through no earthly intermediary. Nothing, they insisted, justified Gregory VII's attempt to depose Henry IV.

The progress of political-ecclesiastical thought appears in the metaphor of the two swords, very commonly used after St. Bernard of Clairvaux popularized it in his *On Consideration*. Bernard insisted that both material and spiritual power belonged to the Church, the latter directly, the former at least indirectly. John of Salisbury held the same view in his *Policraticus*. Translated into feudal terminology this theory led the popes to attempt to reach a position of feudal overlordship over the princes of Europe, and on this issue occurred the first of many clashes between the popes and the Hohenstaufen emperors.

Hohenstaufen Aspirations.   Although Frederick I Barbarossa (1152–1190) embodied the ideals of Germanic feudal society, he nevertheless cherished Roman traditions and was supremely conscious of his imperial office. The use of the adjective "holy" to describe his empire and the canonization of Charlemagne by one of his antipopes reveal Barbarossa's exalted estimate of his dignity. He desired nothing less than the restoration of the ancient Roman Empire within its Christian framework.

The disparity between Frederick I's actual authority and his aspirations was particularly obvious in regard to Lombardy which the Investiture Controversy had wrenched from German control. Furthermore, Barbarossa felt that the Eternal City, too, should acknowledge the jurisdiction of its emperors as should the Norman kingdom, the third political unit of the Italian peninsula. Thus Barbarossa's romantic dreams lured him into fatal Italian ventures and precipitated a headlong struggle with the papacy, for under the circumstances the realization of Barbarossa's schemes would have entailed the subjection of the spiritual as well as temporal power of the papacy. His highhanded treatment of the bishoprics of Germany presaged the fate of the popes if they fell under Barbarossa's domination, since his principles of government were taken from the absolutism of the Justinian Code. Hence, even though the long conflicts between the popes and the Hohenstaufen dynasty often appear on the surface to be a struggle mainly for temporal dominions, at their roots lay the question of the subjugation or independence of the popes in the spiritual as well as temporal area, since the two were interdependent.

Barbarossa and Adrian IV.   Initial contacts between Frederick and Pope Adrian IV (1154–1159) were friendly, since each required the other's services: the king could be crowned emperor only by the pope, and Adrian was threatened by the rebellious Roman Republic and the Normans in the south. Furthermore, the Greek Emperor, Manuel Comnenus, was preparing to invade Italy to the detriment of all concerned. By the

Treaty of Constance in 1153 Barbarossa and Adrian exchanged vows of friendship. Nevertheless their first meeting three years later was not without incident, for Barbarossa refused to perform the customary ceremony of holding the pope's stirrup and took umbrage at a painting in Rome that implied that the emperor was the pope's vassal. However Adrian crowned him and Frederick in turn suppressed the Roman Republic.

In 1156 Adrian concluded a treaty with King William I of Sicily who acknowledged his feudal dependence on the pope and freed the Church in southern Italy from a number of vexatious restrictions. Barbarossa complained of this as a violation of the Treaty of Constance and of his own alleged imperial rights in southern Italy. Adrian denied the emperor's charges and sent legates to the Diet at Besançon in 1157 to protest an attack by German knights on the Archbishop of Lund who was taken prisoner while returning to Sweden through Germany from a visit to Rome. Cardinal Roland Bandinelli read the pope's message which, after a reference to Adrian's bestowal of the imperial crown, stated that "we would be glad to confer even greater benefits (*beneficia*) on you if that were possible." When the emperor's minister translated the word *beneficia* he rendered it by its technical meaning "fief" rather than by the general sense of the word. Immediately a protest was made that the empire was not a fief from the pope, to which Cardinal Roland replied: "From whom then does the emperor hold the empire if not from the pope?" But for the emperor's intervention the duke of Bavaria would have slain the cardinal on the spot, and the diet ended in confusion. After an exchange of acrimonious letters Adrian finally calmed the storm by explaining that the unobjectionable classical sense of the troublesome word had been intended.

The Lombard towns, the States of the Church, and the Norman Kingdom comprised the three divisions of Italy whose conquest was envisaged by Barbarossa. In 1158 the emperor crossed the Alps in strength to impose his will on the Lombards. At a great diet at Roncaglia he attacked their independence as mere usurpation and asserted his own claims in the words of the code of Justinian: "The emperor's will is the law." Whatever opposition showed itself was quickly crushed. The temporal rights of the papacy were evidently in danger but Adrian's death postponed the impending crisis.

Alexander III and the Schism.   Two parties existed among the cardinals on the issue of co-operation or resistance to Barbarossa. The anti-imperial majority proclaimed Cardinal Roland, an eminent canonist and the emperor's adversary at Besançon, as Alexander III (1159–1181), while a minority of three chose Cardinal Octavian as Victor IV. Riots in Rome made the city unsafe for either candidate, and Victor took refuge with the emperor. Frederick shrewdly withheld his own decision. Proclaiming his right as emperor to summon general councils, he called an ecclesiastical assembly to Pavia in 1160, but few prelates except his own vassals attended. Alexander denied this Council's competence but Victor submitted his case and won recognition. With a few significant exceptions the German bishops followed Victor and Emperor Frederick into schism.

After excommunicating the emperor and the antipope Alexander fled by sea to France. Although Henry II of England and Louis VII of France acknowledged Alexander, the pope was hard pressed to prevent their extorting concessions in return. The zealous support of the Carthusians and Cistercians did much to insure Alexander III's success, but it was the resistance of the Italian cities, encouraged by Alexander, that turned the tide. In 1167 Barbarossa conquered Rome and installed Paschal III, his latest antipope, in St. Peter's, but a terrible plague ravaged his army and carried off thousands of the German troops. Frederick hastened back to Germany while the Italians rejoiced at this "divine intervention." To concert their resistance the cities organized the Lombard League and espoused the cause of Alexander III. When Frederick returned on his fifth Italian expedition in 1176 the League's army inflicted a decisive defeat on the Germans at the battle of Legnano.

No choice remained to the emperor but to make peace. Preliminary terms were worked out with the pope at Anagni and then incorporated into the general Peace of Venice in 1177 and the definitive Peace of Constance in 1183. Frederick gave up his seventeen-year-old schism, promised to restore all papal temporal rights in the States of the Church and in other disputed territory, and agreed to protect the Church in every respect.

The English Imbroglio. While Alexander III resisted Frederick Barbarossa, the archbishop of Canterbury, St. Thomas Becket, crossed swords with King Henry II of England. The foremost of the many issues involved was the immunity of the clergy from the jurisdiction of secular courts, what medieval men called "benefit of clergy."

During the anarchy of King Stephen's reign (1135–1154) the customs that had isolated the English Church from outside influences had almost entirely disappeared and English prelates enjoyed as much freedom from royal control as any continental bishop. When Henry II (1154–1189) ascended the throne he proposed to re-establish the monarchy by re-claiming lapsed prerogatives, including control of the Church, through a return to the situation that had prevailed in St. Anselm's time. In addition, Henry II's interest in legal matters brought him to consider the possibility that his subjects might escape condign punishment for breaches of the law by virtue of being in ecclesiastical orders. Such offenders were judiciable only in ecclesiastical courts which inflicted less severe penalties than secular courts. To the king's suggestion that clergy, examined and degraded by episcopal courts if guilty, be turned over to royal judges for punishment, the archbishop of Canterbury replied that double punishment for a single offense was prohibited by canon law. The Constitutions of Clarendon (1164) in sixteen articles embodied Henry II's ecclesiastical policies, including his view concerning criminous clerks, and almost all English prelates except the archbishop accepted them.

St. Thomas of Canterbury. The critical element in the English situation was the character of Becket. Having served the king as a devoted, somewhat worldly chancellor, Becket was rewarded with the archbishopric by Henry II who hoped to further his ecclesiastical policies through a thoroughly pliable primate. But Becket quickly revealed a new facet of his personality by becoming a rigid ascetic as completely dedicated to defending the liberties of the Church as he had formerly been to extending the power of the crown. After wavering indecisively at first, Becket adamantly opposed the Constitutions of Clarendon. So bitter were his relations with Henry that Thomas fled to safety in France. Pope Alexander III hesitated to intervene for fear of driving the king into the camp of the emperor's antipope; besides, the canonical aspects of the issue were not wholly clear. In 1170 the archbishop and the king were personally reconciled but as soon as Becket returned he began punishing bishops who had taken Henry II's side. In a rage the king expressed a desire to be rid of the archbishop. Four knights of the royal household took him at his word and murdered Becket in his cathedral.

Public opinion regarded St. Thomas as a martyr and his tomb soon became the most popular shrine in England. Becket's murder entirely upset the king's program. Henry hastened to exonerate himself with Pope Alexander but the king had to promise to allow appeals from England to the papal court, to cease encroachments on the rights of the Church, and to relinquish claim to jurisdiction over criminous clerks. Henry also swore to go on crusade as penance.

Italy After the Peace of Constance. In Italy again Barbarossa salvaged what he could of his schemes and found that the Lombard victory left him still firmly entrenched in Italy. Across the north central section of the peninsula stretched a tier of lands, Tuscany, Romagna, Ancona, and Spoleto, whose ownership was in dispute with the papacy but which the settlement at Constance left temporarily in the emperor's hands. Frederick's master stroke, however, was the betrothal of his son Henry to the heiress of the Norman kingdom, Constance, aunt of the reigning William II. The marriage was celebrated in 1186, and four years later Henry VI laid claim to both Empire and Kingdom.

Too late the popes — five aged, politically incapable pontiffs ruled after the unusually long reign of Alexander III — awoke to the danger of encirclement by the Hohenstaufen. Henry VI (1190–1197), an unscrupulous, ambitious and very shrewd emperor, threatened the papacy more seriously than anyone since Henry IV. He refused point-blank to render homage to the pope for the Norman Kingdom, he held one half of Italy and all Germany tightly in his grasp, and his diplomatic ventures reached from Westminster to Constantinople. When he imprisoned Richard the Lionhearted, a crusader under the Church's special protection, the pope did not even dare protest. But death struck Henry VI at the age of thirty-two and three unexpected events completely changed the Italian scene: a nationalistic Italian uprising against the Germans, a disputed election to the Empire, and the accession of the most powerful pope of the entire middle ages.

Pope Innocent III. Because he was able to express in actual deeds the moral ascendancy of the papacy which his predecessors had laboriously formulated in words and theories, Innocent III (1198–1216) is usually called the greatest medieval pope. In both temporal and spiritual matters Innocent's will prevailed over Europe more completely than any pope before or after him, as much because of the force of his own personality and ideals as from the fortuitous circumstances of his reign. Four kingdoms acknowledged him as feudal suzerain: Sicily, Aragon, Portugal, and England. Spiritual motives guided Innocent's every act but as a capable politician he did not shrink from the mundane means required to attain religious goals. Nor did he permit his means to obscure the noble ends for which he struggled. Problems of every sort beset him constantly yet he managed to make the papacy the international arbiter of European affairs.

Trained in theology at Paris and in law at Bologna, Innocent III was pre-eminently a canonist rather than a theologian. Church-State relations he described by analogy with the sun and moon: "As the moon receives its light from the sun and is inferior to the sun, . . . so the royal power derives its splendor and dignity from the spiritual authority." "No king can rule justly unless he devoutly serves Christ's vicar."

The Disputed German Election. At Rome both the prefect and the leading senator of the city held office from Innocent, although it took ten years to quell all factional opposition. Revolts against the German dukes such as adventuresome Markward von Anweiler whom Henry VI had established in central Italy enabled Innocent to reclaim these lands for the States of the Church and place them under responsible officials.

The most direct menace to the Church's independence, German encirclement, subsided with Henry VI's death, since the hereditary part of his dominions, the Norman lands, passed to his three-year-old son Frederick, while a double election to the imperial dignity occupied the Germans. Young Frederick's mother died in 1198 leaving the orphan Innocent's ward, and Frederick could not have found a more tenacious defender of the authority of the Sicilian monarchy. Although there was some sentiment in Germany for recognizing Frederick as his father's heir, this did not come about. Instead some of the princes elected Philip of Swabia, Frederick's uncle, while others chose Otto of Brunswick, head of the anti-Hohenstaufen Guelf family. Both announced their election to Innocent and requested his approbation.

For three years Innocent postponed taking sides but finally in 1201 he declared against Philip, who was nevertheless personally more suitable than Otto and was supported by the better and more numerous German princes. Three considerations, Innocent declared, influenced his decision: (1) Philip had been under sentence of excommunication at the time of his election, (2) the impression must be avoided that the Empire is a hereditary dignity, (3) Philip is "a persecutor and a scion of a race of persecutors." When Otto promised to concede everything Innocent desired in central Italy, there was hardly any doubt whom the pope would support.

Opposition to Innocent's Intervention. Few German princes beyond Otto's small circle admitted the pope's right to a voice in the election. They contended that the choice of the emperor-elect was their own affair entirely; the fact that their candidate had to receive the imperial crown from the pope did not subject his election to the possibility of a papal veto. Innocent countered with the assertion that Pope Leo III's action of freely bestowing the crown on Charlemagne left with Leo's successors the privilege and obligation of judging both the character and the legal right of the princes' choice before granting or withholding the imperial title.

Innocent now threw all his energy into the struggle but papal legates, letters of admonition, even excommunications availed little against the superior resources of the Hohenstaufen candidate. By 1206 it was apparent that Philip's cause would triumph, so Innocent opened negotiations with him and was on the point of recognizing him when Philip was assassinated in 1208. Immediately Innocent's flexible diplomacy switched back to Otto whom the Germans, exhausted by the civil war, now unanimously accepted.

In 1209 Otto came to Rome for his coronation but as soon as this was completed he treacherously forgot all his oft-repeated promises and adopted the traditional Hohenstaufen policy of German consolidation in central Italy. When Otto headed southward in 1210 to annex Sicily Innocent excommunicated him and took steps to bring about his deposition. Innocent proposed that the princes elect the only likely candidate, his former ward Frederick, king of Sicily. The princes agreed and the young man snatched at the proffered crown. On his northward journey Frederick visited Rome to assure Innocent that, once established in Germany, he would renounce his Sicilian title in favor of his infant son and thus preclude the dreaded encirclement of the Patrimony. After the decisive battle of Bouvines in 1214 Frederick II's position was secure.

Innocent III and the National Kings: France.   Innocent III clashed with the kings of France and England also. With Philip II of France (1180–1223) it was a question of the enforcement of the Church's marriage laws. The king had married Princess Ingeborg of Denmark in 1193 and repudiated her the day after the wedding. French bishops annulled the marriage on grounds of a very distant affinity. Ingeborg appealed in vain to Pope Celestine III but Innocent III lost no time in championing her cause. He denounced the action of the French bishops and ordered Philip to set aside Agnes of Meran, whom he had meanwhile married, and take back Ingeborg. When the king refused Innocent placed France under interdict for six months during 1200. Complicating the issue was an attempted mediation by Innocent of a French-English war; Philip insisted that the pope's intervention had not been asked and his decision would not be accepted. At length Philip broke off his relationship with Agnes but it was thirteen years before he restored Ingeborg to her rights as wife and queen.

King John of England. The death of Archbishop Hubert Walter of Canterbury in 1205 set the stage for Innocent III's dispute with King John of England (1199–1216). John wanted to nominate a successor, the suffragans of Canterbury insisted on their right to vote, and the monks of the cathedral chapter thought that the election belonged to them alone. While the bishops dispatched a messenger to argue their case before the pope, the monks proceeded to elect their subprior Reginald and sent him to Rome for confirmation. As soon as John learned that his prerogatives had been ignored he rushed to Canterbury and forced the monks to elect his nominee, John de Grey. A third delegation representing the king set out for Rome. Innocent III requested delegates of the chapter to come also and then he rejected both Reginald and John. At Innocent's suggestion the Canterbury canons then in Rome elected a learned English cardinal, Stephen Langton, whom the pope promptly confirmed. John rejected Stephen and the battle began.

In 1208 Innocent placed England under interdict, hoping to goad John's subjects to rebellion by denying them the sacraments. The king confiscated Church property in retaliation. Next Innocent excommunicated the king, but John seized children of powerful noble families as hostages against revolt and, to set an example, crushed to death a clerk who complied with the excommunication by quitting the king's service. Finally in 1212 Innocent declared John deposed by releasing all Englishmen from their oath of allegiance and commissioned Philip of France to attack his old enemy. With discontent rife in England and a French expeditionary force preparing to cross the Channel John capitulated. He accepted Langton, agreed to compensate the Church for its confiscated revenues (almost 100,000 pounds sterling), issued a charter of liberties for the English Church, and surrendered his kingdom to the pope to receive it back as a fief and hold it thenceforth on condition of an annual tribute.

John's humiliation could hardly have been more complete but he now enjoyed Innocent III's support when his barons revolted and forced him to sign the Magna Charta. Innocent annulled the charter because it was extorted by force and censured the barons, including Stephen Langton who had joined the rebels. When the French invaded England, partly in response to the pope's earlier mandate, the pope threatened to excommunicate them and helped save the throne for John's infant son.

Honorius III and Frederick II. It is one of the ironies of history that Pope Innocent III's own protégé turned out to be such a bitter foe of the Church. That Frederick II was marvelously talented cannot be denied but as a ruler he was a forerunner of the despots of the Renaissance, autocratic, unscrupulous, faithless, cruel, and morally a libertine. Whether or not he was a heretic or freethinker as popular rumor alleged, Frederick had much less than the customary medieval respect for the Church, especially when political issues were involved. His absolutism and the fatal Hohenstaufen chimera of a united Italy menaced the Church's freedom and the existence of the Papal State. Caesaro-papism underlay his idea of the position of the Church in society.

Three flaws in his armor left Frederick II vulnerable in his relations with the papacy: (1) his solemn engagement to Innocent III and to Honorius III not to unite both Sicily and the Empire under his own rule; (2) the crusader's vow which he made publicly and voluntarily in 1215 on the occasion of his coronation as king; (3) the feudal suzerainty of the pope over the Norman kingdom which put Frederick legally in the wrong in most of his direct conflicts with the popes.

Honorius III (1216–1227), Gregory IX (1227–1241), and Innocent IV (1243–1254) were the popes who had to deal with Frederick II. Honorius had been one of his tutors and was moreover personally a mild man willing to concede much for the sake of peace. Honorius reluctantly permitted Frederick to change the original scheme of partitioning his two realms by assigning Germany to his young son while he himself governed the Norman Kingdom and retained the imperial title. To secure the support of the powerful ecclesiastical lords of Germany Frederick in 1220 granted them by the document called the Alliance with the Ecclesiastical Princes wide immunities from royal control and almost complete jurisdiction within their own fiefs. This charter marked a significant advance toward the territorial sovereignty of the bishops and abbots and the creation of those ecclesiastical principalities in Germany which lasted until the time of Napoleon.

In regard to Frederick's crusading vow Honorius insisted time after time that the emperor depart for the Holy Land or for Egypt where the fifth crusade was vainly awaiting his arrival. After setting a date for departure some half a dozen times and then always excusing himself at the last minute, Frederick finally agreed with the pope that he would depart in 1227 or suffer automatic excommunication. Honorius mediated the emperor's Lombard war lest this impede his crusade. Early in September of the appointed year Frederick embarked, only to return three days later because of an illness, whether real or feigned no one knows. Gregory IX, pope since March, promptly announced the emperor's excommunication to all the princes and bishops of Christendom.

Frederick II's Wars With the Papacy. Gregory IX, a nephew of Innocent III, differed radically from his long-suffering predecessor. He was a man of wide experience as a canonist, impatiently ready to have recourse to the sword, irritable and uncompromising. When Frederick II went to Palestine in 1228 in spite of his excommunication Gregory renewed his sentence and worked to ruin his efforts in the Holy Land. Frederick's officials struck back by an invasion of the Papal State, to which Gregory replied by dispatching a papal army under John de Brienne into the Kingdom. As soon as the emperor returned in 1229 the pope's forces retreated in a rout and the emperor advanced toward Rome. When Gregory could find no allies to pull his chestnuts out of the fire he had to make peace. Yet in the Treaty of San Germano it was Frederick who yielded on every point, promising to allow free ecclesiastical elections, to compensate all whom he had punished for siding with the pope and to grant a general amnesty. Gregory lifted the excommunication.

For nine years after San Germano a semblance of peace prevailed in papal-imperial relations but actually it was a period of considerable friction. Frederick did not fulfill all the terms of the treaty, he imposed new taxes on the clergy, robbed churches of their endowments, held bishoprics vacant to collect their revenues, and obstructed the work of papal legates. The city of Rome seethed with discontent and Gregory suspected the emperor of fomenting revolt against him.

On the other hand, Gregory IX assisted the Lombard League after the opening of Frederick's new campaign against them in 1236. Frederick could not forget the Hohenstaufen will-o'-the-wisp of a united Italy. When he published a statement of his claims against the Lombards and the papacy, Gregory fired back a strongly worded assertion of independence and supremacy of the pope over the emperor. Gregory realized full well the fate of the Church if Frederick succeeded, and the slaughter of the Lombard army at Cortenuova in 1237 seemed to forecast a quick imperial triumph. When Frederick laid claim to Sardinia, which the popes considered a part of the States of the Church, Gregory excommunicated him anew (March, 1239) and placed under interdict every place in which he should stay. The papal legate in Germany, Albert of Behaim, was instructed to preach rebellion and excommunication of all Hohenstaufen partisans, orders which Albert dared not obey since many bishops remained loyal to Frederick.

In 1240 Frederick marched on Rome where Gregory IX was again insecurely established but the citizens this time defended the pope. Gregory decided to summon a general council to rally the lukewarm support of the whole Church. Frederick warned the pope and the bishops not to come into Italy while war was raging. He blocked the Alpine passes and closed the highways but the city of Genoa offered to transport the prelates by sea. The emperor's fleet, under the command of his natural son Enzio, captured the Genoese ships and took prisoner three cardinals and over 100 bishops. With the emperor advancing on Rome a second time Pope Gregory IX breathed his last.

First General Council of Lyons.   After the fifteen day reign of Pope Celestine IV the cardinals scattered. They were divided among themselves and deadlocked for twenty months over the choice of a new pope. Not until Frederick II released his three cardinal prisoners at the urging of Louis IX of France was the election of Innocent IV completed. Innocent IV was a lawyer politician, adamant, unscrupulous in his use of spiritual power for political ends, and convinced of the absolute supremacy of the Church and its right of direct intervention in secular affairs — precisely the man to curb the ambitions of Frederick II. With the Romans wavering and some members of the Sacred College in opposition, Innocent fled into Gaul. To Lyons, the papal residence for six years, a free imperial city comfortably close to the friendly protection of Louis IX of France, Innocent summoned a general council in June, 1245.

The thirteenth ecumenical council, attended by about 225 bishops, had for its primary purpose the consideration of papal charges against the emperor. When Frederick made a feint at marching on Lyons Louis IX frightened him off. Thaddeus of Suessa, Frederick II's envoy, frantically tried to prevent action but, on the basis of charges of perjury, sacrilege, violation of the rights of clergy and laity, and suspicion of heresy, the Council voted to depose the emperor. Innocent's ringing bull of excommunication and deposition called on the German princes to elect a successor. The war against Frederick was declared a crusade, all who enlisted receiving the indulgences of a pilgrimage to the Holy Land.

Papal Triumph.   By 1250 Frederick II was dead and Germany and Italy on the verge of chaos. But the Holy War continued because Innocent

IV had sworn to exterminate the whole "viper breed of the Hohenstaufen" and Frederick's sons Conrad and Manfred, and his grandson Conradin had one by one to be destroyed. Last to fall was Conradin, a promising youth of sixteen, captured and then beheaded after the massacre of his army at Tagliacozzo in 1268. New rulers suitable to the papacy had to be found for Empire and Kingdom. A succession of foreign phantom kings paraded about Germany until the promotion of Rudolph of Hapsburg in 1273 at Pope Gregory X's insistence, while the Norman kingdom finally devolved upon Louis IX's brother, Charles of Anjou. By this time Innocent IV was long since in his grave, Alexander IV (1254–1261), Urban IV (1261–1264), Clement IV (1265–1268), and Gregory X (1271–1276) put the finishing touches to his projects.

Conclusions. The grim struggle of the papacy against the Hohenstaufen emperors and the lesser conflicts with national kings were waged to secure medieval standards of freedom for the Church. They represented simply a further stage in the long process of emancipation from secular domination. Had the Hohenstaufens succeeded the papacy would have been reduced to the degraded position of the patriarch of Constantinople.

Unfortunately too much energy had to be expended on this negative task. Often the Church's leaders appear in an unfavorable light — as mere politicians, ambitious, merciless, perverters of spiritual powers to secular ends. The constant tendency to assert the supremacy of the *sacerdotium* over the *regnum* or *imperium* obscured the real causes of conflict and often offended medieval as well as modern opinion. Even St. Louis IX of France denied Innocent IV's right to depose Frederick II and refused aid in what he regarded as papal secular politics. Pressed for funds to wage their wars the popes resorted to dubious financial expedients which, especially in England, produced violent anti-papal demonstrations. Papal overlordship of England and the annual tribute were needless sources of irritation even though the ideals which motivated Innocent III were noble ones. In short, in achieving their greatest apparent triumphs the popes were also paving the road to decline.

REVIEW AIDS

1. Discuss medieval concepts of the relations between Church and State.
2. What political aim of Frederick I brought him into conflict with the papacy?
3. Describe the clashes between Frederick I and Popes Adrian IV and Alexander III.
4. Explain St. Thomas Becket's fight with Henry II of England.

5. Summarize the political activity of Pope Innocent III in regard to Germany and England.
6. Show how the factor of personality entered into Frederick II's conflicts with the various popes.
7. What were the effects on the Church of the long Hohenstaufen wars?

SUGGESTIONS FOR FURTHER READING

For the ideological background see Robert W. and A. J. Carlyle, *History of Mediaeval Political Theory in the West*, 6 vols. (London: 1928–1936), Vols. 4 and 5. A general sketch that is still worth reading is Ugo Balzani, *The Popes and the Hohenstaufen* (London: 1901). Paul J. Knapke, *Frederick Barbarossa's Conflict with the Papacy* (Washington, D. C.: 1939), treats its topic thoroughly. Biographical sketches of all the popes of this period can be found in volumes 10 to 14 of H. K. Mann, *Lives of the Popes in the Middle Ages* (St. Louis: 1914–1928). A popular life of a very important pope is Joseph Clayton, *Pope Innocent III* (Milwaukee: 1941). Two other biographies that are well done are E. Almendingen, *The English Pope (Adrian IV)* (London: 1925), and William H. Hutton, *Thomas Becket, Archbishop of Canterbury*, rev. ed. (Cambridge: 1926). For the effects of the political problems of the papacy see Arthur L. Smith, *Church and State in the Middle Ages* (Oxford: 1913), especially sections 4 and 5, although the picture is somewhat overdrawn. A more judicious survey is John Tracy Ellis, *Anti-Papal Legislation in Medieval England (1066–1377)* (Washington, D. C.: 1930).

DOCUMENTS

1. Not all aspects of papal policy during the long papal-imperial conflict redounded to the honor of the Church. As politicians the popes made enemies. Even the common people heard rumors injurious to the Church which originated in the political struggle. The Chronicler Matthew Paris has preserved some samples of the current public opinion about Pope Innocent IV. *Chronica majora*, translated by J. A. Giles, 3 vols. (London: 1889), III, 101–102.

In the same week in which Pope Innocent the Fourth departed this life, a wonderful vision was seen by a certain cardinal, whose name is suppressed for caution's sake. It appeared to him that he was in heaven before the majesty of the Lord, who was sitting at the judgment-seat, and on whose right hand stood the blessed Virgin his mother, whilst on his left there appeared a woman of noble person and venerable mien. The latter, with arm extended, carried in her left hand a kind of temple, on the front of which was written in letters of gold, "The Church." Before the Divine Majesty was prostrated Innocent the Fourth, who with clasped and upraised hands, and on bended knees, was asking pardon, not judgment. The noble lady, however, spoke against him, saying, "Oh! just judge, give judgment aright, for I accuse this man on three points. Firstly, when you founded the Church on earth, you gifted it with the liberties which proceeded from yourself: this man has rendered her a most abject slave. Secondly, the Church was founded for the salvation of sinners, to gain over the souls of the wretched; but he has made it a money-changer's table. Thirdly, the Church was founded on the firmness of faith, on justice, and on truth; but this man has caused faith and morals to waver, has done away with justice, and overshadowed truth; render me, therefore, a just judgment." Then said the Lord, "Go, and receive your reward according to your deserts," and then he was taken away. Terrified at this dreadful sentence, the cardinal awoke crying aloud with fear, and became like one beside himself, and all indeed thought that he was mad; however, as his grief became less he began to narrate the particulars of his vision in full, and it became public in that part of the country. This vision (we know not whether it was a creation of fancy or not) greatly alarmed many people, and God grant that it may take effect and chasten and amend their ways.

2. The medieval Church enjoyed numerous privileges which often aroused the wrath of secular rulers striving to enhance their power. Benefit of clergy was one such privilege. In attempting to restrict benefit of clergy, Henry II of England in his Constitutions of Clarendon imposed serious restrictions on the Church's freedom, as evident in the following excerpts from the University of Pennsylvania *Translations and Reprints*, I, 6, 27–28.

3. Clergymen charged and accused of anything, when they have been summoned by a justice of the king shall come into his court, to respond there to that which it shall seem good to the court of the king for them to respond to, and in the ecclesiastical court to what it shall seem good should be responded to there; so that the justice of the king shall send into the court of holy church to see how the matter shall be treated there. And if a clergyman shall have been convicted or has confessed, the church ought not to protect him otherwise.

4. It is not lawful for archbishops, bishops, and persons of the realm to go out of the realm without the permission of the lord king. And if they go out, if it please the lord king, they shall give security that neither in going nor in making a stay nor in returning will they seek evil or loss to the king or the kingdom.

8. Concerning appeals, if they should occur, they ought to proceed from the archdeacon to the bishop, from the bishop to the archbishop. And if the archbishop should fail to show justice, it must come to the lord king last, in order that by his command the controversy should be finally terminated in the court of the archbishop, so that it ought not to proceed further without the assent of the lord king.

Chapter 15

CATHOLIC LIFE IN THE
HIGH MIDDLE AGES

WHATEVER the issues involved, the disputes between popes and princes summarized in the preceding chapter were only incidental to the fundamental goals of the Church: the Christlike life and eternal salvation of mankind. More directly related to those ends were the institutional and interior aspects of Catholicism to which we now turn, and we notice at once that the century from Frederick I to Frederick II was one of intense activity. Several of the greatest popes guided the affairs of the Apostolic See as the centralization of ecclesiastical administration in Rome continued, each generation had its own ecumenical council, unparalleled success greeted the newest religious orders, the intellectual and artistic life of Catholic Europe attained its medieval peak, and steps were taken to check the spread of heresy.

The Papal Monarchy. The elaborate supervision exercised by the Holy See over every aspect of ecclesiastical policy or administration, one of the striking features of modern Catholicism, developed in the twelfth and thirteenth centuries. Papal primacy, always admitted, lacked for centuries the administrative machinery for its day-to-day exercise. The general conditions of the early middle ages rendered impossible close contact between Rome and the rest of Christendom. Only with the Gregorian reform, when churchmen began looking for means to eradicate the evils of lay domination, were the potentialities realized of a strong, independent papacy as a counterbalance to the forces of corruption. Since this entailed greater papal surveillance of local affairs, the popes from

Gregory VII onward assumed many functions formerly handled locally in order to protect the Church from abuses.

This centralizing tendency can be observed in many ways. In 1215 the Fourth Lateran Council reserved to the pope the right of certifying the genuineness of new relics. The same decree restricted bishops in granting indulgences, especially plenary indulgences, which hereafter generally originated from Rome. During the twelfth century the right of canonization was recognized as belonging properly to the pope alone rather than to every bishop. Certain grave sins were reserved to the papacy for absolution. All crusaders became special wards of the pope and papal sanction protected their property during their absence. When the bishops could not cope with the pernicious Albigensian and Waldensian heresies Pope Innocent III intervened and Gregory IX organized the special papal tribunal of the Inquisition. At the same time the scope of papal intervention in episcopal elections gradually broadened, either through direct restrictions on local rights or as a result of appeals in disputes; Innocent III's share in the elevation of Stephen Langton will be recalled. Appeals to Rome in judicial matters were always encouraged and resulted in almost complete dependence on the pope in all major and many minor causes.

To bind the Church more closely together and see that the will of the pope was obeyed, papal agents were sent out from Rome in increasing numbers. Some of these were tax collectors while others were ambassadors or legates, general representatives of the pope with limited or plenipotentiary jurisdiction over specific matters. These were of three types: *legati nati*, i.e., legates by virtue of holding a see such as Toledo or Lyons to which the honor was permanently attached; *legati missi*, diplomatic representatives of the ordinary type; and *legati a latere*, special ambassadors, always cardinals, employed for the most important missions. Just the opposite method of furthering centralization and supervision of local affairs was the obligation of periodic *ad limina* visits to Rome by all bishops, an obligation that was becoming general. No archbishop's installation was complete until he received from the pope the pallium, a woolen stole-like vestment which was customarily bestowed personally on the occasion of a special journey to Rome.

Canon Law. So many centripetal forces operating at once created a need for papal officials and administrative organization. Of basic importance was an adequate legal framework, for which the foundation had been laid by Gratian's *Decretum*. Canon law continued to evolve and training in it came to be a prerequisite for ecclesiastical advancement in Rome. It is customary to classify the popes of the high middle ages as monk popes and lawyer popes to illustrate the traits characteristic of their approach to the Church's problems. The former, Gregory VII pre-eminently, were ascetics or mystics whose zeal sprang from the heart rather than the brain, while the latter, such as Alexander III, Innocent III, Gregory IX, and Innocent IV, great canonists all, tempered their zeal with their intellect and fortified the Church with legal distinctions, argumentation, and rationalization. Gregory VII is a more attractive personality than Innocent III or Innocent IV — and he has been canonized while they have not — yet the Church had need of the talents of each according to the circumstances of the times.

Five collections of decretals followed the *Decretum* to keep it up to date, of which the third, issued in 1210 by Innocent III, is the oldest official, papally approved collection of legislation for the Roman Church. Innocent's work, however, was superseded by the *Decretals of Gregory IX* in 1234, a thorough reworking of all earlier sources that was carried out by the Dominican scholar St. Raymond of Penafort. The elaboration of canon law continued for another century until the additions of Pope John XXII (1316–1334) completed the Code of Canon Law which remained in use until 1918.

The Papal Curia. The Roman Curia served as the governing body of the Church in the same way that the court of a feudal king assisted the monarch in ruling his kingdom. Papal infallibility was not defined during the middle ages since it was not questioned. The cardinals, the most responsible assistants of the pope, met with him in public or secret consistory for all phases of curial business and to advise the pope on particular matters. The cardinals' origin as the most important local Roman clergy was still evident in the requirement that medieval cardinals reside in Rome, yet they were chosen from all European nationalities. Since the election decree of 1059 the distinctions between the three orders of cardinal bishops, priests, and deacons slowly disappeared, particularly after they were all recognized as having an equal voice in papal elections by the Third Lateran Council in 1179. The same Council specified the need for a two-thirds majority in papal elections to avoid schisms such as those under Innocent II and Alexander III. Although the maximum number of cardinals possible was fifty-two, the Sacred College usually averaged below thirty in the twelfth and early thirteenth centuries. Expanding activity of the Curia necessitated a division of labor among the officials; in the thirteenth century three administrative departments are in evidence: the chancery, the *camera* or apostolic chamber, and the judicial tribunals. The chancery consisted of a cluster of offices charged with the preparation of routine papal correspondence through every stage from preliminary drafting to filing copies in the registers. The extent of the chancery's work can be seen from the approximately 4800 letters preserved in the registers of Innocent III, and these are only those letters on significant matters which have survived. Innocent III laid down elaborate regulations governing format and style of papal documents so that forged material could be easily detected. The name "bull" as applied to papal documents was derived from the seal (*bulla*) attached to them.

Financial business was the province of the apostolic chamber and its head the chamberlain or camerarius, one of the most important curial officials. Because financial matters were world-wide and were closely connected with the established rights of the Church everywhere, the chamberlain was in the best position to keep informed on political developments throughout Europe. He has been aptly called the medieval secretary of state. Clerks of the chamber handled the pope's political and confidential correspondence.

A more active papacy needed more money and much attention had to be paid to this knotty problem. Sources of papal revenue were numerous and varied. From the States of the Church the pope collected revenues comparable to those of any feudal lord from his estates. But local income was insufficient to support a universal papacy, so fees had to be garnered from all of Christendom. The census consisted of a nominal payment by exempt monasteries to express their dependence on the pope. Before becoming pope Honorius III drew up the *Liber censuum* to regularize these fees, and he also included in his book accounts of tribute paid by the papal vassals such as the kings of England and Sicily as well as the Peter's Pence collected in England, Scandinavia, and Poland. In 1199 Innocent III imposed property and income taxes on the clergy to support the crusades. "Voluntary" gifts, procurations, chancery fees, legacies, services, and visitation taxes provided further income for the Curia. At all periods the financial status of the papacy was so precarious that every crisis raised serious difficulties, while the Hohenstaufen wars threw the papacy into the clutches of the Italian banking houses.

The origin of the various curial courts is obscure. At this time the consistory functioned as the supreme court of the Church; although the pope officially made the decisions much of the preliminary investigation was handled by cardinals to whom the pope referred particular questions.

Cases involving financial transactions came within the competence of special courts in the apostolic chamber. Sometimes the pope appointed local ordinaries to serve as judge-delegates when the litigants could not come to Rome. Another papal tribunal functioning outside Rome was the Inquisition.

The Fourth Lateran Council. The series of ecumenical councils in the West both enhanced and manifested the expanding jurisdiction of the papacy. They followed a general pattern, i.e., the councils met in connection with crises that were often of a political nature, and they concerned themselves chiefly with a wide variety of disciplinary measures rather than with doctrinal problems such as had evoked the eastern councils.

Two and a half years before the twelfth general council met at the Lateran in 1215, Innocent III sent out advance notices calling on the clergy to begin their preparations. In his letter the pope declared the twofold purpose of the Council to be the external problem of the recovery of the Holy Land and the ever recurring domestic subject of discipline and reform of abuses. An attendance of 412 bishops, 800 abbots and priors, many proctors and representatives of lay rulers made the Fourth Lateran Council the most impressive religious assembly of the middle ages, a fitting climax to the work of Innocent III. In three sessions the Council passed seventy decrees which Innocent had prepared in advance and submitted merely for discussion and approval.

The two most celebrated canons of the Fourth Lateran Council were the first, a profession of faith directed against Albigensian and Waldensian heretics which stated concisely the fundamental Catholic doctrines and gave official sanction to the term "transubstantiation," and the twenty-first which imposed the obligation of annual confession and communion at Easter time for all members of the Church. The disciplinary decrees covered all sorts of detail. Certain specific minor heresies were condemned; new religious orders were forbidden unless they used one of the monastic rules already recognized; relations between the laity and the Church in regard to taxation and ecclesiastical property were regulated; proper procedure in suits under canon law and in ecclesiastical elections was established; four canons limited the civil rights of Jews and commanded them to wear a distinctive dress; a dozen or so decrees concerned moral lapses of the clergy; all monastic orders were ordered to hold triennial general chapters after the Cistercian manner. In the nonreligious field, Frederick II received recognition as emperor, and elaborate preparations were undertaken for a new crusade.

The New Religious Orders. The monasticism of the thirteenth century differed greatly from the older orders, all of which concerned themselves primarily with the personal sanctification of the individual monk through withdrawal from the world. Their numerous contributions to society were incidental to their purpose. Exactly the opposite approach was taken by the Dominicans and Franciscans: service to man was their way of serving God and of promoting the welfare of their own souls. Instead of fleeing into deserts or wildernesses the friars sought out human society in crowded cities to leaven it with their spirit of the Beatitudes. They were not isolated within walled monasteries. What are now called social services, pastoral labors, missions, and education were the areas in which they distinguished themselves. Although the canons regular had already set themselves roughly the same ideals, the friars were the most successful in attaining them.

Franciscans. St. Francis of Assisi (1182–1226) is the most appealing figure in medieval history. The intensity of his love for God and man, his total detachment from the world, and the lyrical *joie de vivre* that characterized his every undertaking have irresistibly attracted men from his own day to the present. Born into a moderately wealthy merchant family, Francis acquired his name (he was baptized John) because of his love for French fashions and especially for the literature of the French troubadours. Under the impact of several misfortunes Francis embraced a life of voluntary poverty and prayer, but after two years as a hermit he dedicated himself to service of others. Followers joined him at once and the Order of Friars Minor came into being.

Pope Innocent III approved Francis' original rule in 1209. Humanitarian labor for the benefit of the poor, sick, starving, and oppressed was the task Francis selected for his Order. Absolute poverty for individuals as well as for the Order was originally prescribed but corporate poverty had to be abandoned because it interfered with the Order's mission. Francis reluctantly accepted this change in the third version of the rule approved by Pope Honorius III in 1223. This program was no complete innovation as far as the Church was concerned; the real novelty lay in the organization of the Franciscan Order. The greatness of St. Francis lay in the fact that he lived so completely the heroic virtues he preached and in his power of inspiring others to the same ideals. Francis placed his Order under the direct authority of the pope and a minister general. St. Clare, under Francis' direction, founded the Second Order of St. Francis for women; he himself organized a Third Order.

The Dominicans. St. Dominic (1170–1221), founder of the Friars Preachers, better known as Dominicans, became a canon of the cathedral of Osma in Spain near his birthplace. Because of his fiery zeal and holiness Dominic was sent into Provence to re-convert the Albigensian heretics. Dominic soon discovered that the ignorance of both clergy and laity concerning the doctrines and moral teachings of the Church was the reason for the spread of the heresy. Since only bishops or their delegates were permitted to preach, and they obviously could reach only a few of the faithful even if they troubled themselves with sermons, it was not unusual for medieval Catholics to be very poorly instructed. Decrees of the Third and Fourth Lateran Councils show that the hierarchy too was beginning to consider the same problem.

To remedy this situation Dominic founded the Order of Preachers specifically dedicated to instructing the people from the pulpit and to teaching in the schools. The rule of the Augustinian Canons provided the groundwork for the Dominican constitution, but Dominic advocated ideals of personal and corporate poverty borrowed from the Franciscans. Every superior was given and urged to use wide powers of dispensation if the Church or the Order could be served by suspension of the rules. A system of democratic elections, representative assemblies and control by a minister general bound the Order together, for the Preachers followed the centralizing tendencies of later monasticism. Dominic also established an order for nuns.

Within fifty years more than 400 Dominican houses were scattered over Europe. The Dominicans conferred immeasurable benefits on the Church and on Christendom in general through their efforts to raise the moral and intellectual level of Europe. Since their objective demanded that the Preachers be trained in theology they were soon found at all the great universities. Mere mention of the Dominican saints Albertus Magnus and Thomas Aquinas indicates the level of the Order's attainments.

Development of the Mendicant Movement. Originally quite different in many respects, the Dominicans and Franciscans gradually drew closer together. Most Franciscans originally were laymen, but soon the proportion of priests matched that of the Dominicans. The Franciscans entered the field of education since they too became popular preachers and hence needed learning. St. Bonaventure, Roger Bacon, and Duns Scotus are among the eminent scholars of the Friars Minor. Both orders engaged in missionary activity in the remote pagan areas of Europe and in Africa and Asia. St. Francis himself had tried to convert the Egyptian sultan and from 1220 Franciscans were to be found in many places in north Africa. In the middle of the century Friars John of Plano Carpini and William of Rubruck even penetrated into Genghis Khan's Asiatic empire.

The popularity of the friars surpassed that of any other monastic or religious order. In England, for example, nine Franciscan friars arrived in 1224 and by 1230 there were Franciscan houses at Oxford, Cambridge, London, Canterbury, Lincoln, Northampton, and ten other places, while the following decade saw the establishment of twenty more. Such progress arose from the fact that the mendicant friars filled a definite need. Society was undergoing vast changes in the thirteenth century; population was shifting to the towns. The established rural diocesan organization could not expand rapidly enough to care for the new concentrations of urban population, but the friars, always more at home among the people than in the countryside, were able to step in at once. Their mobility adapted them to every kind of employment. The mendicants were democratic compared to the aristocratic older orders, thus providing an outlet for the religious impulses of all men. Both orders became intimately associated with the papacy and served well the general centralizing tendencies; in return they were carefully protected by the papacy against the jealous opposition of the secular clergy and the older orders.

Heresy: The Waldensians.   The religious impulse toward Christian poverty and a life of apostolic simplicity which at last found orthodox expression in the mendicant friars had, in the preceding twelfth century, usually been perverted into heresy. Arnoldists, followers of Arnold of Brescia, and the Lombard Patarines and Humiliati all hovered on the verge of error in their theories concerning Church ownership of property and clerical poverty. The largest group of this type was the Waldensians, founded by a wealthy merchant of Lyons, Peter Waldo, who in 1173 distributed his wealth and formed a group of itinerant lay preachers called the Poor Men of Lyons. They appealed directly to the Gospel and advocated reading of the Bible by all. Pope Alexander III gave them permission to preach provided they obtained the consent of the bishop of the diocese.

Originally the work of the Waldensians had been conceived in the spirit of protest against corruption and negligence among the clergy, but as the movement expanded some of its members adopted heretical ideas and incurred excommunication by Pope Lucius III in 1184. From criticism of unworthy priests they advanced to the Donatist heresy of denying the validity of sacraments administered by bad clergy and then to an open attack on the place of the clergy within the Church. Anticipating Protestantism they preached the priesthood of the laity and private interpretation of the Scriptures.

The Albigensians. A much more serious menace to Catholicism and to society were the Cathari, i.e., the "pure," also known as Albigensians from their stronghold at Albi in southern France. Here they were heavily concentrated but the sect was to be found throughout the Mediterranean area and into Bulgaria, the apparent source of the heresy.

Albigensian teachings represented a revival of the ancient Manichean heresy. All the strange beliefs which Pope Leo I had long ago unearthed among the Roman Manichees were again brought to life. Dualism lay at the root of their teaching, the division of creation into the good things of the spirit and the essentially evil things of the flesh or matter. The soul, imprisoned in the flesh, can be liberated only through extreme ascetic practices and renunciation of all material, physical, and sexual contacts. Suicide represented the logical culmination of Albigensian doctrine; starvation was the approved method. As with the ancient Manichees, the extreme condemnation of all things of the flesh led paradoxically to the collapse of morality, especially in regard to sex. There were two groups of Albigensians: the "perfect," who strove to fulfill rigidly the precepts of Catharism; and the "believers," who only promised to do so at some future date. By refusing to take oaths the Cathari threatened to undermine the political structure of Europe since the feudal system rested on oaths of homage or fidelity.

Popular opinion reacted violently to the Cathari. In 1022 King Robert of France burned thirteen of them; Emperor Henry III hanged several; in 1075 and 1114 mobs lynched Cathari at Cambrai and Strassburg. Eventually heresy became a capital offense under the civil laws of many governments. Nevertheless Catharism flourished and even ensnared bishops and clergy. Under the circumstances the normal procedure for coping with such problems in episcopal courts failed completely. Pope Innocent III therefore inaugurated the practice of sending special envoys to investigate and to win back as many as possible by preaching. Without the support of the secular authorities — Count Raymond VI of Toulouse dallied with Catharism as did various lesser nobles of Languedoc — the missionaries made no headway. When one of the papal legates, Peter of Castelnau, was murdered in 1208, Innocent III preached a crusade against the Albigensians. Under Simon de Montfort the crusaders devastated Languedoc but resultant political squabbles limited the religious effectiveness of the crusade. Gregory IX then originated the papal Inquisition.

The Inquisition. According to the inquisitorial machinery set up by Gregory IX in 1233 and elaborated by Innocent IV and later popes, the inquisitors, either Dominicans or Franciscans, visited towns under suspicion and called on all heretics to appear or for people who knew of heretics to denounce them secretly. Children were encouraged to inform on their parents if they suspected them. Once accused, a person found it almost impossible to prove himself innocent, but if he immediately admitted error and accepted a penance he suffered no harm. Those who denied that they were heretics might be tortured until they confessed, or those who admitted their heretical beliefs and refused to recant could be tortured to persuade them to change their opinions. The most obstinate heretics and those who afterward retracted their confessions were handed over to the secular government for punishment, which meant burning at the stake.

The Inquisition is totally repugnant to modern standards of just legal procedures and toleration. No Catholic historian attempts any longer to defend it. Its major defects were the lack of protection for the innocent and the difficulty of preventing abuses of power by overzealous inquisitors. While many of the friars inquisitors conducted themselves in a manner above reproach, others violated natural justice and Christian charity in outrageous fashion. A Dominican named Robert le Bougre, himself a reformed heretic, caused the burning of about 180 heretics on a single day in 1239, but he was later suspended from his office. By way of a fair appraisal of the Inquisition it must be noted that abuses were on the whole comparatively rare and a relatively small number of victims suffered death. At the same time, the procedure and the intolerance that motivated it were considered entirely equitable at the time and in harmony with the standards of the religiously homogeneous middle ages. In short, it was a case of churchmen failing to rise above the barbarities of their environment.

The Apogee of Medieval Learning. The alliance between Christian revelation and Aristotelian philosophy cemented in the thirteenth century has endured to the present. Contact with Aristotle's logic during the twelfth century whetted the appetite of western thinkers for his ethical, metaphysical, and scientific writings. Since these first appeared in Europe through translations and commentaries of the Arabian philosophers, some apprehension was aroused by the non-Aristotelian accretions, but through the labors of the friars become theologians Aristotle was baptized and put to the service of the Church.

Two Dominicans, St. Albert the Great (1206–1280) and his pupil St. Thomas Aquinas (1225–1274), dominated the scholastic system in the thirteenth century. Albert, a German educated at Padua, was a versatile scholar exceptionally learned in the physical sciences as well as theology, hence well qualified to expound a unified view of the universe and of man's place in it that did justice to the genius of Aristotle himself. Aquinas stemmed from Norman Italy and studied at Monte Cassino before joining the Dominicans. At the University of Paris and at Cologne he studied under Albert. Most of his mature teaching (1252–1259 and 1268–1272) was done as a professor at the great school of theology at the University of Paris. Aquinas' two major works, the *Summa contra Gentiles* and *Summa Theologiae,* the latter unfinished at the time of his death, mark the climax of constructive medieval philosophy and theology.

In establishing an Aristotelian base for Christian theology, Albert and Thomas critically rejected those ideas of the Greek philosopher which they deemed unsatisfactory. They sought to establish a unified synthesis of all human knowledge with the teaching of Christianity. They drew a distinction between philosophy and theology in terms of method rather than object, the former examining natural truths by the light of reason, the latter analyzing the supernatural order as revealed by God, hence from the point of view of authority. Yet the object of each was truth and therefore the two sciences could not be incompatible or mutually contradictory since truth cannot contradict itself. The scholastic concept of philosophy as an auxiliary science serving theology is evident in Aquinas' use of Aristotelian metaphysics, the source of the theory of act and potency which Aquinas used to fix the bases of theology, for he explained God in terms of pure act and creatures in terms of a combination of act and potency.

Although the Dominican scholars dedicated themselves to the new learning, it proved impossible, even undesirable, to eliminate the Platonic element in Catholic theology since this was firmly embedded in the writings of all the ancient Fathers, especially Augustine. The more conservative Franciscan theologians spent their efforts in defending and developing this older tradition. St. Bonaventure (1221–1274) founded the Franciscan school of theology. He taught at Paris before his appointment in 1257 as minister general of his order removed him from academic circles. True to the Platonic tradition, Bonaventure excelled as a mystic rather than as a speculative thinker, and while the works of this "Seraphic Doctor" have always been popular as devotional literature, they are below the intellectual attainments of Aquinas.

Gothic Church Architecture. In the century between 1170 and 1270 it is calculated that Gothic cathedrals or churches of equivalent size arose in Europe at the rate of one every two months, a stupendous material expression of the faith of the thousands of unknown laborers and artisans of every class whose combined skill produced the great structures. Gothic, the style of the high middle ages, developed out of the earlier Romanesque pattern. Romanesque buildings were characterized by a low, massive appearance due to heavy walls, barrel vaults, round arches and few windows. The perfection of the Romanesque was attained in the Cluniac monastic churches, although the cathedral of Mainz is a particularly fine example.

Gothic architecture, however, which appeared in the eleventh century, emphasized height. While the monastery church of Cluny set the record of ninety-eight feet for Romanesque churches, the Gothic cathedrals of Reims and Amiens attained 126 and 144 feet in height. Notre Dame and the Sainte Chapelle at Paris, York, and Cologne cathedrals are other classic Gothic churches. Through the use of pointed arches and buttresses the weight of the roof and sides of Gothic buildings was broken, permitting the opening of the walls by stained glass windows and a generally lighter interior. Whatever existed of the lesser arts of sculpture, painting, metalwork, and the like was usually also the result of ecclesiastical patronage and hence generally religious in theme.

The Later Crusades. Little remained of the Latin Kingdom of Jerusalem when Innocent III became pope but this great pontiff cherished as his dearest project the recovery of the lost possessions. As never before the elaborate diplomatic machinery of the papacy was put into motion to urge Europe to take up the cross for the fourth great crusade. New indulgences were proclaimed, papal legates strove to mediate Europe's feuds to release man power for the holy war, and for the first time a general tax was levied by the pope on all church property everywhere to supply the necessary funds.

But the fourth crusade (1202–1204) was a disappointment. Whether seduced by Venetian or German intrigue, the crusaders attacked Christian Hungarian territory and incurred papal excommunication before going on to capture Constantinople from the Byzantines and establish the Latin Empire of Constantinople. Again Innocent pronounced excommunication for those responsible but soon he accommodated himself to the situation in the hope of a reunion of the Greek Church with Rome. Nothing of the sort happened; the Greeks would have nothing to do with the Latin patriarch and his clergy who were sent from Europe. An arrogant, tactless papal legate ruined all chances of reunion. The fall of the Latin Empire in 1261 left the religious division as before, except that the Greeks hated the Latins more than ever.

At the Fourth Lateran Council Innocent III launched the fifth crusade (1218–1221) but he was dead before it met disaster in Egypt, largely owing to the incompetence of Cardinal Pelagius who, as papal legate, fancied himself supreme military commander as well. The sixth, Frederick II's crusade, was the strangest of all since Frederick was under excommunication at the time for having failed to depart on schedule. With the friars everywhere denouncing him, with no co-operation from the Latins or the military orders, Frederick won by diplomacy alone the cities of Jerusalem, Bethlehem, and Nazareth. The sultan relinquished these by the Treaty of Jaffa in 1229 on the condition that toleration be granted to Moslems living there. But in 1244 the Moslems re-entered Jerusalem, which called forth the two crusades of St. Louis of France (1248–1254 and 1270). In these expeditions some of the old religious zeal is again evident, due solely to the remarkable king who led them; militarily they were debacles. With the fall of Acre in 1291 the Latins were deprived of their last foothold in the Levant. Although later popes continued to exhort Christians to renewed offensives, and at times with some success, it was a hopeless task. With crusades being preached against the pope's enemies in Europe, the Baltic pagans and the Spanish Moors, there was no real incentive to cross the sea.

Conclusion. However significant they may be, institutional achievements such as the papal government, canon law, and papal victories over political aggressors are unsatisfactory guides to a proper estimate of the success of the Church. No historian can examine the spiritual realm in which alone lies the proof of the Church's accomplishment of its task. Yet external indications provide the only clues available. Therefore if we consider the number of enthusiastic members of the Dominican and Franciscan Orders, the concern for the purity of the Faith which led people to accept the Inquisition, the intellectual zeal for a deeper and truer knowledge of the Faith, and the lives of the eminent saints of the times, there seems sufficient justification for judging this period one of the most flourishing ages of the Catholic Church.

REVIEW AIDS

1. Indicate the evidence for the increasing papal centralization of the affairs of the Church, and analyze the good and the bad features of this development.
2. Describe the three major departments of the papal Curia and their part in the administration of the Church.
3. Enumerate some of the leading canons of the Fourth Lateran Council.
4. What was the fundamental difference between the new religious orders of the thirteenth century and the older communities?
5. In what ways did the Dominicans and Franciscans differ and in what ways did they resemble each other?
6. What explanation can be given for the great success of the friars?
7. Summarize the teachings of the Waldensians and Albigensians.
8. Discuss the papal inquisition from the medieval and from the modern viewpoint.
9. Explain the intellectual achievements of the mendicant scholars.
10. What are the chief characteristics of Romanesque and Gothic architecture?
11. Briefly summarize the later crusades.

SUGGESTIONS FOR FURTHER READING

An excellent discussion of the papacy is to be found in the brief essay by Marshall W. Baldwin, *The Medieval Papacy in Action* (New York: 1940). The following treat of different aspects of the papal government: William Lunt, *Papal Revenues in the Middle Ages*, 2 vols. (New York: 1934); Reginald L. Poole, *Lectures on the History of the Papal Chancery* (Cambridge: 1915); Eric W. Kemp, *Canonization and Authority in the Western Church* (Oxford: 1948). An intelligent attempt to trace the carrying out of the decrees of the Fourth Lateran Council is Marion Gibbs and Jane Lang, *Bishops and Reform, 1215–1272* (Oxford: 1934). J. R. H. Moorman, *Church Life in England in the 13th Century* (Cambridge: 1955), gives a complete picture of the Church in action on the lower levels. For an intimate picture of medieval Benedictine monasticism and the problems of monks and abbots there is available a translation by H. E. Butler of *The Chronicle of Jocelin of Brakelond* (London: 1949), a primary source of extreme value and charming candor.

Biographies of some of the important people of this period are Bede Jarrett, *Life of St. Dominic* (Westminster, Md.: 1947); Joseph Clayton, *Pope Innocent III and His Times* (Milwaukee: 1941); and Johannes Jörgensen, *Saint Francis of Assisi* (New York: 1912). A series of scholarly studies rather than a biography is Pierre Mandonnet, *St. Dominic and His Work*, 3rd ed. (St. Louis: 1948). Steven Runciman, *The Medieval Manichee* (Cambridge: 1947), discusses the problem of heresy. Among the thousands of books on the Inquisition the most intelligent Catholic treatment is E. Vacandard, *The Inquisition*, trans. by Bertrand L. Conway (New York: 1926).

DOCUMENTS

1. The legislation of the Third and Fourth Lateran Councils covered a wide variety of topics, indicative of the multifarious interests of the medieval Church at the peak of its prestige and influence. Canon 18 of the Third Lateran Council, 1179, indicates, for example, the Church's role in medieval education. From H. J. Schroeder, *Disciplinary Decrees of the General Councils* (St. Louis: 1937), p. 229. Used by permission.

The Church of God as a devoted mother is bound to provide for those in need, not only in the things that pertain to the body but also in those that pertain to the good of souls. Wherefore, that the opportunity of acquiring an education may not be denied to the poor who cannot be aided by their parents' means, let some suitable benefice be assigned in every cathedral church to a master who shall teach *gratis* the clerics of that church and the poor students, by means of which benefice the material wants of the master may be relieved, and to the students a way opened to knowledge. In other churches also and in monasteries, let it be restored if in times past something of this sort has therein existed. For permission to teach, no one shall exact a fee or under pretext of custom ask something from those who teach; nor shall anyone who is qualified and seeks a license be denied the position to teach. Whoever acts contrary to this shall be deprived of his ecclesiastical benefice. For it is proper that he have not the fruit of his labor in the Church of God, who through cupidity endeavors to impede the progress of the churches by the sale of permission to teach.

2. Canon 3 of the Fourth Lateran Council in 1215 concerns the episcopal inquisition used to uproot heresy. It also indicates how the medieval Church insisted that Catholic secular princes use the material force at their disposal to compel their subjects to accept the Church's teachings. *Ibid.*, pp. 242–244.

Secular authorities, whatever office they may hold, shall be admonished and induced and if necessary compelled by ecclesiastical censure, that as they wish to be esteemed and numbered among the faithful, so for the defense of the faith they ought publicly to take an oath that they will strive in good faith and to the best of their ability to exterminate in the territories subject to their jurisdiction all heretics pointed out by the Church; so that whenever anyone shall have assumed authority, whether spiritual or temporal, let him be bound to confirm this decree by oath. But if a temporal ruler, after having been requested and admonished by the Church, should neglect to cleanse his territory of this heretical foulness, let him be excommunicated by the metropolitan and the other bishops of the province. If he refuses to make satisfaction within a year, let the matter be made known to the supreme pontiff, that he may declare the ruler's vassals absolved from their allegiance and may offer the territory to be ruled by Catholics, who on the extermination of the heretics may possess it without hindrance and preserve it in the purity of the faith. . . . Catholics who have girded themselves with the cross for the extermination of the heretics, shall enjoy the indulgences and privileges granted to those who go in defense of the Holy Land.

We add, moreover, that every archbishop or bishop should himself or through his archdeacon or some other suitable persons, twice or at least once a year make the rounds of his diocese in which report has it that heretics dwell, and there compel three or more men of good character or, if it should be deemed advisable, the entire neighborhood, to swear that if anyone know of the presence there of heretics or others holding secret assemblies, or differing from the common way of the faithful in faith and morals, they will make them known to the bishop. The latter shall then call together before him those accused, who, if they do not purge themselves of the matter of which they are accused, or if after the rejection of their error they lapse into their former wickedness, shall be canonically punished. But if any of them by damnable obstinacy should disapprove of the oath and should perchance be unwilling to swear, from this very fact let them be regarded as heretics.

SECTION III: APOGEE OF MEDIEVAL CATHOLICISM

A.D.	POPES	WRITERS	HERESY	THE CHURCH	THE WORLD	SECULAR RULERS
1000	Sylvester II			Simony, Neglect of Clerical Celibacy, Lay Investiture Cluniac Congregation Monastic revival Camaldolese monks	Normans in S. Italy	St. Henry II Henry III
1025	Benedict IX	Peter Damian Humbert of Moyenmoutier		Synod of Sutri		
1050	Leo IX			Leo IX's travels Cerularius and Greek schism		Edward the Confessor
	Nicholas II			Election decree Papal-Norman alliance Lanfranc reforms English church	Norman invasion of England Recovery of Spain begins	William the Conqueror
	Alexander II					
1075	Gregory VII	Lanfranc		Investiture Controversy Canossa German schism	Seljuk Turks in East	Henry IV
	Urban II	Ivo of Chartres Publicists		Council of Clermont	Crusades Jerusalem taken, Kingdom set up	Comneni in Constantinople
1100	Paschal II	Wm. of Champeaux Anselm		Anselm vs. Henry I of England Paschal's weakness Cistercians Canons Regular	Revival of town life and commerce Germans expand eastward	
	Callixtus II	Abelard Bernard of Clairvaux		Concordat of Worms LATERAN COUNCIL I Premonstratensians Carthusians Age of Bernard of Clairvaux	Civil war in England	
125	Innocent II	Roland Bandinelli			Second Crusade	
	Eugene III			Anacletus' schism Military monasticism LATERAN COUNCIL II	Roman Republic of Arnold of Brescia	
150	Adrian IV		Patarines			Henry II of England
	Alexander III	Peter Lombard Gratian		Conflict with Barbarossa	Diet of Besançon Diet of Roncaglia	Frederick II, Barbarossa
175			Waldensians	Thomas Becket vs. Henry II of England LATERAN COUNCIL III	Lombard League Battle of Legnano	Saladin
			Albigensians (Cathari)		Turks recapture Jerusalem	
	Celestine III			Conversion of Livs, Letts, and Estonians begins	Third Crusade	Richard the Lionhearted
200	Innocent III			Albigensian crusade Franciscans and Dominicans LATERAN COUNCIL IV	Disputed imperial election Papal intervention Fourth Crusade Latin Empire of Constantinople England a papal fief	John Frederick II
	Honorius III					Henry III of England
225	Gregory IX	Raymond of Penafort		Papal Inquisition	Frederick II's crusade	
				Teutonic Knights convert Prussians Conflict with Frederick II COUNCIL OF LYONS I	Frederick seeks to rule all Italy	Louis IX
	Innocent IV				Tartar invasions Turks re-enter Jerusalem German interregnum Crusades of Louis IX	
250		Alexander of Hales Albertus Magnus Thomas Aquinas Bonaventure Roger Bacon		Mendicant popularity Augustinian Hermits Carmelites Franciscans visit China		
	Gregory X			COUNCIL OF LYONS II Temporary Greek reunion		Edward I
275						

THE IMPACT OF A CHANGING WORLD

Chapter 16

THE AGE OF TRANSITION

TOWARD the end of the thirteenth century Europe entered upon a new stage in its historical evolution. This is the period of the later middle ages, an era that bridged the gap between medieval and modern times. It is an age of transition. While numerous elements of medieval civilization waned and disappeared, others survived into later centuries but only after a desperate struggle with the changing environment. Such institutions as the Church which outlived the middle ages did so only with difficulty, for the new forces shaping Europe were dynamic and powerful. Unless the transitional character of the period be kept always in mind, the story of the Church from its victory over the Hohenstaufen to the outbreak of the Protestant revolt must be incomprehensible. So perfectly had the Church adapted itself to the feudal world that the advent of a new political, social, and economic climate threatened to sweep away the ecclesiastical along with the feudal structure of society. This chapter examines the new tendencies and their results for the Church which are particularly manifest in the troubles of Pope Boniface VIII.

Effects on the Church. On the whole the later middle ages was a time of great difficulty for the Church. It was too much to expect that the high level of achievement climaxing in the thirteenth century could be sustained indefinitely. Decline is the obvious keynote in the history of the Church as it is of most of the medieval world, for the human element in the Church is not immune to the influences that determine secular society.

During this period there occurred the crises of the attack on Pope Boniface VIII, the Avignon papacy, the Great Western Schism, and the Renaissance. Yet these crises in themselves do not suffice to explain the decline. Earlier popes had suffered physical violence; there were previous schisms and disputed papal elections; the Renaissance prelates were no worse than those of the pre-Gregorian period. It is too facile an explanation to see in these successive tribulations the causes of the decay within the Church. They aggravated existing ills rather than created them. Their significance cannot be minimized but neither must it be exaggerated for they are external symptoms of deeper troubles.

The root of the matter was the assault on the whole traditional order of Christendom by those economic, social, intellectual, and political factors which characterized the transition from the medieval to the modern world. In consciously or unconsciously making the adjustments to the new spirit popes and bishops faced the task of distinguishing between essential prerogatives of the Church and medieval accretions which could be surrendered if necessary. The disasters of Boniface VIII's reign show that unyielding insistence on the established position was not the answer, but on the other hand there have always been those who denounce any compromise as departure from the original purity of the Church's teachings.

It is possible to single out four fundamental attributes of this period which undermined the established position of the Church: (1) a shift in the economic basis of society; (2) a gradual secularization of society; (3) the weakening of the ecclesiastical monopoly over education and the educated class; (4) birth of national sentiment in the midst of general political centralization.

Economic Factors. Feudalism as an economic system rested on land as the measure and source of wealth. In order to maintain itself the Church had acquired land in tremendous quantities as endowment for the various ecclesiastical offices and functions. The eleventh-century revival of commerce and industry brought about a more flexible economic organization and a return to a money economy. Inevitably the Church felt this change just as did secular institutions, for it was faced with decline in its land values and a concurrent need for ready cash at the very time its functions were becoming more complex and consequently more costly.

As the largest landholder in Europe, the Church's economic basis was seriously weakened. A change-over to new methods of finance had to be made if the Church was to survive as an influential element in society. Hence from the thirteenth century onward the clergy on all levels engaged in a constant struggle for funds, a struggle that was intrinsically necessary, that matched similar efforts by secular governments, yet which was frequently undignified and subject to serious abuse. Moreover, the Church's concern for wealth was obvious to all while the reasons for it were not. Papal use of facilities of Italian banking houses and adoption of businesslike methods of finance indicated degeneration to some observers and shrewdness to others. None the less, in all the years from 1250 to 1517 nothing caused more dissatisfaction and criticism — often justified — or contributed more to the decay of Catholicism than this unremitting search for gold.

Social Changes.   Concomitant with and in many ways consequent on economic developments a new secularistic or lay spirit gradually pervaded Europe. The accumulation of wealth turned society from its medieval otherworldly orientation to concentration on the present. Seldom was there genuine irreligion or atheism in the new secularism. It expressed itself rather in a greater awareness of this world, of nature, and of human experiences as well as of the comforts and refinements the world contained for those with the ability and desire to attain them. The relative rather than the absolute role of religion in life changed.

Ascetic renunciation of the world, the ideal of earlier centuries, held little attraction for the mentality of the later middle ages. The evident decadence of later medieval monasticism testifies to the attenuation of the ascetic impulse. Even the mendicant orders, representing a compromise between older monastic ideals and the newer urban spirit, lost much of their attraction for later generations.

Ecclesiastics as well as laymen succumbed to the new environment. Although they simply mirrored the times in their personal tastes and material interests, the penetration of the secularistic spirit among the clergy bore disastrous consequences for religion. In the 1300's it was an attitude of "sleepy, slack routine, the comfortable exploitation of endowments" on the part of the clergy; however, this spirit led inevitably to moral decadence in the next century. Persistent demand for reform "in head and members" was voiced at the councils. Anticlerical tendencies appeared. Chronicles and documents abound with evidence of the damage inflicted on the moral prestige of the Church by secularism boring from within.

The repulsive monks and nuns of Chaucer's *Canterbury Tales* are types of their age.

The Intellectual World. Equally portentous trends emerged in the intellectual sphere. The salient features are on the one hand a decline in the caliber of Catholic philosophers and theologians and on the other the spread of education among the laity. The Church lost its monopoly of talent.

By 1300 the greatest of the scholastic philosophers and theologians were dead. In 1277 both the bishop of Paris and the archbishop of Canterbury condemned certain propositions of Aquinas as heretical. Although the Dominicans defended him and the Augustinians largely accepted him, St. Thomas did not dominate the centuries after his death. With amazing rapidity William of Ockam's pernicious nominalism displaced the scholastic synthesis despite the efforts of university authorities, paving the way for logical skepticism. There were still important but no longer remarkable thinkers in the scholastic tradition. Gerson and d'Ailly, eminent at Paris a century after Aquinas, were pale shadows compared to their predecessors. Theology and especially canon law continued for a while on a high plane, but their philosophical basis had been ruined. Only at the very end of the middle ages did a reversal of the trend set in but by then it was already too late. The scorn of the fifteenth-century humanists for philosophers and theologians was deserved and indicates how the mighty had fallen.

Vernacular languages, coming into their own in the fourteenth century, provided the medium for Chaucer, Langland, Dante, and others who, while entirely Catholic in spirit, employed their talents for nonecclesiastical purposes. Indeed, it was not a cleric but a layman — Dante in his *Divine Comedy* — who expressed in its most perfect literary form the Catholic culture of medieval Europe. Princely patronage and humanism in the Renaissance further emphasized the lay element in the literary world. This indicates, when contrasted with the decline of philosophy and theology, that the best minds were no longer engaged directly in the service of the Church. As the laity became more educated they became more aware of the ignorance of many of the clergy and more critical of clerical shortcomings.

Politics. From the viewpoint of immediate repercussions, political developments of the later middle ages presented the most immediate and trying problems for the Church. Forms of government are essentially no concern to the Church, yet it cannot be denied that certain forms offer a healthier climate than others. The feudal regime had been peculiarly favorable to the Church. Political units had been small, weak, and jealously at odds with one another. The concept of political unity embodied in the Empire, although accepted by all theorists, was hardly more than a fiction. As the only real universal authority amid a welter of particularistic, local jurisdictions, and as the only genuine unifying factor in Europe, the Church had been in a good position to exert the maximum influence — provided, of course, that its machinery of control was adequate for its theoretical jurisdiction, as it had been after the Gregorian reform.

Now, however, with the collapse of the feudal system, the stronger territories were expanding along vaguely nationalistic lines, and the modern map of Europe was assuming recognizable shape. National states were emerging along with a rudimentary national sentiment, i.e., a consciousness of the differences dividing national groups, a desire for separation on the basis of these differences, and antipathy toward those who were "foreigners." While still in its incipient stages, this sentiment came to be a rallying point around which gathered the public opinion of the citizenry. All claims of the emperors to leadership of a unified Christendom lapsed; the national kings inherited the imperial claims in their own realms.

Destruction of its secular counterpart and the consolidation of the national monarchies imperiled the universal authority of the Church. Nationalism was a sentiment never before encountered by the Church, born and bred as it was in the Roman tradition of universalism. That any Catholic should contest papal claims simply because the pope was not of his nationality, or hesitate to pay a papal levy for fear of aiding another nation, or refuse to accept an ecclesiastical appointee merely on the grounds of his being a foreigner — these were inconceivable to the ecclesiastical mind of the middle ages. Nevertheless the next centuries produced such examples. A universal Church in the midst of a nascent system of national states could scarcely hope to avoid serious conflict. From its beginnings in the thirteenth century to the present day nationalism has been a Pandora's box of problems for the Church.

A second political characteristic of the age was the trend toward centralization of all authority in the hands of the sovereign. Subjects must be amenable to the ruler's control to the fullest extent. Royal bureaucracy, a royal army and new sources of revenue promoted the process. It was a complete reversal of the medieval dispersion of public authority.

Naturally such wide exemptions as the clergy enjoyed from control by the local government aroused distrust. As early as the Constitutions of Clarendon there had been attempts to limit jurisdiction of episcopal courts. Clerical immunity from civil courts, freedom from certain secular taxes, appeal of cases to Rome from the local bishop's court, and like prerogatives came under fire from ambitious rulers. When supported by popular national sentiment encroachments on ecclesiastical privileges were difficult to withstand. Buttressed by the absolutist principles of revived Roman Law, justified by Aristotelian political theory which recognized the state as a natural organ stemming from the nature of man, encouraged by shrewd legists educated along these novel lines, the national kings and their centralized power were formidable adversaries.

Heretofore in conflicts with kings or emperors the popes had found stanch allies among the lay aristocracy and to a lesser extent among the bishops, but from 1270 onward these allies were unreliable. Allegiance to the new national monarch took precedence over loyalty to a distant pope. Demands of the national state took precedence over claims of a supranational Church.

The Sicilian War. It would be many years before the full impact of the new era was felt by the Church. History evolves slowly and imperceptibly. In 1270 only a very discerning eye could have perceived any sign of an unhappy future for the Church. What problems existed then did not seem to differ significantly from those of preceding decades.

Most pressing for the papacy was the settlement of the affair of southern Italy. After the defeat of the Hohenstaufen, a new vassal prince had to be found to hold the Norman Kingdom from the pope. St. Louis IX of France, diffident toward the purely temporal concerns of the papacy, declined the proffered crown but finally permitted his brother Charles of Anjou to accept it. The native population soon discovered that it cared less for French than for German overlords. In 1282 the people of Sicily massacred all Frenchmen on their island and invited the king of Aragon, related by marriage to Frederick II, to come and rule them. As rebels against a papal vassal the Sicilians incurred the pope's wrath. Successive pontiffs supported Charles and his descendants, excommunicated his enemies and preached a holy war against them, deposed the king of Aragon and sent French crusaders into Spain. For twenty years this War of the Sicilian Vespers raged until Boniface VIII in 1302 acknowledged the loss of Sicily and accepted a compromise.

No spiritual questions were involved in this conflict. It was a war for temporal rights of the popes as feudal sovereigns. As against Frederick II the damage done to papal prestige by the use of spiritual weapons to enforce temporal rights against princes who might otherwise claim to be good Catholics, fruitless diplomacy, defeats, waste of money, and diversion of interest from more important objects was more serious than contemporaries realized.

One reason why the Sicilian war dragged on so long was the short reigns and frequent, protracted vacancies of the Holy See. Twelve popes reigned between 1254 and 1294, three in the one year of 1276. Vacancies of thirty-four and again of twenty-seven months reveal grave dissensions among the cardinals, which stemmed from the rivalry of French and Italian interests. French influence in the Curia gradually increased as a result of the French orientation of papal policies.

Fourteenth Ecumenical Council. The Second Council of Lyons, summoned by Pope Gregory X for 1274, highlighted ecclesiastical developments in these years. The death of Aquinas en route to Lyons and of St. Bonaventure during the sessions lends an added significance to the Council. Three matters demanded attention: the situation of the Holy Land, the Greek schism, and disciplinary problems.

To revive concern for the precarious Syrian states, elaborate plans were laid at the Council as at Innocent III's Council in 1215. But this time no armies set out and in 1291 the last Christian outpost at Acre fell to the Turks. In the new world of national states there was no place for international enterprises on the scale of the great crusades.

For reasons more political than religious the Byzantine Emperor Michael VIII, following the expulsion of the Latins from Constantinople in 1261, opened negotiations with the pope for the end of the Greek schism. After much discussion, during which John Beccos, Patriarch of Constantinople, was converted to the Roman cause, a formula of agreement was achieved whereby the Greeks acknowledged papal primacy and Catholic teaching on the procession of the Holy Spirit. Byzantine delegates at Lyons accepted the agreement and the end of the schism was joyfully proclaimed; however, the reunion proved unpopular with the Greek population and was repudiated when Emperor Michael died.

Among the decrees of the Second Council of Lyons two are significant. Canon 2 sought to prevent delays in papal elections by providing for a secret conclave of the cardinals within ten days after the pope's death. Unless they agreed upon a new pontiff quickly the cardinals' diet was to be reduced to bread, water, and wine. Civil officials of the place of the conclave were charged with the execution of the scheme. Promulgated against the cardinals' opposition, the decree was soon suspended, then annulled entirely, but finally re-enacted in 1294 by Celestine V.

The Fourth Lateran Council's prohibition on the establishment of new religious orders was renewed. The tremendous success of the Dominicans and Franciscans had called into existence a bewildering variety of imitators, either entirely new groups or older ones reorganized along mendicant lines. Moreover, the popularity of the mendicants exacerbated the long-standing enmity between regulars and seculars. In 1253 the theologians at Paris had even voted to expel all friars from the University and had petitioned the pope to suppress them entirely. Armed with many com-plaints, the bishops at Lyons determined on drastic action. In its final form the conciliar decree suppressed all mendicant orders except the Dominicans and Franciscans, although a decision was withheld on the Carmelites and Augustinians pending further examination. These latter two eventually were permitted to continue also, but the Friars of the Sack, Pied Friars, Crutched Friars, Williamites, and other little known groups either disappeared according to the terms of the canon or amended their rule to escape condemnation.

Boniface VIII and the National Monarchies.   Twenty years after the Council at Lyons Pope Boniface VIII (1294–1303), the last great medieval pope, ascended the Chair of Peter. His nine year reign unmis-takably marked the beginning of the decline of papal prestige in European affairs. It was his misfortune to have as contemporaries Edward I of Eng-land and Philip IV of France, both national monarchs of the new stamp, both numbered among the great kings of their respective countries. Boniface, embodying perfectly the medieval concept of papal power, was fated to clash with these representatives of the new absolute, nationalistic political spirit.

For his high office Boniface VIII was excellently qualified. He was an expert in canon law with wide experience in the diplomacy of the Curia. He had good family connections and considerable wealth derived from some sixteen benefices. But there were corresponding defects: a legalistic mentality that failed to grasp the broader social aspects of issues; an attitude of unconcealed arrogance; an irascible temper that turned opponents into bitter enemies.

Boniface was in a weak position to engage in major disputes since enemies within the Curia hampered him at every step and the Sicilian war steadily drained his resources. The unusual events of his predecessor's reign and his own desire to enhance his family's fortunes plagued him throughout his pontificate.

Pope Celestine V (July 5–December 13, 1294) was certainly a saint — he was canonized as St. Peter Celestine in 1313 — but he was completely unversed in those secular matters of vital and valid concern to the papacy. His election came unexpectedly after a twenty-seven month dead-lock of the cardinals. Aware of his own incompetence Celestine abdicated and Boniface was elected. To prevent the very real possibility of a schism should the naïve hermit fall into the hands of enemies of the Church, Boniface kept Celestine under virtual arrest until his death. Malicious slander had it that Boniface had preyed upon Celestine's conscience, tricked him into resigning, procured his own election and then removed the guileless old man by murder.

An ambitious scheme for making his family, the Gaetani, great landholders in the vicinity of Rome brought Boniface into conflict with the powerful Colonna clan. He degraded two cardinals of this family, preached a crusade against their strongholds and destroyed the Colonnas' wealth. Implacable enmity filled the hearts of the ex-cardinals who found refuge at the French court where they spread against Boniface charges of heresy and usurpation of the papal throne.

Clericis Laicos.   The privileged position of the Church imposed a serious check on the new monarchies. As ever, ecclesiastical independence served as "a barrier in the path of despotism." That a considerable portion of the wealth of the kingdom and a sizable group of citizens should be beyond royal control irritated rulers such as Edward I and Philip IV. They sought to introduce innovations to eliminate these exemptions; Boniface VIII conservatively defended the established order recognized by medieval law.

Land held by the clergy in feudal tenure paid the usual assessments such as aids and relief, and the newer taxes levied as a result of the changing economic system. But the clergy enjoyed other income designated as "spiritualities": endowments providing for the care of souls, various fees, offerings, tithes and such. These were subject to no secular obliga-tions and could be touched only with papal consent. Since 1199 the popes themselves had taxed this property with increasing frequency to subsidize crusades to Palestine or papal crusades in Europe. Often popes permitted kings to collect this papally-imposed tax on the basis of vague crusading schemes. Thus in France a tithe for six, four, three, and two years respec-tively had been granted by the popes to the kings in 1274, 1284, 1289, and 1294. Always the funds were diverted to the ordinary expenses of the realm. In England the situation was similar. On one occasion Edward I demanded half of the annual revenue of all "spiritualities."

Trouble began when England and France went to war, for their monarchs demanded subsidies from the clergy from their exempt possessions. Here was no pretext even of a crusade, only the demand to contribute to the common defense. No protest came from the cowed bishops, but in France the abbot of Citeaux refused to pay and appealed to the pope. Boniface' reply was the bull *Clericis laicos* (February, 1296) reiterating the canon law of no taxation without papal consent. He added a single new element, a clause decreeing automatic excommunication for anyone demanding or paying unauthorized levies. Without hesitation the kings took up the challenge: Edward outlawed the clergy who refused to pay; Philip forbade the export of money outside his realm to strike at the papal purse. The latter also approached the University of Paris for opinions on the legality of Celestine V's abdication, hoping to contest Boniface's election.

Pope Boniface was taken by surprise by the furor provoked by his bull, for it only repeated in sharper form what everyone had long acknowledged. With his own conflict with the Colonnas about to begin, the pope neither desired nor dared quarrel with the kings. Moreover, the episcopate in both countries, with the exception of Archbishop Winchelsey of Canterbury, let it be known that they would not take a stand against their monarchs. Boniface then issued a series of bulls gradually weakening the tone of *Clericis laicos*: voluntary extraordinary levies were permitted, they might be imposed in time of emergency, and the king himself could be the judge of the emergency. The kings had won the first round. While maintaining the principle of exemption of ecclesiastical property, Boniface opened so many loopholes that, in France at least, the king's discretion was given free reign.

Boniface and King Philip IV. The second phase of Boniface VIII's conflict with the national monarchs concerned another clerical prerogative, the exemption of clergy from trial in secular courts. In 1301 Philip IV's agents arrested and imprisoned Bernard Saisset, bishop of Pamiers. Although the bishop was a persistent, indiscreet troublemaker, his unjust trial and condemnation made a mockery of justice to say nothing of benefit of clergy.

Boniface VIII was not the man to hesitate in the face of so obvious a violation of the law. Moreover, the first Jubilee Year, celebrated in

1300, had shown in the crowds of pilgrims to Rome that the masses of Europe were as loyal as ever to the Church. Boniface's personal problems also were temporarily solved. Two carefully composed bulls were soon on their way to France: *Salvator mundi*, revoking all privileges granted to Philip IV and reinstating *Clericis laicos*, and *Ausculta fili*, a personal letter to the king enumerating the pope's grievances. Saisset was to be turned over to the Curia; Philip should cease oppressing the Church; the French bishops were summoned to Rome for a synodal examination of the state of the French church.

Had Boniface stuck to the issue of the violation of benefit of clergy, his position would have been incontestable, but he carried the matter into the theoretical areas of Church-State relations. *Ausculta fili*, for example, read: "Let no one persuade you that you have no superior and that you are not subordinate to the head of the ecclesiastical hierarchy, for he is a fool who thinks thus." Other statements of this same sweeping nature followed, seemingly transferring the issue from the religious to the political field. Saisset was practically forgotten.

Immediately the French chancellor Peter Flotte denounced Boniface for attempting to infringe on the royal authority. By playing on national sentiment he procured from the French Estates General a solid demonstration of support for Philip IV. The insolence and disrespect toward the supreme pontiff displayed by the French and the dishonesty of the king's advisers in counterfeiting papal letters impugn the integrity of the whole French court.

Unam Sanctam.   Boniface replied on November 18, 1302, in the bull *Unam sanctam*, said somewhat inaccurately to be the most extreme statement ever made of papal claims to domination over the temporal power. Actually it presented no novel theories. The bull is couched in general terms with no explicit reference to the current dispute. *Unam sanctam* enunciates two principles: the distinction between temporal and spiritual power in St. Bernard's two swords metaphor, and the innate superiority of the spiritual in Gelasian terminology. As Christ's vicar the pope claims to exercise this supreme power on behalf of the Church. Hence, he concludes, "We declare, state, define and pronounce that it is altogether necessary for salvation that every human creature be subject to the Roman pontiff."

The difficulty is that it is impossible to determine whether this statement was supposed to mean that the pope's authority extends directly or only indirectly over purely temporal matters. The ancient concept of indirect control, the Gelasian theory, held that even kings are subject *ratione peccati* to the moral authority of the pope in the same way as any other Christian. This is and always will be the teaching of the Church.

On the other hand, since the days of Innocent IV canonists had veered toward the idea of direct control whereby the pope in virtue of his superiority might govern affairs of state in any respect whatsoever, irrespective of question of sin. Whether or not Boniface VIII had this extreme concept in mind, it is certain that some of his lawyers did go this far in their contributions to the pamphlet warfare engendered by the dispute. Among these were the Augustinians Giles of Rome and James of Viterbo, both of whom were rewarded with archbishoprics for their efforts. The French also interpreted *Unam sanctam* in this light and a violent explosion of anti-papalism resulted.

Although some French writers such as Peter Dubois and John of Paris attempted to answer the papalists' arguments, and in doing so they usually went to the opposite extreme of subordinating Church to State, the official reply to *Unam sanctam* was an emotional campaign of personal denigration against Boniface. Philip's legists charged the pope with simony, heresy, murder, sorcery, idolatry, and sacrilege. At a meeting of the royal council in June, 1302, in the presence of twenty-six bishops and eleven abbots, the charges were presented and an appeal made to a general council to judge the pope. In all France only the abbot of Citeaux and the bishop of Autun protested; they were arrested at once.

Boniface now prepared to pronounce formal excommunication against King Philip. Word of the pope's intention reached William of Nogaret, Philip's agent in Italy. To forestall the ban Nogaret gathered a band of desperadoes who attacked Anagni, Boniface's native town where he was then staying, and took the pope prisoner (September 7, 1303). Probably the Frenchman intended to carry Boniface back to France to place him on trial there, but after two days papal supporters rallied and expelled Nogaret. Boniface, broken in mind and body, returned to Rome where he died three weeks later.

The Sequel. Two cardinals had stood by Boniface VIII in his hour of humiliation. One of them succeeded him as Benedict XI. How to capitalize on the feeling of revulsion that swept Europe at the news of the outrage at Anagni without further endangering the authority of the Holy See: that was the new pontiff's problem. Benedict adopted a flexible attitude; he made known his willingness to pardon whoever acknowledged his guilt and repented. Philip IV was permitted to extricate himself and to receive back former privileges. Only Nogaret and those directly involved in the attack on Boniface remained unreconciled when Benedict died after seven months.

Clement V, chosen after eleven months of wrangling by the cardinals, never departed from his native France. Unable to resist pressure from Philip, he granted concession after concession. Since only an ecclesiastical condemnation of Boniface could save the king's reputation, that became the aim of the royal diplomacy. Clement having weakly temporized as long as possible, yielded finally and allowed formal hearings to commence in what might be called the case of Philip the Fair *vs.* Boniface VIII. Nogaret, boldly acting as prosecutor, presented charges ranging from heresy to debauchery against the deceased pontiff. Philip, who was using the trial partly to force Clement to suppress the Knights Templars, finally withdrew his charges. With a sigh of relief the pope quashed the proceedings, wrote the king praising him for his pious motives and zeal for the welfare of the Church, and granted conditional pardon to Nogaret. Officially Boniface was exonerated, yet so thoroughly had his maligners blackened his name that even today it is difficult to obtain an unbiased, honest appraisal of this last of the great medieval popes.

REVIEW AIDS

1. Show how the economic and social changes taking place in Europe in the later middle ages affected the Church.
2. How did the intellectual atmosphere of Europe contribute to the decline of the Church?
3. Explain the concepts of nationalism and political absolutism. Why were these to play so profound a role in the problems of the Church?
4. What was achieved by the Council of Lyons?
5. In what way did Boniface VIII's personality influence his policies?
6. What were the circumstances that led Boniface to issue *Clericis laicos?*
7. Analyze the bull *Unam sanctam.*
8. Trace the steps by which Benedict XI and Clement V resolved the dispute between Boniface VIII and Philip IV.

SUGGESTIONS FOR FURTHER READING

The best summary of the position of the Church in the age of transition is the article by Wallace K. Ferguson, "The Church in a Changing World: A Contribution to the Interpretation of the Renaissance," *American Historical Review,* LIX (October, 1953), 1–18. Also helpful, although dealing with politics only, is J. R. Strayer, "The Laicization of French and English Society in the Thirteenth Century," *Speculum,* XV (1940), 76–86. Philip Hughes, *A History of the Church,* III, 1–101 is well done. H. J. Schroeder, *Disciplinary Decrees of the General Councils* (St. Louis: 1937), describes the Council of

Lyons. *Boniface VIII*, by T. S. Boas (London: 1933) is without doubt the best biography of the pope, although Vol. XVIII of H. K. Mann, *Lives of the Popes in the Middle Ages* (St. Louis: 1932) is also good. Volume V of R. W. Carlyle and A. J. Carlyle, *History of Mediaeval Political Theory in the West*, 6 vols. (London: 1928–1936), analyzes Boniface' theories and ties them in with the general position of the popes before his time. See also Daniel-Rops, *Cathedral and Crusade*, Chapter XIV.

DOCUMENTS

One of the most famous documents of the medieval papacy is Pope Boniface VIII's bull *Unam sanctam*. Although issued on the occasion of the pope's dispute with King Philip IV of France, the bull does not mention that particular issue; rather, it is couched in general terms for universal application. This tendency to appeal to the fundamental principles instead of negotiating on the specific matters in dispute is characteristic of the medieval papacy and it rendered it difficult to settle arguments amiably. Text in H. Denzinger, *Enchiridion Symbolorum*, 24–25th ed. (Barcelona: 1948), pp. 218–220.

Faith compels us to believe and to accept one, holy, catholic, and apostolic Church. This we believe and openly confess, nor is there salvation or remission of sins outside it. . . . Therefore there is one body of the one unique Church, and one head, not two like a monster, that is, Christ and Peter the vicar of Christ, and the successors of Peter, according to Christ's words to Peter: "Feed my sheep." "My sheep," He said, speaking in general and not referring specifically to these or those. By this we understand that all were entrusted to him (Peter). If therefore the Greeks or others say that they were not entrusted to Peter and to his successors, they necessarily admit that they are not Christ's sheep. For as the Lord said according to John, "There is one fold and one shepherd."

The Gospel teaches us that there are two swords in the Church's power, the spiritual and the temporal. . . . The latter is used on behalf of the Church, the former by the Church. The former belongs to the priest, the latter is used by kings and soldiers but according to the will and discretion of the priest. However it is proper that one sword be above the other, that the temporal authority be subject to the spiritual. . . . We ought to admit that the spiritual power surpasses the temporal in dignity and nobility just as spiritual things surpass temporal things. . . . For truly the spiritual power has the right to institute the temporal power and to judge if it is good. . . . Therefore if the temporal power errs it will be judged by the spiritual, but if a lesser spiritual power errs it will be judged by a superior; and if the supreme power errs it can be judged by God alone, not by man. For the Apostle says: "The spiritual man judges all things but he is judged by no one." This authority, even though given to a man and exercised by a man, is not human but rather divine. It was given by God to Peter and it was confirmed to him and to the successors of him whom the Lord confessed to be a rock, when He said to

Peter, "Whatsoever you shall bind, etc." Whoever therefore resists this power ordained by God, resists the ordinance of God, unless like a Manichee he imagines that there are two principles — which we judge to be false and heretical since according to Moses, "God created heaven and earth in the beginning," not, "in the beginnings." Wherefore we declare, state, define and pronounce that it is altogether necessary for salvation that every human creature be subject to the Roman pontiff.

Chapter 17

THE AVIGNON PAPACY

FROM 1309 to 1376 the capital of Christendom was Avignon, a city situated on the east bank of the lower Rhone, now French but then still part of the imperial fief of the County of Provence. The chief feature of these seventy some years is the growing French influence at the papal Curia which, while less than is often believed, was nevertheless evident enough to evoke nationalist reactions. This was a clear indication of changing times, as was also the dismal papal conflict with Emperor Louis IV. Yet the splendor of the Curia, the better than average caliber of the popes, the absence of serious heresy, and the many influential saints of the fourteenth century induced a false sense of security that obscured the fact that the tenor of life was changing in the direction of secularism.

The Papacy at Avignon. The fundamental reason for the papal sojourn at Avignon was the insecurity of Rome and of all Italy. Rome itself was always a turbulent city in the middle ages and now the meaningless conflicts between the Guelfs, nominally pro-papal, and the Ghibellines, nominally anti-papal, both factions the heritage of the Hohenstaufen wars, tore Italy asunder. Under such circumstances it was natural that the popes would do as they had often done before, that is, seek temporary refuge elsewhere. That Avignon became the site of the papal residence was largely accidental. Pope Clement V was elected in 1305 while archbishop of Bordeaux; his poor health and the press of negotiations with Philip IV of France prevented his going to Rome immediately. In 1309 he visited Avignon and stayed there almost until his death as guest of the Dominicans. Pope John XXII was bishop of Avignon and his dispute with the emperor persuaded him to stay where he was safest. By that time the Italian wars had become so acute that the journey to Rome seemed too dangerous and was again postponed. In 1348 the pope purchased Avignon and built a papal palace. Yet all seven of the Avignon popes realized and admitted the necessity of returning to Rome as soon as it could safely be done.

French Influence.   The prolonged papal absence from Rome was not unprecedented. It has been calculated that of the 205 years from 1099 to 1304 the popes spent 122 years away from Rome. However, the continuous residence in one place and the air of permanence that went with it were new features, but what made the greatest difference was the fact that men of the fourteenth century were beginning to view events with eyes clouded by that national sentiment which so sharply distinguishes the modern from the medieval world.

Englishmen, Germans, and Italians found it difficult to believe that a French pope surrounded by mostly French cardinals and living across the Rhone from France would not favor France at the expense of other nations. And the French took pride in their pre-eminence at the Curia and looked to pope and cardinals alike to promote French interests. Everyone, therefore, tended to read ulterior motives of a nationalist nature into anything connected with the papacy which aroused his disfavor. In short, a pope residing at Avignon could not, it was felt, be the neutral and objective head of the Catholic Church that a pope at Rome could be. Whether the assumption was valid or not, Europeans of the fourteenth century accepted it and spoke and acted accordingly.

The actual extent of French domination of the papacy was considerable but it has been greatly exaggerated. All seven of the Avignon popes were French as were seventy-five per cent of the cardinals whom they appointed, and Avignon lay only a stone's throw from the French kingdom. Certainly Clement V submitted all too readily to pressure from the French king, but this unfortunate pope was dealing with Philip the Fair, an extraordinarily difficult, ruthless monarch. Clement could just as easily be accused of excessive complaisance toward Edward I of England. John XXII also leaned heavily on Louis X and Philip V during his conflict with Emperor Louis, and to keep their friendship he excommunicated their enemies in Flanders. French rulers were allowed to tax ecclesiastical property heavily, but the popes lent money to both English and French kings.

Nevertheless, the conduct of the Avignon popes toward France was on the whole far from obsequious. Legates interfered frequently in the Anglo-French war whether advantageous to France or not. Benedict XII peremptorily forbade Philip VI to conclude an alliance with Louis of Bavaria, to mediate between Scotland and England, or to confiscate Guienne from a troublesome vassal. Gregory XI protested vehemently in 1372 when Charles V encroached on the jurisdiction of ecclesiastical courts. In many instances where papal diplomacy supported that of France or sought to cultivate French good will the explanation lay in the fact that such action seemed best for the Church under prevailing circumstances. Benefits accruing to France were often of only secondary concern. Thus while the popes argued with the German emperor it was only natural that they should strive to keep in particularly good graces with France; this had been papal policy ever since Gregory III appealed to Charles Martel against the Lombards.

Character of the Avignon Popes. Personally the Avignon popes present all the variations of temperament and personality that any group of seven successive pontiffs would reveal. Some were reformers, two have been beatified, some showed great strength of character and others little. Clement VI was a prodigal nobleman and John XXII an ascetic. Five of these pontiffs were renowned as canonists. Most of them could claim to be scholars and to be actively interested in education. Urban V shared in the establishment of the Universities of Cracow, Vienna, and Orange. All the Avignon popes strove to stimulate crusading enthusiasm and to settle the Hundred Years' War. Finally, the whole group was characterized by administrative ability of the highest order.

Petrarch first gave Avignon the name "Babylon," an appellation from the *Apocalypse* which furnished him many an invective with which to denounce the city and the Curia for the corruption supposedly rampant there. He described Avignon as "the hell on earth, the sink of vice, the sewer of the world," yet he spent many years there himself living from the generosity of ecclesiastical patrons. He was a disappointed Italian patriot and his description is not accepted as accurate. Reformers such as the extremist wing of the Franciscans to whom all material possessions smacked of sin also heaped abuse on Avignon. It is true that the tenor of life at Avignon was not always conducive to spirituality. The papacy was a great power and as such subject to corruption because of the human element involved. Yet derogatory statements of biased contemporaries must always be examined in the light of the particular frame of reference of those who uttered them.

Reign of Pope Clement V (1305–1314). Three significant events occurred during the reign of the first Avignon pope, Clement V: (1) the end of Philip the Fair's action against Boniface VIII, (2) the suppression of the Knights Templars, and (3) the fifteenth ecumenical Council held at Vienne. All revolved around the fundamental question of Boniface VIII; in order to persuade the king to drop his accusations against Boniface the Templars were sacrificed and the council was summoned chiefly to consider their dissolution.

The suppression of the Templars as a religious order revealed clearly to all Europe how thoroughly Clement V was dominated by the king of France. The final loss of the Holy Land in 1291 raised the question of the fate of the military orders. The Hospitallers maintained a tenuous foothold on the island of Rhodes; the Teutonic Knights transferred to Prussia; the Templars were left with nothing but the European financial undertakings in which they had become involved on a very large scale. Moreover they were richly endowed. Philip IV, having expelled the Jews and Lombards from France as an excuse for confiscating their wealth, eyed the Templars' endowments covetously.

False accusations of heresy, idolatry, and other crimes were fabricated and circulated in France by the king's agents. Philip then arrested all Templars in his domain — a violation of their clerical immunity — and tortured them until they confessed to whatever he desired. Pope Clement was offered the choice of a canonical investigation of the order or a renewal of Philip's demands for the condemnation of Boniface VIII; he chose the former, and summoned a general council to hear the matter. A commission of the Council reported that the order could not be judged until the Knights had been allowed to speak in their own defense. Clement then simply issued a decree dissolving the order without exonerating or condemning it. Although its property was to pass to the Hospitallers, King Philip managed to lay hold of most of it in France. The grand master was burned as a relapsed heretic when he recanted his forced confession and stoutly protested the pope's action.

Since the official acts of the Council of Vienne have not survived, little is known directly about that assembly. Three sessions in all were held between October, 1311, and March, 1312. About 300 members of the hierarchy attended. In addition to the case of the Templars, consideration was given to the Franciscan Spirituals and the Beghards, and to plans for a new crusade. The Council enacted various disciplinary decrees, of which those seeking to mitigate the discord between the secular clergy and the friars, those concerning episcopal visitations, and those dealing with lax clergy deserve mention.

John XXII and the Franciscans. Circumstances surrounding the election of Pope John XXII presaged a troubled reign. He was frankly a compromise candidate chosen because of his advanced age after two years of wrangling among the cardinals. Nevertheless John XXII reigned for eighteen vigorous years and died at the age of fourscore and ten — the longest reign and the oldest pope of the Avignon line.

Schism within the ranks of the Franciscans immediately presented a formidable problem. Quite early in the order's history two groups had taken shape, the Spirituals and the Conventuals, differing on the question of a more or less rigid interpretation of the rule of poverty. St. Bonaventure and Pope Nicholas III had attempted unsuccessfully to resolve the difficulty in the last century. The Council of Vienne and Clement V's bull based on its investigation had likewise proved abortive. John XXII found a radical group among the Spirituals, the Fraticelli, resorting to force to overcome their more liberal brethren. John threatened the Fraticelli with excommunication and a temporary lull set in.

In 1322 the friars' general chapter precipitated a new crisis by declaring in vindication of the Spirituals' views that it had always been a matter of faith that Christ and the Apostles had lived in absolute poverty. Pope John condemned this opinion as heretical and imprisoned Bonagratia of Bergamo, the impassioned Franciscan representative at Avignon. Most of the friars acquiesced in John's declaration and in the changes he ordered in the Franciscan constitution. However, Michael of Cesena, the Minorite minister general who had been summoned to Avignon, quarreled violently with the pope in 1328 and fled, taking with him Bonagratia and William of Ockam, another Franciscan under suspicion for his teachings at the University of Paris. These three, plus a few remaining dissidents, found a powerful protector in Emperor Louis IV.

John XXII and the Empire. Nowhere is the transitional character of the Avignon period more obvious than in the last of the major conflicts between pope and emperor which erupted at this time. In many respects the quarrel of John XXII and Louis IV paralleled earlier disputes: the papal claims to jurisdiction over the Empire, the imperial invasion of Italy, the nomination of an antipope, the excommunications, the intransigence of the original contestants, the literary activity on both sides. Yet in other respects there lay important differences: the Empire was moribund and only its corpse was at stake; the popes won a victory but ten years later meekly surrendered the principle they had been fighting for; a semblance of national German resistance to the papacy manifested itself; and the political theories enunciated by the imperialists betrayed an entirely new concept of the position of the Church in society.

Basically the popes aimed at preventing a resurgence of the Ghibelline power south of the Alps. Italy was the key to their policy. Possibility of imperial authority again exerting itself there raised the specter of a new "viper breed" laying violent hands on the Papal State and called forth extreme measures of defense.

The facts in the dispute can be briefly enumerated. A double election occurred in 1314 between Frederick of Austria and Louis of Bavaria and it was not settled until Louis defeated his rival after eight years of civil war. Pope John XXII had remained neutral but when the victorious Louis showed an interest in the affairs of northern Italy John declared him a usurper on the ground that no man might exercise the rights of emperor without papal approbation. When Louis refused to countenance such a claim the pope excommunicated him. The emperor received support from Marsilius of Padua and the disaffected Franciscan minority, among whom were John of Jandun and William of Ockam, both university professors, and Michael of Cesena, all of whom Louis sheltered at his court. These came to Louis' defense by accusing John XXII of heresy because of his refusal to accept the Spirituals' ideas on the poverty of Christ, and later because of the really strange views on the Beatific Vision which the pope preached in a private sermon. On a visit to Rome in 1328 Louis set up a Franciscan friar as antipope but this maneuver collapsed quickly. The German clergy, ignoring the pope's threats, opposed or aided Louis as their personal interests dictated.

After Pope John's death efforts at compromise between Louis and, successively, Benedict XII and Clement VI failed over the insurmountable obstacle of the papal claim to the right of approving German elections. Initially Louis had the support of many German princes, lay as well as ecclesiastical, before whom he posed as champion of German interests against a usurping papacy. In 1338, the princes announced by the Declaration of Rense, confirmed as imperial law the next year, that their votes alone were sufficient to elect the emperor, that papal approval was not necessary to add validity to their act, and that John XXII's measures against Louis had been unjust. However, Louis, a weak, vacillating man, gradually alienated many of his friends, especially when he attempted to set aside by imperial decree the Church's marriage laws for his dynastic advantage. In 1346 the electors chose a new emperor in the person of Charles of Moravia who had first secured papal approval by visiting Avignon and promising whatever Clement VI demanded.

Charles IV's Golden Bull. When Louis died in 1347 it seemed as if the *sacerdotium* had again won a decisive victory over the *imperium*. Yet ten years later the principle for which Louis had fought was firmly fixed as the uncontested law of the Empire. Charles IV (1347–1378), who owed his office to the efforts of his former tutor Pope Clement VI, blandly ignored the Holy See after his election. An uneasy truce ensued. Then in 1356 Charles issued his famous Golden Bull to regulate all phases of the electoral process and of the rights of the electors. He did not disclaim the role of the pope in the procedure, he simply ignored it. The seven electors were to cast their ballots and the candidate with the majority was thereby emperor-elect. No mention was made of any necessity of securing or even asking for the pope's approval. Pope Innocent VI, apparently realizing the hopelessness of the situation, protested only feebly. But in tacitly renouncing imperial pretensions in Italy, the Golden Bull did end for good and all the threat of German domination south of the Alps. This, in the final analysis, was the main, if unmentioned, source of all the trouble.

New Political Theories. The literary aspects of this last papal-imperial imbroglio disclosed distinctly the advent of a new age. Whereas the defenders of the papacy reiterated the old arguments of earlier centuries, the imperialists developed bold new ideas, many of which were considerably in advance of the times. Rather than merely trying to defend the power of the prince against papal claims to temporal authority, they attacked even the spiritual power of the pope. William of Ockam wielded his powerful pen to show that John XXII had usurped powers not belonging to him and proposed a general council as the means to check papal absolutism. Marsilius of Padua, former rector at the University of Paris, collaborated with John of Jandun on the truly revolutionary work entitled *Defender of Peace*.

Defender of Peace was antipapal in that it denied the pope any superiority over other bishops, except in a purely administrative sense. It was anticlerical in foreshadowing the later Protestant concept of the priesthood of all believers, and proposing an assembly representing all the faithful as the supreme authority in disputed matters of faith. It was secularistic in reducing the Church to an arm of the State, advocating state control over the Church in everything except the administration of the sacraments, i.e., in such matters as ownership of property, deciding who should or should not be ordained, and practically abolishing canon law as distinct from civil law. Strange to say, the papal side produced no champion to disprove adequately Marsilius' work and, in spite of John XXII's condemnation, it survived, was translated into the vernaculars, and seventy years later was in part accepted by respected Catholic thinkers. But not until the sixteenth century were all these ideas again so blatantly advocated.

Centralization Continues. All Avignon popes were able administrators and under their guidance the process of centralization and consolidation of ecclesiastical government in the papacy reached its medieval peak. Urban V issued new regulations for the apostolic chamber. The chancery functioned more smoothly than ever. Further steps were taken to subdivide judicial work; the special court known as the Rota is clearly in evidence after 1336. It handled cases arising from disputes concerning the holding of benefices whose collation was in the pope's hands. A fourth major administrative agency, the apostolic penitentiary, was given a comprehensive set of rules by Benedict XII in 1338; it functioned to put an end to the effects of ecclesiastical censures of all kinds, to give absolution in reserved cases, to remove various canonical irregularities, and to grant dispensations from impediments to marriage.

Papal Provisions. Clear indication of the extent of centralization was the papal assumption of the right to appoint to all benefices throughout Christendom. Through a series of bulls beginning with Clement IV in the thirteenth century patrons were deprived of their right of nomination and chapters lost the right of election as more and more offices were filled by direct papal provision. By the time of Urban V (1362–1370) few ecclesiastical benefices remained that the popes did not claim, although their actual control was often limited by compromises with secular authorities.

Everywhere this extension of papal control encountered lively opposition. In Germany where ecclesiastical lords and corporations were particularly well entrenched papal appointees were physically mistreated when appearing to assume office. Very bitter resistance in England produced numerous complaints in Parliament and culminated in the Statute of Provisors (1351) declaring papal provisions illegal. Two years later the Statute of Praemunire forbade appeals from England to the papacy without royal consent.

Nevertheless the papal policy gradually prevailed since some improvements in personnel did result. It should also be noted that the system of free election had generally broken down by this time anyway and all too often factional fights and wrangling disgraced the Church. Papal provisions can be regarded as an effort to amend this situation.

Finances. All European monarchs in the fourteenth century, likewise striving to build up centralized governments, had to face the problem of finance. The papacy was no exception. This problem was especially acute with the papacy separated from its accustomed Italian revenues and because of the inflation in Europe in the later fourteenth century. In fiscal matters the Avignon popes, John XXII primarily, showed great ingenuity, reshaping or creating a vast financial structure designed to produce sufficient revenue for the Holy See. Numerous and diverse were the levies projected. One group consisted of those collected directly at the Curia. Upon appointment the members of the hierarchy were assessed a sum equal to one third of the annual revenue of their benefice; a list was maintained on file of the assessed value of every bishopric to facilitate this payment. A host of fees surrounded every transaction with the Curia in the form of "gratuities" to personnel, charges for preparation of documents, charges payable at the time of *ad limina* visits, and fees for the reception of the pallium.

A second group of taxes were those collected locally, for which purpose a network of papal tax agents covered Europe. These included the tithe, annates (the entire revenue of a benefice the first year after it had been bestowed), the right of spoil by which papal collectors received all movable property of deceased bishops, and the right to all revenues during vacancies of benefices.

These were all levies on Church property or churchmen, but they were felt by all Catholics. Taxes are never popular and in the fourteenth century, with the devastation of France and heavy impositions of English and French kings during the Hundred Years' War, with the ravages of the Black Death from 1348 to 1350, with the general scarcity of money, coupled with objectionable methods of collection, these taxes were considered oppressive.

One reason why people objected to papal taxes was the common suspicion that the Avignon papacy was squandering its revenue on luxury and frivolity. St. Bridget of Sweden wrote some harsh words to Clement VI on this subject. Much pomp and material splendor pervaded Avignon during Clement's reign since he came from a high aristocratic family and like most medieval nobles he was inclined to financial prodigality. There were scandals of one sort or another to fire the popular imagination. But the situation varied considerably from one pope to another. A modern study has shown that under John XXII the three largest charges on the papal treasury were military affairs, Curial expenses, and alms, in the sums of 63 per cent, 12 per cent, and 7 per cent respectively of the annual revenue.

Reform Efforts. Although abuses existed at times, reform projects of diverse types also appeared sporadically. Benedict XII (1334–1342) and Innocent VI (1352–1362) drove away some of the hangers-on at the Curia, compelled absentee bishops and clergy to return to their duties, and tried to prevent the appointment of laymen as commendatory abbots. Benedict especially concerned himself with the religious orders. Cistercians, Benedictines, Augustinian Canons, Dominicans, and others were subjected to review and correction by this monk pope. Clement V earlier had legislated for the Benedictines. Disciplinary decrees of Clement V and John XXII eventually found their way into the Code of Canon Law under the title of *Clementines* and *Extravagantes*. Unfortunately the disruption of normal life by the terrible Black Death and then by the great schism, in addition to the natural tendency to resist change, vitiated many of these measures.

Popular Mysticism. If papal reform efforts often failed to percolate downward, many sincere individuals were striving on a lower level and in their own fashion to sustain the spiritual life of the Church. Some of these popular reformers lost their bearings and found themselves under ecclesiastical censure. In Germany the Flagellants and Brethren of the Free Spirit fell into heresy as had the Fraticelli in Italy. On the other hand, numerous outstanding figures contributed to making the fourteenth the greatest century of Catholic mysticism. The new mysticism represented a transformation from the older monastic type to a more popular form, expressed in less philosophic terms and preached or written in the vernacular languages.

In Italy St. Catherine of Siena (1347–1380) holds the first place; her reputation was such that even the popes respected her opinions. St. Bridget of Sweden (d. 1372) spent her mature years in ascetic exile in Rome. Bl. Giovanni Valle organized the Reform of the Strict Observance to revive in orthodox fashion the pristine spirit of the Franciscans. In northern lands the Preaching Friars played an integral part in the popular mysticism of the Rhineland and the Low Countries. Master Eckhart, Bl. Henry Suso, and John Tauler, all Dominicans, enjoyed tremendous followings between 1280 and 1360. The Friends of God and the Beguines, laywomen ascetics living community life, were much influenced by them. Also in the lower Rhine area Bl. John Ruysbroeck (d. 1381) occupied an important place, while Gerard Groote (d. 1384), a figure of great significance in the religious history of the later middle ages, was just approaching the summit of his short life during the reign of the last Avignon pope.

All these figures and their many followers shared a desire for change of emphasis in their religious life, a change away from the theological intellectualism so highly regarded in the thirteenth century toward a rediscovery and re-emphasis on the role of man's will in his religion. There is much ambiguity and obscurity in their writings. They avoided precise definitions and dogmatic exactitude and this has caused some to see in them distant and accidental Protestants; however this is entirely unfair since none of the mystics had any inclination to break from Catholicism.

The Missions.   One of the glories of the Avignon period is the missionary labor of the mendicant friars. By this time few areas of Europe remained in paganism so the missionary scene shifted to more distant parts of the world. The most famous of the missionary friars is the Franciscan John of Monte Corvino who reached China before 1300 and preached in Peking before the Great Khan himself. According to John's report he baptized about 6000 converts despite opposition from Chinese Nestorians. In 1307 Pope Clement sent ten Minorite bishops to his aid with orders to consecrate John archbishop of Peking. Benedict XII also sent reinforcements. Three Christian churches were constructed in a see at Zaiton on the Pacific coast of China. Bl. Odoric of Porderone is said to have converted 20,000 Chinese. Mission stations even dotted the overland route between Europe and Peking. Samarkand was erected as an episcopal see by John XXII. India, Ceylon, Borneo, and Java were also penetrated.

Dominicans were particularly active in Persia where John XXII in 1318 organized the metropolitanate of Sultaniyah with ten suffragans. In north Africa Raymond Lully, a Franciscan tertiary, labored with more enthusiasm than success. At Raymond's urging Clement V and the Council of Vienne ordered the universities of Paris, Oxford, Bologna, and Salamanca to teach courses in Greek, Hebrew, Chaldean, and Arabic to student mis·

sionaries. This marked the beginning of a scientific approach to missionary effort.

However, a revolution in China in 1368 and Tamerlane's conquest of Persia closed these areas to Christianity. Although Franciscans were still heard of in Peking for a few more decades a curtain of silence soon fell over the Church in the Orient that was not lifted until the Jesuits reached India and China in the sixteenth century.

The Return to Rome. Consciously if not steadfastly the Avignon popes prepared for the day of their return to the city on the Tiber. To establish order in Rome, to expel the usurpers from the Patrimony, and to aid the Guelfs everywhere: these comprised the threefold program by which they hoped to make that return possible. War raged constantly in Italy until 1334, with Pope John XXII hesitating neither in the use of arms nor in the use of excommunication and interdict to accomplish his goals, but all in vain. The Italians were becoming so accustomed to papal fulminations that they paid no heed to ecclesiastical censures. After 1350 new efforts produced greater success when the papal army was led by the brilliant Spanish statesman and soldier Cardinal Albornoz. Finally in 1367 Urban V deemed the situation favorable and returned to the Patrimony only to be practically driven back to Avignon by new rebellions after the death of Albornoz. By 1375 eighty cities in the States of the Church were in league to achieve their independence.

But now a new force came upon the scene in the person of St. Catherine of Siena. Catherine journeyed to Avignon in person to exhort Gregory XI in God's name to overcome all obstacles raised by his cardinals and his relatives and show himself in Rome. Gregory could not resist Catherine's pleas. Sending Cardinal Robert of Geneva by land with a new mercenary army, the pope himself sailed from Genoa. By January, 1377, he was in the Vatican. Papal forces checked the revolt of the cities with excessive brutality and commensurate success but Gregory XI died the following year before a permanent peace was concluded. The Avignon period had come to a close but a crisis of far vaster proportions was its legacy to the Church.

Conclusion. The unmistakable lesson of the Avignon period is the absolute necessity for the papacy to dissociate itself from specific nations and states. In an age of inchoate national feeling the Church had to protect its supranational character. Looking backward, the events of this time justify the papal defense against Hohenstaufen encroachments; for the future they map out the policies that resulted finally in the creation of the independent state of Vatican City.

REVIEW AIDS

1. In what respect can it be said that the Avignon period marked a stage in the decline of the Church?
2. What reasons can be alleged to explain the papal residence in Avignon?
3. Describe the work of the Council of Vienne.
4. Indicate some of the permanent achievements of the Avignon popes.
5. What were the reasons for dissatisfaction with the papal residence in Avignon on the part of the different states of Europe?
6. How did developments within the papacy at this time parallel contemporaneous developments among the states of Europe?
7. Explain the significance of John XXII's conflict with Louis of Bavaria.
8. Who were some of the mystics of the fourteenth century, and what was the significance of the group?

SUGGESTIONS FOR FURTHER READING

The classic survey has finally been translated: G. Mollat, *The Popes at Avignon* (London: 1963). Continuing useful is Helen Jenkins' monograph, *Papal Efforts for Peace Under Benedict XII, 1334–1342* (Philadelphia, 1933). A view of the troubled state of Italy is to be found in the second volume of Johannes Jorgensen, *Saint Bridget of Sweden*, 2 vols. (London: 1954). The same author's *St. Catherine of Siena* (New York: 1939) is also helpful in this respect as well as giving an insight into fourteenth century mysticism. The English reaction to the Avignon papacy is presented in John Tracy Ellis, *Anti-Papal Legislation in Medieval England* (1066–1377) (Washington, D. C.: 1930). Goeffrey Barraclough's monograph, *Papal Provisions* (Oxford: 1935) is important. For the religious orders at this time, from the point of view of England, see David Knowles, *The Religious Order in England* (1216–1485), 2 vols. Cambridge: 1950–55). A. C. Moule, *Christians in China before the Year 1550* London: 1930) takes up missionary activity in a scholarly fashion. Specific articles in the *Catholic Encyclopedia* can be consulted profitably.

DOCUMENTS

1. In his *Defender of Peace* Marsilius of Padua summed up his chief tenets in the form of handy conclusions. The half dozen reproduced here show how far Marsilius departed from the orthodox interpretation of the position of the pope and other bishops within the Church. Carl Mirbt, *Quellen zur Geschichte des Papsttums und des römischen Katholizismus*, 2nd ed. (Tübingen: 1901), p. 150.

2. Only a general council of all the faithful or the greater number or part of it ought to decide doubtful passages of the divine law, especially in regard

to those things which are called Articles of Faith and other things which must be believed for salvation's sake; and no other partial body or single person of whatever condition has the power to determine such matters.

5. No mortal can dispense from the divine commands or the prohibitions of the new law; only a general council or the Christian human legislator can forbid what is permitted under penalty of guilt or punishment in the present world or in the next.

7. Decretals or decrees of the Roman bishop or of any bishop whatsoever either as an individual or as a member of a group bind no one under pain or punishment unless promulgated with the consent of the human legislator.

17. All bishops are of equal authority directly from Christ, nor can it be proved from divine law that any are above or below the others in spiritual or temporal affairs.

22. It is the exclusive right of the ruler, in accordance with the laws of the faithful, to regulate the number of churches or temples and the number of those who minister in them — priests, deacons, and other officials.

25. No individual bishop or group of bishops as such can grant license to teach or publicly to practice an art or profession; that is the sole right of the Christian legislator or of one ruling by its authority.

NOTE: Marsilius refers the term "legislator" to the body of all the faithful.

2. During Emperor Louis the Bavarian's dispute with the papacy, the German princes gathered at Rense on July 16, 1338 and published a statement of their veiws. This Declaration of Rense upheld the emperor. It reveals faintly the first stirrings of nationalist sentiment which rallied the princes to the emperor's defense, against all traditions of feudalistic particularism, in the face of alleged encroachments by a foreign pope. Mario Krammer (ed.), *Quellen zur Geschichte der deutschen Königswahl und des Kurfürstenkollegs*, Heft II (Leipzig: 1912), pp. 91–92.

In the name of the Lord, Amen. Be it known to all by this present public enactment that in the year of the Incarnation 1338 . . . the venerable noblemen and lords have assembled in the orchard located beside the town of Rense on the Rhine where the electoral princes of the holy Roman Empire usually meet to discuss electoral or other business of the Empire. . . . they pronounced their judgment and definition that this is the law and approved ancient custom of the Empire: After anyone has been elected king of the Romans by the electors of the Empire or by the majority of them in case of dispute, he does not need the nomination, approbation, confirmation, assent or authorization of the Apostolic See for the administration of the goods and laws of the Empire or for taking the royal title. For these things the man elected has no need of having recourse to the same See. It has been the custom, observed as long as anyone can remember, that those whom the electors of the Empire elect either unanimously or by a majority, as stated above, have taken the royal title and have administered the goods and laws of the Empire, and they could and can do this legally by law and custom, without having received or obtained the approbation or permission of the said Apostolic See for doing so.

Chapter 18

THE GREAT WESTERN SCHISM
AND THE MENACE OF
CONCILIARISM

IMMEDIATELY following the pope's return from Avignon a grave constitutional crisis occurred within the Church. First came a schism in the papacy enduring for forty years, and from the schism arose a theory of ecclesiastical government that denied the plenary power of the Vicar of Christ and vested it instead in ecumenical councils. For thirty years more the popes struggled to recover their authority. All this distracted attention from the Church's primary function of guiding the moral conduct of Christendom and permitted further inroads by the State on the jurisdiction of the Church.

The Election of Pope Urban VI.   Pope Gregory XI died on March 27, 1378. Ten days afterward, as provided by canon law, the sixteen cardinals in Rome went into conclave. Present were eleven Frenchmen, four Italians, and a Spaniard. The French controlled the necessary two-thirds majority but they were split hopelessly into two stubborn factions. Obvious prospects of a deadlock caused the electors to canvass among themselves immediately after Gregory's death for a compromise, non-French candidate and some evidence indicates that they had reached a decision before the conclave began.

As the cardinals made their way into the Vatican for the election on the evening of April 7, they encountered a large, enthusiastic crowd of people clamoring for "a Roman pope, or at least an Italian." Having the papacy in their midst again after seventy years the Romans wanted no more French popes for fear of a return to Avignon. Throughout the period of the conclave the mob roamed the area, consuming wine rifled from the papal cellars and shouting soon for a Roman only. The din penetrated into the conclave. On the afternoon of the 8th the crowd even succeeded in forcing its way past the guards into the very conclave. Hastily the cardinals clothed in the papal robes the aged Cardinal of St. Peter's, one of the two Romans in the Sacred College, and persuaded him to show himself to the populace to pacify them and save the cardinals from insult or injury. In the midst of the confusion the cardinals scattered, some fleeing the city, others taking refuge at the papal citadel in the Castle of St. Angelo. For they had not fully yielded to the people's wishes; they had already unanimously elected a Neapolitan, Bartholomeo Prignano, Archbishop of Bari — an Italian, but not a Roman — who took the name Urban VI.

When the tumult of the election subsided and the cardinals returned, they ratified their action and acknowledged the new pope. They informed their absent colleagues of Urban's election. They celebrated the Holy Week services with Urban, asked and received favors, benefices, and the like from him, and in every way treated him as pope.

Pope Urban's Personality. The cardinals thought they had every reason to be satisfied with Prignano. A decade of service at the Curia at Avignon had provided him with experience and had apparently made him a Francophile. His ability had gained him the important position of papal vice-chancellor. Personally free from simony or any trace of avarice, the archbishop enjoyed an unsullied reputation. Peter Corsini, cardinal bishop of Porto, in a personal letter written six days after the election, spoke of Urban as follows: "We firmly believe and hope that, on account of his knowledge, his blameless life, his numerous great virtues, his wide experience, and with the help of Him whose vicar he is, he will rule the universal Church profitably, according to the will and justice of God, and that the whole Christian people will be comforted and consoled."[1]

There existed, however, one serious flaw in Urban's character, hitherto well concealed but now to prove his undoing. He was entirely lacking in prudence and tact, virtues indispensable for a successful ruler of any kind. Extravagant statements about his unlimited power escaped his lips. Altercations with curial officials and unrestrained outbursts against the

---

[1] Walter Ullmann, *The Origins of the Great Schism* (London: Burns, Oates and Washbourne Ltd., 1948), p. 31. Used by permission.

cardinals disgraced the Curia. Urban denounced individual cardinals in public and to their face as liars, traitors, and simoniacs. It seemed as if Urban, himself of humble family, suddenly released a long pent-up dislike of the proud aristocrats who surrounded him and who had raised him to the heights of authority in expectation of easily dominating him. Some historians have asserted that the sudden responsibility of his office upset Urban's mental balance since it is difficult to explain rationally some of his actions as pope.

Soon the cardinals began to regret having elected the former Archbishop of Bari and to feel that they had made a grievous mistake. Even if Urban deserves to be considered a genuine reformer zealous in the cause of the Church — as his contemporary St. Catherine of Siena believed — he certainly began in the worst possible way. Any attempt to amend the sacred college would have encountered opposition; Urban's uncouth actions provoked violent resistance. The cardinals were princes of the Church, accustomed to treatment of a far different sort. Any pope who so completely misunderstood the machinery of the Roman Curia must, in their eyes, be unsuitable to occupy the throne of Peter. Although a pope could not be deposed except for heresy, canon law recognized that fear or compulsion at the time of election invalidated that election. The riots of the Romans during the conclave seemed to have impaired the cardinals' freedom sufficiently that they might claim that Urban never had been truly pope.

The Schism. Having deserted Rome at the end of May because of hot weather, the cardinals assembled gradually at Anagni. From here they issued a manifesto, dated August 2, proclaiming to the world that Urban VI was not true pope since his election had been brought about only from fear of violence at the hands of the Roman mob. Since Urban refused to step down, as he was bidden, the cardinals went into conclave on September 20 and chose a Frenchman, Cardinal Robert of Geneva, as Pope Clement VII. Every one of the cardinals forsook Urban and adhered to Clement. The former, however, appointed a new college and excommunicated Clement and his followers; Clement reciprocated in kind. The Great Western Schism had begun.

Historians on the whole now agree that Urban VI was the legitimate pope. A mass of evidence has been unearthed and examined to substantiate this opinion. Even if the election itself had been invalid, the fact that the cardinals subsequently acknowledged Urban in public acts and in private correspondence and also requested and accepted favors and benefices (which they later refused to resign, even though denying Urban's right to bestow them) confirmed his right to the apostolic see.

But contemporaries lacked the evidence that is now available. All they knew was that Urban VI had been chosen only to be unanimously repudiated three months later. Each pope argued his case in the most convincing manner. Ultimately political interests largely determined the decision of the states of Europe. France readily accepted the Frenchman Clement and England just as readily declined to desert Urban. France's ally Scotland and the Spanish kingdoms, too, adhered to the Avignon line, while Italy, Scandinavia, and most of the Empire and eastern Europe accepted the Roman cause.

Canonized saints are found for both factions, likewise on a national basis: St. Vincent Ferrer and St. Collette, Spanish and French respectively, supported Avignon; St. Catherine of Siena and St. Catherine of Sweden zealously supported the Roman line of popes. Religious orders split within themselves; the Franciscans came to have two generals, one for each cause. Learned doctors and canonists were similarly divided. The ordinary Catholic layman, or clergyman too for that matter, had no choice but to accept the decision of an authority that seemed reliable and pray that his pope was not the schismatic and excommunicate.

The Cardinals.   Whatever may be alleged as causes for the schism it is clear that full responsibility for it rests with the cardinals. It is not necessary to impugn their motives but some light is thrown on their decision if the history of the Sacred College be kept in mind. And that history is a gradual evolution of administrative authority to the point where it had, by 1378, become a vested interest anxious above all to preserve if not to extend its jurisdiction.

Nicholas II's electoral decree of 1059 inaugurated the political rise of the cardinals. A checkered career, with much depending on the personality of the popes, brought them increased responsibilities paralleling the over-all increase in the business of the Curia. Their numbers were small — hardly ever more than twenty-five and often considerably less — creating a feeling of close comradeship and community of interest. They resided wherever the pope happened to be except when serving as legates on the most important missions, and often as legates cardinals showed an arrogant consciousness of their power. The corporate unity of the Sacred College was furthered when it was assigned definite revenues and a fixed share in the papal income. Normally the cardinals' opinions were asked and respected in matters of great import. Scions usually of proud aristocratic families, they were accustomed to command and to live on a grand scale, as truly princes of the Church as any duke or count was a prince of the State.

The Avignon period had augmented the role of the cardinals considerably. In fact, much of the scandal of this time stemmed from the deportment of prominent cardinals rather than from the pope. Even the secular rulers found it advantageous to curry favor with individual cardinals for the protection of their interests at the Curia. Nevertheless, the lack of solid guarantees of their power thwarted their advance. While they were coming to conceive of the government of the Church in oligarchical terms, tradition and law vested the plenitude of powers in the pope alone and saw the cardinals as subordinate rather than co-ordinate with him. This they were anxious to change. Even during the pontificate of Boniface VIII, a strong pope brooking interference from no one, Cardinal Johannes Monachus, a canonist of repute, asserted in his gloss on the *Sext* that the pope could enact nothing without the cardinals' consent. Further expressions of the same sentiment can be found. When Urban VI in 1378 threatened to reverse the trend he only added fuel to the cardinals' discontent.

Roman line	*Avignon line*	*Pisan line*
Urban VI	Clement VII	Alexander V
(1378–1389)	(1378–1394)	(1409–1410)
Boniface IX	Benedict XIII	John XXIII
(1389–1404)	(1394–1417)	(1410–1415)
Innocent VII		
(1404–1406)		
Gregory XII		
(1406–1415)		

Popes and Antipopes during the Great Western Schism

This tendency to guard jealously and expand if possible the prerogatives already theirs makes the Sacred College a formidable element in the history of the Church from now on. Reforms of every sort seem always to shatter on the granite-like resistance of the cardinals to any diminution of their privileges. Much of the trouble lay in the personnel of the College. Although there were notable exceptions, all too many of those who wore the red hat in the fourteenth century were unworthy of their office and incapable of understanding their responsibilities.

Attempts to End the Schism. Once the schism began it proved exceedingly difficult to heal. The French pope found an available capital at Avignon whither he repaired after a futile effort to capture Rome. When Urban and Clement died their respective Colleges at once picked successors. Neither they nor their popes were magnanimous enough to put the welfare of the Church above their own petty quarrels and ambitions in spite of the most solemn promises and oaths by all concerned. The two problems that seemed to attract all the popes' attention were: How to keep the various princes faithful and where was the money coming from? Canon law offered no solution. The latest precedent was the disputed election of Innocent II and Anacletus II in 1130 but then Europe had had Bernard of Clairvaux to decide the question by his moral persuasion alone.

Nor could either side vanquish the other by force. Bishop Despenser of Norwich led a crusade into France on Urban's behalf. Much warfare and diplomatic maneuvering centered on the Kingdom of Naples. But temporal weapons failed as dismally as spiritual. The secular states provided little effective leadership. At various times during the schism England was ruled by a childish king, France by an insane king, and the Empire by a chronic drunkard.

Could the learned world proffer any solution? From the beginning the theological faculty of Paris, foremost school of theology in Europe, interested itself in the problem. At first the theologians split equally between Urban and Clement but pressure from the French government soon brought the entire University to a reluctant acceptance of Clement. When the schism dragged on, however, and no end came in sight the University in 1394 canvassed its doctors and graduate theologians for a thorough census of opinion. Three possibilities were suggested: both popes should abdicate (*via cessionis*); a committee of arbitration should be appointed and its decision bind both obediences (*via compromissi*); a general council should assemble to tackle the problem (*via concilii*).

Voluntary resignation was the preferred solution, but the popes rejected the idea. The regents of France then tried to force the issue. In a national synod in 1398, closely controlled by the government, the French hierarchy voted to withdraw obedience from the Avignon pontiff and remain neutral. For five portentous years the Catholic Church in France acknowledged no head at all. But Benedict XIII refused to be coerced and in 1403 France again recognized him.

Hope of both popes' resigning was finally dashed in 1408. Benedict XIII and Gregory XII had each agreed to fulfill his oath to abdicate if his opponent would do the same. A meeting was arranged in northern Italy to smooth the way and amid the most complicated intrigue the two Curias moved toward the designated town of Savona. Benedict arrived but Gregory stopped short fifty miles away. Endless discussions, continuous negotiations, and streams of legates effected no results. The fact was that Gregory, at the insistence of his relatives, had changed his mind and Benedict had never been sincere. Exasperated, Gregory's cardinals now abandoned him. France again declared neutrality and Benedict's Curia also cut loose. Each College summoned the bishops of its obedience to a joint council of reunion at Pisa in 1409. Thus for a second time the cardinals deserted their chosen pontiffs.

The Council of Pisa. Pisa ushered in the conciliar epoch, that period of about forty years during which the theory of the supremacy of a general council over the pope was widely advocated and expressed in a multitude of councils. The failure of the popes to heal the schism naturally led to the thought of a council as the only expedient to save the Church from ruin. A council must sit in judgment over the recalcitrant pontiffs. But the conciliarists advanced a step further once the opening wedge had entered. Not only in the present emergency but at all times a general council is superior to the pope. The Church is not just the Holy Father but all the faithful in whom as a corporate entity ecclesiastical sovereignty resides. Popes administer the Church not with absolute power but subject to the greater authority of the faithful. Just as a parliament or diet represents a king's subjects, a general council represents the faithful members of the Church. The Church is not monarchical in its constitution but rather oligarchical or, with extreme conciliarists, democratic.

William of Nogaret and Marsilius of Padua had advanced the conciliar theme in their attacks on Boniface VIII and John XXII. The exigencies of the schism now lent an air of respectability to the theory and the University of Paris had urged it as a possible solution. So desperate was the situation after the failure of the way of abdication that all eminent writers accepted the conciliar idea. Among these were Cardinal Peter d'Ailly, John Gerson, Chancellor of the University of Paris, and Cardinal Zabaralla, the greatest canonist of the day.

Nevertheless the Council of Pisa failed to heal the schism. Its twenty-two cardinals and eighty-four bishops pronounced the deposition of Benedict XIII and Gregory XII and then proceeded to elect Alexander V who soon died and was replaced by John XXIII. As might have been anticipated, Benedict and Gregory did not recognize their deposition; they pointed to the simple fact that according to canon law only the pope could summon a legitimate general council. Three contenders now stood forth claiming to be the true successor of St. Peter.

John XXIII's cause deteriorated rapidly. Personally he was a poor choice and serious political trials beset him. At this juncture, Sigismund, the new German king, decided to intervene. Obsessed with his duty as temporal head of Christendom, mindful of the role of Constantine and ancient emperors in the early ecumenical councils, and finding John XXIII helpless in adversity, Sigismund forced him to convoke a new council to meet at Constance in November, 1414.

The Council of Constance. The Council of Constance was a truly remarkable assembly — for its size, its duration, its accomplishments, and its failures. Its fifty-five sessions spread in almost continuous sequence over three and a half years. Twenty-nine cardinals, 186 bishops, over 100 abbots, and about 300 doctors of theology and law attended the largest sessions. Since it was a revolutionary assembly, some question surrounds the validity of many of its acts. Sigismund, Gerson, and d'Ailly were the leading figures. Three obvious tasks presented themselves: extinction of the schism, extirpation of heresy, and reformation of the Church "in head and members."

John XXIII brought a crowd of Italian bishops faithful to himself in order to control a majority of the votes. Popular opinion, however, preferred to treat all three popes alike rather than merely confirming the action of the Council of Pisa. To forestall Italian dominance a novel scheme of voting was established whereby all delegates were lumped into four "nations," English, French, German, and Italian, each nation casting a single ballot in plenary sessions. After considerable vacillation Pope John suddenly fled in disguise, hoping to disrupt the assembly — and he almost succeeded. Rallying amid strong antipapal sentiment the Fathers passed five decrees, the famous Articles of Constance, enacting the superiority of a council over the pope and declaring their own competence. Sigismund's troops pursued John, captured and imprisoned him. In May, 1415, the Council declared him deposed. John ratified the decision without even trying to defend himself.

The Roman pope was easily disposed of, for Gregory XII resigned voluntarily after being allowed to convoke the Council in his own name. Benedict XIII proved more recalcitrant. Protracted negotiations and the withdrawal of support by the Spanish monarchs failed to move him. After a lengthy process the Council deposed him in July, 1417, for perjury, schism, and heresy. In November of that same year the cardinals, assisted by thirty delegates of the Council, elected Martin V as the first universally acknowledged pope in forty years.

Heresy: Wyclif and Hus. While the Fathers themselves formulated novel ideas of the government of the Church they were averse to any attempt to subvert the dogmatic content of Catholicism. Under cover of the schism and as a result of a strong current of anticlericalism in the later fourteenth century, reformers seized the opportunity to propagate their opinions. Several of these radicals were examined at Constance. Gerard Groote and his disciples were exonerated but the Fathers condemned John Wyclif and John Hus.

Wyclif, the foremost heretic of medieval England whom Protestants have hailed as "the morning star of the Reformation," first attracted attention while teaching at Oxford because of his attack on unworthy clergy. His career has much in common with the Waldensians. Carried away by his zeal and protected by John of Gaunt, the king's uncle, Wyclif became increasingly radical. To end clerical preoccupation with material things he advocated confiscation of all ecclesiastical property by lay lords. After 1380 he advanced to a denial of transubstantiation and of auricular confession, and an affirmation of predestination. The Bible, he asserted, was the sole rule of faith. Wyclif organized an active propaganda and wrote voluminously. His disciples, the "poor priests," spread his heresy over central England.

A provincial synod in London in 1382 condemned Wyclif's teachings but the only disability he suffered was expulsion from the University. He died two years later still in possession of his parish church but by then his ideas had been disseminated widely and came to be known as Lollardy. The Council of Constance re-examined Wyclif's arguments and confirmed the heresy of his writings.

Wyclif's books found their way to Bohemia and the University of Prague where they were taken up by an eloquent preacher John Hus. A strong Czech nationalist movement complicated the issue for the people regarded the condemnation of Hus by the University faculty, mostly Germans, and by the German archbishop of Prague, as motivated by hostility to the native population. King Wenceslas vacillated between fear of heresy and desire to protect his Czech subjects. In hope of vindicating himself Hus journeyed to Constance under safe-conduct from Emperor Sigismund. Refusing to recant his obvious errors he and his associate

Jerome of Prague died at the stake. Immediately Hus became a martyr to the Bohemians; his death stimulated rather than checked the spread of his opinions.

Reform. Disappointingly little positive reform was achieved at Constance although three different committees studied the subject. Too many of the Fathers were ecclesiastical politicians willing to improve others but not themselves. Their interests were reflected in various decrees in 1417 and 1418 limiting papal fiscal exactions and reaffirming rights of local ordinaries threatened by papal centralization. The forty-third session accepted seven general but insignificant decrees and Martin V negotiated special concordats with the various nations in lieu of further conciliar action.

In the opinion of many the revolutionary conciliar theory was itself the chief reform and offered the best remedy for all the Church's ills. The most zealous leaders at Constance strove to secure a sanction for this idea. They had lost confidence in the papacy. A major dispute in the last months concerned the question of election of a new pope before or after consideration of reform. According to the decree *Frequens* (Oct. 5, 1417), councils must be convoked periodically lest a reinvigorated papacy escape the implications of conciliarism by silently ignoring it. But in relying on a false program the Council doomed itself to failure in the matter of a reformation "in head" as well as "in members."

Pope Martin V. Although Martin V (1417–1431) himself rejected conciliarism, he hesitated to condemn it despite its obvious contradiction of the divinely established primacy of St. Peter. So strong was the current of conciliar sentiment, especially in learned circles north of the Alps, that Martin feared a new schism if he took a firm stand and therefore he temporized. *Frequens* provided for a general council five years after Constance. Martin summoned it to Pavia in 1423, transferred it to Siena, and then dissolved it as soon as he felt safe in doing so. A second council was supposed to meet seven years later. Reluctantly Martin announced Basle as the site and mid-1431 as the time for the next council but before it convened Pope Martin had died.

Had Martin V possessed more than mediocre ability he might have undertaken a vigorous reform program and given the lie to those who expected nothing but selfish concern for the *status quo* on the part of the Curia. As it was, Martin dreaded conciliarism so heartily that he equated all reform with that theory and consequently did nothing.

Reorganization of the government of the Papal State was his only accomplishment.

Council of Basle. The Council of Basle (1431–1449) had a long and confused history. Partly this was due to the vacillating policy of Pope Eugene IV (1431–1447) who dissolved the Council after a few months and then reconvoked it; who worked to undermine it while professing his support; who neither obeyed nor denounced its peremptory summons to himself to appear before it and be judged. Much confusion stemmed also from the fact that the Council of Basle represented the logical development of the conciliar theory. From an aristocratic government of bishops the conciliarists here advanced to a democratic concept on a republican basis. Comparatively few bishops attended, and those who did found their voices drowned out by the lesser clergy and often by laymen, mere bachelors in theology, all of whom enjoyed a vote equal to that of members of the hierarchy. Nicholas of Cusa and John of Segovia were the theoreticians of the Council although Nicholas deserted it when the radicalism inherent in his own writings became apparent.

Under the presidency of the Cardinal-legate Cesarini, the Council achieved one significant success, the settlement of the Hussite heresy. After Hus's death Bohemia fell into turmoil of civil war and militant heresy. Crusades against the heretics, called Utraquists or Calixtines because of their demand for the chalice in Communion, suffered ignominious defeat. Concessions were necessary if the Hussites were to be won back. By the Compacts of Prague (1433) the Hussites received from the Council permission to have Communion under both species, while they modified their other demands sufficiently to be again considered Catholics.

Jubilantly the Council turned to the subject of reform. Some decrees, as those against clerical concubinage, neglect of canonical obligations, and misuse of ecclesiastical censures received papal approbation. Others, aggressively attacking the pope and cardinals, depriving them of most of their revenues and reaffirming the pre-eminence of councils exhausted Eugene's patience. In 1437 he transferred the Council to Ferrara. All cardinals but one and most bishops obeyed but a few prelates and many inferior clergy remained at Basle, deposed Eugene and elected Felix V, the last antipope. Until 1449 they held out in schism but by then they had lost all secular support. Felix resigned and the schismatics disbanded after recognizing Nicholas V, the legitimate pope since 1447. Thus the active phase of conciliarism came to an end. In 1460 Pius II's bull *Execrabilis* formally condemned the theory although it lingered on as a favorite tenet of Gallicanism and of the religious rebels of the sixteenth century.

The Greek Reunion. Meanwhile the ecumenical section of the Council reconvened in 1438 at Ferrara, from which it too was subsequently transferred to Florence and finally to Rome. One major topic occupied its attention: the reunion of the dissident eastern Churches. Political adversity again impelled the Byzantine emperor to offer the bait of reunion as a means of gaining aid against the Turks who were now pressing Constantinople on every side. Eugene IV welcomed the opportunity for new discussions and even paid the expenses for the delegation of over 700 Greeks en route to Italy and for their seventeen-month sojourn there. Four points were debated: the procession of the Holy Spirit, papal primacy, purgatory, and the use of unleavened bread at Mass. At length a satisfactory accord was reached and on July 6, 1439, the reunion of the Churches was solemnly proclaimed.

Patriarch Joseph II of Constantinople, Bishop Bessarion of Nicaea, and Isidore of Kiev sincerely labored for reunion — Pope Eugene even promoted the two latter to the rank of cardinal — but the motives of the other Greeks were dubious. Just as after the attempted reunion at the Second Council of Lyons, so now too the factious Greek population repudiated the work of their hierarchy. Spurning spiritual submission to Rome, Constantinople fell in 1453 into total thralldom to the Ottoman Turks.

Saints and Religious Orders.   High ecclesiastical politics of the Schism and councils can easily mislead the student of history to overlook the more humble aspects of Catholicism during this age. Despite the general turmoil some important saints flourished and signs were not wanting of the divine life of the Church.

Joan of Arc, divinely summoned from her obscure bucolic home, played her mysterious role and in 1431 died a martyr to the corruption within the Church — death at the stake through the efforts of a political bishop of a French see to prove his devotion to the cause of England. Less obtrusive, St. Colette reinvigorated the French Poor Clares. Vincent Ferrer (d. 1419) preached to great throngs in Spain and France. The Observant branch of the Franciscans revived some of the glory of the Minorites through the work of SS. John of Capistrano, Bernardine of Siena, and James of the March. Bernardine "cleansed all Italy from sins of every kind" and gained the title "Apostle of the Holy Name" by his missionary campaigns. Capistrano also preached to huge crowds; he led a section of the Christian army on the crusade against the Turks that won a great victory at Belgrade in 1456.

Bl. Raymond of Capua and Bl. Giovanni Dominici, Gregory XII's cardinal confessor, reinvigorated the Friars Preacher. The Dominican archbishop of Florence, St. Antoninus (d. 1459), whose *Summa Theologica Moralis* marked a new development in moral theology, offers an example of a model bishop in an age renowned for shepherds who fleeced rather than fed their flocks.

Periodically new religious foundations have appeared — Cluny, Citeaux, the friars — to rescue the Church from tribulation and instill new life into its tired members. These troubled times of the Schism demanded such a group but the need was answered only in part. While the mendicants recovered in their Observant branches, the few new groups that arose were of limited, often local significance, like the Alexian brothers in Germany or the Bridgittines in Sweden. Christendom lacked the interior vigor to institute a European-wide ascetic movement.

The last outstanding manifestation of the medieval corporate religious spirit was the Brethren of Common Life in the region of the lower Rhine, the product of the vibrant mysticism of that area which is known collectively as the New Devotion. Gerard Groote, founder of the Brethren, was Ruysbroeck's disciple. Deventer and Zwolle in the Netherlands were centers of its large lay wing — groups living the community life but bound by no vows. Care for and education of youths provided their chief work. A monastic branch of the Brethren began with the establishment by more ascetic-minded members of the Congregation of Augustinian Canons at Windesheim about 1380, the start of an organization that eventually included nearly eighty priories in northwestern Europe. A vast quantity of solid works of devotion and private piety emanated from the Brethren. The *Imitation of Christ*, at least partly the work of Thomas of Kempen, is only one of their achievements, albeit that of widest renown.

Conclusion. Although this chapter thus closes on a sanguine note, the age it encompasses was disastrous for the Church. The Schism was healed, heresies checked, and conciliarism officially repudiated, but the spirit of Christendom had changed from happier days. Constructive reform remained unaccomplished and new evils such as abuses of indulgences were cropping up. Papal authority and prestige sustained another tremendous shock. The unity of Christendom was weakening perceptibly as the supranational role of the papacy declined. Secular states had learned to plunder the rights and property of the Church on a grand scale in defiance of distraught popes. A more critical attitude toward the Church was evident.

REVIEW AIDS

1. Describe the election of Pope Urban VI.
2. What were the causes and the occasion for the Great Schism?
3. Show how the political situation of Europe influenced the course of the Schism.
4. Explain the position taken by the Cardinals to justify their action in 1378 and the possible subconscious motives that probably influenced them.
5. What efforts were made to heal the Schism by the popes or by others?
6. Explain the conciliar theory and its significance; show how this theory operated at the Councils of Constance and Basle.
7. How well did the Council of Constance succeed in its three aims?
8. Why were no constructive steps in the direction of reform taken in the first half of the fifteenth century?
9. Describe the New Devotion and the Brethren of Common Life.

SUGGESTIONS FOR FURTHER READING

No study of the Schism can even begin without Walter Ullmann, *The Origins of the Great Schism* (London: 1948), whose interpretation has been followed in this chapter. An older book that treats the entire course of the Schism is Louis Salembier, *The Great Schism of the West* (New York: 1907). A general survey of this entire period that is very critical of the Church is Alexander C. Flick, *The Decline of the Medieval Papacy*, 2 vols. (New York: 1930). John N. Figgis gives a concise and accurate account of "The Conciliar Movement and the Papalist Reaction," part 2 of his *Studies of Political Thought from Gerson to Grotius 1414–1625* (Cambridge: 1907). Brian Tierney's new book, *Foundations of the Conciliar Theory* (New York: 1955), traces the conciliar idea down to the Schism.

For the Councils of this period, short accounts are to be found in H. J. Schroeder, *Disciplinary Decrees of the General Councils* (St. Louis: 1937). Two worthwhile monographs on the Council of Constance are: George C. Powers, *Nationalism at the Council of Constance* (Washington, D. C.: 1927), and John P. McGowan, *Pierre d'Ailly and the Council of Constance* (Washington, D. C.: 1936). The standard life of Wyclif is Herbert Workman, *John Wyclif*, 2 vols. (Oxford: 1926). Albert Hyma has done a study of *The Brethren of the Common Life* (Grand Rapids: 1950) that gives an enthusiastic Protestant viewpoint. Two new monographs on a long-neglected subject are Joseph Gill, *The Council of Florence* (London: 1958) and O. Halecki, *From Florence to Brest (1439–1596)* (Rome: 1958).

DOCUMENTS

1. Dietrich of Niem, an employee in the curia of the Roman pope in 1410, wrote a book on the *Ways of Uniting and Reforming the Church*. Sincerely desirous of ending the schism and reforming abuses in the Church, he advocated the conciliar theory as the best means to those ends. This excerpt from Dietrich's book shows conciliarism in its full-blown form. Translated in Matthew Spinka, ed., *Advocates of Reform from Wyclif to Erasmus*, Vol. XIV, The Library of Christian Classics (Philadelphia: Westminster Press, 1953), pp. 159–160. Used by permission.

. . . the summoning of a general council in no way belongs to the pope, even though he be the sole universal and undoubted pope. It does not even belong to him to preside as judge or to define anything having to do with the state of the Church. This [prerogative] belongs primarily to the bishops, cardinals, patriarchs, secular princes, communities, and the rest of the faithful. A man of ill report cannot and must not, from the point of view of what is right, be a judge, particularly in his own case, when, for the sake of the common welfare, the resignation and deprivation of a private individual's advantage and honor is the aim. . . .

It (the council) is superior in authority, dignity, and function. The pope himself is bound to obey such a council in all things. Such a council can limit the power of the pope. To such a council, as it represents the Church Universal, the keys of binding and loosing were granted. Such a council can take away the papal rights. From such a council no one can appeal. Such a council can elect, deprive, and depose the pope. Such a council can set up new laws, and destroy old ones. The constitutions, statutes, and regulations of such a council are immutable and cannot be set aside by any person inferior to the council.

The pope is not and has not been at any time able to make dispensations contrary to the canons passed by general councils unless a council has specifically granted this power to him for some important reason. The pope cannot change the acts of a council; indeed he cannot interpret them or make dispensations contrary to them since they are like the Gospels of Christ, which admit of no dispensation and over which no pope has jurisdiction. In this way there will be among the members the unity of the spirit in the bond of peace. . . .

Thus a general council, representing the Universal Church, if it desires to see a thorough union, if it desires to repress schism, if it wishes to bring an end to schism, if it wishes to exalt the Church, should before all else limit and define, according to the example of the holy Fathers who preceded us, the coercive and usurped power of the popes.

2. When the cardinals deserted Pope Urban VI, they issued a "Declaration" to the Catholic world explaining their action. They endeavored to justify themselves by describing Urban's election in such a way that no one could doubt that it was invalid. This is their description. Quoted from

Walter Ullmann, *The Origins of the Great Schism* (London: Burns, Oates and Washbourne Ltd., 1948), pp. 71–72. Used by permission.

Thus, when the cardinals were about to go into the conclave they had difficulty in entering the palace, because the square in front of it was thronged with people, many of whom were armed. Moreover, a huge crowd entered the palace together with the cardinals, and the doors had to be kept open throughout the night, because the crowd would not allow them to be shut. The whole palace was surrounded by armed men, so that nobody could go in or out without the mob's permission. . . . Just when the cardinals were about to begin the election, the bells of the capitol and of St. Peter's began to ring, as if to summon the people, and immediately afterward the cries "Romano lo volemo o al manco Italiano," became more furious than ever before. The cardinals were advised by some of the guards (some of whom were ultramontane, and some Romans) immediately to elect a Roman or an Italian, if they wanted to safeguard their own lives. For this reason the ultramontane cardinals condescended to the election of an Italian, only in order to escape the danger of death, as they then declared — in no other circumstances would they have agreed to it. Moreover, some of the Italian cardinals declared that, if they happened to be elected, they would not accept the election, because of the obvious pressure. Since they all were anxious to escape danger, they hastily nominated the Archbishop of Bari without any discussion of his merits. They immediately elected him pope, as he was well known to them and, they trusted, greatly experienced in the business and customs of the curia, though later experience plainly proved the belief erroneous.

Chapter 19

THE RENAISSANCE AND THE
CLOSE OF THE MIDDLE AGES

IN THE decades following the collapse of the conciliar movement the Church felt the full impact of secularism, individualism, humanism, and nationalism. These attitudes had, of course, not blossomed out overnight but the Church had not yet clarified its point of view toward them. Now, in the age of the Renaissance, the question remained whether the Church would be molded into the image of the new social forces or whether they could be adapted to suit the needs of the Church and become a means of serving rather than impeding the salvation of mankind.

The Renaissance. The rebirth of the culture and civilization of ancient Greece and Rome which the Renaissance represented was nothing new to the Church, itself the most obvious relic of antiquity, since the Church had been the intermediary through which classical culture had been preserved and passed on to the barbarian conquerors of Rome. Earlier centuries had witnessed the gradual unfolding of the ancient traditions under Alcuin, Gerbert, and Aquinas; the fifteenth merely climaxed this development. It was to be expected, therefore, that the Church would take an active interest in the intellectual achievements of the Renaissance.

There was, to be sure, a significant new element in the latest rebirth. A basic ingredient, at least of the Italian aspect of the Renaissance, was a new set of values epitomized in the word "secularism." Renaissance man's interests centered on the present rather than on the next world. Although he usually did not overlook entirely the prospect of eternal life he did relegate it to a subordinate or purely formal role in determining present conduct. Theology was dethroned as queen of the sciences. Monasticism came under heavy attack since secularism always stands at the opposite pole to asceticism and monastic self-denial. Anticlericalism too waxed strong. Nevertheless there were no attacks on religion as such or on the Church as an institution. Outwardly the humanists' lives conformed to at least the minimum standards of Catholic deportment, and one of them, Thomas More, is a canonized saint.

Nature, the physical world, and the natural powers of men, all highly esteemed by the humanists, certainly deserved better treatment than medieval man had customarily accorded them. However the corrective advocated by the humanists amounted to a virtual deification of nature. From one extreme they simply moved to its opposite. Their boundless optimism clashed with the Catholic teaching of original sin and its consequences. Unrestrained admiration of the cult of antiquity all too often resulted in deportment patterned after the materialistic paganism of the ancients. Herein lay serious defects in an otherwise remarkable period of human endeavor.

Yet it would be erroneous to regard the Renaissance as fundamentally inimical to Catholicism. The greatest humanists remained loyal to the Church, and most of them took a profound and sincere interest in the Faith. The patronage so liberally bestowed by popes and prelates on the practitioners of the new arts and letters indicates that they at least saw much that was admirable in these achievements.

Christian Humanism.   Some humanists were corrupted by the pagan and immoral content of the classical literature they cherished; others became skeptical toward the Church because of their scorn for the utilitarian Latin style of ecclesiastical writers, the lack of education among the clergy, and the realization that some at least of the documents used by the Church such as the Donation of Constantine and the False Decretals were forgeries.

But there were also many humanists who burned to apply the new learning to a reform of the Church and their program is known as Christian Humanism. Literary education was the key to this scheme. Latin, Greek, and even Hebrew, diligently mastered, should introduce the student to the sources of Christianity in the New Testament and the Church Fathers. Better understanding of these would stimulate genuine piety and sense of duty among the clergy. Knowledge of the primitive Church would reveal the deficiencies of fifteenth-century Catholicism and gradually induce that reform in head and members so earnestly desired.

In Italy Petrarch, Cardinal Bessarion, and the pedagogue Vittorino da Feltra represented this ideal although Christian Humanism developed chiefly outside Italy where the Renaissance had a more sober, religious basis. In Spain the Franciscan Cardinal Ximenes founded the University of Alcala to train the clergy in the classical languages as well as in theology and law. The Complutensian Polyglot edition of the Old Testament was one of the monuments of the new learning that emanated from Alcala. A steady improvement in the Spanish clergy in the next decades attests to the efficacy of Ximenes' work. In London John Colet, dean of St. Paul's established the Westminster School after first lecturing at Oxford on the Pauline Epistles. St. Thomas More and St. John Fisher belonged to the circle of English humanists. Lefevre d'Etaples at Paris produced works of textual criticism such as his Quintuplex Psalter, five versions of the psalms in parallel columns.

German humanism sprang directly from the schools of the Brethren of Common Life and the pietistic New Devotion. Here occurred the sharpest break with the scholastic tradition because of a famous argument between Reuchlin, an eminent German Hebrew scholar, and the conservative Dominican theologians of Cologne. The friars championed efforts to destroy all Hebrew books as inimical to Christianity while Reuchlin denied the validity of such blanket condemnation. Scholastic philosophy and theology and the religious orders suffered from the satire of the humanist supporters of Reuchlin.

Erasmus. Greatest of the Christian humanists was Erasmus of Rotterdam (1466–1536) whose genius gave Christian Humanism its final form. Books such as *Handbook of a Christian Soldier* and *Education of a Christian Prince* served to explain his concept of the role of religion in life. In his *Praise of Folly* Erasmus satirized the shortcomings of the clergy, theologians, and philosophers as well as popular religious practices. Mechanical, formal observance of religious duties without interior spirituality was the particular object of his scorn. Erasmus saw in his contemporaries the same faults which Christ had criticized so severely in the Pharisees. Indefatigably he attacked the relic craze, pilgrimages, and superstitious veneration of saints, insisting that these practices distracted Christians from the fundamentals of Catholicism. Study of the New Testament and of the Fathers were much more important than the accidental accretions of the medieval period. Using his thorough knowledge of Greek and Latin Erasmus issued in 1516 the first modern edition of the Greek New Testament, which had sixty-nine printings before his death. He also published editions of both Greek and Latin Fathers.

Erasmus' contempt for philosophers and theologians, so characteristic of the humanists, rested on his own lack of understanding of theology as a science. He preferred the literary type of education of the ancient world to the medieval system which rested on philosophy. In naïvely advocating a return to the simple, "natural" Christianity of the primitive Church Erasmus unwittingly became the precursor of the sixteenth century revolutionaries yet he himself always remained a loyal if misunderstood Catholic. Pope Paul III offered him a cardinal's hat but he declined.

The Renaissance Papacy. From its earliest beginnings the Renaissance had been patronized by the popes. Avignon saw its beginnings and Pope Clement VI was the first prince pope of the Renaissance type. Many struggling humanists found employment in the Roman Curia where capable Latinists were always in demand. Outstanding figures like Salutati, Poggio, and Bruni worked as papal secretaries. For the rebuilding of Rome after the neglect of the French period and the destruction of the Schism the popes commissioned painters, architects, and sculptors. The cardinals emulated the popes in patronizing humanists to lend luster to their own entourage.

The early Renaissance popes were pretty much above reproach. Nicholas V (1447–1455) was the first humanist to become pope and his major ambition was to make Rome the intellectual capital of Europe. "All the scholars in the world came to Rome in the time of Pope Nicholas, partly of their own accord, and partly at his request, because he desired to have them there," wrote one of Nicholas' admirers with some exaggeration. Nicholas V built the papal library, collected manuscripts, and commissioned translations of Greek works into Latin to make them generally available for study. He undertook repairs on St. Peter's, the Vatican palace, and churches throughout the city and the Patrimony. Fra Angelico, the Dominican artist, decorated many of these structures.

Pius II (1458–1464), probably the best writer ever to wear the tiara, was one of the prominent men of the century. Intrigue won him the papal throne despite unsavory incidents in his youthful days, but he resolutely turned his back on his past and made a sincere effort to fulfill the obligations of the papal office. He devoted himself to the project of a crusade to stem the Turkish tide after the fall of Constantinople in 1453.

The della Roveres, Sixtus IV (1471–1484) and Julius II (1503–1513); the Borgia, Alexander VI (1492–1503); and the de Medicis, Leo X (1513–1521) and Clement VII (1523–1534), continued to patronize writers and artists. Rome grew splendid under the brush and chisel of Bramante, Michelangelo, and Rafael. The Sistine Chapel and the new St. Peter's are monuments to the Renaissance popes. Julius II, perhaps the finest type of the age and a really remarkable man, humanly speaking, was also exemplary in his personal life. Speaking of Julius the Venetian ambassador reported: "Everything about him is on a magnificent scale."

Corruption at the Curia. But beneath the material beauty moral decay set in under the popes of the high Renaissance. If some of them were monsters of iniquity they were a small minority. Jovial company, "enlightened" conversation, and splendid banquets do not necessarily denote decadence, yet there was sufficient corruption to have kept tongues wagging ever since. Innocent VIII (1484–1492) was the first pope publicly to recognize his illegitimate children. Sixtus IV involved himself in a plot to assassinate the Duke of Florence. Unblushing simony secured the tiara for Alexander VI; this pope's numerous progeny are well known, especially his son Cesare who pocketed the funds collected for the Holy Year in 1500. Pastor, the historian of the popes, said of Leo X that "an insatiable thirst for pleasures was his leading characteristic."

Nepotism, the bestowal of office on members of one's family without regard for merit, spread corruption through the entire Curia. Many of the cardinals were millionaires who squandered their wealth on luxury. Much of the pornographic literature of the Renaissance emanated from the pens of papal secretaries. A popular saying was that "Everything can be bought in Rome." Never has the gap yawned more widely between the divine character of the Church and the human nature of its administrators.

The reason for such abuses is that the popes and cardinals accepted the standards of the age for men of rank and position in society without understanding that their own ecclesiastical character made a difference. Churchmen were always expected to be leaders rather than followers in setting moral standards. However, apologists for the Church have always pointed out that the unworthiness of persons does not compromise the character of the institution and that the dogmatic content of Catholicism remained unscathed throughout the Renaissance period. There is also, of course, the other side of the picture. Careful investigation has revealed considerable genuine concern for the state of religion on the part of pontiffs popularly known for their failings. Among the cardinals Bessarion, Nicholas of Cusa, Cajetan, Ximenes, and Caraffa more than offset Cesare Borgia, Bibbiena, and their notorious colleagues.

The States of the Church. In their capacity of Italian princes there was little to distinguish the popes from their secular counterparts — so little, in fact, that many people in the fifteenth century thought of the popes primarily in this secular role. Preoccupation with local political affairs caused the pontiffs, too, to forget their higher dignity. Defeats sustained in the less important political arena inevitably damaged the spiritual authority of the Vicars of Christ. A popular satire described the exclusion of Julius II from heaven after his death since St. Peter, guarding the gates of Paradise, failed to recognize the doughty warrior before him for the pope that he was. Through their military and political activity the prince popes of the Renaissance made no friends, acquired little territory, bankrupted their treasury, and aroused suspicion and distrust among all the ruling families of Europe. But they did preserve the independence of the Papal State.

Just as in their wars with the Hohenstaufen emperors of Germany, the popes adhered to the principle that their spiritual freedom could be guaranteed only by political independence. The Italian political scene in the fifteenth century featured consolidation of the numerous petty principalities into a half dozen larger units. Venice was the leading aggressor against papal land but ambitious *condottieri* had also usurped the rights of government in many cities within the Papal State. The popes strove to regain these lost prerogatives. Then when France invaded Italy in 1494 to contest with Spain for ownership of Naples and Sicily the Italian wars were transformed into all-European conflicts. A third-rate power such as the Papal Government had to labor mightily to keep from being trampled by the giants.

Because of the frequent changes of occupants of the Holy See consistency was lacking in papal politics. Shifting alliances won a reputation for treachery. Thus in 1508 the League of Cambrai brought Pope Julius II into alliance with the German emperor, France, and England to despoil Venice, but four years later Julius formed the Holy League which welcomed Venice and turned against France. This proved disastrous since the French won a great victory at Marignano in 1515, and as a result Pope Leo X had to accept the Concordat of Bologna. Significantly, the Concordat did not deprive the pope of any of his Italian territory but it made over to Francis I of France control of the French Church. The year 1527 brought the climax: the armies of Emperor Charles V captured Rome and subjected it to months of pillage and brutality that surpassed the ferocity of Vandals and Visigoths.

Church and State. A fundamental fact in the history of the Church at the close of the middle ages was that the Church was slowly losing control of its own organization. This is evident in two areas: in relations with the secular governments of Europe and in regard to its own administrative machinery. Since Boniface VIII the tendency had been for the State to dominate more and more over the Church. By 1500 the Church stood everywhere on the defensive, striving vainly to restrict the State to temporal matters only. The revived Roman Law, political absolutism, and above all the new national spirit pressed the Church closely on every front. Blinded by national sentiment the native clergy worked with their secular rulers against the papacy. Cardinal Wolsey in England and Archbishop Mendoza in Spain typify the great ecclesiastical politicians of the age; their fame rests solely on their services to their kings, not to the Church. As supranational feeling waned during the age of transition the concept of national churches controlled by absolute kings crystallized gradually in some men's minds.

France. *Gallicanism* is the word that designates the French desire for an autonomous Church which, in practice, signified a Church under royal domination. Roots of Gallicanism stretch back to the Great Schism and beyond, even to Boniface VIII, but the popularity of the conciliar theory nurtured it into full bloom. Conciliarism and Gallicanism eventually became almost synonymous.

While the Council of Basle in 1439 debated the deposition of Pope Eugene IV, King Charles VII summoned the French hierarchy to Bourges where the Pragmatic Sanction was drawn up. This document, prepared by the prelates and promulgated by the king as domestic law, reiterated several dozen antipapal decrees of Constance and Basle: *Frequens, Sacrosancta*, abolition of papal taxes, denial of appeals to Rome, and substitution of royal for papal interference in elections. At one stroke the French church removed itself from papal jurisdiction; by posing as the champion of true Faith Charles VII greatly augmented his political power. The popes objected strenuously but when Louis XI agreed in 1461 to abrogate the Pragmatic Sanction, widespread protest in France compelled him to halt. Certainly some of this opposition was sincere for the popular mind equated reform with royal domination, and corruption with papal control.

Franco-papal relations approached a crisis in 1511 when Louis XII contrived to convene a schismatic general council at Pisa, for which Pope Julius II excommunicated him. After the decisive French victory at

Marignano King Francis I and Leo X agreed on the Concordat of Bologna in 1516. Three major provisions were incorporated into the Concordat: (1) the unilateral Pragmatic Sanction was revoked; (2) the king should nominate and pope confirm archbishops, bishops, and abbots in France, (3) the extreme statements of conciliarism and other so-called reform decrees were abolished either specifically or tacitly. Being a mutual arrangement the Concordat was more satisfactory than the Pragmatic Sanction, but royal control of the Church in France remained unchecked. It could not be otherwise as long as French Catholics wanted it that way.

Spain. Using the pretext of reform Ferdinand and Isabella, busy establishing an absolute government, extended their control over the Spanish Church. Little by little they deprived the hierarchy of its political, military, and financial power. In 1482 the sovereigns wrung from the pope the right of supplication in favor of their nominees to bishoprics; Charles V expanded this into the right of presentation. In the recently acquired Kingdom of Granada as in the New World ecclesiastical patronage was vested entirely in the crown. A decree of 1493 prohibited publication of papal bulls without royal consent. After 1497 the decisions of the Spanish Inquisition could not be appealed to Rome and this tribunal under the notorious Dominican Torquemada degenerated into a nefarious instrument of the government. At the time the Spanish Church benefited from royal despotism since Queen Isabella's influence secured the primatial see of Toledo for her confessor Ximenes, a zealous and saintly Franciscan who accomplished much good. Nevertheless the dangers were obvious.

The Empire. Within the Holy Roman Empire the liberty of the Church, never very great, was similarly assaulted. Here there was no all-embracing national monarch but rather a congeries of princely jurisdictions, each bending its energies in pursuit of absolute power. To preserve its own prerogatives the Roman Curia joined hands with the princes to exploit the resources of the German Church. The Concordat of Vienna in 1448 guaranteed payment of annates to Rome and protected papal reservations. Yet in the day-to-day administration of religious functions secular influence knew no bounds. When Nicholas of Cusa became bishop of Brixen by papal appointment and tried to reform his diocese the Count of the Tyrol imprisoned and then expelled him. Duke John of Cleves was jestingly called "Pope John," so strictly did he control his clerical subjects.

At the same time the archbishops of Mainz, Trier, and Cologne were numbered among the Electors of the Empire and governed extensive areas as independent prince-bishops. Numerous important bishoprics and monasteries also possessed territorial sovereignty and this caused princely families to fight constantly to introduce their own members into such lucrative positions. At one time the family of the count of Mörs dominated all northwest Germany by holding the sees of Cologne, Paderborn, Münster, Osnabrück, and Utrecht. Ecclesiastical princes of this type seldom concerned themselves with anything but their secular power; ecclesiastical authority merely provided means for achieving secular goals.

England. The great ecclesiastical offices of England continued to fall to clerks of the king's ministerial class as they had since the Statutes of Praemunire and Provisors in the fourteenth century. On the whole the Church in England was not plagued with as many problems as on the continent. Royal influence was not exercised odiously but it was a well-established tradition which explains the facility of the subsequent transfer of the English Church completely into royal hands.

Administrative Anarchy. As with any government the organization of the Catholic Church had to meet certain standards of administrative procedure in order to function properly. In particular there should have been clear patterns of responsibility and control between inferiors and superiors, along with sound financial practices. The centralizing tendencies which had been begun by the Gregorian reformers as a means of repressing abuses had created a top-heavy system that placed full responsibility for ecclesiastical organization in the hands of the pope. This had been done by bypassing the older order whereby bishops administered their dioceses through visitations and local synods, and were in turn responsible to Rome. As long as the popes were capable and able to bear the increasing burdens of a centralized, monarchical system all went well. However the breakdown that occurred during the Schism was not repaired during the conciliar or the Renaissance periods and the encroachments of the lay power raised additional barriers. As a result the head of the Church was largely severed from the body of the faithful and this in turn opened the doors to moral decline.

Bishops were unable to fill the gap because they were no longer masters of their sees. Every diocese contained monasteries, priories, congregations, and communities free from episcopal supervision and endowed with their own revenues, jurisdiction, and prerogatives. In Germany even cathedral chapters opposed or simply ignored their bishops. In Paris the bishop appointed only 20 per cent of the city's pastors, while 21 of 392 parishes in the diocese of Lyons answered to the archbishop. At another place a bishop who entered an exempt church on a canonical visitation was bodily thrown into the street by the monks. And if the bishop were a political appointee, he probably would not even want to bother with visitations at all. Constant litigation between jealous jurisdictions clogged the ecclesiastical courts and disgraced all concerned.

Exemption from local control had provided the means by which Cluniacs, the friars, and other such groups had been able to achieve their goals, but they had always remained responsible to Rome. And the papacy had taken an active interest in the religious orders. But when schism, Renaissance, and Italian wars distracted the popes' attention, exempt bodies found themselves independent of all ecclesiastical and even civil authority. Left to themselves they often were unable to resist the corrupting influences of the age.

Similar disintegration of control characterized the Orders. During the fifteenth century the Cistercians, for example, fell apart as Spanish, Portuguese, Tuscan, and Lombard houses cut themselves adrift from the authority of the General Chapter. A prolonged fight between Citeaux and Clairvaux injected a further element of weakness. Commendatory abbots, nonresident and often laymen interested solely in gathering monastic revenues, got control of Cistercian as well as other monasteries.

Anarchy in the Roman Curia. Even the Church's central governmental machinery suffered from administrative confusion. Practices had developed which rendered it impossible to control adequately the large Roman curial bureaucracy. Many officials had purchased their positions from popes threatened with bankruptcy; one sixth of Leo X's revenue came from this source. Yet men who bought positions in the Curia looked on them as investments from which a goodly profit might be realized, even though the resultant corruption hurt the Church. Nepotism introduced a spirit of faction into the Curia. Humanists with notorious standards of personal conduct as well as of literary propriety were tolerated for their technical competence. Cardinals, too, betrayed the Church and the papacy; Cardinal Petrucci's plot to assassinate Leo X was an extreme case, while the schismatic Council of Pisa in 1511 was less violent but no less serious. If the popes could not control their own official family, how could they effectively govern the universal Church?

Abuses. Many of the specific abuses most often complained of in the literature of the fifteenth century were administrative in character: pluralism, absenteeism, provisions, and reservations. As the number of educated laymen increased, more complaints were heard of ignorant clergy. The medieval Church had never developed a satisfactory method of education and training for the clergy. Resulting from the decay of disciplinary machinery was a decline in clerical morality that was most evident in the matter of celibacy. A Parisian synod in 1429 declared that the laity no longer regarded offenses against the sixth commandment as mortal sins because so many priests were guilty of them. A German writer described how the laity of Schlettstadt pelted with rotten eggs the known concubines of priests.

Financial scandals of one kind or another form a special category of gravamina, even though they often arose from the truly desperate financial position of the papacy. Simony was widespread and the "sale" of indulgences and relics caused sporadic protest. The disparity between the princely incomes of some of the hierarchy and the miserable lot of the lower clergy did not escape notice. In Italy and Germany an "ecclesiastical proletariat" existed because of an oversupply of priests.

Fifth Lateran Council, 1512–1517. With considerable reluctance Pope Julius II summoned the eighteenth general council to meet at the Lateran in 1512. Few non-Italian prelates attended, which partly accounts for its limited success, for the Council's achievements were piddling. It condemned Averroist philosophy; approved the latest of the friars' social endeavors, the *montes pietatis* or pawn shops under ecclesiastical supervision for making small loans to the poor; provided for the censorship of books by local ordinaries; and tried again to end the perpetual feuds between the regular and the secular clergy.

In the matter of reform the Council failed dismally. Although the bishops took cognizance of abuses in the Curia, the episcopate, and the lower clergy, they devised no remedies beyond weakly restating disciplinary decrees of earlier councils. A sincere will to reform was conspicuously lacking. The decree ordering preachers to desist from public criticism of the hierarchy reveals the extent of their reforming zeal. The selfish vested interests of the assembled prelates overrode their concern for the welfare of the Church which could be protected only at their own expense.

Popular Piety and Reform. Despite all that has been narrated popular religion continued to flourish at the close of the middle ages. Externals such as the large number of religious books produced on the new printing presses, including editions and translations of the Bible, the many new churches being erected in all parts of Europe, the sacred themes of much of the magnificent art of the age, and the numerous pious bequests testify to the hold of religion on the people's lives. The Carthusians, severest of all orders, showed the least signs of decay, while the Observant Franciscans were everywhere displacing laxer Conventuals.

Reforms on a limited scale produced very satisfactory results. Ximenes improved the mendicants in Spain as well as the cathedral chapters; the great Spanish saints of the next generation are his spiritual children. Under commission from Pope Alexander VI in 1501 Cardinal d'Amboise undertook a vigorous administrative and moral reconstruction of the friars throughout France. Somewhat earlier Cardinal Nicholas of Cusa had visited and reorganized monasteries and chapters in central and north-western Germany, and John Busch of the Canons Regular of Windesheim continued his work. By 1515, 136 abbeys scattered throughout Germany were organized in the Bursfeld Congregation, a league of reformed Bene-dictine monasteries for liturgical and disciplinary unity. The Oratory of Divine Love originated in Genoa in 1497 to promote the personal sanctity of its clerical members through prayer, the sacraments, the works of charity. St. Francis of Paula founded the Order of Minims in 1457 and they soon spread from Italy into France and Spain.

Best known of the popular preachers is Jerome Savonarola, a Dominican ascetic, fanatic, and visionary who boldly challenged the mundane spirit of the Renaissance in its very citadel, the city of Florence. For four years he held sway as a spiritual dictator until a clash with Pope Alexander VI brought about his downfall and execution. His startling albeit ephemeral success indicated the common readiness to respond to reform; his ultimate failure only proved the practical inadequacy of his type of conservative, essentially medieval program.

In contrast with Savonarola, Christian humanism offered a sounder prospectus in its attempted fusion of the vital elements in the current intellectual atmosphere with genuine piety. On this foundation the Jesuits within a few years erected their great educational system. The first steps toward the urgently needed rehabilitation of theology were taken when the Dominicans in 1484 decided to discard Peter Lombard's *Sentences* as the basic theological text in their institutions and substituted instead the writings of Aquinas. Within a few years the Preachers' generals Cajetan and Francis de Sylvestris of Ferrara completed the classic commentaries on the Angelic Doctor's two *Summas*.

Conclusion. For more than a century the call for reform in the Church had been heard from all parts of Europe. There can be no doubt that Catholicism still held its appeal for the vast majority of the people, but leadership was lacking both to give effective direction to the demand for reform and to carry out that reform from within. The hierarchy on all levels had simply abdicated their responsibility. Rather than influencing society as they had done for centuries they now let society influence them. They compromised with dangerous tendencies instead of firmly opposing them, either because that was the easier thing to do or because they failed to realize the consequences. Statistics indicating the failure of the Church's leaders, the bishops, themselves, to live up to their position are provided by the number of bishops whom the Church has canonized. In the period 1049 to 1270 there were seventy-four bishops later canonized; from 1270 to 1370 only four; and from 1370 to 1520 only three — an average of one every three years, every twenty-five years, and every fifty years respectively.[1] Certainly conditions were no worse than they had been in the tenth century and by the medieval reformation the Church had rescued itself. Christ's own words left no reason to question the possibility of another genuine reform. and it did finally come, but whether or not it could have come without a tremendous shock is a moot question.

---

[1] Philip Hughes, *A History of the Church*, Vol. III (New York: Sheed and Ward, 1947), p. 212, n. 1.

REVIEW AIDS

1. Explain the concept of the Renaissance and show its relation with the Church.
2. What is Christian Humanism? Who are some of its originators?
3. Describe the condition of the papacy in the late fifteenth century.
4. What effect do the lives of the Renaissance popes have on the Church?
5. Why was it possible for state attacks on the Church's independence to be so universally successful during these years?
6. Give examples of secularism and nationalism in this period and show their impact on the Church.
7. Define "administrative anarchy," and show how it caused the decline of the Church.
8. Describe and explain the abuses in the Church.
9. Compare conditions of the Church in the fifteenth century with conditions in the tenth century.
10. What was accomplished by the Fifth Lateran Council?
11. Discuss the evidence of continued Catholic spirituality during this period.

SUGGESTIONS FOR FURTHER READING

A good summary of the Church in the Renaissance is to be found in chapters VI–VIII of Myron P. Gilmore, *The World of Humanism 1453–1517* (New York: 1952). Philip Hughes does a fine job in Vol. III, pp. 361–497, of his *A History of the Church* (New York: 1947). The first eight volumes of Ludwig von Pastor's *History of the Popes* (St. Louis: 1906 ff.) contain a mass of information. Two thorough works by Protestant authors are Mandell Creighton, *A History of the Papacy from the Great Schism to the Sack of Rome*, revised edition in six volumes (London: 1919), and Alexander C. Flick, *The Decline of the Medieval Church*, 2 vols. (New York: 1930), of which volume II is pertinent. Flick's work however does not give a full picture since it stresses only signs of decay and makes little attempt to see the better side of things. For the very important concept of administrative confusion the only English work is Pierre Janelle, *The Catholic Reformation* (Milwaukee: 1949), Chapters I and II. Albert Hyma has written *The Christian Renaissance* (Grand Rapids: 1924), to draw attention to Christian Humanism. A handy biography of Erasmus is Margaret Mann Phillips', *Erasmus and the Northern Renaissance* (London: 1950). Peter Partner, *The Papal State Under Martin V* (London: 1958) explores a neglected area.

DOCUMENTS

Many of the evils afflicting the Church in the fifteenth century stemmed from corruption among the bishops and other important ecclesiastical dignitaries. Pope Pius II has left a description of one such late medieval bishop: Ambroise de Cambrai, Bishop of Alet. Pius' candid narrative leaves no doubt of the urgent need for reform. *The Commentaries of Pius II*, translated by Florence Alden Gragg, annotated by Leona C. Gabel, *Smith College Studies in History*, XXX (1947), 315–318. Used by permission.

There was in the Roman Curia the above-mentioned Bishop of Alet, a sly and crafty man ready for any trick, a supreme artist in simony, a practiced orator, a handsome fellow, agreeable in address, a lavish spender, and bent on making money, for since he spent all he had on banquets and mistresses, he did not fear to lie or perjure himself for gain. He concealed his vices however with remarkable skill so that, though his falsehoods were myriad, he still appeared truthful and a lover of truth and virtue. Therefore since his real character was not known, he had obtained the post of referendarius in the Curia. When he heard the Count's suit (for dispensation to marry his own sister), he was overjoyed to find a bird to pluck. He wrote him that what he asked could be obtained, but not for less than 24,000 ducats. . . . Negotiations began in the first year of Calixtus' pontificate and continued till his last. The Bishop had three interviews with Calixtus, hoping to smooth down the greedy old man with money. When his efforts were fruitless, he had recourse to deception, thinking perhaps he might find someone in the palace who could be bribed to forge the dispensation. . . . (Eventually the matter was found out.) In the case of the Bishop infamous and enormous crimes were uncovered: simony, perjury, lies, adultery, incest, murder, treason, sacrilege. The murder he said he had committed by accident. Two cardinals however asserted that it was deliberate. . . . The Bishop was removed from his bishopric, sentenced to life imprisonment, and banished to the brethren of Monte Oliveto twelve miles from Siena. There he wore himself out by vigils and prayers till he convinced the monks of his reformation and then, as he was carelessly guarded, he escaped over the high cliffs and fled to France.

SECTION IV: THE IMPACT OF A CHANGING WORLD

A.D.	POPES	WRITERS	HERETICS HERESY	THE CHURCH	THE WORLD	SECULAR RULERS
1275	Gregory X	Eckhart			French in Naples and Sicily	Charles of Anjou Edward I Philip IV
1300	Celestine V Boniface VIII	Henry Suso		*Clericis laicos* 1st Jubilee Year *Unam Sanctam* Outrage at Anagni	Model Parliament End of Latin Kingdom French Estates General	
	Clement V	Dante John Tauler		COUNCIL OF VIENNE Abolition of Templars Papacy at Avignon	Swiss Confederation	
1325	John XXII			Schism among Franciscans		
		William Ockam	Fraticelli			
	Benedict XII	Marsilius of Padua		Last papal-imperial dispute	Hundred Years' War begins	Edward III Louis of Bavaria
	Clement VI	Petrarch		Mysticism flourishes		
1350				Peak of papal centralization		Emperor Charles IV
	Innocent VI			Franciscans visit China Dominicans in Persia Provisors Praemunire	Black Death Jacquerie Golden Bull Turks enter Europe Hanseatic League	
	Urban V					
1375	Gregory XI Urban VI		Wyclif Lollards	Catherine of Siena Return to Rome Great Schism Brethren of the Common Life	Marco Polo English Peasants' Rebellion	
1400	Boniface IX				Union of Poland and Lithuania	Richard II
	Innocent VII	Gerson d'Ailly Zabarella	Hus Jerome of Prague	Council of Pisa COUNCIL OF CONSTANCE Decree *Frequens* Conciliarism Hussite wars	Feudalism in decay	Sigismund
	Gregory XII Martin V		Hussites			
1425	Eugene IV	Conciliarists Nicholas of Cusa		COUNCIL OF BASLE-FERRARA-FLORENCE Compacts of Prague Greek reunion	Joan of Arc saves France	
1450	Nicholas V	Thomas of Kempen Aeneas Sylvias Bessarion Antoninus of Florence		Pragmatic Sanction of Bourges Mendicant preachers in Italy Concordat of Vienna Minims	Growth of Absolutism and Nationalism The Renaissance Fall of Constantinople to Turks Portuguese explore African coast	Ivan the Great
	Pius II					
	Paul II			Cusa reforms German church	War of Roses Italian Despots	Louis XI
1475	Sixtus IV			Bursfeld Union The Renaissance Papacy	Battle of Bosworth Spanish Inquisition French invade Italy Columbus discovers America	Charles the Bold Henry the Navigator Henry VII Ferdinand and Isabella
	Innocent VIII			Savonarola		
1500	Alexander VI	Ximenes Cajetan Francis de Sylvestris Reuchlin Erasmus		Papal wars in Italy LATERAN COUNCIL V Christian humanism	India reached by sea	Henry VIII Francis I
	Julius II					
	Leo X	Thomas More		Concordat of Bologna		Charles V

PART TWO

PART TWO

THE PROTESTANT REVOLT
AND CATHOLIC REFORM

Chapter 20

THE PROTESTANT REVOLT
IN GERMANY

ON HALLOWEEN of 1517 an Augustinian monk, Martin Luther by name, posted ninety-five theses on the church door at Wittenberg in Saxony. In them he attacked the Church's handling of indulgences and the exactions levied by the Italian Curia on the Church in Germany. A child born in this year might have lived to see half of Europe lost to the Catholic faith. Most of the northern German states and the Scandinavian countries adopted Lutheranism within a generation. Calvin's reformed religion was established in Holland, Scotland, and a large part of Switzerland, and it made considerable headway in certain parts of almost all other European countries. The Anglican religion was established in England, and various minor sects, such as the Anabaptists and Zwinglians were scattered in various places throughout Europe.

Causes of the Protestant Revolt. The indulgence controversy started by Luther seemed hardly spark enough to set off such a revolution as the Protestant Revolt of the early sixteenth century. More menacing in 1517 in the eyes of the pope and almost all Catholics was the danger of the Turk coming into Hungary and threatening the capital of the Empire. Indeed, ever since the fall of Constantinople in 1453 Catholics had been urged by the papacy to undertake common European action against the Turkish invader. More important than the Lutheran affair at first, moreover, seemed the task of working out a synthesis of the new humanism and the old Christianity. Even more important than the indulgence controversy in the eyes of Pope Leo X, was the coming imperial election which would affect the interests of the Church in the German Empire and the general balance of political power in Europe.

On the surface there was reason for not taking Luther's protests seriously at first. Such protests had frequently been made in the past. Such heretical doctrine as Luther was soon to preach publicly had been held by men like Wyclif and Hus — and the Church had weathered each storm apparently without serious damage. As we shall see, the Church was ridden with innumerable grave abuses which evoked popular support for anyone who called out for their correction. But there had been abuses before, and they had never caused any widespread successful revolt from the Church.

What Pope Leo X and other leaders in the Church did not realize is that there existed in Europe a concatenation of political, social, economic, cultural, and religious factors which, combined with serious abuses in the Church, furnished the combustible material for spreading and perpetuating this incendiary movement sparked by Luther's protest. This, indeed, is what happened. It is impossible to account for either the rapid spread of the Protestant Revolt or its permanent success on religious grounds alone. We must remember that the early sixteenth century was an age of revolution in Europe. A geographic revolution had swung the center of trade westward, had sent ships around Africa to the Orient, and had resulted in the discovery of the new world twenty-five years before Luther posted his theses on the church door at Wittenberg. Germany suffered seriously from this swing of trade lines westward.

An economic and social revolution had given the middle class new wealth and power in western Europe. The victory of money over goods as the medium of exchange had created innumerable problems for State and Church alike. Taxes in money replaced payment in goods, and the change to the new economy was done clumsily and with many abuses. The growth of urban communities had produced a new class with a new mentality — and it was chiefly among this class that the new religious ideas took root. A political revolution had promoted the power of the king against the nobility and the clergy, and the new absolute prince was anxious to control the religion of his realm. A cultural revolution had stressed the creative achievement of the individual at the expense of his Creator and his fellow men. It was an age of revolution, then, of which the Protestant Revolt was the religious aspect. Restlessness was in the air at the beginning of the sixteenth century, affecting all classes and permeating all parts of Europe.

More specifically, "modern" developments which had been progressing at an accelerated pace through the preceding two centuries had by 1517 created a state of mind and a desire for power among the ruling classes which predisposed them to support an attack on the "Roman controlled" Catholic Church. The old struggle between secular and religious authority took a new turn with the coming of the absolute prince. This new type of ruler, personified in a Ferdinand of Aragon or a Henry Tudor of England, resented the Church's limitations on his absolute power. He was anxious to control the personnel and the revenue of the Church so that he could render it ineffective as a brake on his ambition. It is worth noting that the Protestant Revolt did not succeed in those states where the monarch had already obtained sizable concessions from the Church, as in France and in Spain, and that it did succeed where the rulers had failed to win such extensive concessions.

By the beginning of the sixteenth century national feeling had grown strong in the various parts of Europe. The pope and the Italian dominated Curia continued to be cosmopolitan in outlook. They seemed not to realize that Germans, Frenchmen, Englishmen, and other national groups came more and more to identify the Church with an Italian papacy. Where the Catholic Church was accidentally identified with national patriotism, as it was in Spain and Ireland and Poland, the Protestant Revolt seemed a treasonable movement and was accordingly shunted aside. On the other hand, where the religious revolution was linked up with national feeling it succeeded. In Scotland, for example, John Knox took advantage of Mary Stuart's being queen of France as well as Scotland and appealed to the Scots' national pride against becoming a mere appendage of France. Lutheranism was successful in large measure because it appeared to be an indigenous German movement, truly *volkstümlich*, directed against a "grasping Italian group" in Rome. In Sweden, again, Archbishop Gustavus Trolle opposed the national rebellion from Denmark and thus encouraged the identification of the successful Swedish revolt with the new Lutheran faith. So, generally, it worked out throughout Europe. The revolt from the Church succeeded where it was identified with national patriotism.

Another secular cause of the rapid spread and ultimate success of the Protestant Revolt is to be found in the condition of the nobility throughout Europe. The noble's income consisted of feudal dues fixed by custom. In this age of rising prices his fixed income continually diminished in purchasing power, and the only means of maintaining his real income was either to discover additional feudal dues or to increase his landholdings. The invitation to confiscate Church lands, when they were offered by Lutheran princes and Henry VIII, was therefore almost irresistible. Thus there was created a class of nobles enriched with Church lands who came to have a vested interest in the permanency of the Protestant Revolt.

The middle class, moreover, had found Catholic teaching restrictive on their commercial activity, and they resented the fact that there was no honorable place for them in the older social arrangements endorsed by the Church. They were therefore predisposed to embrace a revolt from the Catholic Church, especially one in the hands of laymen and directed to the middle class's mentality, as was the case with Calvinism. Finally, it should be remembered from previous chapters that the Renaissance had produced a new secular, critical state of mind which predisposed the individual to question and to judge the claims of religious authority. Such a state of mind caused the individual to consider himself a competent judge of the claims of competing religious groups and to make an "independent" choice as to which was correct. Protestantism pushed individualism, already triumphant in the philosophical field, into the realm of theology.

The nonreligious causes of the Protestant Revolt, then, cannot be ignored if we are to account for its success. But neither can the serious abuses in the Church be overlooked. In many ways the organization of the Church had become obsolete by the beginning of the sixteenth century. Because exemptions from episcopal authority had multiplied since the Great Schism, many parishes were in the hands of patrons, and the bishops' authority was frequently evaded. Moreover, religious orders were largely exempt from episcopal control. Such defective organization tangled up the lines of authority and responsibility. Consequently, clerical discipline suffered. The papacy and Curia had connived at this defective organization and the abuses growing out of it, for the popes and their Roman associates found in them a sorely needed source of additional revenue. Although successive popes from Martin V to Leo X recognized the need for reform within the Church, we shall see later that sometimes prudence and always financial need postponed their taking decisive action. Reform could come only from those having a vested interest in the abuses. Hence it was put off.

Nepotism was one of the most serious of the abuses in the Church. Relatives were given preference by popes and bishops for two principal reasons: first, it was a means of bestowing on needy relatives position, honor, and income; second, it seemed a method of securing nominees who would be loyal to the authority appointing them. *Pluralities* were a kindred abuse whereby an individual was dispensed from canonical prohibitions and allowed to hold more than one high ecclesiastical office. The granting of *dispensations* was an important source of revenue to the papacy, and the holding of additional offices meant additional income for the incumbent. Plural holdings naturally resulted in the evil of *absenteeism*. Frequently the office holder failed to obtain a substitute to take his place and thus many parishes were without priests. Pope Julius II obviously could not personally direct the affairs of the archdiocese of Avignon, the dioceses of Bologna, Lausanne, Coutances, Viviers, Mende, Ostia, and Velletri, and the abbeys of Nonantola and Grottaferrata, besides presiding as Bishop of Rome and head of the Church universal. Nevertheless he held title to and enjoyed the income from all these offices. The archiepiscopal see of Sens, to cite one other example, never saw Archbishop Antoine du Prat until he was carried into his cathedral for burial.

Monetary abuses were general and serious, both in the handling of church patronage and the dispensing of favors. Popes collected money for crusades against the Turk, but for various reasons no crusades materialized. A price was attached to canonical dispensations and exemptions; the giving of alms was frequently linked to the obtaining of indulgences and sometimes even to the reception of sacraments. Moreover, monetary abuses grew worse because of the clumsy method of collecting each tax or donation. They seemed worse, too, because of the lavish lives lived by many of the hierarchy and the way they spent money freely on such secular pursuits as patronage of the arts or even in public gambling.

There were serious abuses in the Church, then, and many good Catholics cried out against them. Attempts at reform had been made, but no effective, permanent reform could be accomplished except through the papacy itself. Popes faced the problem of reform, but they shied away from it when cardinals and bishops having a vested interest in the abuses threatened to revive the conciliar movement. The popes were mortally afraid of a fresh schism, and they were concerned with establishing their temporal authority against the new absolute princes of Europe. They therefore condoned abuses year after year, admitting them as evil and hoping the time would come when they could be abolished. Meanwhile they concentrated on other matters.

Ecclesiastical abuses were more serious in Germany than elsewhere in Europe. The weakness of secular authority in the Empire enabled members of the hierarchy to assume more power than elsewhere and to perpetuate abuses without hindrance from the emperor. Money exactions by the Curia were more frequent and severe in Germany because the emperor was not in a position to oppose them. Clerical exemption from secular courts was consistently abused. The power and the wealth of ecclesiastics caused an increasing number of nobles to embrace the religious state for nonreligious reasons. Under the control of a frequently unfit hierarchy was a host of lesser ecclesiastics, some of whom were exemplary men while others were ignorant, irresponsible, and in no wise fit for the religious life.

The rapid expansion of the Lutheran heresy cannot be adequately accounted for without adversion to this factor of ignorance on the part of ecclesiastics and laymen throughout the Christian world in 1517. We must remember that Luther's teaching dealt with the difficult problem of nature and grace, a problem not clearly defined until the Council of Trent. Moreover, many of the universities were in a state of confusion on unsettled theological points such as this, and thus it was possible for theologians in large numbers to believe that Luther was right. Worldly bishops and lower clergy — both diocesan priests and friars — were not well educated, and it was possible for them to look upon Luther as a "reformer" rather than a "heretic," at least until 1541 when the new religion was consolidated.

The Indulgence Controversy. This is the setting in which the Lutheran revolt took place in Germany. The incident which set off the movement was the famous indulgence controversy brought about by nepotism, pluralism, and something very close to simony. Elector Joachim of Brandenburg had obtained the archbishopric of Mainz for his younger brother Albert. The latter, although only twenty-five years of age, already held the archbishopric of Magdeburg and administered the see of Halber-stadt. He therefore had to obtain papal dispensation both for plural holdings and for being under canonical age for holding an archbishopric. Pope Leo X was anxious to cultivate the good will of the Brandenburgs who held two of the seven votes in the imperial elections. Moreover, he was anxious to obtain funds for St. Peter's basilica which he was building in Rome.

The pope, therefore, granted the requested dispensations, for which Albert was to give the Holy See 24,000 ducats. Albert was to raise the money through the preaching of an indulgence in his three dioceses. Half the income from the indulgence mission was to go to the Holy See, the other half to repay the Fugger banking house for money it had advanced to Albert. The Dominican John Tetzel was selected to preach the indulgence. Tetzel was a man of good morals and sound doctrine, and he preached the orthodox Catholic doctrine on indulgences. Theologians agreed that one had to be in the state of grace to gain an indulgence for oneself, but there was difference of opinion on this point when indulgences for the dead were in question. A common opinion, which Tetzel preached but the papal bull on indulgences did not sanction, was that indulgences for the dead could be gained simply by performing the required good work and saying the specified prayers. One did not have to be in the state of grace. In his enthusiasm Tetzel seems to have emphasized the giving of alms as the good work for obtaining such an indulgence.

Martin Luther had been opposed to the emphasis on good works for some time, and he looked on Tetzel's mission as a particularly vulnerable instance of making a good work the purchase price of grace. He therefore posted his ninety-five theses to the church door at Wittenberg, the general tenor of which was inimical to a mediatory priesthood and in favor of justification by faith alone. The key thesis was the sixth: "The pope cannot remit any guilt, except by declaring that it has been remitted by God and by assenting to God's remission."

Luther sent a copy of his theses to Archbishop Albert. The latter forwarded them to Rome where Leo X took prompt action to check Luther. He referred the Augustinian monk's theses to the outstanding theologian in Rome, Cardinal Cajetan, who reported in December on Luther's errors. At this point neither the pope nor Cajetan thought the matter to be anything more serious than a theological dispute between Augustinians and Dominicans. Nevertheless, on February 3, 1518, Leo directed the vicar-general of the Augustinians, Gabriele della Volta, to remonstrate with Luther either by letter or by envoy. By the time the Augustinians met at Heidelberg in April to hear Luther defend himself, his theses were generally known throughout Germany where their strong anti-Italian bias won them a favorable hearing.

At Heidelberg Luther ably defended himself before his Augustinian brethren, and his views were forwarded to the pope with an explanatory letter from his superior Staupitz. In these *Resolutions* Luther told of existing abuses and reiterated his stand on indulgences. But at the same time he insisted he was an obedient son of the Church. "I cast myself at the feet of your Holiness," he wrote, "with all that I have and all that I am. Quicken, kill, call, recall, approve, reprove, as you will." There was, consequently, still no reason for Rome to believe that Luther would not retract his errors when they were convincingly pointed out to him.

In Germany, meanwhile, Tetzel had answered Luther with a long list of countertheses which Luther, in turn, answered to the general satisfaction of his German supporters. In the early months of 1518 he rapidly became the champion of all who held a grievance against the Roman Curia, or of those who opposed abuses in the Church, or those who felt German resentment against Italian domination of the Church. The papal censor Prierias had examined Luther's original ninety-five theses and had argued that he was a heretic in refusing to accept papal authority in matters of faith and the interpretation of Holy Scripture. Luther answered Prierias by denying the headship of the pope over the Church universal.

Early in July, 1518, the papacy took action by ordering Luther to appear in Rome within sixty days. Elector Frederick of Saxony, in whose state the University of Wittenberg was located, decided to protect Luther. For political reasons the pope changed the citation to have Cardinal Cajetan pass judgment on Luther's doctrine in the German city of Augsburg. Cajetan was ordered not to be drawn into dispute with Luther but rather to listen to his arguments and pass judgment on their orthodoxy. Cajetan received Luther graciously in several interviews in which the Cardinal reduced Luther's heretical theses to the smallest number possible and insisted that he retract only these. At this point, however, Luther insisted on two principal heretical propositions: (1) that the pope is not supreme in matters of faith and morals and the interpretation of Scripture; and (2) that the faith of the participant is the only decisive element in the administration of the sacraments. Luther departed unreconciled and arrived at Wittenberg on October 31, 1518, where in the years to come he was to enjoy the protection and the support of Elector Frederick.

Luther's Revolt From the Church. To understand the development of Lutheran doctrine one must remember that Luther was a heretic before the indulgence controversy occurred and that the force of argument against Catholic defenders of the faith pushed him into holding further heretical propositions. As a young novice Luther had been abnormally worried about his salvation. At length he had arrived at the consoling theory that man is justified solely by trust in God. Good works are unnecessary. Thus Luther shifted the burden of salvation from the individual's shoulders to Christ's alone. He had taught this doctrine in the seminary at Wittenberg before the indulgence controversy, and it was in its defense that he denied papal authority and within a few months the authority of a general council in matters of faith and morals and the interpretation of Scripture. The Bible came to be the sole authority in these matters, and each individual was to interpret the Bible himself. Logically, then, there was no need for a mediatory priesthood in the Lutheran system. Five of the seven sacraments were denied — baptism and the Holy Eucharist alone being considered valid — and the Catholic doctrine of transubstantiation was replaced by Luther's theory of consubstantiation.

In the summer of 1519 the Catholic champion, John Eck, engaged one of Luther's friends, Carlstadt, in a public disputation at Leipzig. Eck clearly had the better of the debates, so Luther appeared to defend his position personally. At Leipzig Eck used more logic than good sense in forcing Luther to hold that councils as well as the pope could err in matters of faith and morals. The Leipzig dispute furthered Luther's popularity as the focal figure for rallying German sentiment against Rome. Humanists like Erasmus temporarily supported him (until his teaching against free will and his theological errors were clearly seen), and young German knights, such as Ulrich von Hutten, made him their champion.

Meanwhile Luther's vacillating policy beguiled Rome into thinking the German problem was not serious. On March 3, 1519, he wrote to the pope that he never intended to attack the authority of the Roman Church or the pope. Leo answered that he was delighted with Luther's repentant submission and invited him to come to Rome to make the retraction which he postponed when before the legate at Augsburg. The papacy was badly misinformed on German affairs. The few who did report accurately on the revolt from the Church, such as Aleander and Morone, were not taken seriously for some time because of the many who insisted the incident would soon be satisfactorily settled. It was believed that the heresy could be quickly ended by a bull of excommunication — if such action became necessary.

Until the autumn of 1519 Rome took no more notice of the Lutheran affair. The pope temporized partly because of his desire not to offend Elector Frederick, then Leo's favorite candidate against the Hapsburgs for the imperial throne. During the summer and autumn of 1520 Luther published three important pamphlets in which he clearly restated his heretical position. *An Open Letter to the Christian Nobility of the German Nation Concerning the Reform of the Christian State* was written in German and appealed openly to German sentiment against Rome. It argued against papal authority and asserted the priesthood of all believers. *The Babylonian Captivity of the Church* struck at the Church's sacramental system. In it Luther asserted that scriptural texts supported only baptism and the Eucharist. *A Treatise on Christian Liberty* developed Luther's theory of the priesthood of all believers and insisted that good works are unavailing for salvation, which depends solely on trust in the merits of Christ.

Meanwhile the Roman Curia moved toward Luther's excommunication, many long consistory meetings being held before the bull of excommunication was finally formulated. Dated June 15, 1520, the bull *Exsurge Domine* listed forty-one Lutheran errors on free will, original sin, the sacraments, faith, grace, sin, penance, confession, good works, purgatory, communion under both kinds, papal primacy, the authority of general councils, and the power of excommunication. Luther was given sixty days from the publication of the bull in which to recant. John Eck arrived in Germany in August with the bull and officially published it in the following month. In December Luther, more a national hero than ever, publicly burned the bull of excommunication, together with books on canon law and some of his adversaries' works; and on January 3, 1521, the papal bull *Decet Romanum Pontificem* pronounced him excommunicated from the Catholic fold.

The Critical Period (1521–1525). From Rome's point of view everything now depended on the young emperor Charles V. Charles, who was only twenty years old, had been crowned emperor four months previously at Aachen. Charles informed the pope's ambassador, Aleander, that he was ready to do whatever was necessary for his faith. But he found many of the German princes in favor of Luther, and he had to cultivate their good will for his impending war with France and for the defense of the empire against the Turk. Charles, therefore, acceded to the demand of Frederick and other princes that Luther be given a hearing in Germany rather than arrested and turned over to the pope. German national feeling was clearly on Luther's side against Rome, especially after the bull of excommunication had been published. Indeed, Aleander wrote to the pope that nine-tenths of Germany shouted "Long live Luther," and the other tenth cried "Death to the Church." It was arranged that Luther should be given a hearing before the

Diet of Worms if he would agree to retract errors proved against him. Luther arrived at Worms on April 16, 1521, where he was examined by the emperor and the Diet. When Luther refused to retract he was placed under the ban of the empire by the Edict of Worms on April 26. He was declared an outlaw in the literal sense of the word and his writings were declared anathema. Enforcement of the edict depended on the many German princes, and they proved unable or unwilling to enforce it against the popular will.

Under the protection of Elector Frederick of Saxony Luther continued to preach and to write. Lutheranism spread in the next few years and its divisive character was soon manifest when extremists like Carlstadt and Zwilling led iconoclastic riots in Wittenberg and preached a truly revolutionary religion. The Diets of 1523 and 1524 showed little willingness to enforce the Edict of Worms against Lutheranism. Its success or failure therefore depended on a host of petty reasons in each principality and ultimately on the decision of each prince. Many of the clergy embraced the new teaching enthusiastically as a way of escaping ecclesiastical discipline, and many of the nobility adopted it as a justification for confiscating church property.

The new pope, Clement VII, received conflicting reports on the seriousness of the Lutheran movement. In answer to Clement's request Aleander prepared a memorandum on how to deal with Lutheranism. In it he suggested the removal of abuses in the Curia and in the German Church, and he exhorted the emperor and the German princes to take strong action against Luther. But Rome still seemed to believe that the Lutheran movement was confined to Saxony and that Aleander overemphasized its seriousness. Nevertheless Clement sent Cardinal Campeggio as his legate to Germany with instructions to reform the clergy. Campeggio set about his reform work, but the papacy did not back him up because political considerations caused by a series of wars between the emperor and the French king came to monopolize Clement's attention.

The Lutheran movement meanwhile reached a critical phase in Germany in 1524 and 1525 when the peasants, moved by a long series of abuses, used the new religion to justify their revolts against the nobility. They saw in the new religion a justification of their social and economic grievances. Although Luther had never preached social or political revolution, his religious innovations were tied in with the Peasants' Revolt. Their program took on a religious coloring when the peasants' leaders demanded that all grievances should be tested by the Word of God and that all men should live according to the Gospel. The revolutionists appealed to Luther's teaching, and thus the new religion was faced with the prospect of being stamped out as a revolutionary movement — as had been the fate of the Albigenses, the Lollards, and the Hussites. Luther saved his religion by denouncing the peasants and encouraging the princes "to slay them like mad dogs." In siding with the princes Luther gave up his role as a national hero to become leader of a sect in Germany and to put control of the new religion in the princes' hands.

From the Peasants' Revolt to the Confession of Augsburg (1530). By 1525 Luther's personal contribution to the Protestant Revolt was practically ended. He spent the rest of his life preaching and pamphleteering, but the success of the new religion depended chiefly on political factors over which he had no control. The emperor was absent from Germany for almost nine years, engaged most of the time in wars with Francis I, anxious to maintain the support of his German princes in these wars and in his trouble with the Turks. Charles' weakened position, combined with the princes' national feeling against Rome and their ambition to use Lutheranism as a lever for gaining land and power, caused the new religion to spread rapidly in the next few years. The princes were hopeful to keep the religious question unsettled in Germany in order to keep the emperor occupied and prevent him from asserting his authority over them. They decided in 1526, at the first Diet of Spires, that each should act on the Edict of Worms in such a way as to be answerable to God and to the emperor according to his conscience — which in effect was a statement of the *cuius regio eius religio* (the ruler chooses the religion of his realm) principle officially to be adopted in 1555.

The real division of Germany into two religious camps may be put at 1529 when the second Diet of Spires voted to prohibit the spread of Lutheranism. Certain German princes, notably the Elector of Saxony, the Landgrave of Hesse, the Margraves of Anhalt and Brandenburg, and fourteen cities protested against this pro-Catholic decision — and from their action comes the label of "Protestant." For a short time it seemed that Charles, now back in Germany, would succeed in stamping out the Lutheran heresy, but the Turks advanced all the way to the gates of Vienna in the autumn of that year and the emperor was forced to turn his attention to the defense of the empire's capital against the invader.

Lutheran doctrine was formally presented by the capable humanist follower of Luther, Philip Melanchthon, at the Diet of Augsburg in 1530. This formulation by Melanchthon became the official statement of Lutheran doctrine in most places. In it he tried to minimize the differences between Lutheranism and Catholic teaching and to stress the points they held in common. Charles was convinced that reconciliation could be effected between the two religious groups on the basis of Melanchthon's profession because it did not specifically deny the supremacy of the pope, the indelible character of the priesthood, or the validity of the seven sacraments. The main points of difference were on communion under both kinds, the marriage of the clergy, and the reform of the canon of the Mass and various ecclesiastical ceremonies. The emperor favored temporizing until a general council decided on these points of difference, on condition that the Lutherans would promise obedience to its decisions. Campeggio and Eck eventually convinced Charles that the Lutherans would not abide by a future council's decision, and consequently the emperor agreed to use force to suppress Lutheranism if the pope and the Italian states would support him. Such support was not forthcoming, and thus the opportunity for suppressing the Lutheran movement passed.

In December of 1530 Lutheran princes and burghers met at Schmalkalden, where they formed a league of mutual defense against attempts to suppress the new faith. Five years later the Schmalkaldic League admitted to its membership all who subscribed to the Augsburg Confession of 1530. Through this league the Protestants bargained for foreign support against the emperor and the Catholic princes who attempted to enforce religious uniformity in the empire. In 1538 the Catholic princes formed the League of Nüremberg, and thus a religious balance of power was set up among the German states of the empire.

The Triumph of the Lutheran Movement (1530–1555). For a quarter of a century after 1530 the Catholic forces in Germany hoped to restore religious unity. The emperor and some theologians, notably Cardinal Contarini, thought that unity could be achieved by discussion and by the removal of abuses through a general council. Hope in this peaceful procedure died out after the failure of the religious colloquy of Ratisbon in 1541, where it was discovered that the doctrinal gulf between Luther and the Catholics was unbridgeable. After 1541 no one could hold that it was abuses in the Church which kept Lutherans out. It was clearly a matter of doctrine and of ecclesiastical jurisdiction.

The Catholic League hoped to repress the movement by armed force. But Charles's wars with France and the latter's support of the Schmalkaldic League enabled the Protestant forces to grow so strong that Charles was unable to crush them when he was able to take action against them in 1546. The Catholic League, moreover, hesitated to help Charles unreservedly lest in crushing Lutheranism it add to the emperor's power.

The first important German states to embrace Lutheranism had been the electorates of Saxony and Hesse. In 1523 the Prussian lands of the Teutonic Order under Albert of Brandenburg adopted the new religion, and in 1534 the important southern state of Würtemberg passed over to the Lutheran camp. The adhesion of ducal Saxony after Duke George's death in 1539 and of Brandenburg in the following year gave the Lutherans sufficient power to resist all attempts to stamp out their new religion.

A settlement was finally effected by the princes of Germany at Augsburg in 1555 by the adoption of the *cuius regio eius religio* principle whereby the ruler was free to adopt either Catholicism or Lutheranism as his established state religion. Ecclesiastical property seized before the Peace of Passau (1552) was to remain in the holder's possession, but no seizures after that date were legal. The Augsburg settlement was not a matter of mutual toleration between the two religious camps but rather a truce agreed on because neither side could overcome the other. Its provisions were not observed faithfully, and further secularization of church property went on throughout the next half century.

Meanwhile, Lutheranism spread into the Scandinavian countries where it was closely tied in with the personal interests of the rulers and the national sentiment of the people. Religious abuses played little part in the Scandinavian revolt. In 1523 the Danish nobility deposed Christian II and elected Frederick I as their new king. Frederick decided to set up a national Danish Church and to consolidate the nobility behind him by allowing them to confiscate church property. Henceforth he imported Lutheran preachers and appointed all Danish bishops without reference to Rome. By the time of his death in 1533 Lutheran teaching had made considerable progress in Denmark. In the struggle for succession to the crown after Frederick's death Catholic forces supported the deposed Christian II; Lutheran forces, including most of the nobility, supported Frederick's son, who was finally crowned king and reigned until 1559. Under him the Lutheran faith was solidly established in Denmark.

The religious revolt in Sweden was inextricably tied in with the Swedish revolt from Denmark. Archbishop Gustavus Trolle bitterly opposed the nationalist movement in Sweden and called upon the Danish king to punish the rebels without mercy. Thus in Swedish eyes the Church was identified with foreign rule and opposed to Swedish national interests. When the Swedish war of independence was successful ten

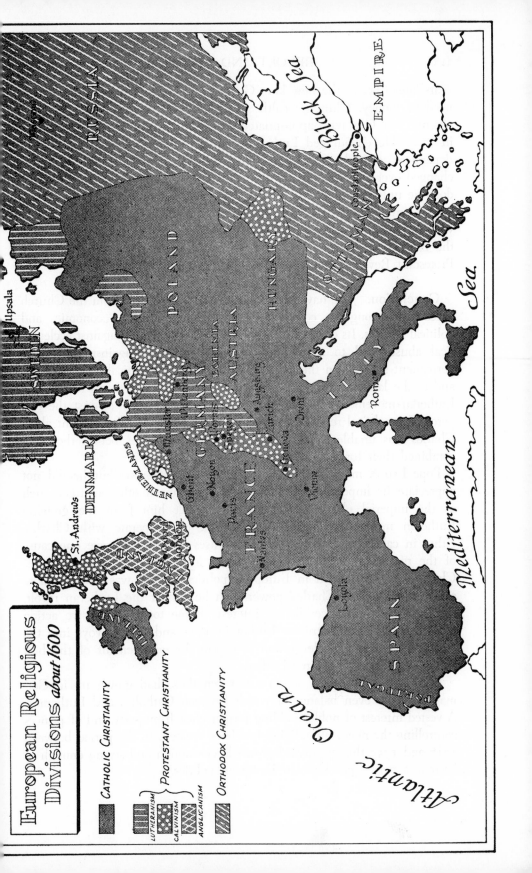

European Religious Divisions *about 1600*

- CATHOLIC CHRISTIANITY
- PROTESTANT CHRISTIANITY
  - } LUTHERANISM
  - } CALVINISM
- ANGLICANISM
- ORTHODOX CHRISTIANITY

Atlantic Ocean

PORTUGAL

SPAIN
Loyola

Mediterranean Sea.

ITALY
Rome

SWEDEN
Upsala

DENMARK
St. Andrews

ENGLAND
London

IRELAND

Oxford

ZETHERLANDS
Ghent
Nogen

FRANCE
Paris
Nantes

GERMANY
Worms
Treves
Wittenberg
Augsburg
Zurich
Geneva
Vienne
Trent

BOHEMIA
AUSTRIA

POLAND

HUNGARY

RUSSIA
Moscow

OTTOMAN EMPIRE
Constantinople

Black Sea

years later (1523) the new king Gustavus Vasa found himself in serious need of money. Church wealth seemed the most vulnerable source of revenue, so Gustavus appropriated all church incomes and properties in 1527. He encouraged Lutheran preachers and took a completely independent attitude toward religion. The Swedish Church gradually changed over to Lutheranism, although there was no official statement of doctrine until 1593. At that time the Swedish Church adopted the Augsburg Confession of 1530 as its official statement of doctrine. Scripture was declared the sole basis of faith, and Luther's catechism was made the basis for religious instruction. In Sweden the sole gainer from the Protestant Revolt was the crown.

Conclusion. We have seen that the Lutheran revolt from the Church succeeded through a convergence of religious, social, economic, and political reasons. Its original popularity was due to feeling against ecclesiastical abuses and to the strong national sentiment against Rome. Its permanent success, on the other hand, was due to political considerations and to the land hunger of the nobility. The German princes saw in the Lutheran movement an opportunity to assert themselves against the emperor. For political reasons alone many of them kept the movement alive. Charles was unable to deal with the German princes before they had combined their forces in the Schmalkaldic League.

Pope Leo X moved to suppress the Lutheran heresy, but he did not appreciate its importance and he therefore allowed other matters, such as the imperial election of 1519, to distract him from the growing Lutheran movement. Clement VII failed to co-operate with Charles, either in calling a council to reform abuses and thus remove one cause of the revolt, or in taking strong action against the Lutheran princes. Clement was embroiled in European politics and he was perhaps more afraid of increasing Charles' power than he was of the Lutheran revolt. As a result of these conflicting interests Rome took no decisive action other than to excommunicate Luther in 1521 and send envoys into the empire to reform the clergy and to secure the enforcement of the bull of excommunication against Luther.

By the time concerted action was taken there had grown up in Germany a fairly even balance of power between Catholics and Lutherans. A vested interest of nobles holding former church property and of princes controlling the new state religion had been created. In the period between 1517 and 1555 this group had grown large enough and strong enough to become a permanent force in European politics.

REVIEW AIDS

1. Explain why a religious revolt occurred in Germany rather than in France or Spain.
2. In what way was the permanent success of Lutheranism promoted by (*a*) the German princes; (*b*) the nobility; (*c*) international politics?
3. Was the Lutheran movement basically a theological matter or a matter of reform? Prove your stand with specific information.
4. List and describe the fundamental tenets of the Lutheran creed.
5. What was the underlying error of all Luther's doctrines?
6. What part, if any, did personal considerations and personalities play in the course of the Lutheran movement?
7. From a close study of Luther's life what psychological explanation can you offer for the development of his doctrine?
8. What did the German bishops do about Lutheranism between 1517 and 1555? the diocesan clergy? the various religious orders?
9. Adduce what reasons you can to explain why most of the northern German states became Lutheran and most of the southern states remained Catholic.

SUGGESTIONS FOR FURTHER READING

The best biography of Luther is Hartmann Grisar, *Luther* (St. Louis: 1914–1917) in six volumes. An excellent one-volume condensation of this work is published under the same title. A more popular Catholic account is Joseph Clayton, *Luther and His Work* (Milwaukee: 1937), which is essentially based on Grisar. A more polemical account from the Catholic point of view is H. Denifle, *Luther and Lutherdom* (Somerset, Ohio: 1917). The most popular Protestant story of Luther's life is Ronald H. Bainton, *Here I Stand: A Life of Martin Luther* (New York: 1950). A less polemical and more objective Protestant work is E. G. Schwiebert, *Luther and His Times* (St. Louis: 1950). Also helpful for understanding Luther in reference to later developments are Jacques Maritain, *Three Reformers* (New York: 1937), and Thomas P. Neill, *Makers of the Modern Mind* (Milwaukee: 1949).

A general view of the Protestant Revolt is given in balanced fashion by Henry S. Lucas, *The Renaissance and the Reformation* (New York: 1934), and in somewhat less satisfactory fashion by E. M. Hulme, *The Renaissance, the Protestant Revolution, and the Catholic Reformation* (New York: 1915). Hilaire Belloc has written the excellent *How the Reformation Happened* (New York: 1954) which was written against the "official" Whig interpretation of the Reformation and is therefore more polemical than balanced. But it is an excellent corrective to this "official" view. Also helpful and easy to read is Belloc's *Characters of the Reformation* (New York: 1937).

The best survey of conditions at the beginning of the Reformation period is the volume in the "Rise of Modern Europe" series by Myron P. Gilmore, *The World of Humanism* (New York: 1952). Valuable for detailed information on political and social events of the period is Volume II of the *Cambridge Modern History*.

DOCUMENTS

1. The Bull *Exsurge Domine* was issued by Leo X on June 15, 1520, after his theologians had given careful study to Luther's writings. The Bull lists Luther's errors and gives him sixty days in which to recant. The selection below includes the more important errors attributed to Luther by the Pope.

Propositions condemned by Pope Leo X in the Bull *Exsurge Domine*.

The following eighteen were among the forty-one propositions condemned partly as heretical, partly as the cause of scandal, and partly as false.

1. It is a heretical, although common, opinion that the Sacraments of the New Covenant confer sanctifying grace upon those who do not place any obstacle in their way.

2. To deny that sin remains in an infant after Baptism is to tread underfoot St. Paul and Jesus Christ.

3. Even though there is no actual sin, concupiscence prevents the soul from immediately entering heaven when it leaves the body.

4. The statement that there are three parts of penance: contrition, confession, and satisfaction, is founded neither on Sacred Scripture nor on the works of the earliest Christian doctors.

6. Contrition, which is inspired by the examination, comparison, and detestation of one's sins, and by which a penitent reviews his past life in the sorrow of his soul, weighing the grievousness, the multitude, and the wickedness of his sins, the loss of eternal happiness, and the penalty of eternal damnation, transforms man into a hypocrite, nay an even greater sinner, because such contrition is derived solely from fear inspired by the law and from the regret of having lost eternal happiness.

11. Do not place any confidence in the fact that you are absolved because of your contrition. . . .

12. A person who, when confessing his sins, is not sorry, or who is absolved by the priest in derision and not in all seriousness, is really absolved if he believes he is absolved.

13. In the Sacrament of Penance and the remission of sin the pope or the bishop does no more than the lowest priest; indeed where there is no priest, any Christian, even if woman or child, may equally do as much.

15. Persons who approach the Sacrament of the Eucharist confident that they have confessed their sins, have not committed any mortal sin, and have made their preparation and recited their prayers, are in profound error. Such persons, indeed, eat and drink their own damnation. But if they believe and are confident that they will receive grace, they will be rendered pure and worthy by this faith alone.

18. Indulgences are a trap set for the faithful, which dispenses them from performing good works. They are to be reckoned among the things that are permissible, but not expedient.

20. To believe that indulgences are salutary and useful is to deceive oneself and to allow oneself to be led into error.

24. Christians should be taught to love excommunications rather than fear them.

25. The Roman Pontiff, the successor of St. Peter, is not the vicar of Jesus Christ, established by Jesus Christ Himself in the person of the blessed Peter over the churches of the entire world.

28. If the pope, together with a large portion of the Church, professed a certain opinion, it would be neither a sin nor a heresy to think the opposite, even though his opinions were true, especially in matters which are not necessary for salvation, until such time as a general council approves one opinion and condemns the other.

29. We are at liberty to dispute the authority of councils, freely contradict their acts, pass judgment on their decrees, and profess without fear anything which seems true to us, no matter whether a council has approved or disapproved it.

31. The just man sins in every good work.

32. A good work, even though well performed, is a venial sin.

35. No one is certain that he is not constantly committing mortal sin, because of the hidden vice of pride.

2. The Peace of Augsburg, September 25, 1555.

The Peace of Augsburg was concluded on September 25, 1555. It settled the war between Lutheran and Catholic princes in Germany on geographic lines that persist, in a general way, till the present time. Failure at Augsburg to recognize Calvinism and continued violation of the clauses on Church property are generally assigned as the causes of the Thirty Years' War (1618–1648), "the last of the religious wars."

15. In order to bring peace into the holy Empire of the Germanic Nation between the Roman Imperial Majesty and the Electors, Princes, and Estates: let neither his Imperial Majesty nor the Electors, Princes, etc., do any violence or harm to any estate of the Empire on account of the Augsburg Confession, but let them enjoy their religious belief, liturgy and ceremonies as well as their estates and other rights and privileges in peace; and complete religious peace shall be obtained only by Christian means of amity, or under threat of the punishment of the imperial ban.

16. Likewise the Estates espousing the Augsburg Confession shall let all the Estates and Princes who cling to the old religion live in absolute peace and in the enjoyment of all their estates, rights and privileges.

17. However, all such as do not belong to the two above-named religions shall not be included in the present peace but be totally excluded from it.

18. And since it has proved to be matter of great dispute what was to happen with the bishoprics, priories and other ecclesiastical benefices of such Catholic priests as would in course of time abandon the old religion, we have in virtue of the powers of Roman Emperors ordained as follows: Where an archbishop, bishop or prelate or any other priest of our old religion shall abandon the same, his archbishopric, bishopric, prelacy, and other benefices, together with all their income and revenues which he has so far possessed, shall be abandoned by him without any further objection or delay. . . .

19. Some of abbeys, monasteries, and other ecclesiastical estates having been confiscated and turned into churches, schools, and charitable institutions, it is herewith ordained that such estates as their original owners had not possessed at the time of the treaty of Passau shall be comprised in the present treaty of peace.

24. In case our subjects, whether belonging to the old religion or to the Augsburg Confession, should intend leaving their homes, with their wives and children, in order to settle in another place, they shall neither be hindered in the sale of their estates after due payment of the local taxes nor injured in their honor.

Chapter 21

THE CHURCH AND CALVINISM

THE divisive nature of the Protestant Revolt soon threatened to weaken the movement and make it possible for the Church to win back the people who had left the faith. In Germany the Protestant princes kept the Lutheran movement from working out its logical individualistic tendencies by insisting on the Augsburg Confession as the statement of Protestant faith and by organizing the Schmalkaldic League to defend their faith. Outside the Germanies, however, new Protestant groups came into being, Zwinglians in Zurich, Calvinists in Geneva, Anglicans in London, and Anabaptists in many parts of the Empire. Attempts to bring the various groups into a single church, such as the attempt by Philip of Hesse to unite Lutherans and Zwinglians, all revealed the divisive nature of Protestantism. Each group insisted on preserving its own autonomy.

The man who saved the Protestant movement from this disintegrating tendency was a French layman, John Calvin, who gave the movement a systematic theology when he published his *Institutes of the Christian Religion* (1536) and infused into it a missionary zeal with his doctrine of the Elect. The success of Calvinism consolidated the Protestant Revolt from the Church and ensured its permanence. Moreover, the followers of Calvin were a more aggressive group than Lutherans, and they played a large part in giving the Western world a new attitude toward life, a new ethic, and a new economic order.

The Rise of Zwinglianism (1519–1531). Ulrich Zwingli was an individualistic Swiss priest who became pastor of the large church in Zurich late in 1518. He was known as a man of irregular life, critical of certain Catholic practices, and vocal as a Swiss patriot. In Zurich he immediately protested against the preaching of indulgences, and he followed Luther's early career sympathetically. Zwingli's open break from the Church occurred early in 1522 when he refused to observe the Lenten regulations because he could find no biblical sanction for them.

Zwingli insisted that the Bible is the sole source of faith. On that basis he abandoned clerical celibacy, declared that the Mass and the Holy Eucharist had only symbolical importance, and formulated the congregational concept of the Church whereby each congregation decided questions of faith for itself. Such an organization of the faithful, which contrasted with the territorial idea of Catholics and Lutherans, fitted in nicely with Swiss political life. The town officials of Zurich embraced Zwingli's ideas. They ordered the clergy to preach only what was found in Holy Scripture. All else was to be swept away as an abuse of the pure faith. Thus fasting, purgatory, the invocation of the saints, clerical celibacy, and other traditional Catholic practices were forbidden, and the Mass was declared to have only a memorial value. On this point, incidentally, Zwingli and Luther could not agree when they met in 1529 at Marburg in the hope of settling doctrinal differences.

Zwinglian teaching spread quickly to the urban parts of Switzerland and to certain places in southern Germany. Inconsistently, Zwingli urged the urban cantons to force his teaching on the other parts of Switzerland, but the forest cantons remained stanchly Catholic. Civil war between Catholics and Protestants followed. In 1531 the second Peace of Kappel provided that each canton should be free to accept the faith of its own choosing, and that all alliances with foreign powers would be null and void. This truce closed the first part of the Protestant Revolt in Switzerland. The second part occurred in the French-speaking part of Switzerland, shortly before Calvin came to Geneva and made it the "Rome of Protestantism."

The Anabaptist Revolt. The sect of Protestants known as Anabaptists, and later as Mennonites, broke off from Zwinglianism in 1523 and came to full development about twenty years later under Menno Simons in the Low Countries. Anabaptism possessed no unity of doctrine, or territory, or leadership. Its only real unity was social: it appealed to the poorer classes and was frequently linked with expectations of a great social upheaval. Anabaptists maintained an extremely literal interpretation of the Bible, on the basis of which they rejected the State's claim to control religious belief. They held union of Church and State an ungodly thing. Generally, they rejected all the sacraments except adult baptism (hence their name), they denied the sacrificial character of the Mass, and they opposed any hierarchical organization of the Church.

Despite its formlessness and the universal opposition of political authority, Anabaptism spread because of the wretched condition of the lower classes throughout central Europe. These poor people seemed ready to accept any movement offering them hope for a better life and salvation hereafter. They were disappointed when Lutheranism and Zwinglianism failed to offer social and economic changes as well as religious innovations. Anabaptist preachers gave new hope to the lower classes by applying scriptural passages to social and political life and thus advocating a radical revolution in European society. The early leaders of the movement were men of position, learned and refined, but as they were executed demagogues took their place. Inhumanly brutal persecution by established political and religious authorities drove the Anabaptists to ever more extreme doctrine, and when they came to power — as they did for a short time at Münster — to extreme social and political action. Thus Anabaptism remained more a social than a religious movement in the sixteenth and seventeenth centuries. Its radical nature precluded the political support necessary for widespread success in any single area.

Protestant Backgrounds in France and Switzerland. The Church in France was regulated by the Pragmatic Sanction of Bourges (1438) and the Concordat of Bologna (1516), which gave the French king control of nominations to high Church offices and thus rather complete control of Church policy. Francis I (1515–1547) favored the humanist reformers who had gathered under the protection of the bishop of Meaux. As humanists, they stressed the importance of Holy Scripture, were suspicious of exterior religious practices, and extremely critical of the clergy and hierarchy.

When Luther's pamphlets circulated in France and aroused reaction among Catholic leaders, the Meaux group did not escape criticism from the Sorbonne and from other theologians who lumped reform and heresy together. (Some members of the Meaux circle, such as Guillaume Farel, did become Protestants, but the greater number stayed in the Church.) At any rate, when Francis was away at war, the Parlement of Paris proceeded against the Meaux group. The reformers were scattered, and several of them obtained the protection of the king's sister, Marguerite of Angouleme. This precipitous action by royal authorities seemed to identify reform and heresy.

The king himself followed a vacillating policy toward Luther's followers in France. Although he did not possess any profound religious convictions, he was interested in reform and encouraged humanist scholars in the country. Francis had no desire to promote a break from Rome, however, because he already had rather complete control of the Church in France. The king's religious policy came to hinge on foreign affairs. Involved in a series of wars with Charles V, Francis played up to the Protestant elements in the Empire. Thus he followed a lenient policy with Protestants at home in order to satisfy the Schmalkaldic League, with which he had made an alliance against the emperor. Occasional outrages against the Catholic religion by fanatical Protestants forced Francis to take a strong stand against heretics and to endorse the policies of the Sorbonne and the Parlement of Paris. Following one such outrage, Francis issued an edict (January, 1535) ordering the complete extirpation of heretics and forbidding the future publication of any heretical literature. But this edict was never systematically enforced.

Among the French reformers of these days who left the Church during one of the brief periods of "persecution" was John Calvin. Born at Noyon, in Picardy, of a solid, middle-class family, young Calvin studied among the humanists and then went to Orleans to take a law degree. Calvin's first writing, a commentary on Seneca's *De Clementia*, shows him to be a thorough humanist in 1532. By the end of the following year, however, he seems to have adopted a position that was essentially Lutheran. Calvin went into hiding when the government took action against Nicholas Cop, rector of the University of Paris, for an address which Calvin helped him prepare.

In the next three years Calvin traveled from place to place, eventually settling at Basel in 1535, where he wrote the first edition of his *Institutes of the Christian Religion*. By this time he had broken off from the humanist reformers and had adopted a purely evangelical form of religion. The first edition of the *Institutes* contains the main outlines of Calvin's mature thought, but his ideas are not well developed until later editions, especially those of 1541 and 1559. Calvin addressed his work to the French king, whom he hoped to convert to his evangelical religion. Although he failed to accomplish his immediate purpose with the *Institutes,* he produced the greatest work on systematic theology by any Protestant and one of the most influential books of modern times.

Meanwhile, the situation in French-speaking Switzerland had grown ripe for a leader of Calvin's ability to assert himself. Guillaume Farel had been winning the French cantons over to Protestantism. A fiery, impetuous man, Farel was eminently successful in identifying Swiss national feeling with opposition to the Roman Catholic Church. By the time he had established his headquarters in Geneva, all the French cantons except Fribourg had been won over to Protestantism. But Farel was not the man to consolidate the movement, a fact which he himself appreciated.

The Protestant Revolt succeeded in Geneva by 1536 because it was identified with communal independence from the Duke of Savoy. The bishop of Geneva appealed to his relatives in Savoy to help conquer the city, and thus Genevans willingly listened to Farel's double exhortation to fight for political independence and to establish a purely evangelical religion. The people of Geneva therefore swore in 1536 that they would live according to the Gospel and stamp out all Catholic practices. This is the Geneva through which Calvin passed on what was to be an overnight visit. Farel convinced him that he had been sent by God to help organize the city and that he would endanger his salvation if he did not stay. Calvin therefore settled in Geneva, where he built the model city of Protestantism, and from which he sent out missionaries of the new faith into all parts of Europe.

Calvinism in Geneva. Calvin's theological system is the first complete and systematic body of thought to be worked out by any Protestant. There was little original thought in Calvin's *Institutes,* but the work is distinctive for weaving the various strands of Protestant thought together and drawing them to logical conclusions. The cornerstone of Calvin's thought is the absolute sovereignty of God and the complete depravity of man. Fallen man cannot earn his justification, but some are predestined by God to salvation. Man's sole function — whether he is one of the Elect or one of the damned — is to glorify God. Calvin held that God's plan for salvation and for the conduct of the world is set forth in Holy Scripture.

Calvin's religion was more extreme and barren than Luther's. He denied all but two sacraments, baptism and the Eucharist, and taught that neither of them is necessary for salvation. For Calvin baptism is only a rite whereby a person is admitted to the Church. In the Holy Eucharist, he claimed, Christ is only dynamically present. Religious service in the new religion was cold and severe, consisting mainly of preaching, hymn singing, and a "memorial service" to commemorate the Last Supper. All "superstitious" practices were ruthlessly eliminated, and the church of the new religion was a plain, unadorned structure.

The Church for Calvin consists of all those who join it and live according to the Scripture. Ministers are appointed by the congregation to interpret Scripture and to preach, but final authority is to rest with all the faithful. Theoretically, the Church cannot punish recalcitrant individuals except by expelling them from the congregation. But the clergy have the right to instruct the State in religious and moral matters and to demand severe punishment for heresy or for "ungodly" living. In Calvin's Geneva there was a rigid regulation of private life in matters of dress, amusements, and the like. And the death penalty was freely administered to those who disagreed with the official Calvinist cult.

Calvin was perhaps a greater legislator than he was a theologian. At any rate, under his direction life at Geneva was soon revised in accordance with his religious teachings. By an ordinance of January 16, 1537, the ideas of Calvin and Farel were adopted by the city of Geneva, and all those who did not comply were to be banished. When an opposition group was elected in 1538, Calvin was forced to live in exile for three years, but in 1541 the town council invited him back and the city was under his control until his death in 1564.

Calvin's new ecclesiastical orders were promulgated in November, 1541. The laws were religious in origin and content, but civil in form and therefore enforceable by secular authority. Genevans were put under four orders that Calvin claimed Christ had instituted for the governance of His Church: (1) ministers, who have charge of most cases of discipline; (2) teachers, who are to teach pure doctrine; (3) a consistory of twelve elders to supervise the conduct of the people; (4) deacons to look after the sick, the poor, and other charitable cases.

Geneva became a city of glass. The laws were harsh, and they were rigorously enforced. Severe punishment was meted out for laughing during a sermon, for dancing or playing cards, for inadvertently using "superstitious" Catholic practices. There was opposition to the Calvinist system in Geneva, but one by one Calvin's opponents were executed or exiled and Geneva was thoroughly puritanized. The city became a refuge for Protestants from other countries, such as England in the time of Mary Tudor (1553–1558), France, Spain and its possessions in the Low Countries. These refugees were trained in Calvinist theology and returned to their native countries to preach the Gospel as they had learned it in Geneva. They influenced religious development in some countries, like England, which had already broken away from the Catholic Church. In others, notably Scotland and Holland, they took advantage of the local political situation to lead more-or-less popular movements against the Catholic authorities and the established religion of the land.

Calvinism in Holland. The spread of Calvinism into Holland was intimately linked to the revolt of the Low Countries from the Spanish rule of Philip II. When Charles V resigned as Emperor, he turned Spain and the Low Countries over to his son Philip II. Whereas Charles had been raised in the Low Countries, Philip II was raised in Spain as a Spaniard. Philip was ignorant of the language, the customs, and the aspirations of people in the Low Countries. His attempts to enforce the Catholic faith through the Inquisition therefore aroused the opposition of natives in this area. They had not taken kindly to Lutheran preachers, but after 1555 many of them listened willingly to Calvinist preachers from Geneva, France, and England.

In 1559 Philip ordered a reorganization of the Church in the Low Countries so as to deal more successfully with heresy. The nobles resented his changes as despotic acts because they were made arbitrarily and were enforced by Philip's Spanish officials. Calvinism, therefore, appealed to some of these people as a method of protesting against Philip's arbitrary rule. Moreover, in these years many Calvinist refugees came to the Low Countries from England during the reign of Mary Tudor and from France during the first of the Religious Wars (1562–1563).

In an attempt to stamp out heresy in the Low Countries Philip appointed the Duke of Alva to act as regent (1567–1573). Alva followed a harsh policy that alienated many people in the Low Countries. The leader of the revolt against Alva's rule, William of Orange, accepted Calvinism, and in 1574 it became the official religion of the revolutionaries. The astute policy of one of Alva's successors, Alexander Farnese, combined with outrages against Catholic practices by some of the extremist Protestants, separated the southern and northern parts of the Low Countries. The section subsequently to be known as Belgium remained loyal to Spain, and the part later called Holland carried on the revolt alone. In 1581 the Dutch Republic formally declared its independence of Spain, and by a truce of 1608 the Spanish government officially recognized Dutch independence and the success of the Protestant Revolt within that country. Philip had found it impossible to put down the revolt in Holland because of English control of the seas and because of French opposition to his sending troops by land from Spain. In Holland, as in Geneva and elsewhere, the Protestant Revolt succeeded largely because it was identified with a successful political movement and because the Catholic Church was identified with an oppressive monarchy.

Calvinism in Scotland. The establishment of the Presbyterian religion in Scotland is closely tied in with foreign relations and with the social organization of the country. The king had little real power in Scotland, a country dominated by the barons and clan leaders of the realm who possessed the power of appointment to most ecclesiastical offices. In order to prevent absorption by England, the Scots had allied themselves closely to England's traditional enemy France. To cement this alliance James V (1513–1542) married Mary of Guise, daughter of the most powerful family in France. Thus, as one historian has put it, "the Scottish royal house was bound to the Catholic cause. Thus the crown, Catholicism, hostility toward England, and the foreign connection with France were all linked together."[1]

When James V died in 1542 he left the crown to his infant daughter, Mary Stuart, who was engaged to the French dauphin, Francis II. Meanwhile, there had grown up in Scotland a certain amount of religious dissent. There had been a few early and ineffectual Protestants, but during Mary Tudor's reign (1553–1558) large numbers of Protestants fled to Scotland from England. Outstanding among them was John Knox, a former Catholic priest who had left the faith in 1545 and had spent some time in Geneva studying under Calvin.

In 1555 Knox returned to Scotland, convinced that the country was ripe for Protestant proselytizing. Mary of Guise had become regent for her daughter in 1554 and national opposition to the French ruler had grown strong. A group of nobles met at Edinburgh to crystallize this opposition to French domination, and they vowed that they would establish the "Word of God" in their land. The nobles were afraid that the regent and queen would subordinate Scottish interests to those of France. Thus Protestantism and Scottish national feeling were identified against Catholicism and the French alliance.

Mary Stuart became queen of France in 1559, and she used French troops to support herself in Scotland. The Scottish nobles therefore appealed to Queen Elizabeth of England for help, because they knew that Elizabeth feared Mary Stuart's claim to the English throne. In the summer of 1560 the Scottish Parliament adopted a Calvinistic religion drawn up by John Knox. They declared the pope's authority in Scotland at an end, repealed all the old laws against heresy, and declared the

---

[1] Henry S. Lucas, *The Renaissance and the Reformation* (New York: 1934), 612.

Mass to be illegal. In the following January the *First Book of Discipline* was adopted.

Meanwhile, Mary Stuart's husband, Francis II, died and in August, 1561, she returned to Scotland. Mary was sincerely Catholic. Despite her vague promise not to alter the state of religion, there was no doubt that if she could prevail she would restore Catholicism. Mary was involved in an unfortunate marriage to her cousin, Lord Darnley, and after his mysterious death she married the Earl of Bothwell. Mary's French connections, her inept rule, and her questionable marital connections all worked to force her abdication in favor of her infant son, James VI, who was raised by Presbyterian divines in preparation for his coming to the throne. Mary Stuart's attempt to recapture the throne failed, and eventually she was executed by Elizabeth as a dangerous contender for the English throne. Henry Lucas sums up the Protestant Revolt in Scotland nicely in these words:[2]

> Nationalist sentiment, which the historian encounters so often in the turmoil of the sixteenth century, aimed at effective direction of the state by its monarch. Mary Stuart failed lamentably, for she proposed to use Scotland as an element in the international Catholic reaction, to the detriment of national welfare. Catholicism and nationalist sentiment were opposed to each other and Catholicism therefore was defeated by the national will. It was but another example showing how secular concerns proved more powerful than religious doctrine.

Calvinism in France. Henry II (1547–1559) followed a more consistent and firm policy than his father had in dealing with Protestants. By the Edict of Fountainbleau (1551) he classified measures against Lutherans and codified the laws dealing with them. Under his repressive policy, however, many important Frenchmen became Protestant. The movement was given unity and direction by Calvin's ministers trained in Geneva and sent back to France. By the end of Henry's reign there were at least twenty Protestant churches staffed from Geneva, and a contemporary estimate is that there were about 400,000 Protestants in the country. At any rate, they held a first national synod in Paris in 1559. Here the Genevan creed and code were adopted. Provision was also made for a national organization with elected pastors and elders, and for provincial and national synods.

This was the situation when Henry II died in 1559. He was succeeded by three weakly sons (Francis II, Charles IX, Henry III) who ruled for

---

[2] *Ibid.*, 620.

thirty years. Their mother, Catherine de' Medici, tried to maintain a balance of power between the Catholic nobility, headed by the Guise family, and the Protestant faction headed by Condé and Bourbon. She was willing to enforce the laws against heresy, but only in so far as not to weaken the throne or increase Guise power. During these thirty years occurred the eight Religious Wars in France. Catholic and Huguenot (the name of the Protestant group in France) leaders were agreed on one thing — that there could be only one religion in France and that the "false" religion had to be completely extirpated.

The court maintained a considerably more moderate policy toward the Huguenots than did the popular Guise family. Extremism on both sides was popular in this age, but eventually a new party came into being, a group known as *Les Politiques* who advanced the new and unpopular idea that Catholics and Huguenots could both live within the same state. The Huguenots were never a large group, but they included many of the influential nobility and a large proportion of the magistrate class.

The Religious Wars in France eventually came to an end when the Huguenot leader, Henry Bourbon, became the sole claimant to the French throne in 1589. Three years later he abjured Protestantism to return to the Catholic Church. In this way he ended religious opposition and could set about unifying the country. In 1598 he settled the religious problem for a time by issuing the *Edict of Nantes*. By this edict — which was very unpopular in France — he allowed Huguenots freedom of religion in all places where it existed and in at least two places in each county. More-over, public money was provided for Huguenot schools and colleges, and they were given complete political and military control of 200 towns. Thus Henry IV created "a state within a state" by granting religious tolera-tion before Frenchmen were willing to practice it and by turning control of part of France over to the Huguenots. Thus by the end of the century a religious truce had been established that recognized a limited Protestant regime within France.

Conclusion. We miss the chief importance of the Calvinist revolt from the Church if we confine our attention only to those Churches which came directly from Geneva. For Calvinism influenced the other Protestant religions and even to some extent Catholic peoples who lived in close contact with reformed Protestants. Calvin's theology and morality ap-pealed along class rather than national lines. His doctrine fitted in nicely with the aspirations and ambitions of the rising middle class, and it is therefore natural that Calvinism should spread along the trade routes,

Third-century statue of
St. Peter
in Grotto of St. Peter's,
Rome.

Excavation under St. Peter's.
In this area lie the
remains of the Prince
of the Apostles.

His Holiness
the late Pope John XXIII

The late Pope Pius XII
with the judges of the
Sacred Roman Rota.

Monte Cassino, before its destruction in World War II.

The central courtyard of Monte Cassino.

"The Coronation of Charlemagne," a painting by Raphael in the Vatican Palace.

Pope Gregory VII.
From a painting by
Raphael in
the Vatican Palace.

Pope Innocent III
approves the rule of
St. Francis.
From the Basilica
of St. Francis
in Assisi.

Peter the Hermit, preaching the First Crusade.

Palace of the Popes at Avignon.

Attack on Castel S. Angelo during the Sack of Rome.

Pope Pius V. Statue in the Basilica of St. Mary Major.

The thirteenth-century Cathedral at Trent, where some of the Sessions of the famous Council met.

The Council of Trent. From a painting in the Louvre.

The death of
St. Francis Xavier.
From the Church of the
Gesu, Rome.

St. Vincent de Paul
visits the foundlings' home.
From the Church of
St. Margaret, Paris.

San Xavier del Bac Mission. Founded for the Indians
of Arizona by Father Kino.

Pope Pius IX
proclaiming the
dogma of the
Immaculate
Conception.

Pope St. Pius X

Pope Leo XIII

Air view of St. Peter's and the Vatican, with Vatican City in the rear.

Pope Pius XI

Pope Pius XI and
six newly consecrated
Chinese Bishops.

center in the cities, and win large numbers of adherents in the commercial areas of Europe.

Calvin's doctrine of the Elect worked out curiously, but logically, to promote wealth seeking for its own sake. Calvin's followers came to believe that prosperity in this life was the best possible objective indication of election for salvation, for certainly God would favor in this life the few He has marked out for salvation in the next. Moreover, the virtues on which Calvin laid great stress were all virtues that made for economic success: hard, unremitting labor, frugality, and industriousness. These virtues make for large income and small spending, in other words for the accumulation of capital. Calvin insisted upon restless activity, and since man is already predestined to salvation or damnation, this activity is naturally to be directed to worldly concerns. That is why R. H. Tawney writes of Calvinism:[3]

> It is perhaps the first systematic body of religious teaching which can be said to recognize and applaud the economic virtues. . . . Such teaching, whatever its theological merits or defects, was admirably designed to liberate economic energies, and to weld into a disciplined social force the rising *bourgeoisie,* conscious of the contrast between its own standards and those of a laxer world, proud of its vocation as the standard-bearer of the economic virtues, and determined to vindicate an open road for its own way of life by the use of every weapon, including political revolution and war, because the issue which was at stake was not merely convenience or self-interest, but the will of God.

Thus the followers of Calvin glorified work as it had never been glorified before. Work was good both as an end in itself and as a means of amassing wealth. English Puritans were insistent on this point. Thus Richard Baxter told his readers: "Be wholly taken up in diligent business of your lawful callings, when you are not exercised in the more immediate service of God. . . . Keep up a high esteem of time, and be every day more careful that you lose none of your time than you are that you lose none of your gold and silver." And John Wesley insisted: "We must exhort all Christians to gain all they can and so save all they can; that is, in effect, to grow rich."

From Geneva, then, Calvin sent out a class of men who were to be important not only in the field of religion but also in creating modern European and American society and in making the world the sort of place it is today.

---

[3] *Religion and the Rise of Capitalism* (New York: 1926), 111.

REVIEW AIDS

1. Luther was a fallen-away Catholic priest. Calvin was a layman, educated as a lawyer. Show how these different backgrounds played a part in different formulations of Protestantism by Luther and Calvin.
2. Why could Calvin logically look upon himself as "God's prosecuting attorney" on earth?
3. A great deal has been made of the connection between Calvin's "Protestant ethic" and the rise of capitalism. Show to what extent Calvinistic theology could logically give impetus to capitalism.
4. Explain how congregational organization of the Church might appeal to the Swiss.
5. Calvin's followers considered their religion "reformed" and "evangelical." Explain why they adopted these two adjectives.
6. Calvin's followers in France numbered some of the most important nobility of the country. Why were they unsuccessful in "converting" the entire country to the Huguenot faith?
7. Explain how Scotland was ideally suited for the successful introduction of Presbyterianism in 1555.
8. The inhabitants of the Low Countries did not take kindly to Lutheran preachers. But half the country in time adopted Calvinism. Explain.
9. Calvinism tended to spread along the trade routes of Europe, whereas Lutheranism spread by country. Explain.

SUGGESTIONS FOR FURTHER READING

The best biographies of John Calvin are those by Albert Hyma, *Life of John Calvin* (Grand Rapids: 1943), and Georgia Harkness, *John Calvin: The Man and His Ethics* (New York: 1931). H. Y. Reyburn, *John Calvin* (London: 1914), is a eulogistic study of the man, and J. Moura and P. Louvet, *Calvin, a Modern Biography* (New York: 1932), is a critical study.

Calvin's thought is analyzed in Etienne Gilson, *Christianity and Philosophy* (New York: 1939), and Thomas P. Neill, *Makers of the Modern Mind.* The connection between Calvinism and economic thought is studied in Max Weber, *The Protestant Ethic and the Spirit of Capitalism* (London: 1930), and modified by R. H. Tawney, *Religion and the Rise of Capitalism* (New York: 1926), and by G. A. T. O'Brien, *An Essay on the Economic Effects of the Reformation* (London: 1923).

The standard works on the spread of Calvinism in France are: H. M. Baird, *History of the Rise of the Huguenots* (New York: 1900), a two-volume study; F. C. Palm, *Calvinism and the Religious Wars* (New York: 1932), a brief, objective work; and the stimulating study of O. Zoff, *The Huguenots* (New York: 1942).

The spread of Calvinism into the Low Countries is handled in two classic but now outdated works: J. F. Motley, *The Rise of the Dutch Republic*, 3 vols. (New York: 1874); and P. J. Blok, *A History of the People of the Netherlands*, Vol. III (New York: 1904). Also useful are Pieter Geyl, *The Revolt of the*

Netherlands, 1555–1609 (London: 1937), and C. V. Wedgwood, *William the Silent* (New Haven, Conn.: 1944).

Most of the accounts of Knox's reformation in Scotland are sympathetic to the movement. Among the better of these works are Andrew Lang, *John Knox and the Reformation* (London: 1905), and A. F. Mitchell, *The Scottish Reformation* (Edinburgh: 1900). Also helpful are the biographies of E. Percy, *John Knox* (London: 1937), and E. Muir, *John Knox* (London: 1929).

DOCUMENTS

Dedication of the Institutes of the Christian Religion
By John Calvin (1536)

The *Institutes of the Christian Religion* was written by Calvin in 1535 and a French translation was published in 1540. This is the most important single writing of the Protestant Revolt, and some historians believe that it saved the movement from collapse. The following selections are from the author's dedication to Francis I and from the general syllabus Calvin prepared to describe the book's contents briefly.

To His Most Christian Majesty, FRANCIS, King of the French, and his Sovereign, John Calvin wisheth peace and salvation in Christ.

When I began this work, Sire, nothing was further from my thoughts than writing a book which would afterwards be presented to your Majesty. My intention was only to lay down some elementary principles, by which inquirers on the subject of religion might be instructed in the nature of true piety. And this labour I undertook chiefly for my countrymen, the French, of whom I apprehended multitudes to be hungering and thirsting after Christ, but saw very few possessing any real knowledge of him. That this was my design, the book itself proves by its simple method and unadorned composition. But when I perceived that the fury of certain wicked men in your kingdom had grown to such a height, as to leave no room in the land for sound doctrine, I thought I should be usefully employed, if in the same work I delivered my instructions to them, and exhibited my confession to you, that you may know the nature of that doctrine, which is the object of such unbounded rage to those madmen who are now disturbing the country with fire and sword. . . .

General Syllabus

The design of the Author in these Christian Institutes is twofold, relating, First to the knowledge of God, as the way to attain a blessed immortality; and, in connection with and subservience to this, Secondly, to the knowledge of ourselves.

In the prosecution of this design, he strictly follows the method of the Apostles' Creed, as being most familiar to all Christians. For as the Creed consists of four parts, the first relating to God the Father, the second to the Son, the third to the Holy Spirit, the fourth to the Church; so the Author distributes the whole of this work into Four Books, corresponding respectively to the four parts of the Creed; as will clearly appear from the following detail: —

I. The first article of the Creed relates to God the Father, and to the creation, conservation, and government of all things, which are included in his omnipotence.

So the first book is on the knowledge of God, considered as the Creator, Preserver, and Governor of the universe at large, and every thing contained in it. It shows both the nature and tendency of the true knowledge of the Creator — that this is not learned in the schools, but that every man from his birth is self-taught it — Yet that the depravity of men is so great as to corrupt and extinguish this knowledge, partly by ignorance, partly by wickedness; so that it neither leads him to glorify God as he ought, nor conducts him to the attainment of happiness — And though this internal knowledge is assisted by all the creatures around, which serve as a mirror to display the Divine perfections, yet that man does not profit by it — Therefore, that to those, whom it is God's will to bring to an intimate and saving knowledge of himself, he gives his written word; which introduces observations on the sacred Scripture — That he has therein revealed himself; that not the Father only, but the Father, Son, and Holy Spirit, united, is the Creator of heaven and earth; whom neither the knowledge innate by nature, nor the very beautiful mirror displayed to us in the world, can, in consequence of our depravity, teach us to know so as to glorify him. This gives occasion for treating of the revelation of God in the Scripture, of the unity of the Divine Essence, and the trinity of Persons. — To prevent man from attributing to God the blame of his own voluntary blindness, the Author shows the state of man at his creation, and treats of the image of God, free-will, and the primitive integrity of nature. — Having finished the subject of creation, he proceeds to the conservation and government of all things, concluding the first book with a full discussion of the doctrine of divine providence.

II. But since man is fallen by sin from the state in which he was created, it is necessary to come to Christ. Therefore it follows in the Creed, "And in Jesus Christ, his only Son our Lord," etc.

So in the second book of the Institutes our Author treats of the knowledge of God as the Redeemer in Christ: and having shown the fall of man, leads him to Christ the Mediator. Here he states the doctrine of original sin — that man possesses no inherent strength to enable him to deliver himself from sin and the impending curse, but that, on the contrary, nothing can proceed from him, antecedently to reconciliation and renovation, but what is deserving of condemnation — Therefore, that, man being utterly lost in himself, and incapable of conceiving even a good thought by which he may restore himself, or perform actions acceptable to God, he must seek redemption out of himself, in Christ — That the Law was given for this purpose, not to confine its observers to itself, but to conduct them to Christ; which gives occasion to introduce an exposition of the Moral Law — That he was known, as the Author of salvation, to the Jews under the Law, but more fully under the Gospel, in which he is manifested to the world. — Hence follows the doctrine of the similarity and difference of the Old and New Testament, of the Law and

Gospel. — It is next stated, that, in order to complete the accomplishment of salvation, it was necessary for the eternal Son of God to become man, and that he actually assumed a real human nature: — it is also shown how these two natures constitute one person — That the office of Christ, appointed for the acquisition and application of complete salvation by his merit and efficacy, is sacerdotal, regal, and prophetical. — Next follows the manner in which Christ executed his office, or actually performed the part of a Mediator, being an exposition of the Articles respecting his death, resurrection, and ascension to heaven. — Lastly, the Author shows the truth and propriety of affirming that Christ merited the grace of God and salvation for us.

III. As long as Christ is separate from us, he profits us nothing. Hence the necessity of our being ingrafted into him, as branches into a vine. Therefore the doctrine concerning Christ is followed, in the third part of the Creed, by this clause, "I believe in the Holy Spirit," as being the bond of union between us and Christ.

So in the third book our Author treats of the Holy Spirit, who unites us to Christ — and consequently of faith, by which we embrace Christ, with his twofold benefit, free righteousness, which he imputes to us, and regeneration, which he commences within us, by bestowing repentance upon us. — And to show that we have not the least room to glory in such faith as is unconnected with the pursuit of repentance, before proceeding to the full discussion of justification, he treats at large of repentance and the continual exercise of it, which Christ, apprehended by faith, produces in us by his Spirit. — He next fully discusses the first and chief benefit of Christ when united to us by the Holy Spirit that is, justification — and then treats of prayer, which resembles the hand that actually receives those blessings to be enjoyed, which faith knows, from the word of promise, to be laid up with God for our use. — But as all men are not united to Christ, the sole Author of salvation, by the Holy Spirit, who creates and preserves faith in us, he treats of God's eternal election; which is the cause that we, in whom he foresaw no good but what he intended freely to bestow, have been favored with the gift of Christ, and united to God by the effectual call of the Gospel. — Lastly, he treats of complete regeneration, and the fruition of happiness; that is, the final resurrection, towards which our eyes must be directed, since in this world the felicity of the pious, in respect of enjoyment, is only begun.

IV. But as the Holy Spirit does not unite all men to Christ, or make them partakers of faith, and on those to whom he imparts it he does not ordinarily bestow it without means, but employs for this purpose the preaching of the Gospel and the use of the sacraments, with the administration of all discipline, therefore it follows in the Creed, "I believe in the Holy Catholic Church," whom, although involved in eternal death, yet, in pursuance of the gratuitous election, God has freely reconciled to himself in Christ, and made partakers of the Holy Spirit, that, being ingrafted into Christ, they may have communion with him as their head, whence flows a perpetual remission of sins, and a full restoration to eternal life.

So in the fourth book our Author treats of the Church — then of the means used by the Holy Spirit in effectually calling from spiritual death, and preserving the church — the word and sacraments — baptism and the Lord's supper — which are as it were Christ's regal sceptre, by which he commences his spiritual reign in the Church by the energy of his Spirit, and carries it forward from day to day during the present life, after the close of which he perfects it without those means.

And as political institutions are the asylums of the Church in this life, though civil government is distinct from the spiritual kingdom of Christ, our Author instructs us respecting it as a signal blessing of God, which the Church ought to acknowledge with gratitude of heart, till we are called out of this transitory state to the heavenly inheritance, where God will be all in all.

This is the plan of the Institutes, which may be comprised in the following brief summary: —

Man, created originally upright, being afterwards ruined, not partially, but totally, finds salvation out of himself, wholly in Christ; to whom being united by the Holy Spirit, freely bestowed without any regard of future works, he enjoys in him a twofold benefit, the perfect imputation of righteousness, which attends him to the grave, and the commencement of sanctification, which he daily increases, till at length he completes it at the day of regeneration or resurrection of the body, so that in eternal life and the heavenly inheritance his praises are celebrated for such stupendous mercy.

Chapter 22

THE ANGLICAN REVOLT

THE Protestant Revolt in England was largely the work of one man, Henry VIII, who was aided and abetted by a greedy new nobility. The masses of Englishmen neither wanted change nor understood that it was taking place. The revolt was an act of State to which men in high places — ecclesiastical and secular — did not put up strong resistance. Most bishops and high-placed laymen did not possess the heroic courage needed to resist Henry's will. Those who did, men like St. Thomas More and St. John Fisher, earned martyr's crowns.

Under Henry the English Church broke away from Rome. Henry took the pope's place as vicar of Christ on earth. By the time that his first two wives died (1536) Henry could have brought the English Church back into communion with Rome. But meanwhile he had created a class of greedy new nobles who had a vested interest in the revolt, for he had enriched them with property taken from the Church. This new class introduced a sweeping change in the English Church under Edward VI and, after the temporary Catholic restoration under Mary Tudor, a second and permanent change under Elizabeth that was a compromise between the Catholic religion and the Protestant religions of the continent.

The same factors that promoted the Protestant Revolt on the continent operated to make the English revolt successful. National feeling was enlisted to identify English patriotism with the new religion. The powerful new nobility and commercial class adopted the new religion because it put much property in their hands and it freed them from some of the restrictions on money-making held by the Catholic Church. There were abuses in the Catholic Church in England, but they were not gross and they seem to have played at most a minor part in stirring up feeling in favor of "reform." The Anglican revolt was primarily an act of State, a series of measures forced on the country by the group of men who constituted the government and who stood to benefit by the religious changes they engineered.

The Church in England did not suffer from the same serious abuses it endured in Italy and Germany. Pluralism had not been a serious abuse before Wolsey, and nepotism had not gone to any great lengths. The bishops and clergy were not without fault, but they were generally good men. The Lollard heresy had been suppressed, but heretics who subscribed to much of Wyclif's teaching could still be found in England at the time Luther posted his theses on the church door at Wittenberg. It is reasonable to conclude, however, that the materials were lacking for a popular religious revolt in England. The impetus and direction of the revolt had to come from the king himself.

Henry's "Question of Conscience." As early as 1527 Henry VIII determined to put away his wife in favor of Anne Boleyn. Henry petitioned that he had been living with Catherine in sin for eighteen years and that his conscience troubled him. The grounds for his complaint were the following. Henry's older brother Arthur had married Catherine in 1502 at the age of 15, and he had died four and a half months later. Henry VII was anxious to complete an alliance with Spain, so he obtained a papal dispensation for his second son, Henry, to marry Catherine. In 1527 Henry VIII argued that the dispensation had been obtained fraudulently and was therefore invalid. As a result he and Catherine had violated the law of affinity which prohibited one from marrying his brother's widow — unless with a dispensation.

There were other facts to which Henry's petition did not advert. Catherine was five years older than Henry, and she had aged rapidly. Moreover, she had failed to bear him a son. Of her five children, only Mary survived early childhood. In short, Henry had grown tired of Catherine and he wanted a male heir to succeed him. He had engaged in adulterous relations with Elizabeth Blount as early as 1519, and somewhat later with Mary Boleyn. He had then come under the attraction of Anne Boleyn. But the latter refused to become his mistress. She would be queen or nothing. To have Anne Boleyn, then, Henry must get rid of Catherine.

Henry's petition put Pope Clement VII in a delicate position. He was at war with Catherine's nephew, Emperor Charles V, and in 1527 he was Charles's prisoner. To make the situation more difficult, Catherine insisted that her marriage to Henry was valid. She claimed that her marriage to Arthur had never been consummated, and a preliminary investigation of the papal dispensation suggested that the subsequent marriage was valid in every respect. Clement was not a particularly forceful man, so he adopted the policy of stalling for time in the hope that the case would somehow solve itself — that one of the parties would die, Henry would tire of Anne, or some other such fortunate development would occur.

On December 23, 1527, Clement issued a bull to Henry providing that he could have his divorce (actually, a declaration of nullity) on the condition that he prove the invalidity of his marriage. Henry had hoped to have full authority for adjudicating his case given to his chancellor Wolsey, but in April, 1528, the pope appointed Campeggio to serve with Wolsey as a commission to examine the case in England. Campeggio was instructed to stall for time, to effect a reconciliation if possible, and at any rate not to issue a final verdict without fresh instructions and faculties from Rome. Campeggio left Rome in July, 1528, but did not arrive in England until the spring of 1529.

From England Campeggio reported to the papal secretary of state, Salviati: "So far as I can see, this passion of the king's is a most extraordinary thing. He sees nothing, he thinks of nothing but his Anne; he cannot be without her for an hour, and it moves one to pity to see how the king's life, the stability and downfall of the whole country, hang upon this one question." Catherine proved stubborn when she appeared before the legatine court. She insisted her marriage with Henry was valid, but the king's lawyers piled up a mass of evidence (some of it fradulent) against her. When it was apparent that proceedings were moving too rapidly, Campeggio suspended hearings until the following October.

By this time Clement had decided to recall the case to Rome. The English people had generally favored Catherine while the case was being heard in England, but now that it was taken to Rome popular feeling began to favor Henry — an indication of strong national sentiment in England and a certain traditional hostility toward Rome. Through the next four years Henry tried every possible means of pressure to bring about a favorable verdict from Rome. Clement continued to postpone making a final decision, but in the face of Henry's threats he grew increasingly firm in his handling of the case.

Henry used every device at hand to force a favorable decision from the pope. Thomas Cranmer solicited opinions favorable to the king from university theologians. Henry pressured the nobles and prelates of England to request the pope to dissolve the marriage. Otherwise, they threatened, the case would be settled in England. Meanwhile, Henry had Parliament pass a series of laws providing for the curtailment or destruction of various Church fees; it remained for the king to enforce these laws, and Henry threatened to do so unless his divorce was granted. The pope answered by threatening to excommunicate Henry and any female marrying him while his divorce case was still pending in Rome.

The English prelates found themselves in a difficult position during this struggle between their king and their pope. Henry forced a general convocation of the clergy to acknowledge him as supreme head of the Church in England — to which the clergy added the saving phrase "so far as the law of Christ permits." Henry also fined the clergy unmerci-fully for their alleged violation of the statute *Praemunire* (which forbade appeals to Rome from Church courts in England) in recognizing Wolsey's jurisdiction as papal legate. Finally, he forced a bill through Parliament, to which the clergy were compelled to submit, providing that no ecclesias-tical laws could be adopted in England without royal approval. By this law Henry became supreme power in Church and State.

Meanwhile it was becoming evident that Henry would not get his divorce from Rome. Therefore, when the archbishop of Canterbury died in August, 1532, Henry chose Cranmer to succeed him with the understanding that Cranmer would grant the divorce. Henry and Anne were secretly married in January, 1533, and in May Cranmer pro-nounced Henry's marriage with Catherine invalid and his marriage with Anne valid.

The Church in England Becomes Schismatic. When Clement VII died (September 25, 1534) the English schism was complete. On March 24 Clement had passed final sentence against Henry in the divorce case. Henry retaliated by having Parliament pass the *Act of Supremacy* and the *Act of Succession*. The former law declared the king supreme head of the Church in England and bestowed on him all papal titles, rights, and incomes. The latter law declared that since the king's first marriage had been invalid, Mary Tudor was illegitimate and ineligible to succeed to the throne. The marriage with Anne Boleyn was held "undoubted, true, sincere, and perfect hereafter," and therefore Elizabeth — who was already born — and Anne's future children enjoyed the right of succession.

At the same time an oath was prepared for all citizens to take if they were suspected of dissatisfaction with the settlement of 1534. The oath required them to accept the succession of Elizabeth, and therewith to repudiate papal authority and accept Henry's position as head of the Church in England. It was because they refused to take this oath that St. Thomas More and St. John Fisher were executed. Most of the clergy took the oath, but a large number of Observant Franciscans and Carthusians resisted and were executed. The execution of More and Fisher moved Pope Paul III to strong measures. He gave Henry VIII three months in which to repent; otherwise England was to be placed under interdict with all the accompanying medieval sanctions, such as releasing subjects from their oath of allegiance. The pope, however, was not able to secure co-operation from Francis I or Charles V in taking measures against the English king. Both rulers sought Henry's favor, since he seemed to wield the balance of power between them.

Papal policy changed in 1536. Early that year Catherine died, and later Anne Boleyn was executed on the charge of adultery. Henry was therefore validly married to his third wife, Jane Seymour, and the pope hoped that the schism would be ended. Jane shortly bore him a son, the future Edward VI. What the pope seems not to have realized is that the religious settlement in England had been complicated by an adventurer, Thomas Cromwell, who had been made vicar-general for ecclesiastical affairs in 1535. Cromwell presented Henry with a complete plan for pillaging the Church in England in order to right royal finances and to reward those who had backed him in his struggle against Rome. The plan was to reduce episcopal income, confiscate half the revenues of the cathedrals, take the first year's income as a tax on all ecclesiastical appointments, and finally to suppress all small monasteries and convents and confiscate their property.

The plan was never fully adopted, but in 1536 the small monasteries were confiscated and in 1539 the larger ones were also suppressed. The suppression of the monasteries created the only crisis Henry had to face in the whole affair. This brought the English religious revolt down to the people for the first time, and it led to a series of riots, especially in the north, which culminated in the Pilgrimage of Grace. The people demanded, among other things, that all heresy be suppressed, the authority of the pope be re-established, and the suppressed monasteries be restored. The pope appointed Cardinal Pole to obtain Francis I's help to co-operate with the rebels and to settle the English matter. It was believed in Rome that two thirds of the people were opposed to Henry and that the movement would succeed. The risings were not as great as Rome thought, however, and Henry managed to suppress them without great difficulty. Cardinal Pole could not obtain the co-operation of Francis I, and thus the attempt to overthrow Henry or bring him to terms ended in failure.

By 1537 Henry had triumphed over all his enemies. As head of the Anglican Church Henry resolutely opposed the introduction of new doctrine or religious practice. He had created the schism because it was the necessary means to get rid of Catherine. During these years many of his supporters, such as Cranmer, were anxious to introduce Protestant elements into the Anglican Church, and by 1537 they had apparently enjoyed a measure of success. Henry therefore set about defining the faith of his new Church. In the *Bishops' Book* of 1537 he made a summary of doctrine and devotional practices which was essentially Catholic on all points. Two years later Parliament passed an *Act for the abolishing of diversity of opinion in certain articles concerning the Christian religion,* better known as the "Six Articles" which asserted the traditional Catholic teaching on the Real Presence, auricular confession, celibacy of the clergy, and communion for the faithful only with bread.

For the rest of his life Henry rigorously enforced the new religion against Protestants and Catholics alike. Lutherans, Zwinglians, Anabaptists, and others who tried to preach new doctrines were hunted down, tried, and executed. So too were Catholics who refused to accept the king's authority in religious matters. By the time Henry died in 1547 the Anglican Church was solidly established, but the daily religious life of the average Englishman must have seemed pretty much the same as it had when Henry came to power in 1509. The quarrel had been about a technical point of jurisdiction, and to the average Englishman it must have seemed a matter that did not concern him in any direct way.

The Protestant Revolution Under Edward VI. By 1547 there was a strong party of men who were intent on bringing about a true religious revolution in England. They were headed by Cranmer, the archbishop of Canterbury, and by the duke of Somerset, the young king's uncle who was made Lord Protector and empowered to rule in the king's name. Cranmer encouraged the preaching of new doctrines and had the government abolish all laws against heresy. In July, 1547, he published a book of sermons which the clergy were ordered to preach. These sermons were Protestant in tone. Toward the end of the next year he finished the first Book of Common Prayer which the clergy were required by the Act of Uniformity (1549) to use in place of the Latin missal. This prayer book was a sort of compromise between Lutheran and Catholic teaching. Essential parts of the Mass are suppressed, for example, but there is no explicit denial of the Real Presence. The clergy were now allowed to marry, and it seems that Cranmer was prepared to introduce other Protestant innovations. But Somerset had proved an incapable ruler, and in 1549 the government fell into the hands of the earl of Warwick, later known as the duke of Northumberland, who was an unprincipled, ambitious man.

Cranmer continued to Protestantize the country during Northumberland's rule of four years. A law was passed ordering the destruction of all Catholic service books; another ordered the destruction of all religious images. Many of the new bishops ordered all altars in their dioceses torn down and stained glass windows destroyed. Two important measures consolidated the Protestant movement of these years. The first was the second Prayer Book — which is essentially the book used in the Church of England today — and the second Act of Uniformity of 1552 which made the new Prayer Book obligatory. The second Prayer Book was unmistakably Protestant in every respect. The second measure was the official statement of the new religion in the *Forty-Two Articles of Religion*.

In the six years of Edward VI's reign, then, the official English Church was thoroughly Protestantized. It is impossible to know how completely these innovations were accepted by the clergy throughout the country. But the changes had been made, and unless there were a Catholic reaction within a short time the government could ensure their permanency. But Edward was a sickly boy and by the end of 1552 it was evident that he would not live long. Northumberland was anxious to secure the succession of a Protestant because he feared that a reaction under Mary Tudor would deprive him and his friends of the tremendous wealth they had taken from the Church. He therefore arranged for a coup whereby Mary and Elizabeth, Henry's remaining children, would be put aside in favor of his daughter-in-law, Lady Jane Gray. His plan failed, however, and Mary Tudor became queen in 1553.

The Catholic Restoration. As Catherine's daughter, Mary was committed to the validity of Henry's first marriage and therefore to a repudiation of the schism he had accomplished and to undoing the Protestant revolution of Edward's reign. Mary was well known as a devoted Catholic, and it was naturally expected that she would use her power to restore the Catholic faith to the position it enjoyed early in her father's reign. But Mary faced serious difficulties. What policy would she adopt in regard to the property which had been taken from the Church? What about men like Cranmer and the Protestant bishops of the land? Were they to be treated leniently or harshly? These were serious problems, because if

Mary did not handle them adroitly she might provoke revolution among the important people of England and find both herself and the Catholic religion forever ousted from the land.

Mary was personally neither vindictive nor intolerant. She published a statement of her religious belief and promised that no one would be troubled about his beliefs until action was taken on the problem by the next Parliament. She released the Catholic bishops who had been imprisoned and restored them to their sees. Foreign Protestants who had entered the country during the last king's reign were given passports to leave the country. The policy of moderation Mary followed had been suggested by her cousin, Cardinal Pole, and by Charles V who advised that she "should adapt herself with all possible gentleness, conforming to the decrees of Parliament and gradually restoring things as best she could, and that she ought to be, above all else, a good Englishwoman."

Unfortunately for Mary and the Catholic cause in England, Charles also advised her to marry his son Philip. Mary's engagement and subsequent marriage to Philip (1554) was her first and most serious mistake. It compromised her rule in the eyes of Englishmen who suspected that England's welfare would be subjected to Spanish foreign policy and to Philip's counter-reformation policies. Mary's second serious mistake was to allow members of her council to exercise imprudent zeal — and perhaps vindictiveness — against their former persecutors. Cranmer and three other bishops were burned at the stake rather than imprisoned, a punishment without precedent in England and an act which Englishmen subsequently held against "Bloody Mary." Mary's third mistake was the result of a scrupulous conscience. She returned to the Church certain properties taken from it and still in royal possession. This frightened many persons in high position, for they feared that she would soon force them all to follow her example and return the Church's property.

Opposition to Mary gradually died down when Englishmen discovered that Philip behaved very properly and made no attempt to exercise undue influence over the English government. Philip consistently urged a moderate policy in the treatment of English Protestants, and he made no attempt to secure rule of the country for himself in case of Mary's death. Nor did the pope cause any trouble about confiscated property. He empowered his legate, Cardinal Pole, to effect a property settlement on the *status quo* basis of 1553. By referring her first episcopal appointments to Rome for confirmation Mary implicitly acknowledged papal authority over the Church in England. This acknowledgment was made explicit by receiving Cardinal Pole as papal legate to England. By the end of 1554 England had formally rejoined the Catholic Church. The clergy had renounced all claim to confiscated ecclesiastical property. Parliament had repealed all the religious legislation of Edward VI's reign, and a few months later the antipapal laws of Henry VIII. Cardinal Pole had held a synod which made plans for thorough reform of ecclesiastical institutions in England, and there was every reason to believe that the religious problem was settled for good.

But such an easy settlement was not achieved. First of all, Mary's early lenient policy did not reckon with the fact that there was a powerful group in the country opposed to the restoration of Catholicism. And second, her advisers were not content with the lenient policy followed in the first year of her reign. Early in 1555 Parliament revived the old laws against heresy, statutes from the reigns of Richard II, Henry IV, and Henry V, which had been repealed for only six years. In the next four years about 273 persons were convicted under these laws and burned at the stake. Such penalties were typical of the sixteenth century, but in this case they failed to achieve their objective, for at the end of Mary's reign the Protestants were still a strong force in the country.

The Protestant tradition in England and America labeled Mary "Bloody" and created a mighty piece of anti-Catholic propaganda out of her reign. What are the facts of the case? First of all, we should remember that heresy stubbornly held was considered the most heinous of crimes, like treason today. Only those who refused to abjure their errors were executed. Second, we should remember that the typical heretic was not a meek person. He was self-educated, argumentative, dogmatic, and intolerant. Moreover, he was willing to send those who disagreed with him to the stake, as indeed Cranmer and other Edwardian bishops had done.

The above-mentioned factors mitigate the seriousness of the charges against Mary's regime. But they do not excuse the Marian persecution. There was nothing in English history to compare to the 273 heretics burned at the stake in the last four years of her reign. But the particular infamy of the Marian persecution derives from the fact that most of its victims could not have been heretics at all. The laws against heresy had been written for a Catholic country and were to apply to lapsed Catholics who held stubbornly to their errors. By 1553 England was a country of religious confusion. Parliament had changed the official doctrine of the English people several times. Priests and bishops had taught one thing one day and denied it the next. How could the average poorly educated Englishman be considered a lapsed Catholic? Certainly he could not have been brought up in the true Catholic faith, understood it and practiced it, and then renounced it in favor of heretical doctrine. Philip Hughes sums the matter up well in these words:[1]

What had happened in England in these years of Mary's reign was not, in fact, the repression by a Catholic government of heresy invading a Catholic country, but the repression of heresy by Catholic politiques in a country where heresy has lately been fully established, a country that is already in great part indifferent to religion: and herein, it seems to me, lies the greatest scandal of the business, and the ultimate reason why it was so easy to exploit it against Catholics in the generation that followed, and to root in it so powerful an anti-Catholic tradition.

In the last year Mary's health failed badly. When it was apparent she would die without issue, she designated her half-sister Elizabeth to succeed her on the condition that Elizabeth faithfully support the Catholic religion. Elizabeth was crowned according to the Catholic rite, swore to protect the Catholic religion, and proposed an alliance with Spain. That is why the Venetian ambassador wrote: "No change can be seen in the churches; no insult has been offered monks and priests visiting London, and her Majesty still hears Mass as before." But at the same time the Spanish ambassador wrote that "every day the queen takes a stronger stand against religion." How were two such different opinions of Elizabeth's ecclesiastical policy possible?

The Elizabethan Settlement. In the first few months of her reign Elizabeth's policy toward religion was guarded. The restoration under Mary had apparently been popular with most people, and Elizabeth was careful not to antagonize popular feeling until she had consolidated her position. Before the year (1558) was out, however, she had appointed Protestant preachers to various positions, and the bishop of Chichester was imprisoned for denouncing a Protestant in December. On Christmas Day the queen left Mass after the gospel when the celebrant refused to obey her command not to elevate the host. Married priests were appointed to court positions. It was evident that Elizabeth favored some kind of Protestant restoration and that her government would present a program to the Parliament of 1559, especially when Elizabeth broke off diplomatic relations with the pope.

By the very nature of things Elizabeth was committed to an anti-Catholic policy. Regardless of her oath to protect the Church, she could not look favorably on the religion that branded her illegitimate and thus made her hold on the throne precarious at all times. It is hard to tell

---

[1] *The Reformation in England*, Vol. II (London: 1954), 303–304.

what religious convictions — if any — she held personally. As queen she seems to have wanted any settlement that would consolidate her royal position. At first, Elizabeth and her advisers proposed only moderate changes. Parliament was told at its opening session of 1559 that it was to decide on a new comprehensive confession of faith and on a common form of worship. But the government's bill proposed only to restore royal supremacy over the Church and to allow communion under both kinds.

The religious settlement of 1559, which is essentially the final settlement of the Protestant Revolution in England, is composed of two main acts. The first is the new *Act of Supremacy*, which restored the anti-papal legislation of Henry VIII that Mary had abolished. By this act England again cut away from the Catholic Church and repudiated the authority of Rome. For political reasons Elizabeth was not designated "head of the Church" but rather "Supreme Governor in all matters ecclesiastical and spiritual." The second law is the new *Act of Uniformity*, which revived the religious settlement made under Edward VI. Religious services were to conform, with certain modifications, to the second Book of Common Prayer of 1552. Everyone was bound to attend the Protestant service every Sunday in his own parish church.

The second Protestant Revolt in England was thus accomplished with surprising ease. Only one bishop accepted the settlement. The others were deprived of their sees and eventually imprisoned. Thus the Catholic hierarchy was removed at a stroke. The mass of the clergy submitted. So too did the mass of lay people, who seem to have been indifferent to the changes taking place. The religious settlement had been engineered by a small minority in the country. Their task now was to enforce the settlement on a Catholic majority and on the extreme Protestant faction of persons dissatisfied with the Elizabethan compromise. The group in control was successful because the Catholic majority was confused, without leadership, and for some time now without sound religious instruction. Elizabeth reigned for almost half a century, more than enough time to insure the permanency of the settlement of 1559 and to create an official historiography which made traitors out of Catholics and patriotic Englishmen out of the greedy group who surrounded "Good Queen Bess."

War with "Catholic" Spain served to increase Elizabeth's popularity and to consolidate the religious settlement of 1559. So too did the various plots to overthrow her and put a Catholic on the throne. Some English Catholics seem to have had a case of conscience as to whether they owed allegiance to their heretical sovereign. It was to relieve their conscience that St. Pius V issued the bull *Regnans in Excelsis* excommunicating the queen and releasing her Catholic subjects from their allegiance to her. The issuance of this bull in 1570 was probably a mistake, because it enabled a hostile government to identify the profession of the Catholic faith with disloyalty and treason. On this matter Philip Hughes has written:[2]

> Whatever the "paper logic" of the matter, the bull never, in fact, made any difference to the loyalty towards Elizabeth of the generality of her Catholic subjects, priests or laymen; and none, in all that time, stirred them, in the name of the bull, to hostile acts against her. But, from the beginning, the bull played into Cecil's hands. He would ignore the patent fact that Catholics were loyal, and insist that they could not, since 1570, be sincerely loyal any longer: he could know better than the Catholics themselves what their religion commanded them.

Until the nineteenth century the story of the Church in England is the story of a tiny group of English Catholics who held to their faith with heroic tenacity. Young men in their families were educated for the priesthood at the English college at Douai University in the Low Countries or at a similar college in Rome. One hundred thirteen priests from Douai were executed during Elizabeth's reign for preaching Catholic doctrine or conducting Catholic services in England. This was the price paid by English Catholics to keep the spark of their faith alive in their native land, for the Catholic religion was never completely extinguished in England. For practical purposes, however, the settlement of 1559 ends the story of the Protestant Revolt in England.

Conclusions. In the last three chapters we have discussed one of the most important events of modern history, the Protestant Revolt from the Church and resulting religious fragmentation of Europe. By the end of the sixteenth century Europe was divided into Protestant and Catholic halves, and the Protestant half was subdivided into the three important sections we have discussed in these chapters. The principle of individual interpretation of Scripture had been introduced, and in time various Protestant religions will continue to subdivide into many sects each. Thus the religious unity of Europe was destroyed by this movement and a process of continual fragmentation was introduced in place of the former single religion of all Europeans.

What can be added to this obvious result of the Protestant Revolt in Europe? First of all, it occurred at a time when Europeans were beginning to explore the rest of the world. Thus the results of the Protestant Revolt

---

[2] *The Reformation in England*, Vol. III (London: 1954), 276.

will be passed on to other areas, such as the English colonies, and the movement therefore assumed a world-wide rather than a local importance.

Second, it occurred at the same time when national states were being solidly established in Europe. We have seen that there was a tendency for the Protestant Revolt to follow national lines. It made national differences deeper and it injected a theological element into international wars, making them more terrible and bitter than they had formerly been.

Third, the Protestant Revolt played a considerable part in building the absolute state, for it enabled the ruler to control the religious as well as the secular life of his citizens. Both Protestant and Catholic leaders were forced to give in to the ruler's demands, and thus they ushered in the next period of Church history, a period of supine dependence of religion on the ruler who made religion another department of State.

Fourth, the Protestant Revolt was in some measure a class affair, and its doctrines were well suited to the temperament and the activity of this middle class. The connection between Protestantism and capitalism is an involved and much disputed subject, but it is safe to say that the two movements worked in harmony, each supporting the other and finding justification in each other.

Finally, the Protestant Revolt prompted and directed the course of reform in the Catholic Church — which we shall discuss in the following three chapters. Reform had already begun in the Church when Luther posted his theses in 1517, but the direction of reform and the definitions of doctrine at the Council of Trent took the form they did because of the Protestant Revolt. A Catholic Church whose leaders had taken things too much for granted for several centuries was forced to take stock of its shortcomings and take strong measures to correct them. It can be said, then, that Catholic reform was prompted and directed by the Protestant Revolt.

REVIEW AIDS

1. Show why the average Englishman would not have appreciated the momentous nature of Henry's antipapal legislation.
2. There was long a serious question about the validity of Anglican orders. In the letter *Apostolicae curae* of 1896 Pope Leo XIII declared Anglican orders invalid. On what lines of reasoning do you think such a decision would be based?
3. Analyze the influence of the continental Protestant groups on the Edwardian formulation of Anglicanism.
4. Many historians believe that St. Pius V's excommunication of Elizabeth in 1570 was a serious mistake. To what extent do you believe they are right or wrong?

5. Suggest three or four reasons why it was impossible for the English Church to stop with the schismatic arraignment of Henry VIII.
6. From reading in outside sources show the personal role played in the revolt of the English Church by (a) Wolsey, (b) Cranmer, (c) Thomas Cromwell.
7. Suggest as many reasons as you can why the Marian restoration of the Catholic religion was not successful.
8. If the majority of Englishmen were Catholics in 1558, why was the Elizabethan settlement of 1559 so easily achieved and so easily maintained?
9. On what principal points of doctrine and religious practice do Anglicans differ from most continental Protestants? from Catholics?

SUGGESTIONS FOR FURTHER READING

The classical work on the English Reformation is the three-volume study of Rev. Philip Hughes, *The Reformation in England* (London: 1950–1954). The first volume, "The King's Proceedings," deals with the reign of Henry VIII, the second with Edward VI's and Mary's reigns, and the last with the reign of Elizabeth. Less objective and scholarly but essentially sound is the work of Gerard Culkin, *The English Reformation* (London: 1954). This small work attempts to boil down the results of Father Hughes' extensive study. Also valuable is G. L. M. Constant, *The Reformation in England* (New York: 1935–1942), a two-volume account that is now superseded by Hughes' work. Most of the portraits drawn by Belloc in his *Characters of the Reformation* are of persons involved in the English movement.

A great many good biographical studies have been made of persons involved in this movement. Among them, the following are both interesting and profitable reading: Theodore Maynard, *Henry the Eighth* (Milwaukee: 1949); William Edward Campbell, *Erasmus, Tyndale, and More* (Milwaukee: 1950); Christopher Hollis, *Thomas More* (Milwaukee: 1934); Evelyn Waugh, *Edmund Campion* (New York: 1935); and the three biographies by Hilaire Belloc, *Cranmer* (Philadelphia: 1931); *Elizabeth* (New York: 1942); and *Wolsey* (Philadelphia: 1930).

DOCUMENTS

A. The Six Articles, 1539

Henry VIII insisted that his schismatic Church maintain Catholic doctrine and practices. When various Protestant innovations were introduced, the king had Parliament pass a law requiring uniformity of religion. The *Six Acts*, given below, indicate how little change was introduced in the Anglican Church in Henry's lifetime.

First, that in the most blessed Sacrament of the altar, by the strength and efficacy of Christ's mighty word (it being spoken by the priest), is present really, under the form of bread and wine, the natural body and blood of our Saviour Jesus Christ, conceived of the Virgin Mary; and that after the consecration there remaineth no substance of bread or wine, nor any other substance, but the substance of Christ, God and man.

Secondly, that communion in both kinds is not necessary *ad salutem*, by the law of God, to all persons; and that it is to be believed, and not doubted of, but that in the flesh, under the form of bread, is the very blood; and with the blood, under the form of wine, is the very flesh; as well apart, as though they were both together.

Thirdly, that priests after the order of priesthood received, as afore, may not marry, by the law of God.

Fourthly, that vows of chastity or widowhood, by man or woman made to God advisedly, are to be observed by the law of God; and that it exempts them from other liberties of Christian people, which without that they might enjoy.

Fifthly, that it is meet and necessary that private masses be continued and admitted in this the king's English Church and congregation, as whereby good Christian people, ordering themselves accordingly, do receive both godly and goodly consolations and benefits; and it is agreeable also to God's law.

Sixthly, that auricular confession is expedient and necessary to be retained and continued, used and frequented in the Church of God.

B. Act Against Catholic Recusants, 1593

The last of the Elizabethan statutes against Catholic recusants, the Five Mile Act of 1593, has been called "the cheapest and most comprehensive method of detention," since it kept all Catholics within five miles of their homes. No one can say exactly how well this law was enforced, but it reveals the way in which Catholics were to be rendered "harmless" in Elizabethan England.

For the better discovering and avoiding of all such traitorous and most dangerous conspiracies and attempts as are daily devised and practiced against our most gracious sovereign lady the queen's majesty and the happy estate of this commonweal, by sundry wicked and seditious persons, who, terming themselves Catholics, and being indeed spies and intelligencers, not only for her majesty's foreign enemies, but also for rebellious and traitorous subjects born within her highness' realms and dominions; and hiding their most detestable and devilish purposes under a false pretext of religion and conscience, do secretly wander and shift from place to place within this realm, to corrupt and seduce her majesty's subjects, and to stir them to sedition and rebellion:

Be it ordained and enacted by our sovereign lady the queen's majesty, and the Lords spiritual and temporal, and the Commons, in this present Parliament assembled, and by the authority of the same, that every person above the age of sixteen years, born within any of the queen's majesty's realms and dominions, or made denizen, being a popish recusant, and before the end of this session of Parliament, convicted for not repairing to some church, chapel, or usual place of common prayer, to hear divine service there, but forbearing the same, contrary to the tenor of the laws and statutes heretofore made and provided in that behalf, and having any certain place of dwelling and abode within this realm, shall within forty days next after the end of this session of Parliament (if they be within this realm, and not restrained or stayed either by imprisonment, or by her majesty's commandment, or by order and direction of some six or more of the privy council, or by such sickness or infirmity of body, as they shall not be able to travel without imminent danger of life, and in such cases of absence out of the realm, restraint, or stay, then within twenty days next after they shall return into the realm, and be enlarged of such imprisonment or restraint, and shall be able to travel) repair to their place of dwelling where they usually heretofore made their common abode, and shall not, any time after, pass or remove about five miles from thence. . . .

And furthermore be it enacted by the authority of this present Parliament, that if any person, or persons, that shall at any time hereafter offend against this Act, shall before he or they shall be thereof convicted come to some parish church on some Sunday or other Festival Day, and then and there hear divine service, and at service-time, before the sermon, or reading of the gospel, make public and open submission and declaration of his and their conformity to her majesty's laws and statutes, as hereafter in this Act is declared and appointed; that then the same offender shall thereupon be clearly discharged of and from all and every pains and forfeitures inflicted or imposed by this Act for any of the said offenses in this Act contained: the same submission to be made as hereafter follows, that is to say:

"I, A.B., do humbly confess and acknowledge, that I have grievously offended God in condemning her majesty's godly and lawful government and authority, by absenting myself from church, and from hearing divine service, contrary to the godly laws and statutes of this realm: and I am heartily sorry for the same, and do acknowledge and testify in my conscience, that the bishop or see of Rome has not, nor ought to have, any power or authority over her majesty, or within any her majesty's realms or dominions: and I do promise and protest, without any dissimulation, or any color or means of any dispensation, that from henceforth I will from time to time obey and perform her majesty's laws and statutes, in repairing to the church, and hearing divine service, and do my uttermost endeavor to maintain and defend the same."

Chapter 23

THE BEGINNINGS OF CATHOLIC

REFORM

THE reform and recovery of the Church in the middle of the sixteenth century has traditionally been called the "Counter-Reformation." This term is somewhat misleading, inasmuch as it suggests that reform in the Catholic Church was simply a reaction to the Protestant Revolt and that its sole aim was the recovery of lost lands and ecclesiastical property. As we shall see, reform had been consistently demanded in Church circles before Luther posted his theses, and it had been initiated in several places by 1517. It is true, however, that Catholic reform was influenced and conditioned by the Protestant Revolt, both in the matter of correcting abuses and in defining certain contested points of doctrine. Reform within the Church, then, was precipitated by the Protestant Revolt and to some extent given direction by it. But it was genuine reform which proceeded independently to correct abuses and shortcomings wherever they could be found.

There was at the same time a Counter-Reformation in the true sense of the term. This was a movement led by the Catholic princes, chiefly Philip II of Spain, to win back to the Church the people lost to Protestantism. The Counter-Reformation was essentially a matter of politics, but it was coupled with real reform and it is often hard to draw the line between the two movements. The Jesuits are an outstanding example of a group that promoted solid reform in the Church and co-operated with princes in the religious wars against the Protestants. Much of southern Germany was rescued for the Church by this combination of real reform and princely support. A better phrase than "Counter-Reformation," then, is "reform and recovery." We shall discuss this twofold movement in the following chapters.

Survival of the Catholic Faith.   The decline of the Church and the subsequent Protestant Revolt ordinarily receive so much attention from historians that we are likely to forget that in its worst years the Church showed tremendous vitality. Abuses were in high places. Everywhere the peasantry continued to practice their religion, partly because they were a conservative class governed pretty much by custom, partly because ecclesiastical abuses were not striking in the rural areas, and partly because the new ideas of the Renaissance had not touched the peasantry and prepared the way for religious change.

We have already seen how Church officials took a lead in the Renaissance and how many of them tried to synthesize the new learning with the Catholic faith. It should be remembered that universities flourished in the fifteenth and sixteenth centuries, that they were centers of religious learning, and that almost all of them remained loyal to the Church when the Protestant Revolt occurred. Early printed books were religious in character. There were at least 98 distinct editions of the Vulgate Bible by 1500, and there were translations into most of the popular tongues. There was intellectual vitality in the Church, then, throughout this age of decline.

There was also a good measure of spiritual vitality. The long list of saintly Italians alone is sufficient proof of the vitality in the Church. From monasteries and convents in Italy in the fifteenth century came 80 canonized saints. The third order of St. Francis had thousands of members. Charitable works and institutions continued to flourish. During the fifteenth century at least 324 hospitals, almshouses, and orphanages were established in Italy. Societies to care for the unfortunate were revived or established, such as the Society of San Roco in 1415, the Good Men of St. Martin in 1441, the Sodality of Dolorosa in 1448, and the Misericordia in 1475.

But there were serious abuses, especially in high places, as we have seen, and there is not a pope or a council in the fourteenth or fifteenth century that did not speak of the need for reform "in head and members." A good deal of reform was accomplished by provincial synods and by individual bishops throughout the fifteenth century. Such reform was spasmodic, however, and generally undone within a generation or two. Among the great reformers of the fifteenth century was Nicholas of Cusa, who was both a reformer and a scholarly humanist. As papal legate in the

Germanies he presided over provincial synods that sought to improve clerical and monastic life. One hundred twenty-seven abbeys accepted his reform statutes, but only about half of them still lived according to Cusa's reformed statutes at the end of the century. It was evident that thorough, lasting reform depended on Rome — and it was Rome which had the greatest vested interest in abuses within the Church.

Reform was therefore postponed from decade to decade. We can summarize the reasons for its postponement in this way: (1) Reformers, numerous as they were, possessed no organization. An individual's reform measures therefore tended to die when death stilled the reformer's voice. (2) Princes consistently interfered with reform measures which they believed would interfere with their "rights" of appointment and control over the ecclesiastical establishments within their jurisdictions. (3) High Church officials were not anxious for reform. Although they admitted its need, they postponed putting it into effect, for they were the ones who would suffer most directly from it. Moreover, the twelve popes of the fifteenth century were mediocre men, and only a strong man could sustain reform within the Church. (4) The Church had but recently recovered from a revolution, the conciliar movement, and the popes had no desire to invite trouble by convoking another council. But thorough reform was impossible except through a council's action. (5) In the age of emerging national states and a changing economy, the popes were too much concerned with establishing their sovereignty over a strong temporal state and securing their financial independence. These were legitimate means toward securing their spiritual independence, but unfortunately the popes of this age concentrated so hard on means that they tended to forget the end. (6) Finally, the humanistic culture of the Renaissance sapped much vigor from religious life. Some few individuals synthesized the new learning and the old faith, but to most humanists the reformers seemed cranks and matters of doctrine or discipline seemed unimportant. For these reasons reform was put off until the sixteenth century.

Reform in the Spanish Church.   Throughout the Middle Ages Spain had been militantly Catholic. The long years of the *Reconquista* were looked upon as a crusade, so that by the time of Ferdinand and Isabella Catholicism was identified with Spanish nationalism. Ferdinand and Isabella had secured absolute control of the Church as well as the State in Spain. They were anxious to promote reform in ecclesiastical life for practical, secular reasons. In 1480 they established the Inquisition to deal with lapsed converts from Judaism and Islamism. They continued reforms of the regular clergy and they appointed good men to ecclesiastical offices. Outstanding among these men was Ximenes de Cisneros who undertook a thorough reform of the entire Spanish Church.

Ximenes had been born of a noble family in 1436. He entered the service of the Church, and for some time he followed a typical ecclesiastical career. He renounced his benefices, however, and joined the strict Observants of the Franciscan Order. Made confessor of the queen in 1492, he was soon provincial of the Franciscan Order, archbishop of Toledo, and primate of Spain. Cardinal Ximenes became chosen adviser of Ferdinand and Isabella, occasionally acting as their regent, and in 1508 he was made grand inquisitor. Thus in one man was concentrated power to corrupt or to reform the Church. A truly spiritual man of unusual perception, Ximenes employed his power for sound reform.

Ximenes effected a drastic reform of the regular clergy on the basis of the rule of the Franciscan Observants. He also forced the regular canons of cathedral chapters to live a religious life in common, and he raised the general tone of spiritual life among the diocesan clergy. Most important of his reforms, however, was the founding of the University of Alcala to train candidates for the episcopacy and other high places in the Spanish Church. The university was divided into a number of small colleges concentrating on theology, law, or languages. In this way Ximenes harnessed the new learning of the Renaissance and used it for the Church. The University of Alcala became a seminary for bishops in Spain, and through it the standards and character of the episcopacy were steadily improved. An outstanding achievement of the young university was the Complutensian Polyglot, a Bible in which the text was printed in the Vulgate and the original languages in parallel columns.

These reforms were completed at the time of Ximenes' death in 1517. They were proof of what could be accomplished when prince and bishop both desired reform and had nothing to lose by it. There was a dangerous tendency latent in such reform, however, the tendency to form a more distinct national church under absolute control of the prince and held to Rome by only tenuous lines of connection. Truly Catholic reform would have to come from Rome and spread from head to members. Nevertheless, the reform of the Spanish Church is an example of action taken by Catholics before the Protestant Revolt. It is proof that they were aware of the abuses and were able to do something about them.

Oratory of Divine Love and the Theatines. There were sincerely religious men in Rome, too, who were aware of abuses and anxious to correct them. Sometime during the pontificate of Leo X, by 1517 at the latest, a group of such men joined together in the Oratory of Divine Love. Their idea was to reform themselves first and then their immediate surroundings. For mutual support in religious renewal, frequent reception of the sacraments, and works of charity they joined together — laymen and clergy — into a loose confraternity. Included in the group were future popes, cardinals, and bishops who would soon be prominent in reforming the Church, men like Caraffa, Sadoleto, Thiene, and Giberti. As R. V. Laurence puts it in the *Cambridge Modern History*: "The ascetic and the humanist, the practical and doctrinal reformer met together and worked in harmony."

Altogether, the Oratory of Divine Love at Rome consisted of 50 or 60 leaders in the Church who sought to harmonize Christianity and the Renaissance and to bring about a true rebirth of spiritual life among Christians. They were scattered after the sack of Rome in 1527, but the Roman Oratory was soon copied in other Italian cities such as Verona, Vicenza, Brescia, and Venice. Important new members were added, men like Contarini and Cortese. But it was soon apparent that the Oratory was limited in its effectiveness because it was merely a fraternity and therefore lacked any strict organizing principle.

The need for a religious order seems to have been sensed chiefly by the fiery Bishop Caraffa and the gentle St. Cajetan. At any rate, these two dissimilar men formed a regular order of clerics who took vows of chastity, obedience, and poverty. "The fundamental idea of the founders," Pastor explains, "was to form a society of devoted priests who should give themselves up entirely to the administration of the sacraments, the work of preaching, and the conduct of ecclesiastical ceremonies so as to set an example before the Church." The Theatines were approved by a papal brief of 1524 and placed directly under the pope.

The new order was composed mostly of prominent members of the nobility who were outstanding for their virtue and zealous for reform. After nine years they numbered only 21, but they were very much loved by the people and were influential out of all proportion to their numbers. The Theatines' chief enemies were the worldly cardinals of Rome, but they were befriended by Clement VII who was himself favorably inclined toward reform. The Theatines devoted themselves entirely to preaching, administering the sacraments, and visiting the sick. They were important, above all else, for the bishops and popes they furnished to the reforming Church in the sixteenth century.

During the disastrous pontificate of Clement VII two other new orders, the Somaschi and the Barnabites, were established in Italy. Other orders were reformed, the most important of these being the Capuchin reform of the Franciscan Order. We shall discuss these developments in a later chapter. Here we wish only to note that they occurred during Clement VII's pontificate.

The Papacy and Reform Till 1534. Church historians usually put 1534 down as the beginning of real reform, for it was in that year that Paul III was elected to succeed Clement VII. But this obscures two facts: (1) there was considerable reform before 1534; (2) Paul III and some of his successors did not break completely and abruptly from the defects and abuses of their predecessors. Even Alexander VI (1492–1503) had recognized the need for reform of the papacy and he had appointed a commission to investigate abuses. But other more pressing concerns prevented him from acting on the commission's suggestions. Julius II made a gesture toward reform in calling the Lateran Council in 1512, but it was only a gesture. Julius enjoyed his revenues too much and played too active a role in secular politics to entertain serious ideas about reform of the papacy. So also it was with Leo X who enjoyed the honors and privileges and cultural connections of his office.

It seemed that reform would come at last with the election of Adrian VI, a Dutchman of saintly reputation who had been professor at the University of Louvain. Adrian stated bluntly: "We know that evil has spread from head to foot, from pope to prelates; we all have deviated from the right way; to abuses in things spiritual are added abuses in the exercise of power; all has been vitiated." Roman scandals, he told the cardinals, are the talk of the world. Adrian had been shocked at the conditions he found in Rome. The cardinals who met him were undistinguishable in dress and appearance from worldly princes. Rome was a motley collection of parasites, prostitutes, armed retainers, and divers hangers-on who all partook one way or another of the Church's revenues. These were the people who, with the pope and cardinals, had a vested interest in the maintenance of abuses.

Adrian ruled for too short a time, little more than a year, to correct the abuses he encountered. He followed the rule of examining candidates for appointments for their morality, their age, and their learning. He excluded the cardinals from the Vatican and forbade their retainers to carry arms. Opposition to the "barbarian from the North" rose up on every side. The simple fact is that the preparatory work for solid reform had not yet been accomplished. Adrian set about his reform in blunt, clumsy fashion. Had he ruled for several decades perhaps he might have been successful — or he might have imposed a reform that would have melted away after his death.

Adrian's successor was the vacillating Clement VII. Clement had been one of the few bishops to put the reform measures of the Fifth Lateran Council into force in his diocese. In 1519 he had founded the Confraternity of Charity for support of the poor, visiting prisoners, and burying the destitute. He favored reform in his heart, but he had been raised in the older school of ecclesiastical politicians and he was timid by nature. His pontificate, moreover, was taken up with other serious matters: the English schism, the threat of the Turk in the Mediterranean, and the wars between Francis I and Charles V. Nevertheless, Clement tried in his ineffectual way to correct abuses at Rome. In 1524 he appointed a commission of cardinals to study reform of the Curia. He also ordered a visitation of the Roman clergy with a view to forbidding those who failed the examination to say Mass.

Clement also issued directions against simony, and occasionally he declared against plural holdings. Various papal decrees were issued for reform of both the regular and diocesan clergy in various Italian dioceses. The enforcement of these decrees was interrupted by war several times, but work was still being done in this direction when Clement died in 1534. These reform decrees were a heartening sign, but they dealt only with particular abuses and they were insufficient to correct evils which had become widespread in the Church.

More significant was the reform work of Clement's secretary, Gian Matteo Giberti, who had been appointed bishop of Verona and obtained Clement's reluctant permission to go to his diocese in 1528. In the previous year Rome had been overrun by an imperial army, and it is commonly said that this sacking of Rome shocked the prelates and made them thoroughly conscious for the first time of their evil ways. At any rate, Giberti went to his diocese where he found matters in terrible shape. Many parishes were tended by unworthy deputies because the pastors lived elsewhere. Many priests could not read Latin, so Giberti had the rubrics translated into Italian for them. Preaching had been abandoned in many places, and the hearing of confessions was irregular.

Giberti instituted a regular visitation of his diocese, conducted periodic examinations of the clergy, and forced them to live according to their clerical vows. Giberti was gentle and understanding, but he was also strong and firm. He used his power of excommunication and demanded public penance in extreme cases, and he dismissed any priest who did not co-operate with his work of reform. Giberti did all he could to restore the secular clergy to their dignity in the diocese. He forbade encroachment by the orders, made people attend parish masses said by the pastor, enjoined weekly confession on all the clergy, published minute instructions on the administration of the sacraments, and required preaching on every Sunday and festival. He insisted on close observance of the ritual so as to achieve dignified services. Giberti seems to have introduced confessionals as we know them today, the keeping of the Holy Eucharist in the tabernacle at the high altar, and the ringing of the bell at the elevation.

Giberti's reforms centered around the saying of Mass and the administration of the sacraments. But they did not stop here. He instituted catechetical instruction for the children on Sunday afternoon. He kept open house for Italian humanists and induced them to apply their talents to the work of reform. Meanwhile, he organized the Society of Charity for the material and moral help of the poor in his diocese. The object of this Society, according to Giberti's biographer, was "that no man should offend God, no man suffer hunger, no man do injury to his neighbor, no man, above all things, commit sin, no man be deprived of the necessities of life; finally that enmity and all hatred and anger should be taken away, so that we, as men once did in the first and happiest days of the Church, should all live with one heart and one soul in the fear and praise of God."

Giberti's work was eminently popular. The distresses and wars of the time gave impetus to reform, and Giberti was imitated by other bishops throughout Italy — in Trent, Brescia, Bergamo, Mantua, Vicenza, Brindisi, Naples, and several other places, and especially by St. Charles Borromeo in Milan. Clement VII supported Giberti warmly in his work of reform. His reforms served as a model for the Council of Trent, and many of his enactments were embodied verbatim in the Tridentine decrees.

Reform Work of Paul III. In 1534 Alexander Farnese was elected in one of the shortest conclaves in history, a matter of an hour or so. He had been recommended for the position by Clement VII as a worthy successor. Farnese was steeped in the humanist culture of the Renaissance. His life had been irregular, and he had accepted many benefices and dignities. In 1518, at the age of fifty, however, he had been converted to a truly spiritual life. He received Holy Orders and turned his remarkable abilities to the reform of the Church. Elected at one of the most serious moments of the history of the Church (Protestantism was successful in Germany, Switzerland, and England, and the Turk had reached the

Danube), Paul III set about effecting solid reform in the Church.

The pope had before him the examples of Adrian's failure and of Clement's timidity. He struck a wise middle course between the two, and he followed consistently, even stubbornly, a moderate course of reform. Most important, he appointed good men from the reform party on whom he could rely to carry out his work conscientiously. As the years went on Paul III freed himself from the older cardinals opposed to reform at Rome, and thus he overcame the chief obstacle to the lasting correction of abuses by giving all the important positions to his new appointees. He himself was guilty of nepotism when he made two of his nephews cardinals in 1534, but when they proved unworthy of the office he reduced them to positions of inconsequence.

At the first consistory Paul announced that he would call a general council, and two years later he published a bull summoning the council to meet in 1537 at Mantua. As we shall see shortly, events over which Paul had no control postponed the meeting of the Council until 1545. Meanwhile, the new pope announced that the pressing question of the time was reform of the clergy in high places. Late in 1534 he said that a reform of the Curia and the college of cardinals must precede reform by a general council. Reform was difficult to achieve because of the entrenched forces in the Curia which were secular in outlook and opposed to any reform at all.

Paul III's appointments took care of this difficulty. In 1535 he made a cardinal of the outstanding advocate of reform from Venice, the layman Contarini, and the following year he gave the red hat to such outstanding reformers as Caraffa, Sadoleto, and Pole. "Never," Philip Hughes has written, "has there been wiser, readier, or more munificent recognition of the combination of talent and virtue. Never did the Sacred College show such an array of personality as during this pontificate."

In 1535 Paul had appointed a commission on reform, and early in 1536 a series of decrees to reform the Roman clergy was published. These decrees ordered the clergy to wear clerical dress and to say their office, to stay away from houses of prostitution, gambling establishments, and theaters, to live in the parish and to say Mass at least once a month. The pope realized that the reform of Rome itself would not be enough. He therefore appointed a Commission of Nine, all of them men dedicated to reform, to survey the problem and to recommend corrective measures. The commission, under the chairmanship of Contarini, made its famous report early in 1537. In it is contained the embryo program of reform adopted at the Council of Trent. In blunt language the Commission laid the blame for abuses in the Church squarely on the papacy itself. The essential evil was the transformation of a spiritual society into a venal administration. The Commission listed more specifically the evils of simony, pluralism, and nepotism. It told the pope that bishops are unable to effect reform in their dioceses as long as exemptions can be freely purchased at Rome.

"There is another abuse," the Commission stated, "which ought not to be in the least tolerated, and by which the whole Christian people is scandalized: it consists in the obstacles which hinder bishops in the government of their flocks, especially in the chastising and correcting of criminals. For, to begin with, wicked men, especially clerics, find many ways to exempt themselves from the jurisdiction of their ordinaries. And again, if they are not exempt, they forthwith fly to the Penitentiary, or to the Datary, where they immediately find a way to impunity, and what is worse, in return for cash."

The Commission ruthlessly decried other abuses. It condemned the scandals so common in religious orders, insisted that monks should not be allowed to buy immunity from clerical attire, and should be regulated in the hawking of indulgences. It condemned the ease with which persons could buy dispensations to marry within near degrees of kindred. It called for the reform and thorough regulation of monastic orders. The report was, all in all, a more severe condemnation of Catholic practices than any made by responsible Protestants. It was therefore used by Protestant propagandists as a confession of fault by Roman Catholics. But the report served the purpose of so publicizing abuses in the Church that they could no longer be ignored or minimized.

When Paul III realized that a council could not meet for some time, he set about reforming the papal administration himself. He therefore appointed a commission of four cardinals, including Contarini and Caraffa, to correct abuses in the curial offices, starting with the Datary. This office bestowed all papal dispensations, privileges, and indults. Originally the charge for such a grant was to cover the clerical expenses involved in handling the case. Charges had come to be adapted to the value of the privilege, however, so that revenue from the Datary amounted to about half the total papal income. This encouraged Datary officials to grant privileges to anyone able to buy them. The office was now reformed so that charges were again strictly for clerical expenses.

Paul III enlarged the Commission of Four to eight and then to twelve so that they could correct abuses in the Rota, the Chancellery, the Penitentiary, and the Courts of Justice. In each case reform was difficult to achieve because of the opposition of entrenched interests. In each case, too, reform diminished papal revenue. But the pope and his associates were not easily discouraged, and by 1541 tangible results had been accomplished. Additional reform would be necessary from time to time, of course, when some of the curial officers slipped back into the old abuses. But it was during Paul III's pontificate that the basic Roman reforms took place.

The pope also attacked the evil of absenteeism. In 1540 he summoned over 80 bishops and archbishops living in Rome and ordered them back to their dioceses. Absenteeism was an evil so deep seated, however, that Paul found it extremely difficult to enforce his orders. He and his successors would have to expel crowds of bishops from Rome time and time again before the episcopacy would once again accept the custom of residence in the diocese. Paul also ordered a set of written rules and instructions drawn up for preachers so that the faithful would receive sound instruction in morals and doctrine.

Meanwhile, as we shall see in a later chapter, the reform movement had renovated many of the orders and had called new ones into existence. Pope Paul III confirmed the Capuchins and the Jesuits, for example, and he encouraged other orders of men and women to expand the good work they were doing. By 1541 reform was solidly established in the Roman Church, the entrenched interest in abuses was crumbling, and the way was prepared for the Council of Trent.

Pope Paul III's great genius lay in his ability to steer a middle course between the two schools that had developed on the question of reform and of dealing with the Protestants. One school was represented by Caraffa, the school of thunder and anathema, whose proponents advocated free use of excommunication and interdict, the Inquisition and armed forces to force true doctrine on the people of Christendom. They insisted vigorously on thorough reform, but at the same time they refused to treat with the Protestants until the latter would humbly admit their heresy and beg forgiveness. The other school was led by Contarini and included such men as Giberti, Sadoleto, and Pole. This school hoped to bring Protestants back into the Catholic fold by a policy of reasonable conciliation, by discussion, by conceding whatever could be conceded. A series of meetings with Protestants, culminating in the Religious Colloquy of Ratisbon in 1541, showed that Protestants were unwilling to belong to a reformed Catholic Church. The result was that the policy of Caraffa and his associates seemed vindicated. Although Protestants were invited to attend the Council of Trent, as we shall see, the Council was strictly a Catholic conclave handling the affairs of the Catholic Church.

Paul III's Preparations for a Council. From the beginning of his pontificate Paul III was determined to call a general council so that a clear statement could be made of issuing Catholic doctrine on various contested points. The need of such a statement was seen to be pressing when such famous preachers as Bernardo Ochino ended up in the Protestant camp. Moreover, abuses in the Church could not be thoroughly eliminated except by the action of a council. In issuing his first call for a council on June 2, 1536, then, Paul said that its first purpose was to handle problems of heresy and its second to effect moral reform in the Church.

The council was to have met at Mantua in May, 1537. But the renewal of war between Charles V and Francis I made it inexpedient and perhaps impossible for the bishops to assemble. The pope then summoned a council to meet in May, 1538, in Vicenza, a town in Venetia. This time the papal legates arrived, but the bishops, abbots, and others who were to make up the council failed to appear. By this time the pope realized that both the emperor and the French king were opposed to a council and that they would do everything to prevent their bishops from attending. Charles insisted that if a council should meet it must confine itself to questions of reform alone, for Charles believed there was a chance to bring Lutherans and Catholics together as long as no definitions of doctrine were officially made by the Church. Francis feared that a general council might interfere with the privileges of the French Church and might, therefore, end his control of the Church in France. If a council should be called, Charles insisted it meet in an imperial city; Francis demanded that it meet in France.

Paul remained obdurate. On June 6, 1542, he called a general council to meet at Trent on the following All Saints' Day. Again the bishops failed to show up because of the opposition of the princes. It was not until after the Peace of Crespy (September 17, 1544) that a council was feasible. Paul therefore issued a new summons for March 15, 1545, and when the appointed time arrived it seemed that the pope's plan had again been frustrated. In December of that year, however, the Council of Trent — destined to be one of the most important ecumenical councils in the history of the Church — began its sessions in a very inauspicious and disheartening manner.

REVIEW AIDS

1. Explain as fully as you can why a good pope would be reluctant to call a council in the first half of the sixteenth century.
2. Show how the system of appointment to high Church offices that had grown up in the Middle Ages was almost certain to end up in numerous abuses.
3. List and discuss as many reasons as you can for the fact that the peasantry, generally speaking, remained loyal to the Catholic faith.
4. Apart from sincere religious reasons, what other motives might such a ruler as Ferdinand or Isabella have in reforming the Church in their country?
5. By consulting a map and reviewing the political history of the time, explain why Trent was an excellent place to hold an ecumenical council.
6. Some historians maintain that Adrian's failure to effect lasting reform proves the necessity of the Theatine Order. Explain the reasoning behind such a statement.
7. In the Catholic Encyclopedia or a similar reference work find the principal facts about each member of the Commission of Nine who reported to Pope Paul III on abuses in the Church.
8. Imagine yourself living in the 1530's and 1540's. Would you have subscribed to Contarini's idea of reform or to Caraffa's? Explain your decision.
9. Explain as fully as you can why Paul III had the ideal temperament to launch the Catholic reformation.

SUGGESTIONS FOR FURTHER READING

The best volume in English covering the matter of this and the succeeding three chapters is Pierre Janelle, *The Catholic Reformation* (Milwaukee: 1949). The first four chapters are pertinent to this chapter. Janelle and the author of this chapter, like everyone else writing Church history in our times, rely heavily on Ludwig von Pastor's *History of the Popes from the Close of the Middle Ages*. Various chapters in Volumes VI to XII inclusive deal with the material of this chapter. Volume V of Rev. Fernand Mourret's *History of the Catholic Church* is on the sixteenth century. Although there are some inaccuracies in this work, it is generally quite useful.

Special studies that should prove helpful for a fuller understanding of the complexities and the accomplishments of this period include the following three works: George V. Jourdan, *The Movement Towards Catholic Reform in the Early XVI Century* (London: 1914); Paul A. Kunkel, *The Theatines in the History of Catholic Reform Before the Establishment of Lutheranism* (Washington: 1941); and R. de Maulde La Clavière, *Saint Cajetan* (New York: 1902).

The student should also consult appropriate articles in the Catholic Encyclopedia, especially those on Popes Adrian VI, Leo X, Clement VII, and Paul III, the Oratory of Divine Love, Cardinal Ximenes, Nicholas of Cusa, Contarini, Reginald Pole, and Bishop Giberti.

DOCUMENTS

The following selection is part of one of the most remarkable documents in modern Church history, the report of the Commission of Nine assigned by Pope Paul III to investigate abuses in the Church. The indictment made by these reformers is as severe as any Protestant charges against abuses in the Church, but it is made by loyal Catholics interested in reform rather than personal advancement or revolution.

The first abuse in this matter [of having a clergy which will perform its duties worthily] concerns the ordination of clerics, and especially that of priests, in which no care is taken and no diligence employed. As a result, it frequently happens that candidates are admitted to holy orders and, worst of all, to the character of the priesthood who are quite untrained, of the very lowest parentage, of bad moral character, and of too young an age. From this there result innumerable scandals, contempt of the clergy, and not merely diminished respect for the divine service but now its almost complete extinction. We therefore believe that it would be a good idea if your Holiness would first assign two or three learned and upright prelates in Rome to take charge of the ordination of clerics. Then you should order all bishops, even under the pain of censures, to do the same in their own dioceses. Nor should your Holiness permit anyone to be ordained except by his own bishop, or with his permission or that of prelates assigned to Rome. Furthermore, you should order that every bishop have an instructor in his churches who, as the law requires, will instruct the minor clerics in both letters and morals.

Another very serious abuse concerns the granting of ecclesiastical benefices, especially those having the care of souls and above all the bishoprics. Here the custom has been established of having regard for the person on whom the benefice is conferred but not for the flock of Christ and for the Church. Therefore, in granting such benefices — those having the care of souls and above all bishoprics — care must be taken that they are conferred on good and learned men so that the recipients will themselves be capable of fulfilling the duties to which they are bound. Moreover, these benefices should be conferred on men who are likely to take up residence. For that reason, a benefice in Spain or England should not be conferred on an Italian, nor vice versa. All this is to be observed not only in granting benefices which have fallen vacant through the death of the incumbent, but also in cases where one man cedes his benefice to another; for at the present time in such instances regard is had solely for the desires of the one making the cession, nothing else being taken into consideration. We think that it would be well to put one or more upright men in charge of handling such cessions.

Another abuse which has crept in in the matter of granting and ceding benefices is the practice of making arrangements for pensions from the revenues of such benefices. Indeed, the man who cedes the benefice sometimes reserves all its revenue to himself. In this matter, caution must be exercised that no pensions may be contracted for except for expending alms on pious uses and for the sake of the poor. For the revenues are attached to the benefice as the body to the soul; therefore, of their very nature they belong to him who holds the benefice so that he can live honorably according to his station and can at the same time sustain the expenses of divine worship and the repair of the church and other sacred edifices, and, if anything is left, support pious causes. . . .

There is another abuse which has established itself: not merely one, but several bishoprics are granted outright or given in commendation to the Very Reverend Cardinals. Holy Father, we think that this is a matter of great concern for the Church of God. First of all, because the office of cardinal and the office of bishop are incompatible. It is the duty of the cardinal to assist your Holiness in governing the universal Church, while it is the office of the bishop to tend his flock, a duty which he can hardly accomplish well and as he should unless he dwells with his sheep, as the shepherd with his flock. Furthermore, Holy Father, this custom sets a very bad example. For how can this Holy See restrain and correct the abuses of others, if the abuses in its chief members are not removed? Nor, we believe, does the fact that they are cardinals give them any special license to break the law; indeed, the very opposite should be the case. For the life of these men should be a law for others; and certainly the Pharisees are not to be imitated, men who speak and do not act. Rather we should follow the example of Christ our Savior who began by acting and then taught. Moreover, this custom does injury in the consultations of the Church, for it foments avarice. The cardinals ambition bishoprics from kings and princes, on whom they become dependent, so that they cannot freely give their opinions. Indeed, if they could and would, they would be deceived in their judgments by perturbations arising from fear and avarice. Therefore we sincerely wish that this custom were abolished and provision made for the cardinals so that they could live honorably in accordance with their dignity, with equal revenues for all. This could easily be done, we believe, if the cardinals were willing to throw off the servitude of Mammon and serve Christ alone.

Chapter 24

THE COUNCIL OF TRENT

THE most noteworthy Council in the history of the Church was held under difficult conditions, in the face of innumerable obstacles, in the imperial city of Trent. The sessions took place in three different meetings between 1545 and 1563. The Council of Trent was the cornerstone of Catholic reform. Its provisions on the conduct and education of the clergy, its regulations on monastic life, its arrangements for episcopal authority are still in effect. Its definitions of doctrine provided an admirable statement of Catholic truth on original sin, justification, the Mass, and the sacraments which cleared the air of doctrinal haziness and made it clear to any thinking person what was Catholic doctrine and what was heretical.

The Council Convenes at Trent. It must have seemed that this Council, which labored under great difficulties at all times, would follow the fate of Paul III's previous attempts and never convene. Interference from the well-meaning but stubborn Emperor Charles V and later from Henry II of France made it almost impossible to assemble a representative number of fathers of the Church. First, there was disagreement over the place of meeting. The pope wanted the Council to meet in an Italian city where it would be free from imperial or French pressure and free also from Protestant armies. Charles insisted that it meet in one of his cities, and the French king demanded that it meet in or near France. The pope finally chose Trent, just inside imperial possessions, not too far from France and with easy access to Protestants if they wished to attend.

Second, there was opposition over the work to be done. The French held that their church did not need reform and refused to co-operate with a Council they thought to be under the emperor's control. Charles demanded that the Council handle only matters of disciplinary reform and that it refrain from discussing or defining doctrine. The pope insisted that definition of doctrine was to be the Council's main work. Eventually, at the suggestion of Campeggio, the council dealt with the two matters of reform and doctrine simultaneously.

Third, sincere Catholics were far from unanimously agreed on the Council's role. With good reason the pope feared that debate on reform might lead to another Basle or Constance and to a fresh emergence of the conciliar theory. Many bishops were suspicious that the pope was not sincere about reform and that his only aim was to tighten slipping Roman authority over the Church. Some cardinals, like Caraffa, had no use for a council; they believed reform could be effected in military fashion from above. Others believed that there was a good deal of truth in the Protestant position on such doctrines as justification and their opposition to such practices as the veneration of relics.

Fourth, it was no easy job for the pope to get a representative number of bishops to the Council. The Council of Trent was an ecumenical council because it was called by the pope and all members of the hierarchy were invited. But it was not universally attended at any time. Only ten bishops were in Trent when the Council was supposed to open in May, 1545. Only 37 members attended the second session on January 7, 1546. A year later the number reached 72. The largest number to attend the second meeting was 59, and the third meeting included as many as 255 at the final session. Even this number represented only a fraction of the Catholic Church.

In some ways these difficulties worked out to papal advantage. Imperial opposition enabled the pope to make this his council. It was presided over by his three legates, Cardinals Del Monte, Cervini, and Pole, and the legates alone had the right to introduce matters for discussion. This enabled them to control the Council's deliberations and keep it from getting out of hand. The pope's summons bound the prelates to attend the Council personally, save in case of serious impediment.

The first two sessions were devoted to organization. It was decided that vote should be by head rather than by nation. This weakened the power of interference by national blocs voting as ordered by the emperor or king. Votes were restricted to bishops, abbots, and the heads of religious orders. No absentee voting was permitted. Theologians and canon lawyers were called upon to discuss various questions, but they were not allowed to vote. The order of business augured well for accomplishing the Council's tasks. Each subject was to be presented by one of the legates. Then it was studied by a group of specially qualified theologians and canonists, where all points of view were presented and where argument was often heated. The subject was then reported back to the congregation of bishops for their consideration. Finally, the decision was embodied in a decree promulgated in a general session. Altogether, 25 general sessions were held in the three meetings.

Accomplishments of the First Meeting (1545–1547). After the Council's organization was settled in the first sessions, the legates turned to the fundamental points of difference between Catholics and Protestants. The first subject considered was the rule of faith. The Nicene Creed with the *filioque* clause was accepted in its entirety. Against the Protestants, Scripture and Tradition were set down as having equal authority. Thus the traditional Catholic sources of knowing religious truth were established against the Protestants' individual interpretation of Scripture.

The next problem considered was an item of discipline — rules for preaching and catechizing. The delicate problem here came to be the relationship of the regular clergy to the bishops, and its discussion resulted in many stormy sessions. The ultimate decision was that bishops were to control the preaching of regular or order clergy in all churches except those belonging to the order. But the discussion of this problem led to another which consumed more time and led to more difficulties than any other — the question of episcopal residence. All parties agreed that the bishop should reside in his diocese and make periodic visitations to all parts of it. But the question arose whether residence is required by divine law or by papal prescription. The champions of episcopal independence from Rome insisted it is *jure divino,* whereas the pope's supporters insisted it is a matter of papal regulation. On the decision of this problem hinged the future organization of the Church. The Council did not arrive at a decision until the third meeting, as we shall see, and then only indirectly.

In defiance of the emperor's demands, the legates next introduced the question of original sin and its effects on human nature. The traditional Catholic doctrine was set down against Protestant teaching of human depravity in the fifth public session on June 17, 1546. Discussion of original sin led to the most important doctrinal consideration of the Council of Trent, the question of justification. This was the fundamental point of doctrinal difference between Lutherans and Catholics. Although the emperor tried to prevent discussion of the subject, the pope insisted that a definition of Catholic teaching be formulated. The decree was finally published in the sixth public session, on January 13, 1547, after six months of work. Only one bishop had argued for the Lutheran view of justification by faith alone, but the precise role of free will and of grace led to much discussion, to drafts, redrafts, and alterations of the statement, until finally a formulation satisfactory to the entire Council was enacted. Its importance lies in that it safeguards the efficacy of good works and the role of free will, while at the same time it states that justification is through Christ alone and that His freely given grace is necessary for salvation. Thus God's omnipotence and man's freedom to co-operate with grace are both safeguarded in the Catholic definition.

The next item for discussion was to be Catholic teaching on the sacraments, particularly on the Holy Eucharist and Mass. But the Council adjourned before making any final statement on these subjects. Meanwhile, the reform decree for the seventh general session (March 3, 1547) dealt with the qualifications for nominees to the bishoprics, the conferring of holy orders, the prohibition of plural holdings, episcopal visitations, and similar matters.

In March, 1547, the Council was removed by the papacy to Bologna. The excuse for this action was an epidemic of spotted fever (*mal di petecchie*) which predisposed most of the bishops to a hasty withdrawal from Trent. The legates had for some time been fearful that war between Charles and the Protestants made a continuance of the sessions at Trent unwise. Charles's success against the Protestants caused Del Monte to fear that the emperor would interfere with the Council in overbearing fashion, and at his request the pope gave the legates permission to move, if necessary, when the majority of fathers present consented. Paul III had complained to the emperor's ambassador Vega: "You have not yet been victorious over the Protestants, and nevertheless your demands are already insupportable; what will your first step be when the emperor is victorious?"

In the face of imperial opposition, then, the legates removed the Council to Bologna. Charles was furious. He ordered the German and Spanish bishops to remain at Trent, but at the same time he told them not to provoke a schism. The group at Bologna held several sessions, but they confined themselves to doing preparatory work for definitions on the sacraments. No decrees were issues from Bologna. At length, in September, 1549, Paul III bowed to the inevitable and suspended the Council. He died a little more than two months later.

The Second Meeting (1551–1552). Cardinal Del Monte was chosen as Paul's successor. The first act of the new pope, who took the name of Julius III, was to reconvoke the Council of Trent. It resumed its sessions on May 1, 1551, under the presidency of the Cardinal Legate Crescenzio. This time difficulties were caused chiefly by Henry II of France. The French king was afraid that the Council might promote religious unity in Germany. Moreover, he was quarreling with the pope over Parma, and he insisted that he would not permit French bishops to attend unless the pope entered into an anti-imperial alliance with him. The Council, therefore, met without the French bishops.

Attendance at the first session was very poor. The second session was set for September 1 to give the German bishops time to arrive. The emperor had been withholding them in the hope of getting permission for Protestants to attend with the right to vote. The pope was willing to allow Protestant theologians to attend, with a guarantee of safe-conduct, and freedom to present their views. But he refused to give them a vote in the Council's deliberations. In this second meeting decrees were formulated on the Eucharist, Penance, and Extreme Unction. Preparatory work was also done on the Catholic doctrine of the Mass, but this material was not published until the third meeting. Meanwhile reform decrees were issued on matters of clerical dress, the bishops' control of priests, and similar matters.

Protestant theologians began to arrive in large numbers in October, 1551, and their presence at Trent showed how wide the breach between Catholics and Protestants had grown and how impossible it was to heal it by discussion. The Council had granted the Protestants letters of safe conduct, a guarantee of free speech and the use of Scriptures in debate, with a promise of no prosecution for anything said at the meetings. But the Protestants refused to participate unless the Council would review all decrees already issued and grant the Protestant theologians a vote. The Spanish bishops were meanwhile pushing Charles's demand that the Council refrain from doctrinal discussions in favor of measures of moral reform. As a result the Council found it increasingly difficult to make any kind of progress.

Emperor Charles V favored suspension of the Council when he heard of the alliance between Henry II and the German Protestants. When Maurice of Saxony neared Trent with his Protestant army, the pope agreed to suspend the Council for two years. The decree of suspension was read at the sixteenth public session, on April 28, 1552, and the bishops at Trent fled precipitately from the endangered city.

Third Meeting of the Council (1562–1563). The second of the three papal legates to the first session of the Council of Trent, Cardinal Cervini, was elected to succeed Julius III in 1555. But the new pope, Marcellus II, lived only 22 days after his election. He was followed by Cardinal Caraffa, Paul IV, who had no use for councils and, as we shall see in Chapter 26, proceeded to effect vigorous and ruthless reform by himself. It was not until Paul IV's death in 1559 that a reconvening of the Council was even considered. His successor, Pius IV, was a temperate person who was anxious for the Council's help in completing the work of reform. He therefore proposed to reconvene the Council as soon as possible.

The pope's chief difficulty lay in getting the unanimous approval of the emperor, the King of Spain, and the French monarch. Ferdinand, Philip II, and Francis II all expressed the desire of a council's meeting, but they laid down such impossible conditions that the pope and his nephew secretary of state, St. Charles Borromeo, temporarily withdrew their plans for reconvening the Council. The French threatened to call a national council, and there was grave danger that a Gallican schism might occur. The pope nevertheless refused to transfer the Council to Avignon, as the French requested, but determined to have it meet at Trent again.

Emperor Ferdinand's demands were the equivalent of vetoing a council. The conditions he set forth included an end of the war between England and France; the representation of all Christian powers, including Denmark, England, and Sweden; the personal attendance of the pope; reform of the clergy before the Council reconvened and permission granted for the clergy to marry; and finally the convocation of the Council at Cologne, Ratisbon, or Constance, rather than at Trent. Pope Pius IV moved shrewdly and carefully among the princes, playing their demands off against each other, and deciding finally to reconvene the Council of Trent rather than call a new one as the princes demanded.

The third meeting at Trent was called for Easter Sunday of 1561. At that time, however, only four bishops were present. Not until November was any sizable number of bishops at Trent, and on January 18, 1562, the Council of Trent solemnly reopened its sessions. The Protestants refused to attend, but Ferdinand and Francis made a number of demands to attract them to later sessions. Among these was a demand for Mass in the vernacular, another for communion under both kinds, one for the marrying of priests, and a series of decrees to undermine or lessen papal authority. The French were even more disruptive in this third meeting at Trent. They continually insisted that the Council be moved to a city

nearer France, and with the Spanish bishops they demanded a restatement
of the conciliar theory of the Council of Constance. The Spanish bishops
feared that Philip II was co-operating with the pope to lessen their
authority and to increase his own over the Church in Spain. They therefore took a strong stand for episcopal power and against papal authority
at all times.

Eventually these disruptive elements were harnassed, largely through
the diplomatic skill of St. Charles Borromeo. The history of the third
meeting of the Council of Trent is mainly the story of skillful diplomacy
by the pope and his secretary of state, whereby they successfully directed
everyone present to the problems of definition of doctrine and statement
of reform that would not constitute a radical departure from Catholic tradition. Attendance increased throughout the sessions of the third meeting.
There were 141 fathers at the second session (the eighteenth of the
Council) of this meeting in February, 1562, and a total of 255 present at
the last session on December 3, 1563.

Work on definitions of doctrine proceeded smoothly. Decrees were
published stating Catholic doctrine on the Mass and on the sacraments of holy orders and matrimony. Decrees were also published on
Purgatory, the invocation of saints, the veneration of relics, and as a
last item, on indulgences. On all these matters there was little difference
of opinion. The problem was that of stating traditional Catholic doctrine
clearly and unequivocally in the light of Protestant errors. The doctrine
of the Real Presence, for example, had to be stated against both Luther's
theory of consubstantiation and Zwingli's denial of any Real Presence
whatsoever.

The greatest difficulty in the third meeting arose on the question of
episcopal residence which had come up in the first meeting. The burning
question came to be whether bishops receive their power from the pope
or from God. The matter was not by any means trivial. Indeed, it was a
question of profound theological importance, and it aroused such intense
strife that one of the fathers wrote that the avoidance of schism was a
miracle. It was also the result of the pope's patience and of St. Charles
Borromeo's skill. The latter's greatest triumph was winning over to
the pope's side the Cardinal of Lorraine and fifteen other French representatives who were originally in favor of the divine-right institution of
residency for the bishops. The Spanish bishops stubbornly resisted a
strong statement of papal authority. The result was that no explicit formulation was made on the relationship between the pope and the bishops.

Indirectly, however, papal primacy was safeguarded in a number of ways. The Roman Church was admitted to be the mother and mistress of all the other churches. All recipients of ecclesiastical dignities were required to promise obedience to the pope. The pope was said to have the care of the whole Church, and it is his prerogative to summon ecumenical councils. Furthermore, the Council's decrees were to have force only subject to the maintenance of the rights of the Roman See. Finally, the Council submitted all its decrees to papal confirmation. It is obvious, then, that St. Charles Borromeo safeguarded papal primacy while avoiding the danger of schism by bringing the matter to a formal statement.

When the doctrinal definitions were on their way to completion, Pius IV turned to the problem of closing the Council. Argument on reform measures could drag on forever, he knew, and he was convinced that the problem was rather for the pope and bishops to enforce the measures already enacted by the Council. Philip II was anxious to prolong the Council, however, so that he could use it as a lever to obtain additional concessions from the papacy. The pope countered with the suggestion that the reform decrees of the Council should be extended to the princes. This was obviously a counter-measure to obtain Philip's agreement for closure of the Council, because such a decree would be almost impossible of formulation in the modern world. At any rate, the pope withheld his approval of Maximilian's election as king of Bohemia until Ferdinand agreed to the closure of the Council. The Spanish bishops continued to intrigue to prolong the Council indefinitely, but all the other bishops agreed to a speedy conclusion when they heard that the pope was seriously ill, for they were anxious to avoid the danger of schism with the college of cardinals electing one pope and the Council another. The Council therefore concluded its sessions hurriedly on December 3, 1563, leaving a number of important projects unfinished.

Reception of the Council's Decrees. The Council requested papal confirmation of its decrees to make them binding. This presented somewhat of a problem, because the officials of the Curia tried to obtain some mitigation of certain decrees that would decrease appeals to Rome and thus cut down their income. Pope Pius IV confirmed the decrees unreservedly, however, and forbade the publishing of any "commentaries, glosses, annotations, and scholia to the said decrees" without the consent of the papacy. On August 2, 1564, he created a Congregation of Cardinals for the interpretation of the Decrees of the Council of Trent.

A number of problems left hanging by the Council devolved upon the papacy. One of these was the publication of a new Index. The original

Index of prohibited books had been compiled under Paul IV, and it was unduly restrictive. The Council pointed out that many of the condemned books were needed by scholars, and a commission was appointed to correct the Index. After the Council's close, the Tridentine Index was again examined in Rome and published by papal authorization in 1564. A second problem was that of drawing up a catechism of Catholic teaching. The Council had proposed such a catechism early in the first meeting; and although an excellent model was later produced by St. Peter Canisius, the Council was concluded without having drafted the catechism. A commission of theologians was appointed in Rome to draw up the catechism — a learned one in Latin for scholars and a popular one in the vernacular for the unlettered and for the young — which was published by St. Pius V as the Catechism of the Council of Trent. The Council also left unfinished the reform of the Missal and the Breviary and the purification of the text of the Vulgate. This work was carried on in Rome. The reformed Breviary and Missal were published by St. Pius V in 1568 and 1570 respectively, but the Vatican edition of the Vulgate was not completed until 1612.

The most difficult problem remained: to persuade the princes throughout Catholic Europe to ratify the decrees enacted at Trent. It was difficult because the princes were accustomed to regard ecclesiastical positions under their control as spoils of office to be passed out to royal favorites regardless of fitness for the position. And the Tridentine decrees put considerable limitations on this prerogative. There was little difficulty in Italy. Elsewhere, there was considerable difficulty. Emperor Maximilian II was anxious to conciliate the Protestants so as to obtain their help against the Turk. He therefore refused to have the Tridentine decrees confirmed at the Diet of Augsburg in 1566. In an effort to conciliate the emperor, St. Pius V allowed communion under both kinds in the empire, but when nothing resulted from the concession it was finally revoked in 1612. Meanwhile, certain Catholic princes in the empire, especially the duke of Bavaria and the three electoral bishops of Mainz, Trier, and Cologne, published the decrees within their jurisdictions and proceeded to effect the Tridentine reforms.

The king of France refused stubbornly to promulgate the Tridentine decrees in his country. This was partly because he feared such action would antagonize the Huguenots during the religious wars, and partly because of the strong Gallican sentiment in France. At length the French church assembly of 1615 acted on its own responsibility and "accepted" the Tridentine decrees and promised to comply with them. Philip II published the decrees in 1564, but "without prejudice to his royal rights." This meant that those reforms which lessened royal power were never enforced in Spain or in territories under Spanish control. In effect, Philip assumed the right of interpreting the Council's decrees and acting, as Pope Pius IV complained, as pope as well as king. Quarrels between the papacy and the Spanish king over the enforcement of Tridentine decrees dragged on throughout Philip's long reign and down into more recent times.

The Significance of the Council of Trent. In his excellent study, *The Catholic Reformation*, Pierre Janelle tells of the conflicting groups at Trent, and then he observes: "Such strength of thought and steadiness of purpose [as the Council showed] would be wholly unaccountable had the Council been merely a scrimmage between contending parties. But in truth all its members shared the same high ideal and had a noble conception of their own duty and of the function of the Church." That is why the Tridentine *Canones et Decreta*, in Janelle's words, exhibit "a striking combination of spiritual ardor and earnestness, and of temperate, sober reasonableness." The reforms of Clement VII and Paul III had borne fruit in the personnel who attended the Council of Trent. They were high-minded men earnest to reform abuses in the Church and to state clearly Catholic teaching on contested points of doctrine. That they did not attend in larger numbers and that they were taken up with national interests was due chiefly to the interference of their princes who had appointed them to office.

The quality of work done at Trent was due in large measure to the unusually capable theologians and canonists who were present. Prominent among these were three companions of St. Ignatius, early members of the Society of Jesus, two of whom served as the pope's theologians — Alphonse Salmeron, James Lainez, and Claude le Jay. Prominent Dominicans included Dominic Soto and Melchior Cano, and among the famous Franciscans of the day were Louis Carvajal, André de Vega, and Bernardine d'Asti, while the Augustinians were represented by their capable theologian, Girolamo Seripando. These men kept discussions on the highest possible theological plane. The generality of the assembly represented the best of Christian humanism, and their conclusions were clearly those of men in the Catholic tradition handling modern problems as Christian humanists could be expected to handle them — with due reverence for God's exalted position and due respect for the human person's individual worth.

The Council of Trent successfully accomplished its two main objectives. In the first place, it clearly defined Catholic teaching on (1) the sources of religious truth, (2) original sin and justification, (3) the nature of Mass and the sacraments, and (4) such contested other points as Purgatory and Indulgences. The importance of these definitions is apt to be lost on the student who benefits from them in the twentieth century. But in the sixteenth century sincere religious thinkers could not know what was true Catholic doctrine. There were all sorts of teachings, and one never knew whether he was a heretic on some of these points until it was too late. Now for the first time Catholic teaching on many of these points was set forth clearly. Now there were definitions against which to check some enthusiastic preacher's sermons.

In the second place, the worst abuses in the Church were removed — absenteeism, simony, pluralism, nepotism, irregular clerical life — and the way was cleared for the removal of others by the pope and the bishops throughout Christendom. The key reform was that which required the personal residence of the bishop in his diocese. Each bishop was required to visit every part of his diocese at least every other year, to reform the morals of the clergy and laity, and to enforce the strict observance of ecclesiastical discipline in his diocese. Pastors were ordered to teach catechism and to give solid instruction in their Sunday sermons. Abuses in monastic life were corrected with a minimum age being fixed for entering the convent or monastery, insistence made on keeping the vow of poverty, and the requirement enforced that nuns stay within the convent.

Trent is significant for the admirable balance it set up between Rome and the bishops throughout Christendom. We have already seen that no doubt was left as to the pope's supremacy over the universal Church. But his abuse of that position — which had been so bad in the past — was made almost impossible by Tridentine limits on the right of appeal to Rome. The whole tenor of the disciplinary decrees was to strengthen the authority of the bishop in his diocese. After Trent he is no longer to be hamstrung by the numberless exemptions which had formerly set his authority at naught. He is left supreme in the matter of ordination and the conferring of benefices within his diocese. By the terms of Trent the pope no longer intervenes in diocesan affairs, and Rome promised to restrict itself to hearing proper cases of appeal to the head of the Church.

The most original creation of the Council of Trent was the provision for seminaries — literally "nurseries" of the clergy where boys from the age of twelve were to be educated for the priesthood. The Council required that each diocese have at least one seminary, and it set down certain requirements for the moral life and the education of the young men in the seminary. This provision was aimed at correcting the worst abuse in the Church — the unqualified and incompetent class of men who were advanced to clerical life after little or no training for the work they were supposed to follow. The development of seminaries lay at the heart of continued Catholic reform since the sixteenth century, and it was one of the crowning accomplishments of the Council of Trent.

REVIEW AIDS

1. Consult a general history of the period to establish the periods of war between Charles V and Francis I; find how far into Europe the Turk had advanced; what religious and political divisions had been established in the Holy Roman Empire.
2. Why was Charles opposed to the Council's handling questions of doctrine? Why did the pope insist that this was the Council's main objective?
3. Consult Pastor's *History of the Popes* to make a list of cardinals appointed by Pope Paul III. Find the role each played at the Council of Trent.
4. Why were the first two sessions of the Council of Trent — which dealt with organization — of tremendous importance for the Council's success?
5. Consult the Catholic Encyclopedia or some other authoritative source to study the article on "justification." Explain the extreme views on this subject and show how the Tridentine definition safeguards both free will and divine power.
6. Explain as fully as you can why the question of episcopal residency was of crucial importance for the Church's organization.
7. Be prepared to state briefly the essence of each of the important doctrinal decisions made by the Council of Trent.
8. The European kings were desirous that Pope Pius IV call a new council into session rather than reconvene the suspended Council of Trent. The pope was insistent that he reconvene the Council of Trent. What difference did it make?

SUGGESTIONS FOR FURTHER READING

Volumes XIII to XVII of Pastor's *History of the Popes* cover the Council of Trent, together with negotiations for its various meetings, in considerable detail. Chapter V of Janelle's *The Catholic Reformation* gives a good summary account of the Council's accomplishments.

The decrees and canons of the Council are published in English and in Latin by Rev. H. J. Schroeder, O.P., *Canons and Decrees of the Council of Trent* (St. Louis: 1941). The catechism which St. Pius V ordered published is in English under the title, *Catechism of Trent for Parish Priests* (New York: 1937), by John A. McHugh, O.P., and Charles J. Callan, O.P.

A fuller understanding of the Council can be obtained by reading the biography of any of its leaders. Among many biographies in English, the following are perhaps the most helpful: Henry O. Evennett, *The Cardinal of Lorraine and the Council of Trent* (Cambridge, England: 1930); Edward Healy Thompson, *The Life of St. Charles Borromeo* (London: 1893); Hubert Jedin, *Papal Legate at the Council of Trent, Cardinal Seripando* (St. Louis: 1947); and Joseph H. Fichter, S.J., *James Laynez, Jesuit* (St. Louis: 1944).

DOCUMENTS

Decrees on Justification

The decrees of the Council of Trent are similar to congressional legislation — the final decision of the Church after sessions of discussion and study on each particular problem. Listed below are part of the decrees on justification, one of the most important doctrinal questions handled by the Council.

I. If anyone saith that man may be justified before God by his own works, whether done through the teaching of human nature or that of the law, without the grace of God through Jesus Christ; let him be anathema.

II. If anyone saith that the grace of God through Jesus Christ is given only for this, that man may be able more easily to live justly and to merit eternal life, as if by free-will without grace he were able to do both, though hardly indeed and with difficulty; let him be anathema.

III. If anyone saith that without the prevenient inspiration of the Holy Ghost and without His help man can believe, hope, love, or be penitent as he ought, so as that the grace of justification may be bestowed upon him; let him be anathema.

IV. If anyone saith that man's free-will, moved and excited by God, by assenting to God exciting and calling, no wise co-operates towards disposing and preparing itself for obtaining the grace of justification; that it cannot refuse its consent, if it would, but that, as something inanimate, it does nothing whatever and is merely passive; let him be anathema.

V. If anyone saith that, since Adam's sin, the free-will of man is lost and extinguished; or that it is a thing with only a name, yea, a name without a reality, a figment, in fine, introduced into the Church by Satan; let him be anathema.

VI. If anyone saith that it is not in man's power to make his ways evil, but that the works that are evil God worketh as well as those that are good, not permissibly only, but properly and of Himself, in such wise that the treason of Judas is no less His own proper work than the vocation of Paul; let him be anathema.

VII. If anyone saith that all works done before justification, in whatsoever way they be done, are truly sins, or merit the hatred of God; or that the more earnestly one strives to dispose himself for grace, the more grievously he sins; let him be anathema.

VIII. If anyone saith that the fear of hell, whereby, by grieving for our sins, we flee unto the mercy of God, or refrain from sinning, is a sin, or makes sinners worse; let him be anathema.

IX. If anyone saith that by faith alone the impious is justified; in such wise as to mean that nothing else is required to co-operate in order to the obtaining the grace of justification, and that it is not in any way necessary that he be prepared and disposed by the movement of his own will; let him be anathema.

X. If anyone saith that men are just without the justice of Christ, whereby He merited for us to be justified; or that it is by that justice itself that they are formally just; let him be anathema.

XI. If anyone saith that men are justified, either by the sole imputation of the justice of Christ or by the sole remission of sins, to the exclusion of the grace and the charity which is poured forth in their hearts by the Holy Ghost and is inherent in them; or even that the grace, whereby we are justified, is only the favour of God; let him be anathema.

XII. If anyone saith that justifying faith is nothing else but confidence in the divine mercy which remits sin for Christ's sake; or that this confidence alone is that whereby we are justified; let him be anathema.

XIV. If anyone saith that man is truly absolved from his sins and justified, because that he assuredly believed himself absolved and justified; or that no one is truly justified but he who believes himself justified; and that, by this faith alone, absolution and justification are effected; let him be anathema.

XVIII. If anyone saith that the commandments of God are, even for one that is justified and constituted in grace, impossible to keep; let him be anathema.

XIX. If anyone saith that nothing besides faith is commanded in the Gospel; that other things are indifferent, neither commanded nor prohibited, but free; or that the Ten Commandments no wise appertain to Christians; let him be anathema.

XX. If anyone saith that the man who is justified and how perfect soever is not bound to observe the Commandments of God and of the Church, but only to believe; as if indeed the Gospel were a bare and absolute promise of eternal life, without the condition of observing the Commandments; let him be anathema.

XXI. If anyone saith that Jesus Christ was given of God to men, as a Redeemer in whom to trust, and not also as a legislator whom to obey; let him be anathema.

XXII. If anyone saith that the justified either is able to persevere without the special help of God in the justice received; or that with that help he is not able; let him be anathema.

XXIV. If anyone saith that the justice received is not preserved and also increased before God through good works; but that the said works are merely the fruits and signs of justification obtained, but not a cause of the increase thereof; let him be anathema.

Chapter 25

REINVIGORATION OF RELIGIOUS
ORDERS

W E SAW how the Benedictines arose in answer to a particular
need in the Church at a given time, and how centuries later
the Franciscans and Dominicans were founded to fill other and
new needs which had developed in the medieval Church. The need for
these orders continued into the sixteenth century, but the original spiritual
zeal had died out in many religious establishments and various abuses
had grown up like fungi in the religious orders. Reform was essential if
they were to perform the work for which they were founded. Moreover,
a general re-examination of purposes and readaptation to the modern
world was necessary if the religious orders were to retain the important
place they had formerly occupied in the history of the Church.

Reform and reinvigoration of existing religious orders was therefore
sorely needed as an essential part of the Catholic reform of the sixteenth century. But it is obvious that the Renaissance had produced
conditions requiring a new kind of regular clergy. The Renaissance was
an age of transition, we must remember, of change from medieval to
modern life in politics, economics, religion, literature, and even spiritual
life. The Franciscan or the Benedictine fit poorly into the individualistic,
aggressive world of a Michelangelo, a Columbus, a Julius II, a Machiavelli.
A new kind of religious was needed, a *condottieri* of religion who would
be free to fight in the new way for his God and his Church, an individual
not too much encumbered by life in common with his brethren but so
trained that he could move in and through the world as an individual
soldier of Christ. A number of new orders were founded to meet modern

needs, as we shall see, and pre-eminent among them in catching the spirit of the times and utilizing it was the Society of Jesus.

Reform of the Older Orders. The reform movement among existing orders had begun as early as the pontificate of Leo X. Successful reform on a wide scale of many orders was made imperative by the Protestant Revolt. The Augustinians were reformed by their general, Egidio Canisio, who had been an outstanding scholar at the Lateran Council; his work was completed by his successor, Girolamo Seripando, who spent several years visiting Augustinian houses throughout Italy, France, Spain, and Portugal. Reform of the Augustinians was particularly difficult because a goodly number of the monks held tenaciously to Luther's view on justification.

Reform of the Dominicans and Franciscans followed a similar pattern. In each case an attempt was made to revive the order according to its old rules and its primitive spirit. The Dominicans were reformed by two visitations during the pontificate of Paul III and by regulations laid down by St. Pius V, who was a Dominican himself. Abuses within the Benedictine and Cistercian orders had multiplied in the fifteenth century because many abbeys were held *in commendam* and were inhabited by monks who made no pretence of following the rules of the order. Reform was directed, therefore, against vested interests which made work slow and difficult. Sometimes armed force was necessary to expel recalcitrant monks! By the end of the century, however, the reform of existing orders had been pretty well accomplished.

Two reforms are of particular importance in the history of the Church in the sixteenth century: the reform of the Carmelites in Spain under St. Teresa and St. John of the Cross, and the Capuchin reform of the Franciscans in Italy under Matteo de Bascio. St. Teresa is best known as the outstanding mystic of the sixteenth century, but she is also important for her reform of the Carmelites. She possessed a great measure of practical efficiency which, combined with her religious zeal and her humility, enabled her to persevere in her course of establishing reformed Carmelite houses in the face of strong opposition from the unreformed Carmelites. In 1567 St. Teresa met St. John of the Cross and persuaded the young man to devote his energies to reforming the Carmelite houses for men. The reform ideas of St. Teresa and St. John of the Cross were eventually adopted by all the Carmelite houses.

Their writings on mystical prayer became classics in the Catholic tradition and have been influential down till the present time. The essential element in their theory of prayer, of course, is the description of the three ways of spiritual life. In the first or *purgative way,* man is converted and cleanses himself of sin. In the second or *illuminative way,* he acquires mystical understanding of God. In the third or *unitive way,* he binds himself to God and gives himself up to divine love, thereby acquiring calm joy in the divine presence. This highest form of prayer was nothing new in the Church, of course, but in the hands of St. Teresa and St. John of the Cross it received a modern formulation and became the ideal for which many people in religious life have striven in modern times.

The Capuchins developed as a reform within a reform of the Franciscan Order. The Observants were the reformed group among the Franciscans, you will recall, who revived the original, strict rule from which the Conventuals had departed in the later Middle Ages. But the Observants were not strict enough for some of the members. One such member was Matteo de Bascio who believed he was ordered by a voice to "observe the rule to the letter." This involved, among other things, the adoption of the pointed hood which has outwardly distinguished the Capuchins from other Franciscans. Matteo's views brought him into difficulty with the Observants. He therefore went to Rome where he laid the matter before Clement VII and begged permission to live according to the original rule of St. Francis. Clement granted his request, but required him to present himself once a year to his provincial as an act of obedience.

During the plague of 1523 at Camerino, Matteo first attracted public attention and came under the protection of Caterina Cibo, duchess of Camerino and niece of the pope. The duchess and Vittoria Colonna befriended Matteo and his early associates when the Observants treated them as apostates and attempted to bring them back by force. Matteo and his associates did outstanding work among the poor during the terrible year of 1527. In the following year Clement VII gave them permission to live according to the original Franciscan rule, to preach to the people, and to live under their own superior. The group soon became known as the Order of Friars Minor Capuchin from the pointed hood which they wore.

The Capuchin movement spread rapidly because it appealed to the neglected poor of Italy. It surmounted serious difficulties caused by the Observants who obtained from several popes decisions which interfered with the recruitment of candidates and the independence of the new group. A serious crisis was overcome when the Capuchins survived the apostasy of their vicar-general, Bernardino Ochino, who married and, together with a number of his brethren, joined the Calvinists. In 1536 Paul III confirmed the Capuchin order as an independent group in the

Church. The Capuchins were largely responsible for checking the progress of the Protestant Revolt throughout northern Italy and across the Tyrol region into southern Germany. They did much to raise the tone of religious life among the lower classes in Italy. They worked among the poor, in the Franciscan tradition, and thus they complemented the work of the Jesuits which, as we shall see, was directed toward the wealthier and more influential classes of Christendom.

New Religious Orders. We have already seen that Caraffa and St. Cajetan established the Theatines, who served as a nursery for bishops and a seedbed for the reform movement within the Church. A number of other orders were established about the same time in Italy to meet particular needs of the Church. All of them had the common aim of mixing in the world and dealing with it more directly and effectively than the older orders could. The Somaschi and the Barnabites were founded about the same time (1528) for similar reasons. The second war between Charles V and Francis I (1526–1529) was fought largely in Italy, and the Italian population was subjected to all the havoc of war — pestilence, destitution, pillaging, and loss of life. The country was soon filled with orphans, starving old men and women, and even unburied bodies in the streets.

The Venetian nobleman, St. Jerome Emilian, played a leading role in performing works of mercy in this setting. He had seen service in the Venetian army, and after a wonderful escape from captivity he had turned to things spiritual. Now he collected orphans into a house near San Rocco, and soon he had established additional houses in Brescia and Bergamo. He gathered a body of pious laymen to help him in his work and established his headquarters in the village of Somasca, near Bergamo. St. Jerome Emilian always looked upon Cardinal Caraffa as his spiritual guide. Although Caraffa refused to become head of the new order, he encouraged the group in its labors and urged it to expand into Milanese territory. It was only in 1568 that the Somaschi became a religious order properly speaking. At this time St. Jerome's successor obtained a papal brief establishing their constitutions and designating them as the Clerks Regular of San Maiolo — a name taken from the church granted to them in Milan by St. Charles Borromeo.

The Barnabites — so called from the church in Milan called San Barnabas — were established in 1530 by an Italian nobleman, Antonio Maria Zaccaria, for essentially the same purposes as the Somaschi. Their chief work was caring for destitute children and teaching religion to

the poorer classes. Their institute was approved by Paul III in 1535, and
in the next few years they expanded rapidly. They specialized in open-air
missions and in public penances by means of which they sought to stir
the masses up to a sense of their sinfulness and need of divine help.
"They took pains to stir the feelings of the ruder sort of people . . .;
they were to be seen, crucifix in hand, preaching in the most crowded
thoroughfares; some carried heavy crosses, others confessed their sins
aloud." The Barnabites spread into the territory around Milan, and
St. Charles Borromeo made extensive use of them in reforming his
diocese.

A number of other new orders were founded to minister to local and
temporary needs of the Church. Among these were the Fathers of a
Good Death or the Camillians, founded by St. Camillus de Lellis to care
for the sick in homes and in hospitals, and the Brothers of Mercy founded
by St. John of God to serve the afflicted. Two orders established for the
religious training and the education of youth were the Society of Secular
Clerics of Christian Doctrine, established by Caesar de Bus, and the
Congregation of Pious Schools, founded by St. Joseph Calasanctius.

Among the orders of women established as part of the Catholic reformation the Ursulines occupy the most important place. During Clement VII's
pontificate St. Angela Merici gathered together a group of young women
to instruct children and to care for the sick. At first she did not intend
to establish an order. The young women lived at home and came together regularly for prayer and other religious services. In 1537 there
were 76 members in the community. They chose St. Angela their superior,
put the community under the protection of St. Ursula, and proceeded to
establish a religious order which was approved by Paul III in 1544. Its
special protector was St. Charles Borromeo, but the group was welcomed
by reforming bishops everywhere.

St. Philip Neri and the Oratorians.   The two most original creations
of the Catholic reformation of the sixteenth century were the Oratorians
and the Jesuits. In many respects they are opposite of each other: an
almost playful freedom is the hallmark of the Oratorians, whereas a military discipline is the distinguishing characteristic of the Jesuits. But in
one respect they are quite similar: both groups were organized primarily
to work in the apostolate. The sanctification of individual members is
important, of course, but the chief end of the organization is to bring
the word of God to the world.

Both orders bear the unmistakable mark of their founders. St. Philip

Neri was born of noble parents in Florence in 1515. He went to Rome at the age of eighteen and worked among the sick and the destitute. Here he met a number of young men of similar character and temperament, and within a few years they formed a confraternity of twelve laymen. Every Sunday they received Communion together and assembled for religious exercises. The movement took on a more formal tone after Philip received holy orders and was appointed to the church of San Girolamo. The group met in Father Philip's rooms for religious exercises he directed. These consisted of readings, pious debates, extempore sermons, and prayers sometimes put to music — hence the name Oratory.

As several of Philip's associates were ordained and settled together at San Girolamo a community began to take shape. It was formally established in 1575 when Pope Gregory XIII granted Philip and his companions the church of Santa Maria in Vallicella. The community was then forced to choose its own form of government. In 1577 Philip was elected provost and five fathers were chosen to be deputies. The final constitution was not approved by the pope until 1612, largely because there were two divergent points of view on what sort of order was to be established. St. Philip prized a considerable freedom of action for his members; he shrank from set rules and tight discipline, and he had no wish to establish a highly centralized order. Some of the fathers, led by Antonio Talpa, wanted the Oratory to become a regular religious order and to expand like the Jesuits.

St. Philip Neri's view eventually prevailed. The Oratorians live in a community, but each member enjoys his own income and contributes to the support of the house. They are bound by no vows. They are secular priests who are free to leave at any time. Their principal obligation is to participate in the religious services of the Oratory. The bishop is the immediate superior of each congregation; the various houses of the Oratory are independent of each other and they have no superior general. Within each house the organization is republican. Emphasis is on the freedom and the equality of all members.

The Oratory was infused with the spirit of its founder, and the main features of his spiritual ideal were humbleness, cheerfulness, and charity. The Oratorians developed a new style of preaching which was especially successful. In contrast to the typical ornate Renaissance style, it was simple, direct, completely free from scholastic verbiage. In contrast to the Brethren of the Common Life and earlier religious groups, the Oratorians stressed the cheerfulness of the saint and the happiness of being good. Oratories were soon established in Germany and Austria, as well as in Italy, and in time they spread to England and the Americas. Among the more illustrious Oratorians of St. Philip's age was the historian Baronius, author of the *Ecclesiastical Annals*. The famous musician Palestrina composed many of their lauds. The influence of the Oratorians was felt especially in their emphasis on learning.

St. Ignatius and the Jesuits. St. Ignatius was different from St. Philip Neri in character and temperament. And he founded a Society that differed in almost every respect from the Oratorians. Stamped with Ignatius' military outlook and his genius for organization, the Society of Jesus became the principal agent of the Catholic counter-reformation. In size and accomplishments it dwarfed all other orders. St. Ignatius had caught both the spirit of the Church and the spirit of the time more completely than did the founder of any other religious order, and the perfect combination of the two does much to explain the amazing accomplishments of the Society. For one must see St. Francis Xavier as both another Paul and another Cortez to understand his labors in the Far East, and one must see St. Peter Canisius as both another Boniface and another Philip II to understand his work in Germany.

St. Ignatius was born in the Basque country of a family that belonged to the lesser nobility. He seems to have had an overpowering ambition to cut a figure in court life and to be an outstanding Spanish grandee. The story of his conversion is well known — how he was wounded in battle, how he decided while recovering that henceforth he would devote all his energies to fighting for God's honor and glory. Ignatius spent about a year at the neighboring town of Manresa where, in 1522–1523, he composed the famous *Spiritual Exercises*. Pierre Janelle tells us that "the *Spiritual Exercises* are at the root of all the surprising results obtained by the Society of Jesus . . . the whole spiritual discipline, the whole action and policy, and the very educational methods, of the Society of Jesus are clearly outlined in the *Exercises*." And a secular historian says of this work, "as a masterpiece of religious literature it easily ranks with anything that Luther or Calvin wrote, and it became the textbook of a militant Catholicism."[1]

The *Exercises* are too complex a work to be analyzed briefly. Here let us only indicate that they provide a course of meditations designed to strengthen the will and to direct it to right purposes. The work reveals St. Ignatius' knowledge of human nature and his practical wisdom in dealing with it. St. Ignatius is concerned with the reader's honoring and

[1] Henry S. Lucas, *The Renaissance and the Reformation* (New York: 1934), 640.

serving God and thereby saving his soul; he allows great leeway of means to achieve this end. The best short description of the *Exercises* is probably the author's own full title: "Spiritual exercises whereby a man may be enabled to conquer himself and so order his life that he is never under the domination of any inordinate affection whatever." The pope gave his unreserved approval to the *Exercises* on July 31, 1548, and their influence soon spread widely outside the Society of Jesus.

For the next five years St. Ignatius tried to find his position in Christ's army. He went to Rome in March, 1523, and after a short stay took ship for the Holy Land. However, he was ordered back to Rome by the Franciscan provincial of the Holy Land. By this time Ignatius had traveled widely. He had found the world sophisticated and full of heresy. Fighting for Christ required the weapons of knowledge and good reasoning. Ignatius therefore decided that he must obtain a thorough education if he were to be influential as a spiritual leader. At the universities of Alcala and Salamanca he ran into difficulties with the Inquisition. In 1528 he went to the University of Paris where he won six devoted companions: Peter Faber, Francis Xavier, Alphonse Salmeron, James Lainez, Simon Rodriguez, and Nicholas Bobadilla. On August 15, 1534, all of them took the vows of chastity and poverty, and agreed to care for sick Christians at Jerusalem and work for the conversion of the Turk. If this were not possible, they agreed to place themselves directly at the disposal of the pope. In effect, then the Society of Jesus was established on this date.

Pope Paul III gave the group permission to go to Jerusalem. But no ships sailed that year. Meanwhile, St. Ignatius and his group found work to do at Rome. On September 27, 1540, Paul issued the Bull *Regimini militantis* which formally established the Society. In it the pope authorized "his beloved sons Ignatius Loyola, Peter Faber, etc., to form a society, known as the Company of Jesus, and to receive therein whosoever, desirous of carrying arms for God and of serving only Jesus Christ our Lord and the Roman Pontiff, His vicar on earth, would be disposed to take the vow of perpetual chastity and to labor for the advancement of souls in the Christian life by preaching, by spiritual exercises, the hearing of people's confessions, and works of charity."

The Jesuits adopted the three ordinary vows of poverty, chastity, and obedience, and a fourth special vow placing them at the pope's service. Daily office was to be said individually rather than in choir, as was the practice with other religious orders. This was to leave the members free to perform whatever work they were called upon to do. The original bull limited the Society to 60 members, but this restriction was withdrawn in 1544. St. Ignatius labored the next three years on the Society's *Constitution*, a remarkable document which exhibits its author's genius as clearly as do the *Spiritual Exercises*. The *Constitution* was adopted by the assembled fathers of the Society in 1550.

The aim Ignatius had in view when he devised the *Constitution* of the Society was the aim common to religious orders, the glory of God and the salvation of men. But he seems to have kept the aim more constantly in view and to have devised his organization as a means of reaching that end without any distractions. Poverty is imposed on the members in such fashion that it cannot be circumvented as was so common in the older religious orders. Obedience, again, is much stricter than in the other orders. It is military in character and it requires an absolute identification of an inferior's will with his superior's. Conditions for admittance to the Society are made incredibly strict, and a sifting arrangement throughout the early years prevents any but the most capable men from becoming fully professed Jesuits. The Society is monarchical in organization. At the top is a general, chosen for life by the votes of the provincials. He is aided and checked by four assistants elected with him. Each province is headed by a provincial appointed by the general.

St. Ignatius devised tactics for his community almost as a general might devise the strategy and tactics of a military campaign. He proposed that his followers pass over the little and unimportant people to concentrate on princes, bishops, and other influential classes. "One ought to prefer such persons and places as, after gaining spiritual improvement, cause the profit to spread to others that obey their authority or follow their directions." Therefore one should concentrate on influential persons "such as princes and lords or magistrates and judges, or to churchmen such as prelates . . . eminent for their learning or authority." These were the tactics followed by St. Peter Canisius in saving a good part of Germany for the Church. By his personal influence he kept the Archbishop of Cologne from turning Protestant. He saved Bavaria for the Church and even talked Duke Albrecht V into championing Catholicism forcefully. He became adviser to the emperor at a time when the Hapsburg ruler thought seriously of turning Protestant. Before long Canisius was establishing colleges, composing devotional literature and, at the emperor's request, writing his famous *Catechism*, which was used in the Germanies for centuries. This same technique of "getting to" the important people has been used by Jesuits throughout their history.

At first bishops did not think well of this military society at the service of the Holy See. But the excellent showing made by the Jesuits at the

Council of Trent caused the bishops in most countries to bid for their services. Only in France did the Jesuits meet strong opposition, partly because of well-organized Catholic groups in that country and partly because of the strong Gallican sentiment of the bishops and the government. By the time St. Ignatius died in 1556, there were twelve provinces, more than a hundred houses with 1600 members, and 65 missions scattered throughout the world. They had missions in Japan, Brazil, Abyssinia, and the Congo. They had houses almost everywhere in Catholic Europe. They had played a considerable part in reforming Italy, Spain, and Portugal. They had played a large role in saving Poland and parts of Germany for the Church, and they had won back certain areas in Germany that had recently slipped into the Protestant fold.

Education and the Catholic Reformation.   The driving power of the Jesuits was due largely to the system of education which the Society adopted and which became one of the chief instruments of the Catholic reformation. Other orders founded schools which did good work in various localities. Good diocesan work was done under the exemplary bishop of Milan, St. Charles Borromeo. The Barnabites and Capuchins established excellent schools in Italy and France. The Oratorians were especially successful in France. But the Jesuit colleges outstripped the others in number and in quality of education.

From the first, the seminaries provided by the Council of Trent were entrusted to the Society of Jesus which alone was able to staff them. St. Ignatius had originally not thought of education as one of the activities for his Society. But he had seen the need of highly trained personnel from the beginning, and the first Jesuit colleges were designed to train members of the Society for their apostolate. Before Ignatius' death in 1556, the Society had undertaken the education of other religious at the Roman College and of the laity at the College of Billom in France. Jesuit colleges spread rapidly, and they played a most important role in the Catholic reformation both in regard to the clergy and the higher placed laity. "Jesuits' colleges," Janelle has written, "swarmed over the whole of Central and Western Europe, and even as far as India; and there were new foundations throughout the sixteenth, seventeenth, and even eighteenth centuries, right up to the suppression of the Society." Three colleges had been established in Poland by 1565. By 1650 about 155 had been established in Germany and 68 in France. Many of these foundations were colleges that had fallen into decay and disrepute, and the Jesuits were called in to revive them. We should also remember that the "college" of these days is about equivalent to the senior high school and junior college of our own time.

Jesuit success was due to the plan laid down by St. Ignatius in the section of the *Constitution* dealing with education and later perfected in the *Ratio studiorum*. Like the *Exercises* and the *Constitution* of the Society, the *Ratio* embodies a blending of Christian wisdom and Renaissance humanism. The aim of the *Ratio* is to build up a strong moral personality, a well-rounded man who is wholly dedicated to the service of God. Stress is therefore laid on activity by the student: he should think independently rather than accept knowledge passively; he should govern himself and his fellows as much as possible so as to acquire a sense of responsibility. Janelle well observes of this system: "Such a conception of education implies psychological insight, wide experience, and an intelligence in advance of the times; in fact it is strikingly modern, and forestalls, in regard to the building of character, the methods of Thomas Arnold and the Rugby School, and in regard to the building of the mind, the teaching practice of the French Lycées."

Both in teaching technique and in curriculum the Jesuits incorporated all that was best of the Renaissance. They used the classical authors in humanist fashion and laid stress on literary and grammatical rather than scientific study. Classes were so arranged that competition between students made them try to excell. The aim of Jesuit education was to train students to think clearly and to argue cogently so as to succeed in later studies or in disputes about their faith. In this sense, there was an apologetic note to Jesuit education that one does not find with Dominicans or Franciscans of days past, who were chiefly interested in truth as the object of study.

The Jesuits were imitated by other orders, especially by the Oratorians in France, whose work was an important aspect of the seventeenth-century religious revival in that country. The Oratorians established 26 colleges in France between 1616 and 1649, all of them modeled on the Jesuit plan. Ursuline schools for girls, which played so important a part in building up a solid class of religious women trained for household management, were also modeled on the Jesuit plan. Religious orders, then, had taken the initiative from secular educators, and they made the Catholic reformation produce lasting results. The seminaries were designed to accomplish this task for the clergy, and the Jesuit style college to accomplish it for laymen.

REVIEW AIDS

1. It has been said of St. Ignatius that he not only established a new order but a new kind of order. What is meant by this statement?
2. What are the principal points of similarity between the Oratorians and the Jesuits? The principal points of difference?
3. Make a list of the factors that explain the tremendous success of the Society of Jesus in its first years.
4. An interesting project — and an instructive one — is to prepare a map of Europe about 1585 to show where the various religious orders had establishments. After preparing such a map try to explain, as fully as you can, why each order spread in the fashion it did.
5. Prepare in parallel columns a list of the new orders, the date and place of their founding, and the purpose for which they were established.
6. Of what particular importance in Church history was each of the following· St. Teresa of Avila, St. Peter Canisius, James Lainez, Matteo da Bascio, Girolamo Seripando.
7. Analyze one of the meditations in St. Ignatius' *Spiritual Exercises* from the standpoint of its sound psychological appeal.
8. Analyze the missionary tactics of the Society of Jesus and attempt to show both their advantages and their disadvantages.

SUGGESTIONS FOR FURTHER READING

There is a tremendous literature on the religious orders, much of it quite uncritical and completely laudatory. Volumes XII, XIII, and XIV of Pastor's *History of the Popes* have a number of chapters devoted to the reform of the older orders and the formation of the new orders. Chapter VI of Janelle's *The Catholic Reformation* treats the subject briefly but well. An excellent study on the *raison d'être* of various religious orders is to be found in Walter Dirks, *The Monk and the World* (New York: 1954). Although this book devotes attention chiefly to the Benedictines and the Franciscans, it has material on the Jesuits, and what it says about these orders is true, *mutatis mutandis*, of the other orders.

Among the many individual studies of religious orders of the sixteenth century, the following should prove most helpful to the average student: For the Capuchins, Father Cuthbert's *The Capuchins, A Contribution to the History of the Counter-Reformation* (New York: 1929). For the Oratorians, *St. Philip Neri and the Roman Society of His Times* (London: 1932), by Louis Ponnelle and Louis Bordet. For the Carmelites, Louis Bertrand, *St. Theresa of Avila* (New York: 1929). A fuller understanding of Spanish mysticism and of St. Teresa can be obtained from reading her own works, among them her autobiography, all of which have been translated into English. Among these works, the following are most important: *The Interior Castle* (London: 1921); *The Way of Perfection* (Philadelphia: 1901); *Book of the Foundations* (London: 1893); and *Minor Works of St. Teresa* (New York: 1913).

The best readable accounts of the Jesuits have been done by James Brodrick, S.J. Among his works, the following are most helpful for this period: *The Origin of the Jesuits* (New York: 1940); *The Progress of the Jesuits* (New York: 1947); *St. Peter Canisius* (New York: 1935); and *St. Francis Xavier* (New York: 1952). The best life of St. Ignatius in English is the translation of the work of Père Paul Dudon, S.J., *St. Ignatius of Loyola* (Milwaukee: 1949), but the work of Cyril Martindale, S.J., *St. Ignatius of Loyola* (London: 1921), is still useful.

DOCUMENTS

Meditation for Second Week, Fourth Day

St. Ignatius' *Spiritual Exercises* are more widely used than any other formula for retreats in the modern world, both for clerics and for laymen. Typical of the *Exercises* and of Ignatian spirituality is the important and decisive "Meditation on the Two Standards."

The meditation on Two Standards, the one of Christ, our sovereign Leader and Lord: the other of Lucifer, the mortal enemy of our human nature.

The usual preparatory prayer.

The first prelude is the history: it will be seen here how Christ calls and desires all under His banner: Lucifer on the contrary under his.

The second prelude is a composition of place, seeing the spot: it will be here to see a vast plain of all the region round Jerusalem, where the Supreme general Leader of all the good is Christ our Lord: and to imagine another plain in the country of Babylon, where the chief of the enemy is Lucifer.

The third prelude is to ask for what I want: it will be here to ask for knowledge of the deceits of the wicked chieftain, and for help to guard against them; and for knowledge of the true life which our Sovereign and true Leader points out, and for grace to imitate Him.

The first point is to imagine the chieftain of all the enemy as seated in that great plain of Babylon, as on a lofty throne of fire and smoke, in aspect horrible and fearful.

The second point is to consider how he summons together innumerable devils, how he disperses them some to one city, some to another, and so on throughout the whole world, omitting not any provinces, places, or states of life, or any persons in particular.

The third point is to consider the address which he makes, and how he warns them to lay snares and chains; telling them how they are first to tempt men to covet riches (as he is wont to do in most cases), so that they may more easily come to the vain honor of the world, and then to unbounded pride; so that the first step is riches, the second honor, the third pride; and from these three steps he leads them to all other vices.

In the same way, on the other hand, we are to consider the sovereign and true Leader, Christ our Lord.

The first point is to consider how Christ our Lord, in aspect fair and winning, takes His station in a great plain of the country near Jerusalem on a lowly spot.

The second point is to consider how the Lord of the whole world chooses out so many persons, Apostles, disciples, etc., and sends them throughout the whole world diffusing His sacred doctrine through all states and conditions of persons.

The third point is to consider the address which Christ our Lord makes to all His servants and friends, whom He sends on this expedition, recommending to them that they desire to help all, by guiding them first to the highest degree of poverty of spirit, and even to actual poverty, if it please His Divine Majesty, and He should choose to elect them to it: leading them, secondly, to a desire of reproaches and contempt, because from these two humility results; so that there are three steps: the first, poverty, opposed to riches; the second, reproaches and contempts, opposed to worldly honour; the third, humility, opposed to pride: and from these three steps let them conduct them to all other virtues.

A colloquy to our Lady to obtain for me grace from her Son and Lord that I may be received under His Standard. And first, in the highest degree of poverty of spirit, and not less in actual poverty, if it please His Divine Majesty, and He should choose to elect and receive me to it. Secondly, in bearing reproaches and insults, the better to imitate Him in these, provided only I can endure them without sin on the part of any person, or displeasure to His Divine Majesty; and after this an *Ave Maria*.

To ask the same from the Son, that He obtain for me this grace from the Father; and then to say an *Anima Christi*.

To ask the same from the Father, that He grant me this grace; and to say a *Pater noster*.

This Exercise will be made at midnight, and again early in the morning; and two repetitions of it will be made at the hours of Mass and Vespers, always finishing with the triple colloquy to our Lady, the Son, and the Father; and the meditation on the Classes, which follows, will be made during the hour before supper.

Chapter 26

THE REFORM POPES AND THE
COUNTER-REFORMATION

THE Catholic reform of the sixteenth century was completed by a series of excellent popes whose principal aim was to put into universal effect the decrees of the Council of Trent. Especially important were St. Pius V (1566–1572), Gregory XIII (1572–1585), and Sixtus V (1585–1590). These men made sure that the Council of Trent would not be sterile in practical results. Against formidable opposition led by the Catholic princes of Europe, they made the decrees of the Council a part of the living Catholic tradition. The Church had lost much ground in the sixteenth century because of the Protestant Revolt, but it emerged from the century a stronger institution internally and one freed from its worst abuses. That these changes were permanent is to the credit of the reform popes of the last half of the century.

Paul IV and Roman Reform. Cardinal Caraffa was elected pope on May 23, 1555, at the advanced age of seventy-nine. Philip Hughes likens Paul IV to a "grim Old Testament figure." "Never was there so iron a will, nor such rigidity, never, it must be added, such intolerance of any will but his own." Age had not diminished his fiery energy. On the very day of his coronation he dispatched two monks from Monte Cassino to reform the Spanish monasteries. Within a few days his austere, harsh zeal was felt in Rome and throughout many parts of the Catholic world. A cardinal was banished from Rome, and a bishop was imprisoned for life — with three months each year on bread and water! Paul IV boasted that not a day passed without his striking at some abuse in the Church.

Paul IV's aims can be summed up as threefold: to rid the Church of heresy; to stamp out all abuses and strengthen ecclesiastical discipline; to free the Church from the control of the princes. All these aims he tried to accomplish by direct and forceful means. To stamp out heresy he relied on the Index and the Inquisition, both of which he strengthened and made unreasonably severe. No discretion was used in putting works on the Index. All of a man's works were put on the Index indiscriminately rather than certain books being selected. Paul IV personally attended the weekly meeting of the Roman Inquisition, extended its jurisdiction to additional crimes, and authorized the use of torture to obtain confessions. He even turned on his old friends in the Oratory of Divine Love — with zealous ferocity — and hailed them before the Inquisition on such charges as dealing gently with heretics. Although Cardinal Morone, for example, defended himself successfully from these charges, he was nevertheless kept in prison until after Paul's death. Cardinal Pole, again, was ordered to appear before the Inquisition for having yielded title to monastic lands in England, but the saintly Englishman died before his case came up in Rome.

Paul's measures were effective. Under him the pagan element that had come into Rome a century before was expelled forever. Dispensations for bishops and monks were abruptly terminated. Cardinals and bishops had to resign all benefices except their proper sees. The 113 diocesan bishops discovered living in Rome were twice ordered back to their dioceses, and within six weeks of the second command they had all fled Rome. Paul ruthlessly solved the problem of the Datary by abolishing all fees — and thereby cutting his own revenue by two thirds at the very time he was preparing for war against Spain. Similar ruthless reform was extended to all branches of the Curia. In making nominations to high offices the pope absolutely refused to listen to the princes' recommendations. Nepotism was ended in dramatic and tragic fashion when the pope found that his own nephews, on whom he had bestowed the management of political affairs of the Papal States, were nothing but scoundrels. In a terrible scene he broke with his nephews and banished them from Rome.

Historians are not agreed on the value of Paul IV's pontificate for the Church. Many believe his measures were entirely too harsh. His pontificate lasted only four years, but it is important for marking a definite break with the abuses of the past. Nepotism had been practiced by his immediate predecessors who, good men though they were, used their office to build up their families' fortunes. Paul was unduly, even unjustly severe. An autocrat by disposition, he refused to call the Council of Trent back into session unless it should meet in Rome under his personal control. A series of such popes would most likely have hurt the Church badly, but Paul's short pontificate served the important purpose of breaking cleanly from the past.

In political affairs he blundered badly — but understandably — in provoking a war with Philip II. Paul IV was a Neapolitan by birth. He had served as nuncio in Spain, and had been archbishop of Naples. Thus he had experienced the rigors and difficulties of Spanish political control over the Church, and he brought to the papacy an abiding fear and hatred of Spain. In fashion reminiscent of Julius II he tried to organize a league to make war on Philip II in order to free Naples and Sicily in the south and Florence and Milan in the north from Spanish domination. Paul entered into a treaty with Henry II to attack Spain. But the promised French forces failed to materialize, and the Duke of Alva moved on Rome without serious opposition. Alva displayed the greatest deference to the pope, and in 1557 the Holy See's military fiasco was ended without great damage to the Church.

Paul IV died in August, 1559. After a delay of more than four months the cardinals finally chose as his successor a man who was known to be moderate, conciliatory, and accommodating. Pius IV was as sincerely devoted to Catholic reform as Paul IV had been, but he hoped to accomplish it through the Council of Trent. We have already seen that this was the main concern of his pontificate. Pius IV also reconciled the Holy See with the Catholic princes and set about accomplishing as much reform work as he could. The new pope refused to abolish any of his predecessor's reform decrees, but he enforced them with a measure of mildness and moderation. He was personally opposed to the Inquisition, for example, and though he did not abolish the institution he used it less vigorously than Paul IV had done.

Reform Measures of St. Pius V, Gregory XIII, and Sixtus V.   In January, 1566, the cardinals chose Michele Ghisleri to succeed Pius IV. The new pope was a Dominican, known for his piety and his austerity. He had been head of the Inquisition under Paul IV. Pius was strong and independent, like Paul IV, and possessed of the same rigorous disposition but he tempered it with true charity and piety. St. Charles Borromeo wrote to a friend explaining why he had worked for Cardinal Ghisleri's election: "Having known the Cardinal of Alessandria for a considerable time and conceived a high esteem for him on account of his singular holiness and zeal, I judged that no more fitting pontiff than he could be found to rule the Christian commonwealth wisely and well."

The new pope, who took the name of Pius V, devoted himself to the twofold task of enforcing the reform decrees of the Council of Trent and leading a Catholic offensive against the Turk and the Protestant. He was extremely stringent in granting dispensations and privileges of any kind, and in his famous bull *Admonet Nos* (1567) he came out unalterably against nepotism. He rigidly enforced the residence requirement on bishops, and he forced priests to live in their parishes. Nuns were required to keep faithfully within cloister. The Tridentine regulations governing relations between bishops and monks were strictly enforced. Within the Papal States, St. Pius V renewed disciplinary measures against shows, banquets, games, and other forms of public entertainment.

The most important of this pope's positive reform measures were the publication of the Tridentine Catechism, the new Breviary, and the new Missal. St. Pius V entrusted the publication of the new catechism to Dominicans, who drew up a compendium that was remarkable for its thoroughness, its theological accuracy, and its simplicity of statement. Bishops and priests were required to use this Catechism to ensure uniformity and accuracy of teaching to the faithful throughout the Church.

Reform of the Breviary and the Missal was long overdue and, as we saw in Chapter 24, the Council of Trent ordained that a revised Breviary and Missal be published as soon as possible. The Breviary had been adapted to humanist vogues during the Renaissance. Clement VII realized it had become more a literary than a religious book, so he entrusted its reform to a Franciscan named Quignonez. The new Breviary went to the opposite extreme of oversimplification. Classical allusions were suppressed, but so also were distinctions between classes of feasts, together with all verses, chapters, and responses. This new Breviary was severely criticized at the Council of Trent as contrary to all Catholic tradition, and Paul III suppressed it. The new reformed Breviary of St. Pius V retained the antiphons and responses of the seventh century, used the Vulgate version of the psalms and lessons, and by eliminating some feasts and reducing others it re-established the liturgical year. The Missal was similarly reformed. The new version made obligatory the recitation of the *Introibo* and *Confiteor* at the beginning of Mass, as well as the *Placeat* and the Gospel of St. John at the end.

Liturgical reform was completed by Gregory XIII. It culminated with the Gregorian calendar, made necessary by the fact that the Julian calendar did not correspond perfectly with the astronomical year. The civic year had fallen ten days behind the astronomical year by 1582, creating confusion in the liturgical as well as the civic year. The Gregorian calendar, now in general use throughout the world, was adopted in 1582 to fix the great Christian feasts in an accurate astronomical cycle. At first the Protestant countries refused to adopt the improved calendar, but by the end of the eighteenth century all large countries except Russia had accepted it. Gregory XIII also had Baronius publish a carefully corrected Roman Martyrology.

Gregory is best remembered as the founder of the modern system of seminaries. The Council of Trent had decreed that there should be a seminary in each diocese, but for a number of reasons the decree was not enforced in very many places. Lack of funds was an important reason. Even more important was the lack of trained personnel to staff an institution devoted to a thorough education of the clergy. Finally, most bishops did not appreciate the critical importance of education in the Catholic reformation. The task of providing seminaries in the spirit of Trent and the Catholic reformation, therefore, devolved upon the papacy. In 1564 Pius IV decided to establish a seminary in Rome, and the commission of cardinals appointed by the pope selected the Jesuits to staff it.

But it was Gregory XIII who put seminaries on a solid basis and made them part of the Catholic system. The Roman College was rebuilt in 1572 and made a college for young men of all nations. Gregory also restored the German College and founded an English College and another for Greeks. In each case the pope showed himself broad-minded and truly interested in the education of the clergy. The Greek College, for example, was staffed by Greek professors. The students wore the caftan and were allowed to use their own rite and their own language in Rome. Gregory also established 23 pontifical seminaries in Germany and other parts of Europe where bishops were unwilling or unable to carry out the Tridentine decree. The Gregorian seminaries were attached to Jesuit colleges, where the students were boarded at papal expense, took classes in the college, and received spiritual direction from Jesuit superiors. Some of the more important seminaries thus established by Gregory were at Vienna, Graz, Dilligen and Fulda, at Braunsberg, Olmütz, and Vilna.

Gregory's financial difficulties led him into political troubles that dimmed his reputation considerably. He spent large sums to subsidize the education of deserving young men for the priesthood, and the establishment of pontifical seminaries drained his treasury. He refused to impose new taxes or to revert to such old abuses as the sale of offices in order to increase his revenues. Finally, he hit upon the scheme of enforcing the feudal law of escheat on the property of nobles in the Papal States. As overlord, he asserted his right to property if the holder failed to fulfill the obligations imposed on him or if the original family line had become extinct. The theory of escheat was logical enough, but nothing was harder to enforce in the sixteenth century and nothing was more likely to stir up a hornets' nest of Roman nobles. All sorts of claims and suits arose. Factions of nobles were soon formed. Many of them insisted they would defend their property by arms. Many others took to banditry. Gregory dropped all his confiscation proceedings, but political life was in a state of turmoil when he died in 1585.

Sixtus V, who succeeded Gregory XIII, was a remarkably capable ruler. Under him the reform of the Church was pretty well completed, and political peace was re-established in the Papal States. Sixtus was a Franciscan noted for his ability and his piety. His first task was to suppress banditry and lawlessness in the Papal States. He accomplished this task by ruthlessly enforcing the law against noble and poor man alike. Even nobles who were caught hiding bandits were given the same punishment of death. The Protestant historian Leopold von Ranke tells us:[1] "No day passed without an execution. Over all parts of the country, in wood and field, stakes were erected, on each of which stood the head of an outlaw. The pope awarded praises only to those among his legates and governors who supplied him largely with these terrible trophies; his demand was ever for heads: there is a sort of oriental barbarism in this mode of administering justice." Bandits' heads were nailed to such prominent places as the bridge of St. Angelo as an example and a warning to the populace. These methods were terroristic; they were also effective.

Back of Sixtus V's ruthless suppression of lawlessness was his fear that conditions might develop in Rome such as had driven the popes to Avignon and prepared the way for the western schism and the conciliar movement. He was anxious that the Papal States be a model of political propriety as well as moral uprightness. Under him Rome was renewed and beautified so that it again looked like the capital of Christendom. He restored the columns of Trajan and Antoninus Pius, built many beautiful streets, finished St. Peter's basilica, and erected many landmarks still prominent in Rome, such as the Piazza di Spagna, the Lateran, and Santa Maria Maggiore.

Sixtus inherited a bad financial setup from Gregory XIII. He increased

[1] *The History of the Popes* (New York: 1901), I, 311.

taxes as much as possible, and then he reverted to the dangerous practice of selling Church offices. The practice did not result in abuses under Sixtus because the price for each office was fixed and the nominee knew what it would cost. Men of proved ability and virtue were chosen for each office. But under weaker popes this dangerous practice could lead back to the old abuses and even to simony.

There is no need to recount the way in which Sixtus executed the reform decrees of his predecessors. He rigorously enforced the measures on residency, the keeping of cloister, episcopal visitation, and the other Tridentine disciplinary measures. His original contribution in this respect was his formulation of the modern requirement of *ad limina* visits to Rome for all diocesan bishops. Sixtus V's reform work was political in character rather than religious. More than anyone else, it is he who gave the government of the Church its modern form of organization. He fixed the college of cardinals at 70 and established fifteen permanent congregations or commissions to deal with ecclesiastical business which had formerly been handled by the pope and his cardinals in consistory. Among the new congregations was that on Rites, which had charge of all liturgical matters, that on Studies, which supervised all Catholic universities, and that on Regulars, which governed all affairs of the religious orders. Every cardinal resident in Rome was required to serve on one or more of the congregations.

By 1590, when Sixtus V died, the papacy had not only reformed itself, but it had also modernized its government of the Church and had established sound temporal rule in the Papal States. The problem of reform is never permanently solved, of course, and pope after pope will have to pull the reins up tight as abuses begin to slip back into the papal government. But the reform had been accomplished by 1590. The problem for the next two centuries is to keep from sliding back into the old abuses. A more serious problem had developed during the Protestant Revolt and the Catholic Reformation: the old problem of Caesaro-papism in new guise, for the Catholic monarchs during sixteenth and succeeding centuries tried to take over the government and control of the Church.

Before we close our discussion of the Catholic Reformation we should see briefly what progress had been made in the closely allied movement known as the Catholic Counter-Reformation.

The Catholic Counter-Reformation.   The popes of this period were less successful in their attempt to inspire aggressive political action by the Catholic princes and to lend their support to warfare against the

Turk and the Protestant. In the last half of the sixteenth century the popes still looked on the Protestant Revolt as a movement that could be suppressed, as the Albigensian heresy had been in the thirteenth century, and thus European religious unity could be restored. Both in objectives and in means to attain them Pius V, Gregory XIII, and Sixtus V were medieval popes who ruled in modern times. All three called upon the Catholic princes for a crusade against the Turk. Only Pius V enjoyed any measure of success in this respect. A combination of religious, economic, and political reasons brought strong support to the pope from Spain and Venice. A combined fleet under Don Juan of Austria defeated the Turks in one of the decisive sea battles of history at Lepanto (October 7, 1571). This defeat spelled the end of Turkish domination of the Mediterranean. Gregory XIII formed a league with Venice and Spain to continue the war against the Turks, but both Venice and Spain found it politically expedient to withdraw from the alliance and make peace with the Turks. Sixtus V formulated grandiose plans which were simply not possible of realization in the sixteenth century. He planned to align with Russia and Persia against the Turk, bring Russia back to the Roman Church and the European group of nations, and finally to open new trade routes by joining the Red Sea and the Mediterranean.

These three popes also participated, with only meager success, in the Catholic counter-reformation on the continent of Europe. Pius V gave moral support to Mary Stuart and encouraged Catholic resistance to Elizabeth whom he excommunicated in 1570. At the time of his death he was thinking about a Catholic expedition to England. Gregory XIII and Sixtus V continued to think of such an expedition. They promised material and moral support to Philip II's projected Armada — but so great was their fear and mistrust of the Spanish king that the help was to be forthcoming only after Philip had landed armed forces on English soil. The plans to retake England by force of arms resulted in nothing, of course, except to increase Anglo-Saxon fear and hatred of the Roman Church.

The popes of the last half of the sixteenth century found themselves in a difficult political position. The leader of the aggressive counter-reformation in Europe was Philip II of Spain, who identified his national policy with the welfare of the Catholic Church. He labored and fought fervently for royal despotism within his lands and for Spanish domination of all Europe. He sincerely tried to stamp out heresy everywhere and to use all means available to enforce both his royal will and the Catholic religion. The popes were anxious to retake lands lost to the

Protestants — but they were almost as anxious not to increase Philip's power over the Church. They complained bitterly and frequently about Philip's control of the Church in Spain and about his too zealous use of the Inquisition for political as well as religious ends. They found it easy to co-operate with him in his struggle against the Turk in the Mediterranean, and with reservations they favored his aggressive policies in Europe.

In these affairs Philip — and with him the Catholic Church — was relatively unsuccessful. Philip's refusal to accommodate himself to certain reasonable requests of his subjects in the Netherlands drove these people to revolt. When they were involved in rebellion against Spain, as we have already seen, they adopted Calvinism. It can be said, then, that Philip's policies cost the Church the important area of Holland. We have seen that his attempt to invade England was a failure. He also tried to intervene in the Religious Wars in France with the double purpose of stamping out the Huguenots and obtaining the throne for his daughter and son-in-law. Frenchmen disliked Philip's interference, and they rallied around his enemy, Henry of Bourbon, who settled the religious problem by giving toleration to the Huguenots in 1598.

The Catholic counter-reformation enjoyed a larger measure of success in central Europe. There seemed every reason to believe in 1550 that the lands of the Hapsburgs would leave the Church, but by the end of the century a generation of zealous, informed, and morally respectable Catholics had grown up among the nobility. Under their aggressive leadership missioners began to win back a good part of southern Germany and even some places in central and northern Germany. Catholic princes supported the missionary and educational work of the Jesuits to bring about a combination of sound reform and political counter-reformation. Similar success was achieved in Poland and Hungary, where through their preaching and their colleges the Jesuits won back the nobility of each country. They were also influential in achieving the Union of Brest (1595), whereby the Ruthenian bishops reunited themselves to Rome in order to reform abuses in their dioceses. This was a notable victory for Catholic reform in Central Europe.

Catholic success in Germany was one of the factors that brought about the Thirty Years' War (1618–1648). This war began when the aggressively Catholic Ferdinand was elected king of Bohemia and Holy Roman Emperor. It began as a religious war, but in each of its four phases it became increasingly political in character. Catholic forces were generally successful in the first two phases of the Thirty Years' War, but the Protestant faction — supported by France, "the eldest daughter of the Church" — was generally successful in the last two phases. The result was to establish a religious as well as a political balance of power in the Germanies. The principle of *cujus regio ejus religio* was adopted by the three-hundred and some sovereign German states, and thus there were created several hundred petty religious tyrannies.

Pope Innocent X protested vehemently against the Treaty of Westphalia which ended the Thirty Years' War in 1648. He objected to the confiscation of ecclesiastical property which the treaty ratified and to many of the absurd religious arrangements it provided. Some bishoprics, for example, were to be held alternately by a Catholic and a Lutheran. At any rate, the Treaty of Westphalia marked the end of a period of history and the beginning of a new arrangement whereby the Catholic Church was one of several Christian churches. International politics were now carried on without reference to Rome. Religion had become pretty much a private affair for each individual. It was driven out of political and social life and put into a separate category labeled "religious." The process of secularization, so characteristic of modern history, was well under way.

Conclusion. The sixteenth century was of momentous importance in the history of the Catholic Church, for in that century the Church's monopoly of religious life in Western society was definitely broken by the Protestant Revolt. Those parts of Europe which were destined to become the aggressive nations of modern times — with the major exception of France — had left the Church in favor of one kind of Protestantism or another. Catholicism remained the established religion among those countries that were destined to play a less important role in modern history. Thus it came to be identified with the "Latin nations" and with an economic and social way of life that was backward as compared to that of the Protestant countries.

Meanwhile, the Catholic Church had undertaken its own reformation, excellently described by Janelle in this way:[2]

> Taken as a whole, the results obtained by the Catholic Reformation appear monumental. We might speak of it almost as a second birth of the Church; a Church, indeed, greatly reduced, at least in Europe, and from which all abuses had not been weeded out; a Church, nevertheless, purified and strengthened, concentrated, more sinewy, more capable of endurance, of bearing persecution at home and abroad, and of expanding in the mission

---

[2] Pierre Janelle, *The Catholic Reformation* (Milwaukee: 1949), 367.

field; a Church with its dogma clearly defined and firmly settled, fit to
serve as a rallying-point; a Church spiritually independent, and apt to play
its part in dealing with great moral, social, and charitable issues; last but
not least, a Church which was supported in its reforming action by literature and art, and which created a cultural movement of lasting value. A
sure sense indeed, of what was best in Renaissance letters and erudition
was found among the Christian humanists who became the Fathers of Trent.
At any rate, they undoubtedly had the leading part in preserving the heritage
of ancient culture, and all that it means for man, while raising it to the level
of the highest spiritual life; and in so doing they may be said to have largely
contributed to the moulding of the modern world.

Unfortunately, the spiritual renovation in the Church was accompanied
by concessions to the Catholic princes which in the seventeenth and
eighteenth centuries were to smother the Church and almost choke the
life from her. Unfortunately, too, so strong a union was established between Church and State under the Catholic princes that many people
in the nineteenth and twentieth centuries came to believe that the only
"natural" political setting for the Catholic Church was a despotic monarchy, and that the Church was somehow committed to reviving the
ancien regime if ever it could command the political conscience of the
people again. The Church enjoyed a short-lived spiritual revival in the
seventeenth century, however, before it settled down in the monarch's
smothering embrace.

REVIEW AIDS

1. Some historians maintain that Paul IV was exactly the kind of pope needed
   in 1555. Explain the line of reasoning behind such a claim.
2. List the five or six reform measures that you consider most important for
   the ending of abuses in the Church in the sixteenth century.
3. Why was it important for the papacy to prepare a Tridentine catechism and
   force bishops to have it used throughout the Church?
4. Consult a political map of Europe in the mid-sixteenth century to explain
   why the popes feared a strong Philip II.
5. Philip's detractors maintain that his primary aim was an increase of his
   personal power and that he subjected religion to this aim. His defenders
   maintain, on the other hand, that he sacrificed everything for the sake of
   the Catholic religion. What conclusions do you reach from your knowledge
   of his reign?
6. Explain how Spanish nationalism and Catholicism were identified with each
   other in the average Spaniard's mind.
7. Follow the career of St. Peter Canisius in some detail to show how solid
   Catholic reform and a political counter-reformation could work hand-in-hand.
8. Of what importance in the history of the Church were the accomplishments
   of the pontificate of St. Pius V? Explain in detail.

SUGGESTIONS FOR FURTHER READING

The reform work of the latter half of the sixteenth century is handled in detail by Pastor in Volumes XVII to XXII of his *History of the Popes*. Every student of modern Church history should make use of these volumes. Chapter XI of Janelle's *The Catholic Reformation* is devoted to this subject, as is the latter part of Mourret's *History of the Catholic Church*, Volume V.

Two biographies which contain the central thread of the story are Lillian Browne Olf, *The Sword of Saint Michael: Saint Pius V* (Milwaukee: 1943); and Joseph Alexander Hübner, *The Life and Times of Sixtus the Fifth* (London: 1872).

Available work on this period of Church history in English is difficult to find. For that reason the student is urged to consult appropriate articles in the *Catholic Encyclopedia*, especially those on the popes of the period, on the Breviary, the Missal, the Gregorian Calendar, and the Liturgy.

DOCUMENTS

Partial Text of the Bull *Regnans in Excelsis*

The following selection is from the Bull *Regnans in Excelsis* in which Pope St. Pius V lists the reasons for his solemn and formal excommunication of Queen Elizabeth. Historians have long argued whether the Bull was a prudential mistake, but there is no doubt of its legal correctness and of the indictment it contains.

. . . This woman having taken possession of the kingdom, unnaturally claims for herself the place, the great authority and jurisdiction of the sovereign head of the Church throughout all England, and has involved in miserable ruin that kingdom so lately recovered to the Catholic faith and piety.

She has forbidden by the strong hand of power the observance of the true religion, overturned by the apostate Henry VIII, and by the help of the Holy See restored by Mary, the lawful queen, of illustrious memory. She has followed after and accepted the errors of heretics. She has driven the English nobles out of the royal council, and filled their places with obscure heretics. She has been the ruin of those who profess the Catholic faith, and has brought back again the wicked preachers and ministers of impieties. She has done away with the sacrifice of the Mass, the Divine Office, fasting, the distinction of meats, celibacy, and the Catholic rites. She has ordered the use of books, containing manifest heresy, throughout the realm, and the observance by her subjects of impious mysteries and ordinances, according to the rule of Calvin, accepted and practised by herself.

She has dared to take away their churches and benefices from the bishops, the parish priests, and other Catholic ecclesiastics, and has given them with other ecclesiastical goods to heretics. She has made herself a judge in ecclesiastical causes. She has forbidden the prelates, clergy, and people to acknowledge the Church of Rome, or to obey its mandates and the Catholic constitutions. She has compelled many to take an oath to observe her wicked laws, to

	ENGLAND	FRANCE	SPAIN	THE EMPIRE
1500	Henry VIII (1509–47)		Death of Isabella (1504)	
1510	Wolsey, chancellor and papal legate (1515)	Francis I (1515–47) Concordat of Bologna (1516)	Death of Ferdinand (1516) Charles I (1516–56)	Charles V (1519–56)
1520	Henry VIII writes against Luther (1521) Henry VIII asks divorce (1527)	*Communeros* uprising (1520–21) War between France and Spain (1521–29) Sack of Rome (1527) Treaty of Cambrai (1529) Treaty of Madrid (1526) with The Empire		War with France (1521–26) The Peasants' War (1524–25) Battle of Pavia (1525) War with France (1527–29) Schmalkaldic League (1530)
1530	St. Thomas More beheaded (1535) Execution of Anne Boleyn (1536) Pilgrimage of Grace (1536)	War between France and Spain (1535–38)		War with France (1536–38) Catholic League of Nüremberg (1538)
1540	Edward VI (1547–53)	Henry II (1547–59)		War with France (1542–44) Schmalkaldic War (1546–47)
1550	Fall of Somerset (1550) Mary Tudor (1553–58) Mary and Philip II married (1554) War against France (1557) Elizabeth (1558–1603)	French capture Calais (1558) Francis II (1559–60)	Philip II (1556–98)	War with France (1552–56) Peace of Augsburg (15 Ferdinand I (1556–64)
	Treaty of Cateau — Cambrésis (1559)			
1560	Peace with France (1564)	Charles IX (1560–74) "Massacre of Vassy" (1562) The Religious Wars (1562–98) Peace and Edict of Amboise (1563)	Beginning of Netherlands' revolt (1567)	Maximilian II (1564–76)
1570		Peace of St. Germain (1570) Massacre of St. Bartholomew's Day (1572) Henry III (1574–89) Catholic League organized (1576)	Battle of Lepanto (1571)	Rudolf II (1576–1612)
1580	War with Spain (1588) Mary, Queen of Scots, executed (1587)	War of the three Henries (1585–89) Henry IV (1589–1610)	Philip II gets Portugal (1580) Defeat of the Armada (1588)	
		War between France and Spain (1589–98)		
1590	England banishes Catholics (1593) Irish Rebellion (1597)	Henry IV's conversion (1593) Religious wars end (1598) Edict of Nantes (1598)	Philip III (1598–1621)	

AND CATHOLIC REFORM

HE CATHOLIC CHURCH	THE PROTESTANT CHURCHES Lutheran	Reformed and Anglican	ECONOMIC, SOCIAL CULTURAL LIFE
s III (1503) ius II (1503–13)			Bourgeoisie gaining power Growth of commerce Unrest, criticism Artists flourishing: Dürer, Holbein, Leonardo da Vinci, Michelangelo, Raphael, Titian, Correggio, Rubens, etc.
th Lateran Council 1512–17) X (1513–21) atory of Divine Love 1517)	Luther posts his ninety-five theses (1517) Discussion at Leipzig (1519)		*The Praise of Folly* — Erasmus (1511) *Utopia* — Thomas More (1516)
rian VI (1522–23) ment VII (1523–34) k of Rome (1527) nry VIII's divorce alled to Rome (1529)	Diet of Worms (1521) Brandenburg adopts Lutheranism (1523)	Zwingli controls state council of Zurich (1525)	Serfdom spreads in central Europe Social unrest evident in peasant rebellions Renaissance architecture Palestrina (1526–94)
ul III (1534–49) undation of the Jesuits 1534) pe appoints commission of ine (1535) st call for council (1536)	Confession of Augsburg (1530) Wurtemberg adopts Lutherism (1534)	Cranmer grants Henry VIII's divorce (1533) Act of Supremacy (1534) Geneva adopts Protestantism (1536) Institutes of Christian Religion (1536) Bishop's Book (1533) Six Articles (1539)	*The Prince* — Machiavelli (1532)
lloquy of Ratisbon (1541) uncil of Trent meets (1545)		Calvin returns to Geneva (1541)	*Book of Common Prayer* (1548–52) Cervantes (1547–1616)
ius III (1550–55) rcellus (1555) ul IV (1555–59) us IV (1559–65)	Peace of Augsburg (1555)	42 articles & 2nd prayer book (1551–52) Catholicism restored to England (1554)	Study of Latin and Greek Education reforms in elementary and secondary levels European expansion Superstition widespread
uncil of Trent adjourns (1563) Pius V (1566–72)		Scottish Parliament adopts Calvinism (1560) *First Book of Discipline* (Scotland) (1561) 39 articles (1563)	Galileo Galilei (1564–1642)
egory XIII (1572–85)		Calvinism officially accepted in Holland (1574)	Johann Kepler (1571–1630) University of Leiden (1575)
lendar reform (1582) xtus V (1585–90) quisition reorganized (1588)			Marlowe and Sidney in England
rban VII (1590) regory XIV (1590–91) nocent IX (1591) ement VIII (1592–1605)		Edict of Nantes (1598)	Spenser — *Fairie Queene* (1590) Shakespeare, Donne, Spenser, R. Bacon, Ben Jonson, etc. becoming popular in England Descartes (1596–1650)

renounce the authority of the Roman Pontiff, to refuse to obey him, and to accept her as the sole ruler in temporal and spiritual matters. She has decreed pains and penalties against those who do not submit to her, and has inflicted them upon those who continue in the unity of the faith and obedience.

She has thrown Catholic prelates and parish priests into prison, where many, worn out by sorrows and their protracted sufferings, have ended their days in misery.

All this being notorious and known unto all nations, and so confirmed by very many grave witnesses, as to leave no room for palliation, defence, or concealment, sin being added to sin, and iniquity to iniquity, the persecution of the faithful, and the ruin of religion daily growing more and more at the suggestion and under the direction of Elizabeth aforesaid, whose will is so obstinate and whose heart is so hardened that she has set at nought not only the charitable prayers and counsels of Catholic princes entreating her to return to a better mind and be converted, but also Our own by her refusal to allow the Nuncios of the Holy See to enter the realm, We, having recourse, by necessity compelled, to the weapons of justice, are unable to control Our grief that We must proceed against one whose predecessors have rendered signal services to Christendom.

Relying then on His authority who has placed Us on this sovereign throne of justice, though unequal to the bearing of so great a burden, We declare, in the fulness of the apostolic power, the aforesaid Elizabeth a heretic, and an encourager of heretics, together with those who abet her, under the sentence of excommunication, cut off from the unity of the Body of Christ.

Moreover We declare that she has forfeited her pretended title to the aforesaid kingdom, to all and every right, dignity, and privilege; We also declare that the nobles, the subjects, and the people of the kingdom aforesaid, and all others who have taken any oath to her, are for ever released from that oath, and from every obligation of allegiance, fealty, and obedience, as We now by these letters release them, and We deprive the said Elizabeth of her pretended right to the throne, and every other right whatsoever aforesaid: We command all and singular the nobles, the people subject to her, and others aforesaid, never to venture to obey her monitions, mandates, and laws.

If any shall contravene this Our decree, We bind them with the same bond of anathema.

THE CHURCH AND THE ABSOLUTE STATE

Chapter 27

SEVENTEENTH-CENTURY REVIVAL AND MISSIONARY WORK

THE reform and recovery of the Church which we have followed in the past four chapters produced two general contrary results in the seventeenth and eighteenth centuries. In the first place, it produced a remarkable revival of the Church in France, a revival which Philip Hughes has termed "in some respects the most brilliant passage of the whole Counter-Reformation epic." This revival produced such great saints as Vincent de Paul, Francis de Sales, Jane Frances de Chantal, and John Francis Regis. It produced new orders for men and women, such as the Vincentians and Sulpicians, the nuns of the Visitation and of the Good Shepherd. In the second place, the Protestant Revolt and the Catholic Reform played into the hands of the king who was becoming an absolute ruler, and in Catholic countries the Church eventually was weakened nearly to the point of impotence as it became more and more a department of state under the monarch's control. The remarkable revival in France, then, was short-lived. It was followed by increasing decadence because of the secularism of the hierarchy and the class of society from which they came, but the good work of St. Vincent de Paul and his associates continued to bear fruit among the French peasantry and even to keep them loyal to the Church during the French Revolution.

In the seventeenth and eighteenth centuries the center of Catholic life shifted from Spain and Italy to France. The country of St. Louis took the initiative in spiritual life formerly held by Spain and by Italy. Under Richelieu and then under Louis XIV France became the center of European life culturally, politically, intellectually, even militarily. Religious life was no exception. In France, too, centered all those movements which were to wreak such havoc in the Church by 1800 — Gallicanism, Jansenism, Quietism, rationalistic deism, and agnosticism. In these two centuries Europe continued to have a certain measure of cultural unity. The hub of this culture was Paris. Its universal language was French. Both the good spiritual accomplishments and the intellectual-religious aberrations centering in France radiated throughout Europe to affect the Church in the Germanies, in Spain and the Italian countries, even in Ireland and in the American missions.

Religious Revival in France. The revival of religious life in France in the first half of the seventeenth century was a remarkable phenomenon. A number of canonized saints and other holy men began, almost simultaneously, to preach missions throughout France, to establish new contemplative or active orders, to organize works of charity, to popularize new devotions, and to set up institutions for the training of an excellent clergy and a devoted laity. These accomplishments were of lasting importance both in France and in the missionary field. Many of them exist down till our own time, despite the persecutions to which they were subjected, and they are part of the paradox of two Frances — the France of the saints and the France which is bitterly anticlerical and anti-religious.

The French Oratory, which has been called "the mainspring of Catholic reformation in France," was founded in 1611 by Peter de Bérulle. His purpose was to restore the priesthood in France to its proper dignity, for the upper classes in that country — including the hierarchy — tended to treat the priests as lowly servants. Bérulle gathered five other priests together to live a life in common in Paris. The Oratory was approved by Pope Paul V in 1613. The papal bull sketched this plan of life for the Oratory: "To live together in a society subject to rules; and, in a spirit of continual humility, to conduct themselves as servants of the Almighty, endeavoring especially to realize in all their acts the perfection of the priestly state; to remain subject to the bishops for the labors of the holy ministry; to devote themselves to the training of the clergy and to have these cultivate learning, not for the sake of learning itself, but for the services it can render the neighbor." Although modeled on St. Philip Neri's Oratory, Bérulle's foundation was somewhat different. The Oratorians were to be under the bishop of each diocese and they were to perform all the priestly functions. No vows were to be taken. The various foundations were under a superior-general and a general assembly which met every three years.

Within a few years the Oratorians found their special place in education. They took over a number of seminaries in France, one of the principal purposes Bérulle had in mind, and by the eighteenth century they ranked second only to the Jesuits in the number of colleges they conducted. From the Oratory came a number of men who were important in reforming and improving the French clergy. Most important of these were Charles de Condren, Adrian Bourdoise, St. John Eudes, and Jean Jacques Olier. These men believed that the welfare and the holiness of the Church was intimately connected with good diocesan clergy. The latter, they believed, should live in common in each parish, observe a life of poverty and of complete devotion to their calling.

Fathers de Condren and Bourdoise continued the work of Bérulle, establishing communities of priests in various places throughout France. They were convinced that the secret of the regular clergy's success lay in the novitiate, and therefore each diocese should provide the equivalent in a seminary for the training of the diocesan clergy. St. John Eudes took the first step toward founding seminaries on a large scale in France. He preached a series of especially successful missions in Normandy, during which time he became more than ever convinced of the need of well conducted seminaries. When his superior-general refused to allow him to establish any, he left the Oratory and founded the Congregation of Jesus and Mary. No special vows were required. The Eudistes, as they were called, confined themselves to the education of the clergy and the preaching of missions. During their founder's lifetime they opened five seminaries. St. John Eudes also founded the Congregation of the Good Shepherd for the saving of fallen girls.

This work of educating the diocesan clergy was continued by Jean Jacques Olier and by St. Vincent de Paul. Olier had come under the influence of St. Vincent de Paul at St. Lazare, had preached missions for him, and then had joined the Oratory at Paris. At de Condren's suggestion Father Olier and two companions set up a "seminary" in a suburb of Paris. Soon they had eight students leading a common life with them. Thus arose the distinctive trait of the Sulpicians — the same rule of life for teachers and students. When Olier became the pastor of St. Sulpice, the "seminary" followed him to his new residence. Gradually the Company of St. Sulpice, or the Sulpicians, came into being. By the time Olier died in 1657 he had established five seminaries which his men staffed.

A generation earlier than St. John Eudes and Father Olier, St. Francis de Sales had made his own great contributions to the revival of the Church in France. St. Francis de Sales became a model priest, spending most of his time preaching and hearing confessions. He undertook the re-conversion of the Calvinist canton of Chablais, and in 1602 he was made bishop of Geneva with his see at Annecy. He became a model for bishops of this age. Together with St. Jane Frances de Chantal he founded the Order of the Visitation. His plan was to establish an active order of women without enclosure, but Roman objections to such a plan forced him to make the order contemplative. Francis de Sales is most important in the history of the Church, however, as a director of conscience and a guide in modern asceticism.

St. Vincent de Paul.   The entire movement of reform and recovery of the Church in France is summed up in the life and labors of St. Vincent de Paul. The founder of two religious communities, a great missionary and director of souls, St. Vincent is even better known for his love of the poor and his work to alleviate their physical as well as their spiritual misery. He was ordained a priest in 1600. On a journey to Rome five years later he was captured by the Barbary pirates and sold as a slave in Tunis. He escaped in 1607 and returned to Paris, where he came under the influence of Father Bérulle.

St. Vincent soon held a place of confidence among the important court people. He was appointed chaplain of Margaret of Valois, tutor to the son of Philip de Gondi, general of the royal galley. In 1617, at Madame de Gondi's request, he preached a mission to the country people of Picardy. When St. Vincent failed to interest either the Jesuits or the Oratorians in Madame de Gondi's plan to have missions preached throughout all the territory dependent on the Gondi family, he undertook the work himself. In every village he established the "Association of Charity of the Servants of the Poor." Meanwhile, St. Vincent worked untiringly for convicts and galley slaves, with the result that he was made royal chaplain of the galleys in 1619.

In 1624 St. Vincent established the Congregation of the Mission.

The purpose of this foundation was to preach on the Gondi estates and later elsewhere in France. The priests of the congregation were to be entirely dependent on the bishop and the pastor in whose parish they were preaching. In 1632 the congregation settled in the priory of St. Lazare in Paris, hence the popular name "Lazarists" for the Congregation of the Mission.[1] Within a few years the congregation took on a new work, teaching in seminaries. St. Vincent began giving retreats to ordinandi as a means of improving the French clergy. In 1632 the archbishop of Paris required all clerics in his archdiocese to make a retreat with St. Vincent and receive two weeks of instruction in their priestly duties before ordination. Thus a regular institution was established, and within a few years the bishops of neighboring dioceses were sending their prospective priests to St. Lazare. St. Vincent felt that something more than a short course of instruction and a retreat was needed to prepare good diocesan priests. First he tried to set up the equivalent of a novitiate in the form of a "minor seminary" attached to the College des Bons Enfants at the University of Paris. When most of the students left without receiving holy orders, St. Vincent decided to set up a "major seminary" for men over twenty. His plan was to receive subdeacons, deacons, and priests. In two or three years they could be trained in priestly virtue and educated in the use of the liturgy and ceremonies. With the help of Cardinal Richelieu the Congregation of the Mission set up such a seminary in Paris. Within a few years several diocesan seminaries throughout France were entrusted to the congregation.

Meanwhile, St. Vincent had worked with Louise de Marillac to establish the Daughters of Charity. These sisters, he insisted, were not to be religious but rather secular, for they were to work in the world. The four or five country girls gathered together in 1633 lived without written rules of any kind for several years. Their work was widespread: in the hospitals and schools, visiting the sick, bringing charity into the world. Thus was established a religious community of women without cloister. The Daughters of Charity were approved by Rome in 1668, eight years after St. Vincent's death.

Judged by concrete accomplishments, St. Vincent de Paul lived one of the most useful lives in the history of Christendom. We do not have space in this survey to describe all his activities. They have been well summed up by one writer:[2]

---

[1] They are generally known as Vincentians in this country.

[2] Quoted by Dom Charles Poulet, *A History of the Catholic Church* (St. Louis: 1940), II, 183.

He reformed the treatment of prisoners; he built free schools for working-class children; he founded houses for deserted children; he arranged vocational training for young lads and girls; he established homes for the aged and anticipated that husband and wife should not be separated, as is the case in most institutions, but should spend their remaining days together. St. Vincent made such adequate provision for the regular relief of the destitute that there was no excuse left for street begging [in Paris], which was accordingly abolished. He recruited and trained what have been called his armies of charity, lay men and lay women, as well as the consecrated Sisters of Charity, to visit and relieve the poor in their homes, and he organized a vast work for relieving the provinces devastated by war.

Additional Foundations of the Seventeenth-Century Revival. The revival of the Church in France involved a number of additional foundations we do not have space to consider in any detail. The Brothers of the Christian Schools were founded by St. John Baptist de la Salle to educate the poor children in a practical way. The Trappists were a reformed abbey founded by Abbot Rancé to practice the most austere life of silence, poverty, prayer, and manual labor. Devotion to the Sacred Heart of Jesus was revived in France by a nun of the Visitation who belonged to the community at Paray-le-Monial in Burgundy. St. Margaret Mary Alacoque was bidden by our Lord in a series of apparitions to establish the practice of honoring His Sacred Heart especially on the first Friday of each month. The new devotion met with general opposition because it fell under the suspicion of Quietism (which we shall discuss in the next chapter), and Father Croiset's book *The Devotion to the Sacred Heart* was put on the Index in 1704. The devotion gradually came to be accepted in Catholic circles in the eighteenth century, however, and in 1765 Pope Clement XIII decreed that the Feast of the Sacred Heart be placed in the liturgical calendar.

The most curious development of this age, however, was the Company of the Blessed Sacrament, founded in 1627 by the Duc de Ventadour. The Company included a number of canonized saints, many priests and bishops and other prelates, but it was under lay control. It was a sort of secret society organized to help every form of Catholic activity. The Company made many of St. Vincent de Paul's ventures possible, and it forced reform on a number of lackadaisical bishops throughout the country. The Company spread rapidly through France. Its members worked as individuals to put down all forms of vice — prostitution, drunkenness, profanity, and the like — and to force virtuous living on the country. Such an organization, which depended only on the religious zeal of its

members, ran the danger of becoming a pious snooping society. The aim
of the Company was always good, but abuses in means to attain its good
purpose caused the Company to fall into ill repute, and in 1663 it was
suppressed by Louis XIV.

Missionary Activity. Missionary activity never completely ceased in
the Church which had been commissioned by God to preach His word
to all nations. The desire to spread the faith was an important motive
for Portuguese and Spanish explorations of the latter fifteenth century.
But the Catholic Reformation gave new impetus to the missionary movement, especially because the renewed vitality of the Augustinians, Franciscans, and Dominicans, and most of all the tremendous zeal of the Jesuits
found expression in this apostolic work. The missionary movement of this
period is perhaps the most important single movement within the Catholic
Reformation of the sixteenth and early seventeenth centuries. It spread
the Catholic faith, which till then was practically coterminous with
Europe, to all corners of the globe. It made the Catholic Church something closer to an actually universal Church. Finally, missionaries spread
European culture throughout the world and protected natives everywhere from some of the worst brutalities of the European colonizers.

From the very beginning, the popes encouraged missionary activity.
Pope Pius V appointed a committee of cardinals for the conversion of
the infidel, and Gregory XIII created a committee to deal with Eastern
rites and the reunion of the Eastern and Western or Roman Churches.
Papal encouragement of the missions was climaxed by the creation, in
1622, of the Sacred Congregation for the Propagation of the Faith, better
known as the Congregation of the Propaganda. This congregation had
ultimate jurisdiction, as it still has, over all missionary activity. By 1622,
however, the new missions abroad were already a century old. They
had been planted — and many flourished — in the Americas, in Africa,
and in various parts of Asia.

These accomplishments are in many ways amazing. They took place
in the face of great difficulties which, it seems today, were not always
solved to the best advantage of the Church. In the first place, the missionary was identified in the native's mind with the European conqueror.
It is true that the missionary was generally the native's sole protector among
Europeans. It is true that the missionary complained of the conqueror's
barbarity and obtained royal decrees to restrain such barbarity. But it
is also true that the missionary was backed by the force of arms, and very
frequently religion was imposed on the native against his will.

In the second place — more serious and more complex in the long run — was the identification of the Catholic religion with Western European culture. The Catholic faith had been so closely intermeshed with European culture for centuries that the two were looked upon by European Catholics as different manifestations of the same basic thing. With the faith, then, the missionaries tried to impose upon the rest of the world the European way of life. Many men who labored in the field understood how this hampered their work and made almost impossible the lasting conversion of native peoples. Especially did the Jesuits in China understand that the Catholic faith should not be identified with any single culture or way of life. Unfortunately, the identification had been so deeply made in European minds that the missionary was psychologically unable to make necessary concessions to non-European cultures. In short, the tremendous success of the missionary activity of this period fell short of its potential greatness because the Catholic faith was not set free from the European culture in which it had been embedded for centuries.

The American Missions.   The first American mission was in 1494 on the island of Hispaniola. Within a few years Franciscans and Dominicans had arrived in sizable numbers, and in 1511 three episcopal sees were established on the islands of Hispaniola and Puerto Rico. The missionaries were hindered by the barbarous way the Spanish conquistadors treated the natives, for "Spanish" and "Christian" were identical in the Indians' mind, and both were equally odious. Dominicans protested to the king as early as 1510, but the king's order to treat the natives kindly was ignored by most Spaniards. In 1515 Bartolomé de las Casas returned to Spain to plead the Indians' cause. He received the support of Ximenes. The Spanish government officially took over the protection of the Indians. Its policy was formulated in the New Laws of 1542, which were humane and just, but which were very difficult to enforce from Spain. However, this new policy both saved the Indians from extinction and rendered Christianity more appealing to them.

Missionaries followed Cortes into Mexico, Franciscans arriving in 1524, Dominicans two years later, and Augustinians in 1533. By 1559 there were about 800 members of the three orders in Mexico, and by 1570 they had established 140 monasteries or foundations. The number of baptisms was astounding. No accurate statistics were kept, but Peter of Ghent tells of baptizing 14,000 daily, and we know that the total number ran into the millions. There is no good reason for doubting the sincerity of these conversions, but there is question whether the Indians could have been well enough instructed in the faith properly to understand it.

The missionaries seem to have been generally conscientious in the matter of instructing their Indian converts. However, their fear that the Indian might carry over some of his pagan beliefs caused the missionary to use Castillian words to convey the concepts of the new religion, and it is likely that these concepts were generally not well understood. Nevertheless, the three orders accomplished wonderful work in these early years. They not only baptized the Indians, but they gathered them into villages, protected them from exploitation by the white man, taught them practical skills, and even established colleges with a surprisingly high degree of scholarship.

The missionaries followed the Spanish conquerors into Peru, Chile, throughout all South America, and into parts of North America as well. Pizarro, the conqueror of Peru, was accompanied by his Dominican nephew, Peter of Valverde, but the extreme cruelty of the conquering Spanish group hampered the work of conversion for some time. The evangelization of Peru was due chiefly to St. Turibius, a Spanish nobleman appointed archbishop of Lima by Philip II in 1580. He preached throughout his diocese, held provincial synods, founded the first American seminary, and established a number of schools and hospitals.

From Peru the Dominicans spread down to Chile and across to Colombia or New Granada. In each province they established a university. Meanwhile, Jesuits had entered the American missionary field in large numbers. They played a large role in the evangelization of Peru and Colombia where St. Peter Claver, the special patron of all the missions to the Negroes, worked untiringly to alleviate the misery of the Negro slaves imported from Africa. Jesuits played the leading role in Brazil and Paraguay. Here they developed the famous *reductions* or villages, from which they excluded Europeans so that they could better control the Indian's spiritual and social life. The villages were models of Christian living in many ways, but unfortunately they became the envy of greedy adventurers and they played some part in the machinations that brought about the suppression of the Jesuits in the eighteenth century.

The conditions under which the American missionaries worked were such that it is impossible to pass any final judgment on their efforts. The ground they covered, the numbers they baptized, and the institutions they founded are all astounding in numbers alone. When consideration is given to the obstacles encountered — the ignorance of the Indian, the language barrier, difficulty of travel, problems presented by the greedy European conqueror — these accomplishments are even more astounding. The work was accomplished almost exclusively by the religious orders. Unfortunately, the Spanish secular clergy who engaged in missionary activity were not exemplary priests, and no substantial native clergy was developed to carry on the work of the regular clergy who set out from Spain and Portugal.

The evangelization of Canada by French missionaries early in the seventeenth century does not appear as tremendous a success at first sight as does the work of Spanish missionaries in South America. But we should remember that the French missionary did not receive the same wholehearted support from the crown that the Spanish missionary did. Moreover, he had to work in the face of English Protestant hostility to the south, and against the French traders who were afraid that their business would be hurt if colonists became too numerous or the native Indians too civilized. The French missionary was part of a bigger movement going on in France in the seventeenth century, the remarkable revival of the faith that we considered earlier in this chapter, and he drew both his inspiration and his personnel from that movement.

Franciscans were the first to arrive in Canada, but it was the Jesuits who enjoyed the greatest success. In 1625 Fathers John Brébeuf and Gabriel Lalemand came to Canada. Within a few years they were followed by a number of other Jesuits. The most famous of these is St. Isaac Jogues who was martyred in 1646 by the hostile Iroquois Indians. From "New France" such famous French missionaries as Father Jacques Marquette and Louis Hennepin traveled westward and southward into the Mississippi valley, and still others came down into what is now Maine. The failure of the French government to push its claims in North America, however, confined successful evangelizing activity to the area along the St. Lawrence River.

Two centers of religious life were set up in New France. The first of these was Quebec, where the Jesuits established a college in 1635, and where the see of the first bishop, Francis de Montmorency-Laval, was established in 1659. Laval built a seminary and established a number of parishes outside the city. The second center of religious life in Canada was Montreal. Here a hospital was built and entrusted to a congregation of sisters established for that purpose, the Sisters of Notre Dame. In 1657 the first Sulpicians came to Montreal, where they worked both as pastors for the colonists and missionaries among the Indians.

Missions in the Far East. Conditions were not as favorable for mass conversions in the Far East as they had been in the Americas. Whereas the American Indian was relatively simple and uncivilized and therefore easily impressed by European culture, the people of the East possessed a culture with a fully developed religion and a philosophy which could not easily be overcome by a handful of missionaries. Moreover, the Portuguese explorers were in no position to protect the missionaries, for they had set up nothing more than a thin line of forts and trading posts throughout the East. Most of the Portuguese, finally, led a scandalous existence and were therefore a poor example of living Christianity.

The evangelization of large parts of the Far East was due very much to the labors of one man — St. Francis Xavier, who has since been made patron of the missions. Eight Franciscans had accompanied Cabral to India in 1500, and in 1510 when Albuquerque took Goa he turned over one of the mosques to the Franciscans. Although Goa was made an episcopal see in 1534, the missionaries labored in this area without much success until St. Francis Xavier arrived there in 1542. Realizing that he could not change the Portuguese inhabitants' scandalous lives simply by preaching, Xavier collected their children for prayer and instruction. Before long he was preaching to thousands of natives in the neighboring towns. His technique was to use interpreters to put the simple prayers into the native dialect and then to teach these essentials to the masses of prospective converts. A few of the most intelligent he instructed more thoroughly, putting his teaching in written form, and these he left behind as catechists to continue the work he had begun.

Xavier labored in the south of India for more than three years. Then he traveled to the Portuguese colonies of Malaya, Malacca, and the Moluccas, where he used the techniques developed in India with great success. After two and a half years of such travel, he returned for another year and a half to Goa. In 1549 he journeyed to Japan where, in two years, he converted about 2000 natives and made a favorable impression on the *elite* of Japanese society. Xavier found it necessary to change his technique in Japan to one of rational disputation and to dress as a person of social consequence. Within the space of twenty years his successors had converted more than 30,000 natives to the faith. Meanwhile, Xavier planned to go to China, the wealthiest, most populous, and most influential country in the East. But he died of tropical fever at the age of 46 before he entered China. Xavier is said to have brought about 700,000 souls to the Catholic faith, but even more important he did the preparatory work for further conversions. Wherever Xavier preached, the Catholic faith continued to prosper, except in Japan where it was stamped out by one of the most severe persecutions in modern times.

Xavier's work in India was continued successfully by the Jesuit Robert de Nobili. Xavier had appealed to the lower castes in India. He failed completely to convert the Brahmins, who looked down on a religion that appealed to the pariahs and whose priests used cow leather and ate cow meat. Father de Nobili overcame these prejudices by living like a Hindu among the Hindus. He allowed his converts to retain whatever national customs he thought were free from superstition and idolatry. He was nevertheless attacked by other missionaries, especially by the Dominicans, but in 1623 Pope Gregory XV sanctioned his actions and decreed that there should be two classes of missionaries in India, one for the Brahmins and another for the lower classes.

Missionary work in Japan progressed after Xavier's death with unusual success. Jesuits, Franciscans, Dominicans, and Augustinians won many converts, especially under Emperor Nobunaga (1565–1582) who favored Christianity. The number of Christians increased to 200,000 by 1582, and forty years later it had reached 600,000. There seemed reason to believe that Japan would become a thoroughly Catholic island. In 1587 the first of the terrible Japanese persecutions began when the new emperor ordered all missionaries to leave the country within twenty days. After a period of comparative peace, a new persecution began in 1610 and was renewed in 1624. Altogether more than 3000 Christians were martyred for their faith. In 1650 Christianity was absolutely proscribed in Japan. A handful of Japanese Christians managed, without priests, to cling to their faith for more than two centuries, and several thousand of them were found still practicing their faith in 1865.

The missions proceeded more tranquilly throughout the area lying between India and China. Led by Father Alexander of Rhodes, missionaries evangelized Laos and Cambodia, Tonkin and Cochin-China. By the middle of the seventeenth century the native Christians in this area numbered about a half million.

The attempt to convert China, which had been Xavier's desire, gave rise to a serious problem which was solved in such a way as to make the conversion of that country impossible in the seventeenth and eighteenth centuries. The first successful missionary work in China was done by the Jesuit Matteo Ricci. Father Ricci combined the methods that Xavier had used successfully in Japan and Nobili had employed in

India. He planned to convert the masses of the people by winning over the class of scholarly mandarins. He therefore dressed as a mandarin and earned their respect through his scientific knowledge. Furthermore, he allowed the prospective Chinese converts to keep every element of their native culture that was not clearly superstitious or idolatrous. He even allowed them to use various native terms for God, although the connotation of these terms was not theologically accurate.

Father Ricci translated the first six books of Euclid into Chinese and he prepared a catechism in such perfect idiomatic Chinese that it was widely accepted among the literate natives of the land as a classic. The missionary found favor with the emperor at Peking and until his death in 1610 he continued to convert a number of important Chinese literati to Christianity. He was succeeded by a Father Longobardi, who was strongly opposed to allowing the Chinese Christians the use of their own rites. The Jesuits were the only missionary priests in China until 1631. When Dominicans arrived in 1631 some were shocked and scandalized to find the Chinese using rites that seemed idolatrous. In 1643 their Father Morales referred the question to Rome, and the Chinese rites he described were condemned by Pope Innocent X in 1645. The Jesuits asked and received permission to present their case for the Chinese rites, and a decree of Pope Alexander VII in 1656 "allowed to the Chinese the said ceremonies, with all superstitions removed, because it seemed that they constituted a rite purely civil and political."

The dispute over Chinese rites continued until Pope Clement XI ended the matter peremptorily in 1704 by absolutely forbidding the Chinese rites and prohibiting the use of all Chinese terms for God except *Tien-chu*. Some of the missionaries appealed the decision on the grounds that their labors in China would be in vain if the Chinese rites were banned. In 1710 the prohibition was renewed, and in 1715 everyone concerned with Chinese missionary work was required to take an oath of obedience to the prohibition of Chinese rites. The Jesuits and other European missionaries obeyed. But the majority of the native clergy apostatized, and the emperor declared that he could not tolerate a religion which ran counter to all native customs. All missionaries were expelled from China and thus came to an end — until the latter nineteenth century — the apostolic work in China.

The question of Chinese rites raised a number of basic problems that continue to confront the Church in mid-twentieth century. It is easier to win converts, of course, if religious practices are adapted to native languages and customs. But such adaptation cannot go so far as to change the essentials of the faith — in creed, code, or cult. Prudent men do not agree in specific cases just where to draw the line between those adaptations which are permissible and those which are not. This gives rise to a further serious consideration: the Catholic Church, which is universal, developed for centuries in a certain culture, that of the Western world, and its ceremonies, its doctrines, and its moral teaching all came to be expressed in the languages of the Western world. The danger, therefore, presents itself of identifying the Catholic Church with a local culture and of believing that the conversion of non-Western peoples involves their conversion to a culture as well as to a faith. The problem of maintaining unity in the Church and not restricting its universality continues down into the twentieth century to be one of the most complex and difficult problems faced by the Church.

The African Missions.   Missionary activity in Africa began as early as the latter part of the fifteenth century, but it was not successful until the nineteenth century. Missionaries had accompanied the Portuguese explorers around the African coast, and in 1491 a Dominican mission went up the Congo river into the interior. The see of San Salvador was erected here in 1595. From it Jesuit and Capuchin missionaries traveled into equatorial Africa.

The most remarkable missionary work in Africa was that done by the Jesuits in Ethiopia. St. Ignatius sent some of his followers there as early as 1546. For a considerable time the missionaries were restrained by the opposition of the Monophysite Emperor Claudius. At length Father Peter Paëz won the emperor's favor, secured his conversion to Roman Catholicism, and obtained his permission to convert several hundred thousand schismatics to the Roman faith. Later missionaries prohibited certain national customs which the church of Ethiopia had long practiced, such as a national liturgy. National feeling was consequently turned against the Roman missionaries, and the new emperor re-established the Ethiopian Monophysite religion and expelled the Jesuits.

Attempts of the Lazarists to evangelize the Barbary Coast and Madagascar were similarly unsuccessful, partly because of Mohammedan opposition, partly because of the bad climate, and partly because the Roman rite did not appeal to the natives. It was not until the nineteenth century, as we shall see later, that any notable headway was made by missionaries in these regions.

REVIEW AIDS

1. Consult the Catholic Directory to find what establishments in this country are conducted by the Lazarists or Vincentians, by the Sulpicians, the Christian Brothers, the Trappists.
2. Show why formal institutions for the training of the diocesan clergy were the essential part of a religious revival in France. If necessary, consult one or two good secular histories to find out the social and political organization of the country which confined the ordinary priest to a lowly position and put the hierarchy out of touch with the country.
3. Show with specific examples why it is correct to call Father Bérulle's Oratory "the mainspring of the Catholic reformation in France."
4. Prepare a list of St. Vincent de Paul's various activities and foundations.
5. St. Francis de Sales is sometimes said to have perfected a "secularized asceticism." What does this mean? In what sense is the statement true?
6. What are advantages and the dangers of an organization such as the Duc de Ventadour's Company of the Blessed Sacrament?
7. Contrast the official Spanish attitude toward the Indian with that of the Englishman. To what extent was the missionary responsible for this attitude?
8. In what way is it true to say that the Portuguese and Spanish missionaries were spiritual conquistadors? In what essential respects did they differ from the secular conquistador?
9. Prepare a list of reasons in favor of the Jesuit missionary technique as practiced by Father Ricci. Prepare a list of dangers involved in such a method.
10. From these lists write an essay on the difficult problem facing the Church in trying to convert peoples of a different culture from that in which the Catholic Church has developed.

SUGGESTIONS FOR FURTHER READING

An interesting discussion of missionary work through the ages is contained in the work of Georges Goyau, *Missions and Missionaries* (London: 1932). There is a voluminous literature consisting of the journals kept by missionaries and their correspondence with people at home. Among the most interesting of these journals is the recently edited work of Matteo Ricci, *China in the Sixteenth Century: The Journals of Matthew Ricci* (New York: 1953). Older but still very interesting is the work of a man who died in 1632, Christoforo Borri, *An Account of Cochin-China* (London: 1744). A general history of missionary work is given in the English translation of Joseph Schmidlin, *Catholic Mission History* (Techny, Ill.: 1933). A good insight into the Chinese missions is contained in Charles Wilfrid Allan, *Jesuits at the Court of Peking* (Shanghai: 1935). A new insight to the Chinese rites problem is given by Malcolm Hay, *Failure in the Far East* (Philadelphia: 1957), who demonstrates from archive sources that the principal opposition to the Jesuit missions in China came from Jansenists who were influential with the Congregation for the Propagation of the Faith. The work of the Jesuits in Canada is revealed interestingly by Daniel Sargent's biography, *Catherine Tekakwitha* (New York: 1936). Spanish missionary work in America can be seen in Louis Anthony Dutto, *The Life of Bartolome de Las Casas* (St. Louis: 1902), and Thomas Francis Cullen, *The Spirit of Serra* (New York: 1935). The Roman viewpoint on missionary work is found in various chapters of Pastor's *History of the Popes*, Volumes XII, XIII, XVIII, XX, and XXVI.

A good general description of the France in which the Catholic revival took place is found in Jacques Boulenger, *The Seventeenth Century* (New York: 1933). The various aspects of the revival can most easily be followed in biographical accounts of the leading actors of the time. Among the many biographies relevant to this subject, the following are particularly worth noting: Edward Healy Thompson, *The Life of M. Olier* (London: 1861); Henry Bordeaux, *St. Francis de Sales: Theologian of Love* (New York: 1929); the three-volume work of Pierre Coste, *The Life and Works of Saint Vincent de Paul* (London: 1934–1935); and the shorter biography of the same saint by Theodore Maynard, *Apostle of Charity* (New York: 1939).

DOCUMENTS

A. Letter of St. Vincent de Paul to Father Claude Dufour, who was thinking of leaving the Congregation of the Mission to become a Carthusian

The following letter of St. Vincent de Paul to Claude Dufour, a member of his Congregation, is valuable for revealing the Saint's idea that there is a vocation to the active priesthood as well as to contemplative life in Holy Orders. Father Dufour wanted to leave the Congregation of the Missions to join the Carthusians, and St. Vincent advises him that his vocation lies in active rather than contemplative life.

I give thanks to God, Sir, for the many blessings He has bestowed on your labors in behalf of the priests and ordinands; and I beg Him to bless in like manner the seminary which you are beginning, and not to permit the temptation, which you experience against your vocation, to trouble the peace of your soul. I know well that the Order of the Carthusians is more perfect in itself, but I do not believe that God is calling you to embrace it, after having called you here and given you the grace to follow His inspirations, by answering this call. In this, His goodness has bestowed upon you a very special benediction, and one that is of such a nature, that if you consider it well, should serve constantly to strengthen you in your vocation, especially if you place yourself in the state in which you would wish to be found at the judgment seat of God. Place in the balance, if you please, the advantages of solitude on the one hand, and on the other, those which our Lord bestows and will continue to bestow more and more upon you, and you will find that the latter outweigh the former. Take also into consideration the conformity of your life at present to that which our Lord led upon earth. Bear in mind that it is in this your vocation consists and that the Church today is in the greatest need of laborers, who will strive to withdraw the greatest number of her children from the ignorance and vice in which they are plunged, and to obtain for her good priests and pastors, which was what the Son of God came on earth to do, and you will esteem yourself only too happy to be employed like Him and by Him in this holy work. You know, Sir, that although the contemplative life is more perfect than the active, it is not however more so than that which embraces both the contemplative and the active, as does yours by the grace of God. But, suppose the contrary, it is certain that God does not call everyone to the most perfect things. All the members of the body are not the head, nor are all the angels included in the first hierarchy; those of the inferior orders do not wish to belong to the superior; they are satisfied with those in which God has placed them: and the blessed in heaven, who enjoy less glory, do not envy those who are in possession of greater. We should likewise be content with the state in which we are placed by the disposition of Providence, and to which God gives His blessing.

B.   Matteo Ricci's description of how the Jesuits were accepted at Peking

Matteo Ricci, who died in 1610, enjoyed remarkable success as a missionary among the Chinese. His technique of accepting and respecting the national culture is exemplified in the following selection, in which Father Ricci explains how the Jesuits got an audience with the Emperor. Unfortunately, his successors did not all use his judicious care in accepting Chinese social customs, and it is not until our own age that missionaries follow his general practices.

Once they began to appear in public, the first care of the Fathers was to see to it that they should never be forced to leave Pekin, and then to go about acquiring all the liberty possible to preach the Gospel, and to this end they endeavored to enlist the interest of the Magistrates of the Court of Ceremonies. These Magistrates in turn were growing tired of having their requests left unanswered, and were ready, in one way or another, to put an end to the whole affair. The revisor of requests intended for the King, being a friend of Father Matthew, was also enlisted in the cause in the following manner. They sent him a very accurately drawn up document, to be presented to the sovereign, in which they informed him that they had been prompted to come here because of the nobility and of the renown of the Chinese Kingdom, that they had been on the way for years previous, and that they had lived here in a way that had won the friendship of everyone, even of the highest dignitaries. Only last year, as they explained, they had come into the Royal City in order to offer a few small presents they had gotten together for the King, the best of which was an image of Christ the Saviour, presented for the conservation of peace in the kingdom, and for the happiness and prosperity of the royal family. These presents they had offered as an evidence of their affection and as a proof of their loyalty to the King. They gave assurance that they were looking for nothing in return, because they were men dedicated to the service of God, celibates, without children or dependents, and so without need of supporting families. They assured him that the only request they were making was that the King should designate some place, in the city or elsewhere, for them to live. This request was no more successful than the others. No doubt, it was not answered because according to the law it should have been presented to the Court of Ceremonies, which had already made its mind known to the King, namely, that they did not wish to have the Fathers in the Court City. Instead of sending a formal written reply to this request, the King expressed his decision verbally, and it reached the Fathers through some of the chief eunuchs. It informed them that they might live in the Capital City in all security, and that he wanted to hear no further talk about their returning to a southern province or to their own country. The Fathers accepted this as an official reply to their petition, and they rejoiced in the Lord that finally with the help of Divine Providence they had overcome the opposition and triumphed over all obstacles. Not only were they granted permission to remain, they were also allotted a subsidy from public funds, to be paid every four months, and amounting to eight gold ecus a month, which in this country is not so small an income as it might appear to be in Europe.

Verily he spoke the truth, who said "Your friends will be many when you are prosperous." All those who had given up their friendship, were now making much of it, throughout the whole city, and they were so numerous, that it can scarcely be doubted that Heaven opened up what had been a narrow entrance into a more ample field for the propagation of the Gospel. The Prefect for Foreigners invited Father Matthew into his court and told him, in a much more courteous way than was his custom, that he was permitted by authority of this court to dwell in the Royal Capital, as long as he desired to, and to live whereever he wished to. He said that Pekin was a big city and could very well afford to add one more foreigner to its population. As the news of this permission was spread about, the number of visitors and of friends increased with every day. We shall mention only a few of the many friends, to prevent a repetitious recital from becoming tiresome.

Chapter 28

DECLINE OF THE CHURCH: THE ABSOLUTE STATE

THE decline of the Church through the seventeenth and eighteenth centuries coincided with the growth of absolute power in the dynastic State. To some extent these two movements were interrelated, for the absolute monarch in Catholic countries looked upon religion as a political concern. Generally interested in purity of morals and doctrine within the Church, the monarch felt that it was his right to control the Church through the power of appointing members of the hierarchy and binding them closely to himself. He resented "interference" from Rome as an illegitimate intrusion of foreigners into his domestic affairs. The popes of these centuries were generally good men, but they were weak and they were anxious to make whatever concessions they could in the interest of peace between Rome and the various Catholic kings.

This tendency we have been describing is known as Gallicanism. It came to a most complete expression in France in the latter seventeenth century, but it was also realized in one way or another in almost every Catholic country. The effect of Gallicanism was to lessen the power and authority of the pope over the Church outside the Papal States, to increase the power of the sovereign, and practically to break up the Catholic Church into a number of national Churches held together by only the most tenuous ties with Rome. The history of Gallicanism became complicated because it was interwoven with Jansenism — a form of Protestantism within the Church — and with such other movements of the time as Quietism. Jansenists occasionally resisted royal absolutism heroically, and thus found themselves, quite accidentally, on the side of

Rome. But generally Jansenists and Gallicans combined to sap the energy and power of the Church through the seventeenth and eighteenth centuries.

Gallicanism. Gallicanism was a program, an attitude, and a doctrine. As a program, it adopted whatever measures increased the independence of the national Church and lessened papal authority in the country. These measures could be directed toward increasing the authority of the national assembly of bishops or, on the other hand, toward increasing royal power over the national Church. Thus a distinction should be made between episcopal Gallicanism and royal Gallicanism. Sometimes these two forms were antithetical, sometimes they were compatible. Episcopal Gallicanism found its justification in the Councils of Basle and Constance; royal Gallicanism built on the doctrine of the legists and the precedents of the Pragmatic Sanctions of Bourges and the Concordat of Bologna. As an attitude, Gallicanism was the religious manifestation of nationalism. It was a tendency to ignore Rome and to develop a peculiarly "national" Church within the country. As a doctrine, Gallicanism held that the pope was subject to a general council and that his authority over the Church in foreign countries was narrowly circumscribed.

When Cardinal Richelieu assumed power as chief minister of France in 1624 he promised Louis XIII that he would make him an absolute ruler. This involved, among other things, the suppression of episcopal Gallicanism and a strengthening of royal Gallicanism. Richelieu ordered the suppression of all literature which argued for papal power or authority, and he forced Jesuits at Paris to repudiate the Roman views expressed in the recently published book of the Italian Jesuit Santarelli. On the other hand, Richelieu found the extreme statement of episcopal Gallicanism by Edmond Richer dangerous to royal power. Richer argued that the pope was only chief executive of the Church, as the bishop is of his diocese, and that legislative power resides in an ecumenical council and ultimately in all the Church. Such a theory gave no place to the king; moreover, there was always the danger it might be applied to political life.

Richelieu advanced instead the claims of political Gallicanism. These claims had been formulated in 1594 by Pierre Pithou in his treatise on the liberties of the Gallican Church. His argument, which was historical and legal in form, held that the king had the right to rule over his clergy and convoke national councils. The pope, Pithou maintained, could not send a legate to reform, judge, or dispense in ecclesiastical matters without permission from the ruler. The pope could not excommunicate the king or his officials, nor could he absolve subjects from obedience to the king. Richelieu commissioned a certain Pierre de Marca to put these arguments in contemporary form. The latter's treatise *De Concordia Sacerdotii et Imperii* (1641) limited the pope's infallibility to those matters which received the consent of the Church, and it defended the right of the king to censure ecclesiastics in his domain when they violated canons or decrees confirmed by royal power. Richelieu toyed with the idea of erecting the Church of France into a Patriarchate with himself at its head, but he died before any action along this line was taken.

Gallicanism reached a crisis under Louis XIV, who began his personal rule in 1660, and who admitted no limitations on his power. Louis believed that he ruled by divine right and that in his person was centered both secular and ecclesiastical authority. His authority was first challenged in 1661 when a Jesuit, Father Coret, defended a thesis that the pope received infallibility from Christ and that it extends to facts as well as law. The thesis was violently attacked as "the new heresy of the Jesuits," and the king declared himself against it. The affair was settled by a negative formula that "it is not the teaching of the faculty that the pope is above the general council; neither is it the teaching of the faculty that the pope is infallible, if the consent of the Church is not added to his definitions."

The next incident was the "affair of the Corsican guards." On August 20, 1662, three partly drunken Frenchmen attached to the household of the French ambassador to Rome got into a fight with some Corsican members of the papal guard. Louis XIV determined to use this incident to push his royal prerogatives to the limit. He expelled the papal nuncio from France, wrote an insulting letter to Pope Alexander VII, and declared Avignon and the county Venaissin annexed to the French crown. He even threatened to send French troops into Italy. Alexander apologized to the French king, punished the Corsican guard, and erected a column to commemorate the event. This event was important because it revealed the anti-papal feeling of most French bishops.

Louis XIV continued in various ways to defy the pope and to usurp his authority in France. This conduct came to a head in the "*regale* affair." The *regale* was the right enjoyed by the king to the revenue of certain bishoprics during their vacancy, and also the right to fill vacant benefices during that time. By a royal declaration of February 10, 1673, the king arbitrarily extended this right to all the bishoprics of France. Two bishops declared that they could not accept this action by the king.

These bishops were supported by Pope Innocent XI, and thus the *regale* affair became a conflict between the pope and the French king.

During the long drawn out quarrel the French bishops sided with the king and expressed their exasperation with the "stubborn" pope. A general assembly of French clergy was called in 1682 to settle the *regale* affair. Bossuet, the brilliant bishop of Meaux, proposed a compromise solution which the French clergy adopted. By it the *regale* was extended to all dioceses in France, but the king was restricted in making appointments to vacancies to naming those who could obtain canonical institution from the proper ecclesiastical authority. The assembly entered on a bitter discussion of the basic question of papal authority. To solve this problem Bossuet drafted the famous Four Gallican Articles of 1682 which were adopted by the assembly and ordered by the king to be taught throughout France.

The Four Articles of 1682 constitute the classic statement of Gallicanism. They declared (1) that neither the pope nor the Church has any power over temporal rulers, and that kings cannot be deposed by spiritual authorities nor subjects released from their oath of allegiance; (2) that, as stated by the Council of Constance, papal power is limited by general councils; (3) that the exercise of papal power is limited by the customs and privileges of the Gallican Church; (4) that, although the pope "has the chief voice in questions of faith . . . yet his decision is not unalterable unless the consent of the Church is given." Philip Hughes comments very well: "The articles had not indeed invented anything new, so far as Catholic thought in France was concerned, but they had given concrete and explicit form to what hitherto was but a vague, though widespread, tendency, and this explicit doctrine was henceforth taught universally to the parochial clergy."

The king gave orders that these articles be taught in the seminaries and formally subscribed to by everyone taking a degree in theology. Pope Innocent XI annulled the proceedings of the Assembly of 1682 and refused to confirm the appointment to a bishopric of anyone who had participated in the Assembly. Louis insisted on nominating only men who had been in the Assembly, and thus a stalemate developed between pope and king. By 1687 more than thirty bishoprics were vacant. Louis tried to intimidate the pope in various ways, such as by abusing the right of asylum enjoyed by the French embassy in Rome. In 1693 Louis was finally forced to yield. He withdrew his edict compelling the acceptance of the four articles, and in return the pope (now Innocent XII) confirmed the king's nominees. All bishops chosen after 1682 signed this retraction: "We profess and declare that we are extremely grieved at what happened in the Assembly of 1682, which is so displeasing to Your Holiness and Your predecessors. Hence we hold and affirm that all declarations issued by that Assembly against the power of the Church and the authority of the pope are herewith rescinded."

The papal victory was more apparent than real. The Gallican articles continued to be taught in the seminaries and generally accepted by the clergy and laity throughout France. Only the Jesuits took a strong "ultramontane" stand — one of the reasons for their suppression in the next century.

Gallicanism, like the other policies of the "Sun King," was adopted by Catholic rulers in the rest of Europe. Doctrine and practice differed somewhat from country to country. A manifestation of Spanish Gallicanism, for example, was an increasing use of the Inquisition for political rather than religious purposes. Genoa and Savoy recalled their ambassadors from Rome; Parma refused to allow money to be sent to the Holy See. In all countries the divine origin of princely power was taught, and the pope was held to be the elected head of the Church limited like a constitutional monarch.

Jansenism.   The Gallican crisis interrupted a pernicious movement in the French Church known as Jansenism. This movement was an insidious and complicated affair that involved some of the high-placed persons in France, involved the Church in a bitter factional quarrel, and injected a Protestant element into Catholic circles in France. It was a movement that occurred within the revival of the French Church we discussed in the previous chapter. Its proponents were, to use the phrase applied to the nuns of Port Royal, angelic in appearance but moved with the pride of Lucifer. Jansenists were ultra-Catholics, men and women holier than the Church. They were Protestant reformers who stayed in the Church because in France there was nowhere else to go.

Jansenism was based on a certain doctrine of justification that proposed rigorous views of human nature and the role of grace in man's salvation. It centered in practice around conditions for any frequency of reception of the sacraments. Jansenists were austere in their morality, and they considered anyone opposed to them as corrupted enemies of God. Their aim was to purify the Church of all accretions since the time of the primitive Fathers. They therefore rejected Scholastic philosophy and theology in favor of Scripture itself and the commentaries of the early Fathers. Jansenistic teaching was condemned many times by the

Holy See, but the Jansenists always managed to evade papal condemnation by various subterfuges and, although opposed by both the pope and the French king, they continued to exist in France down till the Revolution of 1789. Philip Hughes terms them "the most shifty casuists of the century." "The history of the heresy," he goes on, "is a history of endless condemnations, of submissions, of subterfuges by which the heretic when condemned submits and then explains away the submission, is recondemned, submits again, appeals, and submits, and always with a fresh reservation, some new loophole through which he escapes to restate — still within the Church — his condemned theory."

Jansenism can be said to have had its origins in the sixteenth century. The Council of Trent had stated that good works meritorious for salvation are the result of both grace and the free will of man, but it did not define the precise role of each factor. Within Catholic circles two general schools of thought developed on this subject. The Jesuits stressed the role of man's free will; the Dominicans stressed the role of supernatural grace. In 1606 Pope Paul V ended the discussion by allowing each side to keep its opinions and forbidding them to accuse the other of heresy.

Meanwhile, a professor of Scripture at the University of Louvain, Michael Baius, had turned to St. Augustine to find what he thought was the true theory of grace and justification. Overstressing one aspect of St. Augustine's thought and neglecting other aspects of it entirely, Baius asserted that the preternatural and supernatural gifts with which Adam was endowed at creation were natural to him and therefore that original sin was more than a deprivation, as taught by the Church — it was a disorderly act which corrupts human nature and renders it incapable of doing good. In other words, Baius took an unduly optimistic view of man before the fall and an unduly pessimistic view of man after the fall. Free will, for Baius, is nothing but concupiscence. In his fallen state man can do nothing but sin. These teachings were condemned by Rome in 1567 and again in 1579, and Baius accepted the decisions. His teachings lingered on in the Low Countries, however, as the answer to the puzzle of grace and free will, and fifty years after his death they were given classic expression in a book called *Augustinus*.

Augustinus was the posthumously published work of Cornelius Jansen, former professor at the University of Louvain and later bishop of Ypres. Jansen had worked closely for a number of years with Jean Duvergier de Hauranne, abbot of St. Cyran, and the organizer of Jansenism in France. The two of them planned a thorough "reform" of the Church, especially in France. Jansen was to furnish the doctrine; St. Cyran was to build an organization for putting the program into effect. This he did through the influential Arnaulds. This large and wealthy family was connected with some of the most important people in France — and it was hostile to Jesuits. One of the daughters, Mother Angélique, was abbess of Port Royal Convent. It was here that St. Cyran established the headquarters of the movement.

As the name of Jansen's book suggests, the new doctrine was supposed to be obtained from the teaching of the great Bishop of Hippo. It was a systematic restatement of Baius' teaching on grace and free will. The Jansenists maintained that Christ did not die for all mankind but only for a few He has predestined for salvation. These cannot resist grace, any more than the reprobate can save themselves. Such a doctrine naturally killed prayer to the saints or to the Blessed Virgin for intercession with God. It also killed the practice of frequent Confession and Communion which the Council of Trent encouraged and which the Jesuits preached everywhere. Jansenists held that the sacrament of Penance is valid only with perfect contrition. They taught that absolution must be withheld until the penance is performed, and they tried to revive the old forms of penance in terms of days, weeks, and years. Holy Communion should be received, they believed, only a few times in a lifetime. No one is worthy to receive Christ. Respectful abstention from Communion honors Christ more than frequent reception. St. Cyran wrote to a nun who was saddened by not receiving that sacrament during her illness: "You will soon understand that you do more for yourself by not going to Holy Communion than by going."

Cardinal Richelieu ordered an investigation into the teachings and practices of the Port Royal group in 1638. As a result of these investigations, Abbot St. Cyran was imprisoned at Vincennes, where he remained until Richelieu's death late in 1642. Meanwhile, *Augustinus* had been published. It was actively opposed by Jesuits, Sulpicians, and Vincentians, and it was formally condemned by the Holy See on June 19, 1643. Meanwhile, the theological faculty of the Sorbonne and the French bishops took official French action against Jansenism. The Sorbonne summed up the fundamental errors of Jansenism in five propositions. Eighty-eight French bishops then signed a petition requesting the Holy See to examine these propositions and pass judgment on them. After lengthy study by a commission of cardinals, Innocent X condemned these propositions in 1653.

The Jansenists accepted the papal condemnation, but they insisted the five propositions could not be found in Jansen's writings. In other words, they agreed that the propositions, as condemned by the Holy See, were heretical, but in the *Augustinus* these statements had a different meaning which was not condemned. To condemn Jansen's writing, they held, was to condemn St. Augustine as a heretic. The French clergy therefore assembled to find a formula to pin the Jansenists down to their heresy. They declared that the five propositions were truly to be found in Jansen in the sense in which they had been condemned by the pope. Then they drew up a declaration which the king enjoined upon all the clergy: "I condemn both in thought and by word of mouth the doctrine of the five propositions of Cornelius Jansen contained in his book *Augustinus*, which the pope and the bishops have condemned; this doctrine is not that of St. Augustine, whose true meaning Jansen has distorted."

At this point the brilliant Blaise Pascal wrote his *Lettres provinciales* against the Jesuits. These were condemned by the Index, and the clergy were again ordered to take the formulary against them. Somewhat later, the king ordered all the clergy to sign without reservation or distinction a similar formula prepared by the Holy See. Four bishops refused to do so on the grounds that the pope is not infallible in matters of fact, and it is a matter of fact whether or not the five propositions condemned by the Holy See are to be found in *Augustinus*. When king and pope decided to take action against the four bishops, nineteen more declared publicly that they agreed with their four colleagues. The crisis was solved by a compromise known as the Clementine Peace. Pope Clement IX was informed that the Jansenist bishops consented to sign the formula. Then the bishops explained away their signing to the clergy of their dioceses. The pope accepted their signing as in good faith and without reservations.

The Clementine Peace lasted thirty years, during which time (1670–1700) the Gallican crisis came to a head and Quietism became a serious problem. In these thirty years Jansenism spread among the diocesan clergy and made inroads even into some congregations, especially the Oratorians. It continued to be the most dangerous movement in the Church at the time because it enlisted many of the wealthiest and most influential persons in France. Through its extremism and its heretical bent of mind, Jansenism threatened to discredit the sound aspects of the seventeenth-century revival the Church was then enjoying in France. During the period of the Clementine Peace Jansenism can be considered an underground movement in the French Church. No party, as such, existed. But countless individuals held Jansen's teaching to be true, and many other Catholics were affected by its austerity and its rigorism. Much of the attitude and many of the practices of the Jansenists rubbed off, as it were, on the other French Catholics.

In 1701 the movement came into the open again when a "case of conscience" became the subject of much discussion among the professors of the Sorbonne. The question was whether absolution could be given to a penitent who maintained a respectful silence on the matter of Jansen's teaching and signed the papal formulary with the mental reservation that the five condemned propositions were not to be found in Jansen. The case of conscience was called to the attention of Pope Clement XI who condemned it in 1703. At Louis XIV's request he formally condemned the attitude of "respectful silence" by the bull *Vineam Domini* of 1705. The bull read, in part: "The meaning condemned in the five propositions of the book of Jansen, which meaning is evident from the words themselves, must be condemned alike by all the faithful as heretical, not only by word of mouth, but also by internal consent; one may not licitly subscribe to the formula with any other dispositions."

Perhaps this decree might have ended the Jansenist trouble had not an ex-Oratorian, Pasquier Quesnel, published his popular *Réflexions morales sur le Nouveau Testament* in 1693. This was a thoroughly revised edition of a work Quesnel had published several times previously. The edition of 1693 insinuated Jansenism into a set of pious reflections made on each verse of the New Testament. The work was quite popular for it reached a class that could never appreciate Jansen's *Augustinus*. Quesnel was careful not to state Jansenistic teaching in blunt formulae but rather to introduce it by insinuation. Moreover, he had secured the approval of de Noailles, then bishop of Chartres, and later, when the difficulty broke out — archbishop of Paris.

Quesnel's *Réflexions* was referred to Rome, and in 1708 it was censured by a papal brief. Cardinal de Noailles accepted the brief. But it was an affront to his pride, since he had made the mistake of approving the condemned work, so he asked for "explanations" in order to save face. At the request of the French king, Pope Clement XI issued the famous bull *Unigenitus* (1713) in which he censured 101 propositions taken from Quesnel's book. For fifteen years the conflict continued. Four French bishops refused to accept the bull. Noailles appealed to a future "pope better informed and to a general council." In return, the pope excommunicated all those who appealed from his decision. Finally, Cardinal de Noailles submitted in 1728, and with his submission Jansenism as an organized movement came to an end.

It lived on in individuals, and it furnished material for the magistrate class in France to harass the Church throughout the eighteenth century. It was also one of the factors that led to the suppression of the Society of

Jesus. Parlementary Jansenism took the form of interference by the magistrates of the *parlements,* or courts, in the affairs of the Church. In 1731, for example, when certain priests in the Orleans diocese tried to make the parishioners subscribe to the bull *Unigenitus, parlement* called their conduct abusive and requested their bishop to restrain them. The most important quarrel, however, was over the giving of last sacraments to those who refused to accept *Unigenitus.* Some priests refused to do so, and the *parlements* took legal action against them. The most extreme case was reached in Paris when Archbishop Christopher de Beaumont was ordered to appear before the *parlement* of Paris because he refused to revoke the regulation requiring subscription to *Unigenitus* for receiving the last sacraments. The archbishop's temporal possessions were confiscated, he was exiled from Paris, and priests were forbidden to refuse the last sacraments to recalcitrants. A compromise was reached in 1756 when Pope Benedict XIV required obedience to *Unigenitus,* but stated that the last sacraments need not be denied to any but notorious public sinners.

A small group of Jansenists broke away from the Church and set up a schismatic group still in existence, the Old Catholics of Holland. The importance of the Jansenist movement, however, lay in the harm it did the Church in France and the way it pitted Catholic against Catholic in an age when growing unbelief called for united front rather than fratricidal strife. Jansenism was a sapping operation that prepared the Church for something close to complete destruction in France by 1800. It had a wider effect also, in that it introduced into Catholic circles a strong puritan note which robbed Catholicism of its richness and its full development wherever the Jansenist influence was strong — as it came to be in certain parts of France, in Ireland, and in the United States.

Quietism. Another heretical movement within the Church in France in the seventeenth century was Quietism. It was a natural but extreme reaction to the stress laid on activity and the role of the will by Jesuits, Vincentians, and others following in the spirit of the Council of Trent. The movement began in Rome, where a Spanish priest, Michael Molinos, had for some time been spiritual director of a group of residents there. In 1685 he was arrested by the Inquisition, and two years later Pope Innocent XI condemned 68 propositions taken from Molinos' book called *A Spiritual Guide.* Both in doctrine and in practical results Molinos and his followers showed the dangerous side of mysticism if it is not truly spiritual and well balanced. Molinos held that man must annihilate his will and all his powers so that God is perfectly free to act in the soul. Men must have no interest whatsoever, he taught, not even in salvation. The perfect state of the soul is one of complete passivity. Molinos went so far as to insist that it is wrong to resist temptation, for this is a positive act of the will. Penances and vocal prayer were abandoned. So too was mental prayer in favor of pure contemplation.

Molinos and his associates put these ideas into practice as men and women "above the law." Their life — there were about two hundred of them — was a strange mixture of contemplative prayer and sexual excesses. After a long trial Molinos was sentenced to imprisonment for life, and the matter might have ended in Rome if it had not been for a certain Madame Guyon, a penitent of one of Molinos' followers. Madame Guyon seems to have been a hypersensitive young widow — she had "visions" when she was five and aspired to martyrdom — who entered impulsively into religious living when her husband died. She had sufficient wealth and connections with enough important people to make Quietism an important movement in France for a couple of decades. She moved from place to place, put her Quietist ideas into writing, and attracted considerable attention. Bishops kept asking her to leave their dioceses until finally, in 1686, the archbishop of Paris had her arrested.

Charges against her moral conduct were never proved, and when she said that her ideas meant nothing to her and she would abandon them as soon as they were declared false, there seemed no reason to fear her orthodoxy. After her release, she met Fénelon, the future archbishop of Cambrai. She and Fénelon found they held much in common. He regarded her as a holy woman in the tradition of St. Teresa and Madame de Chantal. When the old rumors about Madame Guyon's character and doctrine circulated again, the bishops decided to examine the case more thoroughly. She was arrested again, while Bossuet, Bishop de Noailles, and the superior of the seminary of St. Sulpice studied the case. After nine months they drew up 34 articles in which her errors were condemned. Fénelon also signed the condemnation.

Quietism did not end when Madame Guyon accepted this condemnation of 1696 because Fénelon and Bossuet continued the dispute. Bossuet brusquely and directly attacked Madame Guyon's ideas, and Fénelon answered him with equal lack of charity. Finally, in 1699, Pope Innocent XII ended the dispute by condemning 23 propositions taken from Fénelon's writings. Fénelon submitted with the famous statement: "Please God, it may ever be said of us that a pastor ought to bear in mind that he must be more docile than the least of his sheep." This put an end to Quietism as a movement in France. It caused the Church considerable damage because it threw additional suspicion on the contemplative life in an age when such a life of prayer was occupying a smaller and smaller part in the Church. Under the Jesuits and other communities religion was becoming more and more a divinely aided effort toward self-perfection in the moral order. Prayer was shrinking in importance before action, and the exposure of Quietism gave impetus to this unhealthy movement.

REVIEW AIDS

1. Explain why the king would consider episcopal Gallicanism a dangerous thing as far as his royal power was concerned, whereas he was strongly in favor of royal Gallicanism.
2. What principle lay back of the contest between the French king and the pope over the former's extension of the *regale* to all the dioceses of France?
3. Explain the practices within the French Church which insured the king of an episcopacy inclined to support him against the pope.
4. Is Gallicanism simply a matter of schism or near-schism, or does it also involve matters of doctrine?
5. Prepare a list of the principal moral and doctrinal teachings of Jansenism.
6. Compare this list with the principal teachings of Calvinism. (See Chapter 20.)
7. Explain why, given the setting of seventeenth-century France, it might be possible for a sincerely religious person to embrace Jansenistic teachings — as was, indeed, frequently the case.
8. Make a brief sketch of the career of Bossuet and see how much of the history of the Church in seventeenth-century France you can connect with his career.
9. From your knowledge of psychology, explain how Quietism could make a strong appeal to a certain type of religious person.
10. Distinguish the doctrines of Quietism from the sound mysticism of a St. Teresa or a St. Francis de Sales.

SUGGESTIONS FOR FURTHER READING

There is surprisingly little in English dealing directly with the subjects of Gallicanism, Jansenism, and Quietism. Each of these subjects is well handled in the *Catholic Encyclopedia,* and a number of articles dealing with each can be found in such Catholic periodicals as *Thought, Catholic World,* and *The Historical Bulletin.* The subjects are also handled in studies of the Jesuits, who opposed all three movements, and biographies of such men as Fénelon and Bossuet.

Considerable treatment of each subject is given by Mourret, *A History of the Catholic Church,* Volume VI; and various chapters of Pastor's *History of the Popes.* Volumes XXX to XXXIX deal with these subjects. All three movements are also treated in the volume in "The National History of France Series" by Casimir Stryienski, *The Eighteenth Century* (New York: 1916). The one specialized study available in English on any of these subjects is Nigel Abercrombie, *The Origins of Jansenism* (London: 1936).

DOCUMENTS

A. The Four Gallican Articles of 1682

At the order of Louis XIV, Bishop Bossuet drew up the Four Gallican Articles of 1682, which became the classic statement of Gallicanism, the theory that sought to limit the authority of the pope over the French Church — a theory adopted by other national groups at later times.

Several persons in these times are endeavoring to oppose the decrees and liberties of the Gallican Church, which our ancestors upheld with so much zeal, and to undermine their foundations, which rest on the holy canons and the traditions of the Fathers. Others, under the pretext of defending these decrees, do not hesitate to attack the primacy of St. Peter and the Roman Pontiffs, his successors, instituted by Jesus Christ, as well as the obedience which all Christians owe to them. . . . In order to remedy this situation, we, the archbishops and bishops assembled in Paris by order of the King, have deemed it necessary to draft the following regulations and to make the following declaration:

I. That St. Peter and his successors, the vicars of Jesus Christ, and the entire Church have received from God power only over spiritual matters which relate to salvation, but not over temporal and civil affairs. Jesus Christ Himself informs us that His kingdom is not of this world, and, in another place, that we must render to Caesar the things that are Caesar's and to God the things that are God's. We must abide by the precept of St. Paul: "Let every soul be subject to higher powers: for there is no power but from God: and those that are, are ordained of God" (Rom. 13:1–2). As a consequence we declare that by the order of God kings are not subject to ecclesiastical authority in matters which concern the temporal order, and may not be either directly or indirectly deposed by the authority of the heads of the Church; that their subjects may not be dispensed from the submission and obedience which they owe them, or absolved from their oath of allegiance; that this doctrine, indispensable for public peace, and just as advantageous to the Church as to the State, must be upheld as being in conformity with Holy Scripture, the tradition of the Fathers of the Church, and the example of the Saints.

II. That the plenitude of powers which the Holy Apostolic See and the successors of St. Peter, the vicars of Jesus Christ, have in spiritual matters is nevertheless such that the decrees of the Holy Ecumenical Council of Constance, contained in sessions 4 and 5, approved by the Holy Apostolic See and confirmed by the practice of the whole Gallican Church, remain in force, and that the Church of France does not approve the opinion of those who attack or undermine these decrees by stating that their authority is not firmly established, that they have not been approved or that they were issued only to meet the emergency of a schism.

III. That the use of the Apostolic authority must be regulated by the canons enacted under the inspiration of God and confirmed by the general respect of all men; that the rules, manners, and constitutions received in the kingdom and in the Gallican Church must remain in force and the customs of our fathers be faithfully preserved; and that, finally, it is a mark of the greatness of the Holy Apostolic See that the laws and customs established by the consent of this See and of the Church be vested with the authority which is rightly theirs.

IV. That, although the pope plays the principal part in all questions pertaining to the faith, and his decrees are intended for all the Churches, and each Church in particular, his judgment is not infallible if the consent of the Church is not given.

B. Some Propositions of Baius Condemned by Pope St. Pius V in his bull *Ex omnibus afflictionibus*

The forerunner of Jansenism was Michel de Bay (Baius), whose teaching was condemned by Pope St. Pius V in the Bull *Ex omnibus afflictionibus* of October 1, 1567. The condemned propositions are grouped under seven headings dealing with: (1) the gifts of the Primitive State, (2) merit, (3) free will, (4) charity, (5) sin, (6) concupiscence, and (7) justification. Below are selections from the condemned propositions.

The elevation of human nature and its exaltation to participation in the divine nature were due to the integrity of its primitive state. Hence this state must be called natural and not supernatural.

The integrity of the first creation was not an elevation gratuitously bestowed upon human nature, but its own natural condition.

The immortality of the first man was not a gift of grace, but his natural condition.

All the acts of infidels are sins, and the virtues of philosophers are vices.

Without the help of God our free will can do nothing else but sin.

It is a Pelagian error to say that free will can make us avoid sin.

Everything the sinner does is sin.

Whoever acknowledges the existence of any natural good, i.e., a good founded on the forces of nature alone, is a follower of Pelagius.

Whatever is done voluntarily, even though it be done necessarily, is done freely.

In all his actions the sinner is obedient to concupiscence, which rules him.

No sin is venial by its nature, but every sin is deserving of eternal punishment.

The bad desires to which reason does not consent, and which man experiences despite his efforts, are forbidden by the Commandment: Thou shalt not covet.

Concupiscence or the law of the members, and its bad desires, which men experience in spite of themselves, are a real disobedience of the law.

In those who have fallen into mortal sin after the reception of the Sacrament of Baptism, concupiscence regains the ascendency, and is a sin just like all other bad habits.

C. Some Propositions of Quesnel Condemned by Pope Clement XI in his bull *Unigenitus*

Jansenism was given new life late in the seventeenth century by Quesnel. Propositions taken from his *Moral Reflections on the New Testament* were condemned by Pope Clement XI in the bull *Unigenitus*, which was published on September 8, 1713.

When at any time or place God wishes to save a soul, the indubitable effect immediately follows in the wake of the divine power.

When God wishes to save a soul, and touches that soul with the interior hand of His grace, no human will can resist Him.

The prayer of the wicked is an added sin, and by the permission of God a new judgment passed upon them.

If anyone abstains from sin because he fears punishment, he commits sin in his heart and is guilty in the eyes of God.

The Church alone has the right to excommunicate through her chief pastors and with the at least presumed consent of the whole body.

The fear of even an unjust excommunication must never prevent us from doing our duty. . . . One is never outside the Church, even though banished by the wickedness of men, as long as one remains attached to God, to Jesus Christ, and to the Church herself through charity.

A person does not rebel against authority or impair unity, but rather imitates St. Paul, when he suffers in silence an unjust excommunication or anathema rather than betray the truth.

It happens too frequently that members who are most tenderly attached to the Church are regarded and treated as unworthy of being in the Church or of already being separated from her. But the just man lives by faith, and not by human opinion.

To be persecuted and to suffer as a heretic, a sinner, and a reprobate, is ordinarily the last and most meritorious of all tests, because it makes us more like Jesus Christ.

Chapter 29

DECLINE OF THE CHURCH:
SECULARISM

THROUGH the seventeenth and eighteenth centuries the initiative in cultural and intellectual life was lost by the Church and taken over by people who, no matter what their religion might be, thought as scientists or economists or artists rather than as Christians. As a result the Church was put on the defensive, and the control of Western culture fell to those who were not directly influenced by the Church. This helps to explain the general phenomenon of modern history which has been labeled "secularism"; or the turning over to worldly institutions various functions formerly performed by the Church.

During these centuries, we should also remember, the popes were not men of unusual ability. They came almost exclusively from families of the Italian nobility, were men of good personal lives, but of only ordinary intellectual ability and force of character. They were not strong enough to give the Church the forceful leadership it needed. The most capable men of the age, especially in the eighteenth century, took up civil careers of one kind or another. With certain exceptions, the apologists of the Church were mediocre men, no match for the Voltaires and the Diderots who held the ancient Christian teaching up to ridicule instead of refuting it directly. Finally, to understand the general trend of these two centuries, we should remember that the aggressive and successful classes were anxious to confine religion to the sacristy, so to speak, and keep it out of the council room and the counting house. Their aim was not so much to destroy the Church as an institution as to render it impotent in everything except the matter of private devotion.

All of these trends added up to a secularizing process whereby religion was pushed more and more out of man's life, out of his social and political life, out of cultural affairs, out of art and literature, and finally out of man's very consciousness except for stated hours of worship each week. In this chapter we can discuss only some of the more important secularizing movements of these two centuries leading up to the French Revolution. France continued to be the most important country in the Catholic orbit, the center in which all these movements seemed to originate and from which they emanated into the rest of Christendom.

Secularist Thought of the "Enlightenment." Religious and social thought of the so-called Enlightenment cannot be easily described in general terms, for each thinker of the age was an individualist who differed in some respects from the others. It is nevertheless possible to make some fairly valid generalizations, as long as the student realizes that they do not apply completely to any one thinker. The term "Enlightenment" is used to refer to French thought from about 1730 until the Revolution of 1789. This thought originated in England in the latter part of the seventeenth century where it took the form of moderate skepticism, deism, and toleration.

Most important among these Englishmen was John Locke, who wrote in favor of toleration of all except Jews, Unitarians, and "Papists," and who gave great impetus to a movement within the Christian religions known as "latitudinarianism" — the idea that only a few essential truths common to all religions are important and that the others should be discarded in favor of a doctrine of the least common denominator held by all religions. This movement of latitudinarianism was taken up by the Freemasons and propagated effectively by them as a means of erasing all established religions in favor of a general religion of mankind. Locke was also important for propagating a sensist psychology, a healthy but clumsy attack on Descartes's theory of innate ideas, which opened the road to the complete sensism and materialism of such Frenchmen as Condillac, La Mettrie, Holbach, and Diderot.

A group of Locke's contemporaries opened the floodgate for secularized morality with their doctrines of moral sentimentalism, deism, and homocentric doctrines on religion and society. Such men as Shaftesbury, Hutcheson, Bolingbroke, and Pope severed morality from religion and from objective reality by setting up the new norms of social approbation, or of personal feeling, as the standard for judging good and evil. Either forgetting or denying the all-important historical fact of original sin, they postulated a man who was essentially good and, because they were in control of social and political life in England, they could conclude that viewed from a timeless pinnacle "whatever is, is right." In Pope's words:

> Respecting Man, whatever wrong we call,
> May, must be right, as relative to all.

Finally, Isaac Newton seemed to solve the mysteries of the universe by his discovery of the law of gravity and other physical laws. Worshipful followers applied the Newtonian concept of the law of nature to man and society, as well as to morality and religion, to develop a new idea of natural law that was divorced from morality and from any religious considerations. They attempted to create a science of ethics on exactly the same pattern as Newton's physical laws.

 When this thought was transported to France it took on a more radical tinge in the writings of such persons as Voltaire, Diderot, Helvetius, and Holbach. Enlightened thought in France varied from the deism of a Voltaire to the materialistic atheism of a Holbach. This thought was best expressed in the *Encyclopédie* published by Diderot and read by all the literati of the age. From France the Enlightenment spread into the Germanies, where it was known as the *Aufklärung,* into Spain, Portugal, the Italies, and other parts of the Western world — even into the Americas.

The Enlightenment has sometimes been called the "Renaissance of the Renaissance." This figure of speech suggests that the individualism, the skepticism, and the homocentric bent of the pagan Renaissance was revived in the eighteenth century. Thinkers of the Enlightenment rejected the claims of any one religion, including the Catholic Church, as the pretensions of a class with a vested interest in propagating ignorance among the people. Some of them admitted the social benefits that came from such an arrangement, but they insisted that "enlightened" persons like themselves could accept nothing more than a "natural religion." Rejecting Revelation, miracles, and a providential God, they tried to create a religion based on truths men could arrive at with unaided reason. These were few: the existence of an ultimate Power or Force that is called God; the obligation all men have to be just in their dealings with each other; the reward or punishment men suffer, either in this life or perhaps in the next, for being good or evil.

The God of these thinkers is necessary because they were logical men and they found no other way to account for creation. But after having created the world and wound it up, so to speak, God must leave it run according to the laws He has set for it at creation. He is not permitted to interfere in man's affairs, either by miracle or by any other intervention with the regularly ordered conduct of things. For some Deists God was a personal being, and they are more properly called Theists. For others He was an impersonal force of some kind. Deists agreed in rejecting the claims of Christ to be the Son of God, and they looked upon the Catholic Church as a body organized to exploit the superstition of the ignorant masses. Their great hope was to reorganize men's thinking by suppressing the Jesuits and by secularizing education, which in the eighteenth century was still a private concern taken care of by families themselves and by religious orders.

Perhaps the most important single member of the Enlightenment in France was Voltaire. One of the cleverest writers of any age, Voltaire poked ridicule at individual bishops and priests and then at the Church as an institution. His importance lay in the fact that he started men laughing at institutions they had held sacred for centuries. Voltaire had an uncanny faculty for finding the weak spots in any enemy's armor. His arguments could not be refuted because they were assertions rather than logical arguments, and no one can refute a joke, a funny story, or a clever analogy. Although Voltaire proved nothing to logical thinkers, he reached a large class of rather superficial people for whom he seemed to demonstrate that the claims of the Church were too absurd for rational people to take seriously.

The great arsenal of the Enlightenment in its attack on the Church, however, was Diderot's *Encyclopédie*. In the preliminary discourse of this work Diderot and his associates frankly stated that they had a twofold aim: (1) to collect and show the interrelationship of all knowledge; (2) to expose prejudices and discredit the authority on which previously held knowledge was based. The *Encyclopédie* was a skillful, vicious attack on old institutions in France, especially upon the fundamental religious, moral, and philosophical system held by the Church and the government — for unfortunately there was a close union between throne and altar in all countries in the eighteenth century. The attack was so skillfully conducted that theologians who were supposed to censor the religious articles seldom realized how deftly traditional beliefs were being undermined. One device was to state objections to religious beliefs strongly and refute them weakly, and then to tack on the traditional teaching for a conclusion which was made to look absurd. Another device was to state the traditional teaching in articles seen by the theological censors and then to undermine it in other articles to which the reader was led by cross references. Jesus, for example, is spoken of with orthodox respect in the religious articles, but in *"Théosophes"* He is called a fanatic, in *"Suicide"* it is intimated that His voluntary death was suicide, and in *"Juifs"* He is called "that absurd and fanatical Jew."

For the Catholic faith Diderot would supply either a natural religion or none at all — it is hard to tell which. For the morality of the old religion he would supply his own strange mixture of moral ideas, the germs of later determinism, behaviorism, and materialism. He rejected free will, but he managed nevertheless to be both determinist and moralist. By creating good environment and having good laws, he believed, society could make man necessarily good. All knowledge and therefore all morality, which he equated with knowledge, depended for Diderot on the senses. Sense pleasure is the norm, he insisted, for deciding whether an act was good or bad.

But it was Helvetius more than Diderot who created the new code of morality in his famous *De l'esprit* and expounded it at greater length in his posthumous *De l'homme*. Helvetius was the father of modern utilitarianism, and because he believed that man is the result purely and simply of his environment and his education, he proposed abolishing the religious orders and making education a monopoly of the State. Since "man is a machine . . . put in motion by corporeal sensibility," "pleasures and pains are the moving powers of the universe." What produces sensuous pleasure is good for Helvetius; what causes physical suffering is evil. Thus Helvetius established a revolutionary new morality which was divorced from religion and from man's responsible will.

More than anyone else, Holbach and La Mettrie were frankly and dogmatically materialistic. In Holbach's *System of Nature* and La Mettrie's *Man the Machine* the secularistic thought of the eighteenth century was brought to a logical conclusion. With them matter is the be-all and end-all of existence. Man, therefore, has neither mind nor soul nor will. "Nature does not make man either good or wicked," Holbach wrote; "she combines machines more or less active, mobile, and energetic." Holbach denied the possibility of God's existence and concluded that religion is the opium of the people. "The religions of the world to come have enabled the priesthood to conquer the present world. The expectation of celestial happiness, and the dread of future tortures, only serve to prevent man from seeking after the means to render himself happy here below." With Helvetius, Holbach would preserve a morality whereby that which increases the pleasures of mankind is good and that which decreases them is wicked. His new moral code contained such advice as this: "Be just, because equity is the support of human society! . . . Be gentle, because mildness attracts attention! Be thankful, because gratitude feeds benevolence, nourishes generosity! . . . Forgive injuries, because revenge perpetuates hatred!" Thus did the thinkers of the Enlightenment seek to preserve a secularized morality after having denied God and rejected religion.

Such "enlightened" thought appealed to the wealthy middle class, who in France and the rest of Europe were becoming the dominant class in society. This is the class that promoted the French Revolution of 1789 and during the course of the nineteenth century took over the economic and political control of almost every country of the Western world. This class was particularly attracted to the romantic thought of Jean-Jacques Rousseau. A deist in religious thought, Rousseau tried to develop a morality based on feeling rather than reason. This carries moral and religious subjectivism to a completely logical conclusion, for Rousseau maintained that "what I feel is right, is right." The romantics who followed Rousseau were in no need of a church or of a priesthood; each of them made direct contact with whatever he thought was God.

French "enlightened" thought spread into the Germanies and the rest of Europe and the Americas. It differed slightly from country to country, but essentially it was the same everywhere. It tended to be antireligious in all countries, to oppose the authority of the priest and the claims of Revelation in favor of each man's individual judgment. It secularized morality by separating it from a personal God and from any religion. Organized religions, including the Catholic Church in some of her members, were to some extent infected with this "enlightened" thought. The apologists of the Church, generally speaking, were not as clever as the "enlightened" thinkers, and in the battle of wits the defenders of religion did rather poorly. By the end of the eighteenth century, therefore, there was a tendency to identify the Church with ignorant peasants and a clerical class who used it to exploit the masses and to keep them subservient to an absolute monarch. Such was one of the serious results of the close Church-State alliance when the aggressive, "thinking" people in society rebelled against established authority. Their revolt against the State involved them, almost necessarily, in a revolt against the Church.

Freemasonry. These ideas of deism, rationalism, and secularized humanitarianism were spread in the eighteenth century by a new organization which soon covered most of Europe and enrolled in its lodges a large proportion of the literate class. The major importance of the Masonic lodges lay in the fact that they furnished the means, in an age before radio or widely circulated journals, to spread the ideas of Voltaire, Diderot, and other "enlightened" thinkers. The aims of the organization seem to have been to end religious differences by establishing a deistic worship of the "Great Architect" and to promote social welfare by adopting the new thought of the Enlightenment. This involved the Masons in revolutionary activity against the established order, especially in France, and therefore against the Catholic Church as well as the political institutions of the time. The movement was veiled in secrecy, in a great amount of ceremony and ritual, and in much vague talk about the welfare of the human species and the benevolence of man for man. As a result, all sorts of persons joined one lodge or another as one joins a benevolent society or a local improvement association today. Many priests and even bishops, as well as such outstanding Catholic laymen as Joseph de Maistre, were enrolled as Masons and apparently saw nothing in the movement hostile to the Church.

The modern origins of Masonry are shrouded in mystery and secrecy — perhaps the chief appeal of the movement. Corporations of Masons had been formed in the middle ages, we know, and they had received certain privileges from the Holy See. But the modern Masonry began in England and Scotland in the seventeenth century. Absolute secrecy was imposed on the members and various oaths were required of them. In effect, they had to put the interests of the Lodge above all other interests and they had to obey the orders of their Masters without question. Masonry was infused with a philosophy and a pseudo religion through its alliance with the Brethren of the Rosy Cross or Rosicrucians, a secret society formed for occult purposes such as the transmutation of metals and the prolongation of life.

The movement spread to France in the early part of the eighteenth century, and shortly afterward into Holland, Spain, Portugal, Italy, the Germanies, and elsewhere in Europe. Members of the nobility, even kings themselves, were enrolled. Generally the Masonic lodges received governmental toleration or even protection in the eighteenth century, although toward the end of the century they fell under suspicion as advocates of revolution. Wherever the lodges spread they propagated the "enlightened" theories of the time, usually tinged with a quasi-mystical thought like that of the Rosicrucians, and always shrouded in mysterious secrecy. The papacy alone seems to have seen the danger to the Church and to human integrity in such a movement. Catholics were warned of the danger on two occasions when popes condemned Masonry for the quasi-religious doctrine it

embraced and for its rigid requirements of secrecy. Clement XII's condemnation was in 1738, and Benedict XIV's in 1751.

Febronianism. The Gallican movement within the Church reached
its climax in the Germanies in a book published under the pseudonym
of Febronius. The author was John Nicholas von Hontheim, auxiliary
bishop of Treves, who had studied under Van Espen, the outstanding
Gallican professor at the University of Louvain. Febronius argued that
the pretended primacy of the pope was a usurpation of powers properly
belonging to the bishops and to the Church as a whole. The pope, he
insisted, was simply the first among equals, and the primacy in the Church
did not necessarily belong to the bishop of Rome. If the Church wished, it
could designate this position to any other bishop, for Roman primacy was
simply an administrative office conferred by the Church on the pope.
Febronius denied papal infallibility and the right of the pope to receive
appeals from the whole Church. Primacy in the Church rests with a
general council, Febronius claimed, and the pope is simply its administrative agent whose powers are limited by its decrees. The abuse of papal
authority should therefore be checked by a general council, by national
synods, and by the secular prince in each country.

The obvious result of such a doctrine was to complete the disruption of
the Church and to place the bishops, independent of Roman authority,
under the complete control of the king. The book was condemned by
Clement XIII in 1764, but translations were speedily made into French,
German, Spanish, Portuguese, and Italian, and Febronius made an abridg-
ment of the work for popular reading. Meanwhile, various Catholic
apologists wrote against this book, and Febronius answered them with a
four-volume *Vindiciae*. Within a few years, therefore, Febronianism was
well diffused throughout Catholic Europe. But its principal effects were
felt in Germany and Austria.

Febronius himself disavowed his doctrines in 1778 at the insistence of
Pope Pius VI, but the prince-bishops of Cologne, Mainz, and Treves
adopted them and tried to put them into effect. They took a stand publicly
against "usurpations" on their jurisdictions by the Curia. Later (1786)
they issued twenty-three decrees, known as the "Punctuation of Ems,"
in which they made strong demands for episcopal "rights" against Rome:
that all exemptions from episcopal authority enjoyed by convents and
monasteries be suppressed; that faculties granted to the bishops every five
years be granted *in perpetuum*; that episcopal permission be required

before papal acts were published in a diocese; and that the episcopal oath of office be replaced by a new one.

Josephinism. The ideas put forth by Febronius proved a justification for the ecclesiastical policy that Emperor Joseph II had in mind when he came to power in 1780. Joseph was a typical "enlightened" ruler who had read the reform writings of the time and resolved to put them into practice. He considered the Church a department of State through which the moral life of the people was to be regulated. He proposed to reform the Church — as he tried to reform all other institutions — in the interests of efficiency, economy, and simplicity. By imperial decree he fixed the number of candles at High Mass, regulated the use of incense, abolished a number of holydays, rearranged the parishes and dioceses in geometric fashion, closed hundreds of convents and monasteries he considered "useless" because they were contemplative, limited pilgrimages and processions, and in various other ways tried to control the Church liturgically as well as politically. Only one Mass could be said daily in each church; the breviary was censored; the rosary was forbidden; and such feasts as that of St. Gregory VII were forbidden.

More basic among Joseph's "reforms" were his attempts to create a national Church with himself its head. By imperial decree he "freed" his bishops from dependence on Rome and placed them under his jurisdiction instead. This "reform" of the Church in the empire threatened to extinguish religious life and replace it with a national institution to control public morals. Pope Pius VI, therefore, took the unprecedented step of visiting Vienna to see whether he could dissuade Joseph from his program, and especially from a formal breach with Rome which he seems to have had in mind. The pope obtained a few vague promises from the emperor who proceeded, until his death in 1790, to enforce his liberal reforms on the Church. These reforms, like his social and economic reforms, were never popular and they were partly undone after his death.

Josephinism was copied by the other "benevolent despots" of Europe. In Tuscany Joseph's brother Leopold attempted to inaugurate reform similar to that of Joseph, and he found in the bishop of Pistoia an ecclesiastic willing to begin the movement. The other bishops refused to co-operate, however, when a synod was called by the bishop of Pistoia. The king of Naples, meanwhile, repudiated the temporal overlordship of the pope, which had been recognized for seven hundred years, and claimed the right to fill vacant sees without papal approval. By 1790 over half the sees in his kingdom were without bishops. In Piedmont, Venice, and

Spain the rulers were asserting the religious independence of their domains, and thus by the time the French Revolution occurred in 1789 the Church enjoyed freedom only in the Papal States and in the missionary country of the United States. Everywhere else it was shackled by the prince who enjoyed the support of an episcopacy he nominated from among the sub-servient nobility he could control. The authority of Rome had been successfully challenged in the years before 1789 partly because the rulers of Europe had combined to suppress the papacy's strongest support in Catholic countries, the Society of Jesus.

Suppression of the Society of Jesus.   By the middle of the eighteenth century the Jesuits had made many enemies within the Church. Gallicans in all countries looked upon them as their foremost opponents. Jansenists considered them their implacable enemies. Many of the other orders admired certain qualities of the Jesuits but thought that they were danger-ously supple and worldly in other respects. Being a Renaissance order with an individualistic temperament, devoted in military fashion to missionary and apologetic work, the Jesuits were almost destined by the nature of things to make many enemies.

In the eighteenth century these enemies, inside and outside the Church, combined to attack the Jesuits and to demand the suppression of the Society. Unfortunately, their natural protector, the papacy, was occupied by weak men at this time, and one of them eventually agreed to suppress the Society of Jesus "for the sake of peace within the Church." The forces combined against the Jesuits had nothing in common except their hatred for the Society. Some of the "enlightened" thinkers, like Voltaire, considered the suppression of the Society of Jesus the necessary first step toward destroying the effectiveness of the Church. Others, like the Bourbons and their Gallican supporters, thought the Jesuits had to be suppressed because they were the strongest bulwark of the papacy. Still others, like the Jansenists and certain sincere Catholics, thought the Jesuits were dangerously loose in their moral teaching, compromisers with the weakness of the flesh and the temptations of the devil, and therefore the Church would be purified by their suppression. This combination of interests proved too much for the Society of Jesus, and within fifteen years (1759–1773) it was progressively suppressed in Portugal, France, Spain, and finally by the pope. Jesuits continued to exist only in Prussia and ultimately in Russia until their re-establishment early in the nine-teenth century.

In the mid-eighteenth century the Jesuits were the largest and the most powerful Community within the Church. They numbered something less than 25,000 members, and they administered 273 foreign missions in addition to their many European establishments. They conducted more colleges throughout Europe than any other lay or religious group; they were confessors to kings and nobles in many countries; they composed the faculty of most of the pontifical seminaries in Europe. In short, they were the last strong element in a Church that was reaching a low point in the middle of the eighteenth century.

The first blow against the Jesuits fell in Portugal. The Portuguese king, Joseph I, a weak debauchee, was completely under the influence of his prime minister, the Marquis de Pombal. The latter was an adventurer who subscribed to the reform theories of the Enlightenment and thought it necessary to suppress the Jesuits. They had long been influential at the court, and Pombal was afraid that through their influence they might undo his secularizing reforms. When the opportunity presented itself, therefore, he trumped up a series of fantastic charges against the Society. In 1750 Portugal obtained from Spain the territory in Paraguay in which were located the Jesuit "Reductions." Pombal denounced the Society to Pope Benedict XIV for engaging in a commercial enterprise, because the Jesuits sold the produce of the Indian "Reductions." The pope consented to Pombal's demand for an investigation and appointed Cardinal Saldanha, archbishop of Lisbon, as visitator of the Society. Within two weeks, without any formal hearing and without listening to the testimony of a single Jesuit, Saldanha found the Society guilty of Pombal's charges.

The Jesuits appealed the decision, but Pombal forged a letter from the pope confirming Saldanha's decision. The forgery was denounced at Rome, but the king was blinded to Pombal's machinations by an attempt on his life — by the husband of a woman with whom he had had an illicit rendezvous. Pombal quickly blamed the attempt on the Jesuits and produced "evidence" to prove that they preached regicide. On January 12, 1759, all the Jesuits in Portugal were arrested. Two hundred twenty-one superiors and other high-placed members of the Society spent the next eighteen years — till Pombal's death — in jail. The others were transported to the papal port of Civitavecchia, where they were unloaded "as a present to the pope." Their houses, colleges, and properties were all confiscated, and when the papal nuncio protested he was expelled and diplomatic relations with Rome were severed.

The next blow fell in France. The king at the time was the weak Louis XV. He was very much under the influence of Madame Pompadour, who hated the Jesuits because they refused to countenance her adulterous relationship with the king. She and other high-placed persons at the court, such as Choiseul, combined with *philosophes* like Voltaire to pick away at the Jesuits and watch for the opportunity to discredit them. The opportunity came in a curious way. The Jesuit mission at Martinique failed financially when its cargoes were captured by the English early in the Seven Years' War (1756). The principal creditor applied for his money to the Jesuit Procurator-General of the Missions. The latter claimed that each house of the Society was solely responsible for its own debts and that the Society was not responsible for the debts of the mission houses at Martinique. This decision was legally correct but it was nevertheless a sad mistake.

The creditor then sued the Society, and the consular courts of Paris and Marseilles found the Society jointly liable with the Martinique mission. Now the Jesuits made their supreme mistake. Instead of appealing to the King's Council, as they had a right to do (or paying the debt), they appealed to the Parlement of Paris, the home of their bitterest Jansenist and Gallican enemies. The Parlement took this opportunity to make an official inquiry into the constitution and statutes of the Society, an inquiry conducted by the Abbé Chauvelin, a confirmed and bitter Jansenist. Parlement found the Jesuits "guilty" of advocating regicide, conspiracies, and other such political crimes. Some eighty books written by Jesuits were condemned as undermining civil authority, and orders were given to all novices to leave the Society by October 1, 1761. With a single exception, the bishops of France insisted that the Jesuits should be allowed to continue as then constituted, but in April, 1762, Parlement decreed that the Society in France should be suppressed.

Such action could not be taken until the king had signed the decree. After more than two years of delay Louis XV signed the decree ordering the suppression of the Society in France and putting its members under the ordinary of each diocese. Pope Clement XIII had meanwhile been most energetic in his support of the Society. He wrote more than 150 letters on behalf of the Jesuits and in January, 1765, he issued his famous protest against the suppression, *Apostolicum pascendi,* in which he gave formal recognition to all the good works of the Society and approved the principles of its constitution. "No greater injury nor more serious offense," he wrote, "could be inflicted on the Catholic Church since the position of those opposed to the Jesuits is tantamount to affirming that the Church has erred disgracefully by solemnly declaring that a wicked and irreligious order was pious and agreeable to God."

The next blow fell in Spain. The suppression in this country, which was the home of the Jesuits and their stronghold, was accomplished in secrecy and under mysterious circumstances. Charles III's minister Aranda was a close friend of the Society's enemies in France and a follower of the "enlightened" thinkers of the age. Aranda seems to have poisoned the king's mind against the Jesuits, and when serious riots occurred in 1766 Aranda convinced Charles that the Jesuits were to blame. An inquiry was conducted in secrecy, no Jesuits were heard, all records of the proceedings were destroyed, and the decision reached was rendered without any reasons given. Sealed orders were dispatched throughout the kingdom with instructions to open them on the night of April 2, 1767. On the next morning every Jesuit in the country and the empire was arrested and transported to the Papal States.

Other Bourbon rulers followed the example of Louis XV and Charles III. The king of Naples, who was the son of Charles III, suppressed the Society in November, 1767, and transported the Jesuits to the frontier of the Papal States. The duke of Parma, Charles's nephew, suppressed them in the following January and marched them to the Papal States. Then the Bourbon rulers combined with Portugal to demand that the pope suppress the remnants of the Society, about 10,000 members in northern Italy, Austria, and the Germanies. Clement XIII resolutely refused to be moved. In an attempt to force the pope's hand, France confiscated Avignon and the Venaissin, two papal enclaves within French borders, and the king of Naples seized Ponte Corvo and Beneventum. Furthermore, the Bourbons threatened to depose the pope and to partition the Papal States. When these threats failed to move Clement XIII, France combined with Spain and Naples in January, 1769, to make a formal demand for the suppression of the Society. Again Clement refused absolutely to meet the demand. The pope died while the Bourbon powers planned to blockade Rome, and the crucial question concerning any successor was his attitude toward the Jesuits.

The ensuing conclave lasted three months. The ambassadors of France and Spain succeeded in excluding twenty-three candidates on the grounds that they were favorable to the Jesuits, and at last Cardinal de Bernis succeeded in having the Franciscan Lorenzo Ganganelli elected as Clement XIV. What the new pope promised — if anything — before his election has always been a disputed matter. At any rate, the Bourbons kept up their pressure on the pope. When such protectors of the Jesuits as Maria Theresa of Austria ceased to uphold them, and others, such as the king of Sardinia, died, the new pope gradually yielded. The Bourbons finally drafted a decree which the pope was willing to sign, and on July 21, 1773, he published the brief *Dominus ac Redemptor* by which he suppressed the Society of Jesus. In this curious document the pope made no charges against the Jesuits, nor did he judge them in any way. The decree simply set forth many accusations which had been made against the Society and concluded that "the Church cannot enjoy true and lasting peace so long as the Society remains in existence."

Jesuits were given refuge first in Prussia and then in Russia when Catherine the Great invited them to establish schools. In 1778 Pope Pius VI countenanced this arrangement, and in 1801 Pius VII declared the Society of Jesus re-established for the whole of Russia. Thus the Jesuits were never entirely suppressed, for through this time they were allowed to accept novices and to live according to the rules of the Society, and when the Society was re-established on a universal basis in 1814 it was able to revive rapidly.

Redemptorists and Passionists. Two bright lights in this otherwise dark picture of Catholicism in the eighteenth century are St. Paul of the Cross and St. Alphonsus Liguori, both of whom founded religious orders to carry on their work, orders which still flourish and add to the richness of Catholic life today. St. Paul of the Cross lived and worked in Piedmont. He developed an intense personal devotion to the Passion of our Lord and founded an Order called the Regular Clerics of the Holy Cross and Passion — popularly known as the Passionists — to preach the meaning of the Passion. The Passionist unites himself to Christ suffering and takes a vow to preach on the Passion wherever he works. The Order was approved by Benedict XIV in 1741.

St. Alphonsus Liguori was a Neapolitan noble who gave up a successful career at law to become a priest and a preacher of missions. In 1732 he established the Redemptorists to preach missions throughout Italy. They received papal approval in 1749. After twenty years of missionary activity, St. Alphonsus took up a literary career and turned out an amazing quantity of religious literature. Much of his writing was on popular devotion and is still widely used, but his most important work is his *Moral Theology* written to combat the rigors of Jansenism. Philip Hughes claims that "none has done more, not merely to rout Jansenism as a system of morals, but to put an end to the Jansenist influence upon certain orthodox Catholic moralists and spiritual directors."

The seeds of the Catholic revival of the nineteenth century can be found in the work of St. Paul of the Cross and St. Alphonsus, for these Orders, especially the Redemptorists, played a large part in that revival which took place in the generation after St. Alphonsus' death in 1787.

REVIEW AIDS

1. On what grounds did the popes condemn Freemasonry? (A good discussion of this subject is in the June, 1927, issue of *Thought*.)
2. Why was the Masonic Order almost bound, by the nature of things, to favor revolutionary movements in all countries?
3. Make a list of the articles of belief stated in the Apostles' Creed. Indicate which of these articles could be subscribed to by a Deist, and which he would reject.
4. Frederick II of Prussia referred to Joseph II as "my brother Sacristan." Explain why Frederick used this derisive appellation.
5. Analyze the doctrine of Febronius (*a*) in the light of the Councils of Constance and Basle; (*b*) as a manifestation of Gallicanism.
6. Make a list of reasons why sincere Catholics might have advocated the suppression of the Society of Jesus.
7. Why did all the enemies of the Church advocate its suppression?
8. Analyze the effects on the Church of the suppression of the Society of Jesus.

SUGGESTIONS FOR FURTHER READING

The general trend of secular thought in the Enlightenment is objectively and sympathetically analyzed by the following works: Basil Willey, *The Eighteenth-Century Background* (New York: 1940); Charles Frankel, *The Faith of Reason* (New York: 1948); and R. B. Mowat, *The Age of Reason* (New York: 1934). The best work on this subject, however, is R. R. Palmer, *Catholics and Unbelievers in Eighteenth-Century France* (Princeton: 1939). The best study of "enlightened" thought on religion is Joseph Edmund Barker, *Diderot's Treatment of the Christian Religion in the Encyclopédie* (New York: 1941).

By the very nature of the subject, there is no good account by a Catholic author of Freemasonry, at least in English. The documents necessary for such a study remain inaccessible. The best study in English, which concentrates on the American scene but is still of some value for European Masonry, is Arthur Preuss, *A Study in American Freemasonry* (St. Louis: 1924).

The best thing in English on Febronianism is to be found in Pastor's *History of the Popes*, Volume XXXVI. Volume XXXIX of the same work handles Josephinism. A fuller treatment of this subject is Sister Mary Clare Goodwin, *The Papal Conflict with Josephinism* (New York: 1938). Joseph II's attitude toward religion is also treated in the biography of Saul K. Padover, *The Revolutionary Emperor, Joseph II* (New York: 1933).

The suppression of the Society of Jesus takes up the greater part of Volumes XXXVI–XXXVIII of Pastor's *History of the Popes*. The first two volumes deal with the suppression in the various Bourbon countries and with the pressure brought on Pope Clement XIII by the Bourbon courts. Volume XXXVIII deals with papal suppression by Pope Clement XIV. The subject is also treated in any general history of the Society, such as Thomas J. Campbell, *The Jesuits, 1534–1921* (New York: 1921). Considerably more detailed information can be found in Daniel A. Hanly, *Blessed Joseph Pignatelli* (New York: 1937).

DOCUMENTS

Correspondence of Ministers of State of the Bourbon Countries on the Suppression of the Society of Jesus.

After the Jesuits were suppressed by the Bourbon governments of Spain and France, these governments tried to bring their combined pressure to bear on the pope in order to have him suppress the Society universally. The following letters are between Bourbon ministers Choiseul of France and Grimaldi of Spain, in which they discuss ways and means of bringing about their objective in Rome.

1) Choiseul to Grimaldi.

You know, Sir, that here we regard the suppression of the Society of Jesus as an event which will be not only useful for the welfare and tranquility of the Church and States, but equally for the advantage of the members who make up the Society. Therefore the king [of France] will willingly adopt the plan that His Catholic Majesty [the king of Spain] proposes for this important object, and he will join with him in the measures he takes to facilitate and accelerate its execution. His Majesty thinks with the king, his cousin, that the success of this project will be impracticable under the pontificate of the present pope [Clement XIII]. It is equally certain that the popes who replace Clement XIII must be better disposed than he to accommodate themselves to the views of the courts that demand the destruction of the Jesuits. . . . In the future attention should be given to the time and circumstances for achieving the project that the three courts propose and realizing that it will be less possible to attain as long as it is only France, Spain, and Portugal that join in this project, while the other Catholic and Protestant powers continue to tolerate and protect these religious in their states.

2) Choiseul to Grimaldi.

As for the Jesuits, I have repeatedly told him [the Portuguese ambassador] that the king will take all the steps that the king of Spain desires of his majesty for the suppression of this society, but I warned him that this object will not be attained except by force, since reasoning has had no effect on the mind of Cardinal Torrigiani. The Comte de Fuentes has written to me to propose that we demand that Rome recalls this Minister [Torrigiani]. I do not know that it would comport to the dignity of the crowns to make a similar demand. . . . It is a declaration motivated by the three crowns that demand the destruction of the Order, and on the part of Spain the sending of the General to Madrid to answer to the accusations which have been made against his Order. In making this demand it should be made clear that if the pope does not send the General he will be carried off from Rome. Certainly the General will not go to Madrid, but fear will cause him and Rome to secularize the Order: companies of Neapolitan Grenadiers will support the demands of the three Courts and the Jesuit Society will be destroyed. You will find, my dear friend, that any other means except those of force, will come to nothing.

3) Grimaldi to Choiseul.

I wish to say that although I agree with you in not demanding the recall of Torrigiani and in believing that we cannot move the pope to proceed to this suppression by means of sweet reasoning, but (I believe) that there is a middle way between sweetness and force. The force of an effective war that Monsieur d'Oeyras wishes in order to occupy the temporal possessions of the pope appears a little too violent. We should make an attempt now to start persuading the court of Vienna to join with the rest of us to make this demand of Rome, and each of the courts should use whatever threats the situation makes possible.

4) Grimaldi to Choiseul.

As regards the conditions for an accommodation (with the Holy See), here we regard the most essential one the extinction of the Society of Jesus. Prelates and juriconsulists have unanimously continued to repeat to the king that there will be no peace in religion or state as long as this order exists in any part of the world, because the followers of their spirited opinions, by the hope of seeing them return to the country from which they have been expelled, always work people up and excite dissentions harmful to the Church and to the government. Starting out with this principle, we think that it will not suffice to second the demand of Portugal on this subject, but that we should keep it in mind as the primary condition for our accommodation with Rome. It is true that there is little hope of obtaining this accommodation from the present pope, but on the other hand, the envoy who is in Rome can end all the disputes not only with the three courts of our Family but also with Portugal and can frighten the pope and his ministers.

Chapter 30

THE CHURCH AND THE FRENCH
REVOLUTION

TWO years after St. Alphonsus died a revolution broke out in France. It caught both the papacy and the French government completely by surprise, for neither pope nor king was aware of the revolutionary forces that had accumulated behind the façade of an outmoded absolutism. The government of both Church and State throughout Europe rested on "divine right" and on an authority which had not been seriously challenged for centuries. We have seen in previous chapters how that authority was undermined in the eighteenth century, especially in France, and how any revolutionary movement was bound to be directed against Church as well as State.

The 1200 delegates who gathered at Versailles to give France a constitution had no thought of despoiling the Church. But within about a year they had confiscated all church property in France, rearranged the dioceses, provided for the election of bishops and parish priests, and, in effect, created a schismatic national French Church. Such interference in ecclesiastical affairs did not seem revolutionary to these delegates because of the Gallican tradition in France. They were only doing a more thorough job of what the kings had long done. About half the French clergy and a great part of the peasantry refused to accept the new Church, however, and thus there came to be two Churches in France. Struggle between the two was bitter. It divided the country into "two Frances," a division which endures even to the present time. And it threw loyal Catholics into the ranks of those who opposed the revolution and worked for the re-establishment of the Old Regime.

Through the nineteenth century small numbers of forward looking Catholics, such as Montalembert and Ozanam, tried to mend the breach between the new France and the old Church. But the chasm was deep, and most Catholics, as well as most supporters of the new government, had no desire to build a bridge across it. They accepted the complete dichotomy of either the new France or the old Church, and they were willing to fight until one or the other was destroyed. This has been the tragedy of the history of the Church in France since 1789.

The revolution was not confined to France. As the French armies marched victoriously into the capitals of Europe from Madrid to Moscow, they served as missionaries converting many Europeans to the ideas of the Revolution. French institutions were forced on those territories that came under French rule, such as Belgium, the Italian states, and a large part of the Germanies. Among these institutions was the secularization or confiscation of church property, the complete control of religious life by the government, and a general persecution of an independent Church. One of the states attacked by France was the Papal States. Pope Pius VI was taken prisoner, and when he died in 1799 the fortunes of the Church were at such low ebb that it was generally felt no successor would be elected. Within a few months, however, a new pope was elected in Venice, and he took the same name as his predecessor.

Within France and elsewhere in Europe a religious revival set in around the turn of the century. This was a "grass roots" movement which showed clearly where the strength of the Church lay. When Napoleon was finally defeated and peace was arranged in 1815, the papacy faced a new Europe with new institutions. The Papal States had been given back to the pope — from a practical viewpoint, unfortunately, perhaps — and the papal government was deceived into thinking it should maintain those relations which had been so disastrous in the eighteenth century. The new forces were hostile to revealed religion, and for several generations leaders in the Church did not give serious thought to accommodating Church policies to them. Pope Pius IX and Frederic Ozanam insisted the Church must convert these men of liberal and secularist thought as it had converted the barbarians who swarmed into the Roman Empire. But the pope's attempt was rebuffed, and it was not until after his death in 1878 that a serious effort was made to accommodate the Church to the changed modern world. Since that date this has been the main theme running through the history of the Church. Even today the leaders of the Church are trying to solve the problems created by the French Revolution.

The French Church in 1789. The Church had lost its hold on the best French minds by the time the Revolution broke out in 1789. The revival of the seventeenth century had spent its vigor, as we have already seen, and religious leaders had settled into a rut. They were mediocre rather than evil men, and they were subservient to the crown. The hierarchy were almost all men of noble birth who had little to do with the "commoners" who were the parish priests throughout the country. High churchmen tended to be active politically and socially, and thus were identified closely with the government. The lower clergy tended to identify themselves with the common people whose spokesmen they were at the outset of the Revolution. Thus the clergy were divided against themselves in 1789, not on morals or dogma, but on political and social policy.

Estimates on the amount of Church holdings in 1789 vary considerably. We can be certain that they were large, and we know that the higher clergy skimmed off about five sixths of the Church's income in France. Cardinal de Rohan's annual income was about $200,000, and the average curé received about $125 a year. The greater part of Church property was devoted to religious and social purposes, and it does not seem to have caused resentment among the French people. What was resented was the tithe, not so much because it was a tax to support the Church, as because of the arbitrary way it was assessed and collected.

The delegates who met at Versailles on May 5, 1789, were to sit in three Estates or houses. The clergy composed the First Estate. Two hundred and five of the 308 clerical delegates were curates; the remainder were bishops or abbots. The critical issue in the first weeks of the Revolution was whether the three Estates should sit separately and vote "by order" or sit together and vote "by head." The latter system would ensure control of affairs for the commoners, since they had twice as many delegates as either the clergy or the nobility. In the contest which ensued, many of the lower clergy sided with the Third Estate. After two months of wrangling the king gave way and ordered the First and Second Estates to sit with the Third as a National Assembly. The lower clergy had thus played the decisive role in creating the body they hoped would reform France.

One of the first acts of this Assembly occurred on the memorable night of August 4–5 when France's social revolution took place. Moved partly by fear and partly by the intoxicating ideas of liberty and equality, members of the nobility and clergy gave up all the hated privileges they had enjoyed since medieval times — such as hunting rights, grist mill taxes, and similar exactions. Among these privileges surrendered in this burst of generosity was the tithe. The question immediately arose whether the Church was to be indemnified for surrendering the tithe. Abbé Sieyès and others pointed out that if the Church were not indemnified the government would have to assume the burden of supporting the clergy. He therefore urged that the tithes be redeemed and the money put aside for the annual support of the clergy. The Assembly, however, decided to suppress the tithe without indemnification and thus the clergy were deprived of their income and bound by the very nature of things to become government charges or else to starve.

The Civil Constitution of the Clergy.   The National Assembly soon ran into financial difficulties. The old taxes had been abolished and the Assembly was reluctant to pass new revenue-raising measures. At this point various elements hostile to the Church — Huguenots, Jansenists, Gallicans, *Philosophes* — combined to suggest that church property should be confiscated to finance the Revolution. Such action would serve many useful purposes besides raising money. It would create a class with a financial stake in the Revolution. Thus it would be insurance against a reaction in favor of the Old Regime, for those who purchased church property would fight any proposal to re-establish the old Church. Anti-clerically inclined persons also favored the confiscation as a means of weakening or destroying the Church. Others saw in the measure an opportunity to enrich themselves by speculating in church lands.

After acrimonious debate an enabling measure was passed whereby the government was permitted to seize and sell church property and to use the funds as security for treasury bonds, called *assignats,* which were later converted into paper money. To allay the fears of prospective buyers the Assembly "released" nuns and regular clergy from their vows and "dissolved" the religious orders. Any member of a religious order who wanted to take advantage of the law was simply to announce his intention of leaving his order before the local civic authority. In return, he would receive a lump sum of money. Those who refused to leave were to be herded together into a few convents and monasteries. Since no orders were permitted to receive novices, the Assembly believed that within a generation there would be no religious orders in France. Monasteries, convents, and similar church properties were then sold at auction throughout France.

As a result of suppressing the tithes and confiscating church property the government had to provide some kind of livelihood for the clergy. This would obviously involve state control of the Church. Gallicans looked on this as a natural and a good arrangement, for they considered religion a department of State. Jansenists saw the opportunity of establishing a simplified, reformed religion that would put an end to inefficiency, laxness, and the ostentatious display they had condemned so bitterly in the established Church of the eighteenth century. The combined attitude of these groups was tersely stated by the Jansenist Camus when he said: "The Church is part of the State; we are a Convention; we have the power to change our religion."

The Civil Constitution of the Clergy was finally passed on July 12, 1790. It put the clergy on the State's payroll and made them subject to the control and the discipline of the State. A pastor had to obtain permission from the civil authority, for example, to leave his parish, or a bishop his diocese. Affiliation with Rome was almost completely severed, and thus the French Church became in effect schismatic. Pastors and bishops were to be democratically elected, with all eligible citizens — Catholic or not — having the right to vote. Bishops were to inform the pope of their election *after* it had taken place and after they had been installed in their see. Finally, diocesan boundaries were completely rearranged so that the dioceses coincided with the new political divisions or *départements*. There were to be 83 dioceses, and there was to be a parish for each 6000 people. Thus the number of parishes was drastically reduced in the interest of economy and efficiency.

The Civil Constitution of the Clergy could not become law until the king signed the bill. After delaying as long as he could, Louis XVI signed the bill and it became law on August 24, 1790. Pius VI was opposed to the Civil Constitution of the Clergy, but he hesitated to condemn it publicly for fear that such action might drive the Assembly to even harsher measures. Meanwhile, most of the bishops and a large part of the clergy throughout France went about their clerical duties as though no change had taken place. Bishops and priests followed the old diocesan boundaries, for example, instead of the newly established ones. The Assembly, therefore, decided to require all bishops and priests to take an oath "to watch over the faithful of the diocese or parish entrusted to him, to be loyal to the nation, the law, and the king, and to uphold by every means in his power the Constitution decreed by the National Assembly and accepted by the king."

Taking the oath meant accepting the Civil Constitution of the Clergy (part of the as yet uncompleted Constitution) and whatever the government might do in the future. It was equivalent to signing a blank check. Only four bishops took the oath. The lower clergy divided about evenly between those who took the oath (the "juring" clergy) and those who did not (the "nonjuring" clergy). It was generally the less well-informed priests in the smaller villages who took the oath, and there is little doubt that many of them did not understand the meaning of what they did.

The Civil Constitution of the Clergy and the required oath divided the Catholic Church in France into the constitutional Church and a Church loyal to Rome. The episcopal succession was secured for the constitutional Church by Talleyrand's consecrating two bishops who, in turn, consecrated others. Those who did not take the oath were denied the use of the churches; they had to say Mass in private chapels or barns or wherever the faithful could gather for worship without interference by the government. Because in many parts of France the people preferred the nonjuring clergy, the government took increasingly severe measures against them. They were given eight days in which to take the oath. Those who refused were listed as suspect. Later they were imprisoned, and still later it was provided that they should be deported from the country.

Persecutions and Recovery of the Church.   As the Revolution progressed it grew more extreme in its religious policy. Among the victims of the September Massacres (1792) were hundreds of priests. Within two hours 120 were dragged out of the prisons of Paris and murdered without trial. Similar scenes were enacted throughout the rest of France, so that by the end of 1792 the French clergy began to emigrate in large numbers to Spain, Germany, England, and the United States. Many stayed in France, however, and worked heroically to keep the faith alive among their flocks. The nonjuring clergy were popular in the country districts and especially in the west which was soon engaged in civil war with the Paris-centered government. Toward the end of 1793 it was provided that any nonjuring clergyman found in France was to be executed.

During the "Reign of Terror" (1793–1794) the juring clergy were also persecuted. The destruction of the Constitutional Church was completed officially when the government established the Religion of Reason. The Gregorian calendar was replaced by a Republican calendar which abolished all holydays and Sundays and instituted natural feast days, such as the Feast of Labor and the Feast of Genius. Notre Dame Cathedral was converted into the Temple of the Goddess of Reason, and a dancing girl was placed on the high altar to impersonate the new goddess.

Resistance to these excesses grew widespread throughout France. When the extreme revolutionary government was overthrown in the Thermidorian reaction (July, 1794) priests came out of hiding to say Mass openly again. The new government followed popular feeling on the matter of religion by decreeing freedom of worship. Whatever churches the government still possessed were restored to the clergy, but the government maintained its right to control religion by such measures as prohibiting priests to wear cassocks in public. For the next few years the constitutional clergy struggled to maintain their position against the popular nonjuring clergy. A great part of the revived Church's energy was therefore consumed in bitter fratricidal strife.

This was the condition of the Church when the extreme revolutionary (Jacobin) element came to power again in 1797. The government began a new persecution by reviving all previous decrees against the Church, by requiring the clergy to take an oath of "hatred for royalty and anarchy," and by empowering the government to deport priests who "disturbed the public peace." Thousands of priests were deported or executed during this persecution, or they escaped to such countries as England and the United States. The persecution of 1797 was especially severe in Belgium, which had been taken by the French after the earlier persecutions and therefore still maintained its religious institutions intact.

The government gave official encouragement to several anti-Christian religions which today seem ludicrous and bungling attempts to concoct a substitute for the ancient religion of France. One of these was a form of Theophilanthropy and another was the Worship of Decadi, the last day of the ten-day week of the new Republican calendar. None of these synthetic religions proved to be popular. The Catholic religion continued to survive in France and Belgium because of the heroic courage of a small band of priests and because of the loyalty of the rural people who clung tenaciously to their religion even when there were no priests to minister to them.

The French government also made war on the pope as a temporal ruler. In 1797, during the course of his first Italian campaign as one of the Directory's generals, Napoleon Bonaparte imposed the Treaty of Tolentino on the pope. By its terms the pope was forced to cede part of the Papal States to a puppet republic Napoleon had organized in northern Italy, pay an indemnity of 330 million francs, surrender 100 works of art, close his ports to English commerce, and promise not to give any help to France's enemies. In the next year General Berthier seized Rome and established the Roman Republic. On the grounds that the pope's presence in Rome might provoke a counterrevolution, the French authorities ordered Pius VI to leave the Vatican. He was escorted to Siena and then across the Alps to France, where he died on August 29, 1799.

The papal conclave eventually gathered on the island of San Giorgio Maggiore, across from Venice, where after three months they elected the bishop of Imola, Cardinal Chiaramonte, who took the name of Pius VII. The new pope was faced with the immediate problem of returning to Rome or of finding some other place where he would not be any ruler's "chaplain" and where he could freely act as head of a universal Church. Meanwhile, the government in France was becoming increasingly unpopular. One of the principal causes of the Directory's unpopularity was its religious policy, for in the last years of the eighteenth century persecution had provoked a widespread religious revival in France.

The Religious Settlement Under Napoleon. No one knew this better than Napoleon Bonaparte who seized power by a *coup d'état* in November, 1799. Napoleon was anxious to settle the religious problem in France for political reasons. He wanted a united country in loyal support of his imperial policies, and he knew that there would never be a single, united France until the religious problem was settled. He was convinced that the people of France, especially in the provinces, were genuinely religious. "I am extremely powerful," he said, "but if I wished to change the old religion of France she would rise up against me and overcome me." Political considerations therefore moved Napoleon to settle the religious problem. A man of no religious conviction himself, he was willing to adopt whatever religion furthered his cause. "It was by turning Moslem that I established myself in Egypt," he explained to a friend, "by turning Ultramontane that I won the Italian mind. If I governed a people of Jews I would rebuild the temple of Solomon." And Napoleon knew he governed a country that was largely Catholic.

After his victory at Marengo (1800) Napoleon, therefore, let the pope know that he was anxious to settle the religious problem in France. Negotiations were begun simultaneously in Paris and Rome. They were made unusually difficult because of the opposition of various groups in France. The Jacobin element, represented by the ex-bishop Talleyrand and the ex-priest Fouché, was unalterably opposed to any settlement with the Church. The royalist element, on the other hand, including most of the *émigré* bishops, opposed any settlement on the grounds that it would help Napoleon and would make a royalist restoration more difficult. The leaders of the Constitutional Church, headed by Abbé Gregoire, were afraid that any settlement would destroy their church created by the Civil Constitution of the Clergy.

Napoleon eventually overcame the opposition of all these groups and speedily negotiated a concordat with Cardinal Consalvi. The story of the negotiations is an account of clever sparring between an unprincipled ruler and a capable diplomat. Consalvi discovered, to cite only a single instance, that the copy of the concordat he was given to sign had been altered in certain important respects from the one he had agreed to on the previous day. Eventually he and Napoleon agreed on terms and the concordat was signed. Napoleon secured its ratification by a series of clever political maneuvers and by publishing with it the "Organic Articles," which modified or contradicted several of its provisions.

The Concordat of 1801 was a personal victory for Napoleon, but it was also a success for the Roman Church. The Roman Catholic religion was recognized as the religion of the majority of Frenchmen. All revolutionary oaths for the clergy were abolished, provision was made for the support of the Church in France, and to all appearances the schism created by the Civil Constitution of the Clergy was healed. The French government was given the right to nominate bishops, and the pope reserved the right of canonical installation as provided in the Concordat of 1516. The papacy accepted the secularization of Church property in return for government support of the clergy, and thus the owners of such property were given assurance that the Church would not contest their ownership in the future.

The difficult problem of the episcopate was adroitly and intelligently handled. There were 82 survivors of the old episcopate on hand. The 83 French sees were occupied by constitutional or juring bishops. Pope Pius VII courageously requested the resignation of all the old bishops, and he deposed those who refused to resign. Napoleon removed all the constitutional bishops. Thus he was free to nominate an entirely new group agreeable to both himself and the pope. His choices were well made. Twelve of the sixty were former constitutional bishops, sixteen were from the old episcopate, and thirty-two were new men. The papacy regularized the status of constitutional priests who had married; the others were accepted into the Church where they assumed their priestly duties alongside the former nonjuring clergy.

Thus it seemed that the Concordat of 1801 settled the problems the French Revolution had created for France. But at the same time Napoleon published the Organic Articles which were drawn up without the knowledge of the Holy See and were promulgated unilaterally as laws regulating the conduct of religion in France. The Organic Articles put all religions on an equal basis and made them subject to the State. They provided that no papal messages or legates could enter France without express consent from the government. Neither could the decrees of an ecumenical council be published in France until the government gave its consent. The Organic Articles also contained numerous provisions regulating the manner of worship, such as those dealing with the ringing of church bells and with clerical dress. Finally, they required that the Four Gallican Articles of 1682 be taught in all French seminaries.

Napoleon's War With the Church. Napoleon's growing power and his even faster growing ambition brought him into conflict with the Church in two principal areas: (1) within France and conquered territories, where he attempted to rule the Church as a department of State;

(2) in the Papal States, which he attempted to govern as an integral part of his far-flung empire. The contest frequently seemed to be about minor matters, such as his younger brother's divorce from Elizabeth Patterson or his own second marriage to Marie Louise, but back of these disputes lay the basic question of whether or not the pope and cardinals were going to allow Napoleon to govern the Church as part of his empire. Eventually, as we know, Napoleon was defeated and Pope Pius VII was returned triumphantly from captivity near Paris to Rome. But in the intervening decade and a half it frequently seemed that Napoleon was at the point of breaking the back of the papacy and driving the remnants of the Church underground.

One of Napoleon's most crushing blows against the Church was the series of changes he effected in the Germanies. He compensated the secular German rulers for lands he took from them by giving them Church property and sovereignty over the lands ruled by the various prince-bishops. Eventually Napoleon deprived these bishops of all their properties, which he turned over to various German lay princes in an attempt to attach them securely to his empire. Altogether, the Church lost about 2000 square miles of territory with a population of three and a half million and a revenue of something like ten million dollars a year. Many of the dioceses remained vacant, and because seminaries, cathedral chapters, and monasteries were deprived of their means of support, they tended to die out and not to be replaced by other Church institutions. Only a skeleton of a Church remained in Germany in 1815.

When Napoleon was crowned emperor in 1804, Pope Pius VII agreed to come to Paris to bestow the crown upon him. The pope hoped, in return, to obtain two important concessions: the revocation or modification of the Organic Articles, and the removal of divorce from the new code of civil laws. Napoleon behaved impudently. He received the pope in his hunting clothes, covered with mud, and at the coronation ceremony he seized the crown from the pope's hands and put it on his own head. Napoleon and his associates had interpreted the pope's coming to Paris as a sign of weakness which they tried to exploit to the full. Pius VII returned to Rome humiliated and without obtaining any concessions from the emperor.

In Rome, the pope stiffened. He refused to annul Jerome Bonaparte's marriage to Elizabeth Patterson, and a little later he refused to annul Napoleon's marriage to Josephine Beauharnais. Despite the pope's refusal, members of the French hierarchy gave the emperor the desired annulments. Political differences between the pope and the emperor became acute after Napoleon's successes at Austerlitz (1805) and Tilsit (1807). After the peace of Tilsit Napoleon was master of the European continent, and he set about defeating his lone remaining enemy, England. His plan was to close all continental ports to English commerce and thus defeat the "nation of shopkeepers" economically rather than militarily. He insisted that the pope must join his "continental system" and close his ports to English commerce.

Napoleon's demand came at an inopportune time. The pope was exasperated by the way Napoleon had twisted Catholic doctrine and worship to support imperial rule in France. A caricature of the catechism had been introduced in the French schools to render Napoleon an almost divine person, and the emperor had insisted that St. Napoleon's day be observed throughout the empire on August 16, thus replacing St. Roch by the obscure and even dubious saint after whom he had been named. At any rate, the pope was in no mood to accept dictation from Napoleon, and he refused to close his ports to the English. The emperor retaliated by occupying part of the Papal States in November, 1807, and three months later he ordered General Miollis to seize the city of Rome. The sovereignty of the pope was ignored by the French, and finally in May, 1809, Napoleon officially annexed the Papal States to his empire. The pope answered by excommunicating Napoleon and all his subordinates who participated in the attack on Rome.

In July the pope was arrested and hurried out of Rome. His trip through northern Italy, across the Alps to Grenoble, and finally to Savona was a severe hardship, for Pius VII was seventy years old and he was severely ill during the tedious journey. Napoleon apparently planned to install the pope somewhere in the environs of Paris, where the head of the Catholic Church was to serve as an imperial chaplain and give spiritual and moral support to Napoleon's imperial policies.

Meanwhile, Napoleon was confident that he could obtain episcopal support from the timid French cardinals and bishops for his war against the pope. But the advisory board presided over by his uncle, Cardinal Fesch, proved less compliant than Napoleon had expected. When asked to judge on the papal bull excommunicating the emperor, they stated that "invasion of ecclesiastical property is a sufficient cause for excommunication," and when asked about the pope's refusal of canonical institution to bishops nominated to the vacant sees in France, they answered that the privation of his freedom was sufficient grounds for the pope's refusal of such institution.

In order to make the French bishops entirely dependent on himself, Napoleon cut their communications with the pope. In the first week of 1811 he wrote to the Governor-General of the Transalpine departments: "As I desire to protect my subjects from the rage and fury of this ignorant and peevish old man, I hereby order you to notify him that he is forbidden to communicate with any church of mine, or any of my subjects. . . . You will take care to have all the pope's papers, books, and documents taken from him." The French bishops were in a difficult position from which they extricated themselves with considerable honor. Thirteen out of twenty-seven cardinals had refused to attend Napoleon's second marriage. They were exiled, forbidden to wear the robes of their office (hence the nickname of "Black Cardinals") and even threatened with death.

Napoleon tried to get authorization from a national council to have bishops canonically invested by the metropolitan if the pope failed to act within a certain time, for the pope's refusal to invest the imperial appointees had created the same embarrassing situation Louis XIV had faced after 1682. The council declared itself incompetent to pass on Napoleon's request and urged him to negotiate directly with the pope. Napoleon sent various subservient bishops to persuade the imprisoned pope to meet the emperor's demands. When Napoleon's envoys failed to break down the pope's resistance the emperor had Pius VII moved to Fontainebleau near Paris. The pope almost died on the journey. Napoleon took advantage of the pope's weakness to visit him personally and to exact from him the abortive Concordat of Fontainebleau (1813) in which Pius renounced the Papal States and conceded that canonical institution of bishops could be made by the metropolitan if the pope did not act within six months. However, Pius VII revoked this concession within twenty-four hours. Napoleon suppressed the revocation, kept the pope isolated, and published the Concordat of Fontainebleau as a valid reconciliation of Church and State in France.

But the sands of Napoleon's fortune were fast running out. His campaign of 1812 in Russia had been disastrous, and in 1813 he was thoroughly defeated in the Battle of the Nations at Leipzig. On January 21, 1814, he gave orders that the pope should be taken back to Savona, and on March 10 he should be restored to Rome. Pius VII refused to accept the Papal States from the man who never had valid title to them. Instead, he returned as rightful ruler to his own states, and he was enthusiastically acclaimed by French and then by Italian crowds on his way back to Rome. In the long drawn out struggle with the mighty emperor the frail and aged Pope Pius VII had emerged victorious.

When the pope returned to Rome he said to the people, "Let us forget the past." Three years later when Napoleon was in exile at St. Helena, the pope wrote to Cardinal Consalvi: "The Emperor Napoleon's family have informed us through Cardinal Fesch that the rocky island of St. Helena is fatal to health and that the poor exile is dying by inches.

[This was not true.] We are deeply distressed to hear this, and you will certainly share our grief; for we must both remember that to Napoleon more than anyone, after God, is due the restoration of our religion in the great Kingdom of France. The pious and courageous initiative of 1801 has long ago effaced the memory of later wrongs. Savona and Fontainebleau were only mistakes due to temper, or the errors of an ambitious man: the Concordat was the saving act of a Christian and a hero." This is perhaps the most charitable estimate ever made of Napoleon's role in the history of the Church.

Conclusion. The assault on the Church by the French Revolution and its child, Napoleon, produced mixed results. The prince-bishop disappeared into the pages of history when Napoleon reorganized the empire and secularized the holdings of the Church throughout middle Europe. This was a good thing without which the tremendous revival of the Church in nineteenth-century Germany could hardly have taken place. At the same time, however, the monastic orders were reduced to near impotency. Their holdings had been confiscated, their houses of studies broken up, and their members dispersed into the world. The Church thus found one of its strongest props weakened. With the decline of the monasteries the liturgical life of the Church grew weak and pallid. Moreover, the universities in which ecclesiastical intellectual life had flourished, had been closed down or were taken over by the State. Thus was the Church's influence on cultural and intellectual life weakened.

Napoleon's Organic Articles had, in perverse fashion, put an end to Gallicanism as a strong element in the Church's life. Catholics after 1815 might argue about papal infallibility, but they were all "ultramontane" in the sense that they were devoted to the pope personally and they looked upon him as the leader of the Church against the secular states. The French Revolution had put an end to the absolute king, although several decades were to pass before general acknowledgment was made of this fact, and thus the Church was free to work out a new set of relationships with the State. Through the nineteenth century Catholics in some states attempted to rest their religious rights on the national constitution and protect them with an organized political party. Another device commonly employed for regulating relations between Church and State was the concordat, a sort of international "peace treaty" between the pope and the head of the state setting forth the terms on which the Church is to function within the State.

The French Revolution was a political and social solvent. It melted down the old institutions, good and bad, into which the Church had been integrated in past centuries, and thus it enabled the pope and bishops to begin afresh, as it were, in creating institutions through which the Church could operate in the new society of the nineteenth century. At the same time, it loosed forces hostile to the Church: a liberalism which was incompatible with ecclesiastical as well as political authority; a nationalism which exalted the nation and sometimes even deified it; a secularism which pushed religion out of worldly affairs to settle men's destinies as though they were creatures without an immortal soul.

The task confronting the Church in 1815 was, therefore, exceedingly difficult. Throughout history the Church has had to adapt itself to changing social and political conditions, but never before had there been such a sudden and complete revolution in European institutions. Never before was there so imperative a need of radically revised policies by the Church, a fact which the pope and the bishops were understandably slow to grasp. The anticlericalism of the new revolutionary spokesmen, unfortunately, made the institutions of the eighteenth century seem good in retrospect, and many leaders in the Church therefore came to look on an alliance with the absolute king — which had done such harm to the Church — as a good and a "normal" thing for the Church. That was perhaps one of the worst results of the French Revolution.

REVIEW AIDS

1. Explain as fully as possible how the Church's established position in France in the eighteenth century predisposed revolutionary leaders to attack it.
2. Describe the critical role played in the first weeks of the Revolution by the lower clergy, and explain why they took the stand they did.
3. Analyze as fully as you can the critical role played by the Civil Constitution of the Clergy on the Church and on the French nation.
4. Make a list of the secularizing measures of the French Revolution.
5. Prepare a list of reasons why (a) Napoleon and (b) Pope Pius VII were anxious to negotiate a Concordat in 1800.
6. Cardinal Consalvi was not a priest. Find out whether he was a cleric. Is it still possible for one not a priest to be made a cardinal?
7. Why did the Concordat of 1801, with which Napoleon and the pope were both pleased, not heal the breach created by the Civil Constitution of the Clergy?
8. Compare the Concordat of 1801 and the "Organic Articles" to discover in what way they were contrary in spirit and in detailed provisions.
9. List the factors which help account for the resistance of large parts of the French population to the revolutionary changes in the Church.
10. Explain why the pope was better able to resist Napoleon after he had lost the Papal States than when he was still their temporal ruler.

SUGGESTIONS FOR FURTHER READING

There is abundant material in French, but very little in English, on the history of the Church during the period of the French Revolution. The outstanding work on the subject is the five-volume study of Pierre de la Gorce, *Histoire religieuse de la Révolution française*. Unfortunately, this work has not been translated into English.

A fairly comprehensive knowledge of Church history during this period can be obtained from reading the standard works on the French Revolution and Napoleon. The best of these are the two volumes of J. M. Thompson, *The French Revolution* (New York: 1945), and *Napoleon Bonaparte* (New York: 1952). The better students will appreciate Crane Brinton, *A Decade of Revolution, 1789–1799* (New York: 1934), and Geoffrey Bruun, *Europe and the French Imperium, 1799–1814* (New York: 1938). These books, which are in the Rise of Modern Europe series, contain excellent annotated bibliographies. Standard one-volume studies of the period are Louis R. Gottschalk, *The Era of the French Revolution* (Boston: 1929), and Leo Gershoy, *The French Revolution and Napoleon* (New York: 1941). Perhaps the most valuable book for the mature student is *A Documentary Survey of the French Revolution*, edited by John Hall Stewart (New York: 1951). This is a collection of documents dealing with the French Revolution, and it contains the text of major measures on religion, such as the Civil Constitution of the Clergy and the Oath required of the clergy.

The lives of the popes in this period are handled in popular fashion by Lillian Browne Olf, *Their Name Is Pius* (Milwaukee: 1941), a study which includes good sections on Pius VI and Pius VII. A gripping account of how the Revolution affected an individual priest is the biographical account of the papal envoy, Msgr. de Salamon, *A Papal Envoy During the Reign of Terror* (St. Louis: 1911). Henry H. Walsh, *The Concordat of 1801* (New York: 1933) is a thorough study of this important subject. Additional light is thrown on papal diplomacy by the excellent study of John Tracy Ellis, *Cardinal Consalvi and Anglo-papal Relations* (Washington: 1942).

DOCUMENTS

A. Excerpts From the Civil Constitution of the Clergy

The Civil Constitution of the Clergy was one of the most important laws passed in French history. It divided Frenchmen, cleric and lay, into "two Frances," and the breach has not yet been closed. The following are typical important clauses of this famous law.

Each and every department shall constitute a single diocese, and each and every diocese shall have the same extent and limits as the department.

A new organization and division of all parishes of the kingdom shall be undertaken immediately, upon the advice of the diocesan bishop and the district administrations; the number and extent thereof shall be determined according to rules to be established.

Dating from the day of publication of the present decree, appointments to bishoprics and curates are to be made by election only.

All elections shall be by ballot and absolute majority of votes.

Proclamation of those elected shall be made by the president of the electoral assembly, in the church where the election was held, in the presence of the people and the clergy, and before beginning the solemn mass which is to be celebrated on such occasion.

The new bishop may not apply to the Pope for confirmation, but shall write to him as the Visible Head of the Universal Church, in testimony of the unity of faith and communion which he is to maintain therewith.

No bishop may absent himself from his diocese for more than fifteen consecutive days during any year, except in case of real necessity and with the consent of the directory of the department in which his see is located.

Likewise, *curés* and vicars may not absent themselves from the place of their duties beyond the term established above, except for serious reasons; and even in such cases the *curés* shall be required to obtain the consent of both their bishop and their district directory, the vicars that of their *curés*.

B.   Articles From the Concordat of 1801

The Concordat of 1801 served as a model for concordats throughout the nineteenth century. It seemed to settle the religious problem in France, but the settlement was more legal than religious or social. Following are the more important provisions of this Concordat.

1. The Catholic, Apostolic, and Roman religion will be freely exercised in France. Its worship will be public, in conformity with the police regulations that the government will judge necessary for public tranquility.

4. The first consul of the Republic, within three months following the publication of the bull of His Holiness, will nominate to the archbishoprics and bishoprics of the new circumscription. His Holiness will confer canonical institution according to the forms established in relation to France before the change of government.

5. Nominations to the bishoprics that will become vacant subsequently will likewise be made by the first consul, and the canonical institution will be given by the Holy See, in conformity with the preceding article.

6. Before entering upon their office, the bishops shall make directly into the hands of the first consul the oath of fidelity that was in use before the change of government, expressed in the following terms.

"I swear and promise to God, upon the holy Gospels, to keep obedience and fidelity to the government established by the Constitution of the French Republic. I promise also to entertain no knowledge, to participate in no counsel, to enter into no league, whether internal or external, which may be contrary to the public tranquillity; and if, in my diocese or elsewhere, I learn that anything is being contrived to the prejudice of the State, I will make the same known to the government."

8. At the end of the divine office the following prayer well be recited in all the Catholic churches of France:

"Domine, salvam fac Rempublicam; Domine, salvos fac Consules."

10. The bishops will appoint the *curés*. Their choice will designate only persons approved by the government.

13. His Holiness, for the sake of peace and the happy re-establishment of the Catholic religion, declares that neither he nor his successors will in any way disturb those who have acquired alienated ecclesiastical property; consequently the ownership of these same properties, together with the rights and revenues attached thereto, will remain indefeasible in their hands and those of their assigns.

14. The government will assure a suitable support (salary) to the bishops and the *curés* whose dioceses and parishes will be embraced in the new circumscription.

15. The government will likewise adopt measures so that French Catholics, if they so wish, may make foundations in favor of the churches.

16. His Holiness recognizes in the first consul of the French Republic the same rights and prerogatives as those enjoyed in relation to him by the former government.

17. It is agreed between the contracting parties that, in the event that any of the successors of the first consul should not be Catholic, the rights and prerogatives mentioned in the foregoing article and the appointment to the bishoprics, will be regulated with regard to him by a new convention.

C. Excerpts From the Organic Articles of 1801

The Organic Articles were passed as French law at the time the Concordat of 1801 was adopted. In many respects these articles nullify the concordat and they were not accepted by the papacy. They had the unlooked for effect of dealing a death blow to Gallicanism, for henceforward Catholic priests had no choice but to be loyal to Rome.

1. No bull, brief, decree, mandate, appointment, signature in lieu of appointment, nor other dispatches from the court of Rome, even concerning merely individuals, can be received, published, printed, or otherwise put into execution without the authorization of the government.

2. No individual calling himself nuncio, legate, apostolic vicar or commissioner, or availing himself of any other title, may, without the same authorization, exercise on French soil or elsewhere any function relative to the affairs of the Gallican Church.

3. The decrees of foreign synods, even of general councils, may not be published in France before the government has examined their form, their conformity with the laws, rights, and liberties of the French Republic, and whatever, in their publication, might alter or concern the public tranquility.

4. No national or metropolitan council, no diocesan synod, and no deliberative assembly can be held without the express permission of the government.

39. There will be only one liturgy and one catechism for all the churches of France.

40. No *curé* may order public extraordinary prayers in his parish without the special permission of the bishop.

	ENGLAND	FRANCE	THE EMPIRE	SPAIN, ITALY, NETHERLANDS
1600	James I (1603–25) Gunpowder Plot(1605)		Protestant union (1608)	
1610	King James version of the Bible (1611)	Louis XIII (1610–43) Regentship of Marie de' Medici (1610–17) Estates-General called (1614)	Matthias (1612–19) Thirty Years' War (1618–48) Ferdinand II (1619–37)	
1620	Charles I (1625–49) Petition of Right (1628)	Richelieu chief minister (1624–42)	Edict of Restitution (1629)	Philip IV of Spain (1621–65)
1630	The Scots' "National Covenant" (1638) The "Bishops' War" (1639–40)	Thirty Years' War: French phase (1635–48)	Ferdinand III (1637–57)	War with France (1635–48)
1640	Puritan Revolution (1642–53) "Rump" beheads Charles I (1649) Cromwell subdues the Irish (1649)	Mazarin chief minister (1642–61) Louis XIV (1643–1715)	Frederick William develops Prussia (1640–88)	Dutch Republic recognized (1648)
		Peace of Westphalia (1648)		
1650	Cromwell subdues Scots (1651)	Peace of Pyrenees (1659)	Leopold I (1658–1705)	
1660	The Restoration: Charles II (1660–85) Conventicle Act (1664) Five Mile Act (1665)	War of Devolution (1667–68)		Charles II of Spain (1665–1700)
1670	The Test Act (1673) The "Popish Plot" (1678)	Dutch War (1672–78)		
1680	James II (1685–88) Declarations of Indulgence (1687–88) William III and Mary II (1689–94) Toleration Act (1689)	Edict of Nantes revoked (1685)	War with Turks (1693–99) Frederick III of Prussia (1688–1713) [King Frederick I after 1701]	William III becomes King of England (1689)
		War of the League of Augsburg (1688–97) (Palatinate)		
1690	William III (1694–1702) The Triennial Act (1694)		Elector of Saxony becomes Polish King (1697)	
		Peace of Ryswick (1697)		

EASTERN EUROPE	THE CATHOLIC CHURCH	ECONOMIC, SOCIAL LIFE	CULTURAL LIFE
...ublous Times" in ...ssia (1605–13)	Leo XI (1605) Paul V (1605–21) St. Francis de Sales founds Visitandines (1607) English oath condemned (1606)	Dutch East India Company chartered (1602) Colonization of Virginia; Jamestown founded (1607) French settlement of Quebec under Champlain (1608)	Calderón (1600–81) Rembrandt (1606–69) John Milton (1608–74) Shakespeare's tragedies (1606)
...tavus II, Adolphus of ...eden (1611–32) ...ael Romanov of Russia ...613–45) ...dinavia bans Catholics ...613)	de Bérulle founds Oratory (1611)		King James Bible (1611)
	Gregory XV (1621–23) Urban VIII (1623–44) Vincentians founded (1625)		Bacon Essay's (1625) Molière (1622–73) Grotius' On Law of War and Peace (1625)
...den enters Thirty Years' ...ar (1630)	Galileo imprisoned (1633) Sisters of Charity founded (1633)		John Locke (1632–1704) French Academy incorporated (1632) Descartes — Discourse on Method (1637)
...ius of Russia (1645–76)	Japanese martyrs (1642) Innocent X (1644–55) Jansenism condemned (1653)	German lands wasted by the Thirty Years' War	Classical school in art and letters G. W. Leibniz (1646–1716)
	Alexander VII (1655–67) Paris Missionary Society (1658)	"Quaker" Movement (1652)	Hobbes' Leviathan (1651) Walton, The Compleat Angler (1653)
...rles XI of Sweden ...660–97)	Clement IX (1667–69) Pax Clementina (1669)		Pepy's Diary (1660–69) Paradise Lost (1667) Dryden — Conquest of Granada (1668)
...n III Sobieski defeats ...urks (1673) ...n III Sobieski of Poland ...674–96) ...odore II of Russia ...676–82)	Clement X (1670–76) Innocent XI (1676–89)		Spinoza's Philosophy (1670) Bunyan's Pilgrim's Progress (1678)
...n V and Peter I ...682–89) ...er I "The Great" of ...ussia (1682–1725) ...n III Sobieski defeats ...urks (1683) ...ssia expels Jesuits (1689)	Bossuet's Gallican Declaration (1682) Molinos condemned (1687) Alexander VIII (1689–91) Alexander VIII vs. Gallicans (1690)	Growth of British commerce overseas	J. S. Bach (1685–1750) Newton's Principia Mathematica (1687)
...er I defeated by the Turks ...1695) ...arles XII of Sweden ...1697–1718) ...gustus II of Saxony ...1697–1733) ...g of Poland	Innocent XII (1691–1700) Bourbons favored, Fénelon's book condemned (1699)		Voltaire (1694–1778) Deism

THE CHURCH AND THE

	ENGLAND	FRANCE	THE EMPIRE	SPAIN
1700	Anne (1702–14) Act of Settlement (1701) Union with Scotland (1707)		Prussia becomes a kingdom (1701) Joseph I (1705–11)	Philip V (1700–46)
		War of Spanish Succession (1702–13)		
1710	Marlborough driven from office (1711)		Charles VI (1711–40)	Spain loses Belgium and Italian territories (171
		Peace of Utrecht (1713–14)		
	George I (1714–27) Jacobite rebellions (1715)	Louis XV (1715–74) Duke of Orleans' regency (1715–23)	Peace of Rastadt (1714) Frederick William I (1713–40) (Prussia)	
1720	Sir Robert Walpole's ministry (1721–42) George II (1727–60)	Mississippi Bubble — John Law — (1721) Cardinal Fleury's ministry (1723–43)		
1730				
	War of Jenkin's Ear with Spain (1739)	War of Polish Election (1733–38)		
1740			Frederick II, "The Great" (1740–86) (Prussia) Maria Theresa (1740–80) (in Austria)	
		War of Austrian Succession (1740–48)		
	Jacobite rebellion (1745)		Charles VII (1742–45) Francis I (1745–65)	Ferdinand VI (1746–59)
		Treaties of Aix-la-Chapelle (1748)		
1750		The "Diplomatic Revolution" (1756)		Charles III (1759–88)
		The Seven Years' War (1756–63)		
		Treaties of Hubertusberg and Paris (1763)		
1760	George III (1760–1820)		Joseph II (1765–90) [Empire] (1780–90) [Empire and Austria]	
1770	Lord North's ministry (1770–82) Irish Penal Laws relaxed (1771) War with 13 Colonies (1776–83)	Louis XVI (1774–92) Turgot's reforms (1774–76)	War of Bavarian Succession (1778)	
1780	India Act (1784) Pitt ministry (1784–1806)	Assembly of Notables (1787) Estates-General (1789)	Frederick William II (1786–97) (Prussia)	Charles IV (1788–1808)
1790	Irish rebellion (1798) War (1793)	National Assembly (1789) Louis XVI beheaded (1793) First Republic (1792–1804) Directory (1795–99) Consulate (1799)	Leopold II (1790–92) Francis II (1792–1806 Francis I of Austria, 1806–35 Emperor of Austria) War (1792) Frederick William III (1797–1840)	

ABSOLUTE STATE

...HER WESTERN EUROPE AND RUSSIA	THE CATHOLIC CHURCH	ECONOMIC, SOCIAL LIFE	CULTURAL LIFE
...t Northern War ...700–21) ...les XII of Sweden puts ...anislaus Leczynski on ...lish throne (1704)	Clement XI (1700–21)	France and Sweden exhausted by wars	John Wesley (1703–91) Benjamin Franklin (1706–90)
	Unigenitus (1713)		Grand Lodge of Freemasonry formed in London (1711)
...erine I (1725–27) ... II (1727–30)	Innocent XIII (1721–24) Persecution in China (1724) Benedict XIII (1724–30) Jansenism condemned (1728)	Growing criticism of Old Regime by European intellectuals	Immanuel Kant (1724–1804) G. E. Lessing (1729–81)
... (1730–40)	Clement XII (1730–40) Freemasons condemned (1738)	John Kay's flying shuttle (1738)	Methodist revival begun (1739)
...VI (1740–41) ...abeth (1741–62) ...between Sweden and ...ssia (1741)	Benedict XIV (1740–58) Chinese rites condemned (1742) Malabar Rites condemned (1744) St. Paul of the Cross founds Passionists (1747)	Reform movements and beginnings of "enlightened despotism" in many countries	A. L. Lavoisier (1743–90) Thomas Jefferson (1743–1826) J. H. Pestalozzi (1746–1827) Goya (1746–1828) Montesquieu's *Spirit of the Laws* (1748)
	Freemasons condemned (1751) Portugal expels Jesuits (1759) Clement XIII (1758–69)	Beginning of industrial revolution (1750) in England	J. W. Goethe (1749–1832) Samuel Johnson's *Dictionary* (1755) W. A. Mozart (1756–91) J. C. F. Schiller (1759–1805)
...r III (1762) ...erine II, "The Great" ...762–96) ...ia wars with Turkey ...768–74)	France expels Jesuits (1764) Spain expels Jesuits (1767) Clement XIV (1769–74)	James Hargreaves' Spinning Jenny (1764) James Watt's Steam Condenser (1769) Richard Arkwright's "water frame" (1769)	Rousseau's *Social Contract* (1762) Beccaria's *Essay on Crimes and Punishments* (1764) *Encyclopaedia Britannica* (1768–71)
...tion of Poland (1772)	Jesuits suppressed (1773) Pius VI (1775–99) Catholic Relief Act in England (1778)	Samuel Crompton's "Mule" (1779)	Ludwig van Beethoven (1770–1827) G. W. F. Hegel (1770–1831) Adam Smith's *Wealth of Nations* (1776) Gibbon's *Decline and Fall of the Roman Empire* (1776–78)
	Missions in Korea (1784) The Punctation of Ems (1786) Synod of Pistoia (1786) Pius VI recognizes Prussia (1788)	Rapid progress of machine industry in Britain Revolutionary discontent in France	Uranus discovered by Herschel (1781) Montgolfier Brothers' balloon (1783)
...tion of Poland (1793) ...tion of Poland (1795) ... (1796–1801)	Civil constitution of the Clergy in France (1790) Napoleon invades Papal States (1796)	Eli Whitney's Cotton Gin (1793)	First ten amendments to the United States' Constitution; Declaration of the Rights of Man and of the Citizen (1791) Jenner's discovery of vaccination (1798)

THE NINETEENTH-CENTURY
REVIVAL

Chapter 31

THE EARLY NINETEENTH-CENTURY REVIVAL

A COMBINATION of factors in the revolutionary age we have been discussing indirectly promoted a revival of the Church in the first half of the nineteenth century. The two popes of the age had borne their privations and sufferings with dignity, and many of the bishops — though not all — seem to have been purified by a quarter century of hardship. As always happens in an age of turbulence, thinking men turned more sympathetically to religion than they had in the age of the Enlightenment. Religion seemed a satisfying thing to them, and among the European religions the Roman Catholic Church appeared most capable of satisfying all a man's complex human needs. Many scholars became converts early in the century, and they became some of the Church's best apologists. There were also saints in this period. By their example and their prayer they both inspired and strengthened the Church in its new life after 1815. Old religious societies revived and took on new vigor; new congregations were founded to meet special new needs. The revival of missionary work, always a good test of the Church's vitality in any age, was a good indication that the Church had cast off eighteenth-century complacency and that new life was coursing in her veins.

The Settlement at Vienna.   When Napoleon was first exiled in 1814 the diplomats gathered at Vienna to arrange a settlement that would insure peace in the nineteenth century. Thousands of claimants were on hand for hundreds of kingdoms and principalities, and none of them had either a perfect or an uncontested claim to his dukedom or kingdom. Among the best claims, of course, was that of the pope to the lands over which he ruled in 1789. And the pope was represented by perhaps the most capable diplomat of the age, Cardinal Consalvi, his secretary of state. Consalvi had no guns or numbers behind him, but he was able to make the most of the moral and legal arguments for his claims. Moreover, he was able to capitalize on the respect and sympathy which even the Protestant rulers accorded Pius VII for his firm stand against Napoleon.

Discussions at Vienna were interrupted when Napoleon returned from Elba in the spring of 1815. But he was quickly defeated at Waterloo and exiled permanently to the island of St. Helena. Then the settlement of Vienna was brought to an expeditious conclusion, despite the many intricate problems that had to be solved. The most complicated of these was in many ways the Italian problem. Italy had been a "geographic" expression from Roman times until Napoleon gave it unity under his control. Some Italians were hopeful that this unity might be made permanent by the Congress of Vienna, together with the social and political modernization which had been accomplished by Napoleon's administrators. Former rulers, including the pope, naturally claimed the territories over which they had ruled in 1792.

The disputed parts of former papal territory were the Legations of Bologna, Ravenna, and Ferrara, the principalities of Benevento and Ponte Corvo, and the enclaves of Avignon and Venaissin. The Legations were held by Austria, and Metternich was anxious to keep them in imperial hands, either directly or through a Hapsburg relative. Consalvi succeeded in retaining for the Papal States all these territories except the two enclaves in France and a small part of Ferrara on the left side of the Po. He lodged a strongly worded protest over these seizures of territory, but he must have realized that from the diplomatic point of view he had done exceedingly well for the Papal States.

As soon as the Vienna settlement was concluded Consalvi hurried back to Rome to help the pope incorporate the Church in the new society of 1815. This involved two sets of problems: (1) the establishment of friendly relations with the various European powers, and (2) the reorganization of the Papal States.

New Diplomatic Relations. Pius VII and Consalvi were in a position to obtain greater concessions from the nineteenth-century governments than the Church had ever obtained in the eighteenth century, for rulers throughout Europe looked upon religion as necessary for peace and order in the country. They were therefore inclined to be friendly rather than hostile to any approaches from Rome.

1. *Negotiations with England.* The first country with which Consalvi entered into negotiations was, strangely enough, England. The English government had adopted a most friendly attitude toward the papacy during the Napoleonic Wars. It was the English who offered the pope asylum when Napoleon invaded Rome, and it was the English who protected him at Genoa during the Hundred Days. It was the English, again, who backed the pope's request for the return of works of art taken from Rome by the French, and who transported these masterpieces back to Rome at their own expense.

When Consalvi went to London before the opening of the Congress of Vienna in 1814 he was given a friendly reception by Prime Minister Castlereagh and by the king himself. He therefore broached the subject of conversations about the rights of English Catholics. These rights had been denied since Elizabeth's time, of course, but the English were willing to discuss restoring them in 1815. The presence of many French clergymen in England during the Revolution had made a favorable impression on the English, and the Romantic writings of Scott, Wordsworth, and others had presented Catholic times in a favorable light. Although negotiations for abrogating the penal laws against Catholics did not terminate in an immediate agreement, nevertheless friendly relations were developed. Four years later the English king accredited a minister to Rome, and in 1829 almost all the penal laws against English Catholics were repealed. The old hostility between Rome and London had diminished. Although suspicion continued through the nineteenth century, relations between the two powers remained better than in the previous three centuries.

2. *Diplomatic relations with France.* The country of St. Louis, Voltaire, and Napoleon continued to be the most important province of the Church in the first half of the nineteenth century. Rome was satisfied with the Concordat of 1801, if the Organic Articles were removed, but when the Bourbons returned to France in 1814 new problems were created. Louis XVIII suppressed the Napoleonic feasts and catechisms, welcomed religious orders back into the country, and sought to suppress the Concordat of 1801 in favor of the Gallican arrangements of the pre-revolutionary age. It was apparent to the pope that the religious policy

of the restored Bourbons aimed at the domination of the Church, and that its zeal in abolishing divorce or supporting the bishops was intended to make such control palatable. The government refused to abrogate the Organic Articles, and it insisted that the Four Gallican Articles of 1682 continue to be taught in the seminaries.

Long discussions were held in the hope of arranging a new concordat between France and the Church. Two such agreements were drawn up, but neither proved satisfactory to both parties. Finally, it was agreed in 1821 that the Concordat of 1801 should remain in force and that thirty new dioceses should be created to take care of the needs of French Catholics. The seductive danger in France was that the papacy should accept state protection and support in return for the surrender of its independence. The anticlerical agitation of French liberals and the possibility of a revival of the persecution inaugurated by the Revolution tempted Church officials to accept the government's "solution" — which was essentially the solution that had almost smothered the French Church in the eighteenth century. We shall see that there was a lively "grass roots" revival in the French Church, but the danger persisted that the official Church might again be identified with an absolute king against the people and their new freedoms. Fortunately for the Church the problem was resolved by the Revolution of 1830, which overthrew the Bourbons and ushered in an anticlerical monarchy with which the Church could never be identified, even by her enemies.

3. *Negotiations with Protestant German states.* The rearrangement of the German states by the Congress of Vienna created a number of problems for the papacy. Hundreds of thousands of Catholics found themselves in a Protestant state; especially numerous were the Rhineland Catholics who were included in the enlarged Prussia. The governments were willing to treat with Rome to establish the status of their Catholic citizens, but they were inclined to accept the Febronian and Josephist views that were general among German ecclesiastics. Fortunately, there were only five bishops in all the Germanies, and four of them were men over eighty. This left the pope a free hand in dealing with the German governments.

Pope Pius VII and Cardinal Consalvi tried to negotiate a concordat with each of these states, modeled after the Concordat of 1801 with Napoleon, in which agreement would be reached on such matters as the method of selecting bishops, their communication with Rome, the drawing up of diocesan boundaries, and the rights of Church and State in the education of the clergy. Most governments tried the Napoleonic trick of publishing the concordat with a set of "organic articles" asserting greater state powers than the papacy had acknowledged in the concordat. In each case this led to difficulties and delays; generally the government withdrew the organic articles and published the concordat as originally drawn up.

Prussia sent its famous historian-diplomat Berthold Georg Niebuhr to Rome to negotiate a concordat, but when agreement could not be reached on several different points, the Holy See and the Prussian government agreed to confine arrangements to setting up new dioceses in Prussia. An agreement was reached in 1821, which Pius VII published as a Bull and the Prussian government as a state ordinance. It set up two archiepiscopal sees, one at Cologne for western Prussia and one at Gnesen-Posen for eastern Prussia. Six bishoprics were established. Provision was made for the election of bishops by the cathedral chapter, with the government having the right to indicate disapproval of any candidate and the pope reserving the right of canonical institution. The Prussian government assumed the obligation of supporting the bishops, clergy, and seminaries within the country. Various difficulties arose in putting all the terms of the agreement into effect, as we shall see later in this chapter, and hostile relations developed between Prussia and the Church.

Representatives of Baden, Würtemberg, Nassau, Hesse, and several smaller states gathered in 1818 with the purpose of negotiating a common concordat with Rome. Their plan was to obtain Rome's help in drawing up diocesan boundaries, and then to issue legislation — "organic articles" — which would assert state control of the Church in each state. The demands of the German states were so excessive that negotiations with Consalvi broke down in 1818. The pope agreed to erect new dioceses and appoint bishops, however, because the need of establishing the Church in these states was so pressing. After long negotiations, the German states finally accepted the papacy's terms, which Pope Leo XII stated in a Bull in 1827.

The terms were similar to those of the Prussian agreement. Chapters were to elect the bishops; the government had the right to strike out names of candidates of whom it disapproved. Chapters and seminaries were to be established in each diocese and were to be under the bishop's control. Bishops were to have free intercourse with Rome. As soon as the pope filled the last of the sees in these states, they published their already agreed upon "organic articles" which gave them control over the Church. Difficulties arose over such matters as elections of bishops, their freedom to issue pastoral letters, control of the seminaries, and the problem of mixed marriages. These difficulties persisted throughout the first half of the nineteenth century and were a continual source of annoyance to the papacy.

4. *Negotiations with Catholic Bavaria.* A concordat was concluded with Bavaria on June 5, 1817, which differed in certain essentials from the agreements made with Protestant states. The king was given the right to nominate bishops, who were to receive canonical institution from the pope and were to be free in the administration of their dioceses. Bavaria was divided into two ecclesiastical provinces with six dioceses. The state guaranteed the Church all the rights derived from her divine constitution and from canon law. The concordat was close to ideal from the papacy's point of view, but the Bavarian government vitiated the arrangement by publishing with it a set of "organic articles" as an "edict of religion" subordinating Church to State.

After long negotiations the king of Bavaria promised that the concordat would have the force of law itself and that the new Bavarian constitution (containing the organic articles) would impose no obligation contrary to the Church's canonical organization. For a while the concordat remained pretty much a dead letter, but better relations were established when Ludwig I ascended the Bavarian throne in 1825. Difficulties occurred over various matters throughout his reign, but there was a general revival of Catholic life in Bavaria at this time and it was possible to settle most of the difficulties satisfactorily.

5. *Diplomatic relations with the other countries.* Pope Pius VII and the tireless Consalvi simultaneously negotiated arrangements for the Church in almost every European country. In 1817 a concordat was concluded with Naples. In it the papacy recognized the secularization of ecclesiastical property that had occurred during the Revolution, and in return bishops were granted freedom to communicate with the Holy See, religious orders were given their rights, and all the faithful were granted the right of appealing to Rome. A treaty with Piedmont embodied similar provisions. Pius VII negotiated a series of partial settlements with Switzerland which his successor completed in 1828. The Swiss Catholics were grouped into five dioceses and provision was made for a sixth in 1845. An agreement with Russia provided for eight episcopal sees in that part of Poland under the Tsar and for an archbishopric in Warsaw.

The results of all these negotiations were more important for the Church, perhaps, than pope or rulers realized at the time. In the first place, they regularized the position of Catholics who found themselves under new governments. Even when the terms of the agreements were violated they were important because the Church had grounds under international law for lodging complaint against the government. Most important, however, these negotiations were an implicit acknowledgment by Catholic and Protestant rulers that the Holy See was the effective head of the Catholic Church. In the last years of Pius VII's reign five states (Russia, Prussia, The Netherlands, Hanover, and Würtemberg) accredited diplomatic representatives to the Holy See. Febronian and Josephist claims in the Germanies were ignored, and nowhere except in France was there a group of bishops who any longer tried to put into practice the now discredited conciliar ideas on the organization of the Church.

Reorganization of the Papal States. We can see in retrospect that the popes were faced with an insoluble problem in their dual role as temporal ruler of a fair-sized state in the modern age and head of a universal Church. For centuries the Papal States had been a clerical state where the citizens were governed by a confusing maze of canon law, civil law, local edicts, ancient customs, all enforced inefficiently by churchmen from the rank of cardinal down to clerks with the rank of anything from subdeacon to monsignor. Papal government had not been unusually harsh, nor had taxes been excessively high. But it was government in temporal as well as spiritual affairs by the clergy over laymen, and naturally enough it generated anticlericalism among the literate laymen which was, in turn, a reaction to the clericalism of the ruling class. Its worst failure was its inefficiency in maintaining law and order. Brigands controlled large parts of the Papal States, and a person was not safe on the streets or highways after nightfall.

For years the Papal States had been part of the Napoleonic empire. Efficient administration had been introduced and the layman was raised to equality with the cleric under civil law. The result was that Pius VII had to find a way to govern a state whose educated people were forever alienated from the old system and in favor of a "liberal" government modeled on that of England or France, a constitutional government with elected representatives and with laymen eligible for both administrative and policy-forming positions. To work out such a system was almost impossible because of the confusion of temporal and ecclesiastical offices, and especially because Italian liberals and patriots favored a united Italy which should have Rome as its capital.

Cardinal Consalvi favored reforms in the Papal States which would modernize the government by adopting the acceptable parts of Napoleonic administration and would, he hoped, satisfy the demands of the people. Other cardinals looked upon any concession as an encouragement to revolution and a sullying of the spotless Church. They formed a party known as the *Zelanti* for the purpose of upholding strict ecclesiastical principles against popular aggression. Backing Consalvi were the *Moderates*, who favored compromise in those areas where it could be achieved without harming the Church. Each group, naturally enough, tried to elect popes and secure the appointment of cardinals who favored their principles.

In 1816 the pope established a new form of government by dividing the Papal States into provinces modeled on the French *départements*. An official, the "delegate," was appointed over each province; he was assisted by a consultive council, the members of which were not elected but were appointed by Rome. Over these provinces was the congregation of cardinals entrusted with the government of the Papal States. The French regulations on taxes and custom duties were maintained, and Consalvi pushed the work of codifying the laws so as to end the confusion created by the Napoleonic Code and Canon Law being simultaneously in force.

No more than a beginning had been made on the reorganization of the temporal power when Pope Pius VII died in 1823 and Consalvi in 1824. During his long pontificate Pius VII had won the respect of the European world for the Church, but he had not built up a large enough party in the Curia to insure that his and Consalvi's policies would be followed after their deaths. The three popes who succeeded Pius VII (Leo XII, Pius VIII, and Gregory XVI) all belonged to the conservative or *Zelanti* party. Leo XII backed rulers against the people everywhere. In the Papal States he sternly suppressed brigandage and tried unsuccessfully to stamp out the secret societies. Leo XII was interested primarily in spiritual matters, however, and he devoted most of his time to reforming the congregations, improving the seminaries, and policing the theaters and the inns.

After Pius VIII's short pontificate, Gregory XVI was elected during the disturbances of 1830–1831. When it was evident that the papal army was unable to put down the insurrection centering in Bologna, an Austrian force was dispatched for the purpose. The French were suspicious of Austrian designs in the Papal States, so they landed a force at Ancona. These rival "protecting" forces remained in the Papal States for six years. Meanwhile, the governments of Europe presented Gregory XVI with a memorandum demanding certain reforms of the temporal power in the interest of general peace. They requested a general amnesty, provision for elective councils, admission of laymen to judicial and civil service positions, and the creation of an assembly of nobles to serve as a council of state for administrative and financial matters.

Gregory XVI adopted some of these suggested reforms in the next few years, but his concessions did not seem to satisfy the insurgents, and fresh revolutionary outbreaks tended to harden the pope against "liberal" reforms. The pope showed himself suspicious of any kind of revolution, even that of the Catholic Belgians from Holland and the Poles against Russia. His dim view of liberal reform probably predisposed him to disapprove of the naïve plan that Lamennais and his associates had made for uniting the Church with the new liberal society. At any rate, from the time Cardinal Lambruschini became secretary of state in 1836 until Gregory's death a decade later the papal government refused to undertake necessary reforms and concentrated instead on forceful suppression of dissent. The temporal rule had suffered from hardening of the arteries, so to speak, for many years when the bishop of Imola, Cardinal Mastai-Ferretti, was elected to the papacy. The new pope, who took the name of Pius IX, was a relatively young man (54) who had earned the reputation of being a truly liberal churchman. The European world watched closely to see how he would liberalize and modernize the government of the Papal States.

The "Romantic" Revival in the Church (1800–1850). The revival of religious life in the Church through the first half of the century was tied in with the general reaction to the rationalism of the preceding century and the surge toward greater freedom among the lower classes. It was in many ways a "grass roots" movement, with all the advantages and disadvantages of any such movement. New congregations were established by ordinary people; laymen participated actively in Church life as they had not previously done in history; converts, saints, parish priests, and members of religious orders all showed an initiative and a zeal exceedingly rare in previous centuries. But unless such a revival was worked into the texture of Church organization by the hierarchy and the papacy it was doomed to only temporary success. Moreover a Romantic revival is almost condemned by its very nature to die out when the feeling behind it grows lukewarm. The Romantic revival of the first half of the century lacked the solid foundations of the later revival of the Church under Pope Leo XIII and his successors, but it gave fresh life to the Church and it promoted new foundations which continue to flourish in our own time.

Chateaubriand was the pioneer of the revival in France. In 1802 he published his epoch-making *Genius of Christianity*. His work had great apologetic value for that time, for it answered Voltaire in his own terms,

and it rode the crest of the Romantic movement to present Christianity
in the most appealing form. The essence of Chateaubriand's argument was
that Christianity must be true because it is so beautiful. In the first pages
of his book Chateaubriand asserts:

> of all religions that ever existed, Christianity is the most poetic, the most
> human, the most favorable to liberty, to the arts and letters; the modern
> world owes it everything; nothing is more divine, nothing more amiable and
> more stately than its dogmas, its doctrine, and its worship; it favors genius,
> purifies taste, develops the virtuous passions, gives vigor to thought, offers
> noble forms to the writer and perfect models to the artist.

Chateaubriand moved men's hearts with his description of the priesthood, the sacraments, and the ceremonies of the Church. And he inspired a group of younger men who were to carry on his apologetic
with a zeal and an enthusiasm they imbibed from him.

Joseph de Maistre did not create the enthusiasm or enlist the following
that Chateaubriand had done, but in the long run he performed a more
lasting work for the Church. Frequently referred to as a "lay doctor" in
the Church, de Maistre used a merciless logic to rip into shreds the
thought of such figures of the Enlightenment as Voltaire, Diderot, and
Rousseau. His famous *Du Pape* was an argument for papal infallibility
in which the Savoyard layman put forth extravagant claims for the papacy
and in which he asserted that it was the cornerstone of European
civilization.

Louis de Bonald was another lay leader in the revival of the Church
in France. His contribution was to stress the value of tradition and the
dignity of man in a world that had been subjected to one revolutionary
change after another for a quarter of a century. In similar fashion a
French priest, *Félicité de Lamennais* showed the need of religion for
every man and for society. His *Essay on Indifference* created a great stir
in France; it was felt that another great doctor of the Church was at
hand to inspire and to guide the religious revival of this age. Great
apologetic work was done against Liberalism by the Spanish priest *Jaime
Balmes* and the layman *Juan Donoso Cortés*. The effect of their writings
was to put the Liberals on the defensive, to show the need of Christianity
for any advanced civilization, and to advance the claims of the pope
as the head of the Catholic Church.

The Romantic revival was perhaps more pronounced in Germany
than anywhere else in Europe. Here the Church benefited from the
revived interest in the Middle Ages and a reaction against rationalism —
which Germans tended to identify in a nationalistic way with France.

There is a great deal of confused thought in this Romantic revival, and occasionally these converts to the Church seem to look on the Church as an institution out of Scott's novels or Grimm's fairy tales. Nevertheless the Romantic revival prepared the way for the later solid life of the Church in the days of Bishop von Ketteler and the Center Party in Germany. This revival is remarkable in that it was exclusively the work of laymen, scholars who joined the Church and promoted its interests despite the lack of ecclesiastical leadership in the Germanies. It is also remarkable in that it did not depend on state support; in fact it rose in opposition to the German governments and was therefore always free from their control. This lay revival forced German bishops to give up their Josephist tendencies and to resist the German prince in obedience to Rome. And from this lay revival were formed centers of Catholicism, notably the Munich circle, that became the cradle of bishops for the latter half of the nineteenth century.

The list of names in the German revival is long and impressive. St. Clement Maria Hofbauer played an inspiring role in its early stages. Novalis did much to emphasize the beauties of the Church; his *Hymns to the Virgin* appealed to the chivalric aspect of Romanticism, and his other writings stressed the warmth of Catholicism as opposed to the cold rationalism of the preceding age. In 1800 the noted Hellenist, Count Leopold von Stolberg, was converted to the Catholic faith, and he combined with another noted convert, Princess Amalia von Galitzin, to acquaint German intellectuals with the glories and beauties of Catholicism. In 1813 Frederick Overbeck was converted, and for half a century he lived in Rome where he was visited by scores of German artists, many of whom joined the faith after their visit to the Eternal City.

Among the most noted of the Romantic German converts was the historian and philosopher, Frederick von Schlegel. Other influential German Catholics of this age were Father John Michael Sailer, later bishop of Ratisbon, whose writings influenced many German intellectuals in favor of the Church; Clement Brentano, Zacharias Werner, Adam Müller, Charles von Haller, Louis Schnorr, the two Schadows, and many others, each of whom made his own distinct contribution to the cultural and social wealth of the German revival in the first half of the nineteenth century. A place apart must be reserved for Joseph Goerres, the journalist, historian, and apologist, who in many ways dominated the intellectual life of the German Church in this age. Goerres was a devotee of freedom and a champion of human dignity. He had sought these things in the Jacobinism of the French Revolution, in devotion to the Prussian state, and finally in the Catholic Church. For the last quarter century of his life (1822–1848) Goerres was the vocal champion of religious freedom for Catholics in Germany. A powerful writer, he published a series of different journals which sounded like trumpet blasts throughout the intellectual circles of Germany, and he created a sensation with such pamphlets as his *Athanasius* in which he championed the cause of the imprisoned bishop of Cologne in the mixed marriage problem.

In 1848 the Romantic movement in Germany culminated in a revolution which almost unified Germany, and though it failed it pointed the way for the more practical Bismarck to create a unified Germany twenty years later. Similarly, in 1848 German Catholics gathered at Mainz to pioneer in a work which has been a concern of the Church in the past century — the securing of social justice. German Catholics seem to have been the first to realize that constitutional government posed a new set of problems and put new weapons in the hands of Catholic voters, which might be summed up under the term "political Catholicism." As voters Catholics were given power, and as Catholic voters they had an obligation to use this power for the good of society. Their obligation, in short, was to protect the rights of the Church and to promote social justice for all men in the State. As Philip Hughes has expressed it: "At Mainz there was founded for the first time a union of Catholics to promote Catholic ideals in social life." The program of the congress stated:

> This association cannot limit itself to the purely educational object of the Church's legal freedom nor to education itself. On the contrary, it must strive to reawaken and to put new life into Catholic public opinion, it must spread this and Catholic moral ideals, must plant these in the whole field of the national life, and so prepare to solve the great problem of the day, the social problem.

Something like a Romantic revival occurred in England. In the decade after 1815 Walter Scott had an influence in England comparable to that of Chateaubriand in France. It did not lead men directly into the Catholic Church, of course, but it did influence them to take a more sympathetic view of those practices which had for long been considered "superstitious" and "papist." The revival in England can be said to have consisted of three parts: (1) the emancipation of Catholics from the penal laws of the sixteenth and seventeenth centuries; (2) the Oxford movement; (3) the re-establishment of the English hierarchy in 1850.

The emancipation of Catholics is always associated with the name of Daniel O'Connell who forced the government's hand in 1829. But emancipation could not have been put off for long. Protestant dissenters had been emancipated in 1828, and the general opinion of the times found political disabilities for religious reasons repugnant to liberal government. The Oxford movement was originally directed by Anglicans interested in a rich liturgy, a fuller ritual, an appreciation of tradition and devotion to the saints. It was an approach, in externals, toward the Catholic Church. Some of its leaders managed to stop short of Rome, but others — notably John Henry Newman and William G. Ward — eventually became Catholics and constituted the intellectual core of the Catholic Church in England for the rest of the century.

The restoration of the Catholic hierarchy by the appointment of Cardinal Wiseman to the archiepiscopal see of Westminster and the division of England into one ecclesiastical province and twelve suffragan dioceses aroused a popular storm of opposition against the Church in England. But many of the best minds in the country opposed this outburst and some of them — such as Henry Edward Manning — entered the Church as a result. Unfortunately, English Catholics spent considerable energy in opposing each other, and it was not until the present century that large numbers of converts came into the Church. But those who came in the nineteenth century were capable men of high repute, and almost everyone of them became an ardent champion of his new faith.

The Mixed Marriage Problem in Prussia.   Two problems facing the Church in the first half of the century are deserving of special notice, both for their intrinsic importance and because they are symbolic of general problems facing the Church in this age: the problem of mixed marriages in Prussia, and the problem of liberal Catholicism in France.

The first of these was typical of the difficulties that arise between the Church and a Protestant state. A Prussian law of 1803 provided that children of mixed marriages were to be raised in the father's religion unless both parents agreed otherwise. Prematrimonial promises to the contrary were invalid. This law did not create any great difficulty for Catholics until 1825, when it was extended to the Rhineland provinces which Prussia had acquired in 1815. Catholics in the Rhineland insisted that Protestant young men were "invading" their lands, wooing their girls, and destroying the Catholic faith. Nevertheless, Archbishop Spiegel of Cologne led the German bishops to accept the Prussian decree and co-operate with it, but they requested permission from the government to submit the problem to the judgment of the Holy See.

Pope Pius VIII went as far as he could in acceding to the Prussian requests without violating canon law, but his concessions did not satisfy the Prussian government. Gregory XVI, who succeeded Pius VIII while negotiations were still in progress, told the Prussian representative that he could not accept their demands. The bishops of West Prussia and the government therefore entered into a secret agreement whereby Catholic priests could officiate at mixed marriages without obtaining the premarital promises required by canon law. But this did not solve the problem, because many priests refused to officiate at such marriages.

Meanwhile Archbishop Spiegel died (1835) and was succeeded by Clemens Augustus von Droste-Vischering, a member of one of the princely families of Westphalia. The new archbishop announced that he would carry out canonical regulations on mixed marriages. He was enthusiastically backed by most of his parish priests when he wrote them to this effect, but his cathedral chapter opposed his "ultramontane" stand. On November 20, 1837, Prussian officials arrested the archbishop, and the government denounced him as a "traitor." The pope denounced this harsh action by Prussia, sent a letter of protest to all the courts of Europe, and praised the courageous loyalty of Archbishop Droste-Vischering.

The arrest of the archbishop was a serious blunder by Prussian officials. Catholics rallied to his cause; a rain of pamphlets attacking the arbitrary action circulated throughout Germany; and bishops elsewhere found themselves almost forced by priests and laymen to oppose State infringement of Catholic rights. The archbishop of Gnesen-Posen, who had submitted to the government's decree, wrote a letter to his priests and ordered them to observe canonical regulations on mixed marriages. He was also arrested, and his entire diocese went into solemn mourning. The Prussian government was clearly coming off badly in the mixed marriage problem when Frederick William IV came to the throne in 1840. He realized that his predecessor's policy was obstructing the unification of Prussia's new domains, and he therefore set about reversing it as expeditiously as possible. He issued a proclamation that the government would not interfere in mixed marriages and that priests were free to officiate or not as they thought proper. The archbishop of Gnesen-Posen was allowed to return to his diocese. The archbishop of Cologne presented a more difficult problem, because he had been accused of treason and could hardly be allowed to return to Cologne a hero. The pope agreed to have a coadjutor appointed for Cologne, although the archbishop retained his title, and the Prussian government withdrew its charges against him.

The mixed marriage dispute proved a boon to Catholicism in Prussia and elsewhere in Germany. It completely discredited the last remnants of Josephism and Febronianism. It attached Catholics more closely to the pope, and it forced bishops to rely on Rome to champion their freedom from the State. Moreover, it provided the element of persecution that drew Catholics in the German states together and infused new life into their religion.

Lamennais and Liberal Catholicism in France. The second problem — Liberal Catholicism — is typically found in Catholic countries. The Revolution of 1830 in France overthrew the Bourbon monarchy and ushered in the Orleanist or July Monarchy. The new government was anti-clerical and liberal. A group of younger Catholics, such as Montalembert, Lacordaire, and De Coux, followed the brilliant priest, Félicité Lamennais, in an attempt to unite the new liberalism and the old Catholicism of France. They selected "God and Liberty" as their motto, and they established a paper, *L'Avenir,* to spread their ideas. Lamennais and his followers realized that the union of absolutism and Gallicanism had almost destroyed the Church in the eighteenth century. They therefore upheld ultramontanism and democracy; they insisted on separation of Church and State; and they denounced bishops and priests who, under the Concordat of 1801, were salaried officials of the government.

L'Avenir fell under the ban of the French bishops and it aroused the hostility of the government. Lamennais and Lacordaire were arrested early in 1801 for articles they had written for *L'Avenir,* but Lacordaire's brilliant defense secured their acquittal. A little later Lacordaire and Montalembert were arrested for violating the law by establishing a private school. This case went to the House of Peers because Montalembert was of the nobility. The two defendants created a stir throughout the intellectual circles of France, and though they were found guilty they won an important moral victory against the government's monopoly of education under the July Monarchy.

Meanwhile, Lamennais and his two young associates, Lacordaire and Montalembert, hit upon the naïve idea of appealing to Rome to endorse their crusade against the conservative French hierarchy. They journeyed to Rome where, after much waiting, they obtained an unsatisfactory interview with Pope Gregory XVI. The three Frenchmen left Rome without obtaining a verdict, but soon afterward the pope rendered his decision in the encyclical *Mirari Vos.* In this letter the pope reproved Gallican ideas, but then he went on to condemn certain specific doctrines found in

L'Avenir. Among these doctrines was the unreserved advocacy of separation of Church and State, the upholding of freedom of religion as an ideal, and a general tendency to accept liberal ideas in unqualified fashion.

The condemnation was too much for Lamennais's pride. Although he submitted at first, he soon left the Church and became one of its bitterest critics. Two years later Gregory XVI condemned him by name in the encyclical *Singulari Vos*. Lacordaire and Montalembert remained entirely loyal to the Church. They were chagrined by the condemnation, of course, but they accepted it in good grace and went on to do excellent work for the Church in France. Montalembert became a foremost Catholic politician who carried on a long struggle for freedom of education, and Lacordaire became the most famous preacher of his day.

L'Avenir was a typical Romantic venture — full of enthusiasm and good intentions, but not carefully thought out, and reckless of the consequences of its policies. In certain respects, these young Frenchmen advocated policies that the Church was later to adopt officially. But their advocacy of these policies was premature, and it lacked the discriminating thought of Catholic thinkers on these subjects since the time of Pope Leo XIII. By their gallant venture, however, Lacordaire and Montalembert — and even more Lamennais — gave concrete expression to the problem that had been facing the Church ever since 1789, and which the bishops had generally refused to face: the problem of adapting the Church to the new society which had come into being with the French Revolution.

One form of adaptation was suggested by Charles Eugene Mazenod, Bishop of Marseille, who founded the Oblates of Mary Immaculate in 1816 "to preach the gospel to the poor." They were also to educate seminarians and other young people, care for prisoners, and later to engage in foreign missions. The Oblates soon spread into several European countries, the Americas, and some of the remotest places on the earth. The order grew rapidly until it became the seventh largest order of men in the Church and the third largest in the missionary field.

REVIEW AIDS

1. A diplomat in the Church has said, "We make concordats with our enemies; we do not need to make them with our friends." Explain what he meant by this statement.
2. From the contents of concordats negotiated after the Congress of Vienna, describe what were the chief problems between Church and State in this period.
3. Explain why statesmen in 1815, no matter what personal religious opinions they held, believed that religion was necessary politically.

4. In retrospect, we can see that many bishops made a mistake in identifying the welfare of the Church with absolute monarchy of the pre-revolution period. Explain how intelligent men could make such a mistake in good faith.

5. List and analyze the special difficulties — over and above the normal problems — that the government of the Papal States faced after 1815.

6. Show why it was a normal thing, after the French Revolution, for laymen to play an increasingly important role in the history of the Church.

7. The revival of the Church in the age of Romanticism has sometimes been called a revival without solid foundations. Explain to what extent this statement is true. Show to what extent the Romantic revival prepared the way for a more solid and lasting revival beginning later in the century.

8. From what you have learned in past chapters show why the mixed marriage problem becomes a critical issue between Church and State for the first time in the early nineteenth century.

9. List and analyze the reasons why *L'Avenir* was condemned. Is it an exaggeration simply to say that Lamennais and Montalembert said the right thing at the wrong time? Explain.

10. Explain why Montalembert and his associates thought freedom of religion and of education would be a good thing for the Church in the France of the July Monarchy.

SUGGESTIONS FOR FURTHER READING

The best general setting for this period is Frederick B. Artz, *Reaction and Revolution, 1814–1832* (New York: 1934). Mourret-Thompson, *A History of the Catholic Church* (St. Louis: 1955, Volume vii) covers the period till 1823. General studies of the history of the Church during the nineteenth century are to be found in Raymond Corrigan, *The Church and the Nineteenth Century* (Milwaukee: 1938), and the two-volume work of James MacCaffrey, *History of the Catholic Church in the Nineteenth Century* (St. Louis: 1909). The best coverage of Catholic social and political problems through the nineteenth and twentieth centuries is *Church and Society* (New York: 1953), edited by Joseph N. Moody.

The Roman story in the first part of the nineteenth century is told intimately by Nicholas Cardinal Wiseman, *Recollections of the Last Four Popes* (New York: n.d.). This story by Cardinal Wiseman covers the period from 1818, when he went to Rome, until the end of the pontificate of Gregory XVI. Also useful is H. L. Hughes, *The Catholic Revival in Italy, 1815–1915* (London: 1935). A general study of the century from a particular point of view is Constantine Kempf, *The Holiness of the Church in the Nineteenth Century* (New York: 1916).

A popular, readable approach to one aspect of Church history in this period is to be found in Thomas P. Neill, *They Lived the Faith* (Milwaukee: 1951). This study of Catholic laymen in the nineteenth century includes analyses of Daniel O'Connell, Charles Montalembert, Pauline Jaricot, Frederic Ozanam, Joseph de Maistre, Joseph Goerres, and Juan Donoso Cortés, all of whom played important roles in the history of the Church in this period. Most typical of these laymen, perhaps, is Frederic Ozanam. Two good studies on him are Louis Baunard, *Ozanam in His Correspondence* (New York: 1925), and Albert Schimberg, *The Great Friend: Frederick Ozanam* (Milwaukee: 1946).

A good study of the Church in France during this period is C. S. Phillips, *The Church in France, 1769–1848* (London: 1929). The most important development of the period is covered by the Hon. W. Gibson, *The Abbé de Lamennais and the Liberal Catholic Movement in France* (London: 1896). The history of the Church in England in this age is handled well by Philip Hughes, *The Catholic Question, 1688–1829* (New York: 1929), and in more detail by the three-volume study of Bernard Ward, *The Eve of Catholic Emancipation* (London: 1911–1912).

DOCUMENTS

Excerpts From the Notre Dame Conferences

The great Dominican preacher, Lacordaire, gave the first Notre Dame Conferences, established at Ozanam's instigation and still given annually in Notre Dame Cathedral in Paris. Lacordaire's conferences were beautifully effective sermons in which he combined French logic and a moving emotional appeal to show the grandeur and glory, as well as the logic of Catholicism. The following excerpt is the conclusion of his sermon on "The Intellectual Public Society Founded by Catholic Doctrine."

We are not the children of violence, of fear, nor of any kind of servitude. See, in the first place, how we were born. If my memory serves me well, we were not born under that stool which men call a throne; we did not open our eyes one day under the robe of the Praetorians at the foot of the Palatine. We were, indeed, under the Palatine, but under its caves, in the catacombs. We were there, tracked like wild beasts from one end of the world to the other; and see how we make proselytes to our faith. A man came from I know not where, who spake strange things; he entered into a great city, walked into a shop, sat down whilst some one mended his sandals, and as the workman labored at that lowly work, the stranger opened his mouth; he announced to the artisan that a God was come to bear to the earth a doctrine of voluntary suffering and crucifixion — a doctrine which humbled pride and scourged the senses. "Comrade," said he to him, "leave thy tools, come with us; we have the Caesars against us, they kill us by thousands, but we have holes under the earth where thou wilt find a bed, an altar, and a tomb. We sleep there, we pray there, we sing there, we die there, and then we are placed between three tiles in the rock, waiting for the day of resurrection, when our remains will appear in honor and in glory. Comrade, descend with us into the catacombs, come and learn how to live and how to die!" The artisan rose up, he went down into the catacombs, and he never more left them, for he had found, underground light and love.

Was this a conquest obtained by the means of autocracy? Ah! when after three centuries of tortures, from the top of *Monte Mario*, Constantine saw the *Labarum* in the air; it was the blood of Christians which had caused it to bud forth in the shade, which ascended like dew even to heaven, and which spread itself out there under the form of the cross triumphant. Our public liberty was the fruit of a moral liberty without example. Our entry into the *forum* of princes was the fruit of an empire, which we had exercised upon ourselves even to death. Men were able to reign after such an apprenticeship to order; they could well cover doctrine with purple, after all the blood which had been shed upon it. The reign was not long, moreover, supposing that that time which elapsed between Constantine and the barbarians might be called by that name, a time so full of combats, during which Catholic doctrine never quitted for a single day the pen and the word. The barbarians then came, and with them a new society to convert. Was it accomplished by means of autocracy? Saint Remy doubtless said to Clovis: "Bow down they head!" But which was the lamb — the bishop or the warrior? Which was the lamb — Clothilde or Clovis?

It is true, in the middle ages, Catholic doctrine appeared to clothe itself in the outward signs of autocracy. I say in the outward signs, for it had passed through its trials; it might think it had the right to protect spiritual unity by the help of civil unity, and, in addition, it never ceased to write and to speak, and to have powerful enemies, even under the crown of the empire. Saint Anselm, Saint Thomas, Saint Bonaventure, then explained and defended the public dogma of Catholicity. There was then no conspiration for extending the light, and destroying the liberty of moral choice. Moreover, this second reign, more complete than the first, was short also; the sixteenth century arose very soon, and after it the eighteenth. You know the rest; all the earth leagued together against the liberty of Catholic doctrine; its goods spoiled; its priests mutilated; its civil authority destroyed everywhere; a deadly war which letters, science, and the arts, have declared against it. And, notwithstanding, it lives, it is sustained, it gains souls, it maintains the immutability of its public dogma, with the same heart, and with the same success. I say its public dogma, for already, you have remarked it, it is not the portion of a single class of men; it calls together all the living elements of humanity. The faith of the poor is the same as the faith of the learned. All believe in and pray to the same God, with the same obligation of humbling their pride, and knowing their nothingness. Science and ignorance become, in the common light, imperceptible shadows, which color unity without corrupting it, and which render more sensible its unalterable splendor.

I recapitulate what I have said, gentlemen; there is no veritable society but the society of minds, and that society is only constituted by ideas which are held in common, which are fundamental, immutable, freely recognized and accepted by men of all ranks. Man, pressed by the need of this unity of minds, has tried many ways to establish it. He has, with this end in view, created the rationalist philosophy, the autocratic philosophy, and the heretical philosophy — three attempts founded on different plans of action, all three filling the world with their efforts, all three powerless to organize in it the republic of minds. Catholic doctrine alone has been able to do this. Why? What is the cause of its success? What is it which has enabled it to succeed where all other doctrines have failed? We must explain this to you, gentlemen, and it will be necessary to draw conclusions from all that you have just heard, conclusions which you doubtless desire, and which will be but the stronger by your having the patience not to require them to-day.

Chapter 32

THE MISSIONARY CHURCH TILL
MID-CENTURY

IN THE first half of the nineteenth century the Church showed unmistakable signs of vitality which had been lacking in the previous
century: men and women distinguished for prayer and holy works,
a number of whom have become canonized saints; several new orders
founded to meet specific needs of the age, flourishing members of the
Church's family of religious institutions today; new vitality in the missions,
with thousands of men and women giving their lives to bring the word
of God to peoples throughout the world. In the decades after 1815 the
Church became Catholic in fact as well as in name, as it had not been
for many years. A renewed piety among the clergy and laity combined with
the layman's increasing role to give the Church a freshness and a vigor
it had not possessed since the reform movement of the sixteenth century
waned. Put in secular terms, the Church resumed the offensive in the
nineteenth century and recovered ground lost in the preceding centuries.

Saints and New Orders. The historian can easily overlook the power
of prayer and sacrifice, the part played in the life of the Church by the
saint who stays in the chapel to pray. We know from Christ's teaching
that the saint who loses himself in love of God promotes the Church's
work as well as does the missionary who endures physical hardship to
bring the Truth to pagan peoples. It is symbolic that the two patrons of
the missions are St. Francis Xavier, who traveled thousands of miles and
preached to millions of people, and St. Thérèse of Lisieux, who lived and
died in the cloistered obscurity of her convent. We must, therefore,

mention at least briefly some of the more important saints of the nineteenth century, for they are an indication of the renewed health of the Church in this age, and they are also partially responsible for its flourishing expansion in the past century.

The number of saints and near-saints in the nineteenth century equals that of any previous period of Church history. Among the unnamed saints are the hundreds of martyrs who died in Korea, China, and Paris. Among the better known canonized saints are three priests of outstanding virtue and accomplishment: (1) St. John Bosco, who founded two religious congregations, and who was a special friend of neglected boys and a protector of the poor; (2) St. John Baptist Vianney, the Curé of Ars, who in his humble way fostered and encouraged various Catholic activities, and tirelessly served thousands who came from all over France to line up before his confessional; (3) St. Clement Maria Hofbauer, the Redemptorist who carried the message of St. Alphonsus into the Germanies, and inspired the revival of the Church in Southern Germany in the first decades of the nineteenth century.

Among the women saints of the century special mention should be made of St. Bernadette Soubirous, a simple French maid who received a number of visions of Our Lady at Lourdes in 1858, and through whose mediation thousands of cures have been effected at the shrine erected to commemorate her visions. Also deserving of special mention is St. Thérèse Martin of Lisieux or the "Little Flower," a Carmelite nun whose life of prayer and devotion came to an end at the early age of twenty-four. Mention should also be made of foundresses of religious congregations, like St. Madaleine Sophie Barat and Blessed Julie Billiart, whose spiritual daughters have played a part in the Church's revival. Many others, like Frederic Ozanam, Pauline Marie Jaricot, and Pope Pius IX, have been presented for canonization and their cases are still to be decided. These saints, martyrs, and near-saints played a powerful but unmeasurable role in promoting the revival of the Church throughout the nineteenth century.

The Church was defended in this period by a group of intellectuals, capable apologists who in various ways asserted the traditional truths of Catholicism and tried to refute the errors of the age. Some of the most brilliant intellectuals in the Church were converts, such as Cardinal Newman, and some were descended from crusaders, such as Montalembert. Some of the Church's most stalwart defenders were laymen, and others were brilliant members of a hierarchy that contrasted so favorably with the bishops and cardinals of the eighteenth century. Men like

Gibbons and Spaulding in America, Wiseman and Manning in England, Dupanloup and Lavigerie in France, Hergenröther and von Ketteler in Germany were both excellent pastors of their dioceses and interpreters of Catholic teaching in a changing world.

Laymen played an especially significant role in the first half of the nineteenth century. Joseph de Maistre wrote convincingly against the rationalist doctrines of the Enlightenment and showed that reason led to faith rather than away from it. His *Du Pape* was a challenging assertion of papal infallibility and a claim that the papacy had done more than any other institution to civilize Europe. Joseph Goerres defended the faith as the deposit not only of truth but also of human liberty, and he tried to show Europeans that true freedom was endangered by political tyrants and by false doctrines rather than by the true faith.

Juan Donoso Cortés played a similar role for the Church in Spain. With his brilliant priest friend, Jaime Balmes, he refuted the liberal and romantic errors of the time, stressed the supremacy of the pope, and asserted that the Catholic Church was the strongest pillar of European culture. Comte Charles Montalembert and Frederic Ozanam took a somewhat different approach in France. They tried to show that the Church was not hostile to true liberty or equality, that it was not bound up irrevocably with monarchical institutions, and that it was the best support for democracy. These laymen all made mistakes, but they performed valuable service for the Church in justifying it to the age. Moreover, their work showed the vitality of the recovering Church, the large amount of intellectual "elbow room" within its borders, and the important role that the new society had thrust upon the layman in the Church's apostolate.

Another manifestation of the Church's new vitality was the revival of the older religious orders and the establishment of many new orders to serve specific needs, especially in the missions and in education. The Jesuits had been dissolved in 1773, and other orders had been largely dispersed when their properties were confiscated after 1790. In 1801 Pope Pius VII restored the Society of Jesus in Russia, and after his return to Rome in 1814 he restored the Jesuits throughout the world. The spirit and the rule of the Society had been maintained by a number of former members who had organized the Fathers of the Faith and the Fathers of the Sacred Heart. These groups affiliated at once with the reconstituted Society of Jesus, and the Jesuits quickly resumed their vigorous activity in educational and missionary work.

A number of new religious orders were established in France in the first years of the century. St. Madaleine Sophie Barat founded the Society of the Sacred Heart as a congregation of women devoted to educating girls according to the tradition of the Society of Jesus. William de Chaminade founded a society of priests and brothers, called the Marianists, who devoted themselves exclusively to education as the means of "increasing the number of true Christians." About the same time (1815) three Parisian priests established the society of the Missionaries of France to preach in the parishes of France and to give retreats. The Brothers of Christian Instruction were founded in 1817 by Jean Marie de Lamennais, and in the same year two French abbés founded the Little Brothers of Mary (Marists) to conduct schools for boys. All of these congregations still flourish in France, and they have many schools in Canada and the United States.

New orders were established for other purposes than education. St. John Bosco, called the best "representative of the Church in the nineteenth century," worked with the poor children of Turin and established the Salesian Society for the care and education of poor boys. In co-operation with Blessed Domenica Mazzarello he founded the Sisters of Maria Conciliatrix to do similar work with girls. The Fathers of the Blessed Sacrament were established by Blessed Peter Julian Eymard in 1857, and a year later he founded a similar society for women, the Servants of the Blessed Sacrament. The purpose of these organizations was to foster and spread devotion to the Blessed Sacrament.

Various forms of piety were promoted by such institutions as the Apostleship of Prayer, the Archconfraternity of Prayer and Penance, and devotion to the Sacred Heart on the First Friday and the Month of the Sacred Heart. Among the host of institutions that reveal the Church's new vitality mention can be made of two typical foundations conceived and established by Frederic Ozanam. The first of these was the Notre Dame Conferences, an annual series of sermons preached by a selected orator at Notre Dame Cathedral in order to "bring light into the darkness." The purpose of this foundation was apologetic, and the Notre Dame Conferences still follow in the tradition established by Ozanam and the first preacher of the conferences, the brilliant Lacordaire. The second foundation was the St. Vincent de Paul Society, organized to bring charity and material goods to the poor. The purpose of this foundation was also apologetic, for it was to prove that Catholicism was not confined to formulas of doctrine but that it was a way of life and that it bore good fruit in charity. A host of similar but less well-known institutions showed that the Church was gaining strength and vitality in an age of increasing skepticism and disbelief.

Revived Missionary Activity. Missionary activity is an integral part of the Church's life, of course, but at the beginning of the nineteenth century the missionary spirit had grown cold and missionary activity had almost died. The suppression of the Society of Jesus had taken 16,000 men out of the missionary field, and the other religious communities had found it almost impossible to maintain both the zeal and the personnel necessary to carry on their work afield. Only a handful of priests were engaged in the missions at the beginning of the century. But a number of developments early in the century revived missionary work so that by the end of the century the Church was spread over the entire world for the first time in its history.

The restoration of the Society of Jesus made thousands of men available for the missions, for the Jesuits had never lost sight of missionary activity as one of their primary objectives. Moreover, the Society of the Foreign Missions was re-established in 1815, and such groups as the Dominicans, Franciscans, Benedictines, and Vincentians renewed their missionary zeal. Rome's renewed interest in the missions was revealed by the fact that the Congregation of the Propaganda was re-established by Pius VII and in 1817 put in charge of mission work throughout the world. The College of the Propaganda in Rome was also reopened in 1817 to supply the Church with priests devoted to missionary work.

These were indications of renewed interest in the missions on the part of the official Church. Three foundations established by laymen and priests showed the "grass roots" interest of Catholics in mission work. The Society for the Propagation of the Faith, the *Leopoldinen-Stiftung,* and the *Ludwig-Missionsverein* gave substantial financial support to the missions and increased the interest of European Catholics in one of the Church's essential functions. A brief account of how these foundations were established is interesting in itself, and it is also revealing of the new way in which Catholic activity came to be promoted in the nineteenth century.

The Society for the Propagation of the Faith resulted from the separate efforts of Pauline Marie Jaricot, Madame Petit, a wealthy merchant named Benoit Coste, and the urging of Bishop DuBourg of Louisiana and the Parisian Seminary of the Foreign Missions. Mlle. Jaricot had organized factory girls in Lyons into groups to reform their loose lives and to teach them to pray. Her brother, who attended the Seminary of Foreign Missions, explained to her groups the desperate need of the missions for financial assistance. Mlle. Jaricot arranged to have each girl contribute a *sou* a week to the support of the missions in the Orient. The girls were combined into groups of tens and hundreds, with a leader in each group responsible for collecting the *sous* and sending them to headquarters.

Three years later a group of Lyons people met to consider the appeal of Bishop DuBourg for support of the American missions. Mme. Petit had been raising funds from among the wealthier people of Lyons for this purpose. At this meeting, however, M. Coste insisted that support of the missions should not be confined to America, but should include missions everywhere. The group adopted Mlle. Jaricot's plan of organization, the name of her society, and agreed to support missions all over the world. This was in 1822. In 1840 Pope Gregory XVI erected the Society for the Propagation of the Faith into a pontifical society. The Society had, from its very beginning, imposed an obligation of daily prayer and weekly alms on its members, and it arranged for the distribution of its funds to properly constituted authorities in the various missions. Thus it had caught the true missionary spirit.

The *Leopoldinen-Stiftung* was established at Vienna at the suggestion of a Cincinnati priest, Father Frederick Rese. It was similar in most respects to the French Society for the Propagation of the Faith: members obliged themselves to say prayers daily for the success of the missions and to contribute a *kreuzer* a week; groups of ten handed their sums over to collectors, and eventually the money reached the bishop through official Church channels. The Vienna organization confined itself to the support of missions in America. The *Ludwig-Missionsverein* was founded at Munich, also at Father Rese's suggestion, and it remained very much under the control of the Bavarian king. No provision was made for spiritual support of the missions, as was the case with the other two organizations, and financial support was confined to Germans in America. Although the Munich group lacked the over-all missionary spirit of the other two societies, nevertheless its financial support of teaching sisters in this country was important in the growth of the American Church.

Missionary activity did not come to full fruition until the latter half of the nineteenth century, as we shall see in Chapter 36, when flourishing new missionary congregations were established and thousands of men and women went out from Europe to every part of the world. But a good beginning had been made before the start of the pontificate of Pope Pius IX in 1846. Once prosperous missions in China, Korea, India, and Japan had just about disappeared, and it was necessary to build them afresh almost from nothing. A more immediate problem seemed to present itself in the United States, where thousands of Irish and German Catholics immigrated to find themselves in a non-Catholic environment, without priests, churches, and schools, and therefore very much in danger of losing their faith within a couple of generations. Man power and financial support were needed to save these immigrants for the Faith — and thus in the first half of the nineteenth century America became the most important area of missionary activity.

The Church in America.   The story of the American Church is one of phenomenal growth in an alien environment. In America the Church had no past, as it did in the European countries, and therefore it was free to create whatever arrangements were both Catholic and American. Catholics had been treated with hostility and suspicion in colonial times, of course, and most states discriminated against them legally. But their conduct during the Revolutionary War disproved these suspicions, and religious discrimination was repugnant to the ideals for which the revolution had been fought. The Constitution was therefore drawn up in an atmosphere of religious tolerance.

The Federal Government quickly adopted a policy of encouraging all religions equally and of discriminating against none. The Constitution stated that "no religious test shall ever be required as a qualification for any office or public trust under the United States," and the first amendment prohibited Congress from making any law "respecting an establishment of religion or prohibiting the free exercise thereof." This forced the Federal Government to take a neutral stand as regards the various religions in America, and allowed it to be benevolent toward all. America was a religious country at the time of its founding, and statesmen did all they could to encourage religious activity. That there was no official American hostility toward the Church in the first half of the nineteenth century is shown by President Polk's opening diplomatic relations with the Vatican in 1846. The various states were left free to regulate religious affairs as they wished. By 1833 they had all disestablished the religions that had formerly been state supported, and they generally tended to follow the federal policy of benevolent neutrality toward all religions.

The unofficial attitude toward the Catholic Church was considerably less friendly. Many distinguished Americans were friendly toward the Church, but Protestant suspicion and hostility toward the Church was widespread in America in the first half of the century, and frequently it gave rise to shameful acts of violence. This animosity against the Church increased because many immigrants were Catholic — Irish and Germans in the first half of the century — and it seemed that these Catholics were not assimilable, that they constituted a "foreign element" who were a danger to American institutions. These immigrants were poor people, and they were ignorant. Thus Catholicism came to be identified with ignorance and poverty, whereas Protestantism seemed to be the religion of the "better sort."

The Church, therefore, faced a series of peculiar American problems — a fact which European Catholics and Roman officials were slow to recognize, and thus they sometimes were as much disturbed and confused by their American Church as they were encouraged by its tremendous energy and its phenomenal growth. The basic problems facing the American hierarchy can be summed up as three: (1) to hold those Catholics already in the fold, especially the immigrant who tended to identify his faith with his way of life and his native language; (2) to educate the Catholic population so that they would become the social and intellectual equals of other Americans — a most important objective in a democratic country; (3) to develop an apologetic adapted to the American scene — which involved raising up a clergy and a laity capable of defending their faith, and establishing papers and magazines through which Catholic teaching and Catholic opinion on current matters could be presented.

To accomplish these objectives the early American bishops had to obtain priests from abroad, establish schools and seminaries to provide a native clergy, build churches, orphanages, and other institutions — in general, to build a Church and organize it into dioceses. These tasks were complicated by geography, for America was far from Rome in those days, and delays of communication created occasional misunderstandings. Moreover, the population was scattered sparsely over wide areas or congregated in a few eastern cities. The small numbers of Catholics naturally caused many mixed marriages and similar difficulties which took up a good deal of the clergy's energy. Despite these difficulties, as we know, the Church took root in early America and grew to mature stature by the end of the nineteenth century.

During colonial times American Catholics had been under the jurisdiction of the Vicar-Apostolic of London. Their position became anomalous when the United States won their independence. Consequently, at the request of American Catholics, Pope Pius VI appointed Father John Carroll bishop of Baltimore in 1789 with jurisdiction over all Catholics in the United States. Bishop Carroll's estimate was that there were only about 25,000 Catholics in America, 15,000 of whom lived in Maryland and 7000 in Pennsylvania. There were only 34 priests in this country in 1790. By the time Archbishop Carroll died in 1815, Baltimore had become a metropolitan see with five suffragans (New York, Philadelphia, Boston, Bardstown, Kentucky, and New Orleans), and the number of Catholics had increased by more than tenfold.

The new American Church, which until the twentieth century continued to be administered by the Congregation of the Propaganda as mission territory, had to adopt measures to regulate local matters under general ecclesiastical law. This involved the calling of diocesan synods and provincial councils. The first diocesan synod met in 1791 at Bishop Carroll's house, and in 1829 the first provincial council was convened at Baltimore under Archbishop Whitefield. By this time, the bishops calculated, the number of Catholics in the country had increased to over half a million. The first provincial council of Baltimore dealt with lay trusteeism, the administration of the sacraments, and the general problem of promoting Catholic literature.

Six more provincial councils were held by 1849, in which the bishops discussed and acted upon their common problems. The council of 1849 petitioned Pope Pius IX to allow American bishops to hold a plenary or national council to legislate on American ecclesiastical matters. The First Plenary Council met at Baltimore in 1852. By this time there were almost two million Catholics in the country. There were 34 dioceses in 1852, and seven more were created the following year. Six archbishops and 26 bishops attended the First Plenary Council of Baltimore. They decreed that parochial schools should be established wherever possible, that a seminary should be erected in each diocese or province, and that pastors must give religious instruction to the young. The Council issued various regulations on diocesan government, and prescribed the Roman Ritual and the Baltimore Ceremonial for the American Church.

The growth of the Church from 1789 till the outbreak of the Civil War was amazing. The number of Catholics increased from about 25,000 to about three million, the number of priests from 34 to 2235, and the number of dioceses had grown from one to 43. Such growth required the construction of thousands of churches and other buildings, a tremendous financial task in a new country of relatively poor people. The young American Church was helped by the mission aid societies mentioned earlier in this chapter, and by large numbers of European Catholics who came to America to labor in these new fields. They created minor problems — French priests and Irish congregations, or German nuns in Irish parishes — but their help was invaluable in a period when money and man power were both in short supply on this side of the Atlantic.

French exiles played an especially important role in conducting the first seminaries in this country. In 1791 the Sulpicians opened St. Mary's seminary in Baltimore. In 1812 and 1829 seminaries were opened at Bardstown and Cincinnati. Colleges were soon established, and by the time of the Civil War there were 29 Catholic colleges or universities in the country. The first of them was Georgetown, established by the former Jesuit, Bishop Carroll, in 1789. It was taken over by the Jesuits early in its history and conducted by them officially ever since their re-establishment in 1814. Within a few years the Jesuits opened St. Louis University, Fordham, Holy Cross, St. Xavier's at Cincinnati, Spring Hill College in Alabama, and many preparatory schools for boys throughout the eastern part of the country. In 1842 the Fathers of the Holy Cross established Notre Dame University. Other early colleges and universities were Mount St. Mary's at Emmitsburg, Maryland, St. Francis at Loretto, Pennsylvania, and Villanova, in Philadelphia. In 1859 the American College was established at Rome to train American priests for certain specialized tasks.

Catholics also established a number of publishing houses, some sixty weekly papers, and a number of Catholic magazines. Catholic authors published more than a thousand books and pamphlets by 1830, and the number increased considerably in the next thirty years. But this growth of the Church in the first half of the century should not obscure the fact that Catholics continued to be a small minority in the country, and they were prone to develop a "ghetto mentality" because they were in some respects different from other Americans, because they were generally less affluent, and because their numbers were being increased largely by the influx of foreigners in larger numbers each decade.

In the first half of the nineteenth century the Church ran into a number of peculiarly American problems. Two of them stand out as the most important: (1) *trusteeism*, which was a problem within the Church, and (2) *nativism*, which was a problem of relations with a hostile social environment.

Trusteeism ultimately resolved itself into the question of whether the bishop or the laymen of each parish are to control the parish. The problem began in Bishop Carroll's time when a Board of Trustees was incorporated in New York City to purchase property for a church site. The trustees were all laymen. They were not content with holding title to the property, but insisted on selecting pastors independently of the bishop and on running parish affairs. The problem was soon complicated and intensified by the fact that America was a land of different nationalities. Each national group wanted a pastor of its own nationality; and on many occasions the bishop's appointees found the doors of their parishes closed on them.

The provincial council of Baltimore, which met in 1829, addressed the problem of trusteeism carefully and seriously. It decreed that no church should be consecrated until title to it was handed over to the bishop, that under no conditions could laymen be given the right to select pastors, that all priests who encouraged trusteeism should be suspended, and that any parish refusing to submit should be placed under the interdict. These regulations set the pattern on which the problem of trusteeism was settled, but the council of 1829 did not by any means end the difficulty. It persisted for a considerable time, until Archbishop Hughes of New York and Bishop Kenrick of Philadelphia (later Archbishop of Baltimore) put an effective end to trusteeism in the east by vigorous action.

Nativism was a more persistent problem, one that has plagued the American Church in one form or another throughout its history. Put in blunt terms, it is a virulent prejudice against Catholics based on the assumption that they cannot be good Americans. Nativists, therefore, proposed various ways of making them second-class citizens or keeping them out of the country altogether. In the 1840's "native" Americans were alarmed at the increasing number of immigrants, by whom, they feared, the Anglo-Saxon, Protestant American would be overwhelmed. Their alarm resulted in legal forms of action, such as petitions to Congress to restrict immigration or lengthen the period preceding naturalization; it also took the form of violent riots in which convents and churches were burned in Philadelphia, Boston, and other cities with sizable Catholic populations.

In the following decade the Nativist movement entered politics in the Know-Nothing Party which sought to elect candidates committed to a Nativist program. For a few years the Know-Nothings were successful. They elected about 75 members to Congress in 1854, and they obtained solid enough control of several state legislatures to secure the passage of a certain amount of anti-Catholic legislation. But within a few years the American tendency toward fair play reasserted itself, and the Know-Nothings faded into obscurity. The Nativist movement did no permanent damage to the growing American Church, perhaps, but it did leave scars and suspicions that made it more difficult for the Church to integrate itself into American society after the Civil War. Moreover, it distracted the leaders of the Church, such as Kenrick in Philadelphia and Hughes in New York, from constructive ecclesiastical work in decades when they had to devote so much of their energies to defending the Church against Nativist charges and against acts of violence.

A last point to be noted about the early American Church is that it took its missionary work seriously from the beginning and thus revealed its Catholic vitality. The Indian population had dwindled to about 400,000 by the beginning of the century, a native population exposed to the wiles and guns of the unscrupulous whites. This made the missionaries' work difficult, and for a time missionary efforts among the Indians almost ceased. Early in the century, however, such bishops as Fenwick, DuBourg, Loras, and Cretin fostered missionary work in and beyond their dioceses. When the Jesuit novitiate was opened at Florissant, Missouri, in 1824, the master of novices restored the Jesuit Indian mission and opened a school for Indian boys. The second provincial council of Baltimore (1833) entrusted all Indian missions west of the Mississippi to the Jesuits. Missionary activity thus became an integral part of Church activity in America, but its results were rather disappointing in numbers of Indians converted — largely because Catholicism was looked upon by the Indian as part of the White Man's culture and destructive of the Indian way of life.

The American Church Outside the United States.   The Church in Canada was in a difficult position at the beginning of the century. Canada remained part of the British dominions when the United States obtained their independence in 1781. Quebec was almost solidly Catholic, and in this province Catholicism was identified with the French language and culture. Elsewhere Catholics were in a minority, much as in the United States, and they were discriminated against both socially and politically. The English Emancipation Act of 1829 was supposed to remove most political discriminations against Catholics, but some of the Canadian provinces refused to apply the law until they were forced to do so. The natural increase of French-Canadians and the large influx of Irish into Canada added considerably to the Catholic population of Canada in the first half of the century. Gradually the government adopted a more tolerant policy, and in 1851 it granted to all Canadian subjects of the crown the "free exercise and enjoyment of profession and religious worship without distinction or preference." Catholicism continued to be identified in most Canadians' minds, however, with the French speaking population of Quebec, and the Church suffered in influence and prosperity because of this identification.

The position of the Church in the Latin American countries was also anomalous. The Spanish and Portuguese colonies of America obtained their independence by a series of revolutions through the first quarter of the nineteenth century. The new governments presumed to keep the privileges formerly possessed by the Spanish and Portuguese kings, especially the right to nominate bishops and to control the publication of papal messages within their domains. This privilege the popes refused to concede to the new governments. Moreover, the new governments were frequently under the control of liberal, anticlerical elements who were willing to keep Catholicism as the established religion but insisted on controlling it even more completely than European kings had done in the eighteenth century.

As a result the Church in the Latin American countries came to be labeled by liberals as an enemy of progress and an opponent of enlightened democracy. The turnover of governments was so rapid in most countries that the Church had difficulty in establishing itself solidly anywhere. Although most Latin Americans in this age were Catholics or else of no religion, nevertheless the bishops and clergy found it extremely difficult to make the more influential classes be Catholic in more than name. A simple piety continued to exist among the poorer classes, however, and through these decades Catholicism continued to thrive among the peasants and working classes in these countries.

REVIEW AIDS

1. Explain as fully as you can why the number of saints and near-saints increased so markedly from the last half of the eighteenth century to the first half of the nineteenth.
2. Compile a list of saints from various walks of life in the first half of the nineteenth century. Explain your reasons for each choice.
3. What functions could laymen perform more satisfactorily than clergy in the nineteenth century? Why did an active laity become more necessary than ever before in the nineteenth century?
4. Why is missionary activity always a good index of the Church's vitality at any period of history? What new difficulties did missionary activity face at the beginning of the nineteenth century?
5. Analyze carefully the provisions as regards religion in Article VI and the First Amendment of the Constitution to determine the constitutional status of the Catholic Church in this country. From your knowledge of American

history show what this country's attitude was toward religion in the first half of the nineteenth century.

6. List and analyze the principal problems facing the Church in America at the beginning of the century.

7. Was Nativism a help or a hindrance to the Church in America? Explain your choice.

8. Trace the career of one of the early leading bishops in this country in order to show the qualities required of a successful Church leader in this age.

9. Explain the difficulties that faced the Indian missionary.

10. In what ways was the Church in Latin America in a more favorable position than in the United States? In what ways was its position less favorable?

SUGGESTIONS FOR FURTHER READING

Most of the works cited at the end of the last chapter are useful as additional reading for this chapter. Especially useful are the studies of Corrigan, Mac-Caffrey, Neill, Kempf, and Moody.

In addition to these works, the student should consult the following studies of mission groups in Europe: Theodore Roemer, *The Leopoldine Foundation and the Church in the United States* (New York: 1933); Theodore Roemer, *The Ludwig-Missionsverein and the Church in the United States* (New York: 1933); and Katherine Burton, *Difficult Star: The Life of Pauline Jaricot* (New York: 1947). A typical life of the founder of a religious order in this period is that by Katherine Burton, *Chaminade, Apostle of Mary* (Milwaukee: 1949). Another such valuable work is Joseph B. Code, *Great American Foundresses* (New York: 1929).

The Church in Latin America is adequately handled by Edwin Ryan, *The Church in the South American Republics* (New York: 1932), and John L. Mecham, *Church and State in Latin America* (Chapel Hill, N. C.: 1934).

The best general study of the missions is still Joseph Schmidlin, *Catholic Mission History* (Techny, Ill.: 1933).

There is an abundant literature in English on the history of the Church in this country. Because the student is likely to be interested in this subject, a number of works are worth citing. A general popular survey is Theodore Maynard, *The Story of American Catholicism* (New York: 1941). This work is not always accurate factually or interpretatively, but it serves as a good introduction to the subject for nonprofessional historians. A more accurate survey is Theodore Roemer, *The Catholic Church in the United States* (St. Louis: 1950). The best readable but scholarly introduction to the subject is John Tracy Ellis, *American Catholicism* (Chicago: 1956).

The early period is adequately covered by the following works: Jules A. Baisnée, *France and the Establishment of the American Hierarchy* (Baltimore: 1934); Frances S. Childs, *French Refugee Life in the United States 1790–1800* (Baltimore: 1940); Peter Guilday, *The Catholic Church in Virginia (1815–1822)* (New York: 1924); Peter Guilday, *The Life and Times of John*

Carroll (New York: 1922); Peter Guilday, *The Life and Times of John England* (New York: 1927); Wilfrid Parsons, *Early Catholic Americana, 1729–1830* (New York: 1939); Thomas P. Phelan, *Catholics in Colonial Days* (New York: 1935).

Other aspects of Church history covered in this chapter are studied in more detail in the following works: Ray A. Billington, *The Protestant Crusade, 1800–1860: A Study of the Origins of American Nativism* (New York: 1938), is the best study of this subject; Trusteeism is well analyzed in Francis E. Tourcher, *The Hogan Schism and Trustee Troubles in St. Mary's Church* (Philadelphia: 1930); American relations with the Papal States are the subject of Leo F. Stock's, *United States Ministers to the Papal States* (Washington: 1933); and three typical accounts of religious orders in this country are James M. Gillis, *The Paulists* (New York: 1932), Charles G. Herbermann, *The Sulpicians in the United States* (New York: 1916), and Gilbert J. Garraghan, *The Jesuits of the Middle United States* (New York: 1938).

DOCUMENTS

The following document is the principal part of the Constitution of the original Society for the Propagation of the Faith. It shows the care with which the practical French founders of the Society arranged the details of structure and responsibility within the Society — a key factor in its successful development.

Constitution of the Society for the Propagation of the Faith

I. A pious Society is founded in France, with the title of the Society for the Propagation of the Faith.

II. Its purpose is to extend the society of faithful Catholics by aiding, with all the means at its command, Missionaries charged with spreading the light of the Faith among foreign nations in both hemispheres.

III. It is composed of the faithful of both sexes whose Christian conduct is such as to call down the blessings of God on its enterprise.

IV. The Society is divided into divisions, hundreds, and sections.

V. Ten members make up a section, ten sections constitute a hundred, and ten hundreds a division.

VI. Each division, each hundred, and each section has a leader.

VII. The leaders of the divisions of a diocese are the council of the administration of the Society in the diocese. They correspond on the one hand with the diocese, and on the other with the leaders of their hundreds.

VIII. The leaders of the hundred are named by the leader of their division. They correspond on the one hand with this leader, on the other with the leaders of their sections.

IX. The leaders of the sections are named by the leader of their hundred, and they correspond with him. Each section leader is empowered to replace any members who drop out of the section.

X. Each leader of a division, a hundred, or a section keeps an exact list of the ten persons under his administration; he is to send this list to his superiors whenever they request it.

XI. Each division, century, and section can have its own meeting.

XII. The principal means by which the Society hopes to achieve its end are prayers and alms.

XIII. In order to call down the graces of God on the Society and on the missions, each Associate is requested to say an Our Father and a Hail Mary every day. It will suffice for this requirement to make the intention of offering the Our Father and the Hail Mary of the morning or evening prayers, and adding the invocation: St. Francis Xavier, pray for us.

XIV. The Society selects as special feasts for particular prayer, the feast of the Discovery of the Holy Cross, the day on which the Society was founded at Lyon, May 3, 1822, and the feast of St. Francis Xavier (December 3), whom it recognizes as its patron. These days should be celebrated with a mass for the success of the work in all cities where councils are established.

XV. Each Associate gives five centimes a week as an alms for the missions.

Chapter 33

POPE PIUS IX AND LIBERALISM

FOR many years English speaking historians treated Pope Pius IX as a reactionary figure, an unfortunate choice as head of the Church who thundered anathemas at anyone who disagreed with him, a pope who absolutely forbade Catholics to think. Such a picture was created because the pope's opponents, inside and outside the Church, wrote so much, and because the movements which he condemned seemed invincible until our times. More recent scholarship has revealed Pope Pius IX to have been a warmhearted person with a good sense of humor, a man who courageously resisted error and promoted sound piety in the Church. Historians agree today that his long pontificate (1846–1878) prepared the way for the positive accomplishments of Leo XIII and his successors. Pius IX was, to use the phrase of his most recent biographer, "creator of the modern papacy."

During this period the Church seemed to suffer one political reverse after another. The pope who had been a popular national leader in 1846 was a prisoner in the Vatican twenty-five years later. But in this same period the Church recovered its internal unity by putting Gallicanism to rest at last, by centralizing the administration of Church affairs without destroying the ordinary power of the bishops, and by evoking a popular affection for the pope such as had not existed previously in modern times. In a purely religious sense, this was a period of great gains. Finally, it was an age in which the head of the Church took issue with current secular heresies and thus prepared the way for the more constructive work of his successors.

Mastai-Ferretti, the "Liberal" Pope. The news of Bishop Mastai-Ferretti's election as pope in 1846 was received by Italians with wild enthusiasm. As bishop of Imola he had earned the reputation of being "liberal." He had criticized the severe policies of his predecessor, Gregory XVI, who had suppressed the revolutionary movements of his pontificate with a stern hand and had turned his back on all proposals for reform. Citizens of the Papal States expected the new pope to establish something like constitutional government at Rome; Italians throughout the rest of the peninsula looked to him as the leader against Austria in the *Risorgimento* — an enthusiastic "reawakening" of Italy that espoused the cause of constitutional government in the various Italian states, and their eventual union in a national Italian state. The new pope was a patriotic Italian, critical of the old conservatism, naturally inclined to be liberal, and willing to effect basic reform in the Papal States.

The problem of Italian unification was basically insoluble — a point which neither the new pope nor the Italian patriots seem to have realized in 1846. Any national state would have to include Rome and the rest of the Papal States. The pope could not resign as a temporal ruler and become an Italian subject, for this would be equivalent to renouncing his effective headship of the Catholic Church and becoming just another Italian bishop. The plan to make the pope constitutional monarch or president of an Italian federation would involve him in national and international politics to such an extent that his role as head of the Catholic Church would be almost certain to suffer. The dilemma was not solved until 1929, of course, and meanwhile the "Roman Question" created difficulties from which the papacy and Italy have not yet entirely recovered.

The new pope's immediate temporal problem, however, was to reform and modernize the government of the Papal States. Within a month of his election Pius IX generously granted an amnesty to more than a thousand persons in papal prisons for political offenses. This amnesty was hailed in Rome and throughout the world as the act of an enlightened ruler. Now the political world watched — liberals expectantly, conservatives apprehensively — to see how he would reform the temporal government. A number of "progressive" measures were quickly undertaken: plans were made for construction of a railroad system, for tariff reform, for lighting the streets of Rome; the criminal courts were simplified, prisons were improved, a more liberal press law was passed, and a general reform of the criminal code was begun.

The most insistent demand of liberal reformers had long been that laymen be admitted to positions in the papal government. Pius IX created a consultive body for the government of Rome, to which laymen were eligible for appointment, and he reorganized the Council of Ministers for the Papal States, admitting laymen to all positions except that of secretary of State. An additional concession to the reformers was the creation of a civil guard to be manned and commanded, reformers expected, by the middle class. In his first measures, then, the new pope showed himself to be on the side of revolutionary reform and opposed to traditional conservatism.

The revolution of 1848, which started in Paris and spread like wildfire throughout all of Europe, forced various Italian rulers to grant their subjects constitutions. On March 15, Pope Pius IX granted a constitution to the Papal States. It followed the pattern of the times, and it made the pope — in his role as a temporal ruler — a constitutional monarch. The events of the following months were exciting and confusing in Rome and throughout Italy. The populace demanded more radical changes, and most of all they insisted that the pope drive the Austrians out of Italy and create a national state. When Pius IX resisted these demands, Mazzini and his radical followers seized Rome and set up a revolutionary government. The pope's prime minister, Pelligrino Rossi, was murdered, and the pope himself had to flee from Rome in disguise.

After the revolutionary forces were defeated by a French army, the pope returned to Rome a disillusioned man. His attempts to reform the Papal States had resulted in murders and revolution. Apparently the policy of Gregory XVI was the only practicable one; apparently, too, Metternich had been right in saying that this new pope did not understand how to rule. Pius IX had learned his lesson the hard way: from now on he would be cautious about reform and he would be on guard against liberals and nationalists who were trying to foment still another revolution and another war with Austria to secure the unification of Italy. In short, Pius IX was converted to conservatism.

The Papacy and Italian Unification.   In the nineteenth century the drive toward national unification in Europe was practically irresistible. Greece, Serbia, and Belgium had become independent national states by 1830. In the Revolution of 1848 an attempt was made by the "professors' parliament" to unify the various German states, and a similar attempt was made by Italian nationalists to create a united Italy. The failure of the revolution did not end Italian hopes for a national state. As a matter of fact, the failure of this revolution consolidated Italian patriots behind the plan of Camillo Cavour to absorb the rest of Italy into Piedmont-Sardinia under the House of Savoy. The other plans — to form a federation

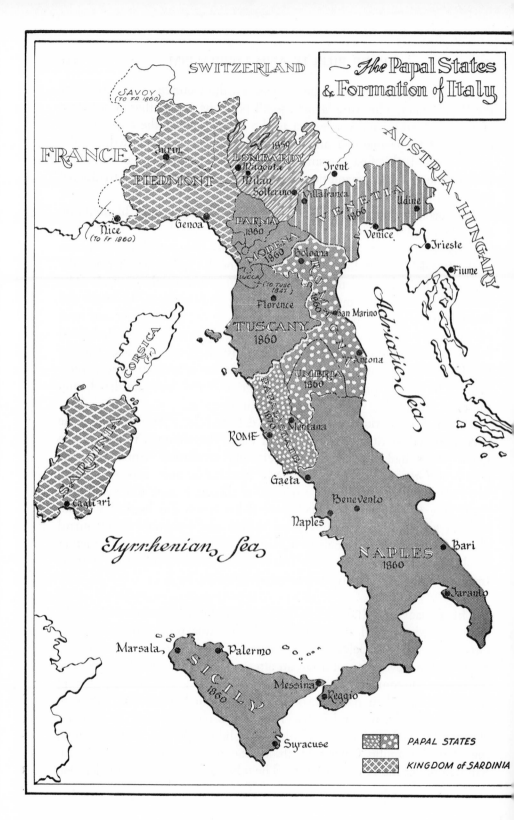

SWITZERLAND

The Papal States & Formation of Italy

SAVOY
(TO FR 1860)

FRANCE

Turin
PIEDMONT

1859

LOMBARDY
Magenta
Milan
Solferino
Villafranca

Trent

AUSTRIA~HUNGARY

VENETIA
1866
Venice

Udine

Trieste

Fiume

Nice
(TO FR 1860)

Genoa

PARMA
1860

MODENA
1860

Bologna

LUCCA
(TO TUSC
1847)

Florence

San Marino

CORSICA
(FR)

TUSCANY
1860

UMBRIA
1860

Ancona

Adriatic Sea

SARDINIA

Cagliari

ROME

PAPAL
STATES

Mentana

Gaeta

Benevento

Naples

Tyrrhenian Sea

NAPLES
1860

Bari

Taranto

Marsala

Palermo

SICILY
1860

Messina

Reggio

Syracuse

PAPAL STATES

KINGDOM of SARDINIA

under the pope, or to form a confederation of republics — had both been discredited by the reluctance of the pope and the excesses of the republicans during the revolution of 1848. All Italian nationalists therefore backed the plan of incorporating the various Italian states into Piedmont-Sardinia.

Cavour planned his campaign carefully and cleverly. Piedmont had a liberal constitution, and it had a king, Victor Emmanuel, who was a patriotic soldier. Cavour built up the strength of his state economically and militarily. He entered into relations with underground organizations in the other Italian states so that, at the right time, they would "spontaneously" demand incorporation into Piedmont. By participating in the Crimean War he put Napoleon III of France in his debt. Thus he had a guarantee of French support against Austria when he was ready to drive the Austrians out of Lombardy and Venetia. But there remained the problem of the Papal States, which lay athwart the Italian peninsula and which would have to be incorporated into any proposed Italian state — if it were truly to be a national state. Cavour had no scruples about making war on the pope, but he had to reckon with the papacy's long-standing claim to Rome and the Papal States, and with Italian respect for these claims.

In 1859 Cavour managed to provoke Austria into a declaration of war. Aided by France, Piedmont defeated the Austrians easily, and when Napoleon III withdrew from the conflict a peace was arranged which gave Lombardy to Piedmont and recognized the validity of local plebiscites to incorporate Parma, Modena, Tuscany, and part of the Papal States into Piedmont. Victor Emmanuel took the title of King of Italy, and the first decisive step toward the unification of Italy had been taken. In 1860 Garibaldi's "Red Shirts" conquered Sicily and Naples. Cavour violated the neutrality of the Papal States by hurrying troops through them to Naples, where Garibaldi saluted Victor Emmanuel as his king.

Rome and surrounding territory remained under the temporal jurisdiction of the pope. But Italian nationalists were not satisfied to make Florence their capital. They could not rest content until all Italian territory was incorporated into the new state, and Rome became its capital. In 1866 they obtained Venetia by siding with Prussia against Austria in the Seven Weeks' War. Several attempts were made by Garibaldi to take Rome by force, but French troops repulsed him each time. Until 1870 the pope maintained precarious control of Rome and its surrounding territory. But in that year France and Prussia went to war, and Napoleon III withdrew the troops that had been protecting the papacy from Italian nationalists ever since 1848. Victor Emmanuel's troops moved on Rome.

Pope Pius IX ordered the papal guard to fire a few shots in token resistance to prove that he had not submitted voluntarily, and then to lay down their arms to prevent unnecessary bloodshed.

Thus the "Roman Question" was created. Rome had been taken from the pope by force. Until the pope would surrender his claim as rightful temporal ruler of Rome, Italy could not have clear title to the city which became the capital of the new Italian state. The pope withdrew to the Vatican as a voluntary prisoner, for he was unwilling to move about Rome as a subject, under Italian law, while he claimed to be a sovereign prince. In November, 1870, the Italian government issued the Law of Guarantees to regulate the pope's new position. This law invested the pope with the personal attributes of a sovereign: immunity from arrest, inviolability of his person, and the same protection enjoyed by the king through the treason laws. The Law of Guarantees also provided that the pope could have a personal military guard, that his communications with bishops and foreign governments would be absolutely free, and that he should have his own postal and telegraph services. He was also given exclusive use — though not sovereign ownership — of the Vatican and Lateran palaces, and the villa of Castel Gandolfo. Finally, in return for his lost territories he was to receive 3,225,000 lire a year (somewhat over $600,000).

Even if the terms had been more generous, Pope Pius IX would have refused to accept the Law of Guarantees. His basic objection was that it was a *unilateral* settlement of the problem, a piece of legislation in which he had no hand and which recognized him only as an Italian subject, even though a special kind of subject. The pope could accept only a *bilateral* or a negotiated settlement that would take the form of a treaty between two sovereign powers. Temporal sovereignty was essential to the preservation of his spiritual independence and his claim to rule over a universal Church.

The "Roman Question" was not settled until 1929. In the intervening years the Italian government faithfully observed its guarantees that the pope would be treated as a sovereign and that he would be free to communicate with bishops and governments throughout the world. Its treatment of the Church in Italy was another matter. Several thousand monasteries and convents were confiscated and the members dispersed; works of charity were secularized; and various Catholic organizations were suppressed. Pope Pius IX tried to counter these anticlerical measures, as well as protest against the basic injustice of the seizure of Rome, by issuing his *non expedit* decree. This decree requested that Catholics refrain from participating in parliamentary elections, either as candidates for office or as voters. Leo XIII changed the request to a command with his *non licet* decree in 1886.

The popes believed that participation in national politics would be tantamount to an implicit acceptance of the Law of Guarantees. These two decrees were sound in principle, but they had sorry practical results in that by withdrawing large numbers of conservative, principled voters from political life they made things easier for the radical, anticlerical elements. These two decrees played at least some part in clearing the way for the development of socialist parties in Italy in these years. In 1909 the Sacred Penitentiary recognized these facts by ordering the decrees suspended in those dioceses where the bishops thought it prudent to do so. Before the outbreak of World War I Catholics were free to vote in most dioceses, a large number of them were elected to the Italian parliament, and an effective Catholic Party was organized. As a result, Catholic principles came to play some part in the struggle against radical elements in Italian political life, and something like a better understanding between Church and State seemed possible.

Definition of the Immaculate Conception. Pope Pius IX's long pontificate can best be understood as a period of transition from the older papacy of post-Reformation times to the modern papacy of the twentieth century. Many administrative changes were made, the Church was soundly centralized, and the pope became the focal point of popular Catholic sentiment. These changes were made possible by the industrial development of the age; they were made easy because of Pius IX's engaging personality, and because he was no longer ruler of a sizable temporal state. It was during this pontificate, moreover, that the pope actively assumed his role as chief teacher in the Church. In a number of encyclicals and allocutions Pope Pius IX analyzed current secular doctrines in the light of the Catholic tradition, and he directed his Catholic children to pray and to worship God in the Church. Pius IX was himself a man of childlike piety, a pope who appeared serene in the midst of violent political upheavals. His devotion to the Blessed Virgin was particularly strong. It is not a mere coincidence that the three most important events of his papacy occurred on December 8: in 1854 he defined the doctrine of the Immaculate Conception; in 1864 he issued the encyclical *Quanta Cura* with an appended "Syllabus of Errors"; in 1869 he opened the Vatican Council.

The full import of the definition of the Immaculate Conception is frequently missed by secular historians. The Bull *Ineffabilis Deus* was something more than a mere definition of doctrine and a pious invocation of our Lady. In the first place, the method by which it was formulated and stated was most important. Second, it was an implicit condemnation of several popular secular doctrines about man and society. Finally, it foreshadowed the "Syllabus of Errors" and the Vatican Council. Ever since the seventeenth century the popes had received occasional requests that the Immaculate Conception be defined as a matter of faith. These requests multiplied after the vision of the Blessed Virgin seen by Catherine Labouré in 1830, for the vision included the inscription: "O Mary, conceived without sin, pray for us who have recourse to thee."

On June 1, 1848, the pope appointed a commission of twenty theologians to study the question whether it would be possible and practical to make this solemn definition. In 1849 he asked the bishops of the Church for their prayers and advice on the subject. Their replies were overwhelmingly enthusiastic, so Pius IX ordered the two outstanding theologians at Rome to prepare drafts of the new dogma. The bishops were invited to Rome for the solemn proclamation on December 8, 1854, and they were allowed to introduce modifications in the text at the last moment. But the pope did not associate himself with the bishops in making the proclamation. The dogma was pronounced on his authority alone. Thus a precedent was established whereby the pope appointed learned theologians to investigate a problem thoroughly, then consulted with the bishops about it, and finally assumed full authority as infallible chief teacher in the Church to make the definition. This is the procedure that Pius XII used in defining the doctrine of the Assumption in 1950.

In the face of a skeptical world, then, Pope Pius IX flatly asserted his traditional claim to infallibility when he speaks *ex cathedra,* as head of the Church on a matter of faith or morals and with the intention of so speaking. For the pope solemnly declared that anyone who dissented from this definition was in error and was excluded from the Church. The doctrine was declared to be in the deposit of the faith, and the case was closed for all time — except, of course, for further embellishments of the doctrine. The decree stated that from the moment of her conception the Blessed Virgin was miraculously exempted from the taint of original sin. The doctrine was stated in these words:

> To the honor of the Holy and Undivided Trinity, to the glory and adornment of the Virgin Mother of God, for the exaltation of the Catholic faith and the increase of the Christian religion, by the authority of our Lord Jesus Christ, of the blessed Apostles, Peter and Paul, and Our own,

We declare, pronounce and define that the doctrine which holds the most blessed Virgin Mary was, by the singular favor and privilege of Almighty God in view of the merits of Jesus Christ, the Savior of the human race, preserved free from all stain of original sin from the first instant of her conception, is a doctrine revealed by God and therefore to be firmly and constantly believed by all the faithful. Wherefore should any presume to dissent in their heart from Our definition, which may God avert, let them know and realize that they are condemned by their own judgment, that they have suffered shipwreck of the faith, and have cut themselves off from the unity of the Church.

The assertion of the Blessed Virgin's miraculous preservation from the stain of sin was an affront to the secular thought of the nineteenth century, for this was an age that thought it had replaced "superstition in miracles" with "solid scientific thought." Even more of an affront was the reverse side of the doctrine. For the pope asserted the fact of original sin to a world that believed in the sinlessness of man, indeed, that did not believe in sin at all. The pope further told the nineteenth century that the Blessed Virgin alone had escaped the taint of original sin; everyone else suffered impaired intellect and weakened will, concupiscence, as the result of original sin.

Liberalism and the Syllabus of Errors. Secular observers seem to have missed the import of the definition of the Immaculate Conception, for it passed almost unnoticed outside the Catholic world. But ten years later the "Syllabus of Errors" caused an uproar in political and intellectual circles — and it is still quoted by those who believe the Catholic Church harbors obscurantism and is opposed to progress. The definition of the Immaculate Conception had been a challenge to the secular world, but it disturbed very few of the faithful because it had been part of the Catholic tradition for so many centuries. The Syllabus, on the other hand, dismayed "liberal" Catholics and seemed to endorse the strongest views of the ultraconservatives.

A close study of the Syllabus shows that it contained nothing new. Every one of the eighty condemned propositions was drawn from one of Pius IX's previous encyclicals or allocutions. But when read consecutively at a sitting, they give the impression of harshness, irritability, unwillingness to accept anything modern. The reader of the Syllabus must understand that it was attached to the encyclical *Quanta cura* and was sent to the bishops as a sort of index of modern errors the pope had previously condemned. Reference was made in each case to the source from which the condemned proposition was taken, and the bishop or priest was naturally expected to read the original document. The Syllabus was never intended to be more than an index to former statements, an *index raisonné*, in Newman's words, but it was soon discussed as an independent document. The ultraconservatives hailed the Syllabus for supporting their views, and many of them wanted to give it infallible authority. On the other hand, bishops in Protestant countries were embarrassed by it, and they tried to minimize its importance as a papal document.

The publication of the Syllabus in the form of eighty tersely stated propositions was probably imprudent. Its purpose of providing a handy index to previous papal statements was forgotten as the Syllabus was heatedly discussed in newspapers and government circles as an independent papal document. The misunderstanding that was bound to occur can be illustrated by looking at a single proposition. The eightieth condemned proposition reads: "The Roman Pontiff can and should reconcile and align himself with progress, liberalism, and modern civilization." Taken by itself, this proposition seems to say that it is wrong for the pope to accept any part of modern progress or civilization. If the reader goes to the allocution *Jamdudum,* from which it was taken, he will find that the pope discusses what many people mean by "modern civilization": attacks on the Church, denial of religion, imprisonment of the clergy, the closing of Catholic schools. Then the pope concludes:

> Can the Roman Pontiff ever extend a hand to this kind of civilization or cordially enter into alliance and agreement with it? Let their real names be restored to things, and this Holy See will be ever consistent with itself. For truly has it always been the patron and nurse of real civilization: the monuments of history bear witness and prove that in all ages from this Holy See have gone forth, even into the most remote and barbarous nations, right and true humanity, moral culture, and wisdom. But if under the name of civilization is to be understood a system devised to weaken, and perhaps even to destroy, the Church — no, never can the Holy See and the Roman Pontiff come to terms with such a civilization.

Bishops and priests using the Syllabus were expected to go to the original documents for a full explanation of each condemned proposition.

No Christian could quarrel with the pope over most of the eighty condemned propositions. Only about a dozen provoked controversy. The first seven concern Pantheism, Naturalism, and absolute Rationalism; the next seven are on modern Rationalism; and the next four are on Latitudinarianism and Indifferentism. Following proposition eighteen is a paragraph condemning Socialism, Communism, and Secret Societies. Up to this point there is nothing to embarrass "liberal" Catholics. The next twenty propositions deal with the Church and her rights, and the following seventeen concern civil society. In these sections the pope clashes with modern liberal thought on the Church-State issue. Propositions 56–64 are on Natural and Christian ethics, and the following ten concern Christian Marriage. Here again there is little one could quarrel with if he admits the Church's claim to her teaching function on moral problems.

The last six propositions concern the pope's civil power and the errors of the Liberalism of the day. It was these propositions, more than any others, which excited heated discussion about the Syllabus and seemed to divide Catholic ranks more widely than ever. Here the pope seems to assert that Catholic countries should not tolerate the practice of other religions, that it is wrong to allow freedom of expression, and that the Church is opposed to progress and to modern political and social institutions. Reference to the original documents reveals that the pope was speaking of Italy and of Italian problems most of the time. But all Europeans and Americans did not associate "progress" with the suppression of convents and monasteries and the closing of Catholic schools, as the Italians did.

The brilliant bishop of Orleans, the liberal Dupanloup, published a pamphlet in which he explained the Syllabus in terms that reconciled the Church with all true progress and with the good aspects of modern civilization. He postulated a famous distinction between the *thèse* and the *antithèse* or *hypothèse*. The former is the ideal, which can be realized only in a perfect society; the latter is what is possible or just in the existing order of things. Since the Church's opponents spoke in absolute terms, Dupanloup pointed out, the pope was required to state the true absolutes. But it does not follow that the failure to attain the true absolute is to be condemned in all circumstances. Separation of Church and State, for example, is not the absolute ideal, but in some countries and under certain conditions it might work excellently.

The pope himself and 630 bishops gave their enthusiastic approval to Dupanloup's explanation of the Syllabus. The idea behind his explanation was far from original or daring. It was part of traditional Catholic teaching, and it had been reasserted as recently as 1863 in the conservative *Civiltà Cattolica* in a discussion of "modern liberties." The Jesuit editor concluded his discussion thus:

> These liberties stated as a thesis, that is, as principles of universal application to human nature and to the divine plan, should be and have been condemned absolutely by the Roman Pontiffs, particularly by Pius VI, Pius VII, and Pius IX. But in the form of hypothesis, that is, an arrange-

ment suitable to the special condition of this or that nation, they may well be legitimate. As such Catholics may love them and defend them. When they employ them as effectively as possible in the service of religion and justice they do a good and useful work.

Thus it became possible to put a much more liberal interpretation on the Syllabus than the ultraconservatives would ever allow.

The furor surrounding the Syllabus has obscured the teaching role that Pius IX performed courageously and effectively throughout his long pontificate. As chief teacher in the Church he addressed many encyclicals and other allocutions to the whole Church and to the bishops and Catholics of various countries. In these addresses he analyzed various contemporary errors and restated traditional Catholic teaching against them. An unfortunate effect of the pope's being so embroiled in Italian affairs is that he seems to have paid little attention to the problems of industrial society that were growing acute in other parts of Europe, and thus the socialists stole a march on him. But in other areas his teaching function was well performed. To Pius IX fell the unpopular but necessary task of condemning errors so that his successors could formulate positive doctrine on modern problems.

The Vatican Council. Exactly five years after he published the Syllabus, Pope Pius IX opened the Vatican Council on December 8, 1869, with more than 700 bishops in attendance. For the first time in the history of the Church representatives to an ecumenical council came from every continent. The fact that 120 of them were from English-speaking countries shows how the national composition of the Church had changed in recent centuries. Protestant and Orthodox representatives were also invited, but of course they did not come. This was, nevertheless, the largest ecumenical council in the Church's history. Of the 1050 eligible to attend, as many as 774 were at some of the sessions. These were cardinals, archbishops, bishops, abbots, and generals of religious orders. For the first time, the Catholic rulers were virtually ignored, and the Church fathers were practically free from outside influence.

The need for a general council had been expressed for some time. No general council had been held since Trent in the sixteenth century, and meanwhile many developments had taken place. New secular heresies had arisen, and many bishops and theologians felt that the time had come for the Church to clarify its teaching against liberalism, naturalism, socialism, evolution, materialism, and various other modern doctrines, just as it had clarified its teaching against the Protestants at Trent. Some leaders in the Church even hoped that a council would enact the greater part of the Syllabus and make it part of the deposit of faith. At any rate, there was rather general agreement that certain disputed points of doctrine should be clarified by a council. Objections to a council centered around the difficulties involved: trouble between France and Germany, which almost wrecked the Council of Trent, seemed likely to prevent harmonious action in a council; the pope, who had only a precarious hold on the remnants of his temporal state, would be imprudent to gather all the bishops into a city that might fall to invading forces any day. But to most bishops these objections did not seem formidable, and steps were taken to prepare for a council to meet at the Vatican palace.

Pius IX sounded out the opinion of cardinals late in 1864 and later the attitude of various bishops. A large majority were enthusiastically in favor of convoking a council. Early in 1865 a congregation of five cardinals was appointed to draw up a tentative agenda. Under this congregation five commissions, composed of theologians, canonists, and other specialists, examined possible material for consideration and from it drew up the schemata to be followed by the council. Eventually these schemata were reduced to two: one on Catholic doctrine, and the other on the organization of the Church. The plan was similar to that followed at Trent. First a set of chapters on doctrine or faith would be handled, and then a set on the Church. The preparatory work was done thoroughly, and thus the Vatican Council was able to accomplish a great deal in the little over seven months it was in active session.

The first public announcement of the forthcoming Council was made on June 29, 1867. It was received by most bishops and Catholic laymen with great enthusiasm, but there were some who feared that the Council would be used to increase the pope's power and even to declare him infallible. The original schemata did not include a chapter on infallibility, but in the months before the Council met discussion in Catholic papers and among Catholic theologians focused on this point. One center of opposition to the definition of papal infallibility was the University of Munich, where the brilliant professor of history and theology, Johann Ignaz Döllinger, attacked infallibility on historical grounds. His articles appeared under the pseudonym of "Janus," and they were answered by the future Cardinal Hergenröther, who wrote under the name of "Anti-Janus."

This set of public debates on papal infallibility had been touched off by a somewhat hysterical letter from Paris which was printed in the Jesuit *Civiltà Cattolica*. The author was apparently concerned with the anti-infallibilist attitude of some of the French hierarchy. He distinguished these "liberal" Catholics from "true" Catholics, asked for a definition of papal infallibility with a minimum of discussion, and prayed for "an explosion of the Holy Spirit" to settle the issue. This inaugurated a public debate in France. Dupanloup led the opposition to the definition of papal infallibility; Louis Veuillot led the forces in favor of it. There was a good deal of bitterness and strong language in the arguments, but both sides were loyal to the pope and to the Church. Dupanloup insisted that it was inopportune to define the doctrine because of the difficulties it would create — and supporting him were some of the best minds in the Church, such as Cardinal Newman.

Pope Pius IX had distinguished three periods in all Church councils: first, the period of the devil, disorderly and troubled; second, the period of men, one of muddled human endeavor; and third, the concluding, glorious period when the Holy Spirit enlightens and purifies proceedings. The historian has difficulty in deciding where one period began and another ended in the Vatican Council. But he can report that the bitterest conflicts occurred before the Council met, that no undue pressure was used by the pope or the majority group to coerce action in their favor, and that the Council deliberated in an atmosphere of tranquillity and security. No attempt was made to rush matters, but the thorough preparatory work made it possible to proceed without unnecessary delay.

The first schemata, on matters of faith, was unanimously adopted on April 24, 1870. This was the most important and most comprehensive work of the Council, and it was accomplished only after intense, heated debate during which the bishops proposed more than five hundred amendments. But the heated discussion did not reveal any serious cleavage of opinion. It centered, rather, around the prudence of attacking Protestant or materialist teaching directly and by name, and the phraseology in which Catholic doctrine should be stated. When these difficulties were settled, there was no question about accepting the traditional Catholic doctrine as defined by the Vatican Council. The Constitution Dei Filius rejected rationalism, naturalism, and pantheism. It reaffirmed Catholic doctrine on the nature of God, of Revelation, of Faith, and of the relation of Faith to Reason. This restatement of Catholic doctrine against the new errors of the age was a most valuable accomplishment of the Vatican Council.

It passed almost unnoticed, however, because of the furor created over the schemata on the Church. This was introduced on January 21, 1870, and the bishops were invited to send in memoranda on the first ten chapters. The schemata on the Church included the controversial issues of the nature of the Church as a "perfect society," the juridical authority of the pope within the Church, the rights and duties of the civil power, and relations between Church and State. But these really controversial issues were not contained in the first ten chapters. Some of the bishops wanted to see the Syllabus of Errors made authoritative and dogmatic; others, like Dupanloup, wanted nothing said about these controversial issues.

Meanwhile, outside the formal sessions, conversation centered chiefly around the question of defining papal infallibility. Two parties had formed: the Infallibilists, headed by Deschamps of Belgium and Manning of England, who wanted the definition made in strong terms; and the Anti-Infallibilists, who opposed the definition. The latter party broke down into two groups: those who thought the doctrine was wrong, and those who believed in papal infallibility but thought its definition was inopportune. The Infallibilists were in a large majority from the very beginning, and there was a strong temptation for such energetic leaders as Manning to use steam-roller tactics on the opposition. They managed to have the chapter on infallibility taken out of order and discussed with the first chapters of the Constitution *De Ecclesia*. But the Council listened to seven weeks of free discussion on the subject, with 164 speeches made for and against the definition.

Three chapters on the primacy of the pope and the one on his infallibility were finally brought to a vote on July 18. Dupanloup and his friends left Rome the preceding day so that they would not embarrass the pope by voting against the doctrine of infallibility. Of the 533 Fathers at the final session, all but two (the bishops of Cajazzo, Italy, and Little Rock, Arkansas) gave their *placet*. After the reading of the decision, the two dissenting bishops knelt at the pope's knees and consented. The remaining bishops throughout the world accepted the decision as true and inspired. Döllinger's supporters in southern Germany refused to accept the doctrine, and they formed a small schismatic group called the "Old Catholics" (not to be confused with the "Old Catholics of Holland") who still persist in Germany.

If the historian is able to discern the Holy Spirit at work in the Council, as Pius IX said He was, it is in the restricted way in which papal infallibility is defined. The definition, of itself, removes almost all the objections offered against it in the arguments of the Anti-Infallibilists, for it does not empower the pope to tell "infallible jokes" or sneeze "infallible sneezes" as some of the opponents seemed to fear the definition would enable him to do. The definition is contained in these measured words of the Council:

Wherefore, faithfully adhering to the tradition handed down from the beginning, for the glory of God our Savior, for the exaltation of the Catholic religion, and the salvation of Christian peoples, with the approbation of the Sacred Council, we teach and we define the divinely revealed dogma that: when the Roman Pontiff speaks *ex cathedra*, that is, when in the discharge of his office as Doctor and Pastor of all Christians, in virtue of his supreme Apostolic authority, he defines a doctrine concerning faith or morals to be held by the whole Church, he enjoys, by the divine assistance promised him in Blessed Peter, that infallibility with which the divine Redeemer willed that His Church would be endowed for the purpose of defining doctrine concerning faith or morals, and therefore such definitions of the Roman Pontiff are irreformable of themselves and not from the consent of the Church.

The Prisoner in the Vatican. Napoleon III had declared war on Prussia three days before papal infallibility was defined. French troops began to leave Rome on August 4, and most of the bishops departed from Rome for their homelands. Rome was occupied by Victor Emmanuel's troops in September, and on October 2, a Roman plebiscite returned a large majority in favor of the annexation of Rome to Italy. The pope retired to the Vatican in protest to this violent action, as we have seen, and remained there a voluntary prisoner. On October 20, 1870, he formally prorogued the Vatican Council which had acted on only the first few chapters of the Constitution *De Ecclesia*. Technically, then, the Vatican Council is still in session, since it is prorogued rather than dissolved, and any future council will be faced with the initial question of whether to continue the schemata of the Vatican Council or officially dissolve it before starting new deliberations.

The dominant note in Church history in the last years of Pope Pius IX's pontificate are the attacks on the Church made by Germany and, in a lesser degree, by other European countries. These struggles were not settled in Pius IX's lifetime, and it is therefore better for us to discuss them in the next chapter.

The historian is tempted to see Providence at work in the selection of each of the last six popes, for each has been exactly the right man for the temper and problems of his pontificate. A just estimate of Pius IX is just now being made, we have suggested, because of the absurd panegyrics of his admirers and the spiteful attacks of his adversaries. He was devoted primarily to the spiritual work of his office; he was a "spiritual" rather than a "political" pope, even though events into which the Holy See was tossed were primarily political. And it was providential that a man of Pius IX's disposition was at the helm of the papacy in these years to keep it at its business — as Renaissance popes, in similar circumstances, had failed to do.

Pius was keenly aware of the danger of modern errors to men's souls. He was a man of large heart rather than of deep intellect, and his absorbing interest in Italy kept him out of touch with social developments elsewhere in the world. He was an emotional rather than an intellectual person, but his feeling was for what was right. His experience in 1848 had turned him against progress and had wed him to the past — a point he well realized. "Let my successor," he advised, "be animated by my love for the Church and my desire to do good. For the rest, all is changed around me; my system, my policy have had their day; but I am too old to change." His system would have been wrong at a later date, but it is doubtful that a better system could have been devised for the years he occupied the Holy See.

REVIEW AIDS

1. Explain fully why, in the age of nationalism, there was no way to resolve the claims of both the papacy and the Italian State unless one or the other sacrificed part of its essential claims.
2. Explain why the pope could not accept the Law of Guarantees without jeopardizing his position as spiritual head of the Catholic Church.
3. Pope Pius IX sincerely tried to effect liberal reforms in the Papal States. Why did these reforms fail?
4. Contrast the implications of the definition of the Immaculate Conception with the Rousseauvian view of man.
5. In what ways can the definition of the Immaculate Conception be said to foreshadow the Syllabus of Errors and the definition of Papal Infallibility?
6. Look through one or two popular prayer books and list the prayers indulgenced by Pope Pius IX. What significance do you attach to his having approved and indulgenced so many prayers?
7. Give a description of the Vatican Council, as to setting, procedure, and personalities, that you can obtain from a biography of one of its participants — Manning, Kenrick, Ullathorne, etc.
8. How can it be said that the Vatican Council finally ended Gallicanism in the Church?
9. Suppose that you have been appointed secretary of the group who believed that it was inopportune to define Papal Infallibility in 1869. Draw up a short memorandum presenting reasons for this stand. Draw up a memorandum answering these reasons from the majority's point of view.

SUGGESTIONS FOR FURTHER READING

The works mentioned in the three previous reading lists, which give a general coverage of the nineteenth century, are also helpful for the pontificate of Pope Pius IX. Especially valuable in this respect is Corrigan's *The Church and the Nineteenth Century.* MacCaffrey's two-volume *History of the Church in the XIX Century* gives the best coverage of Church history in the various countries, and Neill's *They Lived the Faith* gives considerable information not otherwise available in English on the activity of laymen in this period. Particularly interesting are the attitudes and activities of Montalembert and Veuillot in connection with the Vatican Council.

The most valuable and best-balanced treatment of Pius IX's pontificate in any language is the recently published *Pio Nono* (New York: 1954), by E. E. Y. Hales. The political problems of Italy and Rome are best handled by G. F.-H. Berkeley, *Italy in the Making* (Cambridge: 1936), and J. F. Maguire, *Rome, Its Ruler, and Its Institutions* (London: 1859).

A great deal of information on Church history can be found in the great biographies done of English cardinals of the period. Among these are Wilfrid Ward's two large studies: *The Life and Times of Cardinal Wiseman* (London: 1897), and *The Life and Times of John Henry Cardinal Newman* (London: 1912). Also valuable are E. S. Purcell, *Life of Cardinal Manning* (London: 1896), and Cuthbert Butler, *The Life and Times of Bishop Ullathorne* (London: 1926).

Information about the Vatican Council can be found in the contemporary issues of the *Dublin Review* and the *Tablet*. Lord Acton gives a hostile account of the Council from Rome, but he could not attend the sessions and he was therefore limited to information obtained through gossip. His account can be found in his *History of Freedom and Other Essays* (London: 1922); it originally appeared in 1870 in the *North British Review*. Without a doubt the best work in English on the Vatican Council is the scholarly work of Cuthbert Butler, *The Vatican Council* (London: 1930).

DOCUMENTS

The "Syllabus of Errors" was attached to the encyclical *Quanta Cura* to serve bishops and priests as a handy guide to errors condemned by Pius IX in previous letters. The condemned errors are taken out of context and were not intended to survive as an independent document, but they soon attracted wide attention in this form. The following are some of the more important propositions condemned as erroneous in 1864.

EXCERPTS FROM THE TEXT OF THE SYLLABUS

V. Errors Concerning the Church and Her Rights

19. The Church is not a true, perfect and entirely free society, nor does she enjoy peculiar and perpetual rights conferred upon her by her Divine Founder; it belongs to the civil power to define what are the rights of the Church and the limits within which she can exercise them.

20. The ecclesiastical power must not exercise its authority without the permission and assent of civil government.

21. The Church has not the power of defining dogmatically that the religion of the Catholic Church is the only true religion.

22. The obligation under which Catholic teachers and writers are bound

applies only to those things which are proposed by the infallible judgment of the Church as dogmas of faith.

23. The Roman Pontiffs and the Ecumenical Councils have exceeded the limits of their power, have usurped the rights of rulers, and have erred even in the definition of matters of faith and morals.

24. The Church has no right to employ force, nor any direct or indirect temporal power.

25. Besides the power inherent in the Episcopate, a further temporal power is granted to it either expressly or tacitly by the civil authority, which power is on that account revocable by the civil authority at its pleasure.

26. The Church has no natural and legitimate right to acquire and possess property.

27. The ministers of the Church and the Roman Pontiff ought to be absolutely excluded from all care and dominion over temporal things.

28. It is not right for Bishops without the permission of the government to promulgate even their apostolic letters.

29. Favors granted by the Roman Pontiff must be considered null unless requested by the civil government.

30. The immunity of the Church and of ecclesiastical persons derives its origin from civil law.

31. Ecclesiastical courts for temporal cases of the clergy whether civil or criminal should by all means be abolished, even without the concurrence and despite the protest of the Apostolic See.

32. The personal immunity exempting clerics from military service may be abolished without violation of natural right or equity; civic progress demands its abolition especially in a society constituted upon principles of liberal government.

33. It does not pertain exclusively to ecclesiastical jurisdiction by any proper and inherent right to direct the teaching of theology.

34. The teaching of those who compare the Roman Pontiff to a free sovereign acting in the universal Church is the doctrine that prevailed in the Middle Ages.

35. There is nothing to prevent the sentence of a general council or the act of the assembled nations from transferring the supreme pontificate from the Bishop and city of Rome to some other Bishop or city.

36. The definition of a national council admits of no further discussion, and the civil administration may regard such an affair as settled.

37. National Churches can be established after being withdrawn and openly separated from the authority of the Roman Pontiff.

38. The arbitrary rulings of the Roman Pontiffs have brought about the separation of the Church into eastern and western divisions.

VI. Errors Concerning Civil Society Considered Both in Itself and in Its Relation to the Church

39. The commonwealth is the origin and source of all rights, and enjoys rights which are not circumscribed by any limits.

40. The teaching of the Catholic Church is opposed to the well-being and interests of society.

41. The civil power, even when exercised by an unbeliever, possesses an indirect and negative right over religious affairs; therefore it possesses not only the right called *exequatur*, but also that called *appellatio ab abusu*.

42. In the case of conflicting laws of the two powers, civil law prevails.

43. Without the consent of the Holy See and even against its protest, the lay power has the authority to break and to declare and render null the solemn treaties, commonly called concordats, concluded with the Apostolic See concerning the use of rights appertaining to ecclesiastical immunity.

44. The civil authority may interfere in matters pertaining to religion, morality, and spiritual government. Hence it has control over the instructions which the pastors of the Church issue for the guidance of consciences and conformable to their duty. Furthermore, with regard to the administration of the divine sacraments, it possesses the power to decree the dispositions necessary for their reception.

45. The entire direction of public schools in which the youth of any Christian state are educated, except to some extent in the case of episcopal seminaries, may and must belong to the civil power; and this in such a way that no other authority whatsoever shall be recognized as having any right to interfere in the discipline of the schools, the direction of studies, the conferring of degrees, and the choice and approval of teachers.

46. Even in ecclesiastical seminaries the method of studies is subject to civil authority.

47. The best theory of civil authority demands that the public schools which are open to the children of all classes, and in general all public institutions intended for the education of youth in letters and higher learning, shall be free from all ecclesiastical authority, government, and interference, and shall be completely subjected to the civil and political authority according to the desires of the rulers and the opinions of the age.

48. Catholics may approve of that theory of education for youth which separates it from Catholic faith and ecclesiastical power, and which is confined exclusively, or at least primarily, to the knowledge of the natural order alone and the purpose of social life on earth.

49. The civil authority may prevent Bishops and the faithful from free and mutual communication with the Roman Pontiff.

50. Civil authority has in itself the right of presenting Bishops, and can demand that they take over their dioceses before they have received canonical institution and the apostolic letters from the Holy See.

51. Furthermore, lay government has the right of deposing Bishops from the exercise of their pastoral ministry, and it is not bound to obey the Roman Pontiff in those things which refer to the institution of episcopal sees and Bishops.

52. The government has the right to change the age prescribed by the Church for religious profession of women as well as of men, and it can require all religious orders to admit no one to solemn vows without its permission.

53. The laws which pertain to the protection of religious bodies and of their rights and duties should be abrogated; moreover, the civil government can assist all those who wish to abandon the religious life and to break their

solemn vows; likewise the government can suppress religious bodies, collegiate churches, and simple benefices, even those of private patronage, and take over their goods and revenues to be administered and disposed of by the civil power.

54. Kings and princes are not only exempt from ecclesiastical rule but are even superior to the Church in disputed questions of jurisdiction.

55. The Church should be separated from the State, and the State from the Church.

IX. Errors Regarding the Civil Power of the Roman Pontiffs

75. Good Catholics dispute among themselves upon the compatibility of the temporal with the spiritual power.

76. The abrogation of the civil power of the Apostolic See conduces in the highest degree to the freedom and happiness of the Church.

X. Errors Concerning Liberalism of the Day

77. In our times it is no longer necessary that the Catholic religion should be the only religion of the State to the exclusion of all others whatsoever.

78. Hence it has been wisely provided by law that in certain regions, Catholic in name, immigrants shall be allowed the public exercise of their own forms of religion.

79. Moreover, it is falsely maintained that civil liberty of every kind of worship and full power granted everybody to manifest openly and publicly any opinions whatever, conduce to corrupt more easily the minds and morals of the people and to the propagation of the plague of indifferentism.

80. The Roman Pontiff can and should reconcile and align himself with progress, liberalism, and modern civilization.

Chapter 34

LEO XIII AND THE CATHOLIC REVIVAL

A LTHOUGH historians entertain different opinions about Pius IX, they agree unanimously that Leo XIII was a great pope. Gioacchino Vincenzo Pecci was sixty-seven when he was elected in 1878, and he guided the Church through the first quarter century of its remarkable recovery in recent times. This was a recovery which had begun earlier in the nineteenth century and had made some headway under Pius IX. But after 1878, due partly to Pius IX's excellent preparatory work and partly to Leo XIII's consummate diplomatic skill and intellectual perception, the Church's revival gained tremendous momentum. This can be seen by such a simple fact as the contrast between world reaction to the pope's death in 1878 and then in 1903. The chamberlains of the papal court had difficulty in burying Pius IX decently and without incident, so great was the hostility to the papacy when he died; but the entire world — Catholic and non-Catholic — paused to pay its respects when Leo XIII died because it knew that a powerful figure in world affairs had passed away. So it has been with Leo's successors.

This recovery, we have suggested, was due partly to Leo's personal qualities. No historian, Father Corrigan has written, "will deny that Leo was in the fullest sense of the word a great pope."

> As a diplomat, as a statesman, as a peacemaker he was superb. He was a progressive pope who never sacrificed principle to expediency. He was a scholar possessed of rare literary ability. He was at home in the field of economics and social theory. He was a promoter of learning and a patron of science, art, history, and philosophy. He could appeal with equal assurance to reason, to revelation, and to the record of his predecessors. He was a providential pope.

Leo had had political experience as governor of Benevento, diplomatic experience as papal nuncio to three European countries, and pastoral experience for thirty years as Archbishop of Perugia. He was prepared for the twofold task that confronted him: (1) accommodating the Church to the modern world without sacrificing principle or any of the deposit of faith – a most delicate task; (2) applying ageless principles and revealed truths to modern problems – the task of teaching anew, which has been one of the great functions of the papacy since the year that Cardinal Pecci was elected pope. We can sketch Leo's pontificate by dividing our survey into his political or diplomatic work and his work as chief teacher in the Church.

The most important diplomatic problems facing the Church in the latter half of the nineteenth century were struggles for her rights in the three states of Germany, Italy, and France. The German *Kulturkampf* took place mostly in the pontificate of Pius IX, and it was settled by Leo XIII. Italian anticlerical legislation began in Pius IX's pontificate and continued throughout Leo XIII's. The French *lois laiques* were passed in the last years of Leo XIII's pontificate and immediately after his death, for his attempts to reconcile the anticlerical French government and the anti-republican French Catholics had failed. It will be convenient, however, to treat all three movements at this time.

The German *Kulturkampf*. This euphemistic title is used to describe a series of laws passed in Germany to weaken the ties between the Church in Germany and the papacy, and to bring the German Church under the control of the absolute State. The *Kulturkampf* began shortly after Bismarck had completed the unification of Germany in 1871. It continued through the 1870's, but within a decade the strength of German Catholics and the diplomatic astuteness of the pope made Bismarck withdraw his anticlerical legislation and come to terms with the Church. The *Kulturkampf* was primarily a Prussian thing which was copied in other German states like Bavaria and Baden. Back of it lay Bismarck's desire to destroy all limitations on the State's absolutism, his fear that Catholics were guilty of divided allegiance between Berlin and Rome, and a Liberal-Protestant-Teutonic idea that the "foreign" element of Roman Catholicism vitiated an otherwise sound Teutonic society.

Two series of events inaugurated the *Kulturkampf*. The first was the growing strength of the Catholic Center Party, which the pope refused to condemn at the German government's request. The second was the protests made by bishops and priests against "Old Catholics" (followers of Döllinger who denied papal infallibility) teaching religion in the universities and colleges. Bismarck mistook the temper of German Catholics and thought that they would support the "Old Catholics" against Rome. He therefore protected them and tried to silence Roman Catholic opposition.

The first measures of the *Kulturkampf* were taken in 1871 when the Catholic section of the Prussian Ministry of Worship was abolished, thus putting government control of the Church entirely in Protestant hands, and priests were muzzled by the "Pulpit Law" which forbade any criticism of the government or the constitution under penalty of a heavy fine and a year's imprisonment. In May, 1873, a series of laws was passed to put the clergy under government control. Candidates for the priesthood had to spend three years in a state university and pass a state examination in various nontheological subjects. Seminaries were put under the control of state inspectors, and the government asserted its right to appoint and dismiss parish priests. In the following year additional legislation made priests liable to military service, provided for the expulsion of recalcitrant priests, declared that any bishop who disobeyed the laws was deposed, and generally tightened the government's control of the Church.

Meanwhile, religious Orders were expelled, first the Jesuits and "affiliated orders,"[1] then all those not engaged in hospital work. Hundreds of priests were fined or imprisoned, and several bishops were deposed, exiled, or imprisoned. After seven years of this "battle for culture" nine bishoprics were vacant, about two thousand priests had been found guilty of disobeying the law, and hundreds of thousands of Catholics were without pastoral care. Bismarck's laws had operated with brutal, mechanical efficiency — and the Church should have been defeated. But Bismarck had not reckoned rightly the toughness of Catholic Germans, nor had he made a correct evaluation of the astuteness of the Center Party's leaders. With each election the Center Party grew stronger, and although they did not constitute a majority they were numerous enough to endanger any legislative plans Bismarck might have for the future. Moreover, there was a feeling among many non-Catholic Germans by 1878 that the *Kulturkampf* was a rather shameful thing and that there was no real justification for it.

Bismarck was realist enough to know that his program to throttle the Church had failed. Moreover, two attempts by socialists on the emperor's life brought home the fact that Socialism was becoming a real danger in

---

[1] There are no Orders affiliated with the Jesuits, of course, but the so-called "affiliated" Orders were the Lazarists, the Redemptorists, the Fathers of the Holy Ghost, and Religious of the Sacred Heart.

Germany, and Bismarck needed the support of the Center Party to curb it. But Bismarck could not lose face politically by suddenly reversing his policy toward the Catholic Church. The coming of the diplomatic Leo XIII to the papacy in 1878 enabled him to revoke the *Kulturkampf* gradually. The day after his election Leo sent Bismarck a personal letter in which he expressed his hope for a speedy end of the religious difficulties in Germany. Bismarck entered into informal conversations with the papal nuncio Massella, and thus began a game of diplomatic hide-and-seek between a clever diplomat and an astute churchman. Bismarck sacrificed Minister Falk, who had written the May Laws, but the pope refused, in return, to require German Catholics to dissolve the Center Party. Leo never gave offense to Bismarck. He showed himself willing to compromise on certain matters, such as the government's claim to appoint to certain ecclesiastical positions, but he stiffly refused to yield on others, especially on the laws which subjected the education of the clergy and the bishops' control of the clergy to the government. The anti-Catholic laws which made up the *Kulturkampf* were gradually modified, and in 1887 the work of revoking them was virtually complete. In that year Bismarck publicly endorsed the laws undoing the *Kulturkampf* and spoke eloquently of the pope as an agent of peace. Leo had astutely avoided humbling Bismarck while obtaining the formal recognition by the German government of the Church's rights in Germany.

The pope was helped by the leaders of the Center Party, who were loyally attached to the Church, who understood the constitutional and theological issues at stake, and who proved themselves consummate politicians in using the social and political situation in Germany to their advantage. Windthorst and his associates in the Center Party perfected a technique that can best be called "political Catholicism." Its basic idea is that modern constitutions guarantee all citizens freedom of religion, and therefore Catholics — like all others — have a constitutional guarantee as citizens that they may practice the Catholic religion freely. The Center Party, therefore, proposed to defend the rights of the Church, not on theological or canonical grounds, but on modern political grounds. The Party would support any government that respected its members' religious rights, and it would make life politically impossible for any government that violated these rights. At any rate, the combined efforts of an astute pope, a loyal and capable party, and a stubborn German Catholic population made the *Kulturkampf* a complete failure, and the result was a strong and active body of Catholics in Germany at the end of the century.

France: Ralliement and Lois Laiques. Leo faced a different situation in France. In this "Catholic" country, "the eldest daughter of the Church," Catholics were in a precarious position when Leo became pope in 1878. He followed the only intelligent policy possible, but it proved futile, and when Leo died in 1903 the Church was in the midst of the French version of Bismarck's *Kulturkampf,* the *Lois laiques* which were more thorough, more vicious, and more successful than their German counterpart.

To understand the French problem we must go back to the Revolution of 1789. We will remember that this Revolution divided France into two "nations": one of them embraced the Revolution and its institutions, was anticlerical, antimonarchical, and thoroughly liberal; the other was Catholic, monarchist, antirepublican, antiliberal, and generally in favor of the institutions of the "glorious old regime" of Louis XIV. The status of the Church was regulated by the Concordat of 1801 and its accompanying Organic Articles — which neither Catholics nor anticlericals endorsed as satisfactory. Events of the nineteenth century made the difference between these two "nations" deeper and more bitter, and the attempts of "liberal" Catholics like Ozanam and Dupanloup failed to bring the two together. By 1875 it was evident that the anticlerical forces would emerge triumphant and the Third Republic would be established. The republican leader, Léon Gambetta, won the election of 1877 on the campaign slogan: "Clericalism, that is the enemy!"

Meanwhile, Catholic monarchists were far from sincere supporters of the Church. To most of them the Church was an instrument to further their political views; they supported the Church because they thought it was the prop of the monarchy and the enemy of the Republic they so hated. Some of them were professed atheists, but for political reasons they insisted all "good Frenchmen" must be Catholics. And the fanatical hatred that most republican leaders bore against the Church confirmed them in their opinion. Among themselves, Catholics were divided into irreconcilable groups, bitterly opposing each other and grasping at revolutionary political schemes that brought nothing but opprobrium on the Church. Meanwhile, the republicans were disciplined and united — agreed that the Church was their enemy and it must be rendered helpless in France.

This was the situation in France when Leo XIII was elected in 1878. He always showed a keen affection for the "eldest daughter of the Church," and he tried to mediate between the conflicting parties by showing that the Church was not committed to any form of government and that Catholics should not try to keep alive political institutions that were antiquated and were repugnant to most of the people in a country. Many French Catholics insisted that the pope did not understand how determined the republicans were to destroy the Church and how, in France, the Church had to oppose the Revolution inasmuch as the two were incompatible. At any rate, the pope took the only possible stand — one to which all but a handful of French Catholics are committed today — but most Frenchmen refused to follow him in 1878.

The Third Republic's war against the Church was fought along the same lines as Germany's *Kulturkampf*. The main battle was over the control of men's minds, and it therefore centered on education. Meanwhile, a number of little skirmishes pushed the Church out of various phases of French life: the clergy were expelled from all hospitals, asylums, and charitable institutions, the administration of which was turned over to laymen; military chaplaincies were abolished; normal schools were laicized; military service was imposed on seminarians (thus cutting down vocations a third); Sunday labor was authorized; and divorce courts were established.

The laicization (*i.e.*, taking over from the Church and giving to the State) of education was accomplished in a series of steps beginning in 1880. In that year the Jesuits were expelled and their twenty-eight colleges were closed. The same measure required that all "nonauthorized" congregations must apply within three months for authorization, submitting their statutes, rules, and number of members. Only those authorized by the government were to continue teaching. In 1882 all religion was excluded from the primary schools, and finally in 1886 all nuns were excluded from government-supported schools, where they constituted over half the teaching body. For about fifteen years the anticlerical program stood still, but in 1901 it was started again with the avowed purpose of finishing the destruction of the Church.

Meanwhile, two developments should have given the government of the Third Republic pause. First, less than three per cent of children attending school were enrolled in the laicized state-supported schools. Apparently this first step in driving the Church out of French life did not meet with widespread support. Second, in 1892 Leo XIII released his encyclical *Au milieu des solicitudes* to the French bishops and their flocks. This was an attempt to end dissensions among French Catholics and to remove all pretexts of anticlericalism among the Church's enemies. Leo's *Ralliement* policy attempted to break up the alliance between French Catholics and the monarchy by showing Frenchmen that they could be loyal to any form of government and that they had an obligation to accept the Third Republic as the duly established government, and to work within it to protect the Church's interests and the common weal. The best Catholics, men like Cardinal Lavigerie and Albert du Mun, enthusiastically accepted Leo's advice, but large numbers of influential Catholics, perhaps a majority, did not.

The conduct of these Catholics in the Dreyfus Affair, beginning two years later, provided the spark that made further anticlerical legislation both possible and — with many — popular. Dreyfus, a Jewish officer, had been accused and twice convicted of selling military secrets to Germany. His persecutors seemed less interested in his guilt or innocence than in the honor of the army, antisemitism, and enmity to the government. Years later Dreyfus was finally proved innocent, and in the publicity attending the affair the army, the monarchists, and the "Church" (the Catholics of the old alliance who refused to follow Leo's *Ralliement* policy) were all discredited. The government then decided to strike while the iron was hot.

Between 1901 and 1905 it enacted a series of anticlerical laws known as the *Lois laiques,* to drive the Church out of French political, social, and intellectual life. An Associations Act of 1901 provided that any religious order wishing to continue work in France must obtain specific authorization from the government and submit to periodical inspection. All remaining Catholic institutions were thus placed under arbitrary government control. A law of 1904 provided that within ten years no member of a religious association could teach in any French school, public or private. Thus the religious were driven out of education. The Separation Act of 1905 was a unilateral abrogation by the French government of the Concordat of 1801. The state support of all priests and bishops (given in return for confiscated property) was terminated, so that the Church, deprived of its properties, had to rely on the generosity of its faithful. Title to all Church property was vested in the State, and the law provided for associations of laymen to administer the property. The purpose of this legislation was obviously to have a fulcrum for the control of the Church's voice in France, and even, with some of the more violent anticlericals, to destroy the Church as a living force in the country. Pope Pius X, recently elected to the Holy See, forbade French laymen to form the associations provided for in the law. The material welfare of the Church was precarious in the next decade: in some places public authorities kept the Church buildings in good repair, and in others they allowed them to fall into such a state of disrepair that they had to be abandoned as unsafe. The law failed to accomplish its full purpose, because popular feeling forced the government to allow the clergy to use churches even if no association of laymen was formed.

Nevertheless, to all appearances the French government's battle against the Church was successfully concluded. It seemed, in 1905, that it only would be a matter of time and the Church would disappear. French Catholics were forced to take heroic measures to keep alive their faith which for centuries most of them had more or less taken for granted, and when World War I was ended Catholics were a smaller but a stronger group than for some time past. Moreover, the exclusion of the religious from the schools freed them for study and writing, so that in the following decades the "advance guard" in Catholic philosophical, theological, canonical, and liturgical speculation was a body of brilliant French religious who might otherwise have spent their lives teaching the rudiments of knowledge to teen-age Frenchmen.

Leo and the Italian Problem. The pope who was most conciliatory with Germany and most understanding with France proved intractable in his dealings with Italy. This seems surprising at first sight, because Leo was a patriotic Italian who sincerely loved the land of his birth. However, his unyielding attitude is explained as a matter of principle, on which he could not yield, and in the insulting, impossible attitude that the Italian government adopted toward the Holy See. By the very nature of the situation, we can see today, Leo's relations with Italy were doomed to a stalemate. Both Leo and his enemies misjudged the connection between the pope's spiritual independence and his temporal position. They had behind them a history of almost two thousand years in which the pope had been one of the princes of Europe, and they were convinced that the pope's spiritual influence was inextricably connected with his political influence, and the latter depended on a sizable state over which he was sovereign. That is why Leo could not have conceived or approved, in his lifetime, of the settlement that was made in 1929.

Leo's stand on the "Roman Question" therefore continued to be essentially the same as his predecessor's. He refused to acquiesce in Italy's act of robbery, and he refused to accept the unilateral Law of Guarantees which treated him like a subject instead of a sovereign. He used the only weapon at his disposal to fight the settlement: public condemnations of its injustice, and the direction to Italian Catholics not to participate in national elections.

Meanwhile, the Church in Italy was subjected to an Italian counterpart of the *Kulturkampf* and *Lois laiques*. The Italian attack on the Church can be summed up under three classes of measures. First, were those intended to annoy and insult the pope and make a mockery of the Catholic faith. On the day of Leo's election the government issued a circular forbidding government officials to attend thanksgiving services for the new pope's election. Then followed in rapid succession a series of measures inspired by an irrational hatred of Catholicism and the person of the pope — possible only in a country recently fallen away from the faith: the wanton attack of government-supported hoodlums on the funeral cortege of Pius IX, when his body was removed in 1881 to the cemetery of San Lorenzo; the permitting of newspapers and magazines to carry (contrary to government law) outrageous anti-Christian blasphemies; the encouragement of antipapal demonstrations beneath the walls of the Vatican; the official celebration of such historical events as the burning of Arnold of Brescia (1155), the Sicilian Vespers (1282), the erection of a monument to Giordano Bruno the "martyr" of papal tyranny — all occasions for stirring up orgies of blasphemous hatred against the Church and the pope. These demonstrations, coupled with the Italian government's attack on Church property and its attempts to control the Church in Italy, caused Leo to think of leaving Rome and he even entered into preliminary negotiations to take up residence in Austria.

The second class of measures against the Church was those against its property. The government suppressed religious orders in Italy and confiscated their "wealth." Late in 1879 it held more than 5600 convents. In 1881 it laid its hands on the Congregation of Propaganda, which possessed considerable revenue-producing properties for the support of missionary activity, by declaring it a minor and taking over control of its property. By another measure the government virtually suppressed Catholic charitable associations in Italy and took over the administration of their properties, which amounted to about two billion lire.

The third class of anticlerical measures was designed to hamstring the Church in Italy and prevent it from carrying out its religious work. The clergy were drafted into the army as soldiers, religious teaching was banned from the schools, the religious oath in the law courts was abolished, and nomination of bishops was hindered so that more than sixty sees were vacant in Italy. Drastic penalties were provided for anyone who attempted to "subject the State or a portion of it to foreign domination," for any priest who should "incite to contempt for the institutions and laws of the State." The regulation of public worship was put under the control of the government, and a Public Safety Act put all religious gatherings under strict police surveillance.

It is not surprising, then, that even the conciliatory Leo XIII found it impossible to deal with the Italian government or to do anything effective toward solving the "Roman Question." All he could do was bear these insulting measures patiently and meanwhile be careful not to do or say anything that might appear to condone these outrages against the Church.

Leo XIII as Teacher. Meanwhile, in the midst of these tribulations Leo performed a function as head of the Church which he and his successors have used for the welfare of Catholics throughout the world and for the prestige of the papacy among well-intentioned non-Catholics. Through a series of masterful encyclicals, he acted as chief teacher in the Church by applying the deposit of the faith to current problems. The *Kulturkampf,* the *Lois laiques,* the Italian anticlerical measures have all been rescinded and they have melted into history. But Leo's encyclicals are still read, studied, and quoted. They are very much a part of contemporary thought, and their effect — never measurable in concrete terms — is felt even in our day. Let us therefore summarize Leo's teaching as chief pastor of the Church.

During his thirty-two years as Bishop of Perugia the future pope insisted that the Church not be isolated from the questions of the day, and he wrote pastoral letters which brought the deposit of Catholic teaching to bear on such current topics as marriage, errors of the day, the temporal power, and the Church and civilization. When he became pope at the age of sixty-seven Leo proceeded to use the Holy See as a professorial chair from which he addressed Catholics throughout the world. For a quarter of a century he issued encyclical after encyclical on spiritual, political, social, and economic subjects. Until his death in his ninety-fourth year, the pope possessed a clear, incisive mind steeped in the wisdom of the ageless Church and practical enough to focus eternally valid principles on problems of the day. Philip Hughes sums up his importance as a teacher in these words:

> Leo XIII did no greater service to the Church than to establish the practice of teaching and guiding it through frequent encyclical letters — veritable treatises on dogma and morals, which applied eternal principles to the ever changing needs of mankind. Here, better perhaps than anywhere else, can the measure be taken of the importance of Leo XIII as the creator of a new age in Catholic history. The great encyclicals are his most enduring memorial.

Within two months after his election, Leo issued the encyclical *Inscrutabili*, a general treatise on "the evils affecting modern society, their causes and remedies." This was a sort of introductory lecture in which the pope discussed briefly many subjects he was to treat more fully in future letters. The important point about this first encyclical is that it was a diagnosis of the ills of modern society from a study of its symptoms, and it was a promise that the pope would spell out his diagnosis in more detail and give the world a scholarly presentation of the truth it had lost. Later in the same year (1878) Leo focused his attention on socialists, communists, and nihilists who proposed to cure the evils of Western civilization by "uprooting the foundations of civilized society." Against these radical groups the encyclical *Quod Apostolici* defended the "right of private property sanctioned by the law of nature."

In *Humanum Genus* (1884) Leo became even more specific in pinpointing the servants of evil and error in the modern world. This encyclical was directed against Freemasonry[2] and other similar secret societies, "which though differing in name, in ceremonial, in form and origin, are nevertheless bound together by a community of purpose." Leo's indictment of Freemasonry rests on two major counts. First, all its tenets can be reduced to a Naturalism which denies God or, at best, makes Him some kind of impersonal force that has no place in human affairs. It is therefore a quasi religion competing against the Catholic Church and other Christian sects for men's allegiance. Second, it has furnished the inspiration and the organization for attacks against the Church. To understand Leo's strong language in making this charge, we must remember that Masons openly led the insulting attacks on the pope and the Church in Rome, that, for example, in the demonstration in honor of Giordano Bruno the red flag of revolution, the green flag of Masonry, and the black flag of Satan were displayed side by side. Leo was convinced, from personal experience and from innumerable reports pouring into the Vatican, that in his day Freemasonry "has found its way into every class of society, and forms an invisible and irresponsible power, an independent government, as it were, within the body corporate of the lawful state."

---

[2] Americans must distinguish the brand of Masonry found in Latin countries from that in the United States. Both are secret societies and both are condemned by the Church. But American Masons tend toward social and business interests, and if they subscribe to Naturalism it is in the same loose way that the average American does. Most Masons in this country tend toward toleration of all religions and benevolence for all institutions helping mankind. The Grand Orient, on the other hand, has been consistently blasphemous, antireligious, and involved in an almost demoniac drive to crush the Church and to control the State. That is why Pope Pius IX had called Freemasonry "the Synagogue of Satan."

Leo condemned the errors and the malpractices of the age in no uncertain terms. The encyclicals in which these condemnations are embodied will in time have merely historical interest, for they are contemporary only as long as the errors they condemn remain alive and vigorous. More important are Leo's positive formulations of Christian teaching on various topics. His four most important treatises are probably *Aeterni Patris*, on scholastic philosophy; *Rerum Novarum*, on the labor problem; *Immortale Dei*, on basic political problems; and *Libertas Praestantissimum*, on liberty, which is "God's most precious gift to man."

Aeterni Patris inaugurated a revival of scholastic thought, based on St. Thomas, which has today probably caused the great medieval Doctor of the Church to be more influential than at any time since his death. In Scholasticism Leo found a system that harmonized faith and reason, and in St. Thomas he found the best systematic treatment of scholastic theology and philosophy that encompassed all being and all knowledge. Leo believed that he went to the heart of social and political, as well as theological reform, in *Aeterni Patris*, for

> . . . a fruitful cause of the evils which now afflict us, as well as those which threaten us lies in this: that false conclusions concerning divine and human things, which originated in the schools of philosophy, have crept into all the orders of the State, and have been accepted by the common consent of the masses.

Leo reasoned that if men thought right, then with the grace of God and good will they would act right and create the right kind of political and social institutions. Human reason, he pointed out, can demonstrate God's existence and can prepare the way for a rational act of faith. The master architect of a system of sound philosophy and theology, properly oriented for human minds and properly directed toward God, is St. Thomas who in his day, "richly endowed with human and divine science, like the sun warmed the world with the ardor of his virtues and illumined it with the splendor of his teachings." *Aeterni Patris* was for Leo the beginning of more than a scholastic revival. It was the first step in the reconquest of the world for Christ, for it should equip clerics and laymen alike with sound principles, clarity of vision, and intellectual acumen with which they could cut through the naturalistic and materialist errors of the day. Moreover, it should serve as a stimulus to remove the errors in society, give religion its true place, reduce the State to its proper role in man's life, and secure justice between man and man.

Leo did not envisage the Thomistic revival as a mere form of apologetics. A good scholar himself, he knew that truth in any form ultimately led to God. He was genuinely interested in promoting any branch of knowledge for its own sake, as he indicated when he opened the Vatican Archives to historians and warned them that their duty was to discover and tell the truth. He encouraged the physical sciences, sound material accomplishments of a practical nature, and all the legitimate new fields of thought. All he required is that each seek after the truth and that none try to pre-empt areas that did not properly belong to it.

One of Leo XIII's longest encyclicals is his closely reasoned treatise on the study of Holy Scripture, *Providentissimus Deus,* wherein the pope shows himself a true scholar in the Christian tradition. He takes issue with the rationalists, pseudo scientists, and "Higher Critics" who in his age thought they had "proved" the Bible to be a tissue of myths, legends, and lies. Leo then goes on to show that there is no incompatibility between truth found in Revelation and truth found by natural reason. Each is a support and an aid to the other. He insists that Holy Scripture is infallibly true, and then he handles the difficult problem of scriptural study, which he encourages competent scholars to pursue in order to develop and extend the knowledge of revealed Truth. But he insists that the Church alone enjoys the prerogative of speaking with finality on this subject, for she is the divinely appointed guardian of Revelation.

In *Rerum Novarum* Leo turned to an area in which truth and justice are not easy to discover, the area of labor relations, and it was almost to be expected that his encyclical would be misunderstood for two or three decades — and even today it is variously interpreted. *Rerum Novarum* condemns Socialism as a solution of the labor problem, and for some time complacent Catholics saw nothing more in it. By the time of World War I it was generally understood to condemn the abuses of the "capitalistic system" as they existed in many countries, and then the pope was called a "socialist." More recently, especially since Pope Pius XI's *Quadragesimo Anno* commemorating the fortieth anniversary of the publication of *Rerum Novarum* in 1891, it is seen as advocating a positive solution of the labor problem. All three views are partially right, for in this encyclical Leo XIII condemns Socialism on the one hand, and the abuses of "Capitalism" on the other, and at the same time he proposes norms for an equitable relationship between capital and labor.

The important initial point about *Rerum Novarum* is that Leo XIII insisted in 1891 that there was a labor problem — a fact which most bourgeois statesmen and many prominent Catholics denied. He then explains why the solution of Socialism is worse than the evils suffered by the workingman in the capitalistic system. Against socialists he defends private property and against capitalists he lays down limits on its use. Leo denies that employer and employee are naturally pitted against each other, and he asserts that "these two classes should exist in harmony and agreement." Justice requires that employers be guaranteed a fair income from their property, and that labor be treated with human dignity, more specifically that hours of labor be not too long, that wages be sufficient to support a family decently, and that special consideration be given to children and women employees. Leo would prefer that such just arrangements be made by capital and labor themselves, but he says that the State has the right to protect workingmen and intervene in the labor problem to secure justice for all. Leo warns, however, that the State cannot absorb individuals, that the workingman has the right to form unions, and that these associations should perform their proper functions for the workingman rather than have the state take them over.

From the vantage point of almost three quarters of a century it is easy to see the historical importance of *Rerum Novarum*. First and most obviously, it was a forthright, courageous analysis of a difficult social problem by the pope at a time when relatively few persons understood that there was a problem. Second, the pope went to the heart of the matter by showing that it was essentially a moral problem, that right principles must be used to obtain a just solution. Third, and perhaps most important, Leo XIII saved the Church from making the same kind of disastrous alliance it had made with the monarchies of the old regime. It was Leo's genius that he resisted the temptation to ally the Church with the bourgeois class. Instead, as Father Corrigan has put it, *Rerum Novarum* "marked a giant step forward toward an alliance of the pope with the workers, of the Church with the common people." More properly, Leo allied the Church with justice, and invited all men of good will to join him.

Immortale Dei stated basic Christian principles on the nature of the State and on relations between Church and State. Like *Rerum Novarum*, it contains teachings that sound like truisms today but which in Leo's time were revealing shafts of light on problems that had become vague and confused. The Church and the State are analyzed as two perfect societies,[3] each sovereign in its own sphere. Between them there is no essential conflict, although in some areas their functions overlap and in many ways they may either help or hinder each other. Leo examined the relations between the two societies historically, philosophically, and theologically. From his examination he showed that the Church was not

---

[3] "Perfect" is used in the philosophical sense, of course, as meaning a society which contains all the means necessary to achieve its ends.

opposed to progress and that "in the temporal order so manifold and great were her services to humanity that the chief end of her existence might seem to be the procuring of earthly well-being." In his own day, he shows, there were widespread errors relative to the State, such as exaggerated notions of "popular sovereignty" and of "liberty." Leo demonstrates that the State is a natural institution and that it has temporal ends assigned to it by the Creator. If the State works for these temporal ends and leaves the Church free to pursue its spiritual ends, then affairs in which there is mixed jurisdiction (such as education) can be harmoniously adjusted.

The fourth of Leo's most important encyclicals is the one on human liberty. *Libertas Praestantissimum* analyzes and condemns wrong notions of liberty current at the time, shows that the Church has always been the friend and advocate of true liberty, analyzes this true liberty, and then discusses the limits to specific liberties of worship, thought, speech, and press. Leo condemns "Liberals" for confusing liberty with license, for giving error equal rights with truth, for seeking to escape from legitimate authority and make each individual the sovereign judge of all things. They

> . . . deny the existence of any divine authority to which obedience is due, and proclaim that every man is the law to himself; from which arises that ethical system which they style "independent" morality, and which, under the guise of liberty, exonerates men from any obedience to the commands of God, and substitutes a boundless license.

The Holy Father analyzes the true notion of liberty in terms familiar to all Catholic students now — as the faculty of choosing means fitted for the end proposed, the faculty belonging to those who have the gift of reason, a gift that entails responsibility for human decisions, and he demonstrates that it needs "light and strength to direct its actions to good and restrain them from evil." Liberty, then, requires law, both natural and human.

> From this it is manifest [the pope concludes] that the eternal law of God is the sole standard and rule of human liberty, not only in each individual man, but also in the community and civil society which men constitute when united. Therefore, the true liberty of human society does not consist in every man doing what he pleases, for this would simply end in turmoil and confusion, and bring on the overthrow of the State; but rather in this, that through the injunctions of the civil law all may more easily conform to the prescriptions of the eternal law.

In a number of other encyclicals Leo XIII developed one or another of the principles discussed in *Immortale Dei*. Among these are *Diuturnum*

Illud, in which the pope rejects the Rousseauvian idea that the State is the result of a human pact, but says that people have the right to choose their form of government. In this encyclical Leo shows himself willing to accept the good elements of modern democracy but insistent on condemning those theories which make the majority "infallible" and omnipotent. Many of these principles are repeated in *Sapientiae Christianae,* on "the chief duties of Christians as citizens."

Less well known are Leo XIII's many encyclicals on spiritual subjects, by means of which he inspired and guided the spiritual revival taking place during his pontificate. Major encyclicals dealt with devotion to the Holy Ghost (*Divinum Illud*) and to the Holy Eucharist (*Mirae Caritatis*); others appeared on such subjects as devotion to the Rosary and the consecration of the human race to the Sacred Heart. These encyclicals on spiritual subjects appeared in the last years of the pontiff's life, most of them after he was ninety, and they can be considered a fitting crown to his remarkable career as chief teacher in the Church.

When Leo XIII died in 1903, the Church was in considerably stronger condition than she had been a century earlier. Internal problems had been handled by the ending of Gallicanism and establishment of the authority and power of the pope. The Church was vigorous and thriving in Germany. In England it was making considerable headway. In Italy, France, and the Latin countries the little people remained loyal and devoted, but there was enmity among the governing class in these countries, among the wealthy people, and it seemed that the Church which had been identified with Latin countries was beginning to develop strength in German and English-speaking countries. Especially hopeful for the Church's future was its vigorous growth in the United States — a fact which did not escape the aged pontiff, and one which gave joy to his last years. The vitality of the Church was also shown by the tremendous expansion of missionary work, which we shall treat in Chapter 36.

The fruit of Leo's pontificate was shown in the large number of Catholic thinkers and writers who began to be influential as Catholics in the field of literature, economic, social, and political work, and in the various sciences and professions. Catholic journals were established in the European countries and America to explain Catholic teaching to the faithful and to comment on current problems. Leo's policy of reconciling the Church with modern times was a difficult and delicate policy to put into effect, and it was almost bound to run into difficulties, but it was beginning to bear good fruit even before he died. Catholic scholars were beginning to win the respect of non-Catholics, and intelligent men came to see that there was no necessary opposition between faith and science or between the Church and progress. Unfortunately, the policy of adapting the Church to modern times was taken up too enthusiastically and without sufficient caution by a small group of clerics and laymen who developed the heresy of "Modernism," which came to a head shortly after Leo's death and had to be handled by his successor.

REVIEW AIDS

1. Contrast the background of the Third Republic's attack on the Church with the background of Germany's attack. In what ways do these differing backgrounds account for the different degree of bitterness in the attacks and the different measures taken?
2. What factors account for the failure of the *Kulturkampf* and the success of the *Lois laiques?*
3. Look up the list of prominent cardinals nominated by Leo XIII. Do you think, from looking over these names, that this is the best and most distinguished set of appointments made by any pope since Paul III?
4. In general diplomatic histories look up the problem of the Caroline Island Dispute and see how Leo XIII settled it. What effects did this settlement have for the papacy?
5. Estimate the importance of *Rerum Novarum* from a perusal of Catholic magazines in 1951 or 1956 commemorating the 60th and 65th anniversaries of the publication of this encyclical.
6. From a reading of *Aeterni Patris* make a list of the reasons that Pope Leo XIII gives for a study of St. Thomas and his synthesis of scholastic thought.
7. Write an essay to show, from the historian's point of view, what the total impact was of Leo's encyclicals (a) in Catholic circles, (b) in the world at large.
8. Contrast the personalities of Pius IX and Leo XIII. In what way is it true to say that Pius IX had to prepare the way for the positive accomplishments of his successor?

SUGGESTIONS FOR FURTHER READING

Leo XIII was a world famous figure, and when he died a number of biographies appeared at once. Among the better were Bernard O'Reilly, *Life of Leo XIII* (Philadelphia: 1903), and Count Charles T'Serclaes de Woomersom, *The Life and Labors of Pope Leo XIII* (Chicago: 1903). Both studies give much information about Leo and his pontificate and show the opinion in which he was held. Better perspective is found in two later works: René Fülöp-Miller, *Leo XIII and Our Times* (New York: 1937); and Eduardo Soderini, *The Pontificate of Leo XIII* (London: 1934). Soderini has also done a helpful study in *Leo XIII, Italy and France* (London: 1935).

Leo's important writings have been collected in various places. The most frequently used collections in English are: John J. Wynne, S.J., *The Great Encyclicals of Leo XIII* (New York: 1903); volume one of *Social Wellsprings*, edited by Joseph C. Husslein, S.J. (Milwaukee: 1940); and *Pope and People*, a publication of the Catholic Truth Society (London: 1910).

Father Corrigan, *The Church and the Nineteenth Century* (Milwaukee: 1938), devotes six chapters to the pontificate of Leo XIII. Three chapters are on the encyclicals, and one each is devoted to relations with Germany, France, and Italy. Rev. James MacCaffrey, *The History of the Church in the Nineteenth Century* (Dublin: 1909), has good chapters in the first volume on the German *Kulturkampf*, and relations with France and Italy. Most of the sixth volume of Reuben Parsons, *Studies in Church History* (New York: 1901), is devoted to the pontificate of Leo XIII. Father Parsons has excellent chapters on the *Kulturkampf*, the anticlerical legislation of the Third Republic, and the difficulties with Italy.

Students in most colleges and seminaries will find Catholic periodicals that appeared during this time, such as *Catholic World*, *Tablet*, and *Dublin Review*. In these periodicals they can find interesting contemporary treatment of many of the subjects covered in this chapter.

DOCUMENTS

A. Excerpt from *Rerum Novarum*

Rerum Novarum, the encyclical on the labor question, is probably the most influential and most quoted document to be published by a pope in modern times. It was published on May 15, 1891, after Pope Leo XIII and scholars in Rome had studied the labor question long and carefully. *Rerum Novarum* was a "policy statement" setting down general principles within which specific economic problems could be settled.

We have said that the State must not absorb the individual or the family; both should be allowed free and untrammelled action as far as is consistent with the common good and the interests of others. Nevertheless, rulers should anxiously safeguard the community and all its parts; the community, because the conservation of the community is so emphatically the business of the supreme power, that the safety of the commonwealth is not only the first law, but is a Government's whole reason of existence; and the parts, because both philosophy and the Gospel agree in laying down that the object of the administration of the State should be not the advantage of the ruler, but the benefit of those over whom he rules. The gift of authority is from God, and is, as it were, a participation of the highest of all sovereignties; and it should be exercised as the power of God is exercised — with a fatherly solicitude which not only guides the whole but reaches to details as well.

Whenever the general interest of any particular class suffers, or is threatened with, evils which can in no other way be met, the public authority must step in to meet them. Now, among the interests of the public, as of private individuals, are these: that peace and good order should be maintained; that family life should be carried on in accordance with God's laws and those of nature; that Religion should be reverenced and obeyed; that a high standard of morality should prevail in public and private life; that the sanctity of justice should be respected, and that no one should injure another with impunity: that the members of the commonwealth should grow up to man's estate strong and robust, and capable, if need be, of guarding and defending their country. If by a strike, or other combination of workmen, there should be imminent danger of disturbance to the public peace; or if circumstances were such that among the laboring population the ties of family life were relaxed; if Religion were found to suffer through the workmen not having time and opportunity to practice it; if in workshops and factories there were danger to morals through the mixing of the sexes or from any occasion of evil; or if employers laid burdens upon the workmen which were unjust, or degraded them with conditions that were repugnant to their dignity as human beings; finally, if health were endangered by excessive labor, or by work unsuited to sex or age — in these cases there can be no question that, within certain limits, it would be right to call in the help and authority of the law. The limits must be determined by the nature of the occasion which calls for the law's interference — the principle being this, that the law must not undertake more, nor go further, than is required for the remedy of the evil or the removal of the danger.

Rights must be religiously respected wherever they are found; and it is the duty of the public authority to prevent and punish injury, and to protect each one in the possession of his own. Still, when there is question of protecting the rights of individuals, the poor and helpless have a claim to special consideration. The richer population have many ways of protecting themselves, and stand less in need of help from the State; those who are badly off have no resources of their own to fall back upon, and must chiefly rely upon the assistance of the State. And it is for this reason that wage-earners, who are, undoubtedly, among the weak and necessitous, should be specially cared for and protected by the commonwealth.

B. Excerpt From *Au Milieu des Sollicitudes*

Au Milieu des Sollicitudes (February 16, 1892) was Leo XIII's letter to the bishops, clergy, and laity of France, a country very dear to him. This letter is famous for its policy of reconciliation which Leo set down for French Catholics when he directed them to support the Third Republic as France's legitimate government and to disassociate themselves from the intransigent Bourbons.

Various political governments have succeeded one another in France during the last century, each having its own distinctive form: the Empire, the Monarchy, and the Republic. By giving oneself up to abstractions, one could at length conclude which is the best of these forms, considered in themselves; and in all truth it may be affirmed that each of them is good, provided it lead straight to its end — that is to say, to the common good for which social authority is constituted; and finally, it may be added that, from a relative point of view, such and such a form of government may be preferable because of being better adapted to the character and customs of such or such a nation. In this order of speculative ideas, Catholics, like all other citizens, are free to prefer one form of government to another precisely because no one of these forms is, in itself, opposed to the principles of sound reason nor to the maxims of Christian doctrine. What amply justifies the wisdom of the Church is that in her relations with political powers she makes abstraction of the forms which differentiates them and treats with them concerning the great religious interests of nations, knowing that hers is the duty to undertake their tutelage above all other interests. Our preceding Encyclicals have already exposed these principles, but it was nevertheless necessary to recall them for the development of the subject which occupies Us to-day.

In descending from the domain of abstractions to that of facts, we must beware of denying the principles just established: they remain fixed. However, becoming incarnated in facts, they are clothed with a contingent character, determined by the center in which their application is produced. Otherwise said, if every political form is good in itself and may be applied to the government of nations, the fact still remains that political power is not found in all nations under the same form; each has its own. This form springs from a combination of historical or national, though always human, circumstances which, in a nation, give rise to its traditional and even fundamental laws, and by these is determined the particular form of government, the basis of transmission of supreme power. . . .

Chapter 35

ST. PIUS X AND BENEDICT XV:
REFORM AND WAR

L EO XIII was in his ninety-fourth year when he died. He retained
his clarity of thought till the end, but in his last years he was
more a teaching pope than an administrator. Hence, reforms of
organization and procedure were needed when he died. The cardinals
went into conclave on July 31. The first two ballots favored Cardinal
Rampolla, Leo's Secretary of State, and it seemed that he would be
chosen on the third or fourth vote. Before the third ballot was cast,
however, Cardinal Puzyna announced that he had been instructed by
Emperor Francis Joseph to exercise the Hapsburgs' ancient privilege to
cast a veto against Rampolla. The conclave refused to accept the veto,
but in succeeding ballots Rampolla lost out to the relatively unknown
Cardinal Patriarch of Venice, Giuseppe Melchiorre Sarto, who took
the name of Pius X.

Cardinal Sarto had been a pastor all his life, as assistant in a little
church, parish priest, Bishop of Mantua, and Cardinal Patriarch of
Venice. He was not acquainted with the inner workings of the Curia
or with techniques of ecclesiastical diplomacy. Nor was he naturally
inclined to diplomatic activity. He was of peasant origin, and all through
his life he approached problems simply and directly. He was a man
of the people more immediately and directly than other popes of modern
times, as was indicated when he gathered his servants about him for an
informal audience shortly after his election, when he preached on Sundays
in simple direct language to the little people of Rome, or ate dinner

with simple priests — all contrary to established protocol. Most of all, however, Pius X was a man of prayer. He was easygoing about such matters as papal etiquette, but he was immovably stern in matters touching dogma or morals. He was, it can be said without presumption, precisely the kind of pope needed at the beginning of the twentieth century: a saintly pope who knew that spiritual vitality depended on the sacraments and prayer, a simple pope who was pastor of Catholics all over the world, a stern uprooter of heresy and energetic reformer of ecclesiastical institutions that had grown antiquated.

St. Pius X (he was canonized by Pope Pius XII in 1954) took for his motto "to restore all things in Christ," a logical sequel to the Leonine program of reconciling Catholicism with modern times. In his first encyclical St. Pius stated:

> We proclaim that the interests of God shall be our interests and for those we are resolved to spend all our strength and our very life. Hence, should anyone ask us for a symbol and an expression of our will, we will give this and no other — to restore all things in Christ so that Christ may be all in all.

In this first encyclical St. Pius briefed the program he would follow for eleven years: the education of children; Catholic teaching on marriage and on the use of property; the need of sound training for priests; the reconciliation of all classes of society according to Catholic principles; the need for the universal practice of charity; and the hope that the Roman Question could be satisfactorily settled. On this last point, the pope concluded:

> The conviction will awaken in all men that the Church, as the institution of Christ, must enjoy the greatest possible liberty and not be subjected to any other power, that our fight for liberty is not merely in defense of the most sacred rights of religion, but also a bulwark for the common welfare and security of nations.

St. Pius X and Modernism. The advance of sciences, especially biology and geology, in the nineteenth century seemed to pose a problem for all the Christian religions of choosing between science and the Bible. Most Protestant religions tended to split into "fundamentalist" and "modernist" groups. The former stuck to a literal translation of the Bible and insisted that modern developments that seemed at variance with Bible were erroneous and evil; the latter tried to adapt religious teaching to modern science, and their tendency was to eliminate doctrine from religion in favor of sentiment and ethical conduct. A group of brilliant but

immature Catholics, known as Modernists, proposed a similar development in the Church. Modernists tried to formulate an interpretation of
Catholic teaching that would be easy for scientists and modern "intellectuals" to accept. By rejecting the objective supernatural character
of Catholic doctrine and making it a matter of subjective religious experience they hoped to present it in attractive form to the age.

Modernism is hard to define because Modernists did not agree among
themselves on what they believed — except, perhaps, that believing was
unimportant, whereas religious experience and pious living were the
essence of religion. Pius X can be said to have given Modernism a creed
when he summed up its teachings under sixty-five condemned propositions.
At this time, in 1907, Pius called it "the synthesis of all heresies." Father
Corrigan has tersely described Modernism in this fashion:

> It was a "synthesis of all heresies." With roots in early humanism and
> individualism and nurtured by the pseudo-enlightenment of the eighteenth
> century, it drew from the vagaries of Kant, Hegel, Schleiermacher and their
> kind a noxious excrescence of Agnosticism, Rationalism, Pantheism, Im-
> manentism, Higher Criticism, Liberalism, and Evolutionism. It was bad
> history, bad philosophy, bad theology. It distorted the idea of faith, dogma,
> the Church, Christ and God.

In his condemnation of Modernism, St. Pius X summed up its errors
under three headings. (1) *Agnosticism,* which asserts that supernatural
truths cannot be known with certainty by human reason. Modernists
wanted to retain Holy Scripture as the norm of faith, but they insisted
that it must be interpreted subjectively and that religious truth was a
subjective experience. (2) *Immanentism,* which holds that Scripture and
tradition do not contain revelations from God but are the expression of
the feelings and inner experience of extremely religious persons. For the
Modernists religion is a purely inner experience that satisfies the psychic
needs of man; any "dogma" that does not evoke such an experience is
not necessary for salvation. (3) *Evolutionism,* which holds that the Church
is the result of a gradual evolution and that it must continue to evolve
in order to adapt itself to changing times. Catholic doctrine and worship,
then, would be not fixed but continually changing things.

Modernists have been described as "officers without an army." The
movement never enlisted more than a small number, but they were
brilliant, vocal men, and they held important positions. Many of them
taught in the seminaries and universities, and there was danger that
within a few decades the movement would spread through most of the
younger clergy. The outstanding Modernists were Abbé Loisy in France and

Father Tyrrell in England. Supporting them were some of the best minds of the Church in England, France, Germany, and Italy. When Pius X was shown the danger that this group constituted he moved quickly and firmly. In the decree *Lamentabili* (1907) he drew up a sort of syllabus of sixty-five condemned propositions taken from Modernists' writings, but did not name anyone specifically as holding the propositions. Later in the same year the pope renewed his condemnation in the encyclical *Pascendi Dominici Gregis*. In this letter he also suggested appropriate remedies for this doctrinal malady in the Church: sound training in the seminaries for the clergy, with emphasis on scholastic philosophy and theology; the careful scrutiny of professors in seminaries and Catholic universities to eliminate those tainted with the Modernist heresy; Catholic journals and newspapers to be brought under careful episcopal control; the creation of a diocesan board of censors to superintend Catholic publications, and a diocesan committee to safeguard the teaching of religion in the schools. In 1910 the pope published a *motu proprio* which required all priests in charge of souls or engaged in teaching to take an explicit anti-Modernist oath.

St. Pius' action against Modernism was stern, and some Catholics felt it was unnecessarily harsh. But such action was needed to prevent another heresy like Jansenism from developing within the Church and poisoning Catholic teaching at its very sources. Most Modernists submitted, but there was bitterness among many of the Church's most advanced theologians and there was confusion among their followers. Many felt that Cardinal Newman was implicitly condemned by *Lamentabili,* for Tyrrell had appropriated Newman's idea of development and insisted on using the great Cardinal's reputation to further his ideas. The pope cleared this matter up by writing a letter to the Bishop of Limerick in which he gave absolute approval to all of Newman's Catholic works. The condemnation of Modernism had one unfortunate — but necessary — effect on Catholic philosophy and theology. It put a temporary check on the work of men who were trying to carry on Leo's policy of further study of Sacred Scriptures to extend our knowledge of revealed Truth. The censure of Modernism and the required oath against it caused most theologians to shy away from original study and simply to repeat the old formulas. But the check was only temporary, and it was salutary because of the danger involved in too rapid and too enthusiastic an adaptation of the Church to modern intellectual developments.

The pope faced a series of similar problems in Catholic organizations trying to put into effect the teachings of *Rerum Novarum.* These problems are sometimes referred to as "Social Modernism." In France an organization and a paper, *Le Sillon,* had been established to deal with economic matters. Its organizer was originally encouraged by some French bishops to keep the movement independent of ecclesiastical authority inasmuch as it dealt with economic problems. Marc Sanguier followed this advice and *Le Sillon* developed as a Catholic movement outside episcopal control. In a letter of August 26, 1910, the pope praised Sanguier and his associates for their good intentions but rebuked them on the grounds that every attempt at Catholic social organization must develop in full accord with the Church's teachings and under the authority of the pope or the bishops. Sanguier made immediate submission. The importance of the movement was the pope's setting down directives for the proper organization of Catholic social work.

A similar occasion for setting forth Church policy on these matters presented itself in Germany and Austria. Catholic unions in these countries had been developing in two ways: those at Cologne, under the patronage of Cardinal Fischer, admitted to membership all men of good will; those at Berlin, under the patronage of Cardinal Kopp, admitted only Catholics to membership. When differences between the two policies became acute, the matter was referred to the pope for a decision. In the letter *Singulari Quadam* of September 24, 1912, Pius X formulated the following set of policies: (1) under certain conditions and in certain circumstances interdenominational unions are to be tolerated; (2) when possible, purely Catholic unions are to be preferred, because interdenominational unions involve dangers to the Faith; (3) the tendency to withdraw social action from the influence of the Church is to be condemned; (4) all Catholic associations should develop in dependence on the bishop. This last statement, implied in *Singulari Quadam,* was made explicitly two months later when Pius censured the publications of the Italian *Societa Editrice Romana,* which had refused to obey the injunctions of the bishops of Lombardy.

Reorganization of the Curia.   At the beginning of Pius X's pontificate the government of the Church was still conducted through the fifteen Congregations created by Sixtus V in 1587. "The result," the Holy Father wrote in 1908, "is that today the jurisdiction or competence of each of them is not quite clear to all nor is it well apportioned." There was much overlapping jurisdiction; some Congregations were overworked, and others no longer had any reason for existence. The pope therefore effected a radical reorganization of the Congregations, abolishing some, creating needed new ones, and assigning each a specific set of tasks.[1]

The *Congregation of the Holy Office* remained the most important office in the Curia. Its prefect is the pope, and it watches over all matters relating to faith and morals, decides questions of heresy, and settles matters relating to indulgences. The next most important office is the *Consistorial Congregation*, also presided over by the pope. It chooses bishops, erects and divides dioceses in areas not subject to the Congregation of the Propaganda. The *Congregation of the Sacraments* was created to handle matters pertaining to the sacraments, which had formerly fallen under the competency of several different congregations. The *Congregation of the Propaganda* watches over the spread of the faith and exercises jurisdiction over areas where a hierarchy is not established or is in its initial stages. At this time the United States, England, Scotland, Ireland, Canada, and Holland were removed from its jurisdiction and placed under ecclesiastical common law. The *Congregation of the Council* was entrusted with the general discipline of the clergy and the laity, handling questions relating to the observance of Church law, the conduct of the clergy, diocesan taxes, and similar matters. The *Tribunal of the Rota* was reorganized and given charge of all contentious questions, such as disputed marriages. Other congregations were given jurisdiction over religious orders, educational institutions, rites, and ceremonies. The net result of this reorganization was a diminution of conflicts of jurisdiction and consequent delays.

In similar fashion, St. Pius X reorganized the papal conclave so as to insure absolute freedom in the election of the pope. A constitution of December 25, 1904, abolished the custom of the veto, and in the following year the pope imposed absolute secrecy on the conclave's deliberations under penalty of excommunication. Closely associated with these reforms were Pius' choice of cardinals. At the consistory of May 19, 1914, he created thirteen new cardinals to give the college an even balance of Italians and non-Italians, including four Americans. For the first time in many centuries the Italians did not have a majority in the College of Cardinals.

Reforms in the Universal Church. Many popes in modern history had spoken of the need for a codification of canon law, but it was a

---

[1] As a result of this reorganization, the Curia was divided into twelve Congregations, three Tribunals, four Offices, and numerous Pontifical Commissions.

tremendous task and none of them thought it feasible during their pontificates. St. Pius X's simple, direct nature was ideally suited to cut the Gordian Knot of codifying many centuries of canons which were overlapping, to some extent contradictory, and to a larger extent antiquated. His work on the codification of canon law has been compared with the Napoleonic Code, and when the work was finished shortly after his death the London *Times* editorialized that he would be known as the greatest legislator of modern times.

In the encyclical *Adruum Sane Munus,* of March 19, 1904, Pius announced his intention of giving the Church a new code. For that purpose he appointed a commission, with himself as president and the able canonist Msgr. Pietro Gasparri its secretary. The pope outlined the steps he wished taken, among them that the commission ask the bishops to consult with their canonists on needed revisions and to send them to Rome to discuss the subject with the commission. The work was long and involved, but it was nearing an end when Pius died in 1914. It remained for Benedict XV to promulgate the new Code of Canon Law on Pentecost Sunday of 1917 and to declare it universally in force a year from that day.

As a result of this codification Canon Law can more easily be known. Various canons have been adapted to modern needs. And the force of law is given to all 2414 canons, some of which had doubtful force until they were promulgated as part of the Code in 1917. The codification renders matters of Church discipline incomparably easier to know and to enforce, and it enables the interested cleric or layman to find his duties clearly stated. (Canon law is still a special field of study, of course, and the average layman must rely on competent canonists to interpret the meaning of each canon. Nevertheless this codification did much to spread a general knowledge of canon law.)

St. Pius X effected a number of disciplinary reforms that proved beneficial for the Church. He transferred the nomination of Italian bishops from a special commission to the Consistorial Congregation, and he issued a set of regulations on the bishops' *ad limina* visits to spread them out by country and to provide the Holy See with full information about each diocese. The pope effected many good reforms in the Italian seminaries, and he supported scholastic philosophy and theology as the best systematic presentation of Catholic thought and the most formidable protector against heresy.

A positive measure in this respect was Pius X's stress on the importance of Christian Doctrine. His encyclical *Acerbo Nimis* (April 15, 1905) was devoted to this subject which he considered most important.

> The intellect is a guide, [he wrote] but if it lacks its companion light, the knowledge of divine things, it will be only an instance of the blind leading the blind . . . whereas Christian teaching not only bestows on the intellect the light by which it attains truth but from it our will draws that ardor by which we are raised to God and joined with Him in the practice of virtue.

The pope therefore urged catechetical instruction for all, especially for the young. "On every Sunday and holy day, with no exception, throughout the year," he ordered, "all parish priests . . . shall instruct boys and girls for the space of one hour from the text of the catechism on those things they must believe and do in order to attain salvation." Finally, the pope ordered the Confraternity of Christian Doctrine canonically established in every parish so that the laity could provide trained helpers in this work of the clergy.

On June 11, 1905, St. Pius X published the letter *Il Fermo Proposito* on Catholic Action. The phrase "Catholic Action" had been used before, but Pius gave it the current definition of the participation of the laity in the apostolic work of the hierarchy. He pointed out that changed times made lay action more necessary than ever before in the history of the Church. "In other times it was the popes and bishops who intervened in defense of their children . . . today it must be the children who will rise up in defense of their father, the laity in defense of the hierarchy." The pope insisted, as his successors would continue to insist, that Catholic Action presupposes saintly living on the part of the actionist. "To carry out this work aright we must have divine grace, and the apostle receives none if he is not united to Christ." Pius urged Catholics to prepare themselves for active political life, to live virtuously, to be invigorated with the apostolic spirit, to be well informed, and then to play their proper role in helping restore all things to Christ.

Spiritual Reforms. St. Pius X is remembered among scholars chiefly for his condemnation of Modernism; the average Catholic knows him more for his spiritual reforms, especially his encouragement of frequent Communion. His canonization in 1954 popularized a fact well known in Roman circles, that Pius X was above all a man of prayer and he believed that a Church which prayed right would have the other things added. Since the time of St. Pius V the Breviary had undergone a series of modifications which tended to disfigure it as the principal book of liturgical prayer. So many saints' feasts had been added that the ferial office had become rare, and it was seldom said except in Advent and Lent. The Psalter was not known in its entirety, while some Psalms were repeated every day. Pius' reform of the Breviary was in the interest of simplicity and making it again serve its purpose of liturgical prayer. The entire Psalter was to be said every week, and Sunday was returned to its traditional place in the liturgical cycle. St. Pius X considered this reform but the first step in a revision of the Breviary which, he said, would take another thirty years.

Pius also gave impetus to the study of Holy Scripture. Leo XIII's encyclical *Providentissimus Deus* had encouraged such study, but it had produced little immediate results, and the Biblical Commission in the Curia had never been assigned any concrete tasks. Pius X ordered that controversies on Biblical passages should be referred to this commission for study and judgment. The same degrees were established for the study of Sacred Scripture as for theology, and by a decree of 1906 the study of Scriptures was imposed on all seminaries. The Holy Father requested Dom Francis Aidan Gasquet to take up the work of correcting the text of the Vulgate, and in 1909 he established the Biblical Institute at Rome, which he entrusted to the Jesuits.

Reform of sacred music had long been discussed, but it remained for Pius X to take the necessary practical steps of putting it into effect. Relying on the intensive studies conducted by the Benedictines of Solesmes, the pope issued a *motu proprio* imposing the Gregorian chant as "the true and only lawful code of sacred music." Choral singing, he decreed, is preferable to solo singing; women are not to form part of the choir because they are incapable of fulfilling a liturgical office; and instruments, except the organ, are not to be used in liturgical services. The organ is to accompany the chant and not to replace choral singing. These reforms were all aimed at making sacred music a form of worship rather than a distraction from liturgical services or an aesthetic delight, as it had become in too many places. St. Pius encountered opposition to his reforms on the part of Catholics who had a sentimental attachment to certain hymns he had excluded and who thought that Gregorian chant was monotonous as compared with various operatic psalms, cantatas, or motets they were accustomed to hear in church.

St. Pius X's most notable spiritual reforms were those relating to the reception of the Holy Eucharist. As a legacy of Jansenism, opinion differed in the Church as to how often good Catholics should receive Communion.

The opinion gradually came to be that reception should be frequent, but no one seemed to know what "frequent" meant nor exactly what condition of soul was requisite for the worthy reception of Christ's Body and Blood. In 1905 Pius issued a decree stating: "Frequent and daily Communion should be open to all the faithful of whatever rank or condition of life, so that no one who is in the state of grace and who approaches the Holy Table with a right and devout intention can lawfully be hindered therefrom." The decree stated that the reception of the Holy Eucharist was not a reward for virtuous living but rather a means of help for such living, and that it was sufficient for reception to be free from mortal sin and have a firm purpose of avoiding sin in the future.

Five years later Pius X issued a decree that children receive their First Communion as soon as possible after reaching the age of discretion — ordinarily about their seventh year. "The age of discretion for receiving Holy Communion is reached," he explained, "when a child knows the difference between the Bread which is the Eucharist and ordinary material bread — not full reason, of course, but incipient reason suffices." The pope set an example by giving First Communion to a child only four when he was satisfied the child fulfilled this requirement. These two decrees on the Holy Eucharist revolutionized Catholic piety in the first half of the twentieth century. They are this saintly pope's most valuable gift to the Church, for they have given the great mass of Catholics a spiritual vitality that could not be obtained except through frequent Communion and the supernatural graces attendant upon its reception.

The Great War and the Papacy. A number of times early in 1914 St. Pius X spoke forebodingly of the "great war" which was coming and which he was powerless to prevent. The war broke out late in the summer of 1914, and within three weeks the pope died. In his pontificate of eleven years he had reorganized the government of the Church which, with minor modifications, still stands. He had taken the first steps toward friendly relations with France and with his own Italy. He had endeared the papacy to Catholics throughout the world as not even Leo had done, and he had inaugurated the distinctively modern work of Catholic Action. Most important, his liturgical reforms restored Church prayer to a purity that had long been lost, and his decrees on frequent and early Communion had opened up the channels of grace to invigorate Catholic spiritual life as it had not been in centuries.

The neutrality of Italy in 1914 proved a providential blessing for the Church, because the cardinals of all nations were free to enter Rome and to deliberate in tranquillity. Fifty-seven cardinals entered conclave on August 31 (Gibbons, O'Connell, and Bégin had not arrived from America, and five others were too ill to attend). Three days later they elected Cardinal Giacomo della Chiesa, Archbishop of Bologna, who took the name of Benedict XV. Cardinal della Chiesa had served for many years as Assistant Secretary of State under Cardinal Rampolla, and for the last seven years he had had pastoral and diocesan administrative experience in the important archiepiscopal see of Bologna.

From the purely human point of view, then, Benedict XV seemed to be the ideal choice for the times, for he was trained in Leo XIII's school of diplomacy — and the problems of the day were chiefly diplomatic. The dominant interest of his papacy was the World War, of course, and it was necessary that the Church steer a course of perfect neutrality, protest violations of the moral law, perform works of charity for suffering humanity, and do what it could to end the conflict and bring the governments to peace. Benedict pursued this fourfold policy with diplomatic skill and with a heart full of charity. Although he was reviled on all sides during the war, his policies were so perfectly maintained that the Church emerged from the World War internally strong, respected in such countries as France and Italy where anticlericalism had been triumphant a few years before, and therefore ready to fight her own "battle for civilization" under popes Pius XI and Pius XII.

Benedict XV carried on the work of his predecessor as well as he could during the war. In November, 1914, for example, he created a pontifical commission on the correction of the Vulgate, and in 1915 he issued an encyclical on preaching. Two years later he created the Congregation for the Eastern Church and set up a pontifical Institute for the Eastern rite. Benedict also enlarged the Roman Academy of St. Thomas, founded by Leo XIII, and reorganized the Sacred Congregation of Universities and Seminaries. Benedict did all he could, under the circumstances of the Great War, to promote the missions. As we shall see in the next chapter, he enthusiastically supported a new organization (Missionary Union of the Clergy) to recruit missionaries, and he published a major encyclical on the missions.

But the pope's absorbing concern was the war, for Catholics were on both sides of this conflict, hatred of nation against nation was systematically cultivated, the normal work of the Church was disrupted, millions of lives were unnecessarily sacrificed, millions of homes were broken up, and countless children were starving — both physically and spiritually. Benedict issued several major statements on the war and its causes, and on the nature of peace. He protested through proper diplomatic channels when outrages were committed, and he performed works of mercy that stagger the imagination when one remembers how meager were his resources how difficult the conditions under which he worked. There is room for us only to outline his major peace appeals and give a general description of his works of mercy.

1. *The encyclical of November 1, 1914.* In the letter *Ad Beatissimi* the pope stated his concern for all mankind, the "other sheep" as well as those in the Catholic fold, and then he analyzed the general unrest in the world that produced the war. He finds four main causes of unrest: a general contempt has developed for authority, mutual love no longer governs human relations, class relations are dominated by injustice, and people are possessed of a universal fever to amass riches. In this inaugural encyclical the pope pleads with the rulers of the warring nations to negotiate a peaceful settlement. "Surely there are other ways and means whereby violated rights can be rectified. Let them be tried honestly and with good will, and let arms meanwhile be laid aside."

The appeal went unanswered, of course, and apparently even unheard. On July 28, 1915, the pope wrote a letter to the belligerent peoples and their leaders in which he exhorted them again to end the conflict and make a just peace. This letter was necessarily written in general terms, but it was a moving appeal for a rational approach to a just settlement of international disputes over which the war was supposedly being waged.

Why not [Benedict pleaded with the belligerents] from this moment weigh with serene mind the rights and lawful aspirations of the peoples? Why not initiate with a good will an exchange of views, directly or indirectly, with the object of holding in due account, within the limits of possibility, those rights and aspirations, and thus succeed in putting an end to the monstrous struggle, as has been done under other similar circumstances? Blessed be he who will first raise the olive branch, and hold out his right hand to the enemy with an offer of reasonable terms of peace. The equilibrium of the world, and the prosperity and assured tranquility of nations rest upon mutual benevolence and respect for the rights and the dignity of others, much more than upon hosts of armed men and the ring of formidable fortresses.

Again the plea for peace negotiations went unanswered.

2. *Protests against violations of moral law.* Throughout the war Benedict XV protested against outrages and atrocities committed during the war. Sometimes the protests were in consistorial allocutions, sometimes in the form of direct protests to the offending government, sometimes in letters to various members of the hierarchy. On several different occasions

he protested against Austria's bombardment of open towns, against the violation of Belgian neutrality, against Germany's deportation of French and Belgian workers, and against methods of warfare which were contrary to international law and humanity. In some minor respects these protests were heeded, as his request that the Central Powers not force prisoners of war to work on Sunday, but generally they only earned him the reputation of giving sympathetic support to the enemy — which charge, made by both sides, is a good indication of his true neutrality.

3. *Works of mercy.* As the belligerent nations converted their factories and farms to their war effort, so Benedict XV converted the Church's organization to the relief of suffering and the minimizing of the hardships attendant upon the war. He wrote more than sixty letters of sympathy to various bishops, mostly in Belgium and France, and sent alms on a munificent scale to help those areas devastated by the war — five and a half million lire from his own purse, and more than thirty million from collections taken up in churches with which he still maintained contact. During the war relief was sent chiefly to the devastated areas of Belgium and France, after the war to Russia and the people of Central Europe.

In December, 1914, the Holy Father set up a Prisoners of War Bureau in the Vatican. Staffed by thirty clerks and helped by four religious communities of women, this Bureau obtained lists of missing soldiers from German and French prisoner-of-war camps and communicated the information to the missing men's families. Arrangements were made through the Bureau for communication between prisoners and their families. The Bureau also made arrangements for the exchange of certain classes of prisoners, such as the seriously wounded, and for the transfer to Switzerland (a neutral country) of those who were fathers of four or more children, or were less seriously wounded. The Bureau also facilitated the exchange of civilian prisoners, and it obtained the liberation of many women, children, men over fifty, physicians, and ministers. Benedict did what he could to alleviate the condition of prisoners of war. Swiss priests were sent to French and German camps, and prisoners in Austrian camps were visited by the Apostolic Nuncio in Vienna.

4. *Benedict's offer to mediate peace between the belligerents.* A stalemate seemed to have been reached in the war in 1917, a certain amount of defeatism had infected the armies and civilian population on both sides, and it therefore seemed a time when negotiations for peace might be welcomed by all nations. Until this time the pope had spoken of peace in general doctrinal terms. But on August 1, 1917, he took the step,

unprecedented in modern times, of sending a diplomatic note to the warring countries "to invite the Governments of the belligerent peoples to bring themselves to agree upon the following points, which seem as though they ought to be the bases of a just and lasting peace, leaving to their charge the completion and the more precise definition of those points." The pope's seven peace points were:

i) The moral force of right should replace the material force of arms.

ii) Simultaneous and reciprocal disarmament.

iii) Acceptance of arbitration, with proper sanctions to punish nations that did not abide by the decisions.

iv) Freedom of the seas.

v) A general and reciprocal condonation as regards damages and the cost of the war.

vi) The reciprocal restitution of territory, "consequently on the part of Germany the complete evacuation of Belgium, with a guarantee of her full political, military, and economic independence as regards all Powers whatsoever; likewise the evacuation of French territory. On the part of the other belligerent parties a similar restitution of the German colonies."

vii) The promise to examine territorial disputes, such as that between Austria and Italy or that between Germany and France, in a conciliatory spirit and taking into account the aspirations of the people concerned.

Benedict's note was not even answered, and the war continued to its bitter conclusion more than a year later. When the armistice was signed, the pope ordered public prayers that the peace be just and lasting. The papacy was excluded from the negotiations at Versailles in deference to Italy's demand, for the Italian government was afraid that the Vatican would bring up the Roman Question and place it on the agenda for discussion. From the Vatican the pope followed the negotiations closely and he managed to obtain modifications in two clauses relating to the disposal of missions in former German colonies. The powers recognized the Holy See as proprietor of the missions and promised to consult with the Holy See about any changes to be made in the missions.

After the peace was signed at Versailles, Benedict XV wrote his encyclical *Pacem Dei Munus* in which he explained that his joy at the signing of peace was tempered "by many bitter anxieties" because "the germs of former enmities remain" and there can be no lasting peace "unless there be a return of mutual charity to appease hate and banish enmity." The pope stated explicitly that Christian peace alone can work a reconciliation that will be just and lasting. In the encyclical he endorsed the League of Nations, but warned that peace could not be maintained by the machinery of the League unless a system of justice and charity be set up anew and all nations be reconciled with each other. Nevertheless, he promised to give the Church's full support to the League and his prayers that it achieve the purposes for which it was founded.

Although the pope was reviled by both sides for "favoring" the other, when the war was over it was generally appreciated that he had followed a strictly neutral and proper course, that he had helped people of all nations and all religions, and that he had been untiring in his efforts to terminate the war and secure lasting peace. The patriotic conduct of Catholics on both sides lessened the fear of "divided allegiance" which anticlericals entertained of Catholics, and resulted in a number of steps in various countries toward reconciling the Church and the government. The pontificates of St. Pius X and Benedict XV had developed a better feeling toward Italy, where Catholics could now participate in national politics. In France the *Lois laiques* were no longer rigidly enforced, and religious orders were allowed considerable freedom. Meanwhile, the Holy See's diplomatic prestige had increased. England appointed an ambassador to the Vatican in 1914, Holland (for the first time in its history) in 1916, and France in 1920. Important political persons, such as the Prince of Wales, the prime minister of England, and the president of the United States made it a point to confer with Benedict XV when they were in Rome. Symbolic of the respect with which non-Catholics were beginning to hold the pope again was the statue of Benedict XV erected in Constantinople by Moslems, Jews, and Eastern Christians. Its inscription read: "To the great Pope of the world tragedy, Benedict XV, a benefactor of peoples without distinction of nationality or religion, the East, in token of gratitude: 1914–1919."

The Church suffered serious material losses during the war. Thousands of priests were taken from their work and drafted into the belligerents' armies; missionary work came almost to a standstill; seminaries were nearly empty in those countries which had long been furnishing the greatest number of priests to the Church; lay organizations had suspended activities in many places; many churches, schools, and other ecclesiastical institutions lay in ruins. But Church organization was sound, and there seemed reason to believe in 1920 that the Church would recover and grow even stronger in the increasingly secularized world.

REVIEW AIDS

1. Explain why St. Pius X thought that at the beginning of the twentieth century Catholic Action was needed as never before.

2. St. Pius X has frequently been referred to as a "spiritual pope," and Benedict
   XV as a "political pope." Show in what way the contrast can legitimately
   be made; also indicate in what sense it is misleading.
3. Indicate by pointing to his reform measures how St. Pius X had a sound
   sense of administration.
4. Show how Pius X's reforms were all directed toward worshiping God according to the traditional notion of sound worship.
5. From an examination of personages and policies show to what extent there
   has been a remarkable continuity in the Holy See since the time of Leo XIII.
6. In what various ways did Benedict XV increase the respect of non-Catholics
   for the papacy?
7. Show how developments between the two World Wars proved that Benedict
   XV acutely diagnosed the shortcomings of the Versailles settlement of 1919.
8. Compare and contrast Benedict's seven points for peace discussions with
   Wilson's "Fourteen Points." Which are more realistic?

SUGGESTIONS FOR FURTHER READING

The best general treatment of this period is to be found in the work of
Orazio M. Premoli, *Contemporary Church History* (*1900–1925*) (London:
1932). Premoli treats the papacy first of all, and then he devotes chapters to
the history of the Church in each of the countries of the world.

There are many good biographies of St. Pius X. These fall into two classes,
those published at the time of his death and those published when his canoniza-
tion was approaching. Among the more helpful works are the following:
Raffaelo Merry del Val, *Memoirs of Pope Pius X* (London: 1939) — a work
originally published by the pope's secretary of state shortly after his death;
Igino Giordani, *Pius X, A Country Priest* (Milwaukee: 1954); Katherine
Burton, *The Great Mantle* (New York: 1950); and F. A. Forbes, *Life of
Pius X* (London: 1932).

Benedict XV has been sadly neglected by the biographers. There is not a
single adequate study of him in English. His messages on behalf of peace are
all collected in the excellent work of Rev. Harry C. Koenig, *Principles for
Peace* (Milwaukee: 1943). An excellent study of his major peace messages is
to be found in Philip Hughes, *The Popes' New Order* (New York: 1944). The
work of the papacy during the war can be followed in any good history of the
period, and since the war dominated the papacy of Benedict XV, this is
sufficient collateral reading on his papacy. His great contribution to the missions
will be analyzed in the next chapter.

DOCUMENTS

Excerpt from *Fermo Proposito*

The following extract is from Pope St. Pius X's encyclical *Fermo Proposito*
(June 11, 1905), in which the Pope outlined a program for the modern
apostolate of the laity. This letter was written to the bishops and it instructed
them on the utilization of lay help in their apostolic work.

The field of Catholic Action is exceedingly vast: from it nothing whatsoever is excluded that in any way directly or indirectly pertains to the divine mission of the Church. Immediately one must recognize the necessity of individual participation, not only for the sanctification of our souls but also to spread and make better known the Kingdom of God in individuals, in families and in society. Let each one, according to his own talents, work for the good of his fellow man, by inculcating revealed truth, by the practice of Christian virtues and by works of charity or of mercy, spiritual and corporal. This is to walk worthily in the sight of God, as St. Paul exhorts us, striving to please Him in all things, producing good fruit and growing in God's knowledge: "May you live as befits his servants, waiting continually on his pleasure; may the closer knowledge of God bring you fruitfulness and growth in all good."

Beyond this duty, however, there are a number of objectives pertaining to the natural order, toward which the mission of the Church is not directly ordained but which flow from it almost as a natural consequence. Such is the light of Catholic revelation which illumines every branch of human knowledge, such is the power of the Gospel maxims, that they confirm and strengthen the very precepts of the natural law. Such is the efficacy of the doctrine and morality taught by Jesus Christ that the material well being of individuals, of families and of society are by them providentially sustained and promoted. The Church, while preaching Christ crucified, to the Jews a discouragement, to the Gentiles mere folly (1 Cor. 1:23), has become the inspirer and primary patron of civilization and culture. Wherever her apostles have spread the Gospel they have also conserved and perfected the best elements of ancient pagan culture, wresting from barbarism the new peoples she has clasped to her breast and educating them in the ways of civilization, giving to whole societies, gradually but surely and progressively, that special mark of culture that has always and everywhere been characteristic of her, just as it is today.

. . . The faithful laity must use all their forces to restore the social order, conscious of the necessity of rolling back the tide of "anti-Christian civilization," and of bringing Jesus Christ back to the family, the school, the whole of society. They must re-establish the principle of human authority as coming from God; they must take intimately to heart the material good of peoples, particularly of those who work for wages. They must not only instill into the hearts of men the teachings of religion, the sole fount of consolation amid the hardships of life, but they must also learn to dry the tears of men, to soften their hard lot, to better economic conditions by positive measures, to bring justice into civil laws, to correct injustices, to defend, in a truly Catholic spirit, the rights of man, of the Church of God.

The whole body of these works promoted and encouraged in large part by Catholic laymen, variously adapted to the particular needs and special circumstances of each nation, is precisely what is meant by the noble expression, Catholic Action, the specific action of Catholics. In every age this has been an enormous boon to the Church; and the Church has encouraged and blessed it.

It is necessary to note, however, that not every procedure that has been useful, indeed most useful, in the past can be set up again in our own age;

radical changes in society and public life develop with the passing of time and new needs must continually be met in new circumstances. The Church, however, in the long course of her history has always and in every case clearly demonstrated that she possesses a marvelous power of adaptation to the varying conditions of civil life: saving always the integrity and immutability of faith and morals, and saving, too, her sacrosanct rights, she easily meets the needs of the hour and accommodates herself in all that is contingent and accidental to the demands of the times and the new exigencies of society.

	ENGLAND	FRANCE	THE GERMANIES	ITALY, SPAIN, BELGIUM, ETC.
1800	Union with Ireland (1800) Slavery abolished to British subjects (1807)	Napoleon dominates Europe: annexes Netherlands, Germany to the Rhine, northwestern Italy; establishes independent states in Switzerland, Poland, Spain, parts of Germany, and parts of Italy. Holy Roman Empire ends (1806)		
1810		Napoleon defeated in Russia (1812) and Germany (1813–14), exiled to Elba (1814), returns, defeated at Waterloo (1815), exiled to St. Helena (1815–21). Congress of Vienna (1814–15) remaps Europe and Colonies. Germany becomes a confederation (Bund) under Austrian presidency. Era of Metternich (1815–48).		
1820	George IV (1820–30) Catholic emancipation (1829) William IV (1830–37) Reform bill of 1832 Poor Law (1834) Victoria (1837–1901)	Restoration: Louis XVIII (1814–24) Charles X (1824–30) July Decrees (1830) Louis Philippe (1830–48)	German Confederation (1815–66) *Burschenschaft* risings (1817, 19) Carlsbad Decrees (1819) Ferdinand I (1835–48) of Austria *Zollverein* (1834)	*Tugendbund,* Carbonari arrive Congress at Verona (1822) Belgium independent (1839)
1840	Irish famine (1845–48) Peel ends Corn Laws (1846) Chartist Movement (1848)	*The Second Republic* (1848–52) "June Days" (June 24–26, 1848)	Frederick William IV of Prussia (1840–61) Revolutions of 1848-49 in Austria, Hungary, Italy, Prussia, Denmark, Holland, etc. Frankfort Assembly (1848) Francis Joseph (1848–1916) of Austria [1867-Austria-Hungary]	Spain: Ferdinand VII (1813–33) Isabella II (1833–68) Republic (1868–70) Pan-Slavic Congress (1848) Victor Emmanuel II of Sardinia (1849–61), of Italy (1861–78) Cavour, Mazzini, Garibaldi, unify Italy (1849–70)
1850	Crimean War (1854–56)	Emperor Napoleon III (1852–70) Crimean War (1854–56) War with Austria (1859)	Revolutions put down (1849)	Sardinia wins Lombardy (1859)
1860	Fenian revolts in Ireland (1866) Reform Bill of 1867 "Church of Ireland" disestablished (1869)	Maximilian's empire falls in Mexico (1867)	William I of Prussia (1861–71) [German Emperor 1871–88]	Italian kingdom annexes Two Sicilies (1860), Venetia (1866), Rome (1870) "Roman Question" (187
1870	Education Act (1870)	Franco-Prussian War (1870–71)		Spain: Alfonso XII (1875–85) Alfonso XIII (1886–1931) Maria Christina (1886–1902) Humbert of Italy (1878–1900)
		Communard revolt in Paris (1871) *Third Republic* (1870–1940)	German Empire (1871) *Kulturkampf* (1870–78) Congress of Berlin (1878)	
1880	Gladstone extends franchise (1884)	Georges Boulanger (1886–89)	Social legislation, imperialism (1882) Frederick III (1888) William II (1888–1918)	Italy joins with German (1883)
1890	Irish Home Rule Bill fails only in House of Lords (1892)	Dreyfus case (1894–1906)	Bismarck resigns (1890)	Spain wars with United States (1898)
1900	Edward VII (1901–10) George V (1910–36) Parliament Act (1911)	Church and State separated (1905)		Victor Emmanuel III (1900–46) Portugal becomes a republic (1910)

CENTURY REVIVAL

...USSIA AND EASTERN EUROPE	THE CATHOLIC CHURCH	ECONOMIC, SOCIAL LIFE	CULTURAL LIFE
...ander I (1801–25)	Pius VII (1800–23) Concordat with France (1801) Pius VII seized by Napoleon (1809)	First Factory Act (1802) *Code Napoléon* (1804) Abolition of Prussian serfdom (1807)	Romanticism Victor Hugo (1802–1885) Wordsworth, Coleridge Schiller's *Wilhelm Tell,* Byron, Scott, Keats, Shelley, Melville, Whitman, "Lewis Carroll," Dickens, Thackery, etc.
...ia repels Napoleon ...812) and annexes Finland and Kingdom of ...land (1814)	Papal States restored (1815)	Adoption of Gold Standard by Britian (1816) Second Factory Act (1819)	Berlin University founded (1810) Dostoevski (1821–81) Richard Wagner (1813–83) Verdi (1813–1901)
...olas I (1825–55) ...lish revolt crushed by ...ussia (1830)	Russia persecutes Catholics (1825) England emancipates Catholics (1829) Leo XII (1823–29) Pius VIII (1829–30) Gregory XVI (1831–46) Portugal expels Jesuits (1834) Spain expels Jesuits (1837)	First high school in United States (1821) Stockton and Darlington Railway opened (1825) McCormick reaper (1834) Goodyear discovers rubber vulcanization (1839)	Herbert Spencer (1820–1903) Louis Pasteur (1822–1895) Tolstoy (1828–1910) Lyell's *Principles of Geology* (1831) Daguerre invents photography (1839)
...sia sends army against ...ungary (1849)	Pius IX (1846–78) Conversion of Newman (1845) Norway tolerates Catholics (1845) Religious toleration in Denmark (1849)	Morse's telegraph in operation (1844) Young Men's Christian Association (1844) Corn Laws repealed (1846) British Navigation Acts repealed (1849)	Rodin (1840–1917) Excavations on site of Nineveh (1846–54) *Communist Manifesto* (1848)
...sia defeated in Crimean ...ar (1854–56) ...xander II (1855–81)	Catholic political parties in France, Prussia, Austria, Spain, England, Holland (1850) Immaculate Conception defined (1854)	Commodore M. C. Perry in Japan (1853–54)	Hawthorne's *Scarlet Letter* First American "Great" literature Romanticism and realism Darwin's *Origin of Species* (1859)
...ncipation of the serfs ...861) ...sh rebellion (1863)	Nagasaki Catholics (1861) *Syllabus errorum* (1864) Vatican Council (Ecum. XX) on papal infallibility (1869–70)	Atlantic Cable laid (1866) Suez Canal opened (1869)	International Red Cross Society; International Workingmen's Association (1864) Mendel's investigation of heredity (1866) Chekov (1860–1904) *Das Kapital;* Joseph Lister introduces antisepsis (1867)
...aty of San Stefano (1878)	Italians seize Rome (1870) Leo XIII (1878–1903) Thomism revived (1879)	Economic crisis (1873) International Postal Union (1874) Bell's telephone patented (1876) Salvation Army (1878)	Schliemann begins excavations on site of Troy (1870) Africa explored by Stanley (1874–77) Edison's phonograph (1877)
...xander III (1881–94)	Vatican archives opened (1883) Freemasonry condemned (1884) Catholic party in Belgium (1884)		De Maupassant, Stevenson, Twain, Tennyson, Kipling, Conrad, Browning, H. G. Wells, Shaw, etc.
...holas II (1894–1917)	Encyclical *Rerum novarum* (1891) Pope supports French Republic (1892) Latin American Council (1899)	Pan American Union (1890) X-rays discovered by Roentgen (1895) Radium discovered (1898)	Hardy, Doyle, Dickinson, Wilde, Crane, etc. First International Peace Conference (1899)
...r with Japan (1904) ...ober Manifesto (1905) ...st Balkan War (1912–13) ...ond Balkan War (1913)	Pius X (1903–14) Czar's Edict of Toleration (1905) Portuguese concordat broken (1910) Spain breaks with Vatican (1910)	Wright Brothers' airplane; Henry Ford manufactures automobiles (1903) Einstein's relativity theory (1905)	Second International Peace Conference (1907)

THE CONTEMPORARY CHURCH

Chapter 36

THE MISSIONARY CHURCH IN MODERN TIMES

PERHAPS the most remarkable development in the past century of Church history is the tremendous expansion of missionary work. This expansion is all the more remarkable because it has taken place in the face of two World Wars, the severest depression in history, the rise of various totalitarian states, the revolt of Asia and Africa from European domination, and the enslavement of a good part of the world by Communism. In the face of these hostile forces, however, the Church has expanded its mission fields, multiplied the number of missionaries, and obtained the wholehearted support of Catholics at home for the missionaries in the field. Pope Pius XII therefore said in 1944, and repeated the statement in 1951 in his encyclical on the missions, *Evangelii Praecones*, "The Catholic missionary movement both in Christian and pagan lands has gained such force and momentum and is of such proportions as perhaps was never witnessed before in the annals of Catholic missions."

The story of this expansion is a story of high adventure, of problems and puzzles, triumphs and discouragements. But underneath the exciting story is another one: the story of a revived Church reassuming its task of teaching all peoples, a Church trying to break out of the shell of

Western culture to be truly Catholic and therefore at home in all nations. The Church of the nineteenth century was made up of Frenchmen, Italians, Germans, Americans, and other nationalities who were tempted to be national as well as Catholic, to treat "native" pagans as inferior people, and to reckon mission success solely in numbers of baptisms. The great missionary movement of the past century has rejected the "paternalistic" approach in favor of the true missionary end of establishing the Church in its fullness in all corners of the globe.

Interest in the missions was fostered by Gregory XVI, as we saw in Chapter 32, and within a few decades missionary work developed as a "grass roots" movement on the part of Catholics who had recaptured the Church's original spirit and purpose. New orders were founded to bring the Gospel to the peoples of Africa and Asia, and the older orders again took up their neglected missionary work. Bishops and diocesan clergy showed zealous interest in missionary activity, and several hundred mission aid societies were established to support the priests in the field. Journals were established to interest the layman in the missions, to get vocations, and to obtain prayers and financial support from the faithful.

The popes after Gregory XVI gave their warm approval to this missionary revival, but it was not until Benedict XV that they were able to take charge of the work as their own, to direct it, and to call for support from Catholics everywhere. The last three popes have made the work their own, for, as Pope Pius XI expressed it in 1923: "The work of the Foreign Missionary Apostolate is properly speaking the whole reason of the Pontificate. . . . The Apostolate is the most precious prerogative of the Roman Pontificate." Each of the past three popes has written a major encyclical on the missions in which he has laid down policy directives, asked for popular support and for mission vocations, and suggested solutions to the major problems confronting missionaries in the field.

The most notable development in the missions of the past century, as we shall see, was a revolutionary change in both missionary spirit and technique. In earlier modern times missionaries went into the field as heroic individuals, usually supported by their respective governments, to win souls for Christ. There was no real organization of missionary activity. Each missioner was a personal extension of the Church and the nation from which he came. It was apparently assumed that there would be a never ending succession of men to take his place, and that the non-European peoples would always remain in a subordinate position in the Church. Under the direction of the past three popes the missioner is obliged to establish the Church in every locale, to develop a local clergy and hierarchy, as well as local lay institutions, and thus to work himself out of a job. The missioner seeks to develop a Chinese Church, an Indian Church, a national Church everywhere, for the Church is at home in all lands. Under papal directive, moreover, the missionaries have made their work scientific. Missiology has become a field of study in Catholic universities; languages, psychology, medicine, anthropology, and other branches of knowledge have been enlisted to aid the missionary in his work and to enable him to establish the Church on solid local foundations. This is a complicated and interesting story that we can only sketch in main outline here.

Progress in the Nineteenth Century. The expansion of missionary activity in the nineteenth century was due primarily to a revival of the Church after 1815 and to its vitality in assuming its traditional apostolic tasks. But it was made possible on a large scale by industrial developments and by the imperialism of the last quarter of the century, which created national "spheres of influence" in Asia and Africa into which the missionary was encouraged to go. As a result of these combined religious and political developments several million converts were added to the Church in Asia and Africa. Between 1800 and 1900 Catholics in India increased from 475,000 to 1,700,000, in Indo-China from 319,000 to over a million, in China from about 200,000 to over a million, and in Africa from a mere 15,000 to well over a million.

French Catholics played a leading role in the expansion of missionary activity in the nineteenth century. A number of missionary congregations were established in France, which was also the cradle of many missionary aid societies and of institutes of mission science. Italy played a secondary role because of local national problems and because the Italian people had no imperialist ambitions until near the end of the century. Most of the French-founded congregations and institutes spread to Germany, Switzerland, Holland, the United States, and other countries in the Catholic world, but the fact is that in the nineteenth century Frenchmen led the way in interest in the missions, in vocations, and in financial support. Only in the twentieth century did the United States make any sizable contributions to the missions.

Even a brief sketch of nineteenth-century progress in missionary activity should not overlook the many martyrs whose blood and prayers nourished the missions. An uncounted number of individual missionaries lost their lives from local diseases; many more were killed in Africa, in China and Indo-China, and in various parts of Oceania. Many of these missionaries were not martyrs in the strict sense of the word because they were killed as hated Europeans rather than for their religion. This identification of the Church with Europe was one of the chief hindrances to missionary activity in the nineteenth century. No matter how detached a missionary may have been, he was still a Frenchman or a German or an Italian who spoke the language of Africans or Chinese with an accent. Moreover, he was protected by his government — which was frequently enough hostile to religion at home — and the missionary himself often believed that an essential part of conversion was to impose European culture on non-European peoples. The missionary can be excused for identifying Europe with the Faith, perhaps, but the identification was incorrect and it hampered missionary activity until three successive popes emphatically condemned it.

Another difficulty facing the Church in the nineteenth century was the tendency of different national groups and various congregations to consider their territories private domains and to resent "interference" by missionaries from other countries or other congregations. Again, the missionary can be excused, for even the saint is not immune from the temper of his age, and this was the age of imperialism when Europeans were convinced that they were bestowing on local peoples the great benefit of European culture and religion — even if it had to be forced on them. Such an approach was contrary to Catholic teaching and the whole tradition of mission work, and many missionary leaders fought heroically against it. Imperialist protection by European governments seemed to make mission work easier and more fruitful, but the gains were short termed and the animosity against the Church continued to increase.[1] That is why Benedict XV took a strong stand against a close alliance between mission work and imperialist policy, a stand reiterated emphatically by Pius XI and Pius XII. In 1926, for example, Pius XI insisted of missionaries that "they hold their sublime commission not from governments, but from Our Blessed Lord." In accepting protection from European governments, he continued, "the Holy See has only in view the safeguarding of her missions from attacks of sheer wantonness, and never, never has had it in mind to allow any of the Powers to make use of the missions for its own political end."

Progress in missionary work in the nineteenth century was due mainly to the regular clergy. The older orders, as we saw in Chapter 32, again

---

[1] Typical of this anti-imperialist movement was the Chinese Boxer Rebellion in which thousands of Catholics were killed, among them 36 bishops who were mostly French, Dutch, and Italian.

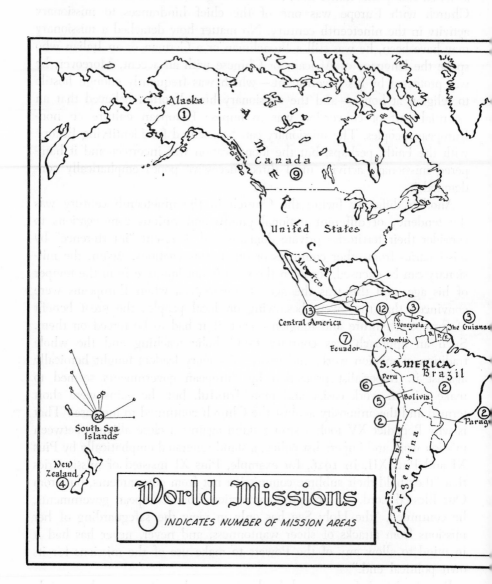

World Missions

○ INDICATES NUMBER OF MISSION AREAS

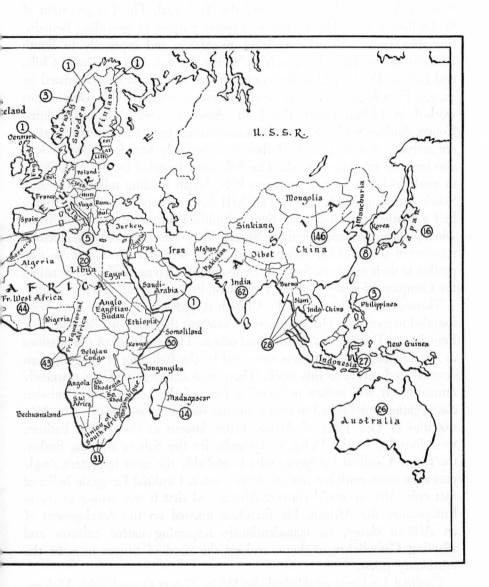

responded to the call of the missions. Benedictines established abbeys in the frontier part of North America, and they worked in Ceylon, Bengal, New Zealand, South America, and the Transvaal. The Congregation of St. Ottilien was established for the express purpose of providing Benedictine missionaries. Franciscans went to Africa, and especially to South America where they did much to revive the missions in Peru, Chile, and Bolivia. By the end of the century there were 5000 friars, assisted by 12,500 Franciscan Sisters, at work on five continents. The Dominicans worked in China, Japan, the Latin American countries, and Belgian Congo. And, as we have seen, the reconstituted Jesuits undertook missionary activity on a large scale. Other more recently founded congregations also took up missionary work. The Salesians, founded by St. John Bosco to work with the poor of northern Italy, began sending missionaries into South America shortly before Leo XIII became pope (1878). Within a half a century they had more than a hundred houses in Asia and Africa where, with the help of their Sisters, they have successfully pursued missionary work. Other congregations have sent out missioners in proportion to their numbers. Servites, Redemptorists, Hermits of St. Augustine, the Company of Mary, and the French Eudists are typical of these groups.

Throughout the history of the Church religious communities have been founded to meet new challenges, as we saw was the case with Benedictines, Franciscans, Dominicans, Jesuits, and others. The challenge of the missions in the nineteenth century was answered by the founding of congregations devoted exclusively to this work. These new congregations are extremely numerous. It will suffice to mention four of the better known mission congregations established in four countries for the same purpose. The Missionaries of Our Lady of Africa, better known as the White Fathers, were founded by the Delegate Apostolic for the Sahara and the Sudan, the future Cardinal Lavigerie, who is probably the most important single person in nineteenth-century missionary work. Cardinal Lavigerie believed that only Africans could convert Africa, and that it was wrong to try to Europeanize the African. He therefore insisted on the development of an African clergy, on conscientiously respecting native cultures and adapting Catholicism to them, and on the need of Sisters to assist the missionary priest.

Cardinal Lavigerie established the White Sisters to work with Mohammedan women and to help the priests take care of children and families in their mission areas. Here he was following the practice of the greatest missionary of all time, St. Paul, who tells us how he was helped by lay catechists and by women who took much of the burden of corporal works of mercy off his hands. The White Fathers enjoyed great success. In 1878 Pope Leo XIII entrusted them with six missionary vicariates he created in the heart of Africa. Since that time the White Fathers have converted several million Africans and have taken great strides toward solidly establishing an African Catholic Church. They now have charge of some thirty districts in which nearly two thousand priests and about the same number of Sisters are at work. Most important for the ultimate success of this work, about one sixth of the White Fathers are African priests, and even a larger percentage of the Sisters are native to the missionary areas.

In 1875 the first German missionary congregation was established in the Dutch town of Steyl by Father Arnold Janssen. The Society of the Divine Word spread rapidly, and before the century was ended it had set up missions in China, Africa, New Guinea, and South America. A house of studies was established at Techny, Illinois, and in the twentieth century the Society of the Divine Word not only worked with Negroes at home but also sent American missionaries into Africa and Asia.

Cardinal Vaughan founded a Foreign Missionary College in 1866 at Mill Hill. This venture started off with one priest and one student, but within a few years members of the Mill Hill Society were working among Negroes in the United States, and then in such places as Afghanistan, North Borneo, New Zealand, and the Anglo-Egyptian Sudan. The Mill Hill Society has grown to include more than a thousand priests, over half of whom are not English, and it has colleges in Holland, Italy, and Austria, as well as in England.

In 1912 Father Price and Father Walsh established the American Society for Foreign Missions, better known as the Maryknoll Missionary Society, to pursue missionary work in the Orient. By 1930 the Maryknollers had fifty-nine missioners in China and Korea, and by 1950 there were more than 600 Maryknoll priests and Sisters laboring in South America as well as in Asia. The new congregations minimize the community aspects of religious life in order to give their members greater freedom of movement as individual missionaries. Moreover, as we shall see, their training includes practical subjects and the formal science of missiology.

Progress in missionary work in the nineteenth century was made chiefly through these new congregations and through the revived older orders. However, the complete story would include chapters on outstanding missionary priests, men like Cardinal Lavigerie, who were true successors of St. Francis Xavier. Prominent among these names are Cardinal Massaia, who worked in Abyssinia for thirty-five years, and interested his government in the spiritual and physical welfare of his charges. Cardinal Massaia introduced vaccination in Abyssinia and established a number of medical clinics. Another prominent missioner was Father Daniel Comboni, who worked in Africa and established the congregation of the Verona Fathers to carry on his work.

In previous ages missionary work was supported by the prince and his government. Such support could no longer be expected in the nineteenth century. A large number of mission aid societies were therefore established to train and support missionary priests and Sisters in the field. The most important of these, of course, was the Society for the Propagation of the Faith organized by Pauline Marie Jaricot. The Association of St. Peter the Apostle was established to collect funds for the education of missioners; the Sodality of St. Peter Claver for the African missions ran a polyglot press and sent hundreds of thousands of books in at least twenty languages to Africa. The Society of the Holy Childhood was organized to rescue pagan children from death or slavery, and it still carries on the support of these children largely by contributions of children. The Catholic Students' Mission Crusade encourages mission vocations among students in Catholic schools and enlists student prayers and alms. There were more than 200 mission aid societies of one kind or another by the beginning of the pontificate of Pope Pius XI. They served as eloquent testimony to the Catholic's revived interest in the missions, and they did much to spread information about the needs and the problems of missions everywhere.

Benedict XV and Missionary Policy. Solid foundations were laid in missionary work by the time World War I began. Popular support had been enlisted, vocations to the missions had increased, thousands of men and women had gone into the field, and millions of conversions had been made. But there were serious problems to be solved. Most of all, firm pontifical direction was needed to make the missions truly Catholic rather than appendages of various national Catholic churches. Confusion on the attitude toward a "native" clergy and hierarchy had to be cleared up, and the very purpose of missionary work had to be clearly defined in the light of Catholic tradition dating back to the first Apostles. This was the task that Pope Benedict XV assumed when the war ended and he could give his apostolic work full attention.

Benedict XV gave his papal benediction to the Missionary Union of the Clergy founded during the war to promote interest in the missions among Catholics everywhere and to co-ordinate missionary work. In 1919 he endowed the Missionary Union with rich indulgences and recommended that the bishops establish it in their respective dioceses so that priests would be able "through this activity, to organize the interests of the faithful in the conversion of so many millions of pagans, and to develop all the works already established and approved by the Holy See for the benefit of the missions."

The pope took the charge of the Oriental Churches from the Congregation of Propaganda, creating a new congregation for this work, so as to free Propaganda for purely missionary activity. He also put the Missionary Union of the Clergy under the control of Propaganda. Finally, and most important, in 1919 Benedict XV wrote the major encyclical *Maximum Illud*, which has been referred to as the *Magna Carta* of the modern missionary movement. In this letter the Holy Father made it clear that missionary work was a duty incumbent upon every Catholic, priest and layman alike, and all were asked to support the work with prayers, alms, and the encouragement of vocations. The pope surveyed the missionary accomplishments of the previous century and concluded that they were great — but not great enough, for there remained a thousand million pagans to whom the Gospel had not been preached.

> It must be confessed [he wrote] that something is lacking, something is wrong or out of gear in the method followed until now with regard to the formation of a clergy destined for foreign missionary work. In order to remedy that defect we do, therefore, ask the Sacred Congregation of Propaganda to take such measures as will seem best suited to each case, for the founding in each country, or group of dioceses, of new Seminaries for Foreign Missions, and to watch over the direction of those already in existence; finally to concern itself specially with the formation of the native clergy in Vicariates Apostolic and other missions.

Benedict XV warned the clergy that they were apostles of Christ and not of any national government. He condemned the occasional failures of missionaries to accept help from other nations or other religious families, and he encouraged them to hold conferences for the exchange of information and mutual instruction. The pope also insisted strongly that

> a native clergy is the one great hope of new missions. For the native priest has all in his favor to command and retain the attention of his own people, birth, mentality, impressions, ideals. Better than anyone else, he knows the ways to their hearts. And it is thus that he can reach many souls who hitherto have proved inaccessible to the European priest.

Native priests, he warned, are not to be considered "as auxiliaries of the Foreign Missionary." They are to be of equal rank, and they are destined one day to be rulers of their dioceses. Put briefly, the successful missioner is one who works himself out of a job, turns his field over to native clergy, and pushes on to still new fields. In *Maximum Illud* Benedict XV described the ideal missionary as a model of piety, charity, and endurance, a man sufficiently learned to be able to answer all objections to the Faith, sufficiently conversant in the local tongue to supervise the instruction in Catholic doctrine and hold his own with the learned men of the country, sufficiently expert in sacred and profane sciences to stand out as a leader in the local community and win the respect of the native people.

Pius XI: "Pope of the Missions." Benedict XV's successor took a lively interest in the missions and did more, perhaps, than any other modern pope to incorporate them under papal leadership and to establish the Church as a native institution in mission lands. His encyclical *Rerum Ecclesiae* (1926) reiterated the policies of *Maximum Illud* of seven years earlier. Pope Pius XI explained his concern with the missions: "As long as it will please Almighty God to leave us in this world, this duty pertaining to Our Apostolic Office, this missionary duty, will be uppermost in our mind. Again and again, the mere thought of that staggering mass of one thousand million heathens prevents us from resting." The pope therefore calls upon all Catholics to pray unceasingly for missionary vocations and to give of their time and their alms to promote the work. He urges the bishops to establish the Missionary Union in their dioceses and to collect donations for such organizations as the Association of the Propagation of the Faith, the Holy Childhood Association, and the Society of St. Peter the Apostle.

The pope then turned to the problem of developing a native clergy. Here he repeats and expands the instructions of Benedict XV. He reminds the faithful that the aim of missions is not merely conversions but the establishment of the Church "throughout the whole of pagan lands." This necessarily involves the creation of a native clergy and hierarchy. Pius XI develops the theological, canonical, and pastoral arguments for this work and then adds the practical political argument that Asiatic and African peoples are tiring of European domination and will soon assert their independence. By that time, he maintains, a native Church must have taken firm root or missionary efforts will have been transient and in vain. Pius XI, therefore, requests that seminaries be established in mission areas and that they provide natives with as good an education as seminarians receive in Europe. For, the pope insists strongly, native priests are not to be mere assistants to foreign missionaries.

> There is no distinction between a native priest and a European priest; no barrier of separation whatever. . . . It is a mistake to imagine that natives are inferior beings and dull-minded. A long experience has proved that Eastern and African races have little to envy the Europeans as regards intellectual gifts and the potential development of the mind.

Pius XI goes a step beyond Benedict XV in urging the establishment of Church institutions in mission areas. He asks for the establishment of congregations of native nuns, and he suggests that contemplative orders should be encouraged especially in the Far East where there seems to be a natural inclination to this type of religious life. He also begs the heads of missions to create institutions to care for the sick and for children as an integral part of the Church's mission in the world.

A few months later Pius XI addressed a letter to the bishops of China in which he dwelt upon the Catholic mark of the Church and repudiated any suggestion that missionaries represented foreign nations or a foreign culture.

> The Church [he wrote] never tolerates in her ministers a worldly spirit, or a national party spirit. Above all never will she tolerate it in those who are sent in her name to preach the Gospel. She has ever considered it as her exclusive prerogative to announce the Gospel, without any political aim whatsoever. She has never allowed her missions to be used as political tools by earthly Powers.

The pope translated these words into acts by personally consecrating six Chinese bishops in 1926, and a year later the first Japanese student to come to the College of Propaganda was consecrated a bishop and entrusted with the see of Nagasaki, which included two thirds of the Catholic population of Japan.

The policies governing missionary activity were clearly set forth in *Maximum Illud* and *Rerum Ecclesiae*, but it remained for the missionary in the field to solve the problems confronting him and to put the Holy See's policies into effect. We can summarize the problems briefly in this fashion:

I. *Disassociating the Faith from European culture.* Despite papal statements to this effect, it remained difficult for Catholics and pagans alike to conceive of the Catholic Faith in any but a European setting. Historical circumstances set the Faith in Europe where it developed and did much to mold European culture. Historically, then, the Catholic Faith has been a Western institution; its theology has been cast in a Western mold, its worship adjusted to the Western temperament, its apologetics formulated for the Western mind. It is, therefore, easy to understand why missionaries must be on guard not to associate their Faith with their national culture and seek unconsciously to Europeanize the African or the Asian in order to establish the Faith afield. It is even easier for the African or the Asian to identify the Catholic religion with a European culture and resent them both as an intrusion into his way of life. Heroic effort is required to see the Faith as truly Catholic — as being for all peoples and all times.

II. *Disassociating the Faith from the white man.* Closely connected with the first problem we have mentioned has been the tendency throughout the world to associate Catholicism with Caucasians who have been the masters of the world for four centuries. During the past several decades the nonwhite races have been in rebellion against this domination, and recent popes have warned that they might reject the Church as a white man's institution. The popes have, therefore, taken every opportunity offered to insist that the Church is Catholic, that it developed in the Mediterranean world because of historical circumstances, but that it belongs to all mankind.

III. *Development of a "native" clergy in the missions.* The chief practical means of proving that the Church is Catholic is to develop a clergy and a hierarchy from among the people everywhere in the world. But this involves a set of difficult problems. Ever since its foundation the Congregation of Propaganda has insisted on the development of local priests and bishops, and the popes have constantly recommended this practice to missionaries. But it is only in recent decades that bishops have been chosen from the local priests and only in recent years that a non-Westerner was appointed to the College of Cardinals.[2] The development of a local clergy has cast the modern missionary in a new role. In many places he has become the auxiliary of the native prelate, and where he has not achieved this position he has failed to reach the goal set for him by the Holy See.

The ultimate goal of missionary endeavor, which should never be lost sight of [Pope Pius XII wrote in *Evangelii Praecones*] is to establish the Church on sound foundations among non-Christian peoples, and to place it under

---

[2] Archbishop Tien of Pekin was named a cardinal in 1945 and Archbishop Gracias of Bombay was raised to this dignity in 1952. Early in 1956 the first native born bishop of Africa, Peter Etoga, was consecrated auxiliary bishop of the Cameroun.

its own native Hierarchy. . . . The magnanimous and noble purpose which missionaries pursue is the propagation of the faith in new lands in order that the Church may ever become more firmly established in them and may, as soon as possible, attain to such a development that it can continue to exist and flourish without the aid of Missionary Organizations.

IV. *Development of a native lay apostolate.* The past three popes have insisted that the Church is in a flourishing condition only if laymen take an active role in Church life. In pursuance of papal instruction, missionaries have established such organizations as the Legion of Mary, Catholic Youth Organizations, Boy Scouts, and the like. Closely connected with this problem is that of establishing contemplative orders, congregations of native women, and other religious institutions which are traditionally an integral part of flourishing Catholic life.

V. *The general problem of adapting Catholic dogma and worship to local cultures.* The problems mentioned above all add up to the delicate but pressing problem of adapting a Faith set in the Western mold to other cultures. The task is difficult and dangerous, but it is demanding and missionaries cannot shun it. Pope Pius XII insisted on this problem being faced when he stated in his encyclical on the missions:

Let not the Gospel on being introduced into any new land destroy or extinguish whatever its people possess that is naturally good, just or beautiful. . . . Whatever there is in the native customs that is not inseparably bound up with superstition and error will always receive kindly consideration and, when possible, will be preserved intact.

This involves a presentation of Catholic dogma in a mode adapted to the non-Western cultures, perhaps the development of rites better fitted than the Roman to their way of life, a general presentation of the Catholic faith so that it belongs to African and Asiatic peoples as naturally as it does to those of the Western world.

Pope Pius XI took many steps toward solving these problems. In the first place, he centralized administration of the missions in Rome, and through the Congregation of Propaganda he brought them under the direct control of the Holy See. He removed the Association for the Propagation of the Faith from Lyons to Rome and placed it in the Congregation of Propaganda. The Society of St. Peter the Apostle and the Society of the Holy Childhood were also attached to Propaganda. Thus all missionary finances were centralized in Rome. Moreover, through his personal representatives, the Apostolic Delegates, the pope maintained direct control of the missions. Pope Pius XI requested Apostolic Delegates to convene national councils of the Chinese Church, the Japanese Church, and the South African Church. Through the Congregation of Propaganda he instructed the superiors of missions to found orphanages, hospitals, and clinics, build chapels and churches, and train competent lay catechists.

Pius XI promoted the missions by interesting Catholics in their work and reminding them continually of their duty to support them. In the Jubilee celebration of 1925 he had the Congregation of Propaganda prepare an imposing mission exhibit which was later made a permanent museum of mission activity in Vatican City. Under Pius XI mission exhibits and conferences took place frequently in Europe and America, and on Mission Sunday the faithful everywhere were asked to contribute their prayers and alms to the success of foreign missions.

More important in the long run, perhaps, was the pope's insistence on modernizing mission activity and making it as scientific and efficient as possible. When he opened the mission exhibit at Vatican City the Holy Father said:

> We have desired that in this exhibition, the scientific, ethnographical, medical, and literary side of mission work should have an important place, because it is ever from the region of ideas that the great incentives to action will come. For we live in an epoch when it becomes more and more evident that all the heroisms and all the sacrifices which accompany missionary work will not suffice without the further help of scientific knowledge. Science must help, it must bring light, point more direct ways, suggest better methods: this is true in industry, in commerce, in everyday manifestations, in practical economics; and the missions cannot and must not be deprived of the practical helps that present times afford.

A medical section had been included in the mission exhibit of 1925 to show what progress had been made in this phase of mission work and to encourage additional action along these lines. Most of the missionary congregations soon included a certain amount of medical training in the preparation of their personnel for work in the field. In 1935 the Congregation of Propaganda issued instructions of Maternity Training for Nuns, even encouraging them to obtain training in midwifery at secular institutions if they could not obtain it in Catholic schools and hospitals. During the pontificate of Pius XI mission work tended to develop more and more as a science. The various auxiliary studies were brought together and utilized for more effective mission work. Special courses in mission work were established in various Catholic universities, and periodic conferences were organized in many countries for missionaries to discuss their problems scientifically.

The growth of mission work — indicated by rough statistics — was most impressive during Pius XI's pontificate. In 1937 Father Philip Hughes claimed that in fifteen years the number of Catholics in mission districts under Congregation of Propaganda had grown from twelve to eighteen million, missionary districts had increased from 330 to 515, and 104 Apostolic Prefectures and 88 new missionary bishoprics were established, most of them in China and Africa. This tremendous growth was due to the solid beginnings made in the nineteenth century, to the energetic leadership of the Holy Father, to the widespread support of the clergy and laity who with their prayers and alms made such expansion possible.

Pius XII: World War II and Recovery. Pope Pius XII was concerned chiefly with World War II for the first six years of his pontificate and, as we shall see in Chapter 39, he carried on the work of Benedict XV and gave to the world the most masterful instructions on the nature of peace ever recorded in history. Even before the war was over, Pius XII had the missions in mind, and in various statements he repeated the policies of Benedict XV and Pius XI and adjusted them to current developments. It can truly be said, without detriment to Pius XII's interest in the missions, that in his pontificate the principal work was to carry on the policies formulated by his two predecessors and to put them into effect. Thus Pius XII created the first Chinese and first Indian cardinals and consecrated the first African bishop. During the pontificate of Pius XII many missionary congresses were held, exhibits were made to acquaint the faithful with the missioners' work, and popular support for missionary work increased tremendously. Especially in the United States has missionary work taken hold of the popular mind, largely because of Bishop Fulton J. Sheen who has been appointed national director of the Society for the Propagation of the Faith and who publishes the excellent magazine *Worldmission*.

In 1951 Pius XII commemorated the twenty-fifth anniversary of *Rerum Ecclesiae* by publishing his encyclical *Evangelii Praecones* on the missions. After reviewing the progress of the intervening years, the pope concludes that "it has become more apparent that the religion of Jesus Christ is really Catholic and that no part of the world is excluded from it." The creation of university chairs of missiology, the multiplication of missionary periodicals, and the many missionary congresses "make it obvious that the work of the apostolate has adapted itself to the changing conditions and growing needs of our times by employing new and more modern methods."

After adverting to the vicissitudes of the Chinese missions under Communist persecution and the existence of a thousand million pagans yet to be converted, the pope explains "the principles and norms that must guide the zeal and activity of Catholic Missionaries." These are essentially the policies that Benedict XV and Pius XI had formulated previously: development of a native clergy and hierarchy; the new role of the missionary as an auxiliary to the native prelate; the need to develop a lay apostolate among the native people; the importance of establishing schools, journals, hospitals, orphanages and similar institutions in each mission area; and the promotion of sound social reforms in each area. Pius XII also issued the same warnings as his predecessors: that missionaries are disciples of Christ and not evangelists of any country, that the various congregations and orders must work together under the Holy See's direction, and that all missionaries must be careful to adapt the Faith properly to native culture in their various fields.

The flourishing missions in China have been expelled from the land or driven underground by the Communist regime in that country. Despite these and other losses, the missionary movement has continued to gain momentum after World War II. This can be seen from a glance at the statistics. Mission areas have grown from 515 to 613 and the baptized persons in them number 31 million instead of 18 million; 26,800 priests labor in the missions, and they are helped by 61,500 nuns, 92,000 lay teachers, and 83,000 catechists. There are almost 50,000 schools and more than 50 colleges in mission lands, and almost a hundred seminaries for the training of native priests. More than 54 million patients are cared for in almost 5000 hospitals, and 1720 orphanages take care of almost a hundred thousand children.

More important is the fact that seventy mission areas are governed by local bishops and clergy exclusively, and fifteen more have native prelates who are assisted by both a native clergy and foreign missionaries. Thus the ultimate aim of missionary work is coming to be realized. The picture is not the same everywhere, of course, for in some parts of Africa phenomenal gains have been made, whereas in other parts hardly anything has been accomplished. So it is in other parts of the world. The progress of the past half century indicates, however, that missionary work has overcome the obstacles it inherited from the nineteenth century, has recaptured the traditional Catholic missionary spirit, and has made great strides toward spreading into the other parts of the world a Church long confined to Western civilization.

REVIEW AIDS

1. Analyze the problems that imperialism would naturally enough create for the missions. What were the obvious short-term advantages that imperialism gave the missionary?
2. From your knowledge of the Catholic Church, try to list the canonical, theological, and practical arguments in favor of a native clergy. Check your reasons with those advanced by the past three popes in their mission encyclicals.
3. From a good biography of St. Paul or from your reading of the New Testament, compare the policies advocated by the past three popes with those of the Apostle of the Gentiles.
4. What advantages do new missionary congregations enjoy over the older religious orders in missionary work?
5. Analyze the reasons why conversions have been so few in Moslem lands.
6. Discover all the reasons you can to explain why there are "pockets" of population that take readily to the Catholic Faith and other "pockets" that resist the missionary strongly.
7. From papal encyclicals and allocutions compose a picture of the ideal missionary.
8. What developments in missionary activity in the past century can give a Catholic reason for optimism? What counterreasons are there for tempering this optimism with a sober pessimism?

SUGGESTIONS   FOR   FURTHER   READING

The most authoritative scholarly work on the missions in English is the translation of Joseph Schmidlin's classical work, *Catholic Mission History* (Techny, Ill.: 1933). More popular, but nonetheless trustworthy, accounts of mission history are Georges Goyau, *Missions and Missionaries* (London: 1932), and Aloysius Roche, *In the Track of the Gospel* (New York: 1953).

Accounts of the work of various mission congregations are numerous. Most helpful to the American student, perhaps, are: Rev. George C. Powers, M.M., *The Maryknoll Movement* (New York: 1920); Rev. John J. Considine, M.M., *Across A World* (New York: 1942); and J. Bouniol, W. F., *The White Fathers and Their Missions* (London: 1929).

Contemporary problems in mission activity, together with valuable insights into missionary history, can be found in the publication of the Fordham University Conference of Mission Specialists since 1953. The 1953 conference was published under the title *The Training of Converts,* and the 1954 conference was *Local Leadership in Mission Lands,* both edited by J. Franklin Ewing, S.J., and published by Fordham University Press. Also valuable on the contemporary problems of missions is the chapter by G. Naidenoff, S.J., "The Present State and the Problems of the Missions of the Catholic Church," in *The Catholic Church in World Affairs,* edited by Waldemar Gurian and M. A. Fitzsimons (Notre Dame, Ind.: 1954).

The three mission encyclicals (*Maximum Illud* of Benedict XV, *Rerum Ecclesiae* of Pius XI, and *Evangelii Praecones* of Pius XII) have all been published in English translation in pamphlet form.

DOCUMENTS

Excerpts From *Evangelii Praecones*

Each of the past three popes has written a major encyclical on the foreign missions. In these three encyclicals is found the Church's revised policies on missionary work. Pope Pius XII published *Evangelii Praecones* on June 2, 1951, in which he summed up and brought up to date the statements of Benedict XV and Pius XI.

With a view to promoting still more effectively the work of evangelization by our missionaries and to prevent one drop of their sweat and blood from being shed in vain, We should like here to explain briefly the principles and norms that must guide the zeal and activity of Catholic Missionaries.

First of all it is to be observed that the person who has been called by God to evangelize distant non-Christian lands, has received a very great and sublime vocation. He consecrates his life to God in order to spread His Kingdom to the farthest ends of the earth. He "does not seek what is his, but what is Christ's." He can apply to himself in a special way those beautiful sayings of St. Paul: "For Christ . . . we are ambassadors." "Though we walk in the flesh, we do not war according to the flesh." "To the weak I became weak that I might gain the weak."

He must, therefore, consider the country he is going to evangelize as a second fatherland and love it with due charity. Furthermore, let him not seek any earthly advantage for his own country or religious Institute, but rather what may help towards the salvation of souls. Certainly he should dearly love his fatherland and his Order, but the Church should be loved with a still more ardent devotion. And let him remember that nothing will be to the advantage of his own Order that is detrimental to the good of the Church.

Moreover, it is necessary that those who are called to this kind of apostolate should not only get the spiritual and intellectual training that befits ecclesiastical students before going out on the mission field, but should learn in addition those subjects which will be most useful to them when they come to preach the Gospel in foreign lands. Hence, they should be given a sound knowledge of languages, especially of those which they will require at some future date. Besides, they should be sufficiently instructed in the sciences of medicine, agriculture, ethnography, history, geography.

The object of missionary activity, as all know, is to bring the light of the Gospel to new races and to form new Christians. Nonetheless, the ultimate goal of missionary endeavour, which should never be lost sight of, is to establish the Church on sound foundations among non-Christian peoples, and to place it under its own native Hierarchy.

In a Letter which We wrote on August the 9th last year to Our beloved son Peter Cardinal Fumasoni Biondi, Prefect of the S. Congregation of Propaganda

Fide, We mentioned the following points among others: "The Church's aim is not the domination of peoples or the gaining of temporal dominions; she is eager only to bring the supernatural light of faith to all peoples, and to promote the interests of civilization and culture, and fraternal concord among nations."

In the Apostolic Letter *Maximum illud* of Our Predecessor of immortal memory, Benedict XV, given in the year 1919, and in the Encyclical Letter *Rerum Ecclesiae*, of Our immediate Predecessor of happy memory, Pius XI, it was laid down that the missions should have as the final goal of their activities the establishment of the Church in new territories. And We Ourselves, as We have said, when We received in audience the directors of Mission Activities in 1944, made the following statement: "The magnanimous and noble purpose which missionaries pursue is the propagation of the faith in new lands in order that the Church may ever become more firmly established in them and may, as soon as possible, attain to such a development that it can continue to exist and flourish without the aid of Missionary Organizations. These Missionary Organizations do not serve their own ends, but it is their task to use every endeavour to realize the lofty purpose We have already mentioned. When that has been attained, then let them be happy to turn to other fields." "Wherefore let the missionary take up no permanent abode in those places where the work of the apostolate has reached full development, since it is up to him to evangelize and sanctify the whole world. The missionary's appointed task is to promote ever more rapidly, in district after district, till the last man in the most remote corner of the earth has been reached, the Kingdom of the Divine Redeemer Who rose triumphant from the dead to Whom is given all power in heaven and on earth."

It is clear, however, that the Church cannot be properly and duly established in new territories unless all is there organized as time and circumstances require and, certainly, unless a native clergy equal to the need has been properly educated and trained. In this connection We should like to borrow the grave and wise directives of the Encyclical Letter *Rerum Ecclesiae*: ". . . While each of you should try to have as large a number of native students as possible, you must further make it your aim to fashion and develop in them sacerdotal sanctity and such an apostolic spirit and zeal for the salvation of their own people that they will be ready to lay down their lives for their fellow-tribesmen and fellow-countrymen."

"Suppose that, owing to war or political upheaval, there is a change of government in some missionary area, and the request is made or a law decrees that the foreign missionaries of a certain country must depart: suppose again a more unlikely case, that the native population, raised to a higher degree of culture and political development in order to gain its freedom, wants to drive out of its territory all governors, armed forces and missionaries belonging to the occupying foreign power and that it cannot do so otherwise than by force. What then, We ask, would be the disaster that would threaten the Church throughout all that territory, unless full provisions had been made for the needs of the Christian populace by a network of native priests throughout the whole country?"

Chapter 37

THE AMERICAN CHURCH COMES
OF AGE

A NEW branch on the Catholic tree has grown large and strong
in the past half century. This is the American Church which has
struck root in its native land and developed somewhat differently
from the various European branches of the Church. American Catholics
have always been closely attached to Rome, even in an age when distance seemed to militate against close connections, and they have been
marked by their loyalty to the person of the pope. They have been singularly
free from intellectual difficulties and from the danger of heresy. They have
developed a practical-minded Catholicism, first building an imposing
network of churches, schools, hospitals, and other institutions necessary
for flourishing Catholic life, then organizing vital institutions of Catholic
Action, and finally in the past two decades developing a fuller spiritual life.

In the course of this development the American Church established
a set of relationships to the State and to non-Catholics that are unique
and have been frequently misunderstood by European Catholics. Taking
advantage of the disestablishment provision of the Constitution and the
government's friendly attitude toward all religions, Catholic bishops
relied upon their people to build a set of institutions in each diocese
that were legally independent, free from political manipulation, and
as free as conceivable from the social opinion of the non-Catholic environment. On most matters Catholic bishops and Catholic lay people
were free to follow their individual persuasions. There was no "Catholic
line" except on matters of dogma or morals that occasionally found
Catholics united against the prevailing American opinion, as on the question of divorce or of birth control. But in most respects the Catholic

Church found the American environment a congenial one in which to grow healthy and strong, for even the persistent nativist prejudice against the Church was social rather than Constitutional or political, and it tended to strengthen the Church internally and in time to win it the respect of most fair-minded Americans.

Under these conditions the Church has enjoyed amazing growth in this country. In 1850 there were about 1,600,000 Catholics in the country, almost half of whom were immigrants. They were scattered over large stretches of territory, divided into language groups, and tended by an inadequate number of priests. Helped by missioners from Europe, American bishops tended their flocks and took care of the immigrants as best they could. By 1950 immigration, a natural increase of the native population, and converts swelled the Catholic population to about 28.6 million, ministered to by 43,889 priests, almost twenty times as many as a century before.

Even more important than quantitative growth is the fact that the American Church grew to maturity in this short time. In 1950 it had four cardinals, its bishops were beginning to play an important part in general Church life, and several Americans were appointed superior-generals of religious orders with headquarters in Europe. Moreover, American contributions of personnel and wealth were growing proportionately larger each decade. The vitality of the American Church in recent years is shown by the tremendous increase of missionary activity on the part of Americans, by the multiplication of retreat houses throughout the country, and by the big increase in vocations, especially to contemplative orders like the Trappists.

But this growth did not take place without difficulty. The problems that Catholics had to face during the past century have been many, but they can perhaps be summed up in this fashion:

1. *Overcoming the "ghetto complex."* Catholics were a small minority in a Protestant country, a minority, moreover, of relatively poor, ill-educated people who had to achieve economic security and social improvement before they could feel equal to "other Americans." This has led to all sorts of problems, as we shall see, and accounts for many strengths and many weaknesses among Catholics today.

2. *Overcoming native bigotry.* American Catholics have had to face the persistent charge that they cannot be good Americans if they are good Catholics. This bigotry has taken more refined forms in recent decades and it seems to be confined to a smaller fraction of the population. But its persistence has done something to shape Catholic developments, and

perhaps it has had the good effect of making Catholics think through Church-State relations and constantly be on guard against any real clash between their interests as Catholics and their interests as citizens.

3. *Shouldering the responsibilities of immigration.* The flood of Catholic immigrants into this country complicated the bishop's pastoral work in many ways. Immigrants were largely Catholic, first Irish and Germans, later Poles, Italians, and other national groups. The pastoral problem was to guide their process of Americanization so that they did not cast off their Catholic religion with their old-world allegiance — and this involved the problem of native-language priests, of disassociating the Catholic Church from their native culture and presenting it as an American institution in this country. The large number of immigrants also burdened the Church with social welfare problems and made Catholicism continue to seem the Church of the poor and the ignorant in the average American's eyes.

4. *Integrating the Church into the American community.* The basic problem, underlying all others, has been the adaptation of the Church to the American environment. This is a delicate problem, for Catholic doctrine and worship must be preserved in their essentials while adaptation is made in accidentals, and there is the intermediate realm of such things as holydays for the American Church or the legal position of Church institutions that must be worked out to the satisfaction of both canon law and American opinion. History shows that wherever a religion has been diametrically opposed to a culture it fails to grow and prosper, and wherever it accepts a culture completely it loses its own identity. The bishops, therefore, had to oppose the various secularist trends in recent American history and show that in opposing them they were good Americans. The underlying harmony between American culture and Catholicism had to be demonstrated to Catholics and non-Catholics alike, and the danger of making too complete an identification between the two also had to be avoided. The Church has done an excellent job in the past century in solving this delicate problem, and Rome has given approval, as we shall see, to the sound solution of Cardinal Gibbons and his successors.

The Nature of the American Church. We have seen that in European countries the Church was enmeshed in the social and political order from the very beginning, and that in many countries it continued to be the established Church after the Protestant Revolt, but in others it was disestablished, its property seized, its clergy expelled, and laws were passed against the public performance of Catholic services. Thus "disestablishment" or "separation of Church and State" in European countries meant persecution of the Church by the State. Disestablishment in this country, we have seen, came about in different fashion and it meant simply that the government could not legally discriminate in favor of one religion against others. As a minority, Catholics had everything to gain from this policy of disestablishment. Cardinal Gibbons expressed general Catholic opinion when he said:

> The separation of Church and State in this country seems to them [American Catholics] the natural, inevitable and best conceived plan, the one that would work best among us, both for the good of religion and of the State. Any change in their relations they would contemplate with dread. They are well aware, indeed, that the Church here enjoys a larger liberty and a more secure position than in any country today where Church and State are united.

Disestablishment freed bishops from political and social functions with which they were encumbered in most countries, and thus it enabled them to concentrate on the religious and social-religious problems of their dioceses. After trusteeism (discussed in Chapter 32) was defeated, each bishop was supreme in his diocese. Men of ability were generally selected for episcopal office in the American Church, and they used their power and their freedom to build solidly in their dioceses. Some bishops had greater vision and greater ability than others, of course, and some made sorry financial mistakes, but their record adds up to one of splendid accomplishment.

Uniformity of policy was achieved in the American dioceses through the bishops' close attachment to Rome and their loyalty in following the pope's directives. More particularly, however, a series of councils held in Baltimore devised ways and means for governing the Church in America, decreed certain common practices about public services and clerical garb, and issued directives on preaching and instruction, on maintaining parochial schools, and on similar pastoral problems. The Second Plenary Council of Baltimore met in 1866. Archbishop Martin J. Spalding, who presided, thought "that at the close of the national crisis, which had acted as a dissolvent upon all sectarian ecclesiastical organizations, the Catholic Church might present to the country and the world a striking proof of the strong bond of unity with which her members are knit together." Nor did events prove him wrong. Matters of faith, as they pertained to conditions in this country, were discussed and published under fourteen headings. These decrees constitute a code of ecclesiastical law for the Church in the United States. The bishops included such matters as the method of presenting candidates for the episcopacy, the creation of new dioceses, and the pressing problem of the spiritual care of the freed Negro population. This last problem was handled by earnestly admonishing all bishops and priests to provide Negroes with the opportunity to attend Mass and receive the sacraments, to be educated properly, and to be taken care of in orphanages and similar institutions. The ways and means of doing this pastoral work were left for each diocese to determine, whether, for example, Negroes were to be segregated into their own schools and churches or to be integrated into the white man's church and school.

The Third Plenary Council of Baltimore met in 1884 under the presidency of Archbishop (later Cardinal) James Gibbons. Fourteen archbishops and sixty bishops deliberated over an agenda that had been prepared the year before by a commission of prelates called to Rome for that purpose. Decrees were formulated on the education of the clergy, and a committee was appointed to arrange for the establishment of a national Catholic university. Most important, however, was the action taken about parochial schools. Bishops had already been instructed by previous councils to establish and maintain parochial schools, but only about 40 per cent of the parishes in the country had schools of their own. The Third Plenary Council of Baltimore decreed: "Within two years after the promulgation of this Council a parochial school must be erected at every church where there is none, and it must always be maintained, unless the Bishop judges that a postponement may be permitted on account of very serious difficulties." The Council further decreed:

> All Catholic parents are obliged to send their offspring to parochial schools, unless they provide adequately and manifestly for the Christian education of their children either at home or in other Catholic schools, or unless for a sufficient reason, approved by the Bishop, and after they have taken suitable precautions and supplied appropriate remedies, they are permitted to send them to other schools.

By the end of the century, however, only about half the parishes in the country had schools.

No plenary council has met since 1884. For many years, however, the archbishops met annually, and in more recent times the bishops of the country meet each November in Washington. The resolutions promulgated at these meetings have only the force of counsel; it remains for each bishop to act on the resolutions as he thinks prudent within his diocese.

The Integration of the Church Into American Society. The flood of immigrants to America furnished the bulk of the Catholic population in this country, but each wave of immigrants proved both burdensome and somewhat embarrassing to the Church. Immigrants in the 1840's were chiefly Irish and German, as we saw in Chapter 32, and nativist opposition to them caused violent outbreaks against the Church. More difficult, perhaps, was the problem of finding enough priests to care for the immigrants and of reducing language problems to a minimum. In the decades after the Civil War immigration increased from about 100,000 a year to almost half a million in 1873. In the decade of the 1880's over five million immigrants entered the country, and almost nine million came in the first decade of the twentieth century. After 1890 a large proportion of the immigrants were Latins and Slavs, poor people who needed social and economic as well as spiritual help in their transition to American citizenship. Until the national quota system was adopted after World War I, immigrants were an increasingly difficult problem for a Church that was already understaffed with diocesan and regular clergy. They were, in effect, a missionary territory set up within the country — people of different languages and traditions who were to be kept in the Faith.

The bishops had fairly well solved the problem of absorbing German and Irish immigrants through the last half of the nineteenth century. Each new wave of immigrants was absorbed by their own national groups who had preceded them to this country and had become Americanized. Moreover, they had a good number of priests of German and Irish origin to help them through their difficult first years in America. But the "new" immigration of Latins and Slavs could not be handled by these methods. They flooded in by the hundreds of thousands, usually unaccompanied by priests from their native lands, and there were no sizable Americanized groups of their national origin to help absorb them. The bishops found that these people tended to identify the Catholic Faith with their native tongue and, having been used to state support of their churches, they were slow to establish and maintain religious institutions in their new home. American bishops appealed to Europe for native priests. The appeal was answered by some diocesan priests and a number of religious congregations as the Salesians, and also by such Sisters as the Missionary Zelatrices of the Sacred Heart. Experience showed, however, that the problem was best solved by American priests who spoke the immigrant's language and understood his traditions and his problems.

The problem posed by these Latin and Slavic immigrants pushed the

Church into various areas of social welfare work. The immigrants settled in the larger cities where they were frequently ill housed, exploited, and confined to language ghettos. Thus they presented a social as well as a missionary problem to many American bishops. Generally speaking, the immigrant himself remained faithful to his religion. The problem was chiefly to provide services for him so that he did not grow indifferent or lax in performing his religious duties. But his children were a more serious problem. In their desire to become completely American the immigrants' children frequently rejected the religion as well as the language and the way of life of their parents. Boys' clubs, parish athletic associations, and other ways of centering social life around the Church were eventually adopted in most cities with a large immigrant population.

The burden of caring for the immigrant Catholic absorbed much of the Church's energy and prevented it from becoming a major cultural influence in their country until about the middle of the twentieth century. It slowed up the integration of the Church into the American social fabric, a task which converts like Orestes Brownson and bishops like John Ireland and John J. Keane considered the most important facing the American Church. These men lived in the last decades of the nineteenth century, and in varying measures they partook of the spirit of the age — a vigorous confidence that America was the land of promise and that it was destined by Providence to lead the world into a bright future, for it was possessed of manly natural virtues. Many Catholic leaders of this generation were convinced that America was naturally Catholic and that it could be brought into the visible body of the Church. They were also convinced that the Latin Church could learn much from Americans in the way of getting business done with dispatch, of putting vigor and economy into its management of affairs, of concentrating on practical matters so as to accomplish the Church's mission in the world.

The Church was represented by a number of outstanding bishops in the last decades of the nineteenth century, men like Ireland and Gibbons and Spalding who earned the respect of non-Catholics for their civic leadership and their patriotism. These bishops took a lead in adopting American democracy and promoting progressive social reform. Their aim was to show that the Catholic Church was not to be identified with Italy or Poland or any other country, that in the United States it was thoroughly American. In some respects, perhaps, one or another of these bishops worked out his adaptation of the Church to the age without sufficient caution. Certainly some of their speeches and writings seemed imprudent endorsements of almost everything in American society. Thus

Archbishop Ireland was thought to praise the public schools and to advocate abandoning the parochial school system required by the councils of Baltimore. A heated controversy on this issue developed among the American hierarchy, which was settled only by a decree from the Sacred Congregation of Propaganda and by a letter from Pope Leo XIII. The decision from Rome upheld the Baltimore decrees on parochial schools but admitted that for sufficient reasons other arrangements could be tolerated.

At the end of the century the American Church was involved in a misunderstanding that has sometimes been called "a phantom heresy." This is a set of attitudes which, if pushed to logical conclusions, would perhaps involve doctrinal errors. These attitudes were summed up under the term "Americanism" — a term which was only partly justified. The controversy over Americanism occurred when the Paulist Father Elliott's biography of Isaac Thomas Hecker, founder of the Paulists, was translated into French by Abbé Felix Klein. This translation became the storm center around which the French clergy debated certain quasi-modernist doctrines and attitudes that they thought were advocated by Father Hecker and leading members of the American hierarchy. Americans were accused of having little esteem for the supernatural, of stressing an *Ecclesia discens* rather than an *Ecclesia docens*, of trying to impose American methods on the Church in Europe, and of being contemptuous of the contemplative life.

Americans were genuinely puzzled at this commotion over Americanism, which was indeed a doctrine of "progressive" French priests rather than Americans. Msgr. Dennis J. O'Connell, rector of the American College in Rome, told Europeans that for Americans

> Americanism is nothing else than that loyal devotion that Catholics in America bear to the principles on which their government is founded, and their conscientious conviction that these principles afford Catholics favorable opportunities for promoting the glory of God, the growth of the Church, and the salvation of souls in America.

Archbishop Ireland summed up the Americanist stand in these words:

> We should speak to our age — of things it feels and in language it understands. We should be in it, and of it, if we would have its ear. . . . Our place is in the world as well as in the sanctuary; in the world, wherever we can prove our love for it or render it a service. We cannot influence men at long range; close contact is needed. Let us be with them in the things that are theirs — material interests, social welfare, civil weal — so that they may be

with us in the things that are ours — the interests of religion. Let us be with them because their interests are ours, and ours are theirs, because nature and grace must not be separated.

This was a sound approach to any society, and it helps account for the successful growth of the Church in this country. But Americanists occasionally made imprudent statements about "active" as opposed to "passive" virtues, and they seemed to urge social action rather than prayer. These were imprudent statements rather than carefully thought out doctrine, such as Archbishop Ireland's declaration that, "An honest ballot and social decorum among Catholics will do more for God's glory and the salvation of souls than midnight flagellations or Compostellan pilgrimages."

French theologians asked Leo XIII to condemn Elliott's *Life of Father Hecker.* The pope refused to do this, and he also refused to censure the activity of American bishops. However, to settle the controversy in France he finally drew up his letter *Testem Benevolentiae,* on "True and False Americanism," early in 1899. Addressing the American bishops in friendly terms, Leo tells them that there are a number of errors "which some comprise under the head of Americanism," errors which he knows American bishops would be the first to repudiate and condemn. Leo explains that the Church can adapt itself to the age, but it cannot modify its essential doctrines. He also warns that while liberty of thought within certain limits is a good thing, it must not set aside the authority or wisdom of the Church. The pope also states traditional Catholic teaching against so-called Americanist ideas on the natural virtues, on the distinction between active and passive virtues, on the value of religious life, and on the adaptation of religion to different cultures.

The American bishops at once proclaimed their loyalty to Rome and their total acceptance of the encyclical. They insisted that they had never held any of the errors condemned by *Testem Benevolentiae,* and they continued to work along the lines they had been following. Archbishop Ireland wrote to a friend that the pope told him to forget the letter on Americanism because it had application only to a few dioceses in France. Three years later the pope praised the American hierarchy and told them: "You have, in your prudent policy, prompted every kind of Catholic organization with such wisdom as to provide for all necessities and all contingencies, in harmony with the remarkable character of the people of your country." This seemed an endorsement of the methods the American bishops had been using so successfully. At any rate, the American bishops accepted the Holy See's warning, and if there had been the slightest possibility of a heresy developing among them it was quickly averted.

Continued Difficulty With Nativist Feeling. The basic idea behind the preaching and the action of Orestes Brownson, Archbishop Ireland, and other Church leaders was to convince Catholics that they could be good Americans and to convince Americans that they should be Catholics. Put another way, they tried to integrate the Church into American society by showing the essential compatibility between the two. They convinced some Americans, but suspicion of the Catholic Church lay deep in American society and it fed on the millions of Latin and Slavic immigrants who flooded into the country between the Civil War and World War I. The fact that these people were Roman Catholics, spoke with an accent, had dirty hands, and ate strange foods all added up to the conclusion that the Catholic Church was un-American. The old nativist fears that Catholics would turn the country over to the pope and his "foreign priestcraft" took on new urgency when as many as half a million Catholic immigrants came to this country in a single year. In 1887 the American Protective Association was formed to save the land from popery, and it obtained a certain amount of popular support when Leo XIII appointed the first Apostolic Delegate to the United States in 1893. The APA issued typical nativist diatribes against the Church, published the "revelations" of apostate priests and "ex-nuns," and stirred up considerable feeling against Catholics among the more ignorant classes. At one time the APA claimed to have about a million members, and it tried unsuccessfully to influence the Republican national convention of 1896. It was never as successful as the earlier Know-Nothings, however, and by the end of the century it had just about disappeared.

After World War I bigotry took a new outward form in the Ku Klux Klan with its violent hatred of Catholics, Negroes, and Jews. This "100 per cent" American movement was especially strong in the Bible-belt through the Midwest and in the South. Klansmen spoke the language of violence, but their actions were confined mostly to threats, burning crosses, holding hooded parades, and occasionally tarring and feathering someone. In 1928 Klan bigotry contributed considerably to the defeat of the Catholic presidential nominee of the Democratic Party, Alfred E. Smith, who was the first Democratic candidate since the Civil War not to carry the "solid South." This vicious campaigning by the Klan was its last significant effort to influence American life — and ironically its conduct tended rather to help the Church in the long run and to discredit the very bigotry it exploited.

Opposition to Smith and to the Catholic Church was conducted on a higher level by better educated Protestants who feared that a loyal and conscientious Catholic could not enforce American law and defend the Constitution. These people pointed to the *Syllabus of Errors* as "Catholic doctrines" that Smith would have to enforce on the country if he were elected president. This fear was the result of ignorance, of course, but it is partly excusable when one remembers that even many Catholics were not very clear about whether there were "conflicts" between Catholic doctrine and American practice and, if there were, how one resolved them conscientiously.

This sincere fear has mixed with bigotry from time to time in the past quarter century to provoke modern versions of nativism. One occasion was President Truman's decision to appoint a representative to the Vatican. This decision provoked a great deal of discussion about "separation of Church and State" and other tangential issues which ultimately boiled down to fear of and hostility against the Catholic Church on the part of many Americans. Similarly, the question of federal aid to parochial schools touched off a reaction that revealed considerable latent bigotry in the country. The wide sale of the works of Paul Blanchard was further indication in the years after World War II that the dream of men like Ireland and Gibbons had not been realized at the middle of the twentieth century. At the same time, bigotry against the Catholic Church was being confined to the ever smaller group of those who had a personal interest in maintaining it and those who were still abysmally ignorant of the Church.

Steady Growth of the American Church. The Church in this country has increased from natural births, immigration, and conversions. Statistics in all three categories are inadequate, and if they are not used carefully they can become very misleading. The important figure each year is of practicing Catholics, but at best this can only be approximated. So it is with converts.[1] Throughout the nineteenth century there was a steady trickle of converts into the Church, some of them persons of wide repute, many of them ministers in various Protestant sects. In recent decades the number of converts has increased considerably. There were 300,000 converts in the 1920's and somewhat more than 500,000 in the 1930's. Through the 1940's the average number of converts was 75,000 a year, in the 1950's it has been about 120,000 a year, and in 1955 the number was 137,310.

---

[1] Statistics have become much more reliable since World War I. Each pastor is strictly enjoined by Canon Law to keep an accurate register of baptisms. The *Catholic Directory* compiles its annual statistics from this source. On the number of baptized Catholics and the number of practicing Catholics, however, estimates vary rather widely.

The Catholic population was about four and a half million in 1870, and there were 3780 priests in the country. Twenty years later the Catholic population had doubled and the number of priests was somewhat over nine thousand. At the turn of the century there were slightly more than twelve million Catholics and twelve thousand priests. Thus in thirty years the ratio of priests to Catholic population had changed from one for every twelve hundred to one for every thousand. By 1940 there was one priest for approximately every six hundred Catholics, who in that year numbered about twenty-two million. In 1955 there was an estimated 32.5 million Catholics in a population of 152 million, and the number of priests had increased to 46,970. Catholics had amounted to something less than 7 per cent of the population in 1850; a century later they were about 20 per cent and they had become the largest single religious body in the country.

Recognition of this growth was given by Rome through the constant increase of dioceses and the organization of the American Church into provinces. Several new dioceses were erected each decade, until in 1955 there were 133 dioceses organized into 26 ecclesiastical provinces. Further recognition of the growth of the American Church by Rome was the appointment in 1875 of the first American cardinal, Archbishop John McCloskey of New York. After 1900 almost all episcopal appointments were made from the American clergy and several members of the American hierarchy were princes of the Church. The American Church was removed from the jurisdiction of the Congregation of Propaganda in 1908 and put under the general jurisdiction of the other congregations — the definitive recognition by Rome of its maturity.

Further evidence that the Church had reached maturity in this country was furnished by the bishops during and immediately after World War I. In 1917 they created the National Catholic War Council to care for the moral and spiritual welfare of hundreds of thousands of Catholics in the armed forces. The Council performed its various duties admirably, and when the war was over the bishops decided to keep their organization intact and to direct its action into peaceful lines. In their joint pastoral letter of 1919 they explained:

> In view of the results obtained through the merging of our activities for the time and purpose of the war, we determined to maintain, for the ends of peace, the spirit of union and the coordination of our forces. We have accordingly grouped together, under the National Catholic Welfare Council, the various agencies by which the cause of religion is furthered. Each of these, continuing its own special work in its chosen field, will now derive

additional support through general cooperation. And all will be brought into closer contact with the Hierarchy, which bears the burden alike of authority and responsibility for the interests of the Catholic Church.

The National Catholic Welfare Council changed its name to the National Catholic Welfare Conference in 1922. It is under the direction of the bishops, who meet annually to select officers and to discuss the program for the year. Participation by the bishops is entirely voluntary, and the NCWC operates only in dioceses where it has the sanction of the local bishops. The functions of the NCWC are divided into departments, each under the chairmanship of a bishop, dealing with such matters as Press, Legal Aid, Social Action, Youth, Lay Organizations, and Education. Since its foundation the NCWC has been the principal unifying organization in the American Church. Its press service furnishes Catholic papers and magazines with reliable information and with translations of papal messages; its various departments publish study material to inform clergy and laity of scholarly Catholic opinion on various social and moral problems; through it the bishops issue an annual joint pastoral letter; by using its central offices the bishops can work in closer unity than if they had to rely on correspondence or occasional *ad hoc* conferences.

Other indications that the Church in America had matured by 1920 or so are not hard to find. The *Catholic Encyclopedia* was proof of scholarship in the Church. This work relied to a considerable extent on European Catholics, of course, but it was edited by Americans and a large number of contributions were by American Catholics. In 1905, two years before the first volume of the *Catholic Encyclopedia* was published, Father Francis Clement Kelley founded the Catholic Church Extension Society to promote the Church in backward and isolated areas in the country. The American Church, which had so recently depended on missionaries from Europe, was now undertaking its own missionary work on an increasingly large scale. The founding of the Maryknoll Society in 1912 indicated that Americans had begun to take foreign missionary work seriously. Within a few years the other general mission aid societies were established in this country, such as the Association for the Propagation of the Faith and the Students' Mission Crusade. An increase in the proportion of vocations to the Catholic population was another indication of increasing Catholic maturity, as also were the additional establishments of contemplative orders. About this time the American Church came to have at least a few respectable journals and some good diocesan papers. Although the level of many Catholic papers and journals was disgracefully low, the fact that at least some were literarily and intellectually respectable showed that the Church was no longer exclusively the Church of illiterate immigrants.

In time it will probably be recognized that the most important accomplishment of the American Church in this period was its strong advocacy of social justice and its putting Catholic moral principles into concrete terms dealing with the American situation. Pope Pius XI has been quoted as saying that the greatest scandal of the nineteenth century was the Church's loss of the working class. The American Church could easily have lost the working class, and thus the future in this country, had the hierarchy not been in such close touch with American society as well as with Catholic teaching.

The initial step in the right direction was taken by Cardinal Gibbons in the famous Knights of Labor controversy. At the insistence of the archbishop of Quebec, Rome had condemned the Knights. Backed by almost all the American bishops, Cardinal Gibbons successfully intervened in Rome to secure a reversal of this ruling. In his famous letter to Rome, Gibbons counseled Church authorities "to acknowledge frankly what is true and just" in the workers' cause, "in order to deter them from what is false and criminal, and thus to turn into a legitimate, peaceable and beneficent contest what might easily, by a course of repulsive severity, become for the masses of our people a dread volcanic force like unto that which society fears and the Church deplores in Europe."

By the very nature of its population the Church in America should have been predisposed to the workers' cause. The fear of socialism and the desire to be thoroughly American, however, made many bishops suspicious of labor unions and hostile to any kind of legislation in favor of workingmen. The decisive event in the Church's stand on the social question was the publication of the Bishops' Program of 1919. This program was introduced with the observation: "The ending of the Great War has brought peace. But the only safeguard of peace is social justice and a contented people." The program, which was considered radical for its day, was a reasoned application of Catholic moral principles to social life. Its most important items were requests for (1) minimum wage legislation, (2) insurance against unemployment, sickness, and old age, (3) prohibition of child labor, (4) legal protection of labor unions, (5) national employment service, (6) public housing for workingmen, (7) effective control of monopolies, (8) prevention of excess profits, (9) participation by labor in management, and (10) a wider distribution of stock ownership. This program was a personal victory for Msgr. John A. Ryan who had been working for two decades to convince the bishops and the laity in the Church that advocacy of these proposals was not an endorsement of the Socialism condemned by the popes. By distinguishing the philosophy of Socialism from its economics and by demonstrating that many so-called "socialistic" measures were practically synonymous with Catholic moral principles, Msgr. Ryan obtained the support of most bishops and a large number of Catholic thinkers and writers for his proposals for social justice.

Since 1919 the American Catholic Church has been a force to be reckoned with in social questions. Papal guidance under the past two popes has taken the same general direction as the Bishops' Program of 1919, and the Social Action Department of the NCWC has disseminated these principles among American Catholics for the past two generations. The courage with which the American bishops faced the social question and worked out concrete proposals from Catholic principles constituted a signal success for the Church in this country. It guaranteed that the working class would not be alienated, as it had been in Europe, and it eventually won the respect of most professional and business people.

Much has been made by Catholic leaders at mid-century of the intellectual backwardness of the Catholic population. Various statistical studies show that the Catholic population is proportionately represented in the armed forces and in the ranks of labor, that it is fairly well represented in such professions as law and medicine, but that it is seriously underrepresented in areas of intellectual leadership, such as professorships in the state universities and membership in learned societies. Catholics formerly blamed this on discrimination against themselves by the majority of Americans. This is one factor, but others are seen to play a part: the fact that most Catholics were immigrants or the children of immigrants put them at a social and economic disadvantage for several generations; a tendency for Catholics to enter better paying professions, such as medicine or law, instead of intellectual pursuits; the heritage of the minority mind that hesitates to join non-Catholic groups and to influence non-Catholic society. The historian can see that this is the normal pattern of development for minorities everywhere, and that Catholics can be expected to be more influential in American intellectual affairs in the future than they have been in the past.

REVIEW AIDS

1. From your acquaintance with a Catholic immigrant family of the past generation or from your reading about immigrant families, list the religious problems faced by the first and second generations of immigrants.
2. What are the principal dangers to be faced and overcome in integrating

the Church into any society? Into the American society of mid-twentieth century?

3. Look through statements by Pope Pius XII in *Catholic Mind* since 1948 to see what he has said on the relationship of Catholics and non-Catholics. Compare these statements with those made by Cardinal Gibbons or Archbishop Ireland.

4. Some people claim that the organization of the Church and the nature of Catholic doctrine make Catholics intellectually passive. Comment knowingly and objectively on this statement.

5. Explain why the Baltimore councils were concerned with (a) the method of nominating bishops, and (b) the establishment of parochial schools.

6. Prepare a sketch of the career of Cardinal Gibbons or Archbishop Ireland in order to show the principal problems they encountered as leaders in the Church.

7. What elements are common to the Know-Nothings, Klansmen, and the POAU?

8. What connection is there ideologically and historically between the Bishops' Program of 1919 and the New Deal? In what ways do they stand in contrast?

SUGGESTIONS FOR FURTHER READING

The student who wishes to read further in American Church history would do well to consult these two excellent bibliographies: John Tracy Ellis, *A Select Bibliography of the History of the Catholic Church in the United States* (New York: 1947); and Edward A. Vollmar, S.J., *The Catholic Church in America: An Historical Bibliography* (New Brunswick, N. J.: 1956).

After John Tracy Ellis' *America Catholicism* (Chicago: 1956), the best single volume text is Theodore Roemer, O.F.M.Cap., *The Catholic Church in the United States* (St. Louis: 1950). This book is arranged by decades, unfortunately, and the story turns into a chronicle rather than a study of the problems and issues faced by the Church in American history. It is an accurate and a worthwhile presentation nonetheless. A more popular account is Francis X. Curran, S.J., *Major Trends in American Church History* (New York: 1946). The current position of the Church is excellently analyzed by Thomas T. McAvoy, "The Catholic Church in the United States," in *The Catholic Church in World Affairs*, edited by Waldemar Gurian and M. A. Fitzsimons (Notre Dame, Ind.: 1954).

The best treatment of nativism in American history is the work of a non-Catholic, Ray Allen Billington, *The Protestant Crusade, 1800–1860. A Study in the Origins of American Nativism* (New York: 1938). The best study of the problem of the Church and immigration is that of Gerald Shaughnessy, *Has the Immigrant Kept the Faith?* (New York: 1925). Americanism has been treated in various journals and touched on in most surveys of American Church history. The fullest treatment is to be found in the recently published work of Abbé Felix Klein, *Americanism: A Phantom Heresy* (Atchison, Kans.: 1951).

Insight into the history of the American Catholic Church can be obtained from the interesting autobiographies of some of its leaders. Among the more interesting and popular are: James Cardinal Gibbons, *A Retrospect of Fifty Years* (Baltimore: 1916); Francis Clement Kelley, *The Bishop Jots It Down* (New York: 1939); and William Cardinal O'Connell, *Recollections of Seventy Years* (Boston: 1934).

Very useful for statistics and official information about the Church is the annual *Catholic Directory*. Also helpful are John Hugh O'Donnell, *The Catholic Hierarchy of the United States* (Washington: 1922); Peter Guilday, *A History of the Councils of Baltimore* (New York: 1932); Peter Guilday, *The National Pastorals of the American Hierarchy* (Washington: 1923); and the *Catholic Historical Review* which, since its inauguration in 1915, has specialized in articles dealing with the history of the Church in America.

DOCUMENTS

Cardinal Gibbons on Church and State

Cardinal Gibbons was one of the great leaders of the Church in America who understood and was understood both by America and by Rome. The following extract is one in which he states the attitude of American Catholics toward the problem of Church-State relationships and the provisions made by the Constitution for freedom of religion in America.

The same Divine Voice, as I have often preached in the discharge of my pastoral office, which gives us the command to render unto God the things of God, gives us the other command, of equally binding force, to render unto Caesar the things of Caesar.

But an objection is repeatedly cast up to Catholics which, repugnant though it is to my inmost feelings of loyalty and reverence towards the Holy Father, I must take into consideration; for utterly impracticable and absurd as it is in our eyes, it seems to haunt the minds of many outside the Church.

Suppose, it is said, the Pope were to issue commands in purely civil matters, should not Catholics be bound to yield him obedience?

The Pope will take no such act, we know, even though it is now a part of Catholic Faith that he is infallible in the exercise of his authority; but were he to do so he would stand self-condemned, a transgressor of the law he himself promulgates. He would be offending not only against civil society, but against God and violating an authority as truly from God as his own.

Any Catholic who clearly recognized this would not be bound to obey the Pope; or rather his conscience would bind him absolutely to disobey, because with Catholics conscience is the supreme law which under no circumstances can we ever lawfully disobey.

* * *

We may put aside, then, as an absurdity the injurious supposition that the Pope would ever interfere with purely civil affairs. But is there not a twilight zone over which both Church and State put forth claims? True: and I grant that here a collision of authorities comes more within the horizon of possibility. But the American concept of government and of liberty puts this hypothesis outside the range of practical affairs.

That concept, as I understand it, is that the Government should leave as large a liberty as possible to individuals and to bodies within the State, only intervening in the interests of morality, justice and the common weal. There are forces at work in the country, I know, that tend to paternalism and Caesarism in Government; but true Americanism recognizes that these forces would bring disaster on American liberties. So long as these liberties, under which we have prospered, are preserved in their fullness, there is, I assert, no danger of a collision between the State and the Catholic Church.

The admission, however, of the merely theoretical possibility of such a collision keeps alive the apprehension of timid Protestants and is sufficient to determine some of them to deprive Catholics forever of the honor of the Presidency. But if no man were to be considered eligible for the Presidency unless we were certain that under no conceivable circumstances would his conscience come into conflict with any possible legislation, then the first consideration to qualify a man as candidate for the office would be that he should have no conscience at all.

"But," many Protestants say, "we obey our conscience, you obey the Pope." Yes; we obey the Pope, for our conscience tells us that we ought to obey the *spiritual* authority of the Pope in everything except what is sinful.

"But," they reply, "we do not believe that any human power should come between the human conscience and duty." Neither do we; but while you believe in private judgment, we believe in a religion of authority which our conscience tells us is our lawful guide and teacher in its own sphere.

You can conceive a State passing laws that would violate your conscientious convictions. Would you accept these laws, or would you resist them as your fellow religionists in England recently resisted an education law of which they did not approve? I think you would not prove false to your religious convictions.

Were the State to attempt to compel Orthodox Jews to accept the Sunday for the Sabbath or to abandon certain Levitical observances which are sacred in their eyes, they would not be worth their salt if they did not resist this encroachment on their rights.

Similarly, for example, if the State should forbid us Catholics to continue our parochial schools we should resist to the uttermost; for we hold that, while the State has the undoubted right to compel her future citizens to receive a certain degree of education, she has no right to deprive them of the daily religious influence which we deem necessary for their spiritual and eternal welfare, as well as for their proper training in the duties of citizenship.

In any such essay by the State to establish Caesarism, Catholics would behave precisely as any other conscientious body would behave. They would not think it necessary to await instructions from any source. We believe in the sacredness and supremacy of conscience; and rulers of the world, from Nero to Clemenceau, have found the Catholic conscience to be a wall of adamant.

*   *   *

In a country wholly or predominantly Catholic, the most desirable relation is the friendly union and cooperation of Church and State, neither power sacrificing its liberty and each acknowledging the other. That this is ideal relation, provided liberty be assured to those not of the established church, no sensible man can deny. The Catholic Church states in form of doctrine what all history shows to be inevitable; that where the Church and State are practically two names for the nation viewed as a body of worshippers and as a political entity, it is impossible to prevent an intimate union.

If my Protestant friends will show me a free nation that really believes in one religion and has no union of religion with the State, I will believe the Catholic doctrine unwarranted. But while the union is *ideally* best, history assuredly does not prove that it is always *practically* best. There is a union that is inimical to the interests of religion, and consequently to the State; and there is a separation that is inimical to the interests of religion, and consequently to the State; and there is a separation that is for the best interests of both.

In our country separation is a necessity; and it is a separation that works best for the interests of religion, as Mr. Howard Taft recently stated, as well as for the good of the State.

I fully agree with him, and I can understand too and sympathize with the great Catholic leader of France, the Count de Mun, who recently exclaimed: "In America separation means the reign of liberty; in France the reign of impiety."

American Catholics rejoice in our separation of Church and State; and I can conceive no combination of circumstances likely to arise which should make a union desirable either to Church or State. We know the blessings of our present arrangement; it gives us liberty and binds together priests and people in a union better than that of Church and State. Other countries, other manners; we do not believe our system adapted to all conditions; we leave it to Church and State in other lands to solve their problems for their own best interests. For ourselves, we thank God we live in America, "in this happy country of ours," to quote Mr. Theodore Roosevelt, where "religion and liberty are natural allies."

Chapter 38

THE CHURCH BETWEEN WORLD
WARS

THE pontificate of Pius XI almost spans the two decades between
World Wars I and II. It was a period of increasing secularism, in
the midst of which the Church grew stronger, healthier, and better
organized. The old problem of adapting itself to the worldly environment
in which it must live plagued the Church throughout this period. By
trial and error a method had been worked out before World War I
whereby the Church could pursue its mission as an unprivileged organization in modern constitutional democracies. But after World War I
democracies gave way in many countries to various totalitarian regimes
that claimed the whole man's allegiance, body and soul, and the papacy
was confronted with the problem of accommodating itself to this new
regime or of "going underground."

This was an age, moreover, in which European countries were of
dwindling importance. The subcontinent of Europe continued to be the
most important area in the world, politically and culturally speaking, but
it was gradually shrinking back to its proportionate size in world affairs
as the Americas and the teeming Asian countries asserted their independence. This change presented the Catholic Church with problems of
disengaging itself from European civilization with which it had been
identified in the past and of making itself geographically Catholic. Thus
it can be said that the Church had the double problem of reorienting
itself politically and geographically so that it could be at home in all
parts of the world.

Throughout these two decades the Church faced a secularistic indifferentism on the one hand and a hostile atheism on the other. The latter force was mostly strongly represented by the Marxist Soviet Union which declared open warfare on all religion and, in its expansionist policy, aimed at "freeing" the entire world from religion as well as from capitalism. The atheistic Communistic Party appealed to many people because of its protest against existing injustices — and Catholics in all countries were therefore obliged for a double reason to take the initiative in crying out against social injustice and proposing reform.

In these trying times the Church was led by a scholar-pope, the librarian and historian, Achille Ratti, who had obtained a few years of diplomatic and pastoral experience before his election to the papal throne in 1922. Pius XI was a vigorous man who brought to the Vatican personal strength and determination. He spoke candidly and directly, whether he was dealing with shortcomings in the Church or the conduct of its enemies. Moreover, he was in every way a modern pope, for he insisted that the Church was as much at home in one age as another, that Catholics should thank God for the good progress that He has permitted men to achieve, and that the Church should encourage and utilize such scientific developments as the radio and new medicines.

As a modern pope Pius XI was particularly interested in Catholic Action, the apostolate especially designed for our times, and in promoting foreign missions so as to incorporate the entire world into the ambit of the Catholic Church. But Pius XI was by no means a "secular" or a "political" pope in the bad sense of those commonly used appellations. Although he insisted that the Church had an interest in political and social conditions, he always stressed the primacy of spiritual interests over temporal. He resumed the role Leo XIII had stressed as chief teacher in the Church by issuing a series of masterful encyclicals on social, political, educational, moral, and spiritual subjects. Finally, as a fitting means for encouraging spiritual life, Pius XI canonized more than twenty-five saints, many of them very much "saints for our times," men and women like the Little Flower, the Curé of Ars, St. John Bosco, and St. Thomas More.

The Church in the New Age.   There was a general feeling, at least among Europeans and Americans, that the war had purged the world of evil and that the countries would settle down to peaceful, prosperous living as soon as peace treaties were signed. Benedict XV had warned that the cessation of armed conflict did not automatically bring peace, and he had suggested that the treaties of Paris left a great deal to be desired. Meanwhile he had set about the task of accommodating the

Church to the new political arrangements in Europe, for old empires had collapsed, new countries had come into existence, some old countries had gained territory while others had lost land. Hungarian bishops, for example, found half their people were in Czechoslovakia, and the Catholics of Transylvania, formerly in Catholic Austria, were transferred to non-Catholic Romania. The preponderantly Catholic states of Alsace and Lorraine, to cite another example, found themselves in anticlerical France, and the French government prepared to apply the Lois laiques of 1901–1907 to these states. Rampant nationalism made these transfers of territory and population pressing problems for the Church. Everywhere governments insisted on a native hierarchy and clergy and on the coincidence of diocesan and national boundaries. Everywhere governments demanded at least some measure of control over education, the press, and various church organizations that have temporal as well as strictly spiritual interests, such as charitable societies or youth groups.

Benedict XV died before the European world had settled down. Pius XI was therefore left with the problem of making a satisfactory settlement with each country so that the Church could pursue its mission without hindrance and so that true peace could be achieved in the world again. The new pope inherited the problems of his predecessor, but he also inherited a generally favorable attitude toward the Church — the result of the three previous pontificates and the loyal conduct of Catholics in all countries throughout the war. Diplomatic relations had been restored with France, and the French government ceased to enforce the more rigorous of the anticlerical laws. The Italian government and the papacy had made a number of friendly gestures toward each other, and there seemed every reason to believe that the bitterness of 1870 had died with the men who were alive at that time. In 1922, then, there seemed a fair possibility that Europe — and with it the rest of the world — could settle down, heal the scars of war, and develop a peaceful Christian society.

Pope Pius XI's first encyclical, Ubi Arcano Dei is a masterful analysis of world conditions, and it should have disillusioned its readers of any fatuous hope of an easily obtained peace. "Nowhere since the catastrophe of the recent war," he wrote, "has man found the peace he seeks for, whether we consider individuals, or groups of nations, that active, fruitful peace which all desire still evades our grasp." The old hatreds and jealousies among nations have not died down, the pope points out, nor has mutual trust developed among them. Moreover, there is no real civil peace within nations, either the defeated nations or the victorious. The root cause of this restlessness and insecurity is the modern world's apostasy from God, for God has been banished from marriage, education, economics, and politics. Pope Pius XI admonishes the world in 1922 that the only true peace is the peace of Christ, and this is possible only in a society over which Christ reigns so that justice is done and charity informs men's actions.

The pope therefore proclaimed the goal of the "peace of Christ through the reign of Christ." In 1925 he established the feast of Christ the King, to be celebrated by the universal Church on the last Sunday of October. The reign of Christ is concerned chiefly with spiritual matters, the pope tells us in *Quas Primas,* for "My kingdom is not of this world." But acceptance of the kingship of Christ will bring order, tranquillity, concord, and liberty to all peoples, for there is no conflict between rulers and ruled when Christian principles are faithfully followed.

So much for a statement of the conditions necessary for peace. As head of the Church the pope also faced the problem of reaching an understanding with various governments as to the respective rights and functions of Church and State in these countries. In the latter part of the nineteenth century Catholics had tended to rely on political action as the most effective means of safeguarding their rights. Most countries had constitutions which guaranteed, among other things, freedom of religion and freedom of political action. In these countries Catholics could insist on their constitutional right to be good practicing Catholics, and they could unite politically to see that their religious rights were respected. The Center Party was the model for this method of securing the Church her freedom of action in a modern, constitutionally governed country.

It was apparent after World War I, however, that the Church could not rely on political action to maintain its rights everywhere. In some countries Catholics were an insignificant minority with no political power; in other countries constitutions were meaningless documents; in still others, there was a tendency to reject party government in favor of a dictator backed by a minority that seized a monopoly of power and dissolved all other parties. Pope Pius XI, therefore, relied on a different device for regulating the Church's position in various countries: the *concordat,* an agreement between the pope as sovereign head of the Church and the proper authority in the given country whereby they outlined the terms on which the Church is to operate within the country. The concordat is, in effect, an international agreement with the status of a treaty under international law. It cannot be lawfully altered except by mutual consent of the contracting parties or according to methods stated in the concordat itself. Mutual agreement by Church and State on various contested points was intended to clarify the legal position of the Church and minimize conflicts between ecclesiastical and governmental authorities. In those countries where the concordats were entered in good faith this salutary result did come about, and in those countries where the concordats were violated consistently, as in Nazi Germany, at least the Church had legal grounds for complaint about the violation of its rights.

Pope Pius XI entered into twelve general concordats (besides six limited ones on specific points) with various European powers. Three were with German states — Bavaria, Prussia, and Baden — and a fourth with Germany as a whole. Four were made with predominantly Catholic states — Italy, Austria, Poland, and Lithuania. Others were made with states in which Catholics were a minority — Latvia, Yugoslavia, Czechoslovakia, and Romania. The arrangements differ from country to country, but certain provisions are more or less common to all twelve concordats. Provision is made in each concordat for the nomination of bishops, and for the first time in history the Church is free from the control of secular governments in the selection and installation of its bishops. All concordats except those with Austria and Germany provide that the pope is free to nominate anyone he wishes to vacant sees, provided only that he choose a citizen rather than an alien and that he submit the nominee's name to the government to make sure he is not politically a *persona non grata*. German and Austrian bishops are chosen by their confreres, who send a list of nominees to the pope, who in turn sends back three choices from which the bishops make the final selection. In all cases, the arrangement protects the pope's freedom of choice and the State's desire that bishops be native citizens.

The concordats of Pope Pius XI provide the Church with a legal autonomy and freedom from secular rulers never before so completely realized in modern times. Every concordat guarantees the Church the free exercise of public worship, and each government recognizes the right of the Church to promulgate laws binding on all Catholics. Moreover, every concordat provides for full freedom of communication between the Holy See and bishops in the country, and between the bishops and their faithful. The *Placet* and *Exequatur*, remnants of the old union of Church and State, are abolished in all countries where they still exist.

Another accomplishment of these concordats is their obtaining official recognition of ecclesiastical organizations and their legal right to acquire and manage property. These organizations are recognized as corporate persons. Each of the concordats also obtains freedom for religious orders to operate as corporate entities within the country. Typical is the provision of the German concordat:

The religious Orders and Congregations shall not be subjected, on the part of the State, to any particular restriction concerning their foundation, their residences, the number and the qualities of their members, their activity in the care of souls, in education, in assisting the sick and in works of charity, in the regulation of their affairs and in the administration of their property.

The concordats also accept the special status of ecclesiastics according to Canon Law, namely, that clerics "are free from military service and from duties and public offices that are unbecoming to the clerical station," and they shall not "accept offices that import secular jurisdiction or duties of administration." Moreover, provision is worked out in most of the concordats for at least some measure of state support for the Church in return for property confiscated in days gone by. Finally, various arrangements are worked out in each country for matters that are a concern to both Church and State, such as education, marriage, the role of Catholic Action groups, and the political activity of the clergy. The Church usually promises that the clergy will not engage in partisan politics, and in return the State recognizes the priests' and bishops' right to discuss the moral aspect of political questions.

The concordats guaranteed the Church the right to follow its divinely appointed mission freely, and in return the Church recognized the legitimacy of certain political and social interests of the State, as education. However, these agreements were soon violated by some of the governments, especially by Nazi Germany when Hitler and his followers fought an undeclared war against the Church. The terms of the concordat gave the pope legal grounds of protest against these violations, but in the period between the wars violation of agreements was so frequent that papal protests attracted little attention. Concordats did achieve their basic purpose of clarifying and delimiting the areas that are Caesar's and God's. The Church had no recourse but to depend on each government's good will in living up to these agreements.

The Lateran Treaty. The settling of the Roman Question in 1929 is generally considered the most important single accomplishment of Pius XI's pontificate, for this settlement was largely his personal work and it ended the 59 years of anomalous existence the Church had endured since 1870. The pope intimated at the beginning of his reign that the Church would accept much less than the city of Rome and that she recognized the unification of Italy as an accomplished fact. All the territory he needed, the pope explained, was a "little corner of the earth" he could call his own so that his spiritual authority would not be compromised. Since the time of Pius X, we have seen, little courtesies on the part of the papacy and the Italian government made for better feelings, and especially throughout the war mutual consideration was shown by the pope and the Italian government. Pope Pius XI's first blessing was made from the outer loggia of St. Peter's, a symbolic gesture that he was willing to negotiate with Italy. His first encyclical closed with an invitation to settle the Roman Question and the very use of the word "Italy" (new in papal documents) intimated that the pope would make large concessions to Italian nationalism.

Mussolini was also anxious to settle the Roman Question. He wanted the solid support of all Italians, and he knew this was impossible until the Church officially accepted the loss of Rome and Italy recognized the papacy as a sovereign state. Mussolini also believed that he could identify Catholicism and Italian nationalism to enhance his own power and prestige rather than have the religious feeling of the Italian people oppose him. "Since the Italian people is almost totally Catholic," he explained, "and Catholicism is the ancient glory and tradition of Italy, the State, which is the juridical organization of the Italian Nation, the representative of its spirit and the heir of its traditions, is not and cannot be aught but Catholic."

Informal negotiations were begun in August, 1926, between Francesco Pacelli, brother of Pope Pius XII, who represented the Holy See, and Domenico Barone, who represented Italy. Both men were eminent jurists, and both were sincerely interested in effecting a settlement. Pacelli and Barone agreed on certain preliminary bases for further agreement: (1) Italy recognized the Holy See's sovereignty and promised to concede it a small strip of territory; (2) the Holy See did not claim the guarantee of foreign powers, such as France or Austria; (3) a concordat regulating the status of the Church in Italy would be signed simultaneously with the settling of the Roman Question; (4) since Italy was a Catholic state, Italian civil law would conform to Canon Law on certain questions such as marriage.

The story of these negotiations is an interesting one into which we cannot enter here. It is enough to remark that Pacelli and Barone had 110 conversations. By November, 1926, they had prepared a draft treaty, and by the following April they had completed the draft concordat. The pope controlled papal negotiations closely, giving Signor Pacelli 129 audiences, many of them several hours long. The last stages of the negotiations were carried on by Mussolini and Cardinal Gasparri acting as plenipotentiaries of the Italian king and Pope Pius XI. Every clause was carefully reviewed, and finally the treaties were signed on February 11, 1929.

The Lateran Treaty consists of three parts: the Treaty proper, a financial settlement, and a concordat. The Treaty is a bilateral agreement entered into by equal sovereign powers. Thus the pope had gained recognition from Italy of his sovereignty, whereas the Law of Guarantees had treated him as a subject. Moreover, the Treaty creates Vatican City, a sovereign state governed by the pope, and an annexed map shows the limits of this tiny state of 108 acres. The usual attributes of sovereignty are guaranteed to the Holy See by the Italian government: full freedom of communication with other states, even those at war with Italy; diplomatic immunity for statesmen accredited to the Holy See, even though they lived in Rome; the inviolable neutrality of Vatican City; and the recognition of cardinals as princes of the Church, who retain their Vatican citizenship even though some of them must live in Rome.

The financial settlement was necessary because the Holy See had lost the Papal States and because a tremendous amount of Church property throughout Italy had been seized since 1870. The Holy See had never touched the money provided by the Law of Guarantees. Italy promised to pay the pope 750 million lire in cash and one billion lire in government stock; the papacy agreed to accept the cash in gradual payments and not to sell the stock which bore 5 per cent interest.

The concordat was very similar to those drawn up with Austria, Poland, and Lithuania. It is a concordat of alliance drawn up with a Catholic state, one which gives the Church a privileged position in the country and incorporates ecclesiastical institutions into civil law. The state pledges itself, for example, to recognize holydays established by the Church, and the Church promises to recite liturgical prayers for the king of Italy and the Italian nation. Again, provision is made for religious education in the primary and secondary schools "according to a program to be settled between the Holy See and the State." In most other respects the Italian concordat follows the general pattern described in the preceding section. Pope Pius XI indicated his personal satisfaction with the Italian concordat when he said that it was "if not the best that could possibly be made, certainly among the best made so far, thanks to which we believe, with deep satisfaction, that we have given God back to Italy, and Italy to God."

Later Political Arrangements. Concordats were the means whereby the Church tried, in the papacy of Pius XI, to clarify relations between

Church and State and to set forth terms on which the Church could operate in various countries. Serious problems arose with some countries that violated the terms of their concordats, such as Germany and Italy, and with other countries with which no concordat was negotiated. In this brief treatment we can sketch the problems faced only with Italy, Germany, France, Spain, and Mexico. Relations with other countries were generally favorable and without incident, as with the United States and England, or they were continually hostile and without noticeable development, as with the Soviet Union.

Italy. The Fascist State was a source of trouble to Pius XI almost from the beginning. Fascist violence could never be condoned, but certain accomplishments of the Fascist government, such as the suppression of secret societies, deserved to be applauded. Again, Fascist protests against materialism were good, but Fascist doctrine of the State was a modern form of idolatry. The pope therefore had to restrict himself to censuring particular Fascist practices and doctrines, and several times during the negotiations for the Lateran Treaty he protested strongly against various Fascist abuses. A few months after the signing of the Treaty, while it was still in process of ratification by the Italian government, the pope flatly took issue with Mussolini's theory of the State. "It is not the function of the State," he said, "to absorb, to swallow up, to annihilate the individual and the family. This would be absurd, contrary to the nature of things, for the family existed before the State, as it existed before society."

Through 1930 and into the spring of 1931 Mussolini conducted an insulting campaign against the papacy and particularly against Catholic Action groups in Italy. Finally, on July 5, 1931, the pope personally wrote the indignant and strongly worded encyclical *Non Abbiamo Bisogno,* which Philip Hughes has described as

> the final damning reply to the lies and bad faith of the Fascist state. . . .
> Through it all there rumbles the deep indignation of an honest man who
> feels he has escaped, and only just escaped, the trickery of rogues, and
> there is the still deeper anxiety and distress that come of the fact that what is
> seemingly at stake is the future of Italian Catholicism.

In *Non Abbiamo Bisogno* the pope described Fascism as "an ideology which openly resolves itself into a true, a real pagan worship of the State." Again, he accuses Fascists of making "a sham of religion" which

> cannot in any way be reconciled with Catholic teaching and Catholic
> conduct. . . . A conception of the State which makes the rising generations

belong to it entirely, without any exception, from the tenderest years up to adult life, cannot be reconciled by a Catholic either with Catholic doctrine or with the natural rights of the family.

Pius XI's strong answer to Mussolini's aggression bore fruit. The decrees against Catholic Action were withdrawn, and through the next eight years many feints were made by Mussolini against the Church but he never dared to declare open war against the Vatican and the Church, as he would like to have done.

Germany. A similar struggle against the State unfolded in Germany, with this difference: Germany was less Catholic than Italy, and it was farther removed geographically from the pope's presence. As a result, Hitler was able to fight his undeclared war against the Church more openly and more successfully. Even before his appointment as chancellor in 1933 various German bishops had condemned both the doctrine and the practices of Nazism. As soon as Hitler came to power he destroyed Catholic Trade Unions and dissolved the Center Party. After 1935 his attack grew more violent and more direct: priests were arrested on flimsy pretexts, Catholic Action groups were dissolved as incompatible with National Socialism, convents and monasteries were closed on the pretext of "immorality" and their property confiscated.

There is reason to believe that for some time the pope did not realize the enormity of this Nazi persecution of the Church. At last he condemned both the doctrines of Nazism and its terroristic activities. His letter of condemnation, *Mit brennender Sorge* appeared in the same month (March, 1937) as his letter against Soviet Communism, *Divini Redemptoris,* and it is written in equally strong language. In this letter the pope describes and rejects, point by point, the doctrinal errors of Nazism, condemns its anti-Christian practices, and warns the faithful not to be taken in by the Nazis' paganized version of "Teutonic" Christianity.

France. We have already noted that postwar relations with France were friendly. Although the French government refused to rescind the anticlerical legislation of 1901–1907, it no longer enforced these laws in a harsh way. Similarly, although the Holy See refused to approve the separation of Church and State, it encouraged Catholics to accept the new *Associations Diocesaines* which met the requirements laid down by Pius X and had the bishop of each diocese as president.

The most important development in the French Church, perhaps, was the condemnation by the pope of *L'Action Française,* an ultranationalist movement that preached hatred of foreigners and aimed at the overthrow of the republic and the restoration of the monarchy. The movement claimed to be Catholic, although its long-time leader, Charles Maurras, was a professed infidel and many of its doctrines were patently anti-Christian. *L'Action Française* had been condemned in 1914, but the condemnation was not published when war broke out between France and Germany. Publication was postponed because *L'Action Française* was the leading organ of anti-Germanic feeling, and its condemnation might be interpreted as papal endorsement of the Central Powers' cause against the Allies. The revival of this intensely nationalist movement provoked a fresh condemnation by Pius XI, which was published in 1927.

Spain. Revolution broke out in Spain early in 1931. From the beginning of the revolution bitter anticlerical and antireligious factions committed depredations against convents, churches, and monasteries. Revolutionary antipathy to the Church grew more intense when some of the Spanish bishops appeared to back the exiled king and to condemn the new republic. In October, 1931, the anticlerical forces led by Manuel Azaña replaced the moderate forces and wrote into the new constitution a bloc of anticlerical and antireligious clauses. The Church's legal rights were abolished; ecclesiastical property was put at the disposal of the State; the religious were excluded from education; and provision was made for the suppression of religious orders. In the next two years the radicals put these constitutional provisions into effect and the Church was driven out of Spanish life. Meanwhile, churches were burned, priests murdered, nuns outraged and slain — while the government watched passively.

In his encyclical of June 3, 1933 — *Dilectissima Nobis* — the pope reviewed and condemned the anticlerical legislation and conduct of the past two years. His letter and a later joint pastoral of the Spanish bishops gave heart to the Catholic groups in Spain and convinced them of the essential rightness of their cause, but the radical elements grew more violent and bitter in their attack on the Church. A survey of Church history cannot enter into the complicated and almost inexplicable development of the Spanish Revolution and the subsequent civil war. Various anarchistic, socialistic, and Marxist forces held in common an intense hatred of the Church, and throughout these years of unrest they used every opportunity to stamp out any manifestation of religion. At the same time, it must be observed that in this land of saints and theologians the Church had somehow lost the loyalty of a large proportion of the working class and especially of the middle class which furnished the anticlerical leaders and the revolutionary "intellectuals." Nor did the conduct of the proclerical forces do anything to win them back.

Mexico. A similar persecution of the Church occurred in Mexico, a persecution conducted by a proportionately small group of middle-class political adventurers whose hatred of the Church was intense. Severe persecution had followed the revolution of 1914 in Mexico. It was renewed in 1924 when Plutarco Elias Calles, sometimes called the "Nero of the Mexican Church," was elected president. Churches were destroyed, priests murdered, nuns outraged. All non-Mexican priests were expelled, all religious schools closed, and the work of the native clergy was severely curtailed. The number of priests was limited to about 4000, and various regulations made it almost impossible for them to perform their ministry. On four different occasions Pius XI protested against these vicious laws, but the persecution of the Mexican Church continued throughout his pontificate.

"The Pope of Catholic Action."   Pope Pius XI consistently and lovingly worked to extend the foreign missions, as we have seen, and also to develop "the mission within the fold" or Catholic Action, which he referred to as "the apple of my eye." His interest in this aspect of the Church's activity came naturally from his modernity and from his realization that priests cannot by themselves adequately perform their apostolic function in the modern secularized world. They need the help of laymen. Pius XI defined Catholic Action a number of times as "the participation of the laity in the work of the hierarchy." It is as old as the Church, he wrote, but it is needed in the twentieth century as never before in the history of the Church. Catholic Action imposes itself on all laymen as an obligation, for the duty to preach the gospel to all people is incumbent on the Church as a whole and not exclusively on the bishops and priests.

Pope Pius XI distinguished Catholic Action associations from simple pious societies on the one hand and from political parties on the other. Pious societies are concerned exclusively with the personal sanctification of their members, whereas Catholic Action groups assume this end and add to it the spreading of the gospel. Its aim, the pope said, was to create "a sacred militia" that would bring true spiritual and moral principles to bear on the problems of the time. Among the specific objectives he listed for Catholic Action were good government, the training of better citizens, the promotion of public welfare, and the instilling of Christian principles into public life.

As individuals, Catholic Actionists have a right to participate in party politics, and that right becomes an obligation when moral questions are involved. But Catholic Action itself takes no part in party politics. "It stands above and beyond all party politics," the pope wrote, "for it aims at the common good of souls rather than at the welfare of particular bodies." Again, "Catholic Action will be careful not to involve itself in politics, for it is by its nature precluded from taking sides in civil government." In his letters on Catholic Action the Holy Father consistently warned that such work must be done under episcopal authorization. Laymen are to be more than errand boys carrying out the bishop's orders, for they are to take the initiative and to maintain an active, sometimes a leading role in Catholic Action. But they are always to remain under the bishops' authority and subject to their jurisdiction.

The pope obtained legal recognition of Catholic Action groups in most of his concordats, and in return he promised that they would not participate in party politics. The growth of Catholic Action groups, especially youth organizations, was one of the most encouraging signs of this pontificate. A large number of exemplary groups developed in France and Belgium, and served more or less as models for other European countries and for groups in the Americas. These Catholic Action associations helped their members spiritually, and did at least something to perform missionary work within the fold, and to make the twentieth-century society a little less secularistic.

Pope Pius XI as Teacher. A scholar himself, Pius XI naturally took a lively interest in Catholic learning. New Catholic universities were established in Poland, Holland, and Milan, and a Pontifical Institute of Oriental Studies was founded in Rome. The standards of learning in Catholic universities and seminaries were carefully examined and raised to uniformly higher levels. Moreover, in thirty encyclicals — some of them very long — the pope revived the teaching role that Leo XIII inaugurated a half century earlier. These encyclicals deal with a wide range of subjects: war and peace, economic and social dislocations and their remedies, education, marriage, motion pictures, Communism, Fascism, Nazism, and various problems of the Church's interior development, such as retreats, missions, the spirituality of St. Francis de Sales, and the intellectual importance of St. Thomas Aquinas.

The encyclicals on the condition of the Church in Spain and Mexico deal with the old liberal aberrations and the anticlericalism they generate. The most important political development of this pontificate, however, was the emergence of the totalitarian State. *Non Abbiamo Bisogno* was a powerful protest against Fascism, uttered "with the fury worthy of a Hildebrand," according to one biographer. So vigorous was the tone of this encyclical that it had to be smuggled out of the country and published in Paris. Pius XI accused the Italian government of attempting to "monopolize all the young, from the tenderest years up to manhood and womanhood, all for the exclusive advantage of a party, of a regime based on an ideology that clearly resolves itself into real pagan worship of the State."

Mit brennender Sorge was an even more incisive indictment of Nazism. This encyclical was smuggled into Germany, delivered to German bishops during the night, and read from the pulpits on Sunday morning — a complete surprise to the Nazis who never thought the pope would dare denounce them so bluntly. In this letter Pius XI denounced the neopagan exaltation of race and blood and the advocacy of collective immorality. The greater part of the encyclical was devoted to the Nazis' violation of the concordat and the systematic destruction of Catholic Action associations in order to monopolize the education of the German youth. The pope demanded that if Hitler youth groups forced Catholics to become members, they must be "purged of all manifestations hostile to the Church and Christianity."

Divini Redemptoris, published three days earlier, was a denunciation of atheistic Communism which "strips man of his liberty, robs human personality of all its dignity, and removes all the moral restraints that check the eruptions of blind impulse." In this encyclical, which is one of the best short analyses and critiques of Communism in any language, the pope condemns its materialism, its advocacy of class struggle, its denial of God and of man's true nature. "It is in opposition both to reason and to divine Revelation," he concludes. "It subverts the social order, because it means the destruction of its foundations; because it ignores the true origin and purpose of the State; because it denies the rights, dignity and liberty of human personality."

Divini Illius Magistri is a classic statement of the Catholic theory of education. "There can be no ideally perfect education," the pope tells us, "that is not a Christian education," for sound education must take into consideration man's final goal in life. It must deal with the whole man, body and soul, with all his faculties, natural and supernatural. Education belongs in the first place to the family and to the Church, which shares the divine teaching office of God Himself. The State has the obligation of protecting these prior rights of parents and the Church, but it also has a right to protect children against their parents' deficiencies and to require sound education for all children in the realm. In this encyclical the Holy Father denounces naturalism, sex instruction, and coeducation as dangerous practices that have grown common in the modern world. He concludes that Christian education forms "the supernatural man who thinks, judges and acts constantly and consistently in accordance with right reason illumined by the supernatural light of the example and teaching of Christ; in other words, to use the current term, the true and finished man of character."

In *Casti Connubii* Pius XI states the traditional Catholic doctrine on marriage. This encyclical has served since its publication in 1930 as the authoritative statement on the nature and purpose of marriage, on its sacramental import, and its part in God's scheme of creation. The second part of the encyclical examines and refutes modern criticisms of Catholic doctrine on marriage and condemns modern distortions, such as birth control, sterilization, and companionate or experimental marriages.

Quadragesimo Anno remains the most widely read and the most important of Pius XI's encyclicals. Issued in 1931 on the fortieth anniversary of *Rerum Novarum,* it reiterates the basic principles of that great work and brings their application up to date. The effect of a message such as this is impossible to measure, of course, but within a few years *Quadragesimo Anno* was known throughout the Western world — by non-Catholics as well as Catholics — and many of its principles became commonplace among sociologists and economists. Moreover, labor leaders and industrialists in our country claim that their thinking has been modified and clarified by this masterful encyclical, and similar tribute has been paid to it in the various European countries.

It is impossible to make a brief summary of so weighty a document. Let us only indicate a few of its leading principles. First, the pope lays down the principle that the Church has the right and duty of exerting its authority in social and economic matters, "not indeed in technical matters, for which she has neither the equipment nor the mission, but in all those that have a bearing on moral conduct." Second, he points out the errors of socialism and communism on the one hand and of rugged individualism on the other. Third, he establishes the right of private property which, however, has a social character and cannot be employed against the common welfare. Fourth, the pope insists that ownership of property entails obligations as well as rights, and then he lists the rights and unjust claims of capital and of labor. Finally, he dwells on the reconstruction of the social order on the basis of vocational groups and respect for the principle of subsidiarity.

Conclusion. The period between the wars seemed one of net gain for the Church. Under Pope Pius XI, as we saw in Chapter 36, the missions were solidly organized and the Church began to spread outside the Western world. Internally it seemed to grow stronger. It made notable gains in Holland, the United States, and generally in the English-speaking world. In the Latin countries it lost ground in some respects, but the core of practicing Catholics in these countries gave rise to the hope that a sound revival of vigorous Catholicism was beginning there.

Pius XI constantly kept the Eastern Church in mind and did all he could to facilitate the reunion of the two Churches. Prayers were ordered for Russia at the end of every Mass. The Oriental Institute in Rome was given strong papal support; a new edition of Eastern writers was begun; a new commission was appointed to codify the Canon Law of the Oriental Churches; and great care was taken to celebrate the centenaries of the great councils in which the Eastern Church played a prominent part. The pope ordered that all seminaries institute courses dealing with the Eastern Church "to help to do away with the mutual ignorance and scorn" that have perpetuated the schism. Finally, the Roman policy on this delicate problem was stated in Pius XI's encyclical *Rerum Orientalium* of 1928.

It was generally recognized by Catholics and non-Catholics that the Church's growing vigor in these years was due in large measure to its earthly leader. When Pius XI died on February 10, 1939, the world respectfully paused to pay tribute to a great man of modern times. An editorial in the New York *Times* voiced the general feeling in this country and in Europe when it said, in part:

> He was a man of ample and various gifts. A humanist, a quiet scholar, fingering lovingly the manuscripts of the Ambrosian and the Vatican, he was a singularly able administrator. A lover of antiquity, he had the modern touch, as he showed in the renovation of the Vatican Library and the installation of radio and telegraph systems connecting his little domain with its widespread spiritual dependencies. Among his larger triumphs his settlement of the so long insoluble "Roman Question" will always be memorable. The Lateran Treaty of 1929 gave the Holy See independence and ended the long quarrel between Church and State. With the characteristic comment, "The Holy See wants independence, not territory," he struck out of the agreement a proposed cession of ground beyond the Vatican confines.
>
> Pius XI made his little domain — larger he would not have — a center of freedom and of the defense of religion against the newer cult of worship of the State. In this defense he was as brave as he was wise. The free men and women whose battles he fought will not forget him.

REVIEW AIDS

1. Review the section of Chapter 36 dealing with missionary developments in the pontificate of Pius XI. Show how they fit into the general policy of his pontificate.
2. Explain in a short essay the significance of calling Catholic Action "the mission within the fold." What is the significance of defining it as "the participation of the laity in the work of the hierarchy"? What are some of the better known Catholic Action associations in this country? In your community?
3. Analyze the postwar situation in central and eastern Europe to explain why concordats were necessary.
4. List the most important gains made by the Church in the concordats. What satisfaction could the various countries take in making these settlements with the Church?
5. From your outside reading about L'Action Française make a list of the reasons why it was condemned by the papacy.
6. In outline form trace the major events in the breaking away of the Eastern Church and its subsequent relations with Rome. What points of difference, besides the "mutual ignorance" of which Pius XI speaks, keep the two Churches apart?
7. Outline the principal reasons why Pius XI opposed Fascism and Nazism. What were his basic reasons for condemning Communism?
8. Outline the principal points made in the encyclicals touched on in this chapter around the concept of "secularism."
9. Summarize the reasons why the non-Catholic as well as the Catholic world considered Pope Pius XI a "valiant man" and a "great pope."

SUGGESTIONS FOR FURTHER READING

A number of biographies appeared near the end of Pius XI's pontificate, when it was apparent that a great pope was nearing the end of his life. The best of these is Philip Hughes, Pope Pius the Eleventh (New York: 1937). Also generally reliable but more popularly written biographies are: Msgr. R. Fontenelle, His Holiness Pope Pius XI (Cleveland: 1939); Lord Clonmore, Pope Pius XI and World Peace (New York: 1938); Edward Vincent Dailey, Pius XI, Pope of the People (Chicago: 1937); and Lillian B. Olf, Pius XI, Apostle of Peace (New York: 1938).

An intimate view of the workings of the papal government can be obtained from Thomas B. Morgan, A Reporter at the Papal Court (New York: 1938). A good treatment of the Roman Question is Wilfrid Parsons, S.J., The Pope and Italy (New York: 1929). Also helpful is the earlier work of Don Luigi Sturzo, Italy and Fascismo (London: 1926). Waldemar Gurian offers a good treatment of the persecution of the Church in Nazi Germany in Hitler and the Christians (New York: 1936).

Most of Pius XI's encyclicals have been published in pamphlet form in various editions by the Paulist Press, the America Press, and the National

Catholic Welfare Conference. They can also be found in *Catholic Mind* and the *Tablet*. Two good collections of his encyclicals are: *Encyclicals of Pius XI*, edited by James H. Ryan (St. Louis: 1927), and *Fourteen Encyclicals of His Holiness Pope Pius XI*, edited by the National Catholic Welfare Conference (Washington: 1937).

A collection of the pope's letters and directives for Catholic Action is *Directives for Catholic Action Expounded by Pope Pius XI*, edited by Rev. James D. Loeffler, S.J. (St. Louis: 1938). Good treatments of this subject are Rudolph G. Bandas, *Catholic Action* (Paterson, N. J.: 1936), and Luigi Civardi, *A Manual of Catholic Action* (New York: 1943).

DOCUMENTS

Excerpt From *Ubi Arcano Dei* (December 23, 1922)

Ubi Arcano Dei was the first encyclical published by Pius XI after his election to the pontificate. In modern times a custom has been established whereby the newly elected pope sums up his view of world and ecclesiastical conditions and states something like a program in his first encyclical. The following selection indicates Pius XI's view of world conditions in 1922.

One thing is certain today. Since the close of the Great War individuals, the different classes of society, the nations of the earth have not as yet found true peace. They do not enjoy, therefore, that active and fruitful tranquillity which is the aspiration and the need of mankind. This is a sad truth which forces itself upon us from every side. For anyone who, as We do, desires profoundly to study and successfully to apply the means necessary to overcome such evils, it is all-important that he recognize both the fact and the gravity of this state of affairs and attempt beforehand to discover its causes. This duty is imposed upon Us in commanding fashion by the very consciousness which We have of Our Apostolic Office. We cannot but resolve to fulfill that which is so clearly Our duty. This We shall do now by this Our first Encyclical, and afterward with all solicitude in the course of Our Sacred Ministry.

Since the selfsame sad conditions continue to exist in the world today which were the object of constant and almost heart-breaking pre-occupation on the part of Our respected Predecessor, Benedict XV, during the whole period of his Pontificate, naturally We have come to make his thoughts and his solutions of these problems Our own. May they become, too, the thoughts and ideals of everyone, as they are Our thoughts, and if this should happen we would certainly see, with the help of God and the co-operation of all men of good will, the most wonderful effects come to pass by a true and lasting reconciliation of men one with another.

The inspired words of the Prophets seem to have been written expressly for our own times: *We looked for peace and no good came: for a time of healing, and behold fear, for the time of healing, and behold trouble. We looked for light, and behold darkness . . . we have looked for judgment, and there is none: for salvation, and it is far from us.*

The belligerents of yesterday have laid down their arms but on the heels of this act we encounter new horrors and new threats of war in the Near East. The conditions in many sections of these devastated regions have been greatly aggravated by famine, epidemics and the laying waste of the land, all of which have not failed to take their toll of victims without number, especially among the aged, women and innocent children. In what has been so justly called the immense theater of the World War, the old rivalries between nations have not ceased to exert their influence, rivalries at times hidden under the manipulations of politics or concealed beneath the fluctuations of finance, but openly appearing in the Press, in reviews and magazines of every type, and even penetrating into institutions devoted to the cultivation of the arts and sciences, spots where otherwise the atmosphere of quiet and peace would reign supreme.

Public life is so enveloped, even at the present hour, by the dense fog of mutual hatreds and grievances that it is almost impossible for the common people so much as freely to breathe therein. If the defeated nations continue to suffer most terribly, no less serious are the evils which afflict their conquerors. Small nations complain that they are being oppressed and exploited by the great nations. The great Powers, on their side, contend that they are being judged wrongly and circumvented by the smaller. All nations, great and small, suffer acutely from the sad effects of the late war. Neither can those nations which were neutral contend that they have escaped altogether the tremendous sufferings of the war or failed to experience its evil results almost equally with the actual belligerents. These evil results grow in volume from day to day because of the utter impossibility of finding anything like a safe remedy to cure the ills of society, and this in spite of all the efforts of politicians and statesmen whose work has come to naught if it has not unfortunately tended to aggravate the very evils they tried to overcome. Conditions have become increasingly worse because the fears of the people are being constantly played upon by the ever-present menace of new wars, likely to be more frightful and destructive than any which have preceded them. Whence it is that the nations of today live in a state of armed peace which is scarcely better than war itself, a condition which tends to exhaust national finances, to waste the flower of youth, to muddy and poison the very fountainheads of life, physical, intellectual, religious and moral.

A much more serious and lamentable evil than these threats of external aggression is the internal discord which menaces the welfare not only of nations but of human society itself. In the first place, we must take cognizance of the war between the classes, a chronic and mortal disease of present-day society, which like a cancer is eating away the vital forces of the social fabric, labor, industry, the arts, commerce, agriculture — everything, in fact, which contributes to public and private welfare and to national prosperity. This conflict seems to resist every solution and grows worse because those who are never satisfied with the amount of their wealth contend with those who hold on most tenaciously to the riches which they have already acquired, while to both classes there is common the desire to rule the other and to assume control of the other's possessions. From this class war there result frequent interruptions of work, the causes for which most often can be laid to mutual provocations. There result, too, revolutions, riots and forcible repression of one side or other by the government, all of which cannot but end in general discontent and in grave damage to the common welfare.

To these evils we must add the contests between political parties, many of which struggles do not originate in a real difference of opinion concerning the public good or in a laudable and disinterested search for what would best promote the common welfare, but in the desire for power and for the protection of some private interest which inevitably result in injury to the citizens as a whole. From this course there often arise robberies of what belongs rightly to the people, and even conspiracies against and attacks on the supreme authority of the State, as well as on its representatives. These political struggles also beget threats of popular action and, at times, eventuate in open rebellion and other disorders which are all the more deplorable and harmful since they come from a public to whom it has been given, in our modern democracies, to participate in very large measure in public life and in the affairs of government.

Chapter 39

THE PONTIFICATE OF
POPE PIUS XII

CARDINAL EUGENIO PACELLI was elected pope in one of the shortest conclaves in the history of the Church. Sixty-two cardinals gathered on the evening of March 1, 1939, and on the third ballot, taken early the next afternoon, they unanimously chose Pius XI's secretary of state to be his successor. The new pope chose the name of Pius XII, an indication that he intended to continue his predecessor's policies of opposing totalitarian encroachments on the Church and promoting peace among nations. On March 3 the new pope made a strong appeal for peace in a radio address to the entire world from the famous Sistine Chapel.

The significance of Cardinal Pacelli's election was not lost on the political world. He was the first secretary of state to be chosen pope since 1775, and the first pope of Roman birth since 1721. The conclave evidently broke tradition because the princes of the Church warmly approved of the policies Cardinal Pacelli had so vigorously enforced in the last years of his predecessor's pontificate. The Nazi press condemned the choice of a "political" rather than a "religious" leader, but the rest of the world — non-Catholic as well as Catholic — hailed the choice as an excellent one. Typical of world reaction was the editorial comment of *America*:

> Humanly speaking, Pius XII is the man of the hour, for the hour is dark. There is not a nation which has not heard thunder on the horizon presaging the storm of war. Worse even than the fear of the scourge of war of man against man, is the fear of the war of man against God. Irreligion, indifference to religion, hatred of religion fostered by atheistic Communism and neo-paganism, merge with the fear of war to make heavy the hearts of men who know that only in the peace of Christ can the world find peace. In his powerful, yet touchingly beautiful and tender address broadcast

to the world on March 3, Pius XII prayed for the establishment of peace, "the sublime gift of heaven, the fruit of charity and justice." These words express the soul of his pontificate.

The new Holy Father seemed to sum up in his person the outstanding qualities of his great predecessors. He possessed the diplomatic skill and experience of Leo XIII and Benedict XV. He had been in charge of the Vatican Information Service and relief work during World War I; he played a key role in Benedict's attempt to mediate peace in 1917; he had negotiated many of the concordats; and as papal secretary of state he had traveled throughout Europe and both Americas, thus seeing more of the world than any previous pope in the history of the Church. Moreover, he was a teacher on the model of Leo XIII and Pius XI, a deeply religious man like Pius X, and a thoroughly modern pope like his immediate predecessor. To these qualities he added a sensitivity to changing social and economic conditions, an awareness of the needs and aspirations of the peoples of the world, and a willingness — almost an eagerness — to adapt the Church to changing conditions. Typical of this attitude was the decision that henceforth all Catholics kneeling before the radio will receive the same plenary indulgence awarded to those physically present at the pontifical blessing *urbi et orbi,* because, the decree stated, the pope is "desirous that the scientific progress of our time may be used to improve and preserve the health of souls."

The three main concerns of this pontificate were (1) peace, (2) protection of the Church's rights throughout the world, and (3) adaptation to changing conditions in the world. The problem of peace concerned the pope both as chief teacher in the Church and as sovereign ruler of the Vatican State. His many messages on peace constitute the best study of this problem made in the history of Western civilization. As pope and sovereign of a small state, Pius XII tried desperately in the first months of his pontificate to prevent the war which he saw coming. During the war he continued to pray and plead for peace. Moreover, he acted energetically as guardian and bishop of Rome, and he employed the Church's world-wide organization to relieve suffering caused by the war and its attendant dislocations.

In the years after the war, Pope Pius XII saw more than 50 million Catholics turned into "the Church of Silence" behind the Iron Curtain in both Europe and Asia. He ordered crusades of prayers for these martyrs in the Church, and he protested formally against the violation of their fundamental human rights.

Meanwhile, the Holy Father guided the Church with a sensitive but firm hand in those regions where it was free — and here the principal note was one of modernity and adaptation to modern conditions. "Certainly the Church is a living organism," the pope said early in his pontificate, "and, therefore, in those things which pertain to the sacred liturgy it grows and develops and conforms itself to the circumstances and requirements of various times, saving and guarding nevertheless the integrity of doctrine." Similarly, he observed that "religious organizations best serve the needs of the times when, on occasion, without giving up their own peculiar spirit, they adapt themselves to changing conditions." In keeping with this attitude on growth and development, spoken of so frequently in his messages, Pius XII guided the Church through more change and development than witnessed by any other generation in modern history.

Peace Efforts Before the War. In the six months between his election and the outbreak of World War II, Pope Pius XII worked and prayed incessantly to avert the conflict he saw coming. In May he launched a crusade of prayer to the Blessed Virgin in the interest of preventing war, and in June he launched a similar crusade of prayer to the Sacred Heart. He addressed groups of pilgrims on various problems connected with the maintenance of the age's precarious peace, and several times he made direct appeals to the leaders and the peoples of the quarreling nations. The most dramatic of these was the radio appeal of August 24, when the pope warned those in power that "nothing is lost with peace; all may be lost with war." On August 31 he made a last desperate effort to postpone armed conflict and to open negotiations to solve the German-Polish dispute. Ambassadors of Germany, Poland, England, France, and Italy were given a diplomatic note which stated:

> The Holy Father cannot abandon hope that conversations now being held may bring about a just and peaceful solution such as the whole world has not ceased to implore. Therefore, His Holiness beseeches, in the Name of God, the governments of Germany and Poland to do everything possible to avoid any incident whatsoever and to abstain from taking any measure capable of aggravating the present tension. He asks the governments of England, France and Italy to support this his request.

During the first six months of his pontificate, while he was making his public appeals for peace, the Holy Father was engaged in quiet but hurried diplomatic efforts to reconcile the great powers. The full story of his diplomatic activity in these months will not be known for many years. But there were many rumors of a "Papal Peace Plan" in the European newspapers in May, and it can now be established that the pope officially proposed the holding of an international conference to settle the outstanding German-Polish and French-Italian disputes. This proposal differed from that made by Benedict XV in 1917 in that it was not made public and it did not include any specific recommendations, for in this way Pius XII thought he had a better chance to get the powers together. Nor was it to be another Munich, for the invitation was to all the great European powers, including the countries directly involved in the disputes. At any rate, by June 2 the pope had been informed that for various reasons the powers had turned down his proposal.

A second attempt seems to have been made in July. A large number of papal diplomats reported to the Vatican in this month, including secretaries of the nunciatures at Belgrade, Madrid, Paris, London, and Bucharest. Msgr. Amleto Cicognani, Apostolic Delegate to the United States, also reported to the Vatican, and Cardinal Enrico Gasparri came to this country on an undisclosed mission. Moreover, the pope stayed in Rome long past the customary time, and it was not until July 24 that he left for his summer palace at Castel Gandolfo. Any chance of bringing the powers together for negotiations was doomed by the successful negotiations secretly going on between Germany and the Soviet Union, and when the Nazi-Soviet pact was signed Hitler could not be stopped from marching on Poland. Papal negotiations had again proved futile.

Meanwhile, Pius XII had been at work on his first encyclical, the instrument by which recent popes have stated their "platform," so to speak, or the policies they intend to follow, and analyzed the dangers confronting the Church and the problems most pressing at the time. Unfortunately, this masterful encyclical was not published until the month after the war began, and it therefore did not attract the attention it deserved. It is still deserving of study as a penetrating critique of the modern world and an assessment of proposed reforms. "What age," the Holy Father asks, "has been, for all its technical and purely civic progress, more tormented than ours by spiritual emptiness and deep-felt interior poverty?" The crisis, which seems to be political and social, is a deep-seated spiritual and moral crisis.

> The moral values by which in other times public and private conduct was gauged have fallen into disuse; and the much vaunted civilization of society, which has made ever more rapid progress, withdrawing man, the family and the State from the beneficent and regenerating effects of the idea of God and the teaching of the Church, has caused to reappear, in regions in which for many centuries shone the splendors of Christian civiliza-

tion, in a manner ever clearer, ever more distinct, ever more distressing, the signs of a corrupt and corrupting paganism: "There was darkness when they crucified Jesus."

The pope explains that two principal errors lie at the source of our troubles. The first is the denial or forgetfulness of the unity of the human race, and the second is the divorce of civil authority from dependence on God. From these errors derive nationalism and the totalitarian State which denies human, family, and even divine rights. Pius XII asserts the Church's obligation to guide mankind in its search for truth and for a new world order which, when the war is over, "must rest on the unshakable foundation, on the solid rock of natural law and of Divine Revelation." Although *Summi Pontificatus* was written in "an hour of darkness," its author maintains a basic Christian optimism about the future, for "God can do all things." The pope therefore urges all Catholics to pray without ceasing and to work for a peace based on justice and charity rather than on vengeance.

The Church Through the War Years (1939–1945). During the war, of course, normal communications within the Church were interrupted, thousands of priests were forced into the armed services, thousands more left their dioceses to serve as chaplains, the missions suffered severely from loss of man power and financial support that could no longer be furnished by a war-torn world, and the Church suffered irreparable losses in thousands of priests killed and billions of dollars of property destroyed. Millions of Catholics suffered for their faith wherever Hitler's forces triumphed, and millions more found themselves behind the Communist Iron Curtain and huddled in the "Church of Silence" by the time the war ended. Leadership devolved on the local hierarchy in these places, for communications with Rome had been cut and each bishop had to gather his flock together and follow whatever policy his conscience dictated. In three strongly worded joint pastoral letters the bishops of Holland protested against the ecclesiastical policies of the German occupation forces, in Belgium Cardinal Van Roey took a strong stand against the Nazis, and in Hungary Cardinal Sereti vigorously condemned various Nazi measures against the Church. Generally speaking, the bishops in occupied countries followed the policy of giving no occasion for persecution but standing up firmly for the Church's rights and for sound morality.

Meanwhile, in Vatican City the pope followed two principal lines of action in regard to the war. Taking advantage of his neutral status — which was respected by all the belligerents — he mobilized the Church's resources for relief work, and he used his moral prestige and his diplomatic service to shorten the war and advocate terms on which a sound peace could be reached. The full story of the Church's relief work has not yet been written, but we know that it assumed gigantic proportions and that its accomplishments stagger one's imagination.

A Pontifical Relief Commission was set up as soon as the Nazis invaded Poland, and within a matter of weeks food, medicine, and clothes were rushed into the devastated areas of that country. New relief stations were set up as the war spread into Belgium, Holland, Norway, Denmark, France, Yugoslavia, and Greece. Food, medicine, and clothing were passed out by Vatican relief workers to people of all creeds and nationalities. Need was the only criterion. The pope obtained resources from those areas with which he could still communicate freely, and the Catholics of the United States were particularly generous in supplying him with goods to dispense among the peoples impoverished by the European war.

After 1943, when the Allies completed their conquest of Africa and began the invasion of Italy, the Holy Father found Rome a particularly pressing problem. Within a short time there were half a million refugees in the city. Papal soup kitchens and emergency ration stations were set up throughout the city, and within a few months they were serving 200,000 soup rations and 50,000 hot meals a day at the cost of about $7,000. Vatican relief services followed closely in the wake of Allied armies as they advanced into German-held areas, for the pope was well informed of conditions in concentration camps and he knew how desperately the inmates needed food, medicine, and the care of doctors and nurses. Papal relief work continued in the years after the war, and through the offices of the Holy See thousands of refugees found new homes, war orphans were protected, and thousands of persons were taken care of until they could find a permanent settlement.

Meanwhile, the Vatican looked after prisoners of war in many countries. After initial rebuffs, Vatican representatives were given free access to prisoner of war camps everywhere except in Soviet-held territory, for it was soon found that the Vatican's aim was purely humanitarian. Vatican representatives concentrated on personal contact with the prisoners, delivering their mail and gift parcels, providing them with literature, conducting recreation programs, and ministering to their spiritual needs. By the end of the war this work was being conducted in almost forty countries.

The Vatican information service was perhaps the outstanding single accomplishment of the Church during the war. The aim of this service was to supply information about missing persons to their relatives, for the spiritual anguish caused by uncertainty is one of the worst sufferings attendant upon war. The Vatican information service started out with two volunteers working in a small room and handling about a dozen messages a day. By 1945 it had a staff of 600 full-time volunteer workers handling tens of thousands of messages daily — a total of more than 5,500,000 inquiries, of which more than seventy per cent were successfully processed. The Vatican information service took advantage of an unofficial network of every bishop and priest in the world, of course, and obtained information that astounded the intelligence services of all the belligerent countries. On several occasions Americans learned of missing personnel through this service rather than through the official American sources.

Throughout the war the pope used his office to mitigate the harshness of the struggle and to urge steps toward an armistice and eventual peace. In 1940, for example, he appealed for a Christmas truce. Various days, such as November 24, 1940, were declared days of penance and prayer for those who died, for those who mourned, and "that true peace may unite as brothers all the peoples of the holy family." May of 1941 was made a crusade-for-peace month, a special prayer for peace was composed by the pope, and every opportunity was taken throughout the war to direct Catholics everywhere to pray for peace. Meanwhile, as we shall see later in this chapter, in a series of Christmas Eve messages and various allocutions Pius XII discussed the principles on which a lasting peace must be based.

As bishop of Rome the pope was faced with a problem similar to that of Pope St. Leo during the barbarian invasions. Rome was clearly a military objective after the Allies invaded Italy, for it was a railroad center and the locale of several airfields and industrial establishments. Pius XII negotiated with both sides to have Rome declared an open city. Allied leaders promised they would restrict bombings to the minimum necessary to prosecute the war, but they could not treat Rome as an open city until the Axis powers withdrew from the city and no longer utilized its facilities. Rome was subjected to several severe bombings and damage was done to some nonmilitary objectives. The pope was one of the first on the scene after each raid, praying for the dying and giving alms to the injured and homeless. Eventually the Nazi command managed to evacuate Rome and it was taken by American troops with a minimum of damage.

The Church and Reconstruction. The Church suffered serious losses in personnel and property during the war. Three bishops and at least 2000 priests had died or been killed in Poland, an estimated 1597 German priests had been killed in action, and similar numbers of religious had lost their lives in the other countries of Europe. Invading Japanese forces had killed many missionaries in China and throughout the Orient, and they had closed many churches, schools, and other establishments. War damages to churches alone were estimated at more than $6 billion. With the defeat of the Nazis persecution had stopped in Western Europe, but a systematic war of attrition against the Church was begun in the countries under Soviet control.

Pius XII set about rebuilding the Church on a world-wide rather than an Italian or European basis. In his first set of appointments to the college of cardinals he spoke of the Church's universal and international character. The college had been reduced to 38 members by 1945, 24 of whom were Italian. Pius XII brought the college to its full complement of seventy by naming 32 new cardinals — the largest group to be appointed in modern times. Only four of these were Italian, and thus for the first time since the Western Schism the Italians did not have a majority in the college. All continents and nineteen countries were represented, and for the first time a native Chinese cardinal sat in the college with European and American princes of the Church.

Seven years later Pius XII named 24 more cardinals to take the places of those who had died since 1946. The new nominations further emphasized the universal character of the Church, for 26 nations were represented in the college of cardinals in 1953. Only 23 of the 70 were Italian. Significant among the nominees were Cardinal Gracias, the first native Indian cardinal, and Cardinal Stepinac who was then in prison for his opposition to the Yugoslavian government's attack on the Church.

In 1946 China was raised from its mission status to be made an integral part of the Church. Twenty metropolitan provinces with 79 suffragan sees were created in China, and plans were made to have the Chinese Church entirely independent of foreign missionaries as soon as possible. This entirely natural development was hurried along because of increasing Chinese nationalism and the Holy See's expectation that foreign missionaries would soon be expelled from the country. In other significant ways the pope emphasized the universality of the Church. On frequent occasions he pointed out that it was wrong to identify the Church with Europe or with Western civilization. In 1946 he published the encyclical *Orientales Omnes Ecclesias* on the 350th anniversary of the reunion of the Ukrainian Church with Rome, and he celebrated the seventh anniversary of his coronation according to the ancient Armenian liturgy. Moreover, the Holy See emphasized the universal character of the Church by employing non-

Europeans on an increasing scale. The pope named Rev. Clemente Neubauer of Milwaukee, minister-general of the Capuchins, for example, and four other congregations chose Americans as their superiors.

The Holy See's efforts to reconstruct the Church on a world-wide basis was thwarted by the Soviet Union. Communists developed a clever strategy in dealing with the Church behind the Iron Curtain. Rather than attack the Church directly, they tried to preserve it as an institution and use it to support the Communist regime. The hierarchy and the priests in all countries behind the Iron Curtain were cut off from Rome, harassed by the government, and limited in their functions. The local bishops were faced with a difficult dilemma: they could co-operate with the Soviet-controlled governments in the hope of keeping the Church alive and ministering to the faithful until these regimes should collapse, or they could stand up defiantly against the Communist governments and die as martyrs for the Faith. Much can be said for and against either choice. Local conditions dictated which choice the bishops and faithful had to make in each country. Meanwhile, the Holy See was powerless to offer more than prayers and encouragement to the faithful in the "Church of Silence," and to protest against such atrocities as were reported by refugees from behind the Iron Curtain. The best estimates are that 53 million of the 425 million Catholics in the world are in this "Church of Silence," and no one knows how long they can preserve their faith in the face of relentless and diabolically clever persecution.

As chief teacher and administrative head of the Church, Pope Pius XII was intimately concerned with postwar reconstruction in Europe. His influence and his guidance was probably the decisive factor in checking Communist advances in Italy in the years after the war. His influence was also felt, though perhaps not so directly or decisively, in such other countries as France where for a time it seemed that Communist parties might take over the government. Moreover, the pope continued to urge social reform as an essential element of reconstruction and international peace. Usually he spoke in general terms, but occasionally he addressed himself to specific proposals or problems. He stressed the need of equable land reform in Italy, for example, and he unreservedly endorsed the Marshall Plan. He also spoke favorably of the United Nations as a step in the right direction of creating international law and international institutions to enforce it. Again, he spoke favorably of plans for a federated Europe and urged immediate action in that direction. Implicit in all these statements is a principle the Holy Father stated explicitly several times: that the Church cannot be unconcerned with the world in which it must live, and that it has the duty of using its influence to achieve a just and abiding peace.

In his annual Christmas Eve addresses and in countless allocutions and impromptu talks the Holy Father dealt with the subject always nearest his heart, the problem of peace. These addresses constitute the most complete analysis of the nature of peace which has been made in the history of Christendom. Here we can only suggest the main outlines of the pope's teaching on peace. Peace, he insists time and time again, is fundamentally a spiritual and moral condition defined by St. Augustine as "tranquil living together in order." The pope therefore emphasizes that peace is a three-fold thing, and that no one aspect of it can be achieved without the other two. It is first of all an interior state of soul and condition of mind within each individual; second, it is a domestic matter within each nation, social peace among the classes within the country; and third, it is a tranquil living together in order by all the various nations of the world.

In his Christmas message of 1939 the pope laid down the essential points of international peace, to which he has returned for further development in various later addresses. These points are: (1) the right to life and independence of all nations, large and small; (2) deliverance from the economic and psychological slavery imposed by large armaments; (3) creation of some international institution to guarantee agreements entered into by the nations of the world; (4) satisfying the real needs and just demands of all nations and all minorities; (5) striving by all peoples and governments to attain justice rather than promoting selfish interests. Underlying these points, the pope has frequently insisted, is the need of mutual trust among all nations, for distrust and mutual suspicion are the ground in which the seeds of war are fruitfully cultivated.

A year later the pope listed certain victories which are preliminary to any lasting peace. These are: (1) victory over the hatred which divides nations in our day; (2) victory over distrust which makes honest understanding among nations impossible; (3) victory over "the dismal principle that utility is the foundation and aim of law, that might can create right"; (4) victory over conflicts arising from an unbalanced world economy; (5) victory over nationalistic selfishness. In various other messages the Holy Father has taught that lasting international peace must be based on justice among nations and among classes within nations, and that its firmest foundation lays in the principles given to mankind by Christ.

The Christmas Eve address of 1942 was devoted to the question of social peace within nations. For, the Holy Father wrote, international relations and internal order are intimately related. International equilibrium and harmony depend on the internal equilibrium and development of the individual States in the material, social and intellectual spheres. A firm and steady peace policy towards other nations is, in fact, impossible without a spirit of peace within the nation which inspires trust. It is only, then, by striving for an integral peace, a peace in both fields, that people will be freed from the cruel nightmare of war.

This message restates and develops the social principles of *Rerum Novarum* and *Quadragesimo Anno*. In it the Holy Father lays special emphasis on the development and perfection of the human person, on the rights of the family, the dignity and prerogatives of labor, and the Christian concept of the State.

The 1944 Christmas Eve message analyzed the connection between democracy in the modern world and the peace of the future. Pius XII suggests that if the people had been allowed to play their proper role in totalitarian countries, "the world would not have been dragged into the vortex of a disastrous war, and that to avoid the repetition of such a catastrophe in the future we must vest efficient guarantees in the people themselves." The Holy Father distinguishes between the true and false concepts of democracy and shows that the sane democracies, accepting right political principles, can solve international problems and promote peace in the world.

Adaptation to a Changing World. Pope Pius XII always showed himself extremely sensitive to changing world conditions, and was deeply concerned with keeping the Church abreast of the times. Little things early in his pontificate indicated that the pope was a very modern man and that, while he respected tradition, he refused to live in the past: as bishop of Rome he took possession of the Basilica of St. John Lateran, the first time the pope had entered this church since 1846; for the first time in seventy years the pope entered the Quirinal Palace when Pius XII visited the King of Italy in 1939; the "March of Time" was allowed to make a movie of life in Vatican City, and the "star" of the movie was the pope himself.

It was not until after the war that the pope could effect changes to modernize certain aspects of ecclesiastical life. Typical of Pius XII's approach to these problems is his address on "Woman's Duties in Social and Political Life" in which he gives a beautiful summary of the traditional Catholic teaching on virginity, on the married state, and on religious life for women who have that vocation. But the pope goes on to explain that in the modern world many women will never be married nor do they have the vocation to enter religious congregations. For them he sympathetically outlines still a third way of life by which they can perfect themselves naturally and supernaturally. Likewise, he explores the vast field of activity that women may follow in civil and political life without failing in their primary duties as wives and mothers.

The pope encouraged women's religious congregations to modernize their dress and to streamline their organizations so that they could more effectively fulfill the purposes of their foundations. In 1952, superior-generals of some 200 women's congregations met in Rome to discuss ways and means of achieving these suggested reforms. Another need created by changing social conditions was recognized by an apostolic constitution on lay persons seeking perfection of spiritual life. A decree of 1947 recognized that groups of lay persons had been springing up in answer to the needs of the times, and that they should not be subject to the canons governing strictly religious communities. The decree therefore laid down norms for such groups and exempted them from canon law requirements for religious bodies.

Most notable to the average laymen in the Church have been the liturgical changes of Pius XII's pontificate. Regulations on fasting before receiving Communion were eased. Evening Mass was introduced in most dioceses, and permission was granted to use the native language for part of the rubrics for the administration of certain sacraments. A decree went into effect January 1, 1956, effecting important changes in the Church calendar and in rubrics governing the recitation of the Breviary. Some minor changes were also made in the Mass. These changes, which carried on the reforms begun by St. Pius X, eliminated the semidouble feasts and took the octave away from all feasts except Christmas, Easter, and Pentecost. Holy Week services were drastically revised in 1956 in the interest of greater participation and fuller understanding of their significance by the faithful. The liturgical services on Holy Thursday, Good Friday, and Holy Saturday were ordered to take place in the afternoon or the evening; the faithful were allowed to receive Communion on Good Friday; and Lent was extended till midnight of Holy Saturday. These changes, like all the other innovations of this pontificate, were made in the spirit of restoring the early practices of the Church so as to make the meaning of Holy Week and its culmination on Easter Sunday more understandable. In October, 1958, the Holy See issued a directive to the Latin Rite Church on lay participation in the Mass. Instructions provided for the recital of many of the Mass prayers by the congregation, and the reading of the epistle and gospel in the vernacular by a narrator, while the priest reads them in Latin.

On November 1, 1950, the pope issued the solemn declaration of the Assumption of the Blessed Virgin into heaven. This was the first dogmatic definition of faith made by the pope alone since 1854, and the first since the solemn statement of papal infallibility by the Vatican Council. As Pius IX had done before defining the Immaculate Conception, so Pius XII solicited bishops' opinions on the subject and had the Church's best theologians study it for several years before he formulated the definition.

Another significant development of this papacy was the unusually large number of persons canonized. The most important of these was the canonization of Pope Pius X, under whom Pius XII served as a young priest and whose liturgical reforms he has tried to continue and extend. The year 1950 was celebrated as a Holy Year, and more than three million Catholics made the pilgrimage to Rome in that year. And 1954 was consecrated to the Blessed Virgin as the Marian Year, and a new feast — the Queenship of Mary — was proclaimed for May 31.

Attracting less attention than the liturgical changes but every bit as important in the long run has been the study of many theologians throughout the Church who seek to develop and expound the deposit of the faith in our day. The Holy See warmly encouraged such study, but in 1950 the pope found it necessary to publish the encyclical *Humani Generis* "Concerning Some False Opinions Which Threaten to Undermine the Foundations of Catholic Doctrine." In this encyclical the pope listed various errors that had crept into the teaching of some few Catholic theologians who were overzealous and imprudent in their attempts to adapt Catholic doctrine to modern science. After discussing these errors, the Holy Father concluded:

> Let them [teachers in ecclesiastical institutions] strive with every force and effort to further the progress of the sciences which they teach; but let them also be careful not to transgress the limits which We have established for the protection of the truth of Catholic faith and doctrine. With regard to new questions, which modern culture and progress have brought to the foreground, let them engage in most careful research, but with the necessary prudence and caution; finally, let them not think, indulging in a false "eirenism," that the dissident and erring can happily be brought back to the bosom of the Church, if the whole truth found in the Church is not sincerely taught to all without corruption or diminution.

Pope Pius XII consistently handled the delicate problem of adapting ecclesiastical institutions and developing Church doctrine by steering a middle course between blind conservatism and rash progressivism. Essentials do not change, he has insisted, and they must be preserved inviolate; but the ways and means of presenting the essentials of Catholic doctrine

THE SOVEREIGN PONTIFF

SACRED CONGREGATIONS

Holy Office

Consistorial

Oriental

Sacraments

Council

Religious

Propagation of the Faith

Rites

Ceremonial

Extraordinary Affairs

Seminaries and Universities

St. Peter's Basilica

TRIBUNALS

Penitentiary

Signature

Rota

OFFICES

Chancery

Datary

Secretariat of State

Secretariat of Briefs

Secretariat of Latin Letters

COMMISSIONS

Biblical

Interpretation of the Code of Canon Law

For the Revision of the Vulgate

S. Archaeology

For the Protection of Historical and Artistic Monuments of the Holy See

Heraldry for the Papal Court

NUNCIOS AND APOSTOLIC DELEGATES

THE HIERARCHY

ORDINARY GOVERNMENT

Archbishops

Bishops

Vicars Apostolic

Prefects Apostolic

Superiors of Missions

Major Superiors in Exempt Religious Communities

EXTRAORDINARY GOVERNMENT

Diocesan Synods

Provincial Councils

Plenary Councils

THE CLERGY

THE FAITHFUL

and worship should be adapted to the age and the culture in which the Church lives. The work of adaptation is delicate and sometimes dangerous, but it cannot on that account be neglected or avoided. For to do so is to put the Church out of touch with the age — and the Church is made for all ages and all peoples.

Pius XII became chief pastor and teacher of all Catholics in a more direct sense than any pope since the earliest days of the Church. During his pontificate he spoke to an estimated fifteen million persons in private and public audiences, delivering 1,386 discourses and numerous shorter speeches. To these groups the Holy Father spoke on countless subjects: the moral aspects of criminology, international law, medicine, obstetrics, atom bombs, modern science, and travel. With special groups, such as historians, philosophers, lawyers, and physicians, he discussed the problems that they face as Catholic professional people. These addresses are published in most of the languages of the world. They add up to such a substantial total that Americans found it wise to establish a journal, *The Pope Speaks,* devoted to publishing the pope's letters and allocutions on various subjects.[1]

The most important papal messages are to be found in the major encyclicals which, in the tradition of Leo XIII and Pius XI, are scholarly dissertations on various subjects. The most important encyclicals of general interest are probably *Mediator Dei* and *Mystici Corporis Christi.* The former is a treatise on the liturgy in which the Holy Father explains the nature and the purpose of liturgical services and encourages active participation in them by the faithful. The latter is an analysis of the Church as the Mystical Body of Christ and a study of the relationship between the Church and its Founder. These two encyclicals, together with *Summi Pontificatus* and the Christmas messages on peace, constitute a fruitful body of doctrine for the faithful to study. To these should be added a number of encyclicals on restricted subjects, such as *Divino Afflante Spiritu* on biblical studies, *Sertum Laetitiae* to the American hierarchy, *Ad Sinarum Gentium* to the Chinese hierarchy and people, and *Orientalis Ecclesiae Decus* on the 1500th anniversary of St. Cyril of Alexandria.

Death of Pope Pius XII. On March 2, 1956, Pope Pius XII celebrated his eightieth birthday and the seventeenth anniversary of his election to the papacy. Catholics and non-Catholics, as well as civil governments throughout most of the world, joined in paying tribute to

---

[1] An excellent summary of the pope's teaching is Robert C. Pollack (editor), *The Mind of Pius XII* (New York: 1955). Papal statements are arranged topically and reference is made to the English source from which each statement is taken.

the octogenarian pontiff as a champion of world peace and a loving pastor of his flock. Two and a half years later, on October 9, 1958, Pius XII died from a stroke suffered at Castel Gandolfo. At the close of his pontificate the Church could look back on the past century with a certain measure of satisfaction and thanks to God for His blessings. A series of remarkably capable and holy men had guided the Church's revival in this century. Under them the Church had grown strong and healthy. Its administration was vastly improved; its spiritual life — as well as mortal man can judge — had grown richer. The missions increased and prospered until they covered a good part of the globe. Papal authority was unquestioned, and the Holy See was freer than ever in the Church's history to choose and communicate with the hierarchy. Moreover, the Church had transcended Western civilization and established itself as a "native" Church in other cultures.

Within the pontificate of Pope Pius XII remarkable changes were inaugurated climaxing this revival and bringing to life the dormant lay portion of the Church. Implementing his encyclicals on the Mystical Body and the liturgy, Pius XII promoted a number of changes making it easier for the laity to receive the sacraments daily, to understand and participate in liturgical services, and to take part in the missionary and apologetic work of the hierarchy and the clergy.

Against these gains were obvious losses in the Communist-dominated countries behind the Iron and Bamboo Curtains, where such remarkable accomplishments had recently been made. About one eighth of the world's approximately 470 million Catholics were suffering persecution behind the Iron Curtain, and newly established dioceses in China seemed about to go into schism. Other Catholics were relatively free to practice their faith, but they had to do this in a world that had become increasingly secularistic and irreligious. The secularism of nonreligious peoples had driven religious leaders closer together, and there was increasing discussion about the possibility of some Protestant and Orthodox groups returning to the Church. At the death of Pope Pius XII Catholics could liken their position to that of the Church in the later Roman Empire. They were a cohesive body in a decadent society, and whether they would become the chrysalis around which the society of the future might form depends on the providence of God, the guidance of new leaders, and how Catholics live and pray.

REVIEW AIDS

1. From a brief summary of Pope Pius XII's life before his election to the papacy indicate his qualifications for this high honor and difficult post.

2. Read the chapter or chapters dealing with the events leading to World War II as presented in any European history text. From this reading summarize the reasons why papal diplomacy failed to prevent war. Was the Vatican in any way responsible for this failure?
3. Explain why the Vatican information service operated so efficiently.
4. Why was the Church interested in postwar social and political reconstruction?
5. To what extent do you think the United Nations is a step in the direction of the pope's blueprint for international peace? Why does the Vatican maintain a representative at the headquarters of UNESCO in Paris?
6. What are the extreme positions on the problem of the Church's adapting itself to the world? Show in what way each extreme is wrong. Indicate criteria for judging sound adaptation.

SUGGESTIONS FOR FURTHER READING

For this last period in the history of the Church the student must rely mostly on periodical literature. The Jesuit weekly, *America,* takes note of the more important developments in Church history as they occur, and most of the Catholic journals have articles from time to time on recent developments. Good coverage is given to the papacy by the London *Tablet,* by some American diocesan papers, and by *The National Catholic Reporter.* This latter paper and the *Catholic Mind* carry the important papal allocutions and encyclicals issued by the NCWC news service.

The most adequate coverage of the pontificate of Pius XII is to be found in Oscar Halecki, *Eugenio Pacelli: Pope of Peace* (New York: 1951), which treats most of the papacy's developments through the Holy Year of 1950. Robert C. Pollock (ed.), *The Mind of Pius XII* (New York: 1955), is an excellent collection of statements by the pope on various subjects. The quarterly, *The Pope Speaks,* serves to keep the student abreast of papal statements.

Special studies of the papacy's dealing with totalitarian powers are: Piet Oudendijk, *Pius XII and the Nazi War Against the Catholic Church* (London: 1944); Camille M. Cianfarra, *The Vatican and the Kremlin* (New York: 1950); and Camille M. Cianfarra, *The Vatican and the War* (New York: 1944).

A number of scholars contributed separate chapters on the Church in various countries in Waldemar Gurian and M. A. Fitzsimons (eds.), *The Catholic Church and World Affairs* (Notre Dame, Ind.: 1954). The Benedictine Dom Aelred Graham has an excellent study of the Church today in *Catholicism and the World Today* (New York: 1952), and Emmanuel Cardinal Suhard's famous pastoral letter, *The Church Today* (Chicago: 1953), analyzes the principal problems facing the Church at this point in history. A valuable work indicating current trends and the purpose of Vatican II is Hans Küng, *The Council, Reform and Reunion* (New York: Sheed & Ward, Inc., 1962).

DOCUMENTS
Extract From *Sertum Laetitiae,* Letter to the American Hierarchy, November 1, 1939

Pope Pius XII wrote his encyclical *Sertum Laetitiae* to the American bishops on November 1, 1939, to commemorate the 150th anniversary of the establishment of the hierarchy in America. The following selection shows the Pope's knowledge of and concern with labor problems in this country.

We desire to touch upon another question of weighty importance, the social question, which, remaining unsolved, has been agitating States for a long time and sowing amongst the classes the seeds of hatred and mutual hostility. You know full well what aspect it assumes in America, what acrimonies, what disorders it produces. It is not necessary therefore that We dwell on these points. The fundamental point of the social question is this, that the goods created by God for all men should in the same way reach all, justice guiding and charity helping. The history of every age teaches that there were always rich and poor; that it will always be so we may gather from the unchanging tenor of human destinies. Worthy of honor are the poor who fear God because theirs is the kingdom of heaven and because they readily abound in spiritual graces. But the rich, if they are upright and honest, are God's dispensers and providers of this world's goods; as ministers of Divine Providence they assist the indigent through whom they often receive gifts for the soul and whose hands — so they may hope — will lead them into the eternal tabernacles.

God, Who provides for all with counsels of supreme bounty, has ordained that for the exercise of virtues and for the testing of one's worth there be in the world rich and poor; but He does not wish that some have exaggerated riches while others are in such straits that they lack the bare necessities of life. But a kindly mother of virtue is honest poverty which gains its living by daily labor in accordance with the scriptural saying: "Give me neither beggary, nor riches: give me only the necessities of life" (Proverbs 30:8).

Now if the rich and the prosperous are obliged out of ordinary motives of pity to act generously towards the poor their obligation is all the greater to do them justice. The salaries of the workers, as is just, are to be such that they are sufficient to maintain them and their families. Solemn are the words of Our predecessor, Pius XI on this question: "Every effort must therefore be made that fathers of families receive a wage sufficient to meet adequately normal domestic needs. If under present circumstances this is not always feasible, social justice demands that reforms be introduced without delay which will guarantee such a wage to every adult working man. In this connection We praise those who have most prudently and usefully attempted various methods by which an increased wage is paid in view of increased family burdens and special provision made for special needs" (Encyclical Letter "Quadragesimo Anno").

May it also be brought about that each and every able bodied man may receive an equal opportunity for work in order to earn the daily bread for himself and his own. We deeply lament the lot of those — and their number in the United States is large indeed — who though robust, capable and willing, cannot have the work for which they are anxiously searching.

May the wisdom of the governing powers, a far-seeing generosity on the part of the employers, together with the speedy re-establishment of more favorable conditions, effect the realization of these reasonable hopes to the advantage of all.

Because social relations is one of man's natural requirements and since it is legitimate to promote by common effort decent livelihood, it is not possible without injustice to deny or to limit either to the producers or to the laboring and farming classes the free faculty of uniting in associations by means of which they may defend their proper rights and secure the betterment of the goods of soul and of body, as well as the honest comforts of life. But to unions of this kind, which in past centuries have procured immortal glory for Christianity and for the professions an untarnishable splendor, one cannot everywhere impose an identical discipline and structure which therefore can be varied to meet the different temperament of the people and the diverse circumstances of the time.

But let the unions in question draw their vital force from principles of wholesome liberty; let them take their form from the lofty rules of justice and of honesty, and, conforming themselves to those norms, let them act in such a manner that in their care for the interests of their class they violate no one's rights; let them continue to strive for harmony and respect the common weal of civil society.

It is a source of joy to Us to know that the above cited Encyclical *Quadragesimo Anno,* as well as that of the Sovereign Pontiff Leo XIII, *Rerum Novarum,* in which is indicated the solution of the social question in accordance with the postulates of the Gospel and of the perennial philosophy, are the object in the United States of careful and prolonged consideration on the part of some men of keener intellect whose generous wish pushes them on towards social restoration and the restrengthening of the bonds of love amongst men, and that some employers themselves have desired to settle the ever-recurring controversies with the working man in accordance with the norms of these Encyclicals, respecting always the common good and the dignity of the human person.

What a proud vaunt it will be for the American people, by nature inclined to grandiose undertakings and to liberality, if they untie the knotty and difficult social question by following the sure paths illuminated by the light of the Gospel and thus lay the basis of a happier age! If this is to come to pass power must not be dissipated through disunion but rather strengthened through harmony. To this salutary union of thought and policy, whence flow mighty deeds, in all charity We invite them, too, whom Mother Church laments as separated brethren. Many of these when Our glorious predecessor reposed in the sleep of the just and when We, shortly after his death, through the mysterious disposition of Divine Mercy ascended the throne of St. Peter; many of these — and this did not escape Our attention — expressed by word of mouth and by letter sentiments full of homage and noble respect. This attitude — We openly confess — has encouraged a hope which time does not take from

	ENGLAND	FRANCE	GERMANY AND CENTRAL EUROPE	ITALY, SPAIN, ETC.
1914	World War I breaks out between Austria-Hungary and Serbia (July, 1914). Germany and h ers) overrun Belgium, northeastern France, Balkans, Russian Poland, but fail to break the super of the Entente Allies: Britain, France, Russia, Italy, etc.			
1917	Russia falls in revolution, makes peace (Brest-Litovsk — December, 1917) and accepts commun trance of the United States into the War (1917) turns the scale. Thus Germany surrenders Peace of Versailles with Germany, and other peace settlements, remap Europe and the colon League of Nations created to maintain the peace.			
1920	Economic crisis Irish Free State (1922) First Labor Cabinet (1924) Baldwin's conservative government (1924–29) General Strike (1926) Total Woman Suffrage (1928) MacDonald's government (1929–35)	Economic crisis French troops occupy Ruhr (1922) Poincaré balances budget and stabilizes franc (1926–31) Maginot line (1927–38)	German Republic (1918–33) Austrian Republic (1918–34) Dawes Plan (1924) Germany agrees to Locarno Pact (1926) and enters League of Nations Hindenburg president (1925) Young Plan (1929)	Mussolini's Fascist dictatorship (1922–43) Rivera dictator in Spain (1923) Lateran Accord with Pope (1929)
1930	Statute of Westminster (1931) Edward VIII abdicates (1936) George VI (1936–52) Chamberlain heads "appeasement" ministry	Stavisky scandal (1934) Popular front (1934) Alliance with Russia (1935) Strikes (1934) Daladier at Munich	Hitler chancellor (1933), then dictator Hitler sends troops into Rhineland (1936) Munich Pact (1938) Germany rearms and annexes Austria (1938), Sudetenland (1938), Czechoslovakia (1939)	Republican revolution in Spain (1931) Spanish Civil War (1936–39) Italy takes Ethiopia (1936) Albania, and allies with Germany (Axis)
1939			German pact with Russia (1939)	
	Hitler's attack on Poland begins World War II (September, 1939). Germany easily overru way, Netherlands, Belgium, fails to defeat Britain under Churchill's leadership and also fails war in 1941 offensive.			
1941	The Japanese attack on Pearl Harbor unites the European and Far Eastern Wars and brings t War (December, 1941). British and American victories in North Africa, 1942–43, the defeat of Italy in 1943, 1944, the Russian victories in eastern Europe, the reconquest of Pacific islands from Japan, bringi powers. A United Nations is set up in 1945 as successor to the League.			
1946	Labor government of Clement Attlee (1945–51) Iron and Steel Act (1949)	German occupation (1940–44) *Fourth Republic* (1946–) Paris Conference (1946) Economic recovery (1945–50)	Germany under military occupation, divided into Western and Russian zones (1945–) "Air lift" (1949)	Italian republic (1946–) De Gasperi's Government (1946–53)
1950	Churchill in with conservatives (1951–) Elizabeth (1952–) England leaves Suez (1954) London Conference (1954)	Economic decline (1950–) European Coal and Steel Community (1952) Saar Europeanized (1954)	Big 4 meeting: England, France, Russia, United States (1954)	Spain trying for Economic Aid (1953) — from U. S Trieste Trouble (1954–) Italy and Yugoslavia
1955	Labor government elected (1964)	Fifth Republic (1958)	German prosperity	

CONTEMPORARY CHURCH

RUSSIA AND EASTERN EUROPE	THE CATHOLIC CHURCH	ECONOMIC, SOCIAL LIFE	CULTURAL LIFE
...ies (the Central Pow-... ...a power and resources	Benedict XV (1914–22) New Code of Canon Law (1917)	War impoverishes Europe but brings temporary boom to industry Panama Canal opened (1914)	Increasing use of air power Shaw, Wells, Maugham, Joyce, Sandburg, Frost, Lawrence, Cather, Mansfield, Anderson, Lewis, O'Neill, Millay, Gorki
...ctatorship, but the en-... ...ovember, 1918. ...orld.	Benedict XV's Peace Plan (1917) U. S. National Catholic War Council (1917) *Non expedit* abolished in Italy (1919)	Russia makes communistic experiment General poverty, inflation, depression, fear, extremism in Europe High tariffs United States emerges as a power	Galsworthy, Eliot, Woolf, Belloc, Coppard, A. Huxley, Morley
...nin's death (1924) ...alin (1924–53)	Pius XI (1922–39) France renews relations with Holy See (1922) Mexico persecutes Catholics (1926) Rumanian Concordat (1927) Lateran Treaty (1929)	Germany in bankruptcy Development of talking pictures "Gilded Age" Dawes Plan (1924) Depression (1929)	Woman Suffrage in United States (1920) Hemingway, Dos Passos, Mann, Santayana, Russell, Chesterton, Pound, etc. Picasso, etc., in art Lindbergh's flight across the Atlantic (1927)
	Encyclical *Quadragesimo anno* (1931) Northern Ireland (1935), Spain (1936), Germany (1937) persecute Catholics Anti-Semitism condemned (1938) Pius XII (1939–)	Reparations and war debts unpaid American New Deal League shows impotency Hard times causes wars and revolutions Rigid controls on imports, currency, etc.	Faulkner, Wolfe, Steinbeck, Marquard, Buck, Farrell, Roberts, Williams, Porter, Auden, etc. Sulfa drugs
...oland, Denmark, Nor-... ...rce Russia out of the		American "lend-lease" to Britain	Huge growth of industry in United States
...nited States into the... ...vasion of Normandy,... ...nal defeat to the Axis	22,000,000 Catholics in United States (1942)	Atlantic Charter (1941) Wartime controls, rationing, wages and prices fixed Conference at Yalta (1945) Potsdam (1945) Atomic bomb used (1945) United States assumes Western leadership	Penicillin and other new drugs Rapid advance of science
...ussia annexes Baltic States and part of Poland and controls most of eastern Europe ...ommunists conquer China (1949) ...ationalism in Asia, Africa		United Nations (1945–) Marshall Plan (1947) Television "Cold War" between East and West Many paper treaties, etc.	Use of atomic energy for peacetime uses
...ommunists invade Korea and the United Nations intervenes (1950–53) ...alenkov (1953–55) ...ommunists conquer Burma, Southern Asia, etc. ...onfusion in Middle East (1954)	Church-State troubles in Czechoslovakia (1950) Pius X canonized (1954)	NATO SHAPE E.D.C. — (killed: 1954) Nationalism in Asia and Middle East Hydrogen bomb (1954) SEATO UN's cultural work	Thomas, Capote, Salinger, etc. Growth of paper-backed literature in U. S. Growth of school enrollment
...rowth of "Polycentrism"	32.5 million Catholics in United States, 458.6 million in world (1955) Vatican Council II (1962–)	Afro-Asian poverty and Western affluence	Ecumenism and the "new theology"

Us, which a sanguine mind cherishes and which remains a consolation to Us in hard and troublous times.

May the enormity of the labors which it will be necessary fervently to undertake for the glory of the Most Benign Redeemer and for the salvation of souls not daunt you, Dearly Beloved, but may it rather stimulate you, whose confidence is in the Divine Help, since great works generate more robust virtues and achieve more resplendent merits.

Chapter 40

VATICAN COUNCIL II:
REFORM AND RENEWAL

THE aristocratic and ascetic Pope Pius XII prepared the way for his successors to lead the Church through an exciting period of reform and renewal aimed at making the Church relevant to the contemporary world. His encyclicals on the Mystical Body and the liturgy were particularly important in giving authoritative support to those who complained that the Church was hampered by outmoded institutions and inflexibly rigid ideas.

The Election of Pope John XXIII. The next Holy Father was different from his predecessor in many ways, and he seemed from a human point of view ideally suited to lead the Church in renewing itself and becoming relevant to the world of the mid-twentieth century. On presumably the twelfth ballot the College of Cardinals chose the Patriarch of Venice, Angelo Cardinal Roncalli, to be the next Bishop of Rome. The new Holy Father, who took John XXIII for his name, was of peasant stock from northern Italy, a man known for his open, democratic ways and jovial disposition. He was a seasoned diplomat, having served as papal representative for ten years in Bulgaria, nine years in Constantinople, and nine in France, before his five-year tenure as Patriarch of Venice. Thus the new pontiff, whose family background and position at the time of his election were similar to those of Pope Pius X, was cosmopolitan in outlook and experience, well versed in diplomatic relations, and extremely popular with men of all faiths with whom he had associated before his election. This personal popularity and tolerant understanding of the position of Protestant and Orthodox churchmen enabled the new Pope to hold audiences with leaders of these other faiths. Within a few months of his election Pope John XXIII had done much, personally and officially, to quicken the ecumenical trend, which the late Rev. Gustave Weigel, S.J., called the "most significant event since the Reformation."

Shortly after his election, Pope John XXIII was reported by newspaper correspondents to have said that as pope he was not bound by tradition, that he was free, so to speak, "to make the rules." He immediately showed himself respectful of, but not bound by, the policies of his predecessor. His first acts revealed his twofold concern with the brotherhood of man and a pastoral rather than dogmatic approach to the faithful. The brotherhood of man gave him a special concern for the needy and the distressed. He granted Vatican employees three monthly bonuses, for example, sent money to the widows of Canadians killed in a mine disaster, and condolences to parents who lost children in a terrible parochial school fire in Chicago. Each year he contributed $1,000 to the UN Children's Fund.

Other specific acts indicated what the Pope meant when he spoke of "opening the window" and the "brotherhood of all men." He revived the custom of personally washing the feet of twelve obscure men, visited prisons as well as hospitals, and ordered the removal from the Good Friday liturgy of the word "perfidious" in reference to the Jews. The new Holy Father thus resembled St. Pius X in his pastoral concern for all souls, declaring himself approachable at all times by all people on the grounds that he never knew when someone might "want to go to confession." He addressed his encyclical *Pacem in Terris* to "all men of good will" rather than just to Catholics, and he gave a private audience to Aleksei Adzhubei, editor of the Communist paper, *Izvestia*.

The new Pope broke tradition within the first month of his pontificate by naming twenty-three new cardinals, thus increasing the College of Cardinals from the traditional maximum of seventy to seventy-five. Of the new appointees, thirteen were Italian and ten non-Italian. Among the latter were Archbishops Richard J. Cushing of Boston and John F. O'Hara of Philadelphia. Among the new Italian cardinals were Archbishop Amleto G. Cicognani, who had just celebrated his twenty-fifth anniversary as Apostolic Delegate to the United States, Archbishop Montini of Milan, and Msgr. Tardini of the papal staff. The two latter new cardinals had refused appointments under Pope Pius XII. Tardini had been named Secretary of State for the Vatican in one of John XXIII's first official acts. In December, 1959, the Holy Father increased the College of Cardinals to seventy-nine by raising eight more to the princely office. Two were Americans, Albert Cardinal Meyer of Chicago and Aloisius Cardinal Muench, formerly Bishop of Fargo and later Papal Nuncio to Germany. In March, 1960, the Pope created seven more cardinals, including the first Japanese, Filipino, and Negro princes in the Church. Early in 1961 four more were raised to the cardinalate, including

Joseph Cardinal Ritter of St. Louis, and two archbishops from Latin America. In 1962 Pope John again increased the number of cardinals in the Sacred College, raising it to a record high of eighty-nine members by creating ten new cardinals.

John XXIII as Teacher.   The new Holy Father continued the tradition of the last six popes of teaching moral and social principles through frequent audiences, allocutions, and encyclicals, but in a tone that was more pastoral than pedagogical, stressing an openness toward and intense love of all mankind. His encyclical on the missions, *Princeps Pastorum*, reiterated the teaching of recent popes and stressed the urgency of missionary work to win back such populations as Latin America while continuing to preach the Gospel to pagan peoples.

On May 15, 1961, the thirtieth anniversary of *Quadragesimo Anno*, and the seventieth of *Rerum Novarum*, Pope John brought the principles of these great social encyclicals up to date and made them relevant to a rapidly changing world in *Mater et Magistra*. Pope John's frequent references to the encyclical while it was in preparation indicated that he considered it one of the most important messages of his pontificate. It was widely acclaimed throughout the world, except by the Soviet press and a few radically conservative journals. *Mater et Magistra* treats social problems in a positive, liberal, and constructive manner. After reviewing the teachings and the social context of *Rerum Novarum* and *Quadragesimo Anno*, the Holy Father considers Catholic social and moral principles in the setting of a world community of interdependent nations and society in which all persons are bound to many others by a complex web of social relationships, and eventually each to all through potential membership in the Mystical Body.

On April 11, 1963, Pope John XXIII published his most famous and widely read encyclical, *Pacem in Terris*. This was the first encyclical addressed not only to Catholics but to "all men of good will." It was applauded by all except those who wanted an explicit condemnation of Communism and other erroneous doctrines. *Pacem in Terris* analyzes the social and political conditions required for man's personal dignity, and adds freedom to truth, charity, and justice as the bases of a well-ordered society. "Human society thrives on freedom," Pope John wrote, "on the use, that is, of means which are consistent with the dignity of its individual members, who, being naturally endowed with reason, assume responsibility for their own actions." The Holy Father also analyzed the interdependence of states in the world community, and the obligation of wealthy states to help poverty-stricken peoples.

Call for an Ecumenical Council. The new Pope announced that one of his principal objectives was to work for Church unity, and another was to make the Church relevant to the contemporary world. As a step toward these objectives he announced that he would convoke an ecumenical council to deal with these and other problems facing the Church in the 1960's. The agenda of the council was not immediately formulated, but in his frequent allocutions the Holy Father hinted at various topics to be discussed. Among these items he continually referred to the ripeness of time for discussing the possibility of reunion, especially with the Orthodox Christians whom he had come to know well at Constantinople. It was made clear that unity could not be a direct aim of the forthcoming council, but it could prepare the way for so momentous a step in the future.

The agenda for the Second Vatican Council was several years in preparation. Not only bishops but also lay groups and even individuals were invited to send the Vatican suggestions about topics they thought should be discussed. These were processed and discussed by various preparatory commissions. From these discussions a preparatory agenda was drawn up and circulated among responsible churchmen for further consideration. From the discussions and comments of bishops throughout the world the preparatory commission composed the schemata to introduce to the council.

On Christmas Day, 1961, Pope John XXIII formally called the Second Vatican Council to convene late in 1962, "on days that will be established according to the opportunity which good Providence may deign to give Us." The tone was set for the council by the Holy Father when he said it was not interested in a dogmatic condemnation of error, but rather in a positive statement of old truths in modern and meaningful language. The key word governing the council's deliberation was to be *aggiornamento* or "bringing up to date."

The Second Vatican Council: First Session. Preparations for the council sessions revealed that the bishops divided into two general schools of thought on what should be done for the good of the Church. The majority believed in the general attitude and program outlined by John XXIII. These bishops were led by Western Europeans, except for the Spaniards and many Italians, and included most of the bishops from North and South America and the missionary countries. The so-called "conservatives," who feared that basic changes were dangerous, were a minority who controlled the Curia and could be expected to block or at least delay measures of reform and renewal.

The first session of the council convened on October 11, 1962, the Feast of the Motherhood of the Blessed Virgin Mary. Present were 2540 council Fathers, who were assisted by their theologians and canon lawyers, as well as invited observers from other faiths and hundreds of reporters. After two months of deliberations, it ended on December 8, with arrangements to reconvene in September of 1963. Non-Romans were handicapped by their unfamiliarity with spoken Latin and the council's failure to provide instantaneous translations, as at the UN. Pope John XXIII's determination that the council should proceed gave the non-Roman bishops heart that their deliberations would bear fruit in future sessions and that schema sent back to preparatory commissions would be returned in improved form.

Election of Pope Paul VI.   Before the second session of the Second Vatican Council convened, Pope John XXIII's death created the crisis of whether his successor would be favorable to continuing the council. The Pope's heroic conduct through his painful illness endeared him to the entire world. Although his pontificate was the shortest in the past century, it soon became apparent that it was a turning point in the history of the Catholic Church. John XXIII had done more than open a window to the outside world. He had gone from Rome into the world, and had literally traveled to Assisi — the first pope to leave Rome in more than a century.

The College of Cardinals convened on June 19, 1963, to choose John's successor. On the sixth ballot they elected Giovanni Battista Cardinal Montini, Archbishop of Milan, who took the name Paul VI. The semi-official Vatican newspaper *L'Osservatore Romano* observed that Paul is "a symbol of ecumenical unity." The new Holy Father had had long experience in the Vatican Secretariat of State, and when he went to Milan he vigorously undertook a renewal of his archdiocese. His reputation was that of a balanced moderate who favored Pope John's *aggiornamento,* but would be less impulsive in achieving it.

In his first public statement, Pope Paul VI assured his listeners that he would recall the council for continued deliberations, and before the council met he addressed the Curia, praising them for their devoted work and pointing out that the Curia needed to be "simplified, decentralized, to enlarge itself and adapt itself to new functions." At various times during the first year of his pontificate Pope Paul VI hinted that perhaps he might create a senate of bishops to advise and assist him.

The Pope of Unity.   The new Holy Father was a scholar who, as a cardinal, had written and spoken about the Church many times. He insisted that the "Church is a mystery," and that theologians and other scholars must ponder it anew to gain better insights into this "continuation of Christ." More than a year passed before he published his first major encyclical, *Ecclesiam Suam*, dated August 6, 1964, the Feast of the Transfiguration of Our Lord. Insisting that he was not passing judgment or stating doctrine, the Holy Father wrote that he wanted to share his reflections about the Church of our time and dialogue with God, Christians, other believers in God, and all men.

During the second and third sessions of the Second Vatican Council, Pope Paul VI saw himself in the difficult position of having to be Pope of the great majority of Council Fathers whose reform and renewal proposals were becoming ever more sweeping, while remaining Pope of those who opposed any basic change. Both groups were disappointed not to receive his complete support. Meanwhile, Pope Paul VI promoted ecumenical feeling by visits to two non-Christian countries. The first was a pilgrimage to the Holy Land, and the second was to the Eucharistic Congress in Bombay. On both trips the Holy Father was received by government officials and by overwhelmingly enthusiastic crowds. On his visit to India he pleaded with the affluential peoples of the word to relieve India's terrifying poverty, as he personally visited destitute Indians and was moved to tears by their poverty. Both visits set many new precedents, indicating that, even more than his predecessor, Pope Paul VI intended to break out of outmoded customs so as to enter into effective communication with the modern world.

Second Session of the Second Vatican Council. The Fathers of the Church assembled in Rome for the opening of the second session of the Second Vatican Council on September 29, 1963. Much had been learned from the first session: the schemata were drastically reduced in number; sessions were more accessible to reporters; some lay auditors were admitted. However, only one important schema was adopted by the council and promulgated by the Pope. This was the Constitution on the Sacred Liturgy. Both Catholics and others interested in the council were disappointed that statements on the Jews and freedom of conscience had been sent back to their respective commissions for revision.

The Constitution on the Sacred Liturgy consolidated the thinking of liturgists of many years' standing and drew up principles and instructions for reforming liturgical worship. The council based its liturgical reforms on Scripture and centered all liturgical worship on Christ. The Constitution has chapters on: (1) General Principles for the Restoration and Promotion of the Sacred Liturgy, (2) The Most Sacred Mystery of the

Eucharist, (3) The Other Sacraments and Sacramentals, (4) The Divine Office, (5) The Liturgical Year, (6) Sacred Music, and (7) Sacred Art. The purpose behind the reforms was to make corporate worship more meaningful and to bring all Catholics into active participation in liturgical services.

A schema on communications media was also adopted and promulgated. Most Fathers and observers felt that it contained nothing significantly new or up to date on the subject.

The Third Session.   There was a general feeling of pessimism among those who favored reform and renewal after the dismissal of the second session on December 4, 1963, feeling that so-called conservative forces in Rome would prevent further action on proposed changes. But Pope Paul's promise that the preparatory commissions would revise the texts of the various schemata in accord with views expressed by the council was realized before the Fathers assembled for the third session on September 14, 1964.

Discussion and debate moved at a hurried pace in this session. As a result, the council passed and the Pope promulgated the most important document of the council, the Constitution on the Nature of the Church, as well as decrees on Ecumenism and the Eastern Churches. It also debated and sent back to the various commissions a number of other statements, the most important of which appeared to be those on religious liberty, the Jews, the lay apostolate, and the Church in the modern world.

Most observers considered the Constitution on the Nature of the Church the most important work of the twenty-first ecumenical council and "a landmark in two thousand years of Christian history." Its full effects will not be realized for many years but its passage by a vote of 2151 to 5 indicates that it expresses the mind of the Church and will be implemented. It is a long document of eight chapters in about fifty pages of Latin. Its purpose is "to unfold more fully to the faithful of the Church and to the whole world its own inner nature and universal mission."

The Church is described as "a mystery," the Body of Christ effectively present on earth. In the second chapter it is called God's "chosen race, a royal priesthood, a holy nation, a purchased people." The important third chapter deals with the "collegiality" of the episcopate, stating that each bishop receives his power from God by consecration rather than by delegation from the Pope. Bishops are to be concerned, with the Pope, with the welfare of the entire Church. The Church on earth is also described as a "pilgrim Church" in union with the Church in Heaven. The last chapter presents a balanced appraisal of the Blessed Virgin's role in the history of salvation, avoiding both the pietistic excesses of some theologians of the recent past and the desire of some "progressivists" who were inclined to move too far in minimizing Mary's unique position.

Rev. Donald R. Campion, S.J., summed up the estimate of most observers in these words: "Perhaps no chapter better manifests the balanced tenor of the council's teaching than that on 'The Blessed Virgin Mary, Mother of God, in the Mystery of Christ and the Church.' In beautiful language, borrowed almost entirely from Scripture and the ancient fathers, it depicts the role and glory of Mary, daughter of Adam, in the life of Jesus and the early Church. At the same time, it sets forth in perfect clarity the divine truth that Christ is our sole Mediator. Its carefully balanced lines can only promote the sort of devotion to Mary proper to the authentic patrimony of Christian life and practice."

The decree on Ecumenism, in effect, announced the end of the Counter-Reformation period of Church history. The Council Fathers ask pardon of God and "our separated brethren" for our offenses against them, and recognize that persons born in separated churches cannot be considered in bad faith. Separated churches are seen as having many endowments present in the Catholic Church, and all Catholics are urged to acquire a more adequate understanding of their theological positions. Special homage is paid to the Eastern churches, and Roman Catholics are called upon to respect diversity in these churches, which have the "power and the duty to govern themselves according to the discipline proper to them."

Conclusion. The third session ended in bitter disappointment for the majority. The relatively small group of "conservatives" managed to hold back final vote on the decree on Religious Liberty, and to send back for review the statement on the Jews. They were also disappointed that the Pope made nine changes, on his own authority, in the decree on Ecumenism before promulgating it. He also announced, as he closed the third session, that he proclaimed Mary "Mother of the Church."

The Holy Father announced that a fourth and final session of the Second Vatican Council would convene as soon as the commissions had amended the remaining texts and had them ready for final consideration by the Council Fathers. Despite these disappointments, the Fathers realized that they had presented the world with a new view of the Church and a new attitude toward other churches. Their thinking was based mostly on Scripture, and it was pastoral in orientation. Individually and collectively they evidenced a new spirit in wanting to make the Church relevant to the modern world, while remaining faithful to the mission entrusted to her by Christ. They could feel, at the close of the third session — when this revision HISTORY OF THE CATHOLIC CHURCH was going to press — that the Constitutions on the Liturgy and the Nature of the Church had effected the *aggiornamento* which Pope John XXIII had set as the goal of the Second Vatican Council when he announced that he would convene the council.

REVIEW AIDS

1. Recall the policies, events, and publications of Pope Pius XII that laid the groundwork for reform and renewal based on Scripture and centered on Christ.

2. In what ways did Pope John XXIII contrast with Pius XII?

3. It has been remarked that the Constitution on the Sacred Liturgy foreshadowed the Constitution on the Nature of the Church. In what respects is this true?

4. In 1964 a book appeared under the title: *Vatican II — Last of the Councils.* What reasoning do you think underlies such a thesis?

5. From newspaper accounts, diocesan or secular, trace any decree or constitution through council proceedings from the time of its introduction to its promulgation.

6. Explain as fully as you can why Pope Paul VI was in a difficult position through the first year of his pontificate.

7. Compare *Pacem in Terris* with *Quadragesimo Anno* to show how new economic, social, and political conditions call for a reformulation of Catholic social teaching.

8. Prepare a list of events to indicate how the work of adapting the Church to modern life was undertaken in the pontificate of John XXIII.

SUGGESTIONS FOR FURTHER READING

The student of contemporary Church history is bewildered by the hundreds of volumes appearing on the subject. His best source of information is the "primary sources" or documents issued by the Vatican, the council, and the bishops in their dioceses. Conciliar constitutions and decrees, as well as all major papal encyclicals are quickly published in English by such publishers as the America Press and the Paulist Press.

Many competent observers have been commenting in weekly papers and journals about council events, and several of them have published books on the subject after each of the sessions.

Other events in recent Church history can best be followed by using bound volumes of such a weekly journal as *America* or a monthly like *Sign, U. S. Catholic,* or *Herder Correspondence,* which now appears in English.

DOCUMENTS

From Chapter I of the Constitution on the Sacred Liturgy

II. *The Promotion of Liturgical Instruction and Active Participation*

14. Mother Church earnestly desires that all the faithful should be led to that full, conscious, and active participation in liturgical celebrations which is demanded by the very nature of the liturgy. Such participation by the Christian people as "a chosen race, a royal priesthood, a holy nation, a redeemed people" (1 Pet. 2:9; cf. 2:4–5), is their right and duty by reason of their baptism.

In the restoration and promotion of the sacred liturgy, this full and active participation by all the people is the aim to be considered before all else; for it is the primary and indispensable source from which the faithful are to derive the true Christian spirit; and therefore pastors of souls must zealously strive to achieve it, by means of the necessary instruction, in all their pastoral work.

Yet it would be futile to entertain any hopes of realizing this unless the pastors themselves, in the first place, become thoroughly imbued with the spirit and power of the liturgy, and undertake to give instruction about it. A prime need, therefore, is that attention be directed, first of all, to the liturgical instruction of the clergy. Wherefore the sacred Council has decided to enact as follows:

15. Professors who are appointed to teach liturgy in seminaries, religious houses of study, and theological faculties must be properly trained for their work in institutes which specialize in this subject.

16. The study of sacred liturgy is to be ranked among the compulsory and major courses in seminaries and religious houses of study; in theological faculties it is to rank among the principal courses. It is to be taught under its theological, historical, spiritual, pastoral, and juridical aspects. Moreover, other professors, while striving to expound the mystery of Christ and the history of salvation from the angle proper to each of their own subjects, must nevertheless do so in a way which will clearly bring out the connection between their subjects and the liturgy, as also the unity which underlies all priestly training. This consideration is especially important for professors of dogmatic, spiritual, and pastoral theology and for those of holy scripture.

17. In seminaries and houses of religious, clerics shall be given a liturgical formation in their spiritual life. For this they will need proper direction, so that they may be able to understand the sacred rites and take part in them wholeheartedly; and they will also need personally to celebrate the sacred mysteries, as well as popular devotions which are imbued with the spirit of the liturgy. In addition they must learn how to observe the liturgical laws, so that life in seminaries and houses of religious may be thoroughly influenced by the spirit of the liturgy.

18. Priests, both secular and religious, who are already working in the Lord's vineyard are to be helped by every suitable means to understand ever more fully what it is that they are doing when they perform sacred rites; they are to be aided to live the liturgical life and to share it with the faithful entrusted to their care.

19. With zeal and patience, pastors of souls must promote the liturgical instruction of the faithful, and also their active participation in the liturgy both internally and externally, taking into account their age and condition, their way of life, and standard of religious culture. By so doing, pastors will be fulfilling one of the chief duties of a faithful dispenser of the mysteries of God; and in this matter they must lead their flock not only in word but also by example.

20. Transmissions of the sacred rites by radio and television shall be done with discretion and dignity, under the leadership and direction of a suitable person appointed for this office by the bishops. This is especially important when the service to be broadcast is the Mass.

III. *The Reform of the Sacred Liturgy*

21. In order that the Christian people may more certainly derive an abundance of graces from the sacred liturgy, holy Mother Church desires to undertake with great care a general restoration of the liturgy itself. For the liturgy is made up of immutable elements divinely instituted, and of elements subject to change. These not only may but ought to be changed with the passage of time if they have suffered from the intrusion of anything out of harmony with the inner nature of the liturgy or have become unsuited to it.

In this restoration, both texts and rites should be drawn up so that they express more clearly the holy things which they signify; the Christian people, so far as possible, should be enabled to understand them with ease and to take part in them fully, actively, and as befits a community.

From Chapter III of the Constitution of the Nature of the Church

On the Hierarchical Structure of the Church and in Particular on the Episcopate

18. For the nurturing and constant growth of the People of God, Christ the Lord instituted in His Church a variety of ministries, which work for the good of the whole body. For those ministers, who are endowed with sacred power, serve their brethren, so that all who are of the People of God and therefore enjoy a true Christian dignity, working toward a common goal freely and in an orderly way, may arrive at salvation.

This Sacred Council, following closely in the footsteps of the First Vatican Council, with that Council teaches and declares that Jesus Christ, the eternal Shepherd, established His holy Church, having sent forth the Apostles as He Himself had been sent by the Father (Jn. 20, 21); and He willed that their successors, namely the bishops, should be shepherds in His Church even to the consummation of the world. And in order that the episcopate itself might be one and undivided, He placed Blessed Peter over the other Apostles, and instituted in him a permanent and visible source and foundation of unity of faith and communion. And all this teaching about the institution the perpetuity, the meaning and reason for the sacred primacy of the Roman Pontiff and of his infallible magisterium, this Sacred Council again proposes to be firmly believed by all the faithful. Continuing in that same undertaking, this Council is resolved to declare and proclaim before all men the doctrine concerning bishops, the successors of the Apostles, who together with the successor of Peter, the Vicar of Christ, the visible Head of the whole Church, govern the house of the living God.

19. The Lord Jesus, after praying to the Father, calling to Himself those whom He desired, appointed 12 to be with Him, and whom He would send to preach the Kingdom of God (Mk. 3, 13–19; Mt. 10, 1–42), and these Apostles (Lk. 6, 13) He formed after the manner of a college or a stable group, over which He placed Peter chosen from among them. He sent them first to the children of Israel and then to all nations (Rom. 1, 16), so that as sharers in His power they might make all peoples His disciples, and sanctify and govern them (Mt. 26, 16–20; Mk. 16, 15; Lk. 24, 45–48; Jn. 20, 21–23), and thus spread His Church, and by ministering to it under the guidance of the Lord, direct it all days even to the consummation of the world (Mt. 28, 20). And in this mission they were fully confirmed on the day of Pentecost (Acts 2, 1–26) in accordance with the Lord's promise: "You shall receive power when the Holy Spirit comes upon you, and you shall be witnesses for me in Jerusalem, and in all Judea and in Samaria, and even to the very ends of the earth" (Acts 1, 8). And the Apostles, by preaching the Gospel everywhere (Mk. 16, 20), and it being accepted by their hearers under the influence of the Holy Spirit, gather together the universal Church, which the Lord established on the Apostles and built upon blessed Peter, their chief, Christ Jesus Himself being the supreme cornerstone (Apoc. 21, 14; Mt. 16, 18; Eph. 2, 20).

Appendix I

THE ECUMENICAL COUNCILS

1. Nicaea (I)	325	Condemned Arianism. Formulated the Nicene Creed.
2. Constantinople (I)	381	Formulated Catholic teaching on the Holy Spirit against various heretics. Completed the Nicene Creed.
3. Ephesus	431	Declared Bl. Virgin to be truly Mother of God against Nestorian heresy.
4. Chalcedon	451	Condemned Monophysitism. Enacted many disciplinary canons.
5. Constantinople (II)	553	Condemned the *Three Chapters*.
6. Constantinople (III)	680	Completed the Church's Christological dogma with the condemnation of Monothelitism.
7. Nicaea (II)	787	Refuted the Iconoclasts.
8. Constantinople (IV)	869	Ended the Photian Schism.
9. Lateran (I)	1123	Ratified the Concordat of Worms and reaffirmed the reform decrees of the Gregorian period.
10. Lateran (II)	1139	Disciplinary measures.
11. Lateran (III)	1179	Regulated papal elections to prevent further disputes. Condemned various heresies, including Albigensianism.
12. Lateran (IV)	1215	Numerous disciplinary decrees. Forbade new religious orders. Annual Communion demanded. Planned a crusade.
13. Lyons (I)	1245	Declared deposition of Frederick II.
14. Lyons (II)	1274	Temporary reunion of the Greeks.
15. Vienne	1311–1312	Abolished the Knights Templars.
16. Constance	1414–1418	Ended the Great Schism; executed Hus. Attempted to give sanction to the Conciliar theory.
17. Basle-Ferrara-Florence	1431–1445	Reconciled Hussites. New reunion with Greeks. Defeat of Conciliarism.
18. Lateran (V)	1512–1517	Considered reforms.
19. Trent	1545–1563	Enacted far-reaching reforms and redefined and restated the entire teaching of the Church. Condemned Protestantism.
20. Vatican I	1869–1870	Defined papal infallibility and condemned many errors of the nineteenth century.
21. Vatican II	1962–	Decrees on the liturgy, ecumenism, and the Church.

Appendix II

THE LIST OF THE POPES

This new list of the Roman Pontiffs was published in the *Annuario Pontificio* for 1964. The dates assigned to the popes of the first three centuries are still not certain. Antipopes are indicated in italics.

St. Peter	–67	St. Julius I	337–352
St. Linus	67–76	Liberius	352–366
St. Anacletus or Cletus	76–88	*Felix II*	355–365
St. Clement	88–97	St. Damasus I	366–384
St. Evaristus	97–105	*Ursinus*	366–367
St. Alexander I	105–115	St. Siricius	384–399
St. Sixtus I	115–125	St. Anastasius I	399–401
St. Telesphorus	125–136	St. Innocent I	401–417
St. Hyginus	136–140	St. Zozimus	417–418
St. Pius I	140–155	St. Boniface I	418–422
St. Anicetus	155–166	*Eulalius*	418–419
St. Soter	166–175	St. Celestine I	422–432
St. Eleutherius	175–189	St. Sixtus III	432–440
St. Victor I	189–199	St. Leo I	440–461
St. Zephyrinus	199–217	St. Hilarius	461–468
St. Callixtus I	217–222	St. Simplicius	468–483
St. Hippolytus	217–235	St. Felix III (II)	483–492
St. Urban I	222–230	St. Gelasius I	492–496
St. Pontianus	230–235	Anastasius II	496–498
St. Anterus	235–236	St. Symmachus	498–514
St. Fabian	236–250	*Lawrence*	498; 501–505
St. Cornelius	251–253	St. Hormisdas	514–523
Novatian	251	St. John I	523–526
St. Lucius I	253–254	St. Felix IV (III)	526–530
St. Stephen I	254–257	Boniface II	530–532
St. Sixtus II	257–258	*Dioscorus*	530
St. Dionysius	259–268	John II	533–535
St. Felix I	269–274	St. Agapitus I	535–536
St. Eutychianus	275–283	St. Silverius	536–537
St. Caius	283–296	Vigilius	537–555
St. Marcellinus	296–304	Pelagius I	556–561
St. Marcellus I	308–309	John III	561–574
St. Eusebius	309	Benedict I	575–579
St. Milziadus or Melchiadus	311–314	Pelagius II	579–590
St. Sylvester I	314–335	St. Gregory I	590–604
St. Mark	336	Sabinianus	604–606
		Boniface III	607

St. Boniface IV	608–615	Sergius II	844–847
St. Deusdedit or		St. Leo IV	847–855
Adeodatus I	615–618	Benedict III	855–858
Boniface V	619–625	*Anastasius*	855
Honorius I	625–638	St. Nicholas I	858–867
Severinus	640	Adrian II	867–872
John IV	640–642	John VIII	872–882
Theodore I	642–649	Marinus I	882–884
St. Martin I	649–655	St. Adrian III	884–885
St. Eugene I	654–657	Stephen V (VI)	885–891
St. Vitalian	657–672	Formosus	891–896
Adeodatus II	672–676	Boniface VI	896
Donus	676–678	Stephen VI (VII)	896–897
St. Agatho	678–681	Romanus	897
St. Leo II	682–683	Theodore II	897
St. Benedict II	684–685	John IX	898–900
John V	685–686	Benedict IV	900–903
Conon	686–687	Leo V	903
Theodore	687	*Christopher*	903–904
Paschal	687	Sergius III	904–911
St. Sergius I	687–701	Anastasius III	911–913
John VI	701–705	Lando	913–914
John VII	705–707	John X	914–928
Sisinnius	708	Leo VI	928
Constantine	708–715	Stephen VII (VIII)	928–931
St. Gregory II	715–731	John XI	931–935
St. Gregory III	731–741	Leo VII	936–939
St. Zachary	741–752	Stephen VIII (IX)	939–942
(Stephen II, died before		Marinus II	942–946
consecration)[1]	752	Agapitus II	946–955
Stephen II (III)	752–757	John XII	955–964
St. Paul I	757–767	Leo VIII	963–965
Constantine	767–769	Benedict V	964–966
Philip	768	John XIII	965–972
Stephen III (IV)	768–772	Benedict VI	973–974
Adrian I	772–795	*Boniface VII* 974;	984–985
St. Leo III	795–816	Benedict VII	974–983
Stephen IV (V)	816–817	John XIV	983–984
St. Paschal I	817–824	John XV	985–996
Eugene II	824–827	Gregory V	996–999
Valentine	827	*John XVI*	997–998
Gregory IV	827–844	Sylvester II	999–1003
John	844	John XVII	1003

---

[1] In the eighth century the date of consecration rather than election was taken to mark the beginning of a pope's reign; hence this Stephen was not counted among the popes. Later custom recognized election as the start of a pontificate, thus giving rise to confusion with later popes named Stephen.

John XVIII	1004–1009	*Callixtus III*	1168–1178
Sergius IV	1009–1012	*Innocent III*	1179–1180
Benedict VIII	1012–1024	Lucius III	1181–1185
Gregory	1012	Urban III	1185–1187
John XIX	1024–1032	Gregory VIII	1187
Benedict IX	1032–1044	Clement III	1187–1191
Sylvester III	1045	Celestine III	1191–1198
Benedict IX		Innocent III	1198–1216
(2nd time)	1045	Honorius III	1216–1227
Gregory VI	1045–1046	Gregory IX	1227–1241
Clement II	1046–1047	Celestine IV	1241
Benedict IX		Innocent IV	1243–1254
(3rd time)	1047–1048	Alexander IV	1254–1261
Damasus II	1048	Urban IV	1261–1264
St. Leo IX	1049–1054	Clement IV	1265–1268
Victor II	1055–1057	Gregory X	1271–1276
Stephen IX (X)	1057–1058	Innocent V	1276
Benedict X	1058–1059	Adrian V	1276
Nicholas II	1059–1061	John XXI[2]	1276–1277
Alexander II	1061–1073	Nicholas III	1277–1280
Honorius II	1061–1072	Martin IV	1281–1285
St. Gregory VII	1073–1085	Honorius IV	1285–1287
Clement III 1080;	1084–1100	Nicholas IV	1288–1292
Victor III	1086–1087	St. Celestine V	1294
Urban II	1088–1099	Boniface VIII	1294–1303
Paschal II	1099–1118	Benedict XI	1303–1304
Theodoric	1100–1102	Clement V	1305–1314
Albert	1102	John XXII	1316–1334
Sylvester IV	1105–1111	*Nicholas V*	1328–1330
Gelasius II	1118–1119	Benedict XII	1334–1342
Gregory VIII	1118–1121	Clement VI	1342–1352
Callixtus II	1119–1124	Innocent VI	1352–1362
Honorius II	1124–1130	Urban V	1362–1370
Celestine II	1124	Gregory XI	1370–1378
Innocent II	1130–1143	Urban VI	1378–1389
Anacletus II	1130–1138	Boniface IX	1389–1404
Victor IV	1138	Innocent VII	1404–1406
Celestine II	1143–1144	Gregory XII	1406–1415
Lucius II	1144–1145	*Clement VII*	1378–1394
Eugene III	1145–1153	*Benedict XIII*	1394–1423
Anastasius IV	1153–1154	*Alexander V*	1409–1410
Adrian IV	1154–1159	*John XXIII*	1410–1415
Alexander III	1159–1181	Martin V	1417–1431
Victor IV	1159–1164	Eugene IV	1431–1447
Paschal III	1164–1168	*Felix V*	1439–1449

[2] There is much confusion concerning popes named John. There was no legitimate Pope John XVI, and no John XX at all.

Nicholas V	1447–1455	Urban VIII	1623–1644
Callixtus III	1455–1458	Innocent X	1644–1655
Pius II	1458–1464	Alexander VII	1655–1667
Paul II	1464–1471	Clement IX	1667–1669
Sixtus IV	1471–1484	Clement X	1670–1676
Innocent VIII	1484–1492	Innocent XI	1676–1689
Alexander VI	1492–1503	Alexander VIII	1689–1691
Pius III	1503	Innocent XII	1691–1700
Julius II	1503–1513	Clement XI	1700–1721
Leo X	1513–1521	Innocent XIII	1721–1724
Adrian VI	1522–1523	Benedict XIII	1724–1730
Clement VII	1523–1534	Clement XII	1730–1740
Paul III	1534–1549	Benedict XIV	1740–1758
Julius III	1550–1555	Clement XIII	1758–1769
Marcellus II	1555	Clement XIV	1769–1774
Paul IV	1555–1559	Pius VI	1775–1799
Pius IV	1559–1565	Pius VII	1800–1823
St. Pius V	1566–1572	Leo XII	1823–1829
Gregory XIII	1572–1585	Pius VIII	1829–1830
Sixtus V	1585–1590	Gregory XVI	1831–1846
Urban VII	1590	Pius IX	1846–1878
Gregory XIV	1590–1591	Leo XIII	1878–1903
Innocent IX	1591	St. Pius X	1903–1914
Clement VIII	1592–1605	Benedict XV	1914–1922
Leo XI	1605	Pius XI	1922–1939
Paul V	1605–1621	Pius XII	1939–1958
Gregory XV	1621–1623	John XXIII	1958–1963
	Paul VI	1963–1978	

GENERAL BIBLIOGRAPHY

This general bibliography is not intended to supplement the lists of readings appended to each chapter. Rather it aims to make available to the student the names of some of the longer, more important works, major collections of sources, and various auxiliary materials with which he should be familiar, and which he will definitely need for advanced work. Since it is impossible to isolate the history of the Church from the secular developments of any age, the standard historiographical works of Potthast, Chevalier, Allison and Dutcher, Gross and Paetow, all of which provide valuable guides to various epochs, and the great national historical collections of England, France, Germany, and Italy, containing much pertinent matter for Church history, should also be consulted as needed.

A. Historiography

Bratke, Eduard, *Wegweiser zur Quellen- und Litteraturkunde der Kirchengeschichte* (Gotha: 1890).

De Smet, Charles, *Introductio generalis ad historiam ecclesiasticam critice tractandam* (Ghent: 1876). These two works are old but they still contain much material that has not been superseded.

Guilday, Peter, *An Introduction to Church History* (St. Louis: 1925). A useful preparatory volume for the study of Church history.

B. Larger Church Histories

Fliche, Augustin, and Victor Martin (general editors), *Histoire de L'Église depuis les Origines jusqu'à nos Jours* (Paris: 1934 –). When completed this co-operative work will consist of twenty-four volumes, of which better than half are already in print. As a masterpiece of sound scholarship it already holds and will continue to hold for a long time the first place among comparable undertakings. The Macmillan Company is publishing the English translation under various titles. Both French and English editions contain extremely full bibliographies.

Hergenröther, Joseph Cardinal, *Handbuch der Kirchengeschichte*, 4 vols., 6th ed. (Freiburg: 1925). Long and deservedly a favorite among German students.

Krüger, Gustav, and E. Preuschen, *Handbuch der Kirchengeschichte für Studierende*, 4 vols., 2nd ed. (Tübingen: 1923–1931). A Protestant work of merit, designed specifically for students and hence well equipped with outlines and bibliography.

Latourette, Kenneth S., *A History of the Expansion of Christianity*, 7 vols. (New York: 1937–1945). Emphasizes growth and missionary activity.

Mourret, Fernand, *History of the Catholic Church*, 8 vols., translated from the French by Newton Thompson (St. Louis: 1930 –). One of the original nine volumes remains to be translated. A large scale work whose usefulness is limited by poor organization and often an unscientific attitude.

Poulet, Charles, *A History of the Catholic Church,* translated from the 4th French edition by S. A. Raemers, 2 vols. (St. Louis: 1948). Very uneven.

Todesco, L., *Corsa de Storia della Chiesa,* 5 vols., 4th ed. (Turin and Rome: 1944–1948). Easily the best Church history in Italian.

C. Handbooks of Source Material

Denzinger, Heinrich, *Enchiridion Symbolorum, Definitionum et Declarationum de rebus Fidei et Morum,* 21–23rd ed. (Freiburg: 1937).

Journel, M. J. Rouet de, *Enchiridion Patristicum* (Freiburg: 1922).

Kirch, C., *Enchiridion Fontium Historiae Ecclesiasticae Antiquae,* 6th ed. (Barcelona: 1947).

D. Patrology

1. Introductory manuals and handbooks

Bardenhewer, Otto, *Patrology. The Lives and Works of the Fathers of the Church,* translated from the 2nd ed. by Thomas J. Shahan (Freiburg: 1908).

Cayré, F., *Manual of Patrology and History of Theology,* 2 vols., translated by H. Howitt (Paris: 1936–1940). A fine piece of work, extending into early modern times.

Quasten, Johannes, *Patrology,* 3 vols. (Westminster Md.: 1950–1960). Extends as far as the Council of Chalcedon. Expertly done in every respect. Indispensable.

Tixeront, Joseph, *A Handbook of Patrology,* translated from the 4th French edition by S. A. Raemers (St. Louis: 1920).

2. Collections of sources

Corpus Christianorum, edited by anonymous Benedictine monks, about 40 vols. to date (Turnholt: 1953 –). A new edition of the Latin Fathers from Tertullian to Bede, planned for 149 volumes. Vast improvement over Migne's texts.

Corpus Scriptorum Ecclesiasticorum Latinorum, edited by the Academy of Vienna since 1866. Seventy volumes have been published to date. Latin text only, but usually the best edition of each of its authors.

Chabot, J. B., I Guidi, *et al.* (eds.), *Corpus Scriptorum Christianorum Orientalium* (Paris: 1903 ff.). The Syriac, Arabic, Coptic, and Ethiopian texts. 100 volumes to date.

Die Griechischen Christlichen Schriftsteller der ersten drei Jahrhunderte, edited by the Academy of Berlin since 1897. 41 vols. Critical editions only and of a high caliber. Includes authors of the fourth and fifth centuries, despite its title.

Migne, J. P. (ed.), *Patrologiae Cursus Completus, Series Latina,* 221 volumes (Paris: 1844–1855). Extends to A.D. 1216. The most complete collection of patristic and medieval texts, but often the editing is poor. Very valuable, however, because of its tremendous scope.

———— *Patrologiae Cursus Completus, Series Graeca,* 161 volumes (Paris: 1857–1866). Extends to 1439. Contains Latin translations of the Greek texts in parallel columns. Unsurpassed in size, although various individual authors have since been better edited in other collections.

Monumenta Germaniae Historica, Auctores Antiquissimi, 13 vols. (Berlin: 1877–1898). Includes many ecclesiastical writers.

Page, T. E., E. Capps, and W. H. D. Rouse (eds.), *The Loeb Classical Library.* Includes many of the Greek and Latin fathers individually edited. Both the original text and an English translation are given.

Pusey, Edward, John Kebel, and John Henry Newman, *Library of the Fathers,* 45 vols. (Oxford: 1838–1888). The fruit of the Oxford Movement. Contains good English translations.

Quasten, Johannes, and J. C. Plumpe (eds.), *Ancient Christian Writers* (Westminster, Md.: 1946 –). The first library of the fathers undertaken by American Catholics. About thirty-one volumes of translations have appeared thus far, every one of the best scholarship. Both Greek and Latin fathers.

Roberts, Alexander, and James Donaldson (eds.), *Ante-Nicene Fathers,* American reprint of the Edinburgh edition, revised by A. C. Coxe, 10 vols. (New York: 1917–1925).

Robinson, J. A. (ed.), *Texts and Studies* (Cambridge: 1891 –). Patristic texts as well as research studies.

Schaff, Ph., and H. Wace, *A Select Library of Nicene and Post-Nicene Fathers,* 1st series in 14 vols. (New York: 1886–1890); 2nd series in 14 vols. (New York: 1890–1900).

Schopp, L. (ed.), *The Fathers of the Church* (New York: 1947 –). A second series of translations by American Catholic scholars. Good but not as scholarly as the Ancient Christian Writers series.

Texte und Untersuchungen zur Geschichte der Altchristlichen Literatur, edited by the Academy of Leipzig, 1st series, 15 vols., 1882–1897; 2nd series, 15 vols., 1897–1906; 3rd series in progress since 1907.

E. Councils

Hardouin, J., *Conciliorum Collectio Regia Maxima,* 12 vols. (Paris: 1714–1715). The earliest general modern collection on which all others depend to a greater or lesser degree.

Hefele, Karl Joseph von, and Henri Leclerq, *Histoire des Conciles d'apres les Documents Originaux,* 11 vols. (Paris: 1907–1949). A revised and enlarged edition in French of Hefele's original 5-volume German work. It is the most readily accessible work, although it contains only French translations of the acts of the general and local councils. Does not get beyond the fifteenth century.

Labbé, P., and G. Cossart, *Sacrosancta Concilia,* 23 vols. (Venice: 1728–1733). A better version of the material in Hardouin.

Mansi, J. D., *Sacrorum Conciliorum Nova et Amplissima Collectio,* 31 vols. to the year 1590 (Florence and Venice: 1759–1798). New edition and continuation, Vols. 32–53 (Paris: 1901 ff.). This is the classic edition of the councils, building on Labbé and Cossart.

Schneemann, Gerard, editor of Vols. I–VI (1682–1870), and Theodore Granderath, editor of Vol. VII (1870–1882), *Collectio Lacensis. Acta et Decreta sanctorum Conciliorum recentiorum* (Freiburg: 1870–1890).

Schroeder, Henry J., *Disciplinary Decrees of the General Councils* (St. Louis: 1937). To the Council of Trent. Text and English translation, the only such available.

───── *Canons and Decrees of the Council of Trent* (St. Louis: 1941). Same plan as the above.

F. The Papacy

Bibliothèque des Écoles Françaises d'Athènes et de Rome, 2nd and 3rd series (Paris: 1884 ff.). Contains the registers of the popes of the thirteenth century edited by various scholars.

Jaffe, P., *Regesta Pontificum Romanorum ad annum 1198,* 2 vols., 2nd ed. (Leipzig: 1885–1888).

Kerr, P. F., *Regesta Pontificum Romanorum (to 1198),* 7 vols. (Berlin: 1906–1925). Corrects errors in Jaffe.

Pflugk-Harttung, J. v., *Acta Pontificum Romanorum Inedita (A.D. 97–1198),* 3 vols. (Tübingen: 1881–1888).

Potthast, A., *Regesta Pontificum Romanorum, inde ab anno post Christum natum 1198 ad annum 1304,* 2 vols. (Berlin 1874–1875). This and the three preceding works contain chronological lists with summaries of all papal documents known at the time, and an indication of where the documents can be found in full. The largest printed collections of papal letters are to be found scattered through Migne's *Patrologiae Latinae.* Cf. above.

Theiner, A. (ed.), *Codex Diplomaticum Dominii Temporalis S. Sedis,* 3 vols. (Rome: 1861–1862). Documents on the history of the Papal State.

G. Monasticism

Holstenius (Holste), Lucas, *Codex Regularum Monasticarum,* new ed. in 6 vols. (Vienna: 1759). A practically complete collection of monastic rules.

H. Hagiography

Baring-Gould, S., *Lives of the Saints,* 16 vols. (Edinburgh: 1914).

Bolland, Jean, *et al., Acta Sanctorum Quotquot Toto Orbe Coluntur,* 65 vols. (Antwerp: 1643 ff.). Arranged according to saints' days, now reaching into early November. A scholarly edition of all the source material for every saint's life. Vol. 62 contains an index for January to October. A periodic supplement, *Analecta Bollandiana* (Paris: 1882 ff.), reports on work in progress by the society of Bollandists who edit the *Acta.*

Socii Bollandiani (eds.), *Bibliotheca Hagiographica Latina Antiquae et Mediae Aetatis,* 2 vols. (Brussels: 1898–1901). A valuable bibliography of hagiographical material.

I. The Hierarchy

Gams, Pius B., *Series Episcoporum Ecclesiae Catholicae,* 2nd ed. (Leipzig: 1931). An attempt to list all known bishops of every episcopal see in the history of the Church, with some bibliographical information. The only such complete work of its kind, although not free from errors.

Eubel, Conrad, *Hierarchia Catholica Medii Aevi et Recentioris Temporis,* 6 vols. (Münster and Padua: 1898–1958). Vols. IV–VI edited by P. Gauchat, R. Ritzler, and P. Seferin. Lists of popes, cardinals, and bishops, with much valuable miscellaneous information, from 1198 to 1730.

J. Auxiliary Works

Baudrillart, A., A. de Meyer, E. Van Cauwenbergh, *Dictionnaire d'Histoire et de Géographie Ecclésiastique* (Paris: 1912 –).

Buchberger, M. (ed.), *Lexikon für Theologie und Kirche,* 2nd ed., 9 vols., (Freiburg: 1957–1964).

Cabrol, F., and H. Leclerq (eds.), *Dictionnaire d'Archéologie Chrétienne et de Liturgie,* 15 vols. in 30 (Paris: 1920–1953).

Catholic Encyclopedia, 16 vols. (New York: 1907–1914).

Hastings, J. (ed.), *Encyclopaedia of Religion and Ethics,* 13 vols. (Edinburgh: 1908–1926).

Hauck, A., *Realencyclopaedie für protestantische Theologie und Kirche,* 3rd ed., 24 vols. (Leipzig: 1896–1913).

Heussi, Karl, and Hermann Mulert, *Atlas zur Kirchengeschichte,* 2nd ed. (Tübingen: 1919).

Jewish Encyclopedia, 12 vols. (New York: 1901–1906).

Marucchi, Orazio, *Manual of Christian Archeology,* translated and adapted by Hubert Vecchierello (Paterson: 1935).

Meer, Frederick van der, and Mohrmann, C., *Atlas of the Early Christian World* (London: 1958).

Paschini, Pio, Celestino Testore, S.J., and A. Pietro Freetaz (editors), *Enciclopedia Cattolica,* 12 vols. (Citta del Vaticano: 1949–1954).

Schaff, P., and Herzog, *Encyclopedia of Religious Knowledge,* 12 vols., new ed. (New York: 1908–1914). Protestant.

Smith, W., and H. Wace (eds.), *Dictionary of Christian Biography,* 4 vols. (London: 1877–1887).

Streit, F. C., *Catholic World Atlas* (Paderborn: 1929).

Vacant, A., E. Mangenot, E. Amann, *Dictionnaire de Théologie Catholique* 15 vols. in 30 (Paris: 1908–1950).

Vigouroux, F., *Dictionnaire de la Bible* (Paris: 1895–1912). Supplements since 1926 by L. Pirot.

K. Periodicals

Catholic Historical Review
Journal of Ecclesiastical History
Revue d'Histoire Ecclésiastique
Revue d'Histoire de l'Eglise de France
Revue d'Histoire et de Littérature Religieuse
Studi E Testi
Studia Catholica
Zeitschrift für Kirchengeschichte

INDEX

Abelard, 201 f

Abuses in Church, listed by Commission of Nine (1537), 364; removed by Trent, 380

Acacius, bishop of Constantinople, 90 f

Acerbo Nimis, encyclical, 567

Adalbert of Prague, St., 173 f

Ad Beatissimi, brief, 571

Administration, of Church, anarchy in, 293 ff; organization of, 67 ff; papal, development, 223 ff; at peak of centralization, 262

Admonet nos, bull, 401

Adoptionism, heresy, among Franks, 151; in 2nd century, 54

Adrian I, pope, and Lombards, 152

Adrian IV, pope, and Barbarossa, 209 ff

Adrian VI, and Church reform, 360 f

Ad Sinarum Gentium, encyclical, 653

Aeterni Patris, encyclical, 551

Africa, ecclesiastical organization, 68 f; *see also* Donatists; Augustine, St.; Tertullian; Cyprian, St.; Carthage

Aistulf, King of Lombards, 139 f

Alacoque, Margaret Mary, St., 418

Alberic, 169

Albert the Great, St., 233

Albigensians, condemned, 227; teachings, 231

Albornoz, Cardinal, 266

Alcala, University of, 358

Alcuin, 151 f

Alexander III, pope, conflict with Frederick I, 210 ff; as legate, 210

Alexander VI, Renaissance pope, 289

Alexandria, archbishopric of, 69; catechetical school, 57 f; theological tendencies, 86

Alva, Duke of, 329

Ambrose, St., 74 f

America, on Pius XII, 639 f

American Church, 509 f; early growth of, 511 f; growth of, 601, 610 f; and immigration, 605 f; modern nativism, 609 f; problems of, 601 f; program of bishops (1919), 613; relation to State, 603;

social teaching of, 613 f; uniqueness of, 600 f

American Constitution, and religion, 509

American government, and Church, 509

Americanism, 607 f

American Protective Association, 609

Anabaptists, 324, 325

Anagni, outrage of, 251

Anglican Revolt, under Edward VI, 344, 345

Anglo-Saxons, 124 ff

Anselm, St., conflict with king of England, 189; and scholasticism, 201

Anthony of Egypt, St., hermit, 100 f

Antioch, archbishopric of, 69; Christianity at, 21; theological school, 58, 86

Anti-papalism, in medieval England, 262 f

Antoninus of Florence, St., 281

APA, *see* American Protective Association

Apologists, defense against Roman persecution, 36; of 2nd century, 37 f

Apostates, readmission of, 56

Apostles, as missionaries, 28 f; role of, 15; selection of, 13

Apostleship of Prayer, 506

Apostolic penitentiary, 262

Apostolicum pascendi, 457

Aranda, and suppression of Jesuits, 458

Archbishoprics, *see* Metropolitanate

Arduum Sane Munus, 566

Arianism, among Germanic tribes, 117 ff; heresy, 58 ff

Aristotle, revived, 201; as used by Aquinas, 233

Arius, condemnation of, at Council of Nicaea, 60; heretic, 58 ff

Arnold of Brescia, 200

Ars, Curé of, *see* Vianney, John B., St.

Art, Christian, *see* Iconoclasm

Articles of Constance, 276

Asceticism, *see* Monasticism

Associations Act (1901), 546

Assumption, definition of dogma, 651

Athanasius, St., and Arianism, 60 ff; and monasticism, 103

Aufklärung, 448